TRIAL EVIDENCE

ASPEN COURSEBOOK SERIES

TRIAL EVIDENCE

Sixth Edition

THOMAS A. MAUET

Milton O. Riepe Professor of Law and
    Director of Trial Advocacy
    University of Arizona College of Law

WARREN D. WOLFSON

Justice of the Appellate Court of the
    State of Illinois (retired) and
    Former Dean and Current
    Distinguished Visiting Professor
    DePaul University College of Law

Wolters Kluwer

Published by Wolters Kluwer in New York.

Wolters Kluwer Legal & Regulatory Solutions U.S. serves customers worldwide with CCH, Aspen Publishers, and Kluwer Law International products. (www.WKLegaledu.com)

To contact Customer Service, e-mail customer.service@wolterskluwer.com, call 1-800-234-1660, fax 1-800-901-9075, or mail correspondence to:

> Wolters Kluwer
> Attn: Order Department
> PO Box 990
> Frederick, MD 21705

Printed in the United States of America.

1 2 3 4 5 6 7 8 9 0

ISBN 978-1-4548-7002-9

Library of Congress Cataloging-in-Publication Data

Mauet, Thomas A., author.
 Trial evidence / Thomas A. Mauet, Milton O. Riepe Professor of Law and Director of Trial Advocacy, University of Arizona College of Law; Warren D. Wolfson, justice of the Appellate Court of the State of Illinois (retired) and former dean and current Distinguished Visiting Professor, DePaul University College of Law. — Sixth edition.
  pages cm. — (Aspen coursebook series)
 Includes bibliographical references and index.
 ISBN 978-1-4548-7002-9 (alk. paper)
  1. Evidence (Law) — United States. I. Wolfson, Warren D., author. II. Title.

KF8935.M28 2016
347.73'6 — dc23
                                                            2015036844

About Wolters Kluwer Legal & Regulatory Solutions U.S.

Wolters Kluwer Legal & Regulatory Solutions U.S. delivers expert content and solutions in the areas of law, corporate compliance, health compliance, reimbursement, and legal education. Its practical solutions help customers successfully navigate the demands of a changing environment to drive their daily activities, enhance decision quality and inspire confident outcomes.

Serving customers worldwide, its legal and regulatory solutions portfolio includes products under the Aspen Publishers, CCH Incorporated, Kluwer Law International, ftwilliam.com and MediRegs names. They are regarded as exceptional and trusted resources for general legal and practice-specific knowledge, compliance and risk management, dynamic workflow solutions, and expert commentary.

SUMMARY OF CONTENTS

CONTENTS

PREFACE

Why *Trial Evidence*? The present legal landscape has numerous evidence hornbooks and treatises, many of which are authoritative and longstanding. What are the gaps in the existing literature that this book seeks to fill?

This book is different from existing ones in several ways. First, it reflects the way judges and trial lawyers in the real world of trials think, or should think, about evidence, using the "three Rs"—relevant, reliable, and right—as its analytical framework. Second, it is structured around the sequential components of a trial—beginning with opening statements and ending with closing arguments—rather than the numerical structure of the Federal Rules of Evidence. Third, it allocates space according to how important the topic is to judges and trial lawyers in the real world of trials, rather than according to the interest level of academicians. For example, party admissions and business records are important topics to trial lawyers, judicial notice and presumptions less so, and the book reflects these realities. Fourth, and most important, the book bridges the gap between evidence as an academic subject in the classroom and evidence as a functional tool in the courtroom. It shows where the evidence rules are commonly used in the real world of trials and how the effective trial lawyer uses them to persuade the judge deciding evidentiary issues.

This book does not claim to do some things. It does not approach evidence from a historical development, social policy, or comparative law perspective. It is neither a critical analysis of the existing rules nor a critique of interpretative case law. It accepts the present evidence rules, the ones lawyers and judges deal with on a daily basis, and analyzes them functionally. It shows how those rules apply in the daily life of the courtroom and how a lawyer can and should use the law as a functional tool to persuade the judge making the evidentiary rulings.

We have not attempted to duplicate the research done by the leading treatises. Instead, we rely on them. The book is principally footnoted to McCormick on Evidence, Weinstein's Federal Evidence, Wigmore on Evidence, and Evidence by Mueller and Kirkpatrick. The citations to these treatises will be much more useful than individual case citations in researching evidentiary issues that arise.

The chapters in the book have law and practice sections. The law sections contain functional overviews of the Federal Rules of Evidence, footnoted to the major treatises. We have relied on these and other treatises as well as the Advisory Committee's Notes. The practice sections contain realistic examples, in commonly recurring fact settings, of how particular rules are used before and during trials, how lawyers should (and sometimes fail to) make proper evidentiary objections, and how judges make rulings. These examples are based on actual federal and state cases. The examples get into the mind of the judge by noting the judge's thoughts, concerns, and reasoning when ruling on objections. We believe this approach is what inexperienced trial lawyers need to learn when bridging the gap between evidence rules as academic subjects and evidence rules as courtroom tools.

Why us? Each of us has been a trial lawyer, professor, and judge. Collectively we have over 25 years of experience as trial lawyers, over 50 years as professors teaching and writing about evidence and trial advocacy, and over 30 years as civil and criminal trial judges. During these years, we have noted a disturbing, recurring fact: Many lawyers, while "knowing" evidence rules, are less capable of using those rules as functional tools to persuade trial judges to rule in their favor. Since we have lived in both the world of academe and the world of trials, we hope that our collective experiences will be useful to those who will, and those who do, use the Federal Rules of Evidence or their state counterparts on a regular basis in the courtroom.

Throughout the book, we have used masculine pronouns to refer to the judges and lawyers. We did this for the sake of simplicity and consistency, and for no other reason.

A book is always the result of more than the efforts of its authors. Our spouses, Gloria Torres Mauet and Hon. Lauretta Higgins Wolfson (retired), have been patient supporters of this effort from its inception. They are both trial lawyers, and their thoughtful suggestions have influenced the book in numerous ways. To our students and staff who have worked with us, we say thanks.

The changes to this sixth edition are principally four-fold. First, we have revised and expanded Sec. 7.1 and other sections dealing with the Sixth Amendment Confrontation Clause, including the Supreme Court's most recent decision in *Ohio v. Clark*, decided in June 2015. Second, we have revised Sec. 10.11 covering electronic communications evidence. In particular, the issue of authentication has become central in determining the admissibility of electronic communications, and the section expands its analysis of this issue. Third, amendments to Rules 801(d)(1)(B) and 803(6)-(8) of the Federal Rules of Evidence became law on December 1, 2014. Rule 801(d)(1)(B)(ii) expands the use of a witness's prior consistent statements "to rehabilitate the declarant's credibility as a witness when attacked on another ground." Rule 803(6)-(8) now make clear that the opponent to the admissibility of business and public records has the burden of showing that the "source of information or the method or circumstances of preparation indicate a lack of trustworthiness." Finally, the text incorporates all Supreme Court decisions through June 2015 affecting evidence rules.

We hope you will find the additions to this sixth edition valuable.

Thomas A. Mauet
Tucson, Arizona

Warren D. Wolfson
Chicago, Illinois

CITATIONS

For ease in citing, the text uses the following abbreviated citations:

McCormick
McCormick on Evidence, Kenneth S. Broun, General Editor (7th ed., Practitioner Treatise Series, 2013)

Mueller & Kirkpatrick
Evidence, Christopher B. Mueller & Laird C. Kirkpatrick (5th ed. 2012)

Weinstein
Weinstein's Federal Evidence, Joseph M. McLaughlin, Editorial Consultant (2d ed. 1997)

Wigmore
Wigmore on Evidence, John Henry Wigmore (Tillers rev. 1983)

TRIAL EVIDENCE

I

AN ADVOCACY APPROACH TO TRIAL EVIDENCE

§1.1.   Introduction

There is something about the way evidentiary rules are learned that works against effective persuasion, the process at trial that finds, using Wigmore's description, "each partisan seeking to move the mind of the tribunal."

In trial advocacy courses, students sit quietly while evidentiary principles are mangled or ignored. Proponents and opponents are at a loss when called on to support their positions.

In actual trials, things are somewhat better, but many lawyers lack the skills needed to obtain favorable rulings for the right reasons. Trial lawyers and judges are required to hear, listen, and analyze quickly. They must guard against being trapped in neat and tidy intellectual compartments, where numbers are substituted for thought and labels obliterate meaningful analysis.

Evidentiary battles are won or lost on the trial court floor. Appellate reversal on purely evidentiary grounds happens, but not very often.[1] Federal Rule of Evidence (FRE) 103 establishes a formidable roadblock to a successful claim of evidentiary error. First, there has to be an erroneous ruling. Second, this has to be brought to the trial judge's attention in an appropriate way, by specific and timely objection or offer of proof. Third, even if the first two hurdles are cleared, the error has to affect a "substantial right of the party," a term of art that is not defined in the Federal Rules of Evidence. Perhaps the most formidable obstacle to an appellate reversal on an evidentiary point is the broad discretion given trial judges by the reviewing courts. In most cases, that discretion is granted great deference by appellate judges.

The challenge for the trial lawyer, then, is to present a case that will "move the mind" of the trial judge. To do that, the advocate must understand the broad

---

1. See M.A. Berger, When, If Ever, Does Evidentiary Error Constitute Reversible Error?, 25 Loy. L.A. L. Rev. 893 (1992), where the author found 30 reversals based on evidentiary error in the federal district courts during 1990 — 17 in civil cases, 13 in criminal cases — from a total of more than 10,000 cases tried.

sweep of the Federal Rules of Evidence. The Rules bring real life, with its strengths and weaknesses, into a courtroom, to be presented, in most cases, to an untrained audience. The audience will create its own version of the story of the case, reflecting each member's life experiences and intelligence.

The law of evidence, then, controls the way rational, decent people conduct a fair and just fact-finding process in an adversary system. The Rules demand that the fact resolver be given reliable evidence that matters, that aids in resolving the dispute, but does not violate constitutional guarantees or desirable social policy or unfairly harm the rights of the litigants.

§1.2.   The three "Rs"

Our goal in this book is to translate the spirit of the Federal Rules of Evidence, or, for that matter, any body of evidence rules, into a workable and effective methodology for trial lawyers, one that correctly encompasses evidentiary rules and policy.

Our approach can best be summarized in terms of relevance, reliability, and rightness — in short, three "Rs." Alliteration alone does not justify the designation, although it should act as an aid to memory. In fact, most evidentiary problems can be quickly and effectively analyzed by a sequential posing of three questions:

1. Is the evidence *relevant* for the offered purpose? If not, the inquiry ends. If the answer is yes,
2. Is the evidence *reliable* for the offered purpose? If not, even though relevant it should not be admitted. If yes,
3. Is it *right* to allow the fact resolver to receive the evidence for the offered purpose? That is, even if the evidence is relevant and reliable, there may be good reasons to keep it out. These include constitutional strictures, matters of social policy, and considerations of unfair prejudice and courtroom efficiency.

Each of the "R" questions must, of course, be fleshed out.

1.   Relevance

Meaningful analysis of the relevance question requires everyone to have a clear idea of the purpose of the offered evidence. Why does the proponent want the fact resolver to hear or see the evidence? No intelligible position can be taken without that understanding. Once an objection is made, opponents cannot resist and judges cannot rule unless they know why the evidence is being offered. One proposing the evidence should be required to bear the burden of explaining its purpose.

Once the purpose of the offered evidence is defined, the opponent can fashion a response, and the judge can rule. If the offered evidence has "any tendency to make a fact more or less probable than it would be without the evidence; and the fact is of consequence to the action," it is relevant within the meaning of FRE 401.

In effect, the evidence must pass two tests in order to be relevant. First, it must be directed to some fact that is important to the issues in the case. That inquiry is really one of substantive law, driven by the pleadings. Second, the evidence must tend to make the existence of that fact more or less probable. That is a purely evidentiary determination, tested in the light of logic, experience, and the ways of human behavior.

If the evidence is relevant, it is admissible *unless* there is some specific reason to keep it out. FRE 402 sets out those reasons — the Constitution of the United States, an act of Congress, other Federal Rules of Evidence, and other rules prescribed by the Supreme Court pursuant to statutory authority. The "unless" provision defines the playing field for most evidentiary disputes. It brings us to the second "R."

2. Reliability

Relevancy, standing alone, is not enough. Evidence should not be admitted unless it is also reliable. There is general agreement that fact resolvers should not base decisions on unreliable evidence. The stakes are too high. Basic fairness is at risk. While steadfast consistency and, certainly, perfection are not attainable in trials, standards of reliability create a way of resolving disputes that has some measure of predictability, order, and rectitude.

The Federal Rules of Evidence are replete with injunctions against unreliability. For example, the Rules include witness competency rules (601-604, 606); opinion testimony rules (701-705); hearsay rules (801-807); authentication and identification rules (901-902); rules concerning the contents of writings, recordings, and photographs (1001-1008); and rules regulating witness questioning (611).

This second "R," reliability, must be analyzed in light of the relevant purpose of the evidence. Thus, the first two questions are entwined. Relevant evidence should not be admitted if the witness offering it does not speak from personal knowledge of the matter, if the expert bases an opinion on unreliable data, if important testimony is elicited by leading questions on direct examination, or if the offered evidence cannot survive challenge by the hearsay rules. That kind of evidence is not reliable, no matter how relevant, and should be excluded.

Most of the specific exceptions to exclusion contained in the hearsay rules (803-804) are based on notions of reliability grounded in law, experience, and logic. They are, the cases say, "firmly rooted." When they are not firmly rooted, hearsay exceptions must contain circumstantial guarantees of trustworthiness in order to achieve evidentiary reliability (807).

3. Rightness

Notions of relevance and reliability are basic to a fair trial. But the inquiry cannot stop here. Evidence might be relevant and reliable for its offered purpose, but one more vital question must be answered: Is it right to admit the evidence?

The Federal Rules of Evidence reflect a policy that prefers admission of relevant and reliable evidence, subject to specific rules of exclusion. The Rules are designed to limit the trial judge's discretion in certain areas. In practice, reviewing courts have tended to give deference to a trial judge's evidentiary rulings. After all, the trial judge was on the scene. The judge could hear, see, and feel the impact of the offered evidence. Appellate courts, by contrast, deal with a cold record.

Discretion ends and error begins when a trial judge excludes competent evidence without a good reason. The evidentiary policy of inclusion does not stand unchallenged. The Federal Rules of Evidence establish two kinds of barriers to the admissibility of relevant and reliable evidence. These barriers represent important statements about the ways cases should be decided. They are the essence of the third "R."

The first barrier consists of rules that reflect social and political judgments. Certain offered evidence might be relevant and reliable, but we run the risk of giving up something important when we allow the fact resolver to hear or see it. We do not want to pay that price. So it is that, in most cases, the Rules bar evidence of subsequent remedial measures (407), compromise and offers to compromise (408), payment of medical expenses (409), pleas or plea discussions (410), liability insurance (411), a rape victim's past behavior (412), and certain privileged communications (501). This first barrier includes violations of guarantees contained in the Fourth, Fifth, and Sixth Amendments to the United States Constitution and parallel provisions of state constitutions.

The second barrier to the admissibility of relevant and reliable evidence, contained in FRE 403, reflects concerns about the ways trials are conducted and the ways juries should and should not reach decisions. Here, the trial judge has virtually unbridled discretion. Reversals are rare when the trial judge conducts the weighing process authorized by FRE 403. This balancing of probative value against likely harm is a way of protecting the integrity of the fact-finding process. We are committed to the principle that juries must not decide cases for the wrong reasons. Evidence must not be misused by the jury, and jurors should not be side-tracked by feelings of anger, outrage, or sympathy.

FRE 403 addresses two areas of concern. One has to do with the integrity of decision making. Relevant evidence may be excluded "if its probative value is substantially outweighed by a danger of unfair prejudice, confusing the issues, or misleading the jury."

The other implicates judicial efficiency. Relevant evidence may be excluded "if its probative value is substantially outweighed by a danger of undue delay, wasting time, or needlessly presenting cumulative evidence." Courtroom efficiency affects the court's opportunity to hear other cases and is important to the judicial system's fairness to other litigants.

The first part of the rule uses key words. Probative value must be "substantially" outweighed. Prejudice must be "unfair." The judge must think, in terms of "danger." The second part of the rule refers to "considerations" aimed at saving time and preventing boredom.

Once the weighing process is begun, there is no simple right or wrong answer. The judge is open to persuasion. Everyone involved in the decision will visualize a balancing scale. That scale, however, is not evenly balanced. It starts out tipped toward admissibility because there is presumptive admissibility of probative evidence under FRE 403. The opponent of the evidence bears the burden of tipping the scale toward exclusion.

On the admissibility side of the scale the judge will place the need for the evidence and the knowledge that it has slight or substantial relevance. If there are other ways the proponent can prove the fact in issue, or if the offered evidence barely passed the relevancy test, that side of the scale will tilt only slightly. When considering probative value, the judge should not use judicial notions of believability. Probative value is judged without assessing the credibility of the evidence. The jury will give it appropriate weight. A fine line, but one that should be drawn.

The exclusion side of the scale reflects a recognition of the nature of the people in the jury box. They are fallible and untrained for their tasks. Some evidence can overly persuade or be misused; other evidence can be repetitive and cumulative. Jurors can be frightened or angered. Our system of law places a premium on the ways important decisions are reached. The integrity of those ways has a great deal to do with the soundness of the decision.

Before any final reading of the scale is made, the judge considers whether a curative or limiting instruction can diminish unfair prejudice, potential confusion, or jury misdirection. Rule 105 recognizes the judge's power to instruct a jury on the limited purpose of evidence. Whether such an instruction effectively protects a litigant's rights depends on the extent of the "danger" posed by admission of the evidence.[2] Our experience tells us that Rule 403 arguments meet with greater success in the trial courts than on appeal.

§1.3.   Using the three "Rs"

How should lawyers and judges use evidence law to argue and decide evidentiary disputes? Using the three "Rs" method is the critical analytical approach. Naming the right rule of evidence at the right time is important. Citing the applicable case law is effective, since trial judges do not enjoy being reversed. In the quest for the right ruling, the lawyer's most effective argument is made in human terms and is directed at the trial judge's willingness to act with a sense of fairness.

Most of the evidentiary disputes that occur during trials cannot be compartmentalized. A mechanical approach to evidentiary principles is a disservice to the carefully constructed fabric of the Federal Rules. The point is best made by examples.

Example 1:

The prosecution seeks to offer police testimony that an anonymous caller reported seeing a man, 5'2" tall and weighing about 300 pounds, rob a woman at gunpoint 10 minutes earlier at the corner of Elm and Maple. The officer who received this information will say he went to that area. One block away from the corner he saw the defendant, who appeared to be 5'2" in height and weigh about 300 pounds.

2. See *Bruton v. United States*, 391 U.S. 123 (1968).

The defendant was arrested and brought to Elm and Maple, where he was identified by the holdup victim.

1. Is the evidence relevant for the offered purpose? The prosecution says the evidence will help the jury understand why the police arrested a previously unidentified man and showed him to the victim. Slight relevance, perhaps, but that is enough in many courts.
2. Is the evidence reliable for the offered purpose? The objection is hearsay, with no semblance of reliability. The prosecution responds that hearsay is not involved. The caller's words are offered not to prove the truth of the matter asserted, but to show why the police officer did what he did. It is the officer's credibility that matters. He is on the stand to be seen and cross-examined. Because the words are not hearsay, the second "R" is satisfied.
3. Is it right to allow a jury to receive the evidence for the offered purpose? Here, the weighing process established by Rule 403 takes place. Is the probative value of the testimony significant? Unless the defendant claims he is the victim of police persecution, the value is minimal. The prosecution does not really need this evidence. On the other hand, the danger is great that the jury will use the caller's words as direct evidence that the defendant in fact committed the holdup. The evidence would be misused, taken for its truth. The risk of unfair prejudice substantially outweighs the probative value of the evidence.

    Well, argues the prosecution, a limiting instruction would solve the problem. Tell the jury the evidence is being admitted for a limited purpose. No, counters the defense, you cannot expect a jury to follow that kind of instruction. The issue is drawn.

Example 2:

The plaintiff sues the Acme Corporation. She claims Acme's negligent construction of a natural gas tank caused an explosion in which she was injured. She tries to offer evidence that Acme had in its files letters complaining of four other explosions of its tanks after faulty welds were observed. Each explosion happened during a two-year period before the plaintiff's injury. The letters say someone was killed in each explosion. None of the writers can be found.

1. Is the evidence relevant for the offered purpose? The plaintiff has the burden of establishing a relevant purpose. She claims that the letters reflect substantially similar circumstances, establishing notice to Acme and the cause of the plaintiff's injuries. The judge first looks to the substantive law. Notice and causation are issues in the case. They are matters of consequence. The letters, as a matter of evidence law, have a tendency to make probable the existence of notice to Acme and faulty welds as a cause of the plaintiff's injuries.
2. Is the evidence reliable for the offered purpose? The defendant contends the letters are hearsay. They are out-of-court assertions offered

for their truth, not subject to cross-examination, not under oath, not in the presence of the jury. The plaintiff answers that the letters are not hearsay at all. They are offered to show that their contents were received and seen by Acme.

One of the plaintiff's stated purposes cannot meet the reliability test. Causation evidence depends on the credibility of the out-of-court declarant. Because the words are offered for their truth, they cannot survive the hearsay objection.

Notice is different. The fact that the words were seen by Acme is all that is required. They are not hearsay. The letters are reliable to show that Acme had notice its tanks could contain faulty welds.

3. Is it right to allow a jury to receive the evidence for the offered purpose? Again, the balancing test appears. The probative value is substantial. The plaintiff's case requires notice evidence, and there is no other way to prove it. The admissibility side of the scale presses downward.

The defendant contends unfair prejudice substantially outweighs whatever probative value the letters have. The jury will misuse the evidence. It will take the letters as proof of faulty welds. Hearing about fatalities in other explosions will inflame the jury, causing it to base a verdict on emotion, not fact. No limiting instruction can cure the unfair prejudice.

The judge has choices. The evidence can be barred. If admitted, the evidence can be limited to its proper purpose by careful instruction. Because there is no need for the jury to hear about the fatalities, information about people being killed in the explosions can be excised from the letters. This is the kind of discretion and trial control authorized by the Federal Rules of Evidence.

§1.4. *Conclusion*

The trial, as envisioned by the Federal Rules of Evidence, becomes a statement of trust. Juries are trusted to reach fair and rational decisions for the right reasons, adhering to instruction from the judge, undeterred by emotion. The lawyers are trusted to know and expound rules of evidence effectively and responsibly, using the best tools of advocacy to persuade the judge that legal and moral rightness supports their position. Finally, the judge is trusted to apply rules of evidence fairly and sensibly, following precedent where applicable, applying the law's broad grant of discretion with reason and humanity.

This book approaches the law of evidence, and its use in the trial courtroom, in the same way. It develops the analytical approach lawyers and judges need in order to understand, and intelligently apply, evidence law in the courtroom. Finally, it focuses on how lawyers should frame evidentiary arguments in court to persuade the trial judge to rule favorably on evidentiary disputes that commonly arise before and during trials.

II

THE ROLE AND POWER OF THE TRIAL JUDGE: EVIDENTIARY OBJECTIONS BEFORE AND DURING TRIAL

§2.1.   Introduction

Our jury trial system is based on a division of labor, with all the participants — judge, lawyers, and jury — carrying out their roles. The judge determines the admissibility of evidence, the lawyers present the evidence, and the jury determines what the facts are. Put another way, the judge decides what evidence the lawyers can present to the jury; the jury decides what weight, if any, that evidence should receive.

The Federal Rules of Evidence represent a broad and virtually limitless grant of power to trial judges to control the admission of evidence. No single rule describes that power. It runs throughout the Rules. Whether the judge rules on admissibility issues from scholarly insight, disciplined reflex, or some notion of fairness, he will be firmly supported by the sum total of the Rules and by appellate disinclination to search for evidentiary errors.

Some judges exert their power more than others. Some manage the course of the litigation more than others. The trial often will be shaped by the way the judge exercises power granted by the Rules. Of course, the ultimate power, that of weighing evidence and making a decision based on that evidence, belongs to the jury. The judge admits; the jury weighs. Theoretically the judge should not be concerned with the persuasiveness of the offered evidence, but reality often intrudes on theory. Judges should not, but often do, weigh the "worth" of proposed evidence.

A lawyer's knowledge of law has to contain, to a large extent, an understanding of judicial behavior. That is, a lawyer must make a fair estimate of what a judge is likely to do in a given situation. Only then can the lawyer who is going to present an argument marshal his theory and authorities. Only then can the lawyer decide what and how many words he will use.

The Federal Rules of Evidence grant the trial judge vast power in the conduct of a trial, but not without purpose. There is a point to it: the rational weighing of relevant and reliable evidence by an impartial decision maker so that morally and factually correct results will be achieved.

§2.2.   Sources of judicial power[1]

The sources of judicial power are principally contained in three of the Federal Rules of Evidence: 102, 611, and 614.

1.   FRE 102

Rule 102.   Purpose

> These rules should be construed so as to administer every proceeding fairly, eliminate unjustifiable expense and delay, and promote the development of evidence law, to the end of ascertaining the truth and securing a just determination.

FRE 102, the "Purpose" rule, is rarely cited and much ignored by lawyers. The rule is a declaration of intent. FRE 102 encourages the judge to construe the Rules in a way that invites admissibility and a firm hand over the proceedings. How else do the courts "administer every proceeding fairly, eliminate unjustifiable expense and delay, and promote the development of evidence law, to the end of ascertaining the truth and securing a just determination?"

No longer do judges sit as silent referees, garbed in black, waiting for the contestants to cry "foul." More judges are "managing" the trial, especially where the issues are complex and the trial lengthy.

2.   FRE 611

Rule 611.   Mode and Order of Examining Witnesses and Presenting Evidence

> **(a) Control by the Court; Purposes.**   The court should exercise reasonable control over the mode and order of examining witnesses and presenting evidence so as to:
>   (1) make those procedures effective for determining the truth;
>   (2) avoid wasting time; and
>   (3) protect witnesses from harassment or undue embarrassment.
> **(b) Scope of Cross-Examination.**   Cross-examination should not go beyond the subject matter of the direct examination and matters affecting

---

1. Wigmore §§487, 497, 587, 784, 861; McCormick §§8, 16-17, 25, 37, 44, 60, 324; Weinstein §§102[01]-[04], 611[01]-[07], 614[01]-[06].

the witness's credibility. The court may allow inquiry into additional matters as if on direct examination.

(c) Leading Questions.   Leading questions should not be used on direct examination except as necessary to develop the witness's testimony. Ordinarily, the court should allow leading questions:

(1) on cross-examination; and

(2) when a party calls a hostile witness, an adverse party, or a witness identified with an adverse party.

FRE 611(a) is aptly titled: "Control by the court." It says that the court "should," not "may," "exercise reasonable control over the mode and order of examining witnesses and presenting evidence." The discretion granted by FRE 611(a) is broad. Judges can allow witnesses to testify out of turn. They can limit the number of expert witnesses a party will present and the time those witnesses will take on the stand, even on cross-examination. They can require the direct testimony of expert witnesses to be presented in the narrative, with time limits.

Of course, that discretion can be abused. It is unreasonable to deprive a party of critical evidence in the name of expediency. FRE 403 provides that considerations of undue delay, waste of time, and needless presentation of cumulative evidence may exclude relevant evidence only when those considerations "substantially outweigh" the probative value of the evidence. Time limits for the presentation of evidence should not be arbitrary; but imposition of limits, although open to a charge of unreasonableness, rarely will result in reversible error.

There are constitutional limitations to the exercise of FRE 611 powers. For example, a criminal defendant's Sixth Amendment right to confront witnesses is violated when minor victims are allowed to testify behind a large screen, preventing the defendant from seeing the victim. Refusal to allow cross-examination of an alleged rape victim on a motive to fabricate the accusation is an error of constitutional dimension. *Olden v. Kentucky*, 488 U.S. 227 (1988).

FRE 611(b) governs the scope of cross-examination, and FRE 611(c) refers to the proper use of leading questions. Nowhere else are specific form objections referred to in the Rules. Presumably those objections—argumentative, asked and answered, narrative, unresponsive, compound, confusing, and so on—are untouched by the Rules. In all matters of evidence, prepared trial lawyers assume their opponents will object to everything and will have at hand the right response—by rule, case, and reason.

Judges differ on how objections and responses to those objections should be made. Some want the objector to state simple grounds—"That is irrelevant," "The question calls for hearsay," "There is no foundation of personal knowledge for an answer to that question." Others want only an announcement of the rule being offended. Some want both. Or neither.

The proponent usually may respond with a brief statement of purpose, but must be cautious about going too far. Almost all judges rightly discourage speeches about the point in the presence of the jury. A lawyer who has more to say for or against the objection should ask to do it out of the presence of the jury. Some call this a "sidebar conference."

Judges have used FRE 611 to overcome a literal interpretation of other rules — for example, FRE 613(b). When impeaching a non-party witness with a prior inconsistent statement, a lawyer no longer is required to question the witness about the prior statement unless the statement concerns a collateral matter. He simply offers it in his case as extrinsic evidence. The only requirement is that the witness be afforded an opportunity to explain or deny the prior statement. That is, the witness is available to be recalled by the party who put him on the stand. Some judges are uncomfortable with eliminating the traditional confrontation requirement. Applying FRE 611(a), and disregarding the clear language of FRE 613(b), they require that the witness be given a chance to explain or deny the prior inconsistent statement before extrinsic evidence is offered. The wise lawyer will learn something about the judge's predilections before the trial begins.

3.   FRE 614

Rule 614.   Court's Calling or Examining a Witness

(a) Calling.   The court may call a witness on its own or at a party's request. Each party is entitled to cross-examine the witness.

(b) Examining.   The court may examine a witness regardless of who calls the witness.

(c) Objections.   A party may object to the court's calling or examining a witness either at that time or at the next opportunity when the jury is not present.

Another broad grant of power to the trial judge — the power to call and question witnesses — is contained in FRE 614. The rule applies to civil and criminal cases. It does not limit the kind of witness the judge may call or question, although the court appointment of expert witnesses is covered by FRE 706. Nor does the rule offer any guidance for the occasion that would trigger the calling or questioning of witnesses by the judge. For example, a judge might call a witness that no party wants to call, for fear of taint by association or because of uncertainty about what the witness will say. Or the judge might feel the parties are depriving the jury of useful information by refraining from calling a witness.

The only restraint on the judge is that the questioning must be conducted in an impartial manner. The judge should not show hostility to either side, nor should he send a clear message to the jury that he does not believe a party or a key witness. He must avoid the appearance of advocacy. Absent a showing of partiality, the judge is free to take an active role in the calling and questioning of witnesses. He can dispel confusion caused by ambiguous testimony or the absence of adequate explanation. He can elicit new information even though a party has omitted the testimony as part of trial strategy.

The rule does not authorize the judge to direct lawyers to call witnesses or to ask certain questions of witnesses already called. However, appellate courts have upheld that exercise of power as inherent.

Questioning by the judge can be extensive, and the questions numerous, so long as impartiality is maintained. It does not ordinarily matter that the questions emphasized key points in a party's case, rehabilitated a witness, explained seeming contradictions developed by the lawyers, or helped or hurt one side. However, the judge abandons neutrality when he proves an essential, but omitted, element of a civil or criminal case.

Reviewing courts often decline to inquire into judicial overreaching when the judge has instructed jurors to treat his questions and the witnesses he has called in the same way they treat the lawyers' questions and witnesses and to decide the case on all the evidence presented, no matter how it was elicited. Reviewing courts will examine judicial intervention more closely in criminal cases.

All parties are entitled to cross-examine witnesses called by the judge. Whether a lawyer will exercise that right depends on the facts of the case and the need for discretion.

The rule recognizes a lawyer's reasonable reluctance to object immediately when a judge calls a witness or asks a question. FRE 614(c) gives the lawyer the option of objecting "at that time or at the next opportunity when the jury is not present." The requirement is that the objection be made at the first opportunity when the jury is not present. But the lawyer must object or face waiver of any error. This is contrary to the general rule that contemporaneous objection is required to avoid a waiver.

§2.3. *Sources of judicial procedure*[2]

Rule 103. Rulings on Evidence

(a) **Preserving a Claim of Error.**   A party may claim error in a ruling to admit or exclude evidence only if the error affects a substantial right of the party and:

(1) if the ruling admits evidence, a party, on the record:

(A) timely objects or moves to strike; and

(B) states the specific ground, unless it was apparent from the context; or

(2) if the ruling excludes evidence, a party informs the court of its substance by an offer of proof, unless the substance was apparent from the context.

(b) **Not Needing to Renew an Objection or Offer of Proof.**   Once the court rules definitively on the record — either before or at trial — a party need not renew an objection or offer of proof to preserve a claim of error for appeal.

(c) **Court's Statement About the Ruling; Directing an Offer of Proof.** The court may make any statement about the character or form of the evidence, the objection made, and the ruling. The court may direct that an offer of proof be made in question-and-answer form.

---

2. Weinstein §§103[01]-[10], 104[01]-[14], 105[01]-[07]; McCormick §§15, 51-53, 59.

(d) Preventing the Jury from Hearing Inadmissible Evidence.   To the extent practicable, the court must conduct a jury trial so that inadmissible evidence is not suggested to the jury by any means.

(e) Taking Notice of Plain Error.   A court may take notice of a plain error affecting a substantial right, even if the claim of error was not properly preserved.

Rule 104.   Preliminary Questions

(a) In General.   The court must decide any preliminary question about whether a witness is qualified, a privilege exists, or evidence is admissible. In so deciding, the court is not bound by evidence rules, except those on privilege.

(b) Relevance That Depends on a Fact.   When the relevance of evidence depends on whether a fact exists, proof must be introduced sufficient to support a finding that the fact does exist. The court may admit the proposed evidence on the condition that the proof be introduced later.

(c) Conducting a Hearing So That the Jury Cannot Hear It.   The court must conduct any hearing on a preliminary question so that the jury cannot hear it if:

   (1) the hearing involves the admissibility of a confession;

   (2) a defendant in a criminal case is a witness and so requests; or

   (3) justice so requires.

(d) Cross-Examining a Defendant in a Criminal Case.   By testifying on a preliminary question, a defendant in a criminal case does not become subject to cross-examination on other issues in the case.

(e) Evidence Relevant to Weight and Credibility.   This rule does not limit a party's right to introduce before the jury evidence that is relevant to the weight or credibility of other evidence.

Rule 105.   Limiting Evidence That Is Not Admissible Against Other Parties or for Other Purposes

If the court admits evidence that is admissible against a party or for a purpose — but not against another party or for another purpose — the court, on timely request, must restrict the evidence to its proper scope and instruct the jury accordingly.

FRE 103, 104, and 105 map the evidentiary territory for lawyers and judges. Lawyers who ignore the clear words of these rules risk losing important evidence or dealing unnecessarily with harmful evidence. On appeal, they face almost certain defeat.

The goals of these three rules suit the purposes of competent judges and lawyers: trial efficiency, the admission of relevant and reliable evidence, considered rulings, and rational decisions by the trier of fact, uncluttered by lengthy interruptions and admonitions to jurors to disregard that which they have heard or seen.

These rules express a clear preference for resolving evidentiary issues out of the presence of the jury, at a time when the judge may reflect and the lawyers have a reasonable opportunity to present their positions. Thoughtful judgments ordinarily are better than hurried judgments, made under the pressure of time constraints. It is a rare judge who does not appreciate the opportunity to consider before ruling.

1.   FRE 104

FRE 104 draws the line between the functions of the judge and the jury. The judge admits or not; the jury weighs. At times, the line is blurry. FRE 104 is a means of ensuring that the jury receives relevant and reliable evidence that does not run counter to some established public or legal policy. It is a screening process. It aims to avoid the indelicate situation where a judge is required to instruct jurors to disregard words they heard or things they saw.

To minimize these indelicate situations, therefore, FRE 104 assumes lawyers will raise evidentiary issues at the appropriate time, which should be as early in the proceedings as possible. Some do it in the form of a motion in limine, although that term is not found in the Federal Rules of Evidence. A motion in limine can be made at any time before or during trial and in writing or orally, although a written motion is the better practice. The motion can be aimed at keeping something out or letting something in. In civil cases, preliminary questions can be raised pursuant to Rule 16 of the Federal Rules of Civil Procedure.

FRE 104 has two principal sections. Section (a) governs the procedure used to determine the competency of offered evidence; section (b) governs the procedure used to determine the conditional relevance of offered evidence. The dichotomy is important because the two sections differ in their procedures, standards for admissibility, application of evidentiary rules to the determinations involved, and instructions to the jury that may follow the judge's rulings.

FRE 104(a) applies when the admissibility of evidence depends on a preliminary factual finding by the trial judge. This determination is made by the judge before or during the trial. The judge alone determines whether the preliminary facts are sufficient concerning "whether a witness is qualified, a privilege exists, or evidence is admissible."

The issues that are handled under FRE 104(a) involve matters of witness competency, factual foundations for testimony, and authenticity of exhibits. For example, the judge decides whether a witness's testimony is barred by the Dead Man's Act, whether a dying declarant had the belief of impending death required by FRE 804(b)(2), and whether there has been a showing of the non-production of an original document required by FRE 1004.

Under FRE 104(a), the judge must consider evidence on both sides of the question of whether the preliminary facts have been established by a preponderance of the evidence. This means that the opponent has the right to voir dire the foundation witness. In fact, the opponent has the right to offer contrary evidence to demonstrate the inadmissibility of the offered evidence. The judge then makes the final determination as the preliminary fact finder.

How the judge hears the evidence to resolve these issues can cause problems. FRE 104(c) provides: "The court must conduct any hearing on a preliminary question so that the jury cannot hear it if: (1) the hearing involves the admissibility of a confession; (2) a defendant in a criminal case is a witness and so requests it; or (3) justice so requires." This process protects the jury from hearing the foundational evidence, which would become a problem if the judge later ruled the evidence inadmissible. The judge would then be in the awkward position of trying to "unring the bell."

When deciding the issues, the judge is not bound by the rules of evidence, except those with respect to privileges. For example, a judge might be asked to make a preliminary ruling that a statement of an alleged co-conspirator is admissible against a defendant because it was made during the course of and in furtherance of a conspiracy. The judge, according to *Bourjaily v. United States*, 483 U.S. 171 (1987), considers all the circumstances, including the co-conspirator's words, to determine whether the statement is admissible under FRE 801(d)(2)(E). The judge may "consider any evidence whatsoever, bound only by the rules of privilege." Id. at 178.

A judge might be asked to determine whether proposed expert testimony satisfies FRE 401, 402, 403, and 702. Presumably, when searching for scientific reliability, the judge considers affidavits, learned writings, published and unpublished studies, and any other testimony or documents that will be helpful to the determination of admissibility. This "gatekeeper" function of a federal judge received new emphasis with the Supreme Court decision in *Daubert v. Merrell Dow Pharmaceuticals*, 509 U.S. 579 (1993).

The rule does not say how much the judge can rely on inadmissible evidence, but a standard of reasonable reliability along with a need to resort to inadmissible evidence seems to be generally accepted. A judge's use of affidavits to determine factual matters is not a new concept. Rule 43(e) of the Federal Rules of Civil Procedure authorizes judges to use affidavits when deciding motions based on facts not appearing of record.

Very often, especially in matters of authenticity and foundation, the jury will have to hear the admissible evidence that supports the ruling. If that evidence is not offered, the opposing party will have the opportunity to object to the admissibility of the disputed evidence. Unsuccessful preliminary objections always should be renewed when the disputed evidence is offered at trial.

When the judge has made the preliminary determination under FRE 104(a), no specific instruction to the jury is necessary. In this case, the judge, not the jury, makes the finding as to the preliminary fact.

FRE 104(b) applies only to conditional relevancy issues. If relevancy of evidence depends on a condition of fact, the trial judge "may" admit the evidence, but the evidence remains in the case only if there is enough other evidence to support a finding that the condition has been fulfilled. For example, the judge "screens" the evidence to determine if there has been a sufficient showing that the speaker in a telephone call was the defendant. If so, the content of the call is admissible.

Under FRE 104(b), the judge considers and determines only if there is offered evidence sufficient to support a finding that the conditional fact exists. If so, the jury later determines if the conditional fact exists and what weight, if any, to give that fact. Only the proponent has the right to present evidence of the existence of the conditional fact (although the opponent may later present contrary evidence). The judge merely screens, rather than weighs, the evidence of the conditional fact; the jury remains the ultimate fact finder.

Under FRE 104(b), the evidence offered to prove the conditional fact must meet all the evidentiary rules. The jury is then usually instructed that the existence of a conditional fact is for the jury to decide and that it should use or ignore the evidence as it sees fit.

The rule's use of "may admit" language impels some judges to informally pretry the existence of the "condition of fact," even though FRE 104(b) does not authorize it. That is, the judge, at times, might not be satisfied with a lawyer's unsupported promise to "connect it up" or "tie it up." He wants some idea of how that will be done. If the promise turns out to be empty, the judge will be in the position of trying to unring bells, since the disputed evidence will be subject to a motion to strike by the party resisting the evidence. For example, the judge may not admit the contents of a letter constituting notice unless the proponent first presents sufficient evidence that the recipient actually received the letter. The efficacy of instructions to disregard can be dubious at times, although appellate decisions show extreme patience with the practice.

An example of how FRE 104(b) operates at trial is found in *Huddleston v. United States*, 485 U.S. 681 (1988). There, the defendant was on trial for possessing and selling stolen videotapes. The issue was whether he knew the tapes were stolen. To prove knowledge, the prosecution offered evidence that the defendant had sold stolen television sets. The Court held the issue was to be decided under FRE 104(b). No hearing outside the jury's presence was required. That is, the trial judge considers the relevancy of the television evidence by examining all the evidence in the case and deciding whether the jury could reasonably find that the televisions were stolen — the conditional fact — by a preponderance of the evidence. The judge does not weigh credibility or find that the prosecution actually proved the conditional fact. That is the jury's function.

FRE 104(b) does not require any particular order of proof. The judge may allow the disputed evidence — such as Huddleston's sale of television sets — to be heard by the jury before a judicial finding that the condition has been fulfilled — by proof that the sets were stolen. However, if it turns out that the condition has not been satisfied, the opposing party should move to strike the already admitted evidence. In that case, the trial judge must instruct the jury to disregard the evidence.

The fact that judges are not bound by any particular order of proof should not dissuade the opponent of the evidence from urging that the condition of fact evidence be offered before the damaging evidence is heard or seen by the jury. This is the safer procedure to be followed and avoids the "unringing the bell" problem all judges prefer to avoid.

If the judge combines FRE 104(a) with FRE 104(b), he must consider only admissible "condition of fact" matters when deciding whether the jury will hear the disputed evidence. That is because the same evidence must be offered again at trial to support admissibility. The question becomes: Is the promised condition of fact evidence sufficient to support a finding that the condition has been fulfilled? Eventually, if the disputed evidence survives objection, it will be for the jury to determine what weight, if any, to give it.

Under both FRE 104(a) and FRE 104(b), the party offering the disputed evidence has both the burden of going forward and the burden of proof when preliminary questions of admissibility are being decided. The analysis is the same in civil and criminal cases.

The standard of proof for admissibility in civil and criminal cases in any FRE 104 analysis is a preponderance of the evidence — that is, whether the proposition is more probably true than not true. That standard also applies to constitutional issues in criminal cases, such as the admissibility of confessions and evidence alleged to have been seized in violation of the Fourth Amendment.

The party opposing the disputed evidence is not required to surrender to it if it is admitted. FRE 104(e) gives the opposing party the right to offer contrary evidence and, presumably, later challenge the weight and credibility of the evidence during closing argument.

There are times when it is hard to see a clear line between FRE 104(a) and 104(b). For example, when the qualifications of an expert witness are challenged, the judge conducts an FRE 104(a) proceeding. He can consider matters not necessarily admissible in evidence, such as a curriculum vitae, the witness's publications, and affidavits of other witnesses. Still, when the expert is allowed to testify, the proponent of his testimony, to overcome objection, must establish the witness's qualifications in the presence of the jury with admissible evidence.

The same is true for matters concerning the authenticity of documents and tape recordings, the foundations for hearsay exceptions such as the existence of an exciting event, the personal knowledge of a lay witness who offers opinions to the jury, or the agency relationship between a declarant and his purported principal.

FRE 104 expresses a strong preference that preliminary questions of evidence be determined out of the jury's presence. FRE 104(c) requires that a hearing on a preliminary question be conducted so that the jury cannot hear it if "(1) the hearing involves the admissibility of a confession; (2) a defendant in a criminal case is a witness and so requests; or (3) justice so requires." When an accused testifies on preliminary matters, he does not, according to FRE 104(d), "become subject to cross-examination on other issues in the case." (However, in *Simmons v. United States*, 390 U.S. 377 (1968), the Supreme Court held a defendant's testimony in a hearing on a motion to suppress evidence could be used to impeach him when he testified at trial on matters directly related to guilt or innocence.)

Most times, however, the jury will be hearing the same foundation evidence the judge is being asked to hear to decide a preliminary question. Since under FRE 611(a) the judge, at trial, can require the foundation evidence to be presented first, there seems little purpose in hearing it twice, particularly when it appears obvious that the proponent will be able to establish the necessary foundation. On these occasions, judges do not bind themselves to fine distinctions between FRE 104(a) and 104(b). They adopt a procedure that best uses courtroom time. The result is that the judge hears the foundation testimony at the same time the jury hears it. It is only when the judge has a serious concern about the proponent's ability to establish a necessary foundation that he will hear the supporting facts out of the jury's presence. In those instances, the lawyer's promise that "I will tie it up" is not convincing.

2.   FRE 103

Appellate reluctance to find abuse of discretion in evidence rulings places the contest directly on the trial court floor. That is where evidence disputes are won or lost. The proponent must offer and the opponent must resist evidence at the right time, for the right reason, in the right way. That is the clear meaning of FRE 103. The failure to adhere to the requirements of FRE 103 invites probable failure in the trial court and almost certain defeat on appeal. Without an understanding of the operation of FRE 103, a trial lawyer will step into a morass of waiver.

FRE 103(a) is a full disclosure rule. Lawyers bear the responsibility of telling the judge and each other why they are offering or objecting to evidence, arguments, and instructions. The judge has the opportunity to reach a considered judgment or to correct a mistake hastily made, and the lawyers may be able to obviate any legal impediment raised to matters they present.

On appeal, the right objection at the right time in the trial court will at least draw the reviewing court's attention to the claimed error, but it will not be considered unless a substantial right is affected by a ruling that admits or excludes evidence. Whether a "substantial right" is affected by an error will depend on the facts and circumstances of the case. Reviewing courts, using the cold record, will make a visceral determination of whether it was highly probable the error had an impact on the outcome of the case. If the court decides it did not, the error will be deemed harmless. The Supreme Court posed the question in *Kotteakos v. United States*, 328 U.S. 750, 765 (1946): Can you say with fair assurance that the judgment was not substantially swayed by the error? If you cannot, you must conclude substantial rights were affected.

FRE 103 does not suggest that the trial judge think in terms of "substantial rights" when ruling on objections. That is an appellate standard. Trial judges, however, know where the "substantial right" territory is. For example, they will show more concern for character trait and other acts evidence than they will for foundations for business records or the original writing rule.

3.   FRE 105

FRE 105 relies on the presumption that jurors will follow instructions to consider evidence for one purpose, but not another, or to consider it as to one party, but not another. It is a rare trial that does not contain some kind of limiting instruction. For example, jurors are told to consider the words not for their truth, but as an explanation for why the listener knew or did something after hearing the words. Admissions of a party are allowed, but jurors are told not to consider them against a co-party. Prior convictions admitted under FRE 609 are limited to the issue of the defendant's credibility. Prior acts under FRE 404(b) are admitted only for their proper limited purpose — to prove intent, for example — but not to prove guilt of the offense charged. The list is long.

Reviewing courts are unwilling to assume jurors will ignore proper instructions, representing, in some cases, a triumph of hope over experience (as well as a substantial body of jury research). This is an area where trial judges have especially broad discretion.

A rare exception to this presumption of juror obedience came in *Bruton v. United States*, 391 U.S. 123 (1968), where the Supreme Court held that a non-testifying co-defendant's confession that implicated the defendant violated the Sixth Amendment's Confrontation Clause despite an earnest attempt to limit use of the confession to the confessor. Nineteen years later, in *Richardson v. Marsh*, 481 U.S. 200 (1987), the Supreme Court held that a co-defendant's confession, edited to omit the defendant's name, was admissible on the giving of a limiting instruction even though the confession only inferred the defendant's guilt.

The difference between the two cases is that the confession in *Bruton* was powerfully incriminating of the defendant and its reliability was suspect, while the confession in *Richardson* was not nearly as powerful. These and other cases establish the kind of sequential analysis trial judges often engage in, consciously or unconsciously, when considering whether to admit evidence for a limited purpose.

Judges consider:

1. Is the evidence relevant for the offered purpose? The party offering the evidence selects the theory of admissibility. Trial judges tend to consider the persuasiveness of the offered evidence for the limited purpose. They understand that limiting instructions, because they appear to run counter to human experience, might not be worth the trouble if the proposed point is not clearly made.
2. Is the evidence reliable for the offered purpose beyond the minimum probability level that FRE 401 requires? If reliability is questionable, judges are more likely to reject the evidence, especially if there is a risk of harm from improper use of the evidence.
3. Is there a risk that the jury will misuse the evidence? That is, is this the kind of evidence that might rebut the presumption of juror obedience? Can the jury accept the proposition that the defendant's prior bank robbery conviction applies only to the question of his credibility in this robbery case?

FRE 403 requires that the probative value of the limited evidence be weighed against the danger of creating unfair prejudice, confusing the issues, and misleading the jury. Might the jury use the evidence for the wrong reason despite the limiting instruction? The degree of potential wrongful devastation has to be placed on the scales. In this weighing process, the judge considers whether the proposed evidence really is needed. Perhaps there is some other way to make the point, not triggering the dangers caused by this evidence.

A showing that the trial judge engaged in this weighing process before giving a limiting instruction most likely will foreclose any further examination of the issue on appeal. The proponent of the evidence must be ready to state its limited purpose in the face of an objection.

Whether a limiting instruction will be given is ordinarily a decision that rests with the opponent of the evidence. For strategic reasons, a lawyer can choose not to ask for a limiting instruction, fearing that it will emphasize the damaging evidence. If he does not ask for the instruction, the issue will be waived on appeal absent a finding of plain error. Declining to ask for a limiting instruction does not waive an objection to the evidence.

Judges, at times, will give a limiting instruction without being asked. That happens when sensitive matters, such as FRE 609 prior convictions and FRE 404(b) other acts, arise. Giving an uninvited instruction and giving an instruction over objection are not considered error on appeal.

FRE 105 is silent on when the request for a limiting instruction must be made. The cases require that the request be timely and specific. It should come as soon as the occasion arises, and it should propose the specific instruction desired. Late requests have resulted in waiver on appeal. If the request for a limiting instruction is timely and specific, the trial judge is required to give it. Refusing to give it is error.

The rule does not dictate any particular time for the giving of the instruction. The best time is when the evidence is heard by the jury. It can be, but is not required to be, given again at the close of the case with the other instructions of law.

There is no particular requirement for the form of the limiting instruction. It can be in the affirmative, simply stating the purpose of the evidence:

> The evidence you are about to hear concerns letters written to the Ajax Company by customers who were injured using the machines at issue in this case. This evidence is offered for a limited purpose. It is offered by the plaintiff as evidence that Ajax had been told its machines were defective.

Or the instruction can add the negative:

> You may not consider these letters as evidence that the machines were in fact defective. That is, you may not consider the letters for the truth of the words contained in them.

The way to get the best possible limiting instruction is to anticipate the need for it and have it ready, in writing, for the judge.

When evidence is admitted for a limited purpose, final argument of the lawyers must be limited to that same purpose. For example, when a prior inconsistent statement is admitted only to impeach a non-party witness, it cannot be argued for its truth.

Curative instructions are not covered by FRE 105, but they raise similar concerns about the efficacy of telling people to forget something they heard or saw. Ordinarily, instructing a jury to disregard something cures any error caused by the offending event.

The law presumes the curative instruction will be followed. The presumption breaks down when a reviewing court finds an overwhelming probability that the jury will be unable to follow the instruction and a strong likelihood that the effect on the injured party will be devastating. In that case, as has been said, the bell cannot be unrung.

§2.4. *Raising and meeting objections*[3]

FRE 103 has two basic requirements for evidentiary objections. First, the lawyer opposing the admission of evidence has a clear obligation: Make a timely objection or motion to strike, stating the specific ground of objection if the specific ground is not apparent from the context. The rule does not define "timely," but it is understood that an objection to evidence must be made as soon as the ground for it becomes known or should have become known.

If the objection is to the question, the objection must be made before the answer is given. When an exhibit is offered, the objection must be made before the judge rules.

There are times when a proper question elicits an improper answer, such as one based on hearsay or inadequate personal knowledge. If the question is proper, but the answer is objectionable, the objection must come when the answer is given, accompanied by a motion to strike the offending answer. If no motion to strike is made, the error is waived.

Second, the objection must state a proper specific legal basis unless the basis is obvious from the circumstances. When the rule refers to a "specific ground" of objection, it means the correct specific ground. Naming the wrong specific ground will waive any claim on appeal based on the right reason. Relevancy objections do not preserve hearsay and foundation objections.

Objections in the presence of the jury should not be speeches or mini-arguments. They should state a legal basis: "Objection, that is irrelevant"; or "I object, the question calls for hearsay." Stating the number of the rule offended is appropriate and desirable. Of course, judges vary in their practices. The wise lawyer learns those practices before the trial begins.

FRE 103(c) expresses a clear preference for taking up evidentiary disputes out of the presence of the jury. Very often more must be said about a point of evidence. Asking to be heard out of the presence of the jury is a useful approach, but must not be overused and should never be used for trivial points. If the judge does not allow sidebar conferences, the objection should be re-raised at the next opportunity out of the jury's presence.

FRE 103 discourages general objections. These are objections made without stating any reason — "I object" or "Objection." Some courts say a general objection raises only a relevance issue; others say it raises nothing.

If a general objection is sustained in the trial court, the ruling will be upheld on appeal if there is any proper ground for the objection. When evidence is excluded by a ruling sustaining a general objection, the offering lawyer should ask the judge to require counsel to state his reasons. It often turns out that whatever the judge had in mind can easily be fixed.

There are times — not many — when a reviewing court will say that the ground for objection was apparent from the context. That means that

---

3. Wigmore §§18-20; McCormick §§51-52, 55; Weinstein §103[01]-[10]; Mueller & Kirkpatrick §§1.3-1.9.

everyone — lawyers and judge — understood the reason for the objection, even if it was not stated. It will take a clear record on the point to bring a reviewing court to that conclusion.

Fear of waiver often impels lawyers to continue objecting to evidence the judge has ruled admissible. After a while, jury resentment becomes a real danger. The objecting lawyer should ask for a continuing objection to the evidence, reminding the judge about it every once in a while out of the presence of the jury.

Until 2000, Rule 103 did not offer guidance on how to preserve an issue for appeal when the judge has made an advance ruling. That is, at or before trial the judge makes a ruling admitting or excluding evidence. Does the loser of that ruling have to renew his objection or offer of proof at the appropriate time in the trial? Appellate decisions have been split on the question.

The 2000 amendment to Rule 103 provides the answer: If the trial judge "rules definitively on the record," a party need not renew the objection or offer of proof to preserve a claim of error. That would be a waste of time. But when the trial judge has reserved his ruling or has indicated his ruling is preliminary or conditional, the objection or offer of proof must be renewed at the appropriate time.

Of course, this assumes the trial lawyer knows when an advance ruling is "definitive." He is obliged to find out. If there is any question about the definitive nature of an advance ruling, the prudent lawyer will object or make an offer of proof at the appropriate time.

The amendment does not change the rule established in *Luce v. United States*, 469 U.S. 38 (1984): A trial judge had held Luce's convictions would be admitted if he were to testify; but if the defendant did not take the stand, any claim of error in the conditional ruling would be waived on appeal.

In addition, renewal of an objection is required to preserve error if the judge changes an initial ruling, definitive or not, or if the other party violates the terms of the ruling.

The rule is well established that a party introducing evidence cannot complain on appeal that the evidence was erroneously admitted. This principle can create a serious dilemma for trial lawyers seeking to obviate or "take the sting out of" damaging evidence that is sure to come. For example, when a trial judge definitively rules the prosecution may use the defendant's prior conviction to impeach on cross-examination, the defense lawyer might think it a good strategy to bring out the conviction during the defendant's direct examination. He can do that, but he then waives the right to claim on appeal that admission of the prior conviction was error: *Ohler v. United States*, 529 U.S. 753 (2000).

When the judge's ruling excludes evidence, the offering lawyer must be sure that the substance of what he was offering is clear in the record. There are two ways to make it clear: by making an offer of proof and by being confident that the substance of the evidence was apparent from the context of the questions. Failure to satisfy one of those two methods will waive the issue on appeal. Relying on the "apparent from the context" alternative is a risk not worth taking.

What is an "offer of proof"? An offer of proof is simply the way lawyers show the trial judge (as well as the appellate court) what the excluded evidence, either witness testimony or exhibits, would have been. Lawyers should not think of an offer of proof as a purely appellate device. Its first purpose is to give the trial judge a chance to reconsider his ruling. Sometimes he will change his mind after an effective presentation of what the evidence would be.

"Offer of proof" is not defined in the rule. It can take various forms. If the witness is available, the safest course is to ask the proposed questions and get the answers of the witness out of the presence of the jury. FRE 103(b) authorizes the trial judge to require the question-and-answer form.

Another method, although second best, is for the offering lawyer to make a narrative statement of the proposed questions and expected answers. That statement can be oral or in writing. It can be in the form of a signed statement by the witness. A general statement by a lawyer, not in question-and-answer form, is a less desirable way of making an offer of proof unless the trial judge agrees it is adequate for the purpose. These offers also are made out of the hearing of the jury.

Making an offer of proof for questions on cross-examination can pose a more difficult problem, especially when the examiner is not sure what the answers will be. Hopefully the purpose of the questions will be apparent from their context. For example: "*Q:* Do you hope your testimony for the prosecution will lead to a lighter sentence for your pending bank robbery charge?" It is apparent from the question that the expected answer is "yes." If the purpose is not apparent, the examiner must do as much as he can to show the judge where he is going and where he hopes to land.

If an exhibit is at issue, it should be marked and made part of the trial court record. In this way, the appellate court, when it reviews the record, will see what the excluded evidence was and will be able to determine if the ruling excluding the exhibit was correct.

The offer of proof, like an objection, should be timely, made when the question arises. If the judge does not rule on it immediately, be sure to get a ruling later, but in any event as soon as possible.

Sometimes a judge will be hostile to the idea of an offer of proof, or he will say: "We will take it up later." Persist. Remind the judge at the next recess. If there is no ruling, there probably is no appeal on the point unless it is clear the judge blocked all efforts to make the offer.

Care must be taken to tailor the offer of proof to proper content and purpose. If inadmissible evidence is mixed with admissible evidence in the offer, the judge may properly sustain an objection. If the wrong reason for admission is stated in the offer of proof, its proponent cannot claim on appeal there was another, better reason.

Hovering over this system for making and preserving objections is the plain error rule contained in FRE 103(d). Reviewing courts may take notice "of plain errors affecting substantial rights although they were not brought to the attention of the court." The question that immediately arises is whether the term "substantial right of the party" in FRE 103(a) means something different than "substantial rights" in FRE 103(d). There must be a difference. Otherwise, whether an objection was made would not make any difference.

FRE 103(a) defines the occasions when reviewing courts will consider a claimed error. It does not control criminal cases where constitutional error occurs. In those cases, a conviction will be reversed unless the preserved error was harmless beyond a reasonable doubt. *Chapman v. California*, 386 U.S. 18 (1967).

The plain error rule of FRE 103(d) is triggered when some grave error, one that affects the fundamental fairness of a trial, takes place. Plain error is found most often in criminal cases, seldom in civil cases. The failure to give limiting instructions on the purpose of highly sensitive evidence, such as FRE 404(b) other acts evidence, has been held to be plain error.

Plain error analysis looks to the strength of the case. It most often comes into play when the evidence is closely balanced, and it is rarely used for some prophylactic purpose. For example, an improper prosecutorial argument will not be considered plain error unless it can be said that the argument had a direct impact on the outcome of the case.

Objections procedure can be summarized as follows:

1. The objection must be timely. It must be made when the occasion arises, that is, when the grounds become apparent.
2. State the specific legal grounds for the objection. A general objection will raise only the question of relevance, unless the grounds are so apparent that no reason need be given. That is a rare occurrence.
3. Be sure you state the correct reason for your objection. You run the risk of waiving grounds not stated.
4. Your objection should not contain a speech and should not argue the evidence. It should not contain statements aimed at inflaming or prejudicing the jury.
5. If you feel more than a simple statement of legal grounds is required to explain your position, ask to be heard out of the presence of the jury. If the judge says he will not hear you now, but will hear you later, accept his invitation. Don't forget.
6. If you make an objection, be sure the record reflects a ruling. Do not let the other side proceed until the judge has ruled. If you hear nothing from the judge, ask for a ruling on your objection.
7. If the judge reserves his ruling, or if evidence is admitted subject to your objection, be sure to renew your objection and ask for a ruling.
8. Some words do not state any grounds for objection. For example: "That's incompetent," He can't do that," or "That's unfair."
9. There is no need to keep objecting to the same thing if the judge's attitude is clear and repetition would only aggravate the situation, tending to prejudice the jury. To be safe, ask the judge for a "continuing objection."
10. When only a portion of an answer, exhibit, or any other evidence is objectionable, your objection must be directed specifically to that part.
11. When the grounds for objection do not become apparent until after the jury has heard the evidence, be sure you not only make a prompt objection, but also ask the judge to strike the evidence and instruct the jury to disregard it. That happens, for instance, when
    (a) An answer to your question is nonresponsive;
    (b) Something the other side has said will be connected up is not connected up;

(c) A count or charge is dismissed after testimony about the count or charge has been admitted;

(d) Your cross-examination demonstrates that an answer given on direct examination was based on hearsay and not on firsthand knowledge.

12. When the other side's objection to your evidence is sustained, be sure you make a proper offer of proof as soon as possible.

III

OPENING STATEMENTS

§3.1.   Introduction

The purpose of an opening statement is to inform the jury of what the parties expect to prove during the course of the trial through witness testimony and exhibits. It is intended to give the jury an overview of the upcoming evidence so that the evidence will make more sense when the jury finally hears it during the parties' cases-in-chief.

The traditional view of opening statements is that they should be brief, state only facts, and avoid anything that might be considered an argument. The more modern view, recognizing the psychological significance of opening statements, is somewhat broader and permits stating themes, theories of the case, characterizations, and even conclusions so long as they are not excessively argumentative. The modern view recognizes that the jury is assisted not only by having a preview of the facts, but also by hearing the parties' points of view about the upcoming evidence. The trial judge has great latitude in deciding the proper scope of opening statements, and substantial differences exist between the various jurisdictions, and between judges in the same jurisdictions, on what is proper to include in an opening statement.

There is no federal rule of evidence, civil procedure, or criminal procedure that governs the permissible content of opening statements. State rules usually are silent. If they address opening statements at all, they usually provide only that the opening statement shall be "a concise and brief statement of the facts which the parties propose to establish by evidence" or similar language.

Ethical rules are similarly general. Model Rule 3.3 prohibits making false statements of material fact or law to a tribunal and offering evidence the lawyer knows to be false. Model Rule 3.4 prohibits a lawyer from alluding to any matter that the lawyer does not reasonably believe is relevant or is not supported by admissible evidence.

Case law discussing what is permissible, and what is not, in opening statements is surprisingly meager and depends as much on the attitudes of a particular jurisdiction, at a particular time, as anything else. Coupled with the wide latitude trial judges have in regulating opening statements, hard and fast specific "rules" are rare. While lawyers regularly make, and trial judges regularly rule on, evidentiary objections before and during opening statements, lawyers infrequently base appeals on erroneous rulings at this stage of the trial. This probably accounts for the meager appellate case law on opening statements.

When a lawyer mentions something improper in an opening statement, the proper procedure is for the opposing lawyer to make a timely objection. If not timely made, any error usually will be deemed waived. If the objection is sustained, a motion to strike and to instruct the jury to disregard the improper comment should also be made. If the improper comment is so egregious that sustaining the objection and instructing the jury to disregard will not cure the error, a motion for a mistrial should be made.

Some lawyers feel they cannot object during opening statements, but that is wrong. Objections and, at times, motions to strike and for mistrial, are essential to preserving the record. Whether to make objections during opening statements is, like other stages of the trial, a balancing act between the need to preserve the record and the risk of offending the jury and judge by making repeated objections. Objections should always have a proper evidentiary basis. It is inappropriate and unethical to object without a good faith basis merely to interrupt a lawyer who is giving an effective opening statement.

In civil cases, a mistrial usually results in the case being tried again at a later time. (The offending party may be required to pay costs incurred by the other parties.) In criminal cases, additional concerns apply. When the defendant in a criminal case moves for a mistrial and the motion is granted, the defendant cannot object to a later retrial on double jeopardy grounds. However, what happens if the defense does something improper, causing the prosecution to move for a mistrial, and the motion is granted over the defendant's objection? Can the defense bar a retrial on double jeopardy grounds? The United States Supreme Court has discussed on three occasions the impact of improper statements made during opening statements in criminal cases.

In *Frazier v. Cupp*, 394 U.S. 731 (1969), the prosecutor, over objection, said in opening statement that a co-defendant who had pled guilty would testify against the defendant, and he set out a summary of the expected testimony. In fact, the prosecutor was uncertain whether the co-defendant would testify. When the co-defendant was called to the witness stand, he refused to testify, invoking his Fifth Amendment privilege. The Court framed the issue in terms of the Confrontation Clause, examining the trial judge's instruction to the jury that an opening statement is not evidence and the likelihood that the jury was influenced by the remarks. The Court, finding that this was not a case of deliberate prosecutorial misconduct, held that the defendant was not prejudiced in a constitutional sense by the opening statement.

Two other Supreme Court decisions concerned improper opening statement remarks by defense lawyers in criminal cases and the implication of a mistrial for the defendant's double jeopardy protection.

In *Arizona v. Washington*, 434 U.S. 497 (1978), the defendant's prior conviction had been reversed because the prosecution withheld evidence. When the second trial began, the defense lawyer talked about the earlier prosecutorial misconduct. When the prosecution objected, the trial judge declared a mistrial. The Supreme Court held that a third trial would not violate the Double Jeopardy

Clause because the trial judge was correct in finding a high degree of "manifest necessity" for the retrial. The trial judge's evaluation of the degree of jury bias caused by the improper comment receives great deference in the reviewing courts.

In *United States v. Dinitz*, 424 U.S. 600 (1976), the defense lawyer in his opening statement insisted on making argumentative comments — "I call this the case of the incredible witness" — and referring to evidence he had no way of producing. Finally, his patience exhausted, the trial judge terminated the opening statement, ejected the lawyer from the courtroom, and, shortly thereafter, declared a mistrial. Holding that the trial judge's action was not motivated by bad faith or a desire to harass or prejudice the defendant, the Court held that there was no bar to another trial. Again, the test was "manifest necessity."

The scope and latitude of opening statements are a matter of trial judge discretion, and some judges will set time limits for them. Appellate reversal for too restrictive time limitations for opening statements is essentially unknown.

As with other stages of a trial, judges usually prefer that anticipated evidentiary problems be raised and decided beforehand whenever possible. If the judge rules, the lawyers must comply with the ruling. If the judge reserves ruling, he may instruct the lawyers to stay away from a topic during opening statements, but it does not mean that this topic is completely out of the case. The judge may want to hear more evidence before he decides. The safe procedure is to raise the matter again, out of the jury's presence, to obtain a ruling on admissibility before attempting to introduce the topic during the trial.

When a lawyer during opening statement mentions what the expected evidence is, the lawyer then becomes obligated to present such evidence during the trial. Lawyers must know their cases and know what evidence they have. When in doubt on the admissibility of that evidence, the safer, professional approach is to avoid the topic or get a ruling from the judge beforehand. Criminal cases have been reversed where a prosecutor promised eyewitnesses and defendant confessions and then failed to present them during the trial.

This chapter will discuss the common evidentiary objections that are made during opening statements and the applicable law and will illustrate the factual settings in which such objections frequently occur. Procedural issues, such as the right to make opening statements, their order, time limitations, and the like, are not discussed, since these are controlled by statutes and by local rules and customs and are usually jurisdiction specific.

§3.2. *Mentioning inadmissible evidence*[1]

1. Law

Opening statements should not mention inadmissible evidence. The standard is one of good faith: Does the lawyer have a reasonable good faith basis to believe

---

1. A.S. Julien, Opening Statements ch. 1A (1982); T.A. Mauet, Trial Techniques and Trails, ch. 4 (9th ed., 2013); R.H. Underwood & W.H. Fortune, Trial Ethics (1988); J.A. Tanford, Trial Process ch. 4 (4th ed. 2009); 75A Am. Jur. Trial §§525, 526, 528.

that the evidence now being mentioned will be admissible later? If so, it is proper to mention it even though the judge later rules that the evidence is inadmissible. The better practice, of course, is to raise any questionable matters beforehand in a motion in limine.

Mentioning inadmissible evidence in the opening statement can be either harmless or reversible error, depending on the nature of the evidence improperly mentioned. If there is a prompt objection and a cautionary instruction is inadequate to mitigate the impropriety, the proper remedy is a mistrial and new trial.

The most common errors in this category are mentioning inadmissible prior bad acts and crimes. These are particularly important because they usually involve significant and highly inflammatory evidence, and improperly mentioning them can result in a mistrial. FRE 404(b) bars other acts evidence if its only probative value is to "prove a person's character in order to show that on a particular occasion the person acted in accordance with the character," commonly called propensity evidence. Such other acts evidence is admissible only if it is probative of things actually in issue, such as knowledge, intent, plan, scheme, identity, and the like.

For example, the prosecutor in a robbery case says, "Only one week before the defendant robbed this store, he was caught trying to steal a car in the same neighborhood." This is improper under FRE 404(b) because it merely shows that the defendant has a previous criminal history, which only shows his bad character. The evidence is admissible only if probative of actual issues, such as intent, knowledge, or identity, none of which is applicable in the case. This comment may result in a mistrial, since the prejudice to the defendant is obvious.

Problems can arise in civil cases as well. For example, the plaintiff's lawyer in a personal injury case says, "Mr. Johnson, the defendant, has been driving for over 20 years. He's had his license suspended two times." This is improper under FRE 404(b). It suggests that the defendant is a bad driver, which is an improper use of other acts evidence. Or the plaintiff's lawyer says, "The defendant received a traffic citation for speeding." The mere fact of a citation, without a later conviction, is inadmissible because it is irrelevant under FRE 401-403.

For example, in a negligence action, the plaintiff's lawyer says, "Was the stairwell negligently maintained? The evidence will be that the owner replaced the carpeting just three days after Mr. Williams fell down." This is an improper use of subsequent remedial measures evidence under FRE 407. Even if the judge previously ruled that evidence of the carpet replacement was admissible for the limited purpose of showing ownership and control, the statement is still improper, since the lawyer was using it to suggest negligence.

Another common error involves mentioning inadmissible character evidence. Character trait evidence is admissible only in limited circumstances under FRE 404 and 608. For example, the defense lawyer in a personal injury case says, "Mr. Johnson stands accused of driving recklessly. However, you will learn that he has always been a careful driver and has always been a safe driver." This is an improper use of character trait evidence, since under FRE 404(a) character evidence cannot be used as circumstantial proof of conduct in civil cases.

Common errors also include violating previous court orders and rulings on motions in limine. Mentioning for an improper purpose evidence that has been ruled inadmissible or evidence that is admissible for only a limited purpose is clearly improper in opening statements. This error is particularly serious, since it frequently eliminates the argument that the error was made in good faith. For example, the defense lawyer in a criminal case says, "The prosecution's star witness, Bobby Wilson, was convicted of burglary 12 years ago." If the court previously ruled that this evidence is inadmissible under FRE 609 to attack credibility, mentioning it in opening statements is clearly improper.

Finally, common errors in this category include mentioning matters that violate the hearsay rules. For example, the plaintiff's lawyer in a personal injury case says, "When Officer Smith arrived at the scene, a bystander told him that the defendant went around that curve too fast." This is hearsay, and no hearsay exception, such as present sense impression or excited utterance, applies.

2. Practice

Issues involving mentioning inadmissible evidence arise more frequently in criminal cases, where evidentiary matters are less likely to be raised before trial. In civil cases, because judges commonly require pretrial statements that set forth each side's expected testimony and exhibits, lawyers are more likely to make motions in limine raising evidentiary objections to the other side's expected evidence, and judges attempt to decide them before trial.

Example 1:

This is an aggravated assault case. In the prosecutor's opening statement, the following happens:

Prosecutor: After the victim called the police, a squad car was sent to the scene, and Officer O'Malley talked to the victim. After getting a description of the assailant, Officer O'Malley knew right away who the assailant probably was. You see, Officer O'Malley has known the defendant for years. He knew that . . .

Defendant: Objection, your honor. This is improper. They're bringing up character evidence and suggesting a prior history.

Judge: Sustained.

Defendant: Move to strike and disregard.

Judge: Very well. The comment is struck. Members of the jury, you will disregard the prosecutor's last comment.

Commentary: Whenever there is evidence that a police officer previously knew a defendant, the jury may think that the officer has previously arrested the defendant or that the defendant has had previous trouble with the law. Such evidence is not admissible in the prosecution's case. In this case, the comment probably is not serious enough to warrant a mistrial.

Example 2:

>   This is an environmental pollution case. The plaintiff claims that the defendant's junkyard polluted the plaintiff's groundwater. In the plaintiff's opening statement, the following happens:

>   *Plaintiff:* How long had the defendant's junkyard been collecting cars, with their gasoline, oil, batteries, and various other chemicals? Over 30 years. Everybody in the area knew about that junkyard. It had the reputation of being the dirtiest . . .
>   *Defendant:* Objection. They're getting into character evidence, your honor. That's inadmissible in civil cases.
>   *Judge:* Sustained. Counsel, move on to something else.

>   *Commentary:*   Character trait evidence is inadmissible, under FRE 404, as circumstantial proof of conduct in civil cases.

Example 3:

>   This is a criminal case. In the prosecutor's opening statement, the following happens:

>   *Prosecutor:* Fortunately, a neighbor, Helen Johnson, saw the defendant crawling into a window of the Smith house and immediately called 911. Mrs. Johnson told the 911 operator that she had seen someone crawling into the house, and she stayed on the line. About one minute later, Mrs. Johnson told the operator that . . .
>   *Defendant:* Objection, your honor. This is hearsay.
>   *Prosecutor:* It's present sense impression, your honor.
>   *Judge:* Overruled.

§3.3.   *Mentioning unprovable evidence*[2]

1.   Law

A lawyer who mentions a specific fact in the opening statement is then obligated to present evidence of that fact during the trial. If you can't prove it, you can't mention it. If the lawyer knows that a fact is unprovable because a necessary witness is unavailable or a necessary exhibit has not been located or cannot be qualified for admission in evidence, that fact cannot be mentioned during the opening statement. For example, the plaintiff's lawyer in a commercial case says, "The records of the shipper the defendant used to deliver the goods from us to them proves that the defendant got the goods." This is clearly improper if the lawyer has not taken steps to reasonably ensure the admissibility of the shipper's

---

2. 75A Am. Jur. Trial §527; J.A. Tanford, Trial Process ch. 4 (4th ed. 2009); A.S. Julien, Opening Statements ch. 1A (1982); F. Lane, Goldstein Trial Technique ch. 10 (3d ed. 1984).

records at trial. These steps include physically obtaining the records, including the records on his list of exhibits in the pretrial memorandum, and having a proper witness from the shipper prepared to qualify the records for admission during trial.

What happens if the lawyer mentions unprovable or, for that matter, unproven facts? The failure to prove facts mentioned in the opening statement will not usually become known until that side has presented its case-in-chief and rested. The other side then has two options. First, it can request the court to instruct the jury that the other party has failed to present evidence it represented it would, so that particular representation in its opening statement should be disregarded. If the omission is serious enough, a motion for a mistrial should be made. Second, the other side can discuss the failure to prove the fact during its closing argument, draw the obvious negative inferences from that failure, and argue that the failure proves a fatal flaw in the other side's case.

For example, the prosecution in an assault case says, "That defendant was seen at the very place where the shooting happened, only 10 minutes before the shooting." If the prosecution offers no evidence during its case-in-chief to support this statement, it is improper. The other side must then decide which of the two approaches discussed above will be more effective.

2. Practice

Issues involving known, but unprovable, facts are best anticipated in advance. A motion in limine will usually result in a ruling, thereby preventing the problem from ever arising during the opening statements.

Example:

This is a personal injury case. Before the opening statements begin, and out of the presence of the jury, the following happens:

Plaintiff: Your honor, we move to bar the defense from mentioning during its opening statement anything about what a witness, Avery Jackson, will testify to. The reason is that we believe that the witness cannot be found, and, therefore, it would be improper to put before the jury testimony that the jury will never hear.

Judge: Counsel, what's the status of this witness?

Defendant: Mr. Jackson was an eyewitness to the collision. He gave a written statement to the police. We listed him on our witness list. About three weeks ago, we attempted to serve him with a trial subpoena, but we were unsuccessful. We've learned that he's out of the country, but is expected back in the next few days. We plan to serve him and call him in the defense case.

Plaintiff: That's just the problem, your honor. They could have, and should have, subpoenaed him earlier. The fact is the witness is not under subpoena and there's no guarantee that he will return, and be timely served, before this trial is over. Under these circumstances, we object to the defense mentioning what he saw during their opening statement.

Judge: I agree. There will be no mention of Mr. Jackson's expected testimony during the opening statements.

Commentary: Judges will normally play it safe in this situation and prevent discussion of such a witness during opening statements. If the witness is later subpoenaed and testifies during the trial, no harm has been done by the ruling.

§3.4. Arguing[3]

1. Law

It is settled law that opening statements should not contain argument. Less clear, however, is what constitutes impermissible argument. Some courts draw the line by stating that opening statements should merely inform the jury and that attempts to persuade the jury are inappropriate. Other courts state that it is proper to tell the jury anything that a witness will say or an exhibit will show during the trial, but that attempts to characterize the credibility of those witnesses and exhibits are inappropriate. The difficulty with these and other distinctions, of course, is that the lines between the proper and the improper are often blurry and are frequently decided by custom in the particular jurisdiction, by the attitude of the particular judge, and by the tone and attitude projected by the lawyer making the opening statement.

For example, the plaintiff's lawyer in a products liability case says, "You will learn that the defendant company did not care about the safety of the lighter that it was selling to the public. It was callously indifferent to safety." Most courts will hold that this lawyer acted improperly by characterizing, rather than stating, the evidence. In a criminal case, the defense lawyer says, "Their star witness, Randy Adams, will lie to you because he has more to gain by lying than by telling the truth." Again, many courts will consider this improperly argumentative. In a criminal case, the prosecutor states that the defendant was "the wolf that goes after the deer." This kind of description is argumentative and improper.

Opening statements also should not contain conclusions. It is for the jury to draw conclusions from facts stated during opening statements. For example, a lawyer can say a car was going "very fast" or "60 miles per hour in a school zone," but cannot say the car was being driven carelessly or recklessly. A lawyer can say, "Jones said he was at home that day at six o'clock, but Shirley Smith saw him downtown that day at that time," but cannot say that Jones lied when he said he was home at that time.

Direct appeals to the bias, prejudice, or other emotions of the jury are improper at any stage of the trial. Direct attacks on the character of the parties and witnesses are improper in opening statements (but may be proper in closing arguments if they are relevant and fair inferences from the evidence). For example, the prosecutor in a criminal case says, "And what did the

---

3. A.S. Julien, Opening Statements ch. 1A (1982); J.A. Tanford, Trial Process ch. 4 (4th ed. 2009).

defendant leave in his wake? A dead victim, but even more. That victim had a wife that loved him. He had three little, beautiful children that adored him." Most courts will consider this an impermissible appeal to sympathy in an opening statement.

Making an improper argument during the opening statement is an evidentiary violation, but is not itself an ethical violation. It becomes an ethical violation only when the argument persists after the trial judge orders the lawyer to stop making arguments or when the argument violates a standing order of the court. Model Rule 3.4(c) makes this clear.

2. Practice

What is argument may be difficult to define, but such discourse usually is recognized when it appears. Argument is based on tone as well as content, and judges and local practices vary in how much latitude the lawyers will be given. Most judges look to see if the lawyer is stating facts, regardless of how persuasively, or if the lawyer is attempting to argue witness credibility and other improper conclusions from the facts. A fine line, but a line that judges look for.

Prefacing an improper argument with the comment "The evidence will show" does not transform an argument into fact. Some lawyers think, incorrectly, that it does.

Example 1:

This is a robbery case. During the prosecutor's opening statement, the following happens:

Prosecutor: That day, May 1, 2015, started out as a perfect day for the victim, Mary Jones. She had gotten up and was walking to catch the bus to her new job. It was a job that Mary had studied hard for, and she was excited about it. She liked the people she was working with. For the first time in her life, Mary thought that she had finally gotten a job with career potential . . .
Defendant: Objection, your honor. This is irrelevant and improper.
Judge: Yes. Counsel, let's stick to the facts of the case.

Commentary: Lawyers frequently try to build up their key witnesses during the opening statements. However, when the basis is character evidence that would be inadmissible during the trial, objections should be sustained.

Example 2:

This is a criminal fraud case. During the prosecutor's opening statement, the following happens:

Prosecutor: So what will all this evidence add up to? It will prove that the defendant was like a virus, contaminating everything that . . .
Defendant: Objection, your honor. This is blatant argument.

> *Judge:* Sustained. Counsel, you will refrain from making comments like
>   that. Is that clear?
> *Prosecutor:* Yes, your honor.

Commentary: Here, the impropriety is clear, and the judge has scolded the offending lawyer in front of the jury.

§3.5. *Stating personal opinions*[4]

1. Law

It is improper for a lawyer to state personal opinions at any time during the trial. Vouching for the credibility, or lack of credibility, of any witness is improper. Stating personal knowledge of facts is improper. Phrases like "I know" and "I believe" are best excised from any lawyer's trial vocabulary. If egregious enough, a motion for mistrial may be warranted. For example, a lawyer says, "I don't think Mr. Johnson will be a credible witness, and neither will you." This is an improper comment on witness credibility. A lawyer says, "I've been down that road myself, as I'm sure you have, and there are potholes all over the place." This is improper because the lawyer cannot be a witness at the trial, yet is representing a fact based on his personal knowledge.

Many courts, however, treat statements such as "I think" and "I believe" as harmless when the statements are linked to the evidence. For example, a lawyer says, "I think the evidence will be that the defendant's car was going way over the speed limit." Many courts permit such comments, since the principal point made is the expected evidence, not the lawyer's opinion about the evidence.

2. Practice

The principal question the trial judge addresses, whenever an objection is made to personal opinions, is whether the lawyer's expression of personal opinion is just an unfortunate use of words or a deliberate attempt to inject his personal beliefs or knowledge into the trial. The former usually is considered harmless, the latter clearly objectionable.

Example 1:

This is a personal injury case. During the defendant's opening statement, the following happens:

> *Defendant:* Folks, when Mr. Driscoll drove south on Main Street during
>   the rush hour traffic, he saw a car stopped in the northbound
>   lane at the Elm Street intersection. Even though that car didn't
>   have its blinker light on, it's been my experience that when a
>   car is stopped in the intersection . . .

4. F. Lane, Goldstein Trial Technique ch. 10 (3d ed. 1984).

Plaintiff: Objection to counsel stating his personal experiences, your
　　　　honor.
Judge: Sustained.
Defendant: Even though that car didn't have its blinker light on, Mr. Driscoll
　　　　assumed that it was trying to make a left turn once the oncoming
　　　　traffic passed.

Example 2:

　　　This is a civil nuisance case brought against the city for permitting raw
sewage to back up into the plaintiff's basement. During the plaintiff's
opening statement, the following happens:

Plaintiff: What did the basement look like? It was right out of a Stephen
　　　　King horror movie. It . . .
Defendant: Objection, your honor, to the characterization. This is
　　　　argument.
Judge: Sustained. Counsel, let's stick to the facts and save characteriza-
　　　　tions for a later time.

　　Commentary: This is a close call but well within the judge's discretion.

§3.6.   Discussing law[5]

1.   Law

Cases frequently state that an opening statement should not discuss or quote the
law. However, an opening statement's purpose is to help the jury understand the
evidence. As a result, it is usually helpful to tell the jury what the applicable law is,
since the jury must later relate the evidence to the law during its deliberations.
Most courts recognize this and permit general references to what a party is
legally required to prove. This is particularly true in statutory or complex
cases. In such cases, the parties are commonly permitted to refer to and read
from the pleadings, paraphrase or summarize the legal elements of the claims
and defenses, and then state what evidence will be introduced to prove them.
However, detailed or lengthy quoting from statutes or elements instructions is
not permitted. In those jurisdictions where the judge instructs the jury on the
applicable law before opening statements, an increasingly common practice,
there will be no need to again state the law in opening statements.
　　Where the applicable law is mentioned, of course, it must be accurately and
fairly summarized. For example, in a jurisdiction where the judge permits some
reference to the law, a lawyer says, "We have to prove that the defendant's
appliance, which caused this injury, was unreasonably dangerous, either because
of a design defect or because the warnings on it were inadequate." This is
proper. In a criminal case, the defense lawyer says, "This is a case of self-defense.

---

　　5. A.S. Julien, Opening Statements ch. 1A (1982); F. Lane, Goldstein Trial Technique
ch. 10 (3d ed. 1984); J.A. Tanford, Trial Process ch. 4 (4th ed. 2009).

The law says that a person can use deadly force to protect himself if he is faced with the imminent use of deadly force." This usually is considered proper.

Can the lawyers talk about the applicable burden of proof in opening statements? Some judges believe that this is an improper comment on the law and is the judge's turf. Such judges may, on their own, prevent lawyers from talking about burdens of proof. On the other hand, it is common practice in criminal cases, especially for defense lawyers, to mention the prosecution's burden of proving guilt beyond a reasonable doubt. This is a topic that lawyers should raise with the judge before trial to determine what references to the law the judge will permit.

2. Practice

The key to avoiding problems in this area is to learn the trial judge's practice before trial. Some judges freely permit references to the instructions of law, others permit only general references, and a few allow no references at all.

Example:

This is a defamation case. The plaintiff claims the defendant, her former employer, defamed her by giving her a poor and inaccurate reference when called by a prospective employer. The defendant denies that the reference was inaccurate and raises the affirmative defense of a qualified privilege. During the defendant's opening statement, the following happens:

Defendant: Members of the jury, not only is what Ms. Hutchinson said about the plaintiff accurate and true, but also she had a legal right to talk about her employee to other prospective employers. That's because the law protects employers in making statements about their employees unless the statement was untrue and was made to injure the employee.
Plaintiff: Objection, your honor, to the defense discussing the law.
Judge: Overruled. Counsel may summarize the applicable law so long as it is done accurately.
Defendant: We will show that when Ms. Hutchinson talked about the plaintiff, what she said was true; that she never intended to injure the plaintiff; and that her statement was legally protected.

§3.7.   *Mentioning the opponent's case*[6]

1.   Law

A lawyer during the opening statement can mention only facts that he in good faith expects to prove with admissible evidence. It follows, then, that a lawyer

---

6. J.A. Tanford, Trial Process ch. 4 (4th ed. 2009).

cannot anticipate and comment on the opponent's case, since he has no control over what that opponent will do in his case. This prohibition is particularly important in criminal cases. Since a defendant has a constitutional right not to present evidence, it always is improper for a prosecutor to mention the defense case. For example, the prosecutor in a criminal case says, "The defense will try to show that. . . ." This is always improper because the defense is not obligated to do anything. Even if the prosecutor expects the defense to present evidence, the comments are improper, since the defense can always change its mind and choose to rest, rather than presenting evidence.

In civil cases, however, if the opponent has committed itself, through pleadings, discovery, or the pretrial statement, to presenting certain evidence at trial, many jurisdictions permit lawyers to comment on that expected evidence. For example, in a products liability case, the plaintiff's lawyer says, "The defendant will claim that this appliance was properly designed and the instructions for use were adequate. But, folks, that's not what the evidence will show. The fact is that Mrs. Johnson read the instructions, followed those instructions, and was injured anyway." Since the defendant already is committed to what it expects to prove, most courts will permit the plaintiff to state those claims before discussing the evidence that will refute them. This allows the opening statements to be more focused and lets the jury know specifically where the parties disagree.

A defense lawyer, civil or criminal, should be able to comment on evidence the plaintiff has just told the jury about. It is no longer the opponent's expected evidence, but rather evidence the opponent has just disclosed to the jury.

2. Practice

Judges become concerned when lawyers in their opening statements talk about what the other side contends or is expected to prove, particularly when the plaintiff in a civil case talks about the expected defense case. However, if the judge is familiar with the case and understands the issues, and if the parties' positions and issues in dispute are clear, some reference to the other side's case usually is allowed.

Example 1:

This is a contract case. The plaintiff claims the defendant failed to deliver certain goods within the time allowed under the contract. The defendant claims it was excused from delivering the goods because other events made delivery impossible. During the plaintiff's opening statement, the following happens:

Plaintiff: Folks, the defendant was required to deliver the goods to us by June 1, 2015. It didn't, and that's why we brought this lawsuit for damages. Now the defendant has claimed, and will claim during this trial, that . . .

Defendant: Objection to what we will claim during the trial, your honor. That's for us to say.

Judge: Well, so long as counsel accurately states the positions raised in the pleadings and during discovery, I'll allow it.

Plaintiff: The defendant has claimed that there was a strike at one of its suppliers that made it impossible to deliver the goods in time. However, that's not what the facts will show.

Commentary: Since the plaintiff always wants to anticipate the defense's position, he commonly discusses the facts that will refute the defense's positions. Most judges will permit the plaintiff to summarize, in general terms, the defense's positions before discussing the facts.

Example 2:

This is a medical malpractice case. In the defendant's opening statement, the following happens:

Defendant: Members of the jury, plaintiff started this lawsuit for one reason, and only one reason. That reason was revenge. You see . . .

Plaintiff: Objection. That's pure argument, and it's improper in any event.

Judge: Sustained.

Plaintiff: Your honor, we ask for a mistrial.

Judge: The jury will be excused for a few minutes while I deal with this legal matter.

Commentary: It always is improper to make disparaging remarks about the other side's claimed motivation in bringing suit. This comment may well result in a mistrial.

IV

DIRECT EXAMINATION OF WITNESSES: BASIC CONSIDERATIONS

§4.1.   Introduction

This chapter discusses the preliminary evidentiary rules that govern various aspects of direct examinations, such as determining witness competency, taking the oath, testifying to firsthand knowledge, offering lay witness opinions, impeaching your own witness, asking leading questions, and refreshing recollection, as well as other rules regulating the calling of witnesses.

These threshold issues rarely are raised on appeal but regularly occur in the course of a trial. The trial judge's rulings on these issues can have a serious impact on the way the trial is conducted.

§4.2.   Witness competency (FRE 601)[1]

1.   Law

Rule 601.   Competency to Testify in General

Every person is competent to be a witness unless these rules provide otherwise. But in a civil case, state law governs the witness's competency regarding a claim or defense for which state law supplies the rule of decision.

---

1. McCormick §§61-67; Weinstein §601[01]-[07]; Mueller & Kirkpatrick §§6.2-6.4; Wigmore §§483-686.

A witness must be competent to testify at a trial. FRE 601 appears to abolish all objections to a witness's competency, except where they are specifically provided for in the other Rules or, in civil cases, where state law supplies the rule of decision with respect to an element of a claim or defense and state witness competency rules apply. Despite the language of FRE 601, however, courts still grapple with issues of witness competency. The presumption of competency is very strong, but it is not absolute.

Qualifications for witnesses are governed by either federal or state competency law, depending on the forum and kind of case involved. In federal criminal cases and federal civil cases based on federal question jurisdiction, the federal competency rules in FRE 601-606 apply (unless the substantive federal statute itself applies state substantive law, as does the Federal Tort Claims Act). In federal civil cases based on diversity jurisdiction, where state law supplies the rule of decision with respect to an element of a claim or defense, the forum state's competency rules apply. (This is because FRE 601 essentially applies the doctrine of *Erie Railroad Co. v. Tompkins*, 304 U.S. 64 (1938), to federal diversity cases.)

Most states have eliminated or sharply reduced the common law disqualifications for witnesses. All have eliminated the common law disqualifications for parties, spouses of parties, felons, and heathens. (These are now considered matters that affect credibility, except for religious beliefs, which are generally inadmissible.) However, some still retain minimum age requirements for witnesses and exclude persons having mental infirmities, such as senility and low intelligence. Some apply them only to criminal cases, others to all cases. Forum-specific research is required here.[2]

Some states still follow some version of the Dead Man's Act, which bars the testimony of interested parties to transactions with the deceased in litigation involving the estate of the deceased. Other states have abrogated the act entirely. Still other states have modified the act in various ways. Forum-specific research is also required here, particularly in diversity cases where the state competency rules apply.[3]

Nothing in the Federal Rules of Evidence specifically addresses the competency of witnesses who are very young, are mentally ill, have low intelligence, or are alcohol or drug abusers. However, case law gives the trial judge discretion to consider such matters affecting witness competency.

On a proper showing, the trial judge may conduct an FRE 104(a) hearing to determine competency. It usually takes a carefully phrased written motion, containing an offer of proof, to trigger the judge's discretion. Otherwise, competency questions become matters of weight for the jury, not issues of admissibility.

Three basic questions cross the trial judge's mind during such a hearing. Does the witness understand the duty imposed by the oath to testify truthfully? Does the witness have sufficient memory to testify to the matter at issue? Does the witness have the ability to communicate what he saw and heard?

---

2. McCormick §62; 81 Am. Jur. 2d Witnesses §§167-173, 211-213, 217-219.
3. McCormick §65; 81 Am. Jur. 2d Witnesses §§563-571.

If these questions can be answered in the affirmative, it does not matter that the witness might be very young, be mentally ill, have a low intelligence, or be an alcohol or drug abuser at the time of the event or at the time of testifying. Even a person who has been found mentally incompetent to stand trial can be a witness if he understands the oath, has enough memory, and can communicate to the trier of fact. The jury, properly instructed, has the ability to give the witness's testimony the appropriate weight. In compelling circumstances, the trial judge has the discretion to order a psychological or psychiatric examination of a witness.

Some judges, faced with serious questions of witness competency, use the FRE 403 balancing test to determine whether that witness can testify. The judge weighs the probative value of the witness's testimony against the danger of creating unfair prejudice, confusing the issues, misleading the jury, or wasting time. This question then becomes one of relevancy, which has little to do with FRE 601.

Sometimes the competency of a hearsay declarant comes into question when the declarant's words are offered under a hearsay exception. For example, the excited utterance of a mentally ill bystander to an event may be offered. In such a situation, lack of competency probably is not a barrier to admission of the statement. In *Idaho v. Wright*, 497 U.S. 805 (1990), the Supreme Court conducted a Sixth Amendment Confrontation Clause analysis of a two-and-one-half-year-old's out-of-court statements under the assumption that the child was not competent to testify.

While nothing in the Rules refers to child witnesses, Congress has addressed the matter in criminal cases: 18 U.S.C. §3509(c) governs a child under 18 who is a victim of physical or mental injury, who has been exploited by child pornography or prostitution, or who has been a witness to a crime committed against another person. That child is presumed competent. The trial judge may conduct a competency examination of the child if there are compelling reasons for it, but age alone is not a compelling reason. The party seeking the examination must make a written motion for the examination, including an offer of proof of incompetency. The examination, conducted by the judge, consists of questions that focus on the child's ability to understand and answer simple questions. No psychological or psychiatric examination to assess the child's competency shall be ordered "without a showing of compelling need."

2.   Practice

Witness competency issues most frequently arise when a party challenges the competency of young children or mentally handicapped or impaired persons. Competency issues usually can be anticipated and should be raised well before trial, or at least before the witness is called to testify at trial.

Example:

In a federal assault case, the defendant is charged with assaulting his wife during an argument in a post office. The prosecution wants to call the defendant's 10-year-old son, who has a history of mental illness and borderline retardation. The defense files a written motion to bar the son as a witness at trial. Before trial, the judge rules that, under FRE 601 et seq., the witness's age, the fact that he has been treated for depression in the past, and his IQ of 75 do not make the witness per se incompetent to testify. The judge defers to the time of trial the issues of whether the witness can properly comprehend the oath and the questions asked and whether he has adequate memory and communication skills, so that the testimony would be relevant and not a waste of time.

At trial, but out of the jury's presence, the son is called to the stand.

Q. (By judge) Bobby, what's your name?
A. Bobby.
Q. And your last name?
A. Johnson.
Q. Bobby, why are you here today?
A. I saw Mommy and Daddy fighting.
Q. Where were they fighting?
A. At the post office.
Q. Do you remember what you saw?
A. Yes.
Q. Bobby, do you know what it means to tell a lie?
A. Yes.
Q. What does it mean?
A. When you say something that's not true.
Q. What happens if you tell a lie?
A. I get punished.
Q. Who does that?
A. My teachers.
Q. How do they punish you?
A. They make me sit in the corner, and they call my mom.
Q. Bobby, where do you live?
A. In our house.
Q. What city is your house in?
A. I don't know.
Q. Do you know the street you live on?
A. Maple Street.
Q. What number is your house?
A. I don't know.
Q. Bobby, tell us about your school.
A. It's a special school.
Q. What are you learning there?
A. We learn reading and counting, things like that.
Q. How are you doing in school?
A. Okay. I like it there.
Q. What grade are you in?
A. Mrs. Robinson's class.
Q. Bobby, you know it's real important today not to tell a lie, right?
A. Yes.
Q. Can you promise me that you'll tell us what happened?

A. Yes.

Judge: I've heard enough. The witness may testify. He appears to understand why he's here and is answering the questions competently.
The jury will be allowed to hear his testimony and give it whatever
weight it feels is appropriate.

Defendant: Let the record show my objection to the competency of this
witness.

Commentary: This example is controlled by 18 U.S.C. §3509(c). The judge
conducted a hearing in accordance with its provisions. The better practice
would be for the judge to refer specifically to the statute when making a finding
of competency.

§4.3.   *Oath or affirmation (FRE 603)*[4]

1.   Law

Rule 603.   Oath or Affirmation to Testify Truthfully

Before testifying, a witness must give an oath or affirmation to testify
truthfully. It must be in a form designed to impress that duty on the
witness's conscience.

FRE 603 requires that all witnesses promise to testify truthfully. This can be
by oath or, if taking an oath is against the witness's personal beliefs, by affirmation. This act subjects the witness to the penalties of perjury if the witness knowingly testifies falsely. There are no magic words to an affirmation. The only
requirement is that it commit the witness to answer truthfully. A witness who
refuses to make a declaration to testify truthfully will be barred from testifying.
If, for some reason, the witness testifies without having been placed under a
proper oath, failure to object waives the error.

2.   Practice

Oath or affirmation issues are rare. When a witness flatly refuses to take any oath,
as sometimes happens with hostile or uncooperative witnesses, the witness will
be barred from testifying. More problematical are situations where a witness will
not swear or affirm on religious grounds.

Example:

Clerk: Do you swear that the testimony you are about to give will be the
truth, the whole truth, and nothing but the truth?

Witness: I refuse to swear. It's against my religious beliefs.

4. McCormick §62; Weinstein §603[01]-[03]; Mueller & Kirkpatrick §6.6; Wigmore
§§1815-1833.

Lawyer: Objection, your honor, to the witness testifying without taking the proper oath.

Judge: Ms. Adams, can you promise us, subject to the penalties for perjury, that your testimony will be truthful?

Witness: Of course.

Judge: Very well. The objection is overruled. The witness may testify.

Commentary: What is important is not the particular form of the oath, but the fact of an oath that will subject the witness to the legal possibility of perjury charges for untruthful testimony. The form of the oath can be modified to meet the religious or ideological needs of the witness.

§4.4.   *Improper witnesses (FRE 605, 606)*[5]

1.   Law

Rule 605.   Judge's Competency as a Witness

The presiding judge may not testify as a witness at the trial. A party need not object to preserve the issue.

Rule 606.   Juror's Competency as a Witness

(a) At the Trial.   A juror may not testify as a witness before the other jurors at the trial. If a juror is called to testify, the court must give a party an opportunity to object outside the jury's presence.

(b) During an Inquiry into the Validity of a Verdict or Indictment.

(1) *Prohibited Testimony or Other Evidence.*   During an inquiry into the validity of a verdict or indictment, a juror may not testify about any statement made or incident that occurred during the jury's deliberations, the effect of anything on that juror's or another juror's vote, or any juror's mental processes concerning the verdict or indictment. The court may not receive a juror's affidavit or evidence of a juror's statement on these matters.

(2) *Exceptions.* A juror may testify about whether:

(A) extraneous prejudicial information was improperly brought to the jury's attention;

(B) an outside influence was improperly brought to bear on any juror; or

(C) a mistake was made in entering the verdict on the verdict form.

---

5. McCormick §§68, 70; Weinstein §§605[01]-[06], 606[01]-[09]; Mueller & Kirkpatrick §§6.8-6.9; Wigmore §§1909-1910.

A judge under FRE 605 may not testify as a witness in the trial in which he is presiding, but the rule is not as obvious as it seems. Clearly a judge presiding at a trial, and, by extension, his law clerk, may not take the stand and testify as a witness. Everyone understands that. If the presiding judge takes the stand, he abandons the appearance and substance of impartiality, and opposing counsel would be hamstrung.

More subtle problems occur when there is a claim that the hearing or trial judge is acting as a witness while remaining in the judge's chair. When a judge uses personal knowledge or experience to find material facts or draw legal conclusions, the integrity of the proceeding is called into question.

The point at which the presiding judge becomes a witness is hard to define. If the judge, or his clerk, gathers facts from outside the record to make a decision, he has crossed the line from judge to witness. On the other hand, the judge is allowed to bring his knowledge and experience to court when assessing evidence. Obviously, instructing the jury on inferences to be drawn or on matters of which the judge has taken judicial notice is proper. Like jurors, judges can use their experiences in life when weighing the credibility of witnesses. However, when a judge, without notice to parties, goes to the scene of the accident during a bench trial, or when he uses his personal experience with the effects of an anaesthetic to rule a confession, made shortly after surgery, involuntary, he has abandoned the role of judge and has become a witness. For example, when a judge states, during a motion to suppress, that "as you come out of a general anaesthetic, you are not accountable for what you do," the judge has improperly become a witness. The question is whether the judge, under the guise of judicial knowledge, uses knowledge he has gained as an individual observer outside the court.

FRE 605 recognizes the difficult position an opposing lawyer is placed in when the trial judge becomes, in effect, a witness. No objection is needed to preserve the point on appeal.

FRE 606 governs the competency of a juror as a witness. FRE 606(a) provides that a member of the jury may not testify as a witness before that jury in which the juror sits as a juror. This rule is confined to the time of trial. It does not apply to the jury selection process or to the judge's attempt to learn whether newspaper accounts have come to the juror's attention during the trial.

FRE 606(b) governs the calling of jurors and grand jurors as witnesses to attack the validity of verdicts and indictments. This section is intended to protect the jury's freedom during its deliberations, to protect the jury from harassment and embarrassment after verdicts, and to protect the finality of verdicts.

Jurors may not testify to events that take place or statements that are made during the course of their deliberations. Nor may they testify to the effect of anything on a juror's mind or emotions that might have influenced the juror to agree or disagree with an indictment or verdict. No juror testimony is allowed concerning a juror's mental processes that led to an indictment or a verdict. FRE 606(b) cannot be circumvented by using a juror's affidavit or someone else's testimony about what a juror might have said.

FRE 606(b) opens the door to attempts to impeach jury verdicts in limited circumstances. A juror may testify "(1) whether extraneous prejudicial information was improperly brought to the jury's attention, (2) whether an outside influence was improperly brought to bear upon any juror, or (3) whether a mistake was made in entering the verdict onto the verdict form."

Again, an exercise in line-drawing is required. The decisions bar inquiry into whether jurors compromised, or considered the presence of insurance coverage, or misunderstood the instructions of law, or misunderstood the evidence. A verdict cannot be impeached by a juror's excessive concern with time pressures or by the fact that the jurors, during deliberations, screamed at each other, used obscene language, or threw chairs. The Supreme Court has held that drug or alcohol use by the jurors during trial is not the kind of "external influence" that may be used to attack a criminal conviction. *Tanner v. United States*, 483 U.S. 107 (1987). FRE 606(b) prohibits the use of a juror affidavit to attack a civil trial verdict where a new trial is sought on the ground that a juror lied during jury selection. *Warger v. Shauers*, 134 S. Ct. 1491 (2014). The Supreme Court left open the possibility that FRE 606(b) would not bar instances of extreme juror attitudes, such as racial or religious bias.

On the other hand, a juror may testify to statements made to the jury by a bailiff or to prejudicial newspaper stories that appeared in the jury room during deliberations. Other permissible areas of inquiry include whether jurors received unadmitted documents improperly put in the jury room, whether jurors went to the scene of the crime during the trial, whether jurors conducted experiments with exhibits during deliberations, whether jurors read unadmitted books, periodicals, or treatises dealing with the issues of the case, and whether jurors made a mistake in entering their verdict on the verdict form.

While jurors may testify about extraneous information or outside influence, the trial judge, not the jurors, weighs the nature and extent of any effect on the jury's deliberations. FRE 606(b) does not touch on the impact of the "outside influence" on jurors. That is a matter for the trial judge to determine under the facts of each case. Trial judges are not enthusiastic about postverdict attacks on the deliberative process. It takes an extreme case of "outside influence" to persuade a judge that the case should be tried again.

Although not expressly covered by the Federal Rules of Evidence, the question of whether a lawyer may testify as a witness while representing a party in a trial comes up from time to time. Rule 3.7 of the Model Rules provides that a lawyer "shall not act as an advocate at a trial in which the lawyer is likely to be a necessary witness except where (1) the testimony relates to an uncontested issue . . . or (3) disqualification of the lawyer would work substantial hardship on the client."

This question often occurs when the lawyer, with no one else present, speaks to a potential witness who then says something different at trial. The lawyer wants to cross-examine the witness on the earlier conversation and, if necessary, take the stand to complete the impeachment. Judges are reluctant to allow lawyers to make an issue of their own credibility before trial.

The wise course is for a lawyer to have another person present during such conversations, so that the other person can be a "prove-up witness" if that later becomes necessary. Otherwise, the best course for the lawyer to take during trial is to ask for permission to question the witness out of the presence of the jury to determine whether the witness will admit making the prior inconsistent statement. If the witness admits it, the question can be repeated before the jury without the lawyer taking the stand. If the witness denies it, the judge then has the discretion to allow the lawyer's testimony to impeach the witness, but it will take a strong showing of urgency to persuade the judge.

2.   Practice

Under FRE 605 and 606, common issues involve whether outside influences affected a jury's verdict and whether a lawyer can call himself as a witness in a trial in which he represents a party. This happens most commonly, and usually without problems, in probate proceedings in which the lawyer testifies briefly about an uncontested matter, as when he identifies the testator's signature on the will or testifies about the will's execution. This is permitted under Model Rule 3.7. In other situations, particularly in the impeachment area, problems can arise.

Example 1:

This is a criminal case in which the defendant was charged with and convicted of arson. One day after the verdict was returned, the case is motioned up before the trial judge, and the following happens:

Defendant: Your honor, when I returned to my office last night, I received a telephone call from one of the jurors, Mrs. Shapiro. She told me one of the other jurors, Mr. Buzzhart, had a book about arson investigation in the jury room during the deliberations. She said he talked to the other jurors about how the book said that most arson fires involve the use of accelerants, just like this case. We're asking that the jurors be brought back to court and a hearing conducted into Mrs. Shapiro's allegations.

Prosecutor: They're trying to impeach the verdict, your honor, by getting into the deliberations in the jury room. They can't do that. Even if they could, they would need a stronger preliminary showing to warrant a full hearing.

Judge: This is the kind of outside influence that is a proper subject of inquiry under Rule 606(b). I believe a hearing would be in the best interest of justice. I will authorize the issuance of subpoenas directed to the jurors.

Example 2:

A plaintiff's witness has just testified on direct examination that he saw the defendant driving "about 60 mph when he struck the plaintiff's car" in a 45-mph zone. On cross-examination, the following happens:

Q. (By defendant's lawyer) Mr. Williams, you talked to me about this case a while ago, right?
A. Yes.
Q. That was in my office?
A. Yes.
Q. Just the two of us?
A. That's right.
Q. During that meeting, didn't you tell me . . .
Plaintiff: Objection, your honor. May we be heard at sidebar?

Judge: Yes, Counsel, please approach the bench: [Lawyers do so.] What's the basis of your objection?

Plaintiff: I believe the defense is going into impeachment with a prior inconsistent statement, and it's obvious that counsel is the only available prove-up witness.

Judge: Was your conversation recorded?

Defendant: No.

Judge: How do you intend to prove up the statement if the witness doesn't admit it?

Defendant: He told me he couldn't really tell how fast the car was going. I'm assuming he'll admit that when asked. If not, I'll call myself as the prove-up witness. Under Model Rule 3.7, this is allowed if an undue hardship would otherwise result.

Judge: Plaintiff, what's your position?

Plaintiff: Your honor, the defense could have avoided the problem by having another witness present during the conversation or recording it in some way. This hardship is of his own making.

Judge: The objection is sustained.

Commentary: This situation points out the perils of not planning how to prove up an out-of-court statement used to impeach if the statement is non-collateral (important) and the witness does not admit making it. In this situation, the defense lawyer should ask the judge for permission to question the witness out of the jury's presence to determine if the witness will admit making the prior inconsistent statement. If he does, the questions can be repeated before the jury. If he does not, that ends the matter. This request is discretionary with the judge.

§4.5.   Who may call witnesses (FRE 614)[6]

1.   Law

Rule 614.   Court's Calling or Examining a Witness

   (a) Calling.   The court may call a witness on its own or at a party's request. Each party is entitled to cross-examine the witness.

   (b) Examining.   The court may examine a witness regardless of who calls the witness.

   (c) Objections.   A party may object to the court's calling or examining a witness either at that time or at the next opportunity when the jury is not present.

   FRE 614 restates the trial judge's common law authority to call and question witnesses. FRE 614(a) allows the judge, on his own motion or at the suggestion of a party, to call witnesses. When the judge does so, all parties are entitled to cross-

6. McCormick §8; Weinstein §614[01]-[06]; Mueller & Kirkpatrick §6.70; Wigmore §§1882-1900.

examine the witnesses. FRE 706 governs the appointment and calling of expert witnesses.

There appears to be little reason for the trial judge to call a non-expert witness. Parties no longer vouch for the credibility of witnesses they call, and FRE 607 permits any party to attack the credibility of any witness, including any witness it calls.

Lawyers sometimes prefer that the trial judge call a witness whose believ-ability will be attacked. That procedure obviates any objection to leading ques-tions. Appellate courts do not question a trial judge's decision to call or not call witnesses.

FRE 614(b) allows the trial judge to question any witness. Judges routinely ask questions to clarify matters for the jury, especially when the witness is an expert or is testifying about some technical matter. The permissible scope of judicial questioning is much broader in trials where the judge is the finder of fact.

While trial judges have the right to ask questions, there are limits. Ques-tioning can be an abuse of discretion where the judge becomes an advocate, shedding the appearance of impartiality. There is no precise formula for the number or kinds of questions that will exceed the limits. The test is whether the judge's conduct created a likelihood of undue influence over the jury. The issue arises from time to time in criminal cases. If, when questioning witnesses or making comments, the judge expresses his view that the defendant is guilty, the reviewing court will find an abuse of discretion, even if the trial judge gave the jury the standard instruction that the jury is not to infer from the judge's conduct during the trial what the jury's verdict should be.

A lawyer is placed in a difficult position when the judge asks questions that harm the lawyer's case. He does not want to object in the jury's presence, for obvious reasons. It looks like the lawyer is fighting with the judge or is trying to block attempts to present important information. For these reasons, FRE 614(c) gives the lawyer the option to object at the time a witness is called or questioned by the judge or to object "at the next opportunity when the jury is not present." If the lawyer does not use either of those opportunities to object, the issue is waived.

2.   Practice

FRE 614 rarely creates issues, since either party can call witnesses and can cross-examine any witnesses the court may call. A related problem does commonly arise, however. Under FRE 611(a), the judge has power to control the order in which witnesses are examined, and lawyers frequently will ask permission to call witnesses out of turn or during the other party's case.

Example:

In a products liability case, plaintiff is presenting her case-in-chief. During a break, the following happens:

Plaintiff: Your honor, before the jury comes back from the morning break, a scheduling problem has come up, and I'd like to address it now.

Judge: Very well, what is it?

Plaintiff: I was just informed by my office that our main liability expert, Dr. Ruth Henderson, has a family emergency. One of her children was rushed to the hospital after a bicycle accident, and his condition appears serious. We were planning on calling her after lunch and resting this afternoon. With the court's permission, we would like to call her the day after tomorrow and then formally rest our case. I realize that this would mean calling Dr. Henderson during the defense case, but I couldn't anticipate that this emergency would happen.

Judge: Defense, what's your position?

Defendant: Your honor, we can hardly oppose the request under these circumstances. However, perhaps we can continue the trial until tomorrow morning. If Dr. Henderson is available, she can testify. If not, I'll be ready to start the defense case. I do object to calling her in the middle of my case. Why don't we just wait until the defense case is completed, and Dr. Henderson can then be the first witness in the plaintiff's rebuttal case?

Judge: That sounds reasonable. Counsel, keep us up to date as you find out what Dr. Henderson's situation is. I will defer any motions for a directed verdict until after she testifies.

§4.6. *Excluding witnesses (FRE 615)*[7]

1. Law

Rule 615.   Excluding Witnesses

At a party's request, the court must order witnesses excluded so that they cannot hear other witnesses' testimony. Or the court may do so on its own. But this rule does not authorize excluding:

(a) a party who is a natural person;

(b) an officer or employee of a party that is not a natural person, after being designated as the party's representative by its attorney;

(c) a person whose presence a party shows to be essential to presenting the party's claim or defense; or

(d) a person authorized by statute to be present.

With a few exceptions, the trial judge must exclude witnesses from the courtroom during the testimony of other witnesses. If there is no request to exclude witnesses, the judge can do it on his own motion. Although FRE 615 refers only to the time when witnesses are testifying, many judges also exclude witnesses during opening statements, offers of proof and discussions about proposed testimony. The purpose of the rule is to prevent later witnesses

---

7. McCormick §50; Weinstein §615[01]-[05]; Mueller & Kirkpatrick §§6.71-6.72.

from being influenced by the testimony of earlier witnesses. The right to exclude witnesses is commonly called "invoking the rule" or "sequestering the witnesses" in some jurisdictions.

The trial judge has the authority under FRE 611(a) to require those persons not excluded from the courtroom to testify at an early stage of the trial before other material witnesses testify. This authority does not extend to the defendant in a criminal case, who, if he testifies at the trial, will often testify as the last witness in the defense case.

There are three exceptions to the exclusion of witnesses. First, the judge may not exclude a party who is a natural person. This applies to civil and criminal cases. A criminal defendant has a constitutional right to remain in the courtroom.

Second, an exception is made when the party is a non-natural person, such as a corporation. In that case, the party's lawyer commonly designates as a representative an officer or employee of the party, who sits at counsel table during the trial. In criminal cases, the government's case agent is usually allowed to assist the prosecutor during the trial.

Third, an exception is made for a person whose presence is shown by a party to be essential to the presentation of the party's case. This exception is most frequently applied to retained experts who will testify at the trial. Whether to exclude a retained expert is a matter of discretion, which can be abused where there is a showing that the expert's presence is essential to a party's case.

The rule does not limit the number of witnesses who will be excepted, but judges usually limit the number to one for each side. Allowing more than one, especially in criminal cases, can be reversible error in the absence of a showing of need.

Although not mentioned by FRE 615, rebuttal witnesses ordinarily are not included in exclusion orders if they are truly rebuttal witnesses. That means that the rebuttal exception cannot be used as a ploy when it was clear from the beginning that the witness would be called. The safe practice is to keep rebuttal witnesses out of the courtroom unless some showing persuades the judge that the witness should remain.

The scope of FRE 615 exceeds its literal terms. Violations of the rule have been found where excluded witnesses are allowed to discuss testimony given in court with witnesses that have already testified and where excluded witnesses have been given transcripts of earlier trial testimony.

Lawyers also may want to discuss a witness's trial testimony with another witness who has not yet testified. Judges should clearly state their view of the scope of the exclusion order. If they do not, lawyers should ask.

FRE 1101(d) lists the various proceedings that are not covered by the Federal Rules of Evidence. These exceptions include fact hearings conducted under FRE 104, such as those held to consider motions to suppress confessions and other evidence. Most judges, however, will apply the rule of exclusion to suppression hearings.

FRE 615 does not contain any sanctions for violations. The appropriate sanction is a matter for the trial judge's discretion. If the violation is willful, the witness can be cited for contempt. Some judges allow the witness to be cross-examined about the violation, and the jury can be instructed to consider the violation when assessing the witness's credibility. In an extreme case, the witness can be barred from testifying. Barring the testimony is a sanction that should be reserved for flagrant and willful violations of the exclusion order.

2. Practice

Issues involving the exclusion of witnesses usually occur in two areas: First, who are persons "essential to presenting the party's claim or defense"? Second, what happens when there has been an unintentional violation of the rule?

Example 1:

In a products liability case, defense counsel before trial requests that the chief design expert for the defense be permitted to sit at counsel table during the trial. Plaintiff objects. At the hearing, the following occurs:

Judge: Counsel, under Rule 615, you have the burden of showing why this expert's presence is essential to the presentation of your case. Why is that so here?

Defendant: Your honor, this case is essentially a war of the experts. Both sides' experts have disagreed in the past, and it is important that Dr. Curtis be present to assist me in cross-examining their experts. Dr. Curtis will also testify, and I need to have him hear the plaintiff's experts so that he can later testify to points of disagreement and why he disagrees.

Judge: Plaintiff?

Plaintiff: Having the expert in court may be convenient and advantageous, but it is hardly essential. They deposed all our experts and got all the discovery they requested, so there is no reason for their expert to be present. This is just another attempt to gain a strategic advantage, since plaintiff presents evidence first.

Judge: I will grant the request. However, plaintiff may also designate one expert to be present throughout the trial, and that expert may later testify in rebuttal.

Commentary: Allowing both sides equal rights under the witness exclusion rule is a common way of dealing with such issues.

Example 2:

In a criminal case, the judge has previously ordered the exclusion of witnesses, except the government's case agent. During the prosecution's case-in-chief, the following happens:

Prosecutor: Your honor, may we approach the bench for a moment?

Judge: You may. [Lawyers come to the bench.]

Prosecutor: I just noticed that the defendant's mother came into the courtroom a few minutes ago while the agent was testifying. She is on the defense's witness list and is subject to the court's

> exclusion order. We request that since she is in violation of your order, she be precluded from testifying.
>
> *Defendant:* Your honor, I told all my witnesses about the requirement of waiting outside until called. I didn't notice her walk in; otherwise, I would have directed her to leave immediately. In any event, all she could have heard was testimony about her son's later arrest, which can't possibly affect her testimony as an alibi witness.
>
> *Judge:* The motion is denied. Counsel, direct her to leave immediately. I will consider her conduct inadvertent. If she violates the order again, she will be barred from testifying.

Commentary: Since the purpose of excluding witnesses is to prevent witnesses from modifying their testimony because they heard another witness testify about the same matter, the important question is whether the violation of the exclusion order was intentional and creates an advantage.

§4.7. *Personal knowledge and opinions (FRE 602, 701)*[8]

1. Law

Rule 602. Need for Personal Knowledge

A witness may testify to a matter only if evidence is introduced sufficient to support a finding that the witness has personal knowledge of the matter. Evidence to prove personal knowledge may consist of the witness's own testimony. This rule does not apply to a witness's expert testimony under Rule 703.

Rule 701. Opinion Testimony by Lay Witnesses

If a witness is not testifying as an expert, testimony in the form of an opinion is limited to one that is:

(a) rationally based on the witness's perception;

(b) helpful to clearly understanding the witness's testimony or to determining a fact in issue; and

(c) not based on scientific, technical, or other specialized knowledge within the scope of Rule 702.

FRE 602, governing the personal knowledge requirement, and FRE 701, governing lay witness opinions, should be read together. Both are grounded in personal knowledge — the observations, experiences, and perceptions of the witness. Their goal is to present the fact finder with reliable evidence from

---

8. McCormick §§10-12, 69; Weinstein §§602[01]-[05], 701[01]-[04]; Mueller & Kirkpatrick §§6.5, 7.1-7.4; Wigmore §§478, 650-686.

witnesses having firsthand knowledge. Neither rule applies to expert witnesses, who are governed by FRE 702-706.

Part (c) of FRE 701 went into effect in 2000. Its purpose, according to the Advisory Committee, is to "eliminate the risk that the reliability requirements set forth in Rule 702 will be evaded through the simple expedient of proffering an expert in lay clothing." It also eliminates the risk that a party will evade the expert witness disclosure requirements of Federal Rule of Civil Procedure 26 and Federal Rule of Criminal Procedure 16.

It is important to note the amendment does not distinguish between expert and lay *witnesses*; it distinguishes between expert and lay *testimony*. Presumably, a witness can testify to some things as a lay witness and then be qualified as an FRE 702 expert for other things.

For example, a police officer can describe the defendant's "suspicious" behavior observed at the site of a drug deal without being qualified as an expert. But he will have to survive an FRE 702 qualification and reliability determination before he uses his specialized knowledge to explain the defendant's use of code words to describe drug quantities and prices or to testify that the defendant's conduct was consistent with that of a drug trafficker.

The intent of the amendment is to make it clear that anything beyond common knowledge is specialized knowledge subject to FRE 702. Still, the argument can be made that a witness need not qualify as an expert unless his testimony is of the type traditionally considered to be within the scope of FRE 702.

Relevancy of the subject being asked about is usually assumed in a discussion of FRE 602 and 701. The real issue is whether the answer called for by the question is reliable enough to be considered by the trier of fact. Because of the wide discretion granted trial judges, there are few appellate opinions where the application of these two rules makes any difference. They do, however, play a major role in the way cases are tried. Objections based on these rules occur frequently in the trial courtroom.

FRE 602 provides that "a witness may testify to a matter only if evidence is introduced sufficient to support a finding that the witness has personal knowledge of the matter." That evidence "may consist of the witness's own testimony." The requirement of "personal knowledge" often is referred to as "firsthand knowledge." The phrase is understood to include a witness's personal observations, experiences, and perceptions.

FRE 701 limits the witness's inferences or opinions to those that are "rationally based on the witness's perception." That is, the witness must have personal knowledge to support the inference or opinion, and the inference or opinion must be one that a reasonable person could draw from that personal knowledge. In addition, FRE 701 requires that the inference or opinion be "helpful to clearly understanding the witness's testimony or to determining a fact in issue."

Both rules, then, require a witness's observations or perceptions as a foundation before sufficient reliability of the witness's answer is established. When faced with ruling on objections based on FRE 602 or 701, trial judges ask: How does the witness know what the witness claims he knows?

The two rules overlap because it often is difficult to separate pure fact from inference or opinion. When a witness testifies that he saw a car going "very fast," it is not useful to stop for an analysis of whether the answer is fact or inference or opinion. It does not matter. Observation and perception matter.

In real life, normal people, in everyday conversation, unconsciously mix facts and opinions when they communicate. Asking such people, when they become witnesses in court, to suddenly adhere to a strict distinction between fact and opinion becomes unworkable. For example, a witness is asked to describe how someone looked after a collision. The witness answers, "She looked scared." Strictly speaking, this answer is not a fact; it is an opinion or inference. The "facts" are the facial expressions and other body language on which the witness bases her "opinion" that the other person looked scared, yet it is obvious that the witness would have a difficult, if not impossible, time trying to describe the "facts" underlying the "opinion."

FRE 701 recognizes these realities and permits such opinions and inferences. So it is that witnesses are allowed to testify that someone looked angry, irritated, in pain, in a hurry, happy, delirious, disoriented, nervous, frightened, or intoxicated. Or they can testify about degrees of light or darkness, sound, size, weight, and distance. These are the judgments people make in everyday life, and FRE 701 permits them when they are based on observation and perception. On the other hand, non-expert witnesses generally cannot testify to what someone else thinks, feels, or intends. No amount of observation or perception by one lay witness can support an inference or opinion about another person's thoughts or inner feelings.

FRE 701 is not intended to allow conclusions to take the place of facts. The "helpful" requirement is intended to encourage testimony about facts, rather than conclusions, where facts are available. A witness should not be able to testify that an accident was "unavoidable" or that the driver "had to speed up because he had no choice." The Rules prefer that the fact finder have the information that would allow it to reach its own conclusions. If the witness cannot offer that information, his conclusions are useless.

Careless questions can cause unnecessary problems. For example, the question. "Why did Jones reach for his gun?" calls for speculation and conjecture, and an objection will be sustained. The lawyer should have asked "What happened then?" — the response being "Smith started walking toward Jones. Smith had a knife in his hand and was saying, 'I'm going to cut your throat.'" The jury can then draw its own conclusion.

There is no perfect agreement among judges concerning the amount of observation or perception needed to support the witness's answer. Ordinarily it is enough of a foundation for the witness to say, "I saw the man holding the gun," before identifying the man with the gun. Admissibility does not require showing the length of time the witness saw the man, the distance between the witness and the man, or the lighting conditions at the time. These are concerns of effective advocacy.

The question of the amount of observation or perception necessary under FRE 602 becomes more difficult when the witness is asked to state whether someone was intoxicated (or to draw some other conclusion that requires some previous experience to be credible). Some judges hold that the opportunity to observe that person is enough. Others require a factual foundation of how the observed person was behaving and whether the witness had any life experience with that kind of behavior.

The trial judge's task is to determine whether a reasonable juror could conclude it is more likely than not that the witness's testimony is based on personal knowledge, experience, or observation. If so, the jury should hear it. On the other hand, when an answer would be based on speculation, conjecture, rumor, inadmissible hearsay, documents not in evidence, or irrational thinking, the jury should not hear it. For example, if a witness's belief that a public official is taking bribes is based on rumors, that belief should not be admitted. No reasonable juror could have a basis to believe the witness.

At times, it turns out later, often through cross-examination, that a witness's answer was not based on a sufficient foundation. When that becomes apparent, the opponent should make an immediate motion to strike the witness's testimony. Otherwise, the point may be waived on appeal.

Trial judges regularly admit, under FRE 801(d)(2)(D), vicarious admissions that would not be admissible under FRE 602 and 701. For example, statements by agents that "the accident was my fault" or "the floor must have been slippery" are admitted against their principals without any showing of personal knowledge. FRE 602 and 701 do not appear to be obstacles to the admissibility of such statements.

Trial judges at times admit hearsay statements under various hearsay exceptions without considering whether the out-of-court declarant had personal knowledge. For example, a statement that constitutes an excited utterance might be admitted without any showing that the out-of-court declarant had personal knowledge. FRE 602 and 701 should be obstacles to the admissibility of such hearsay statements.

There is some disagreement over whether personal knowledge is something a trial judge decides under FRE 104(a) or 104(b). In practice, judges do not want to take the time to conduct an FRE 104(a) hearing on the existence of adequate observation or perception. A lawyer will rarely be able to persuade a judge that the admissibility of an expected answer bearing on a material point is a "preliminary question" under FRE 104(a). Strictly speaking, FRE 104(b) does not apply to this issue, since that is a conditional relevancy rule, not a foundation rule.

Most judges allow the issue to play out before the jury. If a reasonable juror could conclude that the testimony is based on personal knowledge, it comes in. If a foundation is lacking, the judge can admit the testimony subject to later establishing personal knowledge, or he can direct the proponent to "establish your foundation." FRE 602 requires that sufficient personal knowledge be "introduced." The party offering the testimony has the burden of proving the existence of a sufficient foundation for an answer.

The form of objection based on FRE 602 and 701 varies from place to place and from lawyer to lawyer. Objections can be made in the words of these rules: "I object, the witness has no personal knowledge," or "I object, the question calls for an inference not rationally based on the witness's perception." Also ordinarily acceptable are objections such as "I object, no foundation," or "I object, that question calls for speculation," or "I object, the question calls for a conclusion." While these objections are not specifically contained in these rules, everyone understands them, and they seem to pose no problems.

The requirement of personal knowledge, experience, and perception to support answers is no greater than the expectations of everyday life. Certainty is not required. Answers that contain qualifiers, such as "I'm not sure, but . . . ," "I believe so," and "my best estimate is . . . ," do not run afoul of FRE 602 and 701.

However, when the witness says, "I guess that . . ." or "I imagine that . . . ," the line is crossed into speculation and conjecture, and an objection should be sustained.

2.   Practice

FRE 602 issues most commonly arise when a question calls for an answer before the personal knowledge foundation is established. Lay witness opinions are routinely admitted at trial, since FRE 701 makes it clear that such evidence, if based on firsthand knowledge and helpful to the jury, is properly admissible.

Example 1:

> This is a personal injury case. An eyewitness is testifying.
>
> Q. (By plaintiff's lawyer) Where were you on June 1, 2015, at 3:00 P.M.?
> A. I was at the corner of Maple and Elm.
> Q. Did you hear anything?
> A. Yes, I heard a loud crunch.
> Q. How fast was the black car going?
> *Defendant:* Objection. No foundation.
> *Judge:* Sustained.
> Q. Did you see the cars involved in the crash?
> A. Yes, one was white, one was black.
> Q. When did you first see them?
> A. A few seconds before the crash.
> Q. How fast was the black car going?
> A. About 50 mph.

Commentary: This objection, while technically correct, accomplished little. The proponent then presented a proper, more persuasive foundation. For this reason, some lawyers elect not to object on foundation grounds when it is obvious that the proponent can overcome the objection.

Example 2:

> In a negligence case, one of the defenses is that the defendant did not regularly do the prescribed therapy. To prove this, the defendant calls a physical therapist.
>
> Q. (By defendant's lawyer) Ms. Wilson, you were one of the therapists who helped the plaintiff during his physical therapy sessions?
> A. That's right.
> Q. Did he ever fail to attend scheduled sessions?
> A. Yes.
> Q. How many sessions did he fail to attend?
> A. With me, five. But I know that he also missed appointments with the other therapists . . .

Plaintiff: Objection, your honor. This witness has no personal knowledge
of what the plaintiff did out of her presence.

Judge: Objection is sustained.

Commentary: The therapist can testify only about the sessions that she
scheduled where the plaintiff did not appear. She cannot testify to the other
sessions missed, even if the missed sessions were noted in the medical records.
The proper way to prove this is to introduce the medical records as business
records under FRE 803(6). This witness may be a competent witness to qualify
the records for admission.

Example 3:

In a personal injury case, plaintiff calls an eyewitness to the collision.

Q. (By plaintiff's lawyer) What did you see next?

A. The defendant's car was going about 40 mph when he started to brake.

Q. What did you notice about the car?

A. It started to slow down. The driver was obviously trying to brake to
avoid the other car.

Defendant: Objection to everything after "slow down." This witness has no
personal knowledge of what was going on in the driver's mind.

Judge: Sustained.

Defendant: We move to strike everything after "slow down" and instruct
the jury to disregard.

Judge: Members of the jury, the witness's answer after "It started to slow
down" has been struck. This means that you must disregard the
rest of the witness's answer.

Commentary: The witness can describe what she saw, but cannot state what
was going on in someone else's mind. The witness has no firsthand knowledge
and is incompetent on that point. If the objection is sustained, the opposing
lawyer should move to strike and disregard. While the jury cannot "unremem-
ber" what it has just heard, it must be instructed to disregard to preserve error
on appeal.

Example 4:

In an automobile negligence case, plaintiff calls an eyewitness to the
collision. She has just testified to seeing the driver get out of the car.

Q. (By plaintiff's lawyer) What did the other driver look like after the crash?

A. Well, he looked nervous, scared, and appeared intoxicated.

Defendant: Your honor, we object. This is opinion testimony, and the witness has not been qualified as an expert. In addition, there is
no factual foundation for his opinion.

Judge: Objection overruled.

Commentary: These are the kinds of opinions permissible under FRE 701.
However, some judges would not be satisfied with the factual foundation unless

it also included time, distance, and ability to observe, particularly as to the opinion on intoxication, where more observations about the driver's appearance would better support the conclusion.

Example 5:

In an income tax evasion case, the prosecution calls a witness who worked with the defendant for years.

Q. (By prosecutor) I'm showing you a check that has been marked Government Exhibit No. 6. Do you recognize the signature on that check?
A. Yes, I do.
Q. Have you seen it before?
A. Yes, a few times.
Q. Under what circumstances have you seen it?
A. When I saw the defendant sign his tax returns.
Q. Whose signature is on Government Exhibit No. 6?
Defendant: Objection. The witness did not see the check signed and is not an expert in handwriting comparisons.
Judge: Overruled. The witness may answer.

Commentary: This standard foundation, governed by FRE 901, is actually opinion testimony used to authenticate a signature. If the witness has seen the signature being written one time, that is enough for the judge. After that, it becomes a credibility issue for the jury.

§4.8.   *Impeaching own witnesses (FRE 607)*[9]

1.   Law

Rule 607.   Who May Impeach a Witness

Any party, including the party that called the witness, may attack the witness's credibility.

Under FRE 607, any party can attack the credibility of any testifying witness, including its own. The Federal Rules have rejected the common law voucher rule, under which a party calling a witness was considered to have vouched for the witness's credibility and therefore could not attack it. This Federal Rule recognizes modern realities: Parties call witnesses because they are necessary witnesses to an event or a transaction, not because they vouch for their credibility.

No problem arises when a party impeaches its own witness with evidence that is otherwise admissible as substantive evidence. If the impeachment is in the form of facts supported by another witness's observations, or an FRE 801(d) non-hearsay prior inconsistent statement, or some hearsay exception, the

---

9. McCormick §38; Weinstein §607[01]-[11]; Mueller & Kirkpatrick §§6.16-6.17; Wigmore §§896-918.

question of whether the examiner has been surprised or damaged by the witness's testimony should not be considered. There is no danger of unfair prejudice. But when the impeachment is in the form of otherwise inadmissible evidence, such as an unsworn prior inconsistent statement, serious problems of potential misuse occur.

A party might call a witness who once made statements favorable to the party's case. Just before trial, the witness tells the party's lawyer he no longer will testify favorably. This situation can happen in any kind of case, but more often occurs in criminal cases. The question becomes: Can the lawyer call the witness, elicit the unfavorable testimony, and then impeach the witness with otherwise inadmissible prior inconsistent statements?

Most courts require a showing that the party calling the witness has been damaged by the in-court testimony before impeachment is allowed, although FRE 607 does not say that. That is, the impeachment must be necessary and in good faith. If the party's case has not been damaged by the testimony, there is no point to the impeachment, other than to place inadmissible evidence before the jury. Courts that require damage refuse to permit impeachment that is used as a subterfuge to get inadmissible evidence before the jury. Reviewing courts have reversed criminal convictions where this kind of impeachment may have caused serious harm to the defendant. When considering whether subterfuge is present, these courts determine whether the calling party truly was surprised by the witness's testimony.

A few courts do not require a showing of surprise or damage before a party impeaches its own witness with inadmissible prior statements. These courts read FRE 607 literally, even where the prior statement directly inculpates a criminal defendant, since the rule does not contain any limitations. Still, some courts are reluctant to allow the impeachment where it is clear the primary or only purpose of the examiner is to get inadmissible statements before the jury, especially where those statements are directed to a material issue in the case. Reviewing courts decide these issues on a case-by-case basis.

When confronted with this situation, trial judges often use the FRE 403 balancing test, weighing the probative value of the impeachment against the unfair prejudice caused by the jury hearing otherwise inadmissible evidence. That kind of analysis avoids the need to examine the proponent's motives and purposes.

Whenever inadmissible evidence is used to impeach a witness, the opposing party may ask for and must receive a limiting instruction as required by FRE 105. Failure to ask for the instruction waives a claim on appeal that the failure to give a limiting instruction was error. However, failure to ask for a limiting instruction does not entitle the proponent to argue the prior statement as substantive evidence.

2. Practice

At times, the party calling a witness will ask about prior inconsistent statements as a way of obviating or blunting anticipated impeachment by the cross-examiner. While this is not, strictly speaking, an "attack" on the witness's credibility, it is within the meaning of FRE 607.

The party calling a witness may attack the witness's credibility in ways other than prior inconsistent statements. By referring to something the witness has said or done, the examiner can establish bias, interest, or motive. Or the witness's character for truthfulness may be attacked with reputation or opinion evidence (FRE 608(a)) or with prior convictions (FRE 609). Use of FRE 608(b) specific acts during direct examination to attack character for truthfulness is unlikely, since that rule applies to "cross-examination."

If the examiner elicits his client's prior conviction during direct examination, he loses the right to claim on appeal that the prior conviction was not admissible under FRE 609. This is true even though the judge has clearly ruled the conviction will be admissible during cross-examination of the witness. *Ohler v. United States*, 529 U.S. 753 (2000). Presumably, the holding in *Ohler* would apply to any witness.

Example 1:

In contract case, the defendant calls a witness in the defendant's case-in-chief.

Q. (By defendant's lawyer) Mr. Johnson, who was present when the contract was signed?
A. Just Mr. Merchant, Ms. Walters, and myself.
Q. That's not what you said when you testified during your deposition, is it?
Plaintiff: Objection. He's impeaching his own witness. There's no showing of surprise or hostility.
Judge: Overruled. The witness may answer.

Commentary: Impeaching any witness is a matter of right. A showing of surprise, hostility, or other circumstances is not required.

Example 2:

In a criminal case, the prosecution calls an eyewitness to testify to seeing the defendant rob the victim. The witness talked to an FBI agent and identified the defendant as the robber. However, before trial, the witness recants and tells the prosecutor that he is disavowing his earlier testimony and will not identify the defendant if called as a witness at trial. Nevertheless, the prosecutor subpoenas the witness for trial and calls him to the stand.

Q. (By prosecutor) You saw the robber, right?
A. Yes.
Q. Look around the courtroom, and if you see the person who did the robbery, point him out.
A. I don't see anyone here who was the robber.
Q. Well, let's talk about what you said to FBI Special Agent O'Brien.
Defendant: Objection, your honor. May we approach?
Judge: Please. [Lawyers come to the bench.] Counsel, what's the basis for your objection?

Defendant: The prosecutor knew that the witness would not identify my client in court. The prosecutor was told that before trial. They called him just to impeach him with his statement to the FBI agent, knowing that testimony would otherwise be inadmissible. Under *United States v. Gomez-Gallardo,* found at 915 F.2d 553, 9th Circuit, 1990, which states the controlling law in this circuit, that's improper.

Judge: (To prosecutor) Did you know before trial that the witness would not make an in-court identification?

Prosecutor: That's what he said, but we didn't know if he was bluffing or not until he got up there.

Judge: The objection is sustained. There will be no further questions directed to this witness about the identification of the robber.

Commentary: Not all jurisdictions would agree with this result.

§4.9. *Leading questions (FRE 611(c))*[10]

1. Law

Rule 611. Mode and Order of Examining Witnesses and Presenting Evidence

(c) Leading Questions.   Leading questions should not be used on direct examination except as necessary to develop the witness's testimony. Ordinarily, the court should allow leading questions:

(1) on cross-examination; and

(2) when a party calls a hostile witness, an adverse party, or a witness identified with an adverse party.

FRE 611(c) provides that a party should not use leading questions on direct examination of a witness "except as necessary to develop the witness's testimony." The use of the word "should" indicates a preference, rather than a command. Trial judges, then, are granted broad discretion when deciding whether to allow leading questions.

The rule is a common-sense guide directed at assuring that the fact finder receives reliable evidence. When the examiner asks a question that contains or suggests the answer sought, it is the lawyer, not the witness, who is testifying.

The rule contains a non-exclusive list of exceptions. Ordinarily, leading questions should be permitted on cross-examination. Here, too, the rule is not firm. For example, a trial judge may prohibit leading questions when a lawyer cross-examines a friendly witness, such as his own client called by an opponent as an adverse witness.

---

10. McCormick §20; Weinstein §611[05]; Mueller & Kirkpatrick §§6.61, 6.64; Wigmore §§769-779.

Leading questions may be used when a party calls a hostile witness, an adverse party, or a witness identified with an adverse party. This category of exceptions includes an opposing party's employees, spouse, children, parents, and anyone else with a relationship close enough to support a reasonable inference of bias.

Not specifically included in FRE 611(c), but recognized as exceptions to the preference for non-leading questions, are people who have difficulty understanding or responding to non-leading questions. These include the young, the old, the forgetful, people with language problems, people with mental disabilities, the frightened, and the reluctant to testify.

In addition, it is well accepted that leading is permitted on preliminary or undisputed matters. Lawyers routinely are allowed to lead when establishing a foundation for an exhibit or when proving up a prior inconsistent statement made by a witness.

The Federal Rules of Evidence make no mention of redirect examination. The method of redirect examination is left to the trial judge's discretion under FRE 611(a). The common practice is to allow the redirect examiner to call the witness's attention to the desired subject matter through a leading question, but to prohibit further leading.

When leading questions are appropriate, such as in the case of a very young witness or a mentally disabled witness, the usual procedure is for the direct examiner to ask the court for permission to lead. The request may come before the witness begins testifying or, if appropriate, after a demonstration of the futility of asking non-leading questions.

Determining when a question is leading is not an exact science. Some questions clearly are leading. For example, "You didn't drive your car over the speed limit, did you?" is obviously leading. However, a question is not leading when it directs the attention of the witness to the subject matter of the inquiry. For example, "Now I call your attention to a point one block before the collision. At what speed were you driving your car?" is a proper question.

Inserting the archaic phrase "if any" into an otherwise leading question does not make the question any better. For example, "How many times, if any, did you fire the gun in order to save your own life?" is improperly leading.

A subject of some confusion is the question that seeks to elicit a negative answer. For example, the question "At any time before the collision did you hear the sound of a horn?" is not leading when the anticipated answer is "no." The question does not contain or suggest an answer. Very often, however, an objection to a question of this kind is sustained because it sounds like a leading question. Some judges recognize the difference. Likewise, a party should have the right to directly deny an accusation made against him during the course of his trial. For example, the question "Did you have cocaine in your hand when the police pulled up?" is proper when another witness has already testified to these facts.

2. Practice

While leading questions rarely become an issue on appeal, objections to leading questions are common during trials. When the objections are to preliminary or undisputed matters, judges, and juries, tend to treat them as an annoyance. Objections to unimportant matters accomplish little if sustained, other than to force the examiner to rephrase the question, usually resulting in a better question.

Judges do take the objection seriously when the leading question concerns an important matter in the case. In that instance, with the examiner supplying the words for the witness, the reliability of the testimony is called into question. The judge's interest in moving the trial along is superseded by his interest in ensuring that the jury receives the testimony of the witness, not the lawyer.

Example 1:

> Q. Ms. Barnes, were you at the Red Dog Tavern on June 1, 2015, around 3:00 P.M.?
> *Opposing Lawyer:* Objection. Leading the witness.
> *Judge:* Overruled. It's preliminary.

Commentary: Just because a question contains specific facts does not make it leading. In this case, the question is technically leading, since the proper non-leading form is: "Where were you on June 1, 2015, around 3:00 P.M.?" It is a rare judge who will sustain this objection because the question can so easily be rephrased.

Example 2:

> Q. Professor Smith, you're a doctor specializing in orthopedics and received your medical degree from Harvard Medical School, right?
> *Opposing Lawyer:* Objection, your honor. Leading.
> *Judge:* Overruled. The witness may answer. Let's move on.

Commentary: Expert qualifications are preliminary matters not in dispute, so judges usually permit leading questions as an efficient way of presenting the qualifications in court.

Example 3:

> The prosecution calls a six-year-old girl to the stand to testify to being sexually assaulted in her home.

> Q. (By prosecutor) Mary, how old are you?
> A. Six.
> Q. Where were you when all this happened?
> A. In my house.
> Q. Mary, tell us what happened.
> A. [No response]
> Q. Mary, what happened to you that day?
> A. [No response]
> *Prosecutor:* Your honor, may I have permission to lead?
> *Judge:* You may.

Commentary: The judge has discretion under FRE 611(c) to permit leading questions if necessary to develop the witness's testimony. A lawyer should ordinarily show need before permission will be granted unless the need is obvious.

Example 4:

The defendant is using a witness to establish a foundation for a business record. On direct examination, the following happens:

Q. (By defendant's lawyer) Mr. Whipple, is that exhibit, Defendant's Exhibit No. 2, a record of your business?
A. Yes.
Q. Was that record made by a person having knowledge of the facts contained in the record?
Plaintiff: Objection, he's leading the witness.
Judge: Overruled. This is foundational.

Example 5:

The witness is being examined on redirect examination when the following happens:

Q. (By plaintiff's lawyer) Ms. Rice, counsel on cross-examination asked you several questions about the way you performed the CAT scan. Please tell the jury why you performed the test the way you did.
Defendant: Objection to counsel leading. This is redirect of his own witness.
Judge: No, it's preliminary. Overruled.

§4.10.   Other form objections[11]

1.   Law

The Federal Rules of Evidence do not set out most of the form objections that are heard during the course of a trial, other than FRE 611, which governs the use of leading questions. No one has suggested these objections no longer are viable. Common form objections include the following:

1. *Argumentative.* These are questions that contain arguments, or factual summaries or inferences, or comments on the evidence. For example, asking "You wouldn't know the truth if it smacked you in the head, would you?" is argumentative.
2. *Asked and answered.* If the witness has answered the question once, it should not be asked again during that examination. This is just an attempt to emphasize an answer by repeating it. This objection is closely related to the "repetitious" objection where the examiner is

---

11. T.A. Mauet, Trial Techniques and Trials ch. 10 (9th ed. 2013); P. Murray, Basic Trial Advocacy ch. 9 (1995).

beating a point to death and taking a long time to do it, and to the "cumulative" objection, where a party is offering multitudinous evidence on the same point in violation of the spirit of FRE 403.

3. *Assuming facts not in evidence.* If the question contains a fact that has not yet been presented at the trial, it is improper. For example, asking "What was the man holding the gun doing?" is improper if no evidence has established the existence of a man with a gun.

4. *Commenting on other witnesses.* It is improper to ask a witness to comment on the truth of another witness's testimony since this is a proper function of the jury. Asking "Did John Jones lie when he told this jury you had a gun in your hand?" is improper.

5. *Compound.* A question that contains two or more questions is improper. The reason is that a simple "yes" or "no" answer will be confusing, since no one knows what part of the question the response was answering. For example, asking "Did you have a gun with you, and did you fire a gun that day?" is improper. The questions should be asked one at a time.

6. *Confusing and misleading.* A question that makes no sense, or is unintelligible, or misstates facts in evidence is improper. For example, asking "Did you, when you reached for the gun, however dark it was, and I assume you did, know that there was something you did not know about?" is objectionable. No witness should be forced to answer such a question. This objection is closely related to the "vague and ambiguous" objection.

7. *Harassing, embarrassing, or personally attacking a witness.* FRE 611(a) directs judges to "protect witnesses from harassment or undue embarrassment." Some lawyers refer to it as "badgering" the witness. Asking a witness "You're just a low-down scum of the earth, aren't you?" is improper. Much depends, of course, on the kind of case and the kind of witness. A turncoat witness who testifies he helped the defendant commit a murder is more open to attack than an unaffiliated eyewitness to an accident.

8. *Narrative.* A question that is so general or open that it provokes a broad and wandering answer, usually of some length, is improper. For example, asking "What happened that day?" or "Will you tell us everything you know about what happened?" is improper. The danger of a narrative answer is that it will contain inadmissible evidence, such as hearsay or conclusions without a foundation of personal knowledge. The trial judge has the discretion to require specific questions.

9. *Non-responsive.* Sometimes a question is appropriate, but the answer does not respond to it. For example, the question "Did you have a gun in your pocket?" is answered with "I was afraid he was going to kill me." Most judges believe only the examiner may object to an answer as non-responsive, since he is the one who has the right to a responsive answer. When the objection is sustained, the examiner may ask the judge to strike the offending answer from the record and to instruct the jury to disregard it. Of course, if the answer contains something that is objectionable on other grounds, such as hearsay, the opponent may object to it.

10. *Speculation and conjecture.* A question that calls for the witness to speculate or guess about some event or condition is improper. For example, asking "Why did the other driver suddenly speed up?" is improper, since there is no way the witness can testify about what is going on in someone else's head.

No doubt there are other form objections, but these are the ones that most often occur during the course of a trial.

2. Practice

Form questions rarely become an issue on appeal, but objections based on the form of a question are common during trial. Objections to unimportant matters accomplish little if sustained, other than to force the examiner to rephrase the question, usually resulting in a better question. However, if the question will confuse the witness or the jury or is being asked to embarrass or harass the witness, a prompt objection should be made.

Example:

On cross-examination, the witness is being questioned as follows:

Q. (By defendant's lawyer) Ms. Burroughs, you were tired that evening and weren't expecting to be in a collision, were you?
Plaintiff: Objection, your honor, it's a compound question.
Judge: Sustained. Counsel, let's ask questions, one fact at a time, so no one gets confused.

§4.11. *Refreshing recollection and recorded recollection (FRE 612, 803(5))*[12]

1. Law

Rule 612. Writing Used to Refresh a Witness's Memory

(a) **Scope.** This rule gives an adverse party certain options when a witness uses a writing to refresh memory:
　　(1) while testifying; or
　　(2) before testifying, if the court decides that justice requires the party to have those options.
(b) **Adverse Party's Options; Deleting Unrelated Matter.** Unless 18 U.S.C. §3500 provides otherwise in a criminal case, an adverse party is entitled to have the writing produced at the hearing, to inspect it, to cross-examine the witness about it, and to introduce in evidence any

---

12. McCormick §§9, 279-283; Weinstein §§612[01]-[07], 803(5)[01]-[03]; Mueller & Kirkpatrick §§6.66-6.69, 8.43; Wigmore §§725-765.

portion that relates to the witness's testimony. If the producing party claims that the writing includes unrelated matter, the court must examine the writing in camera, delete any unrelated portion, and order that the rest be delivered to the adverse party. Any portion deleted over objection must be preserved for the record.

  (c) Failure to Produce or Deliver the Writing. If a writing is not produced or is not delivered as ordered, the court may issue any appropriate order. But if the prosecution does not comply in a criminal case, the court must strike the witness's testimony or—if justice so requires—declare a mistrial.

Rule 803(5).   Recorded Recollection

  (5) *Recorded Recollection.* A record that:
    (A) is on a matter the witness once knew about but now cannot recall well enough to testify fully and accurately;
    (B) was made or adopted by the witness when the matter was fresh in the witness's memory; and
    (C) accurately reflects the witness's knowledge.
If admitted, the record may be read into evidence but may be received as an exhibit only if offered by an adverse party.

FRE 612 recognizes the well-established courtroom reality that witnesses frequently forget things they are asked to testify about. When that happens, the examiner uses something, usually a writing, to jog or refresh the witness's memory. The item used to refresh memory does not have to be admissible. In fact, it often would be inadmissible under some other rule of evidence. For example, the prosecution uses a police report to refresh the officer's memory about the events surrounding an arrest. There is no requirement that the writing be made at or near the time of the event the witness is testifying about.

  The rule assumes the existence of the practice, but is directed at determining the integrity of testimony based on the refreshed memory. FRE 612 is a reliability rule, aimed at detecting whether testimony has been fabricated or is the product of undue suggestion.

  When a witness, at any kind of "hearing," uses a writing to refresh his memory, "an adverse party is entitled to have the writing produced at the hearing, to inspect it, to cross-examine the witness about it, and to introduce in evidence any portion that relates to the witness's testimony." Only the adverse party has the option of introducing the writing in evidence under FRE 612.

  Because the writing being used does not have to have been made by the witness, the opponent, in rare circumstances, may successfully attack the integrity of the refreshed memory. This could happen when the witness's memory is refreshed by a fraudulent document or by notes made only for the purpose of the litigation.

  Few problems arise when the writing is used to refresh the witness's memory while he is testifying. The examiner cannot claim privilege or work product when the documents are used at trial. But the rule also provides for the production of writings used to refresh the witness's memory "before testifying" at the hearing. In that instance, the opponent has no automatic right to production of the writing. FRE 612 requires disclosure of the prehearing writing only "if the court decides that justice requires the party to have those options."

Most courts will order production of a writing examined before the hearing if it clearly was used to refresh the witness's memory. Problems arise when the writing is covered by some privilege, such as the attorney-client privilege, or by the work-product protection of Rule 26(b)(3) of the Federal Rules of Civil Procedure. In such an instance, almost every trial judge will use a balancing test, weighing the necessity for disclosure against the need to protect the writing. This weighing process includes consideration of the probative value of the writing and whether the evidence can be obtained in some other way. A few courts have held that the act of showing a writing to a witness to refresh his memory automatically waives any privilege or work-product protection.

While FRE 612 is an evidence rule, not a discovery rule, it applies to writings shown to a witness during a deposition if the purpose is to refresh his memory.

In any instance where production is requested, the examiner has the right to contend that portions of the writing are not related to the witness's testimony. In that case, the trial judge will examine the writing in camera, redact anything found irrelevant, and order delivery of whatever remains.

FRE 612(b) begins by stating that it does not apply to Section 3500 of Title 18 of the United States Code. That section of the Code, commonly called the Jencks Act, covers the production of witness statements in criminal cases. But Rules 26.2 and 17(h) of the Federal Rules of Criminal Procedure seem to cover the same ground as Section 3500. If Section 3500 no longer is viable, the words of FRE 612(c) — "If a writing is not produced or is not delivered as ordered, the court may issue any appropriate order. But if the prosecution does not comply in a criminal case, the court must strike the witness's testimony or — if justice so requires — declare a mistrial" — take on additional importance in criminal cases.

FRE 612 refers to a "writing" used to refresh memory. However, it is commonly accepted that anything, even a physical object or a leading question, can refresh a witness's memory.

The rule does not say exactly when the opposing party must be given the opportunity to inspect the writing being used to refresh memory. It does not require that the writing be shown to opposing counsel before it is shown to the witness, but that is the common practice in most courts. Showing it first to the opposing lawyer gives him the opportunity to make an objection before there is any risk of tainting the witness's testimony with an improper document.

Nothing in FRE 612 suggests the proper foundation for the use of a writing to refresh memory. A simple "I don't remember" from the witness can be enough to trigger use of the writing. Some judges require more, such as asking "Is your memory exhausted on the subject?" or "Is there anything that would refresh your memory?" When produced, the writing or other item being used should be marked as an exhibit.

The usual practice is to show the writing to the witness and then let him read it silently. The writing should not be read to the jury if it has not been admitted into evidence under some other rule. Once the witness has read the document, the lawyer most often will remove it from the witness's sight. That will avoid the risk of the witness simply reading or repeating the words on the document. His memory must be truly refreshed; the testimony should be the product of independent and present recollection. Otherwise, an objection to the testimony is likely to be sustained.

Most trial judges, however, take a realistic view of the need for some witnesses to keep their writings in front of them for occasional reference. Police officers, treating doctors, and retained experts, for example, are not expected to remember the details of such things as investigations, treatments, and other lengthy or complicated matters. Strict adherence to the requirement that the witness not refer to the writing while testifying would unduly lengthen the witness's time on the stand, while doing little to protect the reliability of the testimony. The trial judge has the discretion to allow some deviation from the usual requirements for jogging a witness's memory.

There are times when, no matter how much it is jogged, the witness's memory cannot be refreshed. In that instance, the next step is to qualify the writing as recorded recollection, a hearsay exception under FRE 803(5). The examiner's questions will have to show that the writing was made or adopted by the witness when the matter was fresh in his memory and that it "accurately reflects the witness's knowledge." If the proper foundation is established, the lawyer or the witness may read the relevant portion of the writing into evidence. The writing itself is not received as an exhibit unless the opposing party offers it. Recorded recollection is discussed further in Sec. 7.12.

2. Practice

Problems commonly arise from attempts to refresh recollection before demonstrating a need to refresh and from other procedural mistakes.

Example 1:

The plaintiff is testifying about his conversation with the defendant concerning a product's design.

Q. (By plaintiff's lawyer) What did Smith say to you?
A. He said his design would be perfect for my purposes.
Q. Did he say anything else?
A. Yes, but I don't remember what he said. It was three years ago.
Q. Is there anything that would refresh your memory about that conversation?
A. Yes. I gave you my written account of that conversation. It would help if I could see it.
Q. Your honor, counsel has a copy of this statement, Plaintiff's Exhibit No. 4. Mr. Jones, I show you Plaintiff's Exhibit No. 4. Please read it to yourself. . . . Have you read it?
A. Yes.
Q. Please give it back to me. Do you now remember what else Smith said to you in that conversation?
A. Yes. He said no other company had any design similar to his.

Plaintiff: I have no further questions.

Q. (By defendant's lawyer) Do you really now remember every word Smith said to you?

A. Well, no.

Q. Were you just repeating the words you wrote on this piece of paper, Plaintiff's Exhibit No. 4?

A. Yes.

Q. Your honor, I move to strike the witness's last answer on direct examination. He did not testify from independent recollection.

Judge: The motion is granted, and the witness's answer will be stricken. Any redirect?

Q. (By plaintiff's lawyer) When did you write Plaintiff's Exhibit No. 4, your account of that conversation?

A. No more than five minutes after Smith left my office.

Q. Where were you when you wrote it?

A. I was still in my office.

Q. Did you accurately record the words Mr. Smith said to you?

A. Yes, I did.

Q. Is Plaintiff's Exhibit No. 4 your original statement?

A. Yes.

Plaintiff: At this time, your honor, pursuant to Rule 803(5), I ask permission to read Plaintiff's Exhibit No. 4 to the jury.

Judge: You may.

Commentary: Some judges believe FRE 803(5) requires that the document be offered into evidence before it is read to the jury. The rule does not appear to impose that requirement, although the exhibit should be given to the clerk to make it part of the trial record. To qualify the exhibit as recorded recollection, Jones did not have to have a total failure of memory, only the inability to "testify fully and accurately."

Example 2:

A plaintiff's witness is testifying about performing chemical tests. During direct examination, the following happens:

Q. (By plaintiff's lawyer) Dr. Wilson, on what date did you perform your chemical analysis of the fluid?

A. It was a few months ago, but I don't remember the exact date.

Q. Would anything help you remember that date?

A. I'm sure the report from our lab would.

Q. Doctor, I'm showing you a report marked Defendant's Exhibit No. 2. Please read it to yourself. . . . Does that report help you remember the date?

A. Of course.

Q. May I have the report back, please. What date did you do the analysis of the fluid?

Defendant: Objection, your honor. The report is not in evidence, and it's not even this witness's report.

Judge: Overruled. The witness may answer.

A. I did the analysis on June 1, 2015.

Plaintiff: Your honor, this testimony involves some lengthy and complex calculations and findings. May the doctor keep the laboratory report in front of him during his testimony and refer to it from time to time? I think that will help move things along.

Defendant: I object to that procedure. He will be reading from a document not in evidence.

Judge: I don't see any point in making counsel march up and back every time he has to refresh the witness's memory. The objection is overruled, and the witness may refer to the report.

Example 3:

The witness is being cross-examined when the following happens:

Q. (By plaintiff's lawyer) Mr. Winters, before coming to court this morning, did you review anything to prepare for your testimony?

A. Yes.

Q. What things?

A. I read over the company's business records on the transaction, read over my deposition transcript, and reviewed my memorandum.

Q. What memorandum is that?

A. It's a two-page memo I made about this transaction.

Q. When did you make it?

A. About two weeks ago, when I was told I would be needed for the trial.

Plaintiff: Your honor, may we approach?

Judge: Yes. [Lawyers come to the bench.]

Plaintiff: Your honor, I've never seen this memo. Under Rule 612, I am entitled to see it.

Defendant: Under the rule, it's discretionary, since he didn't use it while testifying, and there's been no showing that producing it is necessary and in the interests of justice.

Judge: I see no reason for him not to produce it. It obviously relates to his testimony. I'm ordering it produced. If the witness has it with him, please obtain it so that counsel can see it. If not, we will continue his testimony so that he can obtain the memo and bring it to court.

Commentary: FRE 612 gives the judge discretion to order the production in court of anything used to refresh recollection, either while testifying or before testifying. If the memo or report has not previously been disclosed during discovery and the witness is important, the judge may order disclosure.

V

DIRECT EXAMINATION OF WITNESSES: RELEVANCE

§5.1. Introduction

Article IV of the Federal Rules of Evidence is aptly titled "Relevance and Its Limits." FRE 401 and 402 begin with the definition of "relevant evidence" and state the proposition that all relevant evidence, with certain enumerated exceptions, is admissible, while irrelevant evidence is not admissible. FRE 403 contains the balancing test that may be used to exclude relevant evidence. FRE 404-415 then describe and regulate specific kinds of relevant evidence, some of which are excluded for reasons having little or nothing to do with relevance. Article IV controls the analysis of relevance unless the Constitution of the United States, an act of Congress, other provisions of the Federal Rules of Evidence, or other rules prescribed by the Supreme Court pursuant to statutory authority also apply.

§5.2. General relevance

1. Law[1]

Rule 401. Test for Relevant Evidence

Evidence is relevant if:
  (a) it has any tendency to make a fact more or less probable than it would be without the evidence; and
  (b) the fact is of consequence in determining the action.

---

1. McCormick §§184-185; Weinstein §§401-403; Mueller & Kirkpatrick §§4.2-4.10; Wigmore §§24-37.7.

Rule 402.   General Admissibility of Relevant Evidence

Relevant evidence is admissible unless any of the following provides otherwise:

- the United States Constitution;
- a federal statute;
- these rules; or
- other rules prescribed by the Supreme Court.

Irrelevant evidence is not admissible.

Rule 403.   Excluding Relevant Evidence for Prejudice, Confusion, Waste of Time, or Other Reasons

The court may exclude relevant evidence if its probative value is substantially outweighed by a danger of one or more of the following: unfair prejudice, confusing the issues, misleading the jury, undue delay, wasting time, or needlessly presenting cumulative evidence.

This section discusses the general relevancy analysis under FRE 401-403.

a.   FRE 401-402

The first stop in any consideration of whether evidence should be admitted is FRE 401. The rule contemplates a pure relevancy analysis. There could be numerous other reasons to exclude relevant evidence. However, there is no need to consider reasons to exclude evidence until a determination is made that the evidence is in fact relevant. Confusing the two matters, relevancy and reasons to exclude relevant evidence, impairs the predictability that should accompany the law of evidence.

FRE 401 provides: "Evidence is relevant if: (a) it has any tendency to make a fact more or less probable than it would be without the evidence; and (b) the fact is of consequence in determining the action."

The repeated use of the word "any" is significant. Slight relevance is enough to satisfy FRE 401. It instructs trial judges not to weigh the believability of relevant evidence. Only the jury weighs believability. In addition, the rule does not distinguish among types of evidence. Whether evidence is direct or circumstantial, or whether it is directed at a preliminary or an ultimate fact, the question is always the same: Does the offered evidence have any tendency to make some matter that is in issue in the case more or less probable? A two-step analysis is required.

i.   What are the matters in issue in the case?

First, is the evidence offered to prove or disprove some fact or matter "of consequence" in the case? It does not have to be a controlling matter. It can be something relatively routine, such as the background of a witness. It does not have to be a hotly contested matter. It can be something that is not disputed. Nothing in FRE 401 limits admissibility to disputed or contested matters in issue, although a judge might use FRE 403 to avoid spending trial time on uncontested matters. The "of consequence" language in FRE 401 encompasses the older label of "materiality," still used in some state jurisdictions.

The pleadings in the case and the substantive law that applies to the case will determine what matters are "of consequence." For example, a simple negligence case requires that plaintiff prove four things: duty, breach of duty, proximate cause, and damages. These four things are usually called the "elements" of the plaintiff's case and are defined by the substantive law. When plaintiff offers evidence, the question of whether the evidence is relevant will be analyzed in the context of plaintiff's pleadings and the substantive law.

ii.   Is the evidence probative of a matter in issue in the case?

Second, assuming the evidence is directed at a fact or matter of consequence, does it have "any tendency" to make the existence of any fact or matter of consequence "more or less probable than it would be without the evidence?" Here, the law of evidence deals in probabilities. Trial judges are to use their experience in life, common sense, logic, and knowledge of human behavior when deciding questions of relevance. If the required probability exists, it should not matter to the trial judge that the evidence does not persuade or convince.

Consider a simple contract case. If plaintiff offers evidence that he was a star athlete in high school, this evidence has no tendency to prove any of the issues — a contract executed by the parties, plaintiff's performance, defendant's non-performance, and plaintiff's damages — involved in a contract case. It is not probative.

Not all evidence is so obviously probative or not probative. For example, consider a robbery prosecution. The prosecution offers evidence that the defendant had recently been fired from his job. Is the evidence probative? To conclude it is probative, the judge must decide that if the defendant lost his job, he must have needed money; if he needed money, he is more likely to have taken money from another person; and if he is more likely to have taken money from another person, he is more likely to be the person who actually robbed this victim. In this situation, the fact to be proved — defendant robbed the victim — is more likely true because of the offered evidence — defendant recently lost his job. The evidence is probative.

On the other hand, evidence of a criminal defendant's poverty or wealth, without more, has little or no probative value when he is charged with seeking some kind of financial gain. Even if economic condition evidence — wealth or poverty — is seen to have some probative value, a persuasive argument can be made that it is substantially outweighed by the danger of unfair prejudice (FRE 403). Of course, probative value would be heightened if there were proof the defendant experienced an abrupt and unexplained improvement in his financial condition immediately following commission of the offense. In that case, the scales most probably would tip toward admissibility.

FRE 401 does not require that the evidence by itself directly establish the fact of consequence. It may be circumstantial, rather than direct, evidence, but that makes no difference. It can be a link in the chain that leads to that fact. The jury can use the evidence to infer other facts that matter. Evidence may be offered for or against the existence of a fact of consequence.

Consider another example. Evidence that the man accused of killing his wife took out a $1 million policy on her life one week before she was killed should be relevant to prove motive. If his wife took out the policy without the defendant knowing about it, relevancy vanishes. If the defendant took out the policy on his wife's life 10 years before her death, the question is closer, calling for a more energetic display of the trial judge's discretion. The relevancy analysis requires inquiry into elements of speculation and remoteness. When speculation exceeds probability, or when remoteness dissipates probability, relevance ceases.

General background information about a witness, such as residence, education, occupation, and marital status, almost always is accepted as evidence relevant to the witness's believability. When the questions reach the witness's winning of the Silver Star for bravery under fire or the backgrounds of the witness's children, the evidence probably will be excluded. When a criminal defendant attempts to testify that he never was arrested before the events at issue, the evidence is usually rejected as improper character evidence, although a few appellate courts have found lack of arrest evidence relevant and admissible.

When analyzing matters of relevancy, the first question that must be addressed is the purpose of the offered evidence. Who is offering it, and why? What matter in issue does it reach, and how does it do it? Until those questions are answered, no responsible conclusion can be reached. The proponent of the evidence must have a clearly defined purpose if he expects to win the point over objection.

There are times when courts find constitutional objections to the exclusion of relevant evidence offered by a criminal defendant. In *Holmes v. South Carolina*, 547 U.S. 319 (2006), the defendant sought to introduce evidence that a third party had committed the murder. The state courts barred the proof because the prosecution introduced forensic evidence that, if believed, would strongly support a guilty verdict. The Supreme Court held the state courts violated the defendant's due process right to have "a meaningful opportunity to present a complete defense."

Once the relevance of the evidence is determined, then, and only then, should the trial judge move on to consider possible reasons to exclude the evidence. The opponent of relevant evidence has the burden of showing why it should not be admitted.

In practice, however, trial judges do not always make pure relevancy determinations before moving on to considerations of exclusion. Weighty relevant evidence is admitted more often than slightly relevant evidence. Clearly reliable relevant evidence is admitted more often than questionable relevant evidence. That is, considerations of probative value, reliability, unfair prejudice, and the best use of courtroom time often are entwined.

For example, the police receive an anonymous telephone call that a 5'5" tall blond man with one arm just stabbed a woman at a street corner. They go to the corner, and there they find a stabbed woman, dead. Nearby they find and arrest the defendant, a 5′5″ blond man with one arm, who denies the stabbing. Is the telephone call admissible? Undeniably it is relevant if offered for its truth. It describes the defendant as the killer. But it is inadmissible hearsay and therefore unreliable. It cannot be admitted to prove the truth of the caller's words. If it is offered as non-hearsay to show why the police went to the scene, it would be a matter of little consequence and therefore irrelevant. Even if some slight relevance to the hearsay were found, its probative value is substantially outweighed by the unfair prejudice that would result. Testimony that a call was received, without going into its contents, would be sufficient to show why the police went to the scene. But a change in the issues can change the analysis. If the defendant is claiming these police officers are framing him because of some prior encounters, the reason they went to the scene becomes a fact of some consequence. Relevance is determined by purpose.

Consider another example. In a civil rights case, a police officer is sued because he shot and killed a robbery suspect. The officer testifies to seeing the suspect make a quick movement with his hand into his coat, "like he was reaching for a weapon." It turns out the suspect did not have a weapon. Is that fact admissible? Since the case centers on the facts known to the officer at the time he fired his gun, whether the suspect actually was armed might not be a fact of consequence. If that is the judge's conclusion, there is no need to go further. But a thoughtful advocate might persuade the judge that the fact the suspect was not armed tends to make it less likely the officer was truthful when he described the quick hand movement. If the judge accepts that purpose, there is some relevance to the fact the suspect had no weapon. But it still might not come in. The opponent of the evidence might persuade the judge that its probative value is substantially outweighed by the unfair prejudice that would be caused. That is, the jury would react emotionally, overvaluing the evidence, deterring the fact finder from a rational consideration of the issues in the case.

Sometimes offered evidence may be "conditionally relevant." Evidence is conditionally relevant under FRE 104(b) if a party first has to prove that another fact exists before the offered evidence will be relevant. For instance, suppose a statute requires that a municipality have actual notice of a dangerous road condition before it will be legally responsible for damages caused by the dangerous condition. Plaintiff brings an action against the municipality, alleging injuries caused by her car hitting a pothole in a city street. To prove the city had notice of the dangerous pothole, plaintiff offers a letter from another driver to the city, dated one month before plaintiff's accident, complaining about the same pothole. This letter is conditionally relevant. It is admissible only if plaintiff first proves the city actually received the letter before plaintiff's accident. That is, the letter's relevance is conditioned on proof of its timely receipt.

The judge has discretion to admit conditionally relevant evidence out of turn, based on the representation that the proponent will "connect it up" by later introducing the additional evidence. If the conditionally relevant evidence is admitted and the proponent fails to introduce the additional evidence that will connect it up, the judge may give the jury a cautionary instruction to disregard that evidence or, if the conditionally relevant evidence does substantial harm, may declare a mistrial.

b.   FRE 403

Just because offered evidence is "of consequence" and has "any tendency" to prove or disprove a matter in issue does not mean it is admissible. FRE 403 must be satisfied if the opponent raises the question. FRE 403 gives the judge discretion to exclude relevant and reliable evidence on two broad grounds.

First, offered evidence may be unfairly prejudicial, confusing, or misleading, and actually hinder, rather than help, the jury in reaching a rational decision. For example, in a murder case where the issue is identification, the prosecution offers color photographs of the victim's mutilated body. The defendant objects. This evidence has minimal probative value, proving only that the victim is dead, a fact that undoubtedly will be established by other evidence; but it is unfairly prejudicial because it primarily inflames the jury's passions. Relevancy increases if the photographs show how the victim was injured and if that is an issue in the case. In the murder case, if the issue is self-defense the victim's injuries may be highly probative on that issue.

Second, offered evidence may cause undue delay, waste time, or be needlessly cumulative. Judicial economy is an important concern, and litigants must be reasonably efficient in presenting proof. For example, in a fraud case, the defendant has already called several character witnesses, each of whom has stated that the defendant is an honest person. When the defendant calls another character witness, the prosecution objects. This evidence, in light of the already existing evidence, adds nothing new and is cumulative and a waste of time.

FRE 403 favors admissibility by providing that relevant evidence is inadmissible only if its probative value is "substantially outweighed" by the countervailing danger of creating unfair prejudice, confusing the issues, misleading the jury, causing undue delay, wasting time, or being needlessly cumulative. The judge should look not only at the offered evidence, but also at the other available evidence that has been or will be admitted, to make intelligent decisions on admissibility.

It is important to distinguish between appellate and trial court considerations in reaching FRE 403 balancing decisions. On appeal, the only real question is whether the trial judge understood he had discretion and then did not abuse it. Appellate courts rarely reverse or even question a trial judge's judgments under that rule, although reviewing courts at times reject other uncharged acts evidence admitted under FRE 404(b) where there is a substantial risk that the jury is being invited to use a forbidden propensity inference. At trial, however, FRE 403 rulings by the trial judge frequently have an outcome-determinative impact on the trial, and judges make these decisions almost all the time. Trial lawyers have to recognize that FRE 403 issues are important and that the key arguments and decisions are made in the trial court, not the appellate court.

Rule 403 is best understood by picturing the apothecary's scales — equal arms with pans hanging below the beam on chains. The scales balance when there is nothing in the pans. The balancing process begins when the probative value of the evidence, including the need for it, is placed in one of the pans. The scales tip. Then the risk of unfair prejudice, confusion of the issues, the potential for misleading the jury, considerations of undue delay, waste of time, or needless presentation of cumulative evidence is placed in the other pan. The judge must determine whether the risk factors substantially outweigh the probative value of the evidence. The judge's exercise of discretion becomes a matter of considered measurement.

The question of whether FRE 403 applies to judges conducting a bench trial does not arise very often, but when it does, the courts hold that it applies only to jury trials. The wording of the rule, singling out the danger of "misleading the jury," does not support that reading. Courts cite to the rebuttable presumption that trial judges use admissible evidence for proper purposes.

In 1997, the United States Supreme Court reminded trial judges there is an outer limit to the exercise of discretion under FRE 403. In *Old Chief v. United States*, 519 U.S. 172 (1997), the defendant was charged with being a convicted felon in possession of a gun. Old Chief's prior conviction was for assault causing serious bodily injury. Contending that evidence of the nature of the prior offense would be unfairly prejudicial, Old Chief offered to stipulate that he had been convicted of a crime punishable by imprisonment exceeding one year. The government declined to accept the stipulation, and the trial judge refused to impose it.

The Supreme Court reversed the conviction for possession of a gun and remanded the case for a new trial. The Court recognized that ordinarily the government is entitled to prove its case in its own way, but here the danger of jury misuse of the evidence was grave when balanced against the probative value of the name of the prior offense. The trial court's broad grant of discretion under FRE 403 had been abused. At the heart of the Court's analysis was the observation that the challenged evidence concerned the defendant's status as a former felon, "an element entirely outside the natural sequence of what the defendant is charged with thinking and doing to commit the current offense." The term "unfair prejudice," as it relates to a criminal defendant, "speaks to the capacity of some concededly relevant evidence to lure the factfinder into declaring guilt on a ground different from proof specific to the offense charged."

Nothing in *Old Chief* prevents the prosecution from proving non-status elements of the crime charged when there is no dispute about those elements. A few courts have allowed an unconditional stipulation by criminal defendants to bar the prosecution from offering evidence on an element of the crime, but it is unlikely that *Old Chief* allows defendants the right to stipulate away non-status elements of the prosecution's case. The FRE 403 balancing test applies whenever the risk of unfair prejudice is an issue.

2.   Practice

Relevance objections are easy for lawyers to raise but often difficult for the judge to decide, particularly before or during the early stages of a trial. This is because the lawyers already know the facts and issues of the case, but the judge does not. For trial lawyers, the message is clear. Relevance issues should be raised before trial whenever possible, by both the lawyer who plans to object and the lawyer who wants the benefit of a pretrial ruling on admissibility. Raising relevance issues early gives the judge an opportunity to become educated on the facts of the case, which is important, since relevance issues cannot be decided in a vacuum. As the trial progresses, the judge learns what the case is about, and relevance issues become much easier to decide. If a relevance objection must be made during trial, the objecting lawyer should ask for a sidebar to explain to the judge why the offered evidence should be excluded.

The trial judge has considerable discretion in ruling on relevance objections, particularly in deciding whether the probative value of the offered evidence is substantially outweighed by its FRE 403 concerns. These rulings are rarely reversed on appeal. The appellate reversals that do occur are primarily the result of erroneous rulings on the question of whether the offered evidence is of consequence to the case, rulings that usually occur when the judge fails to understand the pleadings and applicable substantive law.

When making relevance objections, lawyers should be careful to identify the actual issues and applicable law and relate their objections explicitly to them, rather than making general objections that the evidence is irrelevant or prejudicial, common objections that hardly induce the trial judge to treat the objection seriously.

Example 1:

In a personal injury case, plaintiff was injured by a power saw. The issue is whether the saw was unreasonably dangerous and had inadequate safety warnings. Plaintiff seeks to introduce photographs of the defendant's manufacturing plant and present testimony about the manufacturing process. Defendant moves before trial to preclude this evidence on relevancy grounds. In a hearing on the motion, the following happens:

Judge: Defense, why should this evidence be kept out?
Defendant: Your honor, the issues in this case are twofold: First, is the power saw's design unreasonably dangerous? Second, are the safety warnings on the saw adequate? Plaintiff seeks compensatory damages only; there is no punitive damages claim. Showing the jury photographs of our manufacturing plant or having a witness describe the plant has absolutely no bearing on either of these issues. It's simply not probative evidence. Moreover, it's pretty obvious that the real reason plaintiff wants to introduce this evidence is to show the jury that we are a large company and can therefore absorb a large verdict. Accordingly, even if this evidence had any probative value, which it doesn't, it is substantially outweighed by its unfairly prejudicial effect: showing that the defendant is a deep pocket.
Judge: Plaintiff?
Plaintiff: Your honor, this case involves a design defect, and surely the jury is entitled to see where the product involved in this case was designed and manufactured. That's relevant and gives the jury a better understanding of the case. Furthermore, there can hardly be anything unfairly prejudicial about this evidence. It's not the kind of evidence that Rule 403 intends to exclude.
Judge: The motion is granted in part. Photographs showing the plant generally and testimony about the size of the plant will be excluded on relevance grounds. However, any photographs that show the area of the plant where the product was designed

and testimony about the design department itself will be admitted. That evidence is directly relevant to the issues in this case.

Commentary: Judges frequently rule on broad relevancy issues by granting motions in part, even though neither party argued for this result.

Example 2:

In a personal injury case involving a collision between plaintiff's and defendant's vehicles, both liability and damages are in issue. Defendant moves before trial to preclude evidence that the defendant was driving a Mercedes sports car or, if that evidence is admitted, to permit evidence that the car was rented. In a hearing on the motion, the following happens:

Defendant: Your honor, this is our motion to bar evidence that the defendant was driving a Mercedes 500 sports car at the time of the collision and, in the alternative, if the court denies that motion, to permit evidence that the defendant rented, rather than owned, the car. First, the evidence should be excluded because the kind of car the defendant was driving is irrelevant to the issue of liability. The plaintiff claims the defendant ran a red light and crashed into the passenger side of the plaintiff's car. The only issue is whether the light was red, as the plaintiff claims, or yellow, as we claim, and the kind of car the defendant was driving doesn't resolve this issue one way or another. Second, the evidence is highly prejudicial, since the jury will conclude that the defendant is likely to be both a hot-rodder and wealthy. If your honor is going to admit this evidence, we ask that we be allowed to introduce evidence that the car was a rental so at least the jury does not assume that the defendant is rich.

Plaintiff: Your honor, I don't see how we can try a collision case without the jury being told about the vehicles involved. The jury needs this information, from both photographs and testimony, to understand the case and learn what happened. The defense hasn't cited one case where such evidence was excluded. Second, whether the car was owned by the defendant or rented has nothing to do with the issues. This is not a case where the defendant claims he drove the car differently because it was a rental or where there is some other issue on which the car being a rental would have some bearing. They want to show the car is a rental to remove any suggestion of the defendant's wealth, but showing the car is a rental doesn't do this, and it's not unduly prejudicial in any event.

Judge: The motion is denied. The jury will be allowed to learn and see what cars were involved in the collision. The fact of the car's rental is excluded because it is not relevant to any issues in the case.

Example 3:

The defendant is charged with murder. The victim was shot, and a .38-caliber bullet was removed from his body. When the defendant was arrested a few days after the shooting, his house was searched for weapons. The search produced a dozen handguns, none of which matched the bullet taken from the victim. Before trial, the defendant moves to preclude evidence of the handguns found in the defendant's house. At the hearing, the following happens:

Judge: Defense?

Defendant: Your honor, if the police had recovered a .38-caliber handgun that matched the bullet taken from the victim, it obviously would be highly relevant and admissible, and we would never have filed the motion. Here, however, the prosecution concedes that there is no match. In fact, of the dozen handguns that the defendant owns, only two are .38-caliber revolvers. All the others are either revolvers or semiautomatics with different calibers. Since none of these could be the murder weapon, they are simply irrelevant to the case. The only reason the prosecution is attempting to introduce these weapons is to paint the defendant as a gun collector or gun lover and turn the jury against him. That's irrelevant under Rule 401. Even if the weapons have some minimal relevance to the issues in this case, that relevance is substantially outweighed by the Rule 403 concerns.

Prosecutor: The only question in this case is identification. Whoever shot the victim did so with a .38-caliber revolver. The fact that the defendant has handguns, and two .38-caliber revolvers, makes it more likely that he had the revolver used in the shooting than would be the case if the defendant had no guns at all. Since there is no suggestion that the guns were illegally owned, there is simply no prejudicial impact under Rule 403 that substantially outweighs the probative value of the defendant's having handguns.

Judge: Evidence that the defendant had the two .38-caliber revolvers will be admitted. Evidence of the other handguns is not admissible.

Commentary: This is a close issue. Some judges might rule that none of the weapons is admissible, others that all the weapons are admissible, on the issue of identification. This points out the importance of forcefully making the best argument when the objection is heard because appellate reversals are rare.

Example 4:

This is a personal injury case in which the plaintiff, a 25-year-old man, was injured in an automobile collision. The plaintiff is called as a witness in the plaintiff's case-in-chief. The direct examination begins as follows:

Q. (By plaintiff's lawyer) Mr. Johnson, good morning. You grew up here, right?

A. That's right.

Q. Where were you raised?

A. I lived with my parents until they died, when I was 14, and then . . .

Defendant: Objection, your honor. May we be heard at sidebar?

Judge: Yes. Approach the bench. [Lawyers approach the bench.]

Defendant: Your honor, this evidence is totally irrelevant to either the issues in the case or witness credibility. It's a clear attempt to get sympathy from the jury. The plaintiff also lived in a foster home until he graduated and went to college. That's irrelevant, so we don't even need to get to the obvious Rule 403 problems.

Plaintiff: Your honor, he's the plaintiff in a personal injury case. The jury needs to size up the plaintiff for purposes of both assessing credibility and determining damages. The fact that, in this case, the plaintiff lost his parents and lived the next four years in a foster home is simply general background information.

Judge: The objection is sustained.

Commentary: Another ruling not all judges may agree on. Judges are usually generous in allowing witness background that has a bearing on credibility, such as that a witness is married, is raising children, is educated, and holds a steady job. These things show responsibility and presumably credibility. And judges often give more latitude when the witness is the plaintiff in a personal injury case or the defendant in a criminal case. However, when the background information seems more designed to curry favor or sympathy, most judges will exclude it.

§5.3. *Special relevancy rules*

1. Character traits[2]

a. *Law*

Rule 404.   Character Evidence; Crimes or Other Acts

(a) Character Evidence.

   (1) *Prohibited Uses.* Evidence of a person' character or character trait is not admissible to prove that on a particular occasion the person acted in accordance with the character or trait.

   (2) *Exceptions for a Defendant or Victim in a Criminal Case.* The following exceptions apply in a criminal case:

   (A) a defendant may offer evidence of the defendant's pertinent trait, and if the evidence is admitted, the prosecutor may offer evidence to rebut it;

---

2. McCormick §§186-194; Weinstein §§404-405; Mueller & Kirkpatrick §§4.11-4.20; Wigmore §§51-82.1.

(B) subject to the limitations in Rule 412, a defendant may offer evidence of an alleged victim's pertinent trait, and if the evidence is admitted, the prosecutor may:

    (i) offer evidence to rebut it; and

    (ii) offer evidence of the defendant's same trait; and

(C) in a homicide case, the prosecutor may offer evidence of the alleged victim's trait of peacefulness to rebut evidence that the victim was the first aggressor.

(3) *Exceptions for a Witness.* Evidence of a witness's character may be admitted under Rules 607, 608, and 609.

Rule 405.   Methods of Proving Character

(a) By Reputation or Opinion. When evidence of a person's character or character trait is admissible, it may be proved by testimony about the person's reputation or by testimony in the form of an opinion. On cross-examination of the character witness, the court may allow an inquiry into relevant specific instances of the person's conduct.

(b) By Specific Instances of Conduct. When a person's character or character trait is an essential element of a charge, claim, or defense, the character or trait may also be proved by relevant specific instances of the person's conduct.

Common experience tells us that a person is likely to act consistently with the kind of person he really is: his "character." For example, an honest person is less likely to commit a theft or fraud than a dishonest person. A person's character can be circumstantial evidence of that person's actual conduct at a particular time. We have all said it: "He is the kind of person who . . . , so he probably. . . ." A person, we assume, will conduct himself consistently with his character.

Common sense also tells us that evidence of character can be misused by a jury. It might improperly use this evidence as proof that a person is a bad person or erroneously conclude that just because a person has a certain character, he must have acted consistently with his character at a particular time and decide the case solely on that basis.

Under certain circumstances, in certain cases, evidence law permits introducing relevant character traits of certain persons. There are two distinct character trait rules under FRE 404 and 405: the "essential element" rule and the "circumstantial evidence" rule.

i.   "Essential element" rule[3]

Character or a trait of character is sometimes, though infrequently, an "essential element" of a charge, claim, or defense. In these circumstances,

---

3. McCormick §187; Weinstein §404[02]; Mueller & Kirkpatrick §4.20; Wigmore §§69.1-82.1.

where character itself is at the heart of a charge, claim, or defense, such evidence is admissible, in both civil and criminal cases, when offered by a proper party at a proper time. When admissible, such evidence is direct evidence because it is being used to directly prove the pertinent character trait in issue.

What determines if a character trait is an essential element of a charge, claim, or defense? Look to the definition of the charge, claim, or defense, and see if it requires proving someone's character trait. A good place to start is with a statutory definition of the charge, claim, or defense and the jurisdiction's established jury instructions.

A character trait is sometimes an essential element of a charge or claim. For example, consider a negligent entrustment case in which the plaintiff claims that the defendant trucking company negligently hired a driver it knew to be an incompetent driver. The plaintiff in his case-in-chief must prove, among other things, that the truck driver had the character of being an incompetent driver. Evidence proving this is admissible to show the company was negligent when it allowed a known incompetent driver to drive its truck. It is not admissible to prove that the driver drove negligently when the collision happened.

Further, in a child custody case, one parent may offer evidence of the violent character of the other parent. It is offered to prove the parent is unfit because the parent is violent. It is not admissible as circumstantial evidence of the parent's conduct at a particular time.

Consider another example. A police officer and the municipality that employs him are sued in a civil rights action brought under Section 1983. The plaintiff claims he was beaten by the officer and the municipality knew or should have known that the beating would happen. The plaintiff offers evidence of the officer's violent character. It is admitted because it has a tendency to prove the officer's violent tendencies and the municipality's knowledge of them. It is not admitted to prove the officer beat the plaintiff at the time in issue. In fact, it is not admissible against the officer.

A character trait is sometimes an essential element of a defense. For example, consider a defamation case in which the plaintiff sues the defendant for saying that the plaintiff is a drug addict and the defense raised is the truth defense. This defense raises the plaintiff's drug addiction as an essential element of the defense. The defendant can offer evidence that the plaintiff is a drug addict.

Further, consider an employment discrimination case in which the plaintiff sues the defendant for wrongfully terminating him because of race and the defense raised is that the plaintiff was actually fired for being incompetent. This defense raises the plaintiff's competency as an essential element of the defense, and the defendant can offer evidence that the plaintiff is incompetent.

A character trait can also be an essential element of a rebuttal case. For example, consider a sale of illegal drugs prosecution where the defense raised is entrapment. This defense raises the defendant's predisposition to commit illegal drug sales, and the prosecution may rebut the evidence of entrapment with evidence of the defendant's character as a preexisting drug dealer. The Supreme Court so held in *Hampton v. United States*, 425 U.S. 484 (1976).

The essential element rule can apply to a charge, claim, or defense in both civil and criminal cases. Because in these types of cases evidence of the pertinent character trait is direct evidence that is frequently crucial and determinative of the case's outcome, FRE 405 permits proving the pertinent character trait in any of three ways:

1. reputation evidence
2. opinion evidence
3. evidence of specific instances of conduct

Reputation is the community's collective belief about the kind of person someone else is. Any member of the person's community who is familiar with and knows the reputation of the person involved is competent to testify to that person's reputation for the pertinent character trait. The community is usually the home community, but most courts permit any other community, such as work, school, or church, in which the person spends substantial time and becomes known by others. The relevant time frame is the time of the event involved in the lawsuit, *not* the time of trial. Reputation can be easily established:

Q. Ms. Smith, have you heard the reputation of Mr. Johnson, in the community where he lives, for peacefulness as of June 1, 2015?
A. Yes, I have.
Q. How have you come to hear his reputation?
A. I've heard dozens of people talk about him over the past 10 years.
Q. What is his reputation for peacefulness?
A. Mr. Johnson is known as an aggressive, violent man.

Reputation evidence, while obviously hearsay, is properly admissible as a hearsay exception under FRE 803(21).

Opinion is one person's personal belief about the kind of person someone else is. Anyone who is personally familiar with the person involved can express an opinion about the person's pertinent character trait. Opinion also can be easily established:

Q. Mr. Smith, do you know Mr. Johnson?
A. Yes.
Q. Did you know him on June 1, 2015?
A. Yes.
Q. How long had you known him on that date?
A. About 10 years. He lives across the street from me.
Q. Do you have a personal opinion as to whether Mr. Johnson was a peaceful person at that time?
A. Yes.
Q. What is it?
A. I think he's an extremely violent, aggressive person.

Specific acts constitute the third way a pertinent character trait can be proven when that character trait is an essential element in a case. Any member of the community who has witnessed the person involved commit an act that would be probative of the pertinent character trait may testify about the act:

Q. Ms. Smith, where were you on June 1, 2015, around 10:00 P.M.?
A. I was in the Tap Root Pub.
Q. Was Mr. Johnson there?
A. Yes.
Q. Tell us what Mr. Johnson did at that time.
A. He was sitting at the bar, and he suddenly started attacking the man on the next stool. He knocked the man out cold.
Q. Did the man do anything to provoke Mr. Johnson's attack?
A. No. He was just sitting there sipping a beer.

When is the proper time to present such character trait evidence where it is an "essential element" in a case? Plaintiff presents such evidence in plaintiff's case-in-chief when a character trait is an essential element of plaintiff's charge or claim. Defendant presents such evidence in defendant's case-in-chief when a character trait is an essential element of defendant's counterclaim or defense. For example, in a case in which the defendant is charged with negligently hiring a driver known to be an incompetent driver, the plaintiff must introduce evidence of the driver's incompetence in the plaintiff's case-in-chief. In an employment discrimination case where the defense is that the plaintiff was fired for being an alcoholic, the defendant must introduce evidence of the plaintiff's alcoholism during the defendant's case-in-chief.

The essential element rule should not be overused. This is an infrequently used character trait rule because most charges, claims, and defenses do not require proving someone's character or a trait of character. For example, a negligence claim does not require the plaintiff to prove that the defendant is a negligent, careless, or bad driver. The plaintiff need only prove that, at the particular time and place in issue, the defendant acted negligently. Another example: In a criminal assault case in which the defendant claims he acted in self-defense, the violent character of the alleged victim is not an essential element of the defense. (The defendant can prove that pertinent character trait of the alleged victim by general reputation or opinion evidence, but not by evidence of specific instances of conduct, under the circumstantial evidence rule.)

ii. "Circumstantial evidence" rule[4]

Even though a character trait is not an essential element of a claim, charge, or defense, evidence of a character trait is admissible under FRE 404(a), in limited situations and limited cases, as circumstantial proof that a person acted consistently with his character at the time in issue in the case. For example, a defendant charged with aggravated assault can introduce evidence that he is a peaceful person, making it less likely that he would have assaulted the victim. This kind of evidence is circumstantial because it requires the fact finder to infer that the person acted in conformity with his character at the time in issue.

---

4. McCormick §188; Weinstein §404[04]-[07]; Mueller & Kirkpatrick §§4.11-4.14; Wigmore §§54.1-68b.

This rule represents one of the "limits" on relevancy. Our life experience tells us that character evidence has some relevancy, since it shows a propensity to behave in a certain way. A careless person is more likely to cause an accident than a careful person. A violent person is more likely to attack someone than a peaceful person. The fear is that the evidence will be overvalued or misused. The probative value of the evidence may be slight, the risk of unfair prejudice great. The trier of fact could be distracted from a careful consideration of what happened on the occasion in question, instead focusing on whether the person is good or bad.

This use of character trait evidence, as circumstantial proof of conduct, is severely restricted by the evidence rules. FRE 404(a)(1) and (2) were amended in 2006 to make it clear that the exceptions to the circumstantial use of character evidence apply only to criminal cases. Before the amendment, some courts were applying FRE 404(a) to civil cases involving intentional torts such as assault, fraud, embezzlement, and RICO claims, on the theory that these were quasi-criminal claims. In another change, FRE 404(a)(2) was amended to make it clear that otherwise admissible evidence concerning a sex offense victim's character should be excluded if exclusion is required by FRE 412.

1. What kinds of character trait evidence can be admitted as circumstantial proof of conduct in criminal cases during direct examination? This depends on the existence of a logical relationship between a character trait and the nature of the conduct charged in the case. Common situations where such a logical relationship exists are "peacefulness" in homicide and assault cases; "honesty" in theft, burglary, and fraud cases; and "truthfulness" in perjury and false statement cases. In each of these cases, the pertinent character trait has probative value as to whether someone, usually the defendant (but sometimes the victim), engaged in the conduct at issue in the case. The question is one of relevance. For example, a defendant's character as a good family man and a kind person is not admissible when is he is charged with bringing an illegal alien into the country. Nor is a defendant's character for bravery admissible in a mail fraud case.

2. What forms of character trait evidence are admissible as circumstantial proof of conduct in criminal cases during direct examination? Only reputation and opinion evidence is admissible; specific instances of conduct are *not* admissible. Note that this is different from the "essential element" rule, which permits all three forms: reputation, opinion, and specific acts. The reason for the distinction is that when a character trait is an essential element of a case, it is often a critical issue, and evidence law is more generous in admitting proof of that character trait.

3. Which party may initiate the introduction of character trait evidence as circumstantial proof of conduct in criminal cases? This choice belongs exclusively to the defendant. The prosecution cannot introduce character trait evidence in its case-in-chief, nor may the prosecution attempt to introduce such evidence during cross-examination of any defense witnesses. If the defendant elects not to introduce character trait evidence as circumstantial proof of his conduct, the prosecution may not either. However, if the defendant does introduce such evidence, the prosecution may rebut with contrary evidence. For example, if the defendant in a murder case elects to introduce evidence that the defendant has a good character for peacefulness, the prosecution in rebuttal may introduce evidence of the defendant's violent character.

A defendant initiates the introduction of character trait evidence by calling a witness to testify, in reputation or opinion form, about the relevant character trait. Merely introducing testimony about the event that brought about the criminal charge is not enough. For example, if the defendant in a murder case testifies that he shot the victim in self-defense, he has *not* offered evidence of his own character, and there is no such evidence for the prosecution to rebut. Most courts also hold that a defendant who testifies to general background information about himself does not thereby "open the door" to the prosecution later rebutting with bad character evidence. For example, a defendant who testifies to holding a steady job for several years is not deemed to have implicitly characterized himself as an honest person, so the prosecution in rebuttal may not introduce contrary character evidence.

When a defendant elects to present evidence under FRE 404(a)(1), it is often said that the defendant "puts his character in issue." That label, however, creates the danger of confusing this circumstantial use of character evidence with the essential element rule, under which character is directly in issue.

There is one exception to the FRE 404 general rule that the defense initiates character trait evidence and only then may the prosecution rebut it: a homicide case where the defendant introduces evidence that the victim was the first aggressor (i.e., offers proof of self-defense). Under FRE 404(a)(2), if the defendant offers evidence that the victim first attacked the defendant, the prosecution may then introduce evidence of the victim's character trait of peacefulness. The reasoning is that this type of proof is necessary in homicide cases involving proof of self-defense, since the victim is dead and unable to testify and there often is no direct evidence to contradict the defendant's version of the event. For example, if in a murder case the defendant (or someone else) testifies that the victim assaulted him and that the defendant shot in self-defense, the prosecution may then, in rebuttal, show through reputation or opinion form that the victim was a peaceful person. This is circumstantial evidence making it less likely that the victim was the aggressor, as the defendant claims.

4. About whom may character trait evidence be admitted as circumstantial proof of conduct in criminal cases during direct examination? Such evidence can be introduced about the defendant, by the defendant, since his conduct is always in issue, and the victim, if the victim's conduct becomes an issue in the case. For example, in a theft case, the defendant's conduct is in issue, and his honesty is a relevant character trait. The defendant can introduce evidence of his honest character. In an assault case, the defendant's conduct is in issue, and his peacefulness is a relevant character trait; if the defense asserted is self-defense, the victim's conduct is also relevant. Therefore, in an assault–self-defense case, the defendant can introduce evidence of both the defendant's peaceful character and the victim's violent character. Note, however, character evidence concerning the alleged victim in a sex offense case is barred by FRE 412.

In this situation, it does not matter that the defendant did not know of the victim's violent character before he acted. The evidence is still proper circumstantial evidence making it more likely that the victim was the aggressor. If the defendant did know or had heard about the victim's violent character, the evidence becomes relevant to the defendant's state of mind, and FRE 404(a)(2) does not apply because the victim's character is not the relevant purpose of the proposed evidence. This distinction is important because FRE

404(a)(2) allows the prosecution to rebut evidence of the victim's violent character with evidence of the victim's peaceful character. The prosecution's response is limited to reputation and opinion evidence. If the evidence is offered only to show the defendant's state of mind, a good argument can be made that the prosecutor should not be allowed to respond with evidence of the victim's peaceful character.

5. What constitutes proper rebuttal evidence to admitted character trait evidence? Rebuttal evidence is exactly what its name implies: evidence that contradicts evidence previously introduced by an opponent. For example, when the defendant introduces evidence of the defendant's good reputation for peacefulness, the prosecution in rebuttal may introduce evidence of the defendant's reputation for violence. If the defendant introduces opinion evidence that the victim is a violent person, the prosecution can rebut with contrary opinion evidence.

Courts differ, however, in determining whether offered evidence is, in particular situations, proper rebuttal evidence. For example, if the defendant introduces reputation evidence about himself, may the prosecution in rebuttal introduce personal opinion evidence about the defendant? May the reverse also occur, so that personal opinion evidence is rebutted by reputation evidence?

Some courts treat rebuttal evidence narrowly, holding that you can rebut only with the same kind of evidence. This means that reputation evidence can be rebutted only by reputation evidence and personal opinion evidence can be rebutted only by personal opinion evidence. Many courts, however, treat rebuttal evidence more broadly, holding that reputation and personal opinion evidence are sufficiently similar, so that evidence of one kind can be rebutted by evidence of the other kind.

The same issue presents itself in situations where both the character of the defendant and the character of the victim are relevant. This happens most often in assault cases involving the defense of self-defense. If the defendant introduces evidence of the victim's violent character, can the prosecution rebut with evidence of the defendant's violent character? The answer, provided in the 2000 amendment to FRE 404(a)(1), is yes. The amendment, according to the Advisory Committee, is "designed to permit a more balanced presentation of character evidence when an accused chooses to attack the character of the alleged victim." Note that the prosecution's evidence about the defendant's character must be of the same trait as that offered by the defendant about the alleged victim's character.

If the defendant introduces evidence of the defendant's character for peacefulness, can the prosecution rebut with evidence of the victim's character for peacefulness? The rule is silent on that question. Most courts, viewing that kind of rebuttal evidence narrowly, bar such evidence, since it does not really rebut the defendant's evidence, but instead introduces new character evidence, which is solely the defendant's election.

6. How do the rules governing the use of character evidence as circumstantial proof of conforming conduct differ from the rules governing an attack on or support of a witness's credibility? FRE 404 and 405 govern character evidence when it is offered as circumstantial evidence of conduct. But FRE 404(a)(3) also authorizes character evidence in all cases, civil and criminal, where the issue is a witness's credibility. Proper use of that character evidence is set out in FRE 608 and 609. The use of character evidence to attack credibility is discussed in Sec.

12.4. FRE 413-415, dealing with evidence of other sexual crimes and acts to prove propensity in sexual assault cases, will be discussed later in this chapter.

7. When a criminal defendant offers testimony of a relevant character trait, he risks triggering a specific instance cross-examination. When character trait evidence is admissible on direct examination, inquiry on cross-examination is allowable into "relevant specific instances of conduct." FRE 405(a).

For example, when a defense witness in a murder case testifies the defendant has a peaceable character, the prosecutor may ask that witness: "Have you heard (or "Do you know") that four weeks before the defendant was arrested in this case he beat a man unconscious with a blackjack because the man stepped on his toes?" If the witness says he had not heard of the blackjack event, his knowledge of the defendant is challenged. If the witness admits hearing of it, his credibility is called into question. Either way, extrinsic proof of the blackjack incident is not allowed. The cross-examiner must accept the witness's answer. This exclusion is not contained in FRE 405(a), but courts consistently enforce it.

The prosecutor must have a good faith basis for asking the question. In all cases, the specific instance cross-examination questions must be relevant to the character trait evidence offered by the defendant. For example, a witness who testifies to the defendant's good character for peacefulness cannot be cross-examined about the defendant's arrests for drunkenness or instances when the defendant told lies. Even when relevant, the prosecutor's questions may be challenged on FRE 403 grounds. When the questions are allowed, the defendant is entitled to an instruction limiting their relevance to the credibility and weight of the character witness's testimony.

b. Practice

The character trait rules are important because this kind of evidence can have a substantial impact on the jury. That impact, and the danger that jurors will misuse or overuse the evidence, accounts for its strict regulation. The character trait rules, although based on logic and experience, are technical and are frequently misunderstood by both lawyers and judges. While it is always preferable to raise any evidentiary issue before trial, many character trait issues cannot be anticipated, and objections must be made during trial. If this becomes necessary, ask for a sidebar conference so that you can, if necessary, make a more thorough argument on the objection.

Example 1:

Plaintiff sues defendant nursing home for an assault committed by a nursing home employee. Plaintiff claims the nursing home negligently hired the employee, without checking his employment history, which would have revealed that he was a violent person. Before trial, defendant moves to bar introduction of evidence that the employee assaulted several patients at a nursing home where he previously worked and was fired for that reason. At the hearing on the motion, the following happens:

Judge: Counsel, why isn't this evidence admissible under the rules?
Defendant: Your honor, this is a civil case, so this evidence is not admissible under the circumstantial evidence rule. If admissible at all, it

would have to fall into the essential element rule of 405(b). We agree that the pleadings raise the defendant's character of being a violent person as an issue, but the plaintiff is trying to prove it with evidence of other assaults and the fact that the defendant was fired from that previous job. All that happened three years ago. That makes it irrelevant and extremely prejudicial, and it should be excluded under Rule 403.

Judge: Plaintiff?

Plaintiff: Under the essential element rule, we are permitted to prove the employee's violent character through reputation, opinion, and specific instances of conduct. In this case, we allege that the defendant could have, and should have, checked the employee's employment history, since the employee listed the previous nursing home on his job application. If they had checked it, they would have learned that the employee had been fired for assaulting several patients in the home only three years ago. The employee's character for violence is the key issue in the case. The evidence we will be introducing, testimony of assaults from patients at the other nursing home, is highly probative on that issue, and any 403 concerns are minimal.

Judge: Counsel, why should the fact of firing be admissible?

Plaintiff: The fact of the firing would, if the defendant had bothered to contact the other nursing home, have put the defendant on notice of the employee's violent character.

Judge: The specific instances of assault, through the testimony of the former patients, will be admitted. The fact of the firing will not be admitted. The fact of the firing is essentially the opinion of the nursing home that the employee is violent, but it's in hearsay form. The fact that the assaults occurred three years ago is not sufficiently remote to make the evidence irrelevant or inadmissible under 403.

Commentary: Some judges might rule that since the only objection to proof of the firing was on relevance grounds, the objection should be overruled. The evidence is not hearsay when offered to prove notice or knowledge.

Example 2:

Plaintiff brings a wrongful termination action against defendant, claiming she was fired because she is a woman, which constitutes gender discrimination. Defendant claims plaintiff was fired for being an incompetent typist. Defendant's pretrial statement lists several witnesses who will testify about plaintiff's typing skills. In addition, defendant, during the depositions of plaintiff's witnesses, asked many questions about plaintiff's typing skills. Plaintiff's pretrial motion asks the judge to bar all such evidence in the plaintiff's case-in-chief. At the hearing on the motion, the following happens:

Plaintiff: Your honor, the only thing we have to prove in our case-in-chief is that the plaintiff was employed by the defendant and that she

was improperly fired for being a woman. The plaintiff's compe-
tence as a typist is part of the defendant's affirmative defense
and is not relevant to our case-in-chief. Therefore, we ask that
you preclude the defense from asking any questions on cross-
examination of our witnesses about the plaintiff's typing skills.
Such evidence would be premature.

Defendant: The only real issue in this case, your honor, is whether the
plaintiff is an incompetent typist. If so, the fact that she is a
woman does not make the firing improper. Just because the
plaintiff's incompetence is the basis of our affirmative defense
does not mean that we cannot elicit any evidence on our
defense when we cross-examine the plaintiff's co-workers in
the plaintiff's case-in-chief. These co-workers are other workers in the typing pool, and they obviously have to talk about
their jobs when they testify.

Judge: The motion is denied.

Commentary: The only issue is not whether the offered evidence is relevant,
but when such evidence becomes relevant. Plaintiff should have made an
explicit additional argument that the proposed cross-examinations of plaintiff's
witnesses would be beyond the scope of the direct examination under FRE
611(b). If the scope objection succeeds, defendant has the choice of recalling
the witnesses in the defendant's case or, with the court's permission under FRE
611(b), examining the witnesses now "as if on direct examination."

Example 3:

This is a murder case. In the defendant's case-in-chief, the defendant
calls a witness to testify to the defendant's reputation for being peaceful.
The following then happens:

Q. (By defendant's lawyer) Mr. Johnson do you know the defendant,
   Avery Smith?
A. Yes.
Q. Do you have an opinion as to whether he is a peaceful person?
A. Yes, I have an opinion.
Q. What is your opinion based on?
A. I've known Mr. Avery for about 10 years. He's my neighbor.
Q. What is your opinion as to whether Avery Smith is a peaceful person?
A. It's great. I know him to be a gentle, quiet, peaceful kind of guy, all the
   years I've known him.
Q. Specifically, Mr. Johnson, what's the basis for concluding that he's a
   peaceful person?
A. Well, I know that one time he . . .

Prosecutor: Objection, your honor. The witness is going into specific
instances of conduct.

Judge: Sustained. Ask another question.

Commentary: When a pertinent character trait is being used as circumstantial evidence of conduct, only reputation and opinion are permitted. Lawyers

frequently try to get around the bar to proof of specific instances of conduct by asking such witnesses the "basis" for their testimony.

Example 4:

This is an assault case. The defense is self-defense. During the defendant's case-in-chief, the defendant introduces evidence of the victim's reputation for violence. The defendant does not testify. In the prosecution's rebuttal case, the following happens:

Judge: Prosecution, call your next witness.
Prosecutor: Your honor, we call Mary Martin.
Defendant: Objection, your honor. May we be heard at sidebar for a moment?
Judge: Counsel, approach the bench. [Lawyers come to the bench.] Defense, what's the basis for the objection?
Defendant: Your honor, I believe that the prosecution is calling Mary Martin to testify that the defendant has a reputation for violence. That's improper. We haven't opened the door to such evidence. We didn't call witnesses to the defendant's character, so there's been absolutely no evidence of the defendant's pertinent character. Consequently, there's nothing for the prosecution to rebut.
Judge: Prosecution?
Prosecutor: They called a witness to testify to the victim's violent character. That directly and obviously implies that the defendant has a contrary character, and we're entitled to rebut that implication through Ms. Martin's testimony.
Judge: The objection is overruled. Rule 404(a)(1) provides that when the defendant offers a trait of character about the alleged victim, the prosecution may offer evidence of the same trait of character of the defendant. Defense, you opened the door.

Example 5:

In a murder case, the defendant testifies that the victim attacked him first and that he shot the victim in self-defense. The defendant is the only defense witness. After the defense rests, the prosecution calls a rebuttal witness. The following then happens:

Q. (By prosecutor) Mr. Jones, do you know a William Smith, the person who was killed?
A. Yes, I do.
Q. How long have you known him?
A. About five years.
Q. Under what circumstances have you known him?
A. He was my next-door neighbor. He became a good friend, and we used to spend a fair amount of time together.
Q. Do you have an opinion as to whether William Smith is a peaceful person?

Defendant: Objection, your honor. They're going into character evidence, and we didn't open the door to it in the defense case.

Judge: The objection is overruled. Rule 404(a)(2) says they can. The witness may answer.

Commentary: This is the murder–self-defense exception in FRE 404(a)(2), which allows the prosecution to rebut evidence that the victim was the aggressor, with evidence of the victim's good character for peacefulness.

Example 6:

Defendant is charged with perjury and testifies as follows:

Q. (By defendant's lawyer) Mr. Laughlin, when you testified before the grand jury, did you knowingly give false testimony?

A. No. I'd never intentionally lie under oath, and I didn't that day.

In the prosecution's rebuttal case, the prosecution calls a witness. The following then happens:

Q. (By prosecutor) Mr. Henderson, have you heard the reputation of the defendant, James Laughlin, for honesty?

Defendant: Objection, your honor. May we approach?

Judge: Please come to the bench. [Lawyers come to the bench.] What's the problem?

Defendant: Your honor, we never put the defendant's character in issue. We never called a reputation or an opinion witness to testify to the defendant's honesty, which is the pertinent character trait in a perjury prosecution. Consequently, there's nothing for the prosecution to rebut.

Prosecutor: The defendant testified, your honor. His truthfulness is now in issue.

Judge: That's correct. Objection overruled.

Commentary: Lawyers frequently confuse the admissibility of character trait evidence as circumstantial proof of conduct, governed by FRE 404(a) and 405(a), with impeachment using bad character for truthfulness, governed by FRE 608(a). Whenever any witness, including the defendant in a criminal case, testifies at trial, that witness's credibility is in issue, and the witness's character for truth-telling may be attacked, in either reputation or opinion form, during the direct examination of a rebuttal witness. The witness's character for truthfulness also may be attacked during cross-examination by the use of reputation, opinion, or specific instances of conduct evidence.

    c. Summary of character evidence

1. When a character trait of a person is an essential element of a charge, claim, or defense, general rules of relevance apply and proof of the character trait may be in the form of reputation, opinion, or specific instances of conduct.

2. When a character trait of a person is offered as circumstantial proof of conduct (i.e., when the essential element rule is *not* applicable), evidence of the character trait is *not* admissible to prove the person acted in conformity with that character trait on a particular occasion. The exceptions to this prohibition are:
    a. In criminal cases, the character of the accused and character of an alleged victim may be offered under the circumstances contained in FRE 404(a)(1) and (2). In civil cases, character evidence is inadmissible.
    b. Character evidence may be admissible against a defendant to prove propensity or conformity in sexual assault and child molestation cases in both criminal and civil cases under FRE 413-415. The sole method of proof is specific instances of conduct.
3. In all cases, civil or criminal, evidence of a witness's truthful or untruthful character may be admitted under circumstances contained in FRE 607-609.
4. When a character witness is cross-examined, the witness may be asked about other specific instances of conduct that are inconsistent with the claimed character under FRE 405(b) and 608(b).

2.   Other crimes, wrongs, and acts[5]

a.   Law

Rule 404.   Character Evidence; Crimes or Other Acts

(b) Crimes, Wrongs, or Other Acts.

(1) *Prohibited Uses.* Evidence of a crime, wrong, or other act is not admissible to prove a person's character in order to show that on a particular occasion the person acted in accordance with the character.

(2) *Permitted Uses; Notice in a Criminal Case.* This evidence may be admissible for another purpose, such as proving motive, opportunity, intent, preparation, plan, knowledge, identity, absence of mistake, or lack of accident. On request by a defendant in a criminal case, the prosecutor must:

(A) provide reasonable notice of the general nature of any such evidence that the prosecutor intends to offer at trial; and

(B) do so before trial — or during trial if the court, for good cause, excuses lack of pretrial notice.

Common experience tells us that a person is more likely to act consistently with the way that person has acted in the past. For example, a driver who repeatedly gets in accidents is more likely to get in accidents in the future. A person who has committed burglaries in the past is more likely to commit burglaries in

---

5. McCormick §190; Weinstein §404[10]-[17]; Mueller & Kirkpatrick §§4.15-4.18; Wigmore §§57-63.1.

the future. People are likely to act, at a particular time, in conformity with how they acted in the past. This past conduct shows a person's character, from which we deduce propensity and likely future conduct. Or so we assume, and there lies the problem. Such evidence has logical dangers.

Subject to proof of reliability and the restraints of FRE 403, FRE 404(b) provides that a party can offer evidence of a person's specific crimes, wrongs, or acts to prove anything relevant to the case, with one important exception: "Evidence of a crime, wrong, or other act is not admissible to prove a person's character in order to show that on a particular occasion the person acted in accordance with the character." FRE 404(b) and the general law of relevance support that simple, but often perplexing, proposition, although inroads into the general prohibition of propensity evidence are made by FRE 413-415, which deal with admissibility of evidence of other sexual crimes and acts in sexual assault cases.

Any analysis of FRE 404(b) must be confined to *other* crimes, wrongs, or acts. That is, the conduct must have been *extrinsic* to the matter being tried, not contained in it, not part of it. Courts also call this extrinsic conduct evidence "other acts" or "uncharged misconduct" evidence. For example, a defendant's prior heroin sale to Adam is extrinsic to the charge that he sold heroin to Baker. The prior sale may be offered to prove the defendant's knowledge or intent in connection with the sale to Baker. It may not be offered as character evidence, that is, to show he is the kind of person who is more likely to have made the sale to Baker.

When the prior conduct is *intrinsic* to the matter being charged, belonging to it, part of it, or, as some cases say, "inextricably intertwined" or a "continuing course of conduct," FRE 404(b) is not implicated, and general principles of relevance apply. Intrinsic conduct can be part of the episode being tried, or it can consist of necessary preliminaries to the matter being tried. It is linked in time and circumstance to the crime or event at issue.

For example, when a defendant is accused of beating his father to death to obtain money to support a cocaine habit, evidence that the defendant bought a large quantity of cocaine right after the murder is admissible under general relevancy rules. It has nothing to do with FRE 404(b) because it was a natural part of the circumstances surrounding the offense. On the other hand, evidence that the defendant attacked his father on prior occasions in attempts to obtain drug money is the kind of extrinsic conduct contemplated by FRE 404(b). It would be offered to prove the defendant's motive for killing his father. It is not admissible to prove the defendant was a violent person and more likely to have killed his father.

Concerns that evidence is being improperly offered as character evidence, to prove a person's propensity to do something, arise whenever extrinsic evidence is being offered on the authority of FRE 404(b). There are more appellate cases on this rule of evidence than on any other. That is because the potential and actual harm of this kind of evidence is obvious. It is admitted for purposes defined by the rule, but the dangers of misuse are palpable. Juries might be confused or sidetracked. They might overvalue the evidence and be distracted from direct evidence concerning the matter in issue. The other conduct might paint the party as a bad person, who should be decided against for that reason. While abuse of discretion remains the standard for appellate review, this is one area of the law of evidence where a trial judge's mistake can and often does result in reversal. For example, where the defendant charged with distribution of a controlled substance denies she knew the package she received contained crack cocaine, evidence that she admitted to personally using crack cocaine on other occasions is inadmissible propensity evidence, resulting in reversal of the conviction. And where the defendant denies he was in possession of a firearm, admitting a photograph showing he bears a tattoo of two crossed revolvers is propensity evidence and is not relevant to the possession charge, resulting in reversal of the conviction.

Most reviewing courts use a four-part test to analyze admissibility of evidence under FRE 404(b): (1) Is the evidence directed toward establishing a matter in issue other than defendant's propensity to commit the crime charged? (2) Does the evidence show that the other act is similar enough and close enough in time to be relevant to the matter in issue? (3) Is the evidence sufficient to support a jury verdict that the defendant committed the other acts? (4) Does the danger of unfair prejudice substantially outweigh the probative value of the evidence?

Some courts have taken another approach. These courts hold that FRE 404(b) specific purpose relevance must be established through a chain of reasoning that does not rely on the "forbidden propensity inference." If the proponent makes a showing of non-propensity relevance, the trial judge then must conduct the FRE 403 balancing test to determine whether the risk of misuse by the jury is too great. When doing the balancing, the trial judge is to consider how much the offered evidence has to do with an actual issue in the case.

FRE 404(b) applies to civil and criminal cases, to parties on both sides, to non-parties involved in the case, and to conduct taking place before and after the matter being tried. There is no exact limit to the time between the event at issue and the prior or subsequent crime, wrong, or act. Passage of three years after the crime charged is not long enough to bar admissions of FRE 404(b) evidence. It most often is used by the prosecution in criminal cases. The specific proper uses listed in the rule are not exhaustive. There can be other purposes, such as the ability to commit a crime and lack of consent.

The other conduct did not have to result in arrest or conviction. In fact, even where the defendant has been tried for and acquitted of the other crime, its use is not barred under FRE 404(b). *Dowling v. United States*, 493 U.S. 342 (1990). The admissibility of other conduct evidence is a matter of conditional relevancy under FRE 104(b), the standard being whether the jury could reasonably find by a preponderance of the evidence that the defendant committed the other crime, wrong, or act. *Huddleston v. United States*, 485 U.S. 681 (1988).

While *Huddleston* held the trial judge may admit the other conduct conditioned on a showing of relevance, nothing in the rule "precludes the court from requiring the government to provide it with an opportunity to rule in limine on 404(b) evidence before it is offered or even mentioned during trial." Advisory Committee's Note to Amended FRE 404(b). The judge, then, may require the prosecution to disclose specifics of the evidence before it is offered, even though the notice provision of FRE 404(b) speaks of providing "reasonable notice of the general nature of any such evidence that the prosecutor intends to offer at trial; and do so before trial — or during trial if the court, for good cause, excuses lack of pretrial notice."

The rule is one of inclusion. It authorizes the admission of a party's conduct that is extrinsic to the matter on trial for any relevant reason other than to prove the party's propensity to do the thing at issue. It would be indulging in fiction to say that admissible other conduct evidence must be completely free of any propensity taint. A reasonable fact finder might entertain that notion no matter how careful the trial judge is in defining the purpose of the evidence. The mere existence of the possibility of misuse is not enough to bar the evidence if it fits within FRE 404(b). It is enough to call on the judge to carefully exercise his discretion.

The test is whether the primary relevance of the evidence is to prove one of the proper elements of FRE 404(b). In fact, some cases hold the conformity bar of FRE 404(b) applies only when the evidence is proof of propensity and little or nothing else. Inevitable spillage into proof of propensity is handled by purpose instructions and careful monitoring of argument. If the evidence has any relevance, its tendency to prove propensity becomes the subject of FRE 403 analysis, the opponent making a case for the substantial danger of misuse of the evidence, or of juror inability to follow a limiting instruction because of the risk of severe emotional reaction to the evidence. A proponent of the evidence will place the importance of and need for the evidence on the probative value side of the FRE 403 scales. Similarity of conduct becomes important when the FRE 403 balancing test is conducted. Where the past act is not substantially similar to the act at issue, or where the past act cannot be proved with specificity or is remote in time, probative value is reduced and the usual FRE 403 presumption in favor of admissibility dissipates.

It is essential that the proponent of the evidence provide a clear statement of purpose when offering other conduct evidence. What matter of consequence will it tend to prove? What is the jury to infer from it? A general laundry list that mixes proper with improper purposes will not do. This is no place for a shotgun approach.

Once the trial judge learns the purpose of the evidence, he can consider the important questions. Is the evidence relevant to prove some matter of consequence in the case? Something other than propensity to commit the crime charged? Or is the proponent trying to smuggle in forbidden character evidence under the guise of FRE 404(b)? How important is the evidence of other conduct? Is it really needed in this case? Is there some other way, not so fraught with danger, that the proponent can make its point? How strong is the proof of other conduct? Can a reasonable jury conclude the defendant committed the other crimes, wrongs, or acts? Is the evidence strong enough to justify the risk? How remote is the evidence in time and place and nature?

Will the jury be able to follow an instruction that defines the proper purpose of the evidence and warns of the impermissible purpose? What are the risks that the jury will misuse the evidence, giving it more weight than it deserves? Will the jury, despite the defining instruction, use the evidence to conclude the defendant is the kind of person who did it before, so he must have done it again? Will the jury conclude from this evidence that the defendant is a bad person deserving of punishment?

Are there any other FRE 403 barriers to the evidence, such as the undue consumption of time or confusion of the issues? Do these considerations substantially outweigh the probative value of the evidence? Turning other conduct evidence into a mini-trial can result in a successful FRE 403 contention.

This weighing process is necessary when FRE 404(b) other conduct evidence is offered. The opponent of the evidence should urge the trial judge to consider these questions. Failure to raise FRE 403 considerations carries the risk of waiving the issue, although in this area plain error has been found where improper 404(b) evidence affects the fairness of the trial. Once the trial judge indicates the evidence is coming in, the opponent has the right to a defining instruction. Again, failure to ask for the instruction poses the risk of waiver, although some courts have held the trial judge has a sua sponte duty to give the instruction.

The judge, in turn, should make specific findings as to why he did or did not admit the evidence. Several reviewing courts have indicated a preference for a statement of reasons from the trial judge.

In *Huddleston*, the Supreme Court held the dangers posed by FRE 404(b) evidence can be obviated by requiring adherence to the FRE 404(b) command that the evidence not be admitted for propensity purposes, requiring that the evidence be relevant for a purpose contained in FRE 404(b), using the FRE 403 balancing test to weigh probative value against unfair prejudice, and using an appropriate instruction.

A controlling question for admissibility of FRE 404(b) evidence is whether the fact of consequence the evidence is directed at really is an issue in the case. Again, a clear statement of purpose is required before the question can be answered.

For example, a defendant is charged with possession of heroin with the intent to distribute. The prosecution has given notice that it will offer evidence of two prior heroin sales by the defendant during the month before the crime charged. If the defendant admits possession, but denies intent to distribute, his intent clearly is in issue. The prosecution is free to offer evidence of the defendant's prior sales of heroin during its case-in-chief to prove intent.

But what happens when the defendant offers to stipulate that whoever possessed the heroin intended to distribute it, but denies he possessed it? Some courts hold that when the defendant unequivocally offers to concede an element of the case, such as intent, and agrees to a jury instruction that the prosecution need not prove that element, that issue is out of the case, barring use of the prior sales to prove that element. Or, they say, the prosecution should wait for its rebuttal case to learn whether intent really is an issue. Other courts, a clear majority, hold that if the formal charge makes intent an issue in the case, the prosecution is free to offer evidence on the point because the prosecution need not accept the offered stipulation. This position is supported by the Supreme Court's decision in *Estelle v. McGuire*, 502 U.S. 62 (1991), where it held that, in federal courts, "a simple plea of not guilty . . . puts the prosecution to its proof as to all elements of the crime charged."

The other conduct evidence is not limited to prior sales. It could include the defendant's prior conviction for a similar offense or a conversation with the defendant where he exhibited knowledge of the drug trade.

A clear statement of the purpose of the evidence will allow the trial judge to determine its relevance to the matters in issue and to determine whether the primary effect of the evidence would be to prove a propensity to act in a certain way, the impermissible use prohibited by FRE 404(b). After the judge finds that the evidence is relevant for a proper FRE 404(b) purpose and then determines that a reasonable jury could find that the defendant was responsible for the extrinsic conduct, the FRE 403 balancing test must be conducted before the evidence is admitted.

If the extrinsic conduct is offered to prove identity of the defendant as the one who committed a crime, there must be a striking similarity, virtually a common signature, between the prior conduct and the conduct at the time of the offense being tried. Mostly generic common features are not enough for admissibility. If the extrinsic evidence is offered to prove the defendant's knowledge of something or his motive or intent to do something, the requirement of similarity is not as strict. Comparing extrinsic conduct to the offense charged first requires an examination of the similarities between them. The dissimilarities become important when the similarities create a close call.

For example, the defendant is charged with bank robbery. The prosecution offers evidence he participated in two other bank robberies. The purpose is to prove identity. If the similarities are no more than the use of a gun and the words "This is a holdup," the common features are generic to bank robberies and should not be admitted to prove the defendant's identity. If, however, the person identified as the defendant wore distinctive clothing in each robbery, used the same unusual weapon in each, and spoke the same distinctive words in each ("I am here to relieve you of other people's money"), this pattern of behavior, a modus operandi, would be admissible as identity evidence. The crimes share distinctive characteristics. To prove identity, the question is: Are the common characteristics distinctive enough to warrant an inference that the same person committed the charged and uncharged acts? Dissimilarities can dilute the similarities, weakening probative value. Enough dissimilarities can swallow the similarities. Note that even where the similarities win the struggle in the relevancy analysis, the FRE 403 weighing process, using the same factors, could produce a different result.

Proof of knowledge, intent, or motive does not require striking similarities or distinctive characteristics. If the extrinsic conduct similarities are relevant to an issue of consequence in the case, and if the legitimate purpose of the evidence is something other than propensity, threshold admissibility is reached.

For example, when a defendant on trial for possessing stolen goods claims he did not know the goods were stolen, the prosecution can offer evidence that twice before the defendant offered to sell goods in large quantities for prices far below their fair market value. When a defendant charged with mailing false pension benefits applications denies he intended to lie, the prosecution can offer evidence that the defendant filled out other documents that contained falsehoods in order to gain something.

The motive to commit burglaries or bank frauds ordinarily is the need for money. The prosecution can prove that need by offering evidence that the defendant had a substantial drug habit or that his other fraudulent enterprises had incurred huge debts.

The relevant purpose that justifies admission of extrinsic other conduct evidence can involve any serious issue in the case. For example, in a Section

1983 civil rights action, the plaintiff claims the defendants, the arresting officers, beat him and deprived him of medical treatment. The defendants say he tried to resist arrest. They offer evidence that six months earlier the plaintiff had been arrested for rape and aggravated kidnaping, had skipped bond on the charges, and had never surrendered. The evidence is admitted not only to show the plaintiff had a motive for resisting arrest, but also to prove his resistance was more probable and the use of additional force by the officers justified. This evidence probably survives the FRE 403 balancing test despite the risk of the jury using it as bad character evidence.

When the defendant interposes an entrapment defense in a cocaine sale case, the prosecution, on rebuttal, may offer evidence that the defendant had sold cocaine on two prior occasions and had been convicted of cocaine-dealing once before. The evidence relates to the defendant's state of mind, his willingness to commit drug crimes. In this case, it does not matter that the evidence might be seen as character evidence, since the defendant has made his character for being law-abiding an essential element of his defense.

In a personal injury damages case involving a claim that speeding caused the accident, evidence that the defendant sped through the accident scene intersection on three prior occasions should be barred as propensity evidence, although an argument can be made that the evidence shows he intended to race through that intersection. Of course, if the defendant was speeding a block from the accident scene just moments before his car struck the plaintiff, that evidence would be intrinsic to the accident and not an FRE 404(b) issue.

Similarly, evidence of a defendant's flight from the crime scene or his making of false exculpatory statements about his role in the crime is highly relevant, but does not implicate FRE 404(b). These matters are part of and intrinsic to the commission of the crime.

Every once in a while, not often, the defense tries to use other crimes evidence to show that some absent third party, not the defendant, is guilty of the crime charged. The circuits are divided, but a thin majority holds FRE 404(b) does not apply to a criminal defendant's evidence of acts of third parties. It is a matter of relevence.

In short, all relevant and reliable extrinsic conduct evidence is admissible unless (1) it is likely to prove character when character is not a fact of consequence in the case, (2) it does not survive the FRE 403 balancing test, or (3) it is excluded by other policy provisions in FRE 407-412.

b. Practice

FRE 404(b) is one of the most important and frequently used rules of evidence. Appellate reversal for the improper admission of other acts evidence is not unusual, particularly when the evidence involves proof of other crimes and wrongs. Because of its significance in criminal cases, FRE 404(b) was amended in 1991 to require that, upon request by the accused, the prosecution, unless excused for good cause shown, give reasonable notice of the general nature of the other acts evidence it intends to introduce at trial.

Whenever possible, issues surrounding the admissibility of other acts evidence should be raised before trial, in accordance with FRE 104. Judges are, and lawyers should be, legitimately worried about appellate reversal for erroneous rulings, and the issues can be considered thoroughly when raised early. This will focus the inquiry on the key issues: Is the evidence being offered for a proper purpose, is the evidence probative of that proper purpose, and is the probative value of the evidence substantially outweighed by the FRE 403 concerns?

Example 1:

The defendant is charged with making a fraudulent loan application in which he knowingly misstated and underreported his debts. The prosecution gives the defendant notice that it intends to introduce evidence that the defendant made two other loan applications at other banks, within six months of the application the fraud charge is based on, and that these loan applications contain substantially different statements of debts. The defendant then files a motion to preclude this evidence. At the hearing on the motion, the following happens:

Defendant: Your honor, this is our motion to preclude 404(b) evidence. The prosecution wants to introduce two other loan applications, made almost six months before the present application, that contain different statements of debts. This, by itself, proves nothing and is irrelevant. It only proves that the defendant made three different loan applications last year, and there's nothing probative in that. I realize that the prosecution will claim that it somehow proves knowledge, but these applications by themselves prove nothing.

Judge: Prosecution?

Prosecutor: The charge requires that we prove the defendant made the loan application knowing that the statement of debts was materially incorrect. Showing that less than six months earlier the defendant made two other loan applications in which he made substantially different statements of debts shows that he had to know that the present application was false.

Defendant: Your honor, for all we know, the present application is accurate and the earlier ones, the uncharged ones, are inaccurate. For all we know, the defendant's circumstances may have changed during those six months.

Prosecutor: We intend to prove, your honor, that the two earlier applications were false when made.

Judge: The objection is overruled, provided that the prosecution, if it introduces the two earlier loan applications, also introduces evidence showing that those applications were false when made. If this is done, the earlier applications will be probative on the issue of knowledge and properly admissible.

Example 2:

Defendant, a male, is charged with sexually assaulting another man. The prosecution gives the defendant notice that it intends to introduce evidence that the defendant's home contained numerous homosexual magazines. The defendant then files a motion to preclude this evidence on FRE 404(b) and 403 grounds. At a hearing on the motion, the following happens:

Judge: Good morning, counsel. Defense, why should this evidence be excluded?

Defendant: Your honor, the prosecution says that this evidence is admissible in the prosecution's case-in-chief because it circumstantially proves intent. The theory apparently is that if the defendant possessed homosexual magazines showing sexual activities between adult males, it somehow proves he is gay, and if he is gay, he is supposedly more likely to sexually assault another man. The prosecution has no other evidence to support these suppositions. The flaws in this evidence are twofold. First, the offered evidence has no demonstrated probative value. Second, even if it has some minimal value, its probative value is substantially outweighed by its prejudicial effect, and it must be excluded under Rule 403. This offered evidence is simple gay bashing. It asks the jury to conclude that the defendant must be gay and to convict him on that basis. That's wrong.

Prosecutor: Your honor, a person who possesses magazines like these is more likely to be gay, and a gay person is more likely to sexually assault someone of the same gender. That's a common-sense deduction, and one that the jury is entitled to make, or reject, as it sees fit. Furthermore, possession of these magazines is not a crime, so the great prejudicial effect the defendant claims exists here is simply not present. The jury is entitled to see this evidence.

Judge: The motion is granted. All evidence of the magazines is precluded from the prosecution's case-in-chief.

Commentary: This is a good example of offered evidence having little, if any, probative value on the specific issue—intent—involved, but its prejudicial effect is substantial, so exclusion under FRE 403 is proper.

Example 3:

The defendant is charged with sexually assaulting a real estate agent. The agent showed the assailant a listed home, and the assault took place in the empty home. The prosecution gives the defendant notice that it intends to introduce evidence that the defendant assaulted three other real estate agents in the same city in the past three years. The defendant then files a motion to preclude this evidence on FRE 404(b) and 403 grounds. At a hearing on the motion, the following happens:

Judge: This is the defense's motion to preclude evidence.

Defendant: Yes, your honor. The prosecution has served notice that it plans to introduce three prior incidents allegedly involving my client.

These three incidents, all sexual assaults, occurred three years, two years, and one year ago. In the first two incidents, the defendant was never charged. In the last incident, the defendant was charged, tried, and acquitted. Now the prosecution is trying to use these earlier incidents, which resulted either in no charges even being brought or in an acquittal, in the present case. Your honor, it's hard to imagine a more prejudicial effect than this on the defendant's right to a fair trial. This is clearly a case where the probative value is low, particularly in the older situations, but the prejudice is enormous. As a practical matter, the jury is going to convict the minute it hears this other acts evidence, even if the real evidence is fatally deficient. It must be excluded under Rule 403.

Prosecutor: The only issue in this case is identification. We have three victims ready to testify that this defendant, posing as a prospective home buyer, arranged to meet the agents at the properties. Once inside, they were raped. Each will identify the assailant. Your honor, this M.O. is so distinctive as to constitute a signature and is exactly the same M.O. as was used in the present case. Its probative value on the issue of identity is extremely high. If it has a prejudicial impact, any such impact does not substantially outweigh its probative value. Finally, the fact that the previous cases either were not charged or resulted in an acquittal doesn't matter. Under *Huddleston*, the only issue is whether we can show by a preponderance of the evidence that the prior rapes happened and that this defendant committed them.

Judge: The motion is denied. I agree that evidence of prior rapes is highly prejudicial, but the probative value of the evidence, because the prior rapes were apparently committed the same way as the rape at issue in the present case, is high. Under Rule 403, the evidence should be admitted. I will wait until trial to determine if the prosecution has met its burden under *Huddleston* to prove these prior crimes to the required preponderance level.

Commentary: This objection was decided under FRE 404(b). However, FRE 413 could make this evidence admissible to show propensity, an argument this prosecutor did not make.

Example 4:

The defendant is charged with embezzling funds from his employer. The defendant testifies at trial and during cross-examination denies that he had a motive to embezzle funds and that he resented or disliked his boss. On rebuttal, the prosecution offers the following evidence:

Q. (By prosecutor) Mr. Torres, on what date did you first detect that funds were being taken from the general account?
A. Around July 1.

Q. Do you do written performance reviews of your employees?

A. Yes, every year.

Q. When do you do them?

A. I complete them by June 1 and give them to my employees when I meet with them individually later that month.

Q. When did you meet with the defendant?

A. On June 25.

Q. Did you give him his written evaluation?

A. Yes, that same day.

Q. Mr. Torres, did you bring a copy of the evaluation with you?

Defendant: Objection, your honor. May we have a sidebar?

Judge: Yes. Since it's almost time for our afternoon break, we'll take it at this time. [Jury leaves courtroom.] Counsel, what's the basis for your objection?

Defendant: It's obvious that the prosecution intends to introduce the job evaluation, and we object. First, the job evaluation is 404(b) evidence and should have been disclosed before trial. We filed a written request for all 404(b) evidence, and the prosecution never notified us that they intended to introduce any job evaluation. The prosecution never asked that its failure to disclose be excused for good cause shown. What they're trying to do now is use this evidence in rebuttal, but 404(b) does not distinguish between the prosecution's case-in-chief and rebuttal. That's improper and unfair.

Prosecutor: Your honor, we didn't think that this evidence would be needed until the defendant was cross-examined and denied that he resented or disliked his boss. The negative job evaluation would logically have affected the defendant's state of mind and shows that his state of mind was likely different from what he now claims. The job evaluation merely proves up what the defendant denied during cross-examination. In addition, this is notice evidence, which is part of the core event of this case, so Rule 404(b) doesn't really apply in the first place.

Judge: The objection is sustained. I think the fact of the job evaluation, and testimony about the meeting in which it was given to the defendant, makes this evidence fall within Rule 404(b). The prosecution has given no reason why this evidence was not disclosed after a request was made. The whole purpose of the notice requirement is to put the defense on notice that the prosecution may use this evidence during trial so that we can deal with it. Since that was not done, the evidence is precluded.

Commentary: This is a close case. Not all judges may agree that FRE 404(b) applies to this evidence. If it does not, there is no notice requirement. Even if the notice requirement applies, many judges take a broad view of the notice requirement and use their discretion to allow late use, especially in criminal cases.

Example 5:

This is a negligence action in which the plaintiff claims the defendant ran a stop sign and caused the collision with the plaintiff. The defendant claims, both in the pleadings and during discovery, that he didn't realize there was a stop sign at that intersection and couldn't see the stop sign because it was obscured by bushes. In the joint pretrial statement, the plaintiff lists as an exhibit the defendant's traffic citation for failing to stop at the same stop sign one year before the collision. The defendant objects to this exhibit. At a hearing on the objection, the following happens:

Judge: This is a hearing on the defendant's objection to certain exhibits. Defense?

Defendant: Your honor, this offered exhibit, a prior citation for the same stop sign, is irrelevant and highly inflammatory. It's irrelevant to the plaintiff's case-in-chief because to make out a prima facie case on liability, the plaintiff need only establish that there was a stop sign and the defendant failed to stop. The evidence of the citation is nothing other than propensity evidence. It suggests that the defendant is a bad driver and is more likely to have been negligent on this occasion. In addition, the citation is hearsay, since it is being offered for its truth.

Plaintiff: The evidence is highly relevant to an issue the defendant injected into the case. They claim that the defendant didn't realize there was a stop sign at the corner and that the sign was obscured by bushes. This claim is totally destroyed by evidence that the defendant was previously cited for running that same stop sign. That's highly relevant, and it clearly prevails over any Rule 403 concerns. The citation is not hearsay, since it is being offered to prove the defendant's state of mind — that he had knowledge of the sign.

Judge: The evidence will be admitted if at trial the defendant continues to maintain that he didn't know or realize that there was a stop sign on that corner. This means that the plaintiff may not introduce the fact of the citation in her case-in-chief, since knowledge is not an element of the plaintiff's case. However, if the defendant introduces evidence of his lack of knowledge, such as through testimony of the defendant, the defendant may be cross-examined on the citation, and the plaintiff may in rebuttal introduce the citation in evidence.

Commentary: The judge has discretion to defer rulings on admissibility. Evidence that may not be admissible in the plaintiff's case-in-chief may suddenly become relevant, and highly so, depending on what the defendant introduces during trial.

c.   Summary of other uncharged crimes, wrongs, or acts

Evidence of other uncharged crimes is admissible if it is relevant for any purpose *other than* to show a defendant's propensity to commit a crime, and the evidence survives the balancing test of FRE 403.

Courts have found other uncharged crimes, wrongs, or acts admissible to prove the following things (the list is not exclusive):

Identity
Modus operandi (usually to prove defendant's identity)
Intent
Knowledge
Motive
Consciousness of guilt
State of mind
Absence of innocent state of mind
Dislike of or attitude toward the victim
Opportunity or preparation to commit the crime
Absence of mistake or accident
To impeach defendant's alibi
Circumstances of defendant's arrest
Circumstances of crime charged when otherwise unclear
Proximity of defendant to time and/or place of crime
Identification of weapon used in crime charged
That charged crime was actually committed

3.   Similar incidents evidence[6]

a.   Law

Similar incidents evidence is governed by rules other than FRE 404(b). General rules governing relevance, personal knowledge, reliability, and considerations of unfair prejudice and trial efficiency govern admissibility of similar incidents evidence. This kind of evidence consists mostly, but not exclusively, of other accidents or the absence of them. It is used frequently in products liability and negligence cases.

Products liability cases focus on the defective conditions of products. Other similar incidents involving a product might be introduced to prove that there was a defective condition or design and that the defendant had notice of the defective condition or design, requiring a better design, or more and better warnings, or an improved manufacturing process.

Similar incidents also tend to prove the magnitude of the danger involved or whether the defective condition of the product in fact caused the plaintiff's injury. The evidence might be admitted to demonstrate the defendant's indifference toward a known risk or the extent of the danger.

In negligence cases, evidence of other incidents usually is offered to prove the existence of a particular danger or hazard or to show the defendant had notice of the dangerous nature of the accident site. Likewise, the absence of

---

6. McCormick §198.

similar incidents might prove that the accident scene was safe or that the defendant could not have known about any potential danger.

Other, but less frequent, similar incidents issues include impeachment of witnesses and establishment of a standard of care.

Once the purpose of the similar incidents evidence is clear and a determination is made that this purpose is relevant to the issues in the case, the trial judge can decide what kind of evidence is reliable enough to support admissibility. The controlling question often is this: How similar does the other incident have to be?

Similar incidents evidence takes several forms. It can come from actual product failures, injuries at a particular location, complaints by users, other lawsuits, private and governmental studies and reports, or other sources. Reliability will depend on purpose.

If notice is the issue, consumer complaints or private studies would not be barred by the rule against hearsay because they would not be admitted for the truth of their contents. The fact that the defendant knew or should have known of these matters is enough to warrant admissibility. A minimal similarity is all that would be required. But if the dangerous nature of a product or location is the issue, or if the evidence is being used to prove causation, more is required.

There has to be proof of substantial similarity to the incident, and the circumstances have to be substantially the same. Substantial, but not exact, similarity is required. However, if the product was different, or if the location had changed materially, relevance is destroyed.

Subsequent similar incidents may be admissible to show the dangerousness of a scene or the defects of a product. They are not admissible as proof of notice of a condition.

Where similar incidents evidence is offered to show causation or the dangerousness of a product or location, firsthand knowledge is required, and the rules against hearsay apply. The proponent of the evidence bears the burden of establishing the proper foundation of relevancy and reliability. When those elements are satisfied, the opponent of the evidence is left with one argument: FRE 403. He may contend that the similar incidents evidence is unfairly prejudicial in that the jury might misuse the evidence, or that the evidence will create collateral issues, or prolong the trial, or confuse the jury, and that these concerns substantially outweigh the probative value of the evidence.

Evidence of the absence of prior similar incidents, offered to prove lack of negligence or dangerousness, is frequently a disputed issue. For example, if plaintiff claims a farm machine that injured him was unreasonably dangerous, evidence that other persons have been injured by the same type of machine is clearly relevant. On the other hand, can defendant offer evidence that it has manufactured and sold hundreds of the farm machines and that no one other than the plaintiff has been injured by them, thereby proving that the machines are safe? This latter negative evidence does not appear to have the same probative level, since the fact that no one has been injured by a machine to date does not prove it is safe. However, courts have usually admitted such negative evidence so long as an adequate foundation is established, showing that the manufacturer keeps track of any injuries, lawsuits, or complaints about its products.

Here, as with virtually all evidence issues, the trial judge must exercise reasonable discretion. Some judges will conduct FRE 104(a) hearings to determine admissibility of other similar incidents. Others will treat the matter as FRE 104(b) relevancy conditioned on fact, allowing the similar incidents evidence to be heard by the jury, but subject to other evidence that establishes relevancy. The safer course is for the matter to be dealt with out of the jury's presence. If the evidence is excluded, reviewing courts will examine the record for a valid reason.

b.   Practice

Because prior similar incidents evidence often has high probative value, it is important to raise issues before trial, when the judge has time to hear the arguments of the lawyers and to conduct a careful and considered analysis of the competing concerns.

Example 1:

This is a negligence action based on plaintiff slipping and falling at the entrance of defendant's store. Plaintiff's claim is based on the fact that there is a one-inch height difference between the floor of the store and the outside sidewalk. Defendant intends to offer evidence that this difference has existed for many years, but that no prior accidents had ever occurred at the store entrance. Plaintiff moves in limine to bar this evidence. At the hearing on the motion, the following happens:

Plaintiff: Good afternoon, your honor. This is our motion to preclude certain evidence defendant intends to offer at trial. Specifically, defendant intends to prove that there have been no other accidents at the store entrance. Our position is that this evidence is irrelevant and would only confuse and mislead the jury.

Judge: Defense, what's your argument?

Defendant: This evidence, the absence of any prior accidents, is admissible to show no notice of any defective condition as well as the non-existence of any defect. Plaintiff's argument is really directed to the weight of this evidence. Weight is for the jury and does not affect admissibility. This evidence undoubtedly has some probative value and should be admitted.

Judge: The motion is denied. The evidence is admissible, provided that a proper foundation from a qualified witness is established at trial.

Example 2:

This is a products liability case brought against the manufacturer of a deep fryer. Plaintiff claims she was burned when a cigarette lighter fell from her shirt pocket into the fryer as she bent over it, causing boiling fat to splash up and burn her. Plaintiff intends to offer evidence that after she was injured, there was a later similar incident involving the same type of fryer in which another person was injured. Defendant moves in limine to bar this evidence. During a hearing on the motion, the following happens:

Judge: Defense, this is your motion to preclude evidence.
Defendant: Yes, your honor. We move to preclude this evidence on two grounds. First, it is irrelevant to any issue of notice or knowledge, since it happened after the event that forms the basis for this case. Second, it is irrelevant generally because the fact that another person may have been injured using the same product does not prove that the product was unreasonably dangerous.
Plaintiff: First, we are not offering it to prove notice or knowledge. We agree it would be inadmissible for that purpose. Second, the evidence is relevant to show the product's unreasonably dangerous design. This evidence will show that another person was injured, using the same product, in a substantially similar way. This other person was injured while using the fryer when she bent over it and two pens fell out of her shirt pocket into the fryer. This will show that the design of the fryer was unreasonably dangerous.
Judge: The motion is denied. The evidence is relevant to the question of design dangerousness so long as the other accident occurred in substantially the same way as in the present case. I will make a final ruling at trial, when I have the opportunity to hear the testimony of this other person.

4. Other acts evidence in sexual assault cases (FRE 412-415)[7]

a. *Law*

Rule 412.   Sex-Offense Cases: The Victim's Sexual Behavior or Predisposition

(a) Prohibited Uses. The following evidence is not admissible in a civil or criminal proceeding involving alleged sexual misconduct:
  (1) evidence offered to prove that a victim engaged in other sexual behavior; or
  (2) evidence offered to prove a victim's sexual predisposition.
  (b) Exceptions.
  (1) *Criminal Cases.* The court may admit the following evidence in a criminal case:
    (A) evidence of specific instances of a victim's sexual behavior, if offered to prove that someone other than the defendant was the source of semen, injury, or other physical evidence;
    (B) evidence of specific instances of a victim's sexual behavior with respect to the person accused of the sexual misconduct, if

---

7. McCormick §193; Weinstein §412[01]-[03]; Mueller & Kirkpatrick §§4.32-4.36; Wigmore §§62, 200, 924a, 934a, 1040.

offered by the defendant to prove consent or if offered by the prosecutor; and

(**C**) evidence whose exclusion would violate the defendant's constitutional rights.

(**2**) *Civil Cases.* In a civil case, the court may admit evidence offered to prove a victim's sexual behavior or sexual predisposition if its probative value substantially outweighs the danger of harm to any victim and of unfair prejudice to any party. The court may admit evidence of a victim's reputation only if the victim has placed it in controversy.

(c) **Procedure to Determine Admissibility.**

(**1**) *Motion.* If a party intends to offer evidence under Rule 412(b), the party must:

(**A**) file a motion that specifically describes the evidence and states the purpose for which it is to be offered;

(**B**) do so at least 14 days before trial unless the court, for good cause, sets a different time;

(**C**) serve the motion on all parties; and

(**D**) notify the victim or, when appropriate, the victim's guardian or representative.

(**2**) *Hearing.* Before admitting evidence under this rule, the court must conduct an in camera hearing and give the victim and parties a right to attend and be heard. Unless the court orders otherwise, the motion, related materials, and the record of the hearing must be and remain sealed.

(d) **Definition of "Victim."** In this rule, "victim" includes an alleged victim.

Rule 413.   Similar Crimes in Sexual-Assault Cases

(a) **Permitted Uses.** In a criminal case in which a defendant is accused of a sexual assault, the court may admit evidence that the defendant committed any other sexual assault. The evidence may be considered on any matter to which it is relevant.

(b) **Disclosure to the Defendant.** If the prosecutor intends to offer this evidence, the prosecutor must disclose it to the defendant, including witnesses' statements or a summary of the expected testimony. The prosecutor must do so at least 15 days before trial or at a later time that the court allows for good cause.

(c) **Effect on Other Rules.** This rule does not limit the admission or consideration of evidence under any other rule.

(d) **Definition of "Sexual Assault."** In this rule and Rule 415, "sexual assault" means a crime under federal law or under state law (as "state" is defined in 18 U.S.C. §513) involving:

(**1**) any conduct prohibited by 18 U.S.C. chapter 109A;

(**2**) contact, without consent, between any part of the defendant's body — or an object — and another person's genitals or anus;

(3) contact, without consent, between the defendant's genitals or anus and any part of another person's body;

(4) deriving sexual pleasure or gratification from inflicting death, bodily injury, or physical pain on another person; or

(5) an attempt or conspiracy to engage in conduct described in subparagraphs (1)–(4).

Rule 414. Similar Crimes in Child-Molestation Cases

(a) Permitted Uses. In a criminal case in which a defendant is accused of child molestation, the court may admit evidence that the defendant committed any other child molestation. The evidence may be considered on any matter to which it is relevant.

(b) Disclosure to the Defendant. If the prosecutor intends to offer this evidence, the prosecutor must disclose it to the defendant, including witnesses' statements or a summary of the expected testimony. The prosecutor must do so at least 15 days before trial or at a later time that the court allows for good cause.

(c) Effect on Other Rules. This rule does not limit the admission or consideration of evidence under any other rule.

(d) Definition of "Child" and "Child Molestation." In this rule and Rule 415,

(1) "child" means a person below the age of 14; and

(2) "child molestation" means a crime under federal law or under state law (as "state" is defined in 18 U.S.C. §513) involving:

(A) any conduct prohibited by 18 U.S.C. chapter 109A and committed with a child;

(B) any conduct prohibited by 18 U.S.C. chapter 110;

(C) contact between any part of the defendant's body—or an object—and a child's genitals or anus;

(D) contact between the defendant's genitals or anus and any part of a child's body;

(E) deriving sexual pleasure or gratification from inflicting death, bodily injury, or physical pain on a child; or

(F) an attempt or conspiracy to engage in conduct described in subparagraphs (A)–(E).

Rule 415. Similar Acts in Civil Cases Involving Sexual Assault or Child Molestation

(a) Permitted Uses. In a civil case involving a claim for relief based on a party's alleged sexual assault or child molestation, the court may admit evidence that the party committed any other sexual assault or child molestation. The evidence may be considered as provided in Rules 413 and 414.

(b) Disclosure to the Opponent. If a party intends to offer this evidence, the party must disclose it to the party against whom it will be offered, including witnesses' statements or a summary of the expected testimony. The party must do so at least 15 days before trial or at a later time that the court allows for good cause.

(c) Effect on Other Rules. This rule does not limit the admission or consideration of evidence under any other rule.

FRE 412 applies only to defendants in criminal and civil cases "involving alleged sexual misconduct. . . ." Its purpose is to prohibit admission of an alleged victim's past sexual behavior or sexual predisposition.

FRE 413-415 represent a severe change in established rules concerning admissibility of propensity or conforming conduct evidence. They apply only to defendants charged with sexual assault or child molestation in criminal and civil cases.

b.   FRE 412

FRE 412, often referred to as the "rape shield rule," is a sweeping prohibition of use of an alleged victim's sexual behavior or sexual predisposition not directly related to the case on trial. Whether relevance of the unrelated conduct is slight or substantial, it gives way to the privacy interests of victims of sexual misconduct. The rule encourages victims to report and pursue their claims with a minimum of humiliation or embarrassment. The authority given to a criminal defendant by FRE 404(a)(2) to prove a pertinent conforming conduct character trait of a victim is withdrawn by FRE 412 in cases involving sexual misconduct.

Operation of the rule does not require an actual charge of a sexual crime; so long as the charge involves sexual misconduct. If a defendant were to take a hostage for the purpose of a sexual attack, the rule would apply even though the actual charge is kidnaping.

Subsection (b)(1) of the rule contains three exceptions to the general rule of inadmissibility of specific instances of sexual behavior by the alleged victim in criminal cases: (1) to prove someone other than the accused was the source of semen, injury, or other physical evidence; (2) sexual conduct with the accused to prove consent to the acts charged; and (3) instances in which exclusion would violate the constitutional rights of the defendant.

The "constitutional rights" referred to in subsection (b)(1)(C) concern the defendant's Sixth Amendment right to confront witnesses and his due process right to present a defense. For example, a defendant charged with rape has the constitutional right to prove the complainant was living with another man to show she had a motive to falsely accuse him of the rape. *Olden v. Kentucky*, 488 U.S. 227 (1988).

Generally, evidence of prior and probably false rape accusations against others should not be excluded by FRE 412, since these are not acts of sexual misconduct. However, some courts have refused to allow testimony that the complainant had falsely accused other men of sexual assaults when sexual conduct with them actually took place, or that the alleged victim had reported and then withdrew sexual assault accusations against family members other than the defendant.

FRE 412(b)(2) provides for admissibility of sexual behavior or sexual pre-disposition of any alleged victim in civil cases, but limits those occasions. First, the evidence must be admissible under the rules, which do not allow conforming conduct character evidence in most civil cases (FRE 404(a)). Second, the defendant must demonstrate the probative value of the evidence substantially outweighs the danger of harm to any alleged victim and of unfair prejudice to any party — a reversal of the FRE 403 balancing test.

The exclusions required by FRE 412 go beyond actual physical sexual con-duct. They include an alleged victim's use of contraceptives, the fact she has an illegitimate child, and that she once had a venereal disease. The way an alleged victim dresses and speaks generally is barred if offered as sexual predisposition evidence; but in a Title 7 sexual harassment case, evidence the plaintiff was sexually provocative in speech or dress in the workplace was held admissible to support the defense claim she welcomed certain sexual advances. *Meritor Savings Bank v. Vinson*, 477 U.S. 57 (1986). On the other hand, evidence a police officer posed naked for magazine photos was not admissible in the sexual har-rassment action she brought against her employer.

Subsection (c) of the rule sets out procedural requirements for a party offering evidence of sexual conduct. A written motion must be filed at least 14 days before trial, unless the court finds good cause to excuse the time limit. In addition to notice to all parties, including the alleged victim, the rule requires specific description of the evidence and its purpose. Then the court must conduct a hearing in camera, where everyone has a right to attend and be heard.

c. FRE 413-415

A principle firmly grounded in Anglo-American jurisprudence is the notion that a criminal defendant should be tried for what he did, not for who he is. That principle is reflected in FRE 404(a), which, with a few exceptions, bars evidence of a person's character when offered to prove he acted in accordance with that character on a particular occasion. The prohibition is repeated in FRE 404(b) which allows evidence of a defendant's commission of other crimes, wrongs, or acts for any relevant purpose other than to prove he acted in accordance with that character on the occasion at issue. That is, FRE 404(b) cannot be used to prove character.

Character evidence is not excluded by FRE 404(a) and (b) because it is irrelevant. It is excluded because it is too relevant. Its potent relevance carries the danger of unfair prejudice and juror misuse. See *Michelson v. United States*, 335 U.S. 469 (1948).

FRE 413-415 are designed to trump the bar against conforming conduct character evidence in sexual assault and child molestation cases, criminal and civil.

FRE 413 provides that in criminal sexual assault cases "the court may admit evidence that the defendant committed any other sexual assault. The evidence may be considered on any matter to which it is relevant." The definition of "sexual assault" includes a broad range of sexual conduct as defined by federal and state law (FRE 413(d)(1)-(5)). The government must give the defendant notice of its intent to use the evidence at least 15 days before trial, unless the court allows a shorter time for good cause.

FRE 414 provides for admissibility of evidence of a defendant's other offenses of child molestation for its bearing on any relevant matter where the defendant is accused of child molestation. The offense of "child molestation" is broadly defined under federal and state law (FRE 414(d)), and the rule contains a notice provision identical to that of FRE 413.

FRE 415 applies to civil cases where relief is predicated on a party's alleged offense of sexual assault or child molestation. Evidence of the party's other offenses of sexual assault or child molestation is admissible in the way provided by FRE 413 and 414 — that is, it may be considered for its bearing on any matter to which it is relevant.

Congress bypassed the ordinary rule-making procedures when adopting FRE 413-415. The rules have met with opposition. A report from the Judicial Conference of the United States observed the opposition of an "overwhelming majority of judges, lawyers, law professors, and legal organizations" to the proposed rules. Report of the Judicial Conference on the Admission of Character Evidence in Certain Sexual Misconduct Cases, 159 F.R.D. 51, 52 (1995).

While there is broad agreement these rules are intended to allow character evidence to prove conforming conduct on the occasion in issue ("He did it before and he did it again, that's the kind of person he is"), other serious questions have yet to be finally resolved.

1. Does the FRE 403 balancing test apply to admissibility of evidence offered under these rules?

Defendants have contended the rules violate their right to due process because they do not contain the balancing test. So far, every circuit court of appeal asked to decide the question has held trial judges are required to apply the FRE 403 balancing test to the evidence. Presumably, there is no need to determine whether a jury can follow limiting instructions, since there is no apparent need for a limiting instruction when evidence is admissible for any relevant purpose. The need for the other offense evidence becomes a crucial factor. Most courts have opted for a strict application of FRE 403 when weighing admissibility of evidence authorized by FRE 413 and 414. These courts find Congress meant that evidence of a defendant's propensity to commit sexual assaults, offered under FRE 413 or 414, is not outweighed by any risk of prejudice or other adverse effects. However, that does not foreclose any FRE 403 attack on other acts evidence admitted under FRE 413 or 414. The defendant still can claim other dangers, such as juror passion or bias, or shock or anger, or feelings that the defendant is a bad person deserving of punishment, or other improper inferences that do not concern propensity.

2. Does the evidence of other offenses require proof the defendant had been charged with or convicted of those offenses?

The rules contain no such requirements. They refer only to "commission" of the other offenses.

3. Must the other offenses be similar in nature to the offense or cause of action being tried?

The answer is unclear. While the titles to FRE 413-415 contain the word "similar," there is nothing in the wording of the rules that requires the other offenses be similar in nature to the offense or cause of action being tried. Presumably, that will be a consideration for the trial judge when applying the FRE 403 balancing test — the less similar, the less its probative value.

4. Is there an age limit to the other offenses?

Apparently not. Appellate decisions have allowed the government to reach back as far as 16, 20, and 30 years for a prior child molestation offense in a case where child molestation was charged.

5. What is the standard of proof for admissibility of other offenses under these rules?

The rules do not refer to the amount of proof required, but it is most likely admissibility will be governed by the same FRE 104(b) conditional relevance standard used in FRE 404(b) cases. That is, the trial judge examines all the evidence in the case and decides whether the jury could reasonably find by a preponderance of the evidence that the defendant committed the other offense. *Huddleston v. United States*, 485 U.S. 681 (1988).

6. Are FRE 413-415 open to constitutional attack?

Claims that use of character evidence to prove guilt in sexual assault cases violates due process and equal protection have been unsuccessful, although there is authority for the proposition that use of other acts evidence as proof of character violates due process in a murder case. See *McKinney v. Rees*, 993 F.2d 1378 (9th Cir. 1993). In Missouri, a statute mirroring FRE 413 was found unconstitutional by the state supreme court. The statute violated the Missouri constitutional provision that a criminal defendant has the right to be tried only on the offense charged. *State v. Burns*, 978 S.W.2d 759 (Mo. 1998).

d. Practice

FRE 412-415 significantly change the admissibility of other acts evidence in both criminal and civil sexual assault and child molestation cases. Since there is no substantial body of interpretative case law, it is particularly important to raise issues before trial. The admissibility of uncharged misconduct in these cases is often outcome determinative.

Example:

This is a child molestation case. The prosecution before trial notifies the defendant that it intends to introduce evidence that the defendant molested two other children in the past. The defendant moves in limine to preclude this evidence. At the hearing on the motion, the following happens:

Defendant: This is our motion to preclude, your honor.
Judge: Yes, I've read your motion. Prosecution, for what purpose are you offering this evidence?
Prosecutor: We're offering it to show that the defendant has a propensity to molest children, your honor. Under Rule 414, we can introduce this evidence for any relevant purpose. There is no question that showing the defendant's propensity for molesting children is highly relevant. Since Rule 414 governs, not Rule 404(b), the evidence is admissible.
Defendant: We agree Rule 404(b) no longer controls the admission of other acts evidence in this kind of case. However, Rule 403

still applies, and our position is that this offered evidence has minimal probative value, but that its unduly prejudicial effect is overwhelming. Therefore, Rule 403 requires that this evidence be kept out.

Judge: I'm going to reserve ruling until just before trial. I'll need to hear the testimony of the other two victims to determine how similar those other events are to the facts of the present case. That's the only way I'll be able to determine the probative weight of that evidence and apply the balancing test of Rule 403.

5.   Habit and routine practice (FRE 406)[8]

a.   Law

Rule 406.   Habit; Routine Practice

Evidence of a person's habit or an organization's routine practice may be admitted to prove that on a particular occasion the person or organization acted in accordance with the habit or routine practice. The court may admit this evidence regardless of whether it is corroborated or whether there was an eyewitness.

Evidence of a person's habit or an organization's routine practice is admissible as circumstantial evidence of conduct at a particular time. While FRE 406 does not define these terms, case law defines "habit" as how someone regularly, almost automatically, responds to a specific recurring situation and "routine practices" as habit evidence in a business or an industry setting. A habit is reflexive, situation-specific repetitive behavior.

For example, you always lock your front door when you leave your house in the morning. Your assistant always seals, stamps, and deposits your letters at the end of every workday in the mail drop in the lobby of your office building. These are habit and routine practice and are properly admissible as circumstantial evidence to prove that you closed your front door on a particular day and that your assistant mailed a particular letter. Habit and routine practice are admissible in both civil and criminal cases. FRE 406 expressly eliminates both the corroboration requirement and the requirement that eyewitnesses be absent before habit evidence may be admitted in evidence.

Habit must be distinguished from character traits. Habit is reflexive, situation-specific repetitive behavior. A character trait is a general personality characteristic that is not situation specific. For example, evidence that a person "always checks her mailbox when she enters her office" is habit evidence. Evidence that a person is a "careful person" is character trait evidence. Other commonly used character traits are honesty, truthfulness, and peacefulness.

Habit evidence is more probative than character trait evidence. For example, if the issue is whether a person received a particular letter, evidence

---

8. McCormick §195; Weinstein §406[01]-[06]; Mueller & Kirkpatrick §§4.21-4.22; Wigmore §§92-99.

that she always checks her mailbox when she enters her office is much more probative than evidence that she is a careful person. Since character trait evidence has low probative value, it is not admissible as circumstantial proof of conduct in civil cases. Because of this, evidence that is actually character trait evidence is sometimes offered as habit evidence. For example, plaintiff offers evidence that she is a "safe driver." This is not habit evidence; it is character trait evidence and, under FRE 404(a), is inadmissible as circumstantial evidence of conduct in civil cases. If plaintiff offers evidence that "she always stops at a particular stop sign," this is situation-specific repetitive behavior and is proper habit evidence. Whether eyewitnesses were at the scene should not affect admissibility of habit evidence.

Routine practice evidence is frequently offered in commercial and products liability cases. This is because such evidence is highly probative and there usually is no direct evidence available. A common use of office routine evidence is to prove mailing. For example, common sense tells us that no company employee will actually remember mailing a particular letter two years ago. If an employee testifies that the company has a routine practice of processing mail and putting a copy of the letter in the correspondence file after the original letter is mailed, this is proper habit evidence that circumstantially proves a particular letter was mailed.

Also common is the use of company procedures to prove standards of care in products liability cases. For example, plaintiff claims she was injured because the product she bought did not have a package insert containing product warnings. Defendant offers evidence that, during the time plaintiff's product was manufactured, the company had in place a procedure under which one employee placed the package insert in each package coming off the production line and another employee sealed each package after checking that both product and package insert were in it.

Some cases describe a tension between FRE 406 and the FRE 404(b) prohibition of conformity evidence. For example, a plaintiff who claims he was wrongfully denied disability insurance coverage offers evidence that the insurance company has a policy of wrongfully denying those claims. FRE 406 would support admissibility if there is enough evidence that the insurance company has a regular and routine practice of wrongful denial. That is, the FRE 404(b) conformity bar does not write FRE 406 out of the rules of evidence.

FRE 406 is silent on how habit and routine practice can be proved. The most common way is through the testimony of a witness with firsthand knowledge of the pertinent conduct. For example, a witness testifies that he car-pools to work with the defendant every day and that the defendant "always makes a complete stop when he comes to the stop sign at Main Street." Judges are comfortable with such factual observations. The specific conduct need not always be identically performed to constitute habit. However, if the specific conduct is not identically performed most of the time, the evidence will not be admissible as habit evidence. For example, evidence that the defendant "usually made a complete stop" may not be sufficient for some judges to qualify it as habit.

Habit also can be proved by introducing specific instances of conduct that collectively are numerous enough to demonstrate a habit. For example, the defendant calls several witnesses who periodically car-pool with the defendant.

They testify that whenever they ride with the defendant, the defendant always makes a complete stop at Main Street. Therefore, the evidence collectively proves a habit. Keep in mind, however, that the judge retains the power under FRE 403 and 611(a) to control and limit witnesses.

Some cases recognize that habit can be proved through opinion evidence. For example, a properly qualified witness can be asked "In your opinion, did the defendant have a habit of stopping at that intersection?" The answer "Yes, he made it a habit of coming to a complete stop" is proper.

b. Practice

Habit evidence is being used more frequently as common law restrictions on its use are eliminated. When evidence of habit is specific, containing a high frequency of repetitive, semiautomatic behavior, it can have substantial impact on the fact finder. It is considered in the same way as any other type of direct or circumstantial evidence. Habit is more commonly used in civil cases, but nothing in FRE 406 bars its use in criminal cases.

Example 1:

In a wrongful death case, the issue is whether the plaintiff's decedent, who had been driving for 30 years, put on his left-turn signal before he made the turn that resulted in the fatal collision. The plaintiff calls a witness who testifies that she rode with the deceased three days a week for about a year before the accident:

Q. (By plaintiff's lawyer) During the times you rode with him, did you observe him do anything before he made a left turn?
A. Yes.
Q. What did you observe?
A. At least 9 out of 10 times he would put his turn signal on about 30 feet from the intersection.
Defendant: I object. Counsel has not established a sufficient factual foundation under Rule 406.
Plaintiff: I have, your honor. She has testified to a regular response to a specific situation. That is enough.
Judge: Objection overruled. It's a matter of weight for the jury.

Commentary: This is the type of conduct that's consistent enough to quality as habit. While the judge is concerned that the witness observed the driver for only a year and that he didn't use his turn signal all the time, that's a matter of weight for the jury.

The examination continues.
Q. Based on your observations of the deceased when he made left turns, do you have an opinion as to whether he had a habit regarding his turn signals?
A. Yes, I do.
Q. What is your opinion?

Defendant: I object. This is not proper habit evidence. Besides, it's cumulative . . . Rule 403.

Plaintiff: Your honor, lay opinion is a proper method of proving habit.

Judge: It is a proper method of proving habit, but we have other evidence
of habit. I think it is cumulative, and for that reason, I will sustain
the objection.

Q. In your opinion, what kind of driver was the deceased?

Defendant: I object, your honor. The question calls for evidence of
character. That is prohibited by Rule 404(a).

Plaintiff: This is habit evidence, your honor.

Judge: No, the question calls for a general character trait. That's not
habit. Objection sustained.

Example 2:

The defendant is a dentist sued for malpractice. The plaintiff claims
the defendant failed to advise her that permanent numbness could result
from the procedure used to remove her wisdom teeth. The defendant, on
direct examination, has no memory of treating the plaintiff.

Q. (By defendant's lawyer) How many times in your professional life had
you performed that procedure before the day you removed the plaintiff's wisdom teeth?

A. Probably once every two or three weeks during the three years I had
been in practice.

Q. When you performed the procedure during those three years, did you
do anything concerning the risk of permanent numbness?

A. Yes. Sometime before the actual surgery I made it my practice to warn
every patient there is always a risk a nerve could be cut, causing
permanent numbness.

Plaintiff: I object, your honor. This is not the kind of automatic behavior
required by Rule 406. Warnings require conscious thought and
can't be proper habit evidence.

Defendant: The rule talks about the conduct of a person, and that's what
these warnings are.

Judge: Objection overruled.

Commentary: The rule covers uniform or semiautomatic behavior. There is
some degree of conscious thought here, but the witness is testifying to the way he
regularly acts in a certain situation, and that's included in habit.

Example 3:

This is a breach of contract case where *A* Corporation sues *B* Corporation for violating an agreement to deliver automotive parts. *A* Corporation
contends, and *B* Corporation denies, that the parts were delivered late
and in a defective condition. Before trial, *A* Corporation moves in limine to
introduce at trial evidence that *B* Corporation "on numerous occasions in
the performance of similar contracts with other companies made late

deliveries of defective parts." At the hearing on the motion, the following happens:

Defendant: I object to this offered evidence, your honor. This is not evidence of a routine practice under Rule 406. The evidence they want to offer is vague and conclusory. We don't know how many other contracts there were where the parts might have been delivered on time and in good shape. We don't know that these other contracts were the same as the one in this case. And we don't know that they have enough instances of late delivery of defective parts to establish an inference of systematic conduct. This is just an attempt to smear *B* Corporation.

Plaintiff: There is no risk of a smear in this case, your honor. We are dealing with a corporate business, not a person. The law does not require any magic number to establish a business routine. This is the way they did business, and the jury has a right to know about it.

Judge: I don't think the number and nature of the other contracts are clear enough to establish a routine practice. This looks like propensity evidence to me. Rule 404(b) prohibits that. Besides, even if it did have some slight probative value as routine practice, that value is substantially outweighed by unfair prejudice and the risk of jury confusion. Objection sustained.

VI

DIRECT EXAMINATION OF WITNESSES: HEARSAY AND NON-HEARSAY

§6.1. Introduction[1]

Trials are a search for reliable and sensible results. It follows, then, that trials should present only reliable information to the fact finder. What evidence is sufficiently reliable? Evidence law has long determined that reliability is enhanced when witness testimony meets three requirements: The testifying witness has firsthand knowledge of the facts about which he is testifying, is sworn to tell the truth, and is cross-examined to expose any weaknesses in his testimony. The rule against hearsay enforces reliability by requiring, in most instances, testimony from the witness having firsthand knowledge, who, in turn, can be effectively cross-examined.

For example, suppose that Smith was an eyewitness to the collision on which the trial is based. Smith tells Johnson what happened during the collision. At trial, the fact finder does not want to hear Johnson repeating Smith's account of how the collision occurred; the fact finder wants to hear directly from Smith, the witness with firsthand knowledge, whose credibility is critical. The cross-examiner, in turn, does not want to cross-examine Johnson, since Johnson did not see the collision; the cross-examiner wants to examine Smith to test the accuracy of Smith's observations and the reliability of Smith as a witness. Applying the rule against hearsay in this situation has two beneficial results: Johnson cannot testify about his secondhand information because it is inadmissible hearsay; Smith, the party with firsthand information, must testify under oath and be cross-examined.

The rules contained in FRE 801-807 reflect the common law's distrust of such out-of-court statements. That distrust is based on three concepts.

---

1. McCormick §§244-253; Weinstein §800[01]-[04]; Mueller & Kirkpatrick §§8.1-8.34; Wigmore §§1360-1366.

First, the fact finder is unable to see and hear the declarant when the statement is made. Our experience in life tells us we want to look at someone who is asking us to believe what he says. We want to look him in the eye, and we want him to look us in the eye. We want to see how he moves, what his expressions are, what his voice sounds like. We want to judge his sincerity and believability. We ordinarily would not buy a used car over the telephone. Why would we rely on out-of-court statements to determine the outcome of a court proceeding? Our assumption that watching a witness testify is a meaningful way to measure his credibility may run counter to social science research, but we believe it anyway.

The fact finder cannot determine how well the out-of-court declarant actually perceived and remembered the subject matter of the statement. Critical questions about the declarant are unanswered: Did he see the event clearly? Does he remember the event? Can he describe the event accurately? Is he an honest person? Is he biased, is he interested in the outcome, or does he have a motive to testify in a certain way? The risks of admitting out-of-court statements are high.

Second, to make matters worse, out-of-court statements ordinarily are not subject to oath or affirmation. We assume the sworn duty to tell the truth means something to most people. They are more likely to understand their obligation to be careful and truthful when under oath. Being subject to perjury laws inhibits some people from making erroneous statements, deliberately or unconsciously.

Third, and most important, the out-of-court declarant ordinarily is not subjected to cross-examination. We place a high premium on cross-examination. Experience has shown us that this is the best way of testing the declarant's honesty and sincerity; of determining his ability to perceive, remember, and report; and of exposing errors and omissions in his statements.

Why, then, given these risks, do we have so many instances where the fact finder is allowed to consider out-of-court statements? Why do the Rules provide for the admission of many out-of-court statements, either because they fall outside the definition of hearsay or because they fall within a hearsay exception? There are two basic, interrelated reasons.

First, we have learned that some out-of-court statements are reliable. They are firmly rooted in logic and experience, or they contain particularized guarantees of inherent trustworthiness. The integrity of the fact-finding process is not compromised by their admissibility.

Second, when the choice is between evidence that bears some risk of unreliability and no evidence at all, necessity sometimes dictates that the evidence be admitted. Otherwise, fair results may not be achieved. Artificial limits, unjustified by human experience, would stifle the fact-finding process.

When reliability and necessity coexist, the presence of the out-of-court declarant, the oath, and cross-examination may be excused.

To accommodate these interests, FRE 801-807 largely adopt the common law approach to hearsay. First, FRE 801(a)-(c) defines hearsay, and FRE 802 requires that hearsay be excluded unless made admissible by the Rules. Second, FRE 801(d) sets out eight exemptions from the definition of hearsay for various kinds of prior statements by witnesses and admissions by parties-opponent. Third, FRE 803, 804, and 807 set out numerous specific hearsay exceptions. Finally, FRE 805 permits the admission of hearsay within hearsay, and FRE 806 allows hearsay to be used to attack or support the credibility of the out-of-court declarant under certain circumstances.

The hearsay rules should not be considered in isolation. They are part of the entire fabric of the Federal Rules of Evidence. FRE 801, 803, 804, and 807 are not rules of admissibility. They merely define hearsay and provide that certain out-of-court statements are not excluded from evidence because of the hearsay rules. There may be, and often are, other evidentiary or constitutional rules that bar admission of the evidence, even though the hearsay barrier has been overcome. See *Crawford v. Washington*, 541 U.S. 36 (2004), holding that hearsay is barred by the Sixth Amendment when it is testimonial, the declarant is unavailable, and the defendant had no opportunity to cross-examine the declarant when he made the statement. Reliability is not part of the analysis.

This chapter will discuss the hearsay rule, non-hearsay, and the exemptions from the definition of hearsay. Hearsay exceptions are discussed in Chapter VII.

§6.2.   *The hearsay rules*

Rule 801.   Definitions That Apply to This Article; Exclusions from Hearsay

(a) Statement.   "Statement" means a person's oral assertion, written assertion, or nonverbal conduct, if the person intended it as an assertion.
(b) Declarant.   "Declarant" means the person who made the statement.
(c) Hearsay.   "Hearsay" means a statement that:
(**1**) the declarant does not make while testifying at the current trial or hearing; and
(**2**) a party offers in evidence to prove the truth of the matter asserted in the statement.

Rule 802.   The Rule Against Hearsay

Hearsay is not admissible unless any of the following provides otherwise:

- a federal statute;
- these rules; or
- other rules prescribed by the Supreme Court.

1.   A "statement"

First, was there a "statement" under FRE 801(a)? There can be no hearsay without a statement by a person. Presumably "person" means a human being. For example, if the prosecution in a drug case offers evidence that a trained dog detected the presence of marijuana, there may be other valid objections to the evidence, but it is not hearsay.

A statement can be oral or written, or it can be non-verbal conduct, but it must be intended as an "assertion." We assert when we state or affirm positively and intend to communicate this to another person.

Ordinarily, when someone says or writes something, he intends an assertion. His purpose is to communicate something. For example, if a person says. "It's cold outside," this is an oral assertion. If a person writes on a piece of paper, "It's cold outside," this is a written assertion. These kinds of assertions, oral and written, are the more common kinds of assertions for purposes of the rule against hearsay.

Some non-verbal conduct is also intended as an assertion. For example, sign language by a deaf person is intended as an assertion. If the police are called to a tavern, the scene of a shooting, and ask, "Who fired the gun?" and the bartender points to someone, that is an assertion. A nod or shake of the head in response to a question is an assertion. A finger pointed at a suspect in a lineup is an assertion.

Most conduct is not intended as an assertion. For example, evidence that a pedestrian stepped back on the curb as the defendant's car went by is a non-assertion when offered to show that the defendant was driving negligently. There was no intent to communicate. Evidence that someone was holding an open umbrella can be offered to prove it was raining at the time, since the person's conduct was not intended as an assertion. Evidence that someone was shivering is not intended as an assertion that the weather was cold. Likewise, the fact that someone was treated in a hospital's AIDS ward is not intended as an assertion by the treaters when offered to prove that the person had AIDS. When conduct is not intended as an assertion, it cannot be a statement, so it cannot be hearsay.

Silence is usually considered a non-assertion. For example, when the presence of smoke in a train car is an issue, evidence that other passengers did not complain of smoke is a non-assertion. When the condition of a store's floor is an issue, the fact that no one complained about slippery floor wax is a non-assertion. The absence of complaints about a product, offered to show it is not defective, is not intended as an assertion. Silence in these situations is not hearsay because there is no assertion, and no statement.

Whether expressions of belief are intended as assertions has been the subject of scholarly debate. When the captain carefully examines his ship before a voyage with his family, this evidence of his belief that the ship is seaworthy is not intended as an assertion. When the child victim of a sexual assault refuses to be alone in the same room with her accused stepfather, that refusal can be offered as non-assertive evidence against him. When police officers who raid a bookmaker's office testify that they received phone calls from people seeking to place bets, the courts treat the evidence as non-assertive expressions of belief by the callers that they are dealing with a bookmaker.

What happens, then, in a case concerning A's competency when evidence is offered that B wrote a letter to A asking for A's views on the current international situation? Obviously the letter is being offered for B's belief that A is mentally competent. FRE 801 treats the letter as non-hearsay, since it is being offered for something other than the truth of the words asserted in the letter. The letter is not being offered for the truth of its words, so it cannot be hearsay.

In practice, there are few cases dealing with the distinction between assertions and non-assertions. Other rules are usually used to resolve disputes. For example, flight by a defendant, arguably a non-assertion, is admitted as an admission. When assertion versus non-assertion issues arise, after a preliminary showing by the proponent of no assertive intent the opponent of the evidence, the one claiming it was intended as an assertion, has the burden of proving inadmissibility, and FRE 104(a) is the appropriate procedural vehicle for resolving these rare disputes.

On occasion courts are required to determine whether out-of-court questions are "statements" and therefore subject to hearsay analysis. The test is whether the declarant intended to make an assertion. Ordinarily, questions are not statements if they are designed to elicit information and a response. When a co-conspirator asks another conspirator, "Are you with Black?", that is not hearsay as to Black. But when a co-defendant, on being arrested, asks, "How did you guys find us so fast?", a statement is intended and is considered hearsay.

2. "Other than one made by the declarant while testifying at the trial or hearing"

Second, a statement can be hearsay under FRE 801(c) only if the statement is "a statement that the declarant does not make while testifying at the current trial or hearing." This question usually is shortened to the following: Was the statement made out of court? The hearsay rule comes into play only if a statement, made out of court, is repeated in court by a witness. For example, if a witness in court says, "The black car was speeding when it struck the other car," she is merely testifying to what she saw. Since she is not repeating in court a statement previously made out of court, no hearsay is involved. By contrast, if the witness in court says, "Bob told me the black car was speeding when it struck the other car," this involves an out-of-court statement, since the witness in court is repeating what Bob had previously stated out of court.

A common misunderstanding involving this second part of the hearsay rule involves the situation where the witness in court repeats his own out-of-court statement. For example, if a witness to an accident attempts to testify that "I told my brother, the day after the accident, that the Cadillac went through the red light," he is testifying to hearsay, even though the out-of-court declarant is on the witness stand and can be cross-examined. This falls within the hearsay definition, since the rule does not care if the witness in court is the same person as the out-of-court declarant.

Consider a Boston vehicle collision case. Mary is in Boston and says to a friend, "It's raining here." If the friend later appears as a witness at trial, the friend cannot repeat Mary's statement if it is offered for its truth because it is an out-of-court statement and falls within the hearsay definition. If Mary herself later appears as a witness at trial, Mary cannot repeat her own out-of-court statement, for the same reason. The result is that Mary is forced to testify not about what she previously said, but about what she previously saw. Mary can testify that she was in Boston and it was raining, but cannot repeat her own earlier statement, "It's raining in Boston." Hearing what Mary remembers seeing, rather than what she remembers saying about what she saw, usually results in more accurate information for the fact finder.

3.   "Offered in evidence to prove the truth of the matter asserted"

Third, is the out-of-court statement being "offered in evidence to prove the truth of the matter asserted in the statement?" Just having an out-of-court statement is not enough. Some of those statements will be hearsay, some not. Whether an out-of-court statement will be hearsay depends on the reason the party is offering the statement. It is hearsay only if it is being offered for its truth. Put another way, the party is offering the out-of-court statement because the party's position is that the statement is true and that because the statement is true, it proves something in issue. Any analysis of an out-of-court statement must begin with this question: What is the *purpose* for offering the statement?

Accordingly, what issue the statement is directed to determines whether the out-of-court statement will be hearsay. If the statement is offered because it is *true*, it is hearsay (it has probative value only because the statement is true). If the statement is offered because it was *said*, it is not hearsay (it has probative value whether or not the statement is true).

For example, consider again the vehicle collision in Boston. Plaintiff claims that defendant was negligent by driving too fast, since the roads were slippery from rain. Plaintiff wants to prove that it was raining when the collision occurred. Plaintiff calls a witness to testify that she called Mary on the telephone and heard Mary say "It's raining in Boston." The only reason plaintiff wants to introduce Mary's statement is for its truth; that is, the statement proves it was raining in Boston when the cars collided. This is hearsay.

Consider the same statement with a different issue. This time the case is a claim on a life insurance policy. The issue is whether Mary died before July 1, when the policy first went into effect. Plaintiff calls a witness who testifies that on July 1 she called Mary on the telephone, and Mary said, "It's raining in Boston." This statement is not hearsay. Why? It is not being offered for its truth. Plaintiff is not offering the statement to prove it actually was raining in Boston (this is not an issue). Plaintiff is offering the statement simply because Mary made it, regardless of whether it is true or not. So long as Mary was heard to speak that day, it proves that she was alive on July 1 (this is an issue). Put another way, whether the statement is factually true or false does not matter. Either way, it proves Mary was alive on July 1. Since the probative value of the out-of-court statement does not depend on the statement being true, it is not hearsay.

The third part of the hearsay rule can then be more functionally stated as follows: Does the probative value of the out-of-court statement depend on the statement's being true or merely on the fact that it was said? If the former, it is hearsay (unless it is exempted from the hearsay definition under FRE 801(d)); if the latter, it is not hearsay.

Apply the rule to another common situation. Plaintiff claims that defendant caused a collision because he drove a car with defective brakes, knowing the brakes were defective. Plaintiff offers the testimony of a mechanic that the day before the collision the mechanic said to the defendant, "Your brakes are defective." Is this statement hearsay? Clearly there is an out-of-court statement. The witness on the stand (the mechanic) is repeating someone's out-of-court statement (his own). Does the probative value of the statement depend on its being true or merely on the fact that it was said? This question can be answered only by asking what's in issue. On the issue of whether the brakes were actually defective, the statement is hearsay because the probative value of the statement depends on its being true. (Put another way, the only reason plaintiff wants to introduce the statement for this purpose is because the statement is true.) On the issue of whether defendant had notice of the brakes' condition, the statement is non-hearsay because the statement has probative value if the defendant heard it. (Put another way, the statement imparts notice to the defendant, regardless of whether it is true or not.)

The same out-of-court statement can be hearsay, then, for one purpose and non-hearsay for another. It all depends on what the issues in the case are and the purpose for which the statement is being offered.

In this situation, the jury is instructed that it can consider the statement only on the issue of notice, not on the issue of actual condition. The question then arises whether the limiting instruction is effective. This is governed by FRE 403. If the probative value for the proper purpose (proof of notice) is substantially outweighed by the danger of unfair prejudice (the jury will use it as proof of defect), the evidence should not be admitted.

In criminal cases, at times the prosecution will offer statements made to a police officer to establish the course of a police investigation. The statements are offered as non-hearsay, not for their truth, but to explain why the officer did what he did to investigate the crime. Whether a limiting instruction will properly confine the evidence to that limited purpose depends on the contents of the out-of-court statement. When an FBI agent testifies he received information from a confidential informant that the defendant may have committed the robbery being tried, the out-of-court statement is inadmissible hearsay and a limiting instruction will not save it.

False exculpatory statements, common in criminal cases, are not hearsay. For example, the defendant says to the police when arrested for robbery, "I was at home when that robbery happened." The police check with the defendant's family and discover that he was not home at that time. The prosecution wants to introduce the defendant's statement because it is false (and can be shown to be false) and its falsity shows a consciousness of guilt. For this purpose, the statement is not hearsay. (Note that if the *defendant* wanted to introduce the same statement to prove an alibi defense, the statement would then be offered for its truth and it would be hearsay.)

Hearsay questions cannot be intelligently framed or decided without knowing the answers to two crucial questions: What is the purpose of introducing the out-of-court statement? For that purpose, does the probative value of the statement depend on its being true?

§6.3.   Non-hearsay

1.   Law

The list of out-of-court statements that are not offered for their truth is virtually limitless, but most fall into a few general categories. In each category, the truth of the words in the out-of-court statement does not matter. The credibility of the out-of-court declarant is not critical. What matters is that the words were said.

Such words are not hearsay (sometimes interchangeably called non-hearsay). These categories are

1. independent legal significance
2. prior inconsistent statements used as impeachment
3. effect on listener's state of mind

a. *Independent legal significance*[2]

Substantive law sometimes attaches legal significance to words merely because they were said. Since the words have independent legal significance because they were said, regardless of whether the words are true, they cannot be hearsay. Common examples are defamation, false representations and fraud, extortion threats, contracts, gifts, and consent. This category is sometimes called "verbal acts" or "verbal parts of acts."

The non-hearsay statements can be complete standing alone, such as in the case of the words of offer and acceptance, or they can have relevance only when associated with some act, such as in the case of the words of a gift. Either way, hearsay is not a consideration.

Defamation is an intentional false communication, made by the defendant to third persons, that injures the plaintiff's reputation or good name. A plaintiff must prove that the defendant made a defamatory statement and communicated it to others. Since the plaintiff is not introducing the statement for its truth — the plaintiff's position is that the statement is false — it cannot be hearsay. For example, plaintiff Jones offers evidence that the defendant said, "Jones is an incompetent doctor." The plaintiff is offering the statement not for its truth, but because it was said. This being the case, the statement cannot be hearsay.

False representation or fraud requires that the defendant make a false representation, which the defendant knows is false when making it, and that the plaintiff believe the representation to be true, rely on it, and be injured. The plaintiff must prove that the defendant made the representation and that it was false. Just like defamation, since the plaintiff is not offering the statement for its truth, it cannot be hearsay. For example, plaintiff offers evidence that he purchased defendant's farm, relying on defendant's representation that "there is well water 20 feet below ground." Plaintiff is offering the statement not because it is true, but because it was said. The statement cannot be hearsay. (It also would be admissible as an admission by a party-opponent.)

Extortion threats are the essence of the crime of extortion. The prosecution must prove the defendant made a threat to the victim. In this case, the prosecution is offering the statement because it was made, not because it is true, so it cannot be hearsay. For example, in an extortion case, the prosecution offers evidence the defendant said, "Give me $10,000 or I'll put a bomb in your house." The prosecution is offering the statement not because it is true, but because it was said. The statement extorts, regardless of whether the defendant meant the words he spoke. The statement cannot be hearsay. (It also would be admissible as an admission by a party-opponent.)

---

2. McCormick §249; Mueller & Kirkpatrick §8.16.

Contract law requires an offer and an acceptance. The actual words of offer and acceptance, whether oral or written, cannot be hearsay; they are being offered because they prove the elements of a contract, not because the words are true. For example, plaintiff offers evidence that she said, "I'll sell you my computer for $200," and that the defendant responded, "I accept." These are the actual words of offer and acceptance and are not hearsay because contract law requires plaintiff to prove only that the parties actually spoke the words of offer and acceptance, not that the words spoken are true (i.e., that the parties actually meant the words they spoke). If the contract is in writing, the contract is not hearsay for the same reason.

A gift of personal property occurs when there is a physical delivery of property accompanied by words of donative intent. Property law requires the accompanying words because the physical act of giving property to someone else, standing alone, is inherently ambiguous. For example, if John hands Mary a watch, what kind of transaction is this? It may be a loan to Mary, it may be the return of Mary's property, or it may be a gift to Mary. Words accompanying the physical transfer are necessary to resolve the ambiguity. If John says, "This watch is now yours," these are words of donative intent, making the transaction a completed gift. The words of donative intent are not hearsay because property law cares only that the words were spoken, not that they are true (i.e., that John actually meant the words he spoke).

Words of authority, permission, or consent may have legal significance. For example, if John says, "Bill, go ahead and take my car," and Bill later is accused of stealing John's car, John's words, being the words of permission, have legal consequences because they were said. Since the statement has value because it was said, regardless of whether the words were true (i.e., that John actually meant the words he spoke), it is not hearsay.

In each of the above situations, the words spoken out of court are not hearsay because their probative value does not depend on the words being true. Rather, their probative value lies in the fact the words actually were said. Accordingly the *actual words* of contract, misrepresentation, extortion, defamation, gift, and permission are never hearsay because the law cares only that those words were uttered, not that they are true.

If the actual words are non-hearsay, then other, later statements may be hearsay. For example, John says, "Mary, this watch is now yours." These words are the actual words of gift and are not hearsay. If John later says to a friend, "Yesterday I gave Mary a watch," these words are hearsay if offered to prove the fact of a gift. In short, only the *actual words* of gift, contract, and so forth are non-hearsay. Later statements may be hearsay if offered to prove a gift, contract, and so forth. (These later statements may, of course, ultimately be admissible if they are non-hearsay party admissions or fall within a hearsay exception.)

b. *Impeachment*[3]

Witnesses who say different things at different times about a subject lose credibility. For instance, assume that a non-party witness at trial says, "The light

---

3. McCormick §§33-50, 251, 324.1; Mueller & Kirkpatrick §8.17.

was red," but shortly after the collision told a police officer, "The light was green." The fact finder, hearing both versions, will be reluctant to accept the witness's trial testimony. Evidence law calls this impeaching a witness with a prior inconsistent statement.

Out-of-court statements of a witness that are inconsistent with the witness's in-court testimony are not hearsay if they are offered only to prove the witness said something different at an earlier time. For example, the witness to an accident testifies that "the light was red for the eastbound traffic at the time of the collision." Evidence that he told the investigating police officer that "the light was green for the eastbound traffic at the time of the collision" is then offered to show that he said something different at an earlier time, thus calling into question his credibility at trial. Admissibility for impeachment purposes does not depend on which statement is true, or if either statement is true. So long as the out-of-court statement is different than the in-court testimony, it impeaches the witness's credibility.

A hearsay objection is never a proper objection to the introduction of a prior inconsistent statement used for the limited purpose of impeaching a testifying witness at trial. The opponent of the evidence is entitled to an instruction limiting the prior statement to its non-hearsay, non-truth purpose. (This assumes, of course, that the witness does not adopt the prior statement as true.) When used to impeach, the out-of-court statement cannot be argued for its truth during closing arguments, and it cannot be used to support or defeat a motion for a directed verdict.

This limited use of out-of-court statements must be distinguished from situations where the rules allow admission of certain prior inconsistent statements as substantive evidence, that is, for their truth. For example, an inconsistent out-of-court statement by a party, offered against the party can be admitted for its truth as a non-hearsay party admission under FRE 801(d)(2). A prior inconsistent statement of a testifying witness given under oath at a trial, hearing, or deposition can be admitted as substantive evidence (for its truth), since it is not hearsay under FRE 801(d)(1). FRE 801(d), which admits certain prior statements as non-hearsay, is discussed in later sections of this chapter.

c.   Effect on listener's state of mind[4]

An out-of-court statement may be non-hearsay if it is being introduced merely to show that the statement affected the listener's state of mind. If so, the statement is being introduced because it was made to and heard by the listener, not because it is true. Since the probative value of the statement depends on its being said and heard, not on its being true, it is not hearsay. Included in this category are words that establish the listener's relevant mental state, such as notice, knowledge, intent, motive, fear, and reasons for acting or not acting in a certain way.

Notice evidence is not hearsay. When a store patron is overheard telling the store manager that "there is a slick spot by the frozen food section," this is evidence the store had notice of the condition that allegedly caused the

---

4. McCormick §249; Mueller & Kirkpatrick §8.18.

plaintiff's injury. Other lawsuits filed against the manufacturer of a product are admissible to show the manufacturer was on notice that its product was defectively designed.

Keep in mind that such state of mind evidence, like any offered evidence, must be relevant to the case. For example, in a dog-bite case, Jones is heard to say to the defendant, "Your dog bit me last week." If substantive law requires that the owner previously be on notice of the dog's viciousness, the statement, when brought out in court through any witness who heard it said, is not hearsay. The statement puts the owner on notice. If, however, notice is not an element of, or relevant to, either liability or damages, such evidence would be irrelevant, and the proper objection is on relevance, not hearsay, grounds.

Fear evidence is not hearsay. For example, in a murder case where the defendant claims self-defense, evidence that Bob, the victim, said to the defendant, "I'm going to kill you if I see you again," is not hearsay. The statement induces fear in the defendant, whether or not Bob actually meant the statement. The statement is relevant because the defendant's fear makes it less likely that he would murder the victim. Evidence in the same case that someone else said to the defendant, "Bob's going to kill you if he ever sees you again," is admissible for the same reason. As long as the defendant heard it, the statement induces fear, and the defendant's fear is relevant to self-defense.

Motive evidence is not hearsay. For example, if a defendant is charged with robbing the victim, a statement made to the defendant that "the victim cheated you in the card game" is not hearsay because it shows the defendant had a motive for later robbing the victim. The fact that a defendant heard that an arrest warrant on a murder charge had been issued for him is non-hearsay evidence of a motive for his leaving town.

Intent evidence is not hearsay. A defendant charged with filing a false income tax return can testify to the advice given to him by his accountant to prove his lack of criminal intent. A defendant charged with possessing a car known to be stolen can testify his cousin told him that the car had just been bought and that it was okay to take it for a ride.

Reasons for acting, shown through out-of-court statements, are not hearsay. For example, when the police go to the scene of a robbery, they can testify they received a radio call telling them of a robbery at that location, since the statement shows why the police acted as they did. If, however, the radio call includes details beyond the relevant non-hearsay purpose, it can cross into hearsay. A radio call that includes the defendant's name crosses the line. When a car dealer claims that the manufacturer improperly canceled the dealer's franchise, the manufacturer can introduce letters of complaint from customers of the dealer to show why the franchise was canceled. The letters are not hearsay when offered to show the basis for the manufacturer's action.

In each of these categories — independent legal significance, impeachment with a prior inconsistent statement, and effect on the listener's state of mind — the out-of-court statement cannot be hearsay. The statement is being introduced because it was said, not because it is true, and the mere fact that the statement was said is relevant to a trial issue. Since the statement is relevant merely because it was said, not because it is true, it cannot be hearsay.

2. Practice

It happens all the time. An objection is made to an out-of-court statement: "I object, that is hearsay." The judge's first reaction is yes, it must be hearsay. It is a conditioned response. We all do it. Only a clearly defined statement of purpose, combined with a strong hold on the hearsay rules, will win the point. That is, "It is not hearsay because. . . ." Or "Yes, it is hearsay, but it is admissible because it comes within the exception in Rule. . . ."

It is a mistake, for both judges and lawyers, to begin any analysis of an out-of-court statement with an assumption that hearsay is implicated and then to search for an applicable hearsay exception. There are too many kinds of out-of-court statements that are not hearsay. Hearsay is an out-of-court statement that is offered for its truth. When an out-of-court statement is offered for any relevant purpose other than proving its truth, it is not hearsay.

Hearsay exceptions should not be considered until four non-hearsay categories are weighed:

1. An out-of-court declarant must intend that his or her oral or written words or non-verbal conduct be an "assertion." If an assertion is not intended, it is not a "statement." If it is not a statement, it cannot be hearsay. The declarant's intent controls the inquiry.

2. Statements that are offered not for their truth, but for some other relevant purpose are not hearsay. These are statements that are offered to prove the words were said or heard. These statements include words that have independent legal significance, such as words of offer and acceptance and gift-giving words; words that are offered only to show that a witness previously said or did something inconsistent with his testimony at trial; and words offered for their effect on the listener, such as words that provide notice or knowledge or otherwise explain the listener's beliefs, motives, or conduct.

3. FRE 801(d)(1) establishes three kinds of out-of-court consistent and inconsistent statements that are not hearsay, but are offered for their truth. In each instance, the declarant must be subject to cross-examination on the statement at the trial or hearing:
   (A) a statement inconsistent with the declarant's testimony if the prior statement was given under oath subject to penalty of perjury at a trial, hearing, or other proceeding or in a deposition;
   (B) a statement consistent with the declarant's testimony, offered to rebut an express or implied charge against the declarant of recent fabrication or of improper influence or motive;
   (C) a statement of identification of a person made after perceiving the person.

4. FRE 801(d)(2) establishes five kinds of admissions by a party that are not hearsay when offered against that party. These admissions do not require that the declarant testify at the trial or hearing or be subject to cross-examination:
   (A) the party's own statement in either an individual or a representative capacity;

    (B)   a statement by another where the party has shown an adoption of or belief in the statement's truth;

    (C)   a statement by a person authorized by the party to make a statement concerning the subject;

    (D)   a statement by a party's agent or servant concerning a matter within the scope of the agency or employment;

    (E)   a statement by a co-conspirator of a party during the course and in furtherance of the conspiracy.

If the out-of-court statement does not fit within one of these four categories, it is hearsay. Then, and only then, is it time to turn to the hearsay exceptions. This section will give examples of the first two categories. The next two sections in this chapter will give examples of the last two categories.

The hearsay rules do not operate in isolation. Even though the hearsay barrier has been overcome, there may be other evidentiary rules that bar the admission of the evidence. For instance, evidence must be relevant to a matter of consequence in the case, and it must be relevant to a proper purpose. After that, the evidence must meet the personal knowledge requirement of FRE 602 and the "rationally based on the perception of the witness" requirement of FRE 701. After that, there may still be other evidentiary objections that will bar the offered evidence, although hearsay is not a barrier.

The question of whether an out-of-court statement is hearsay or non-hearsay can usually be anticipated before trial and should be raised in a motion in limine. This will give the judge time to consider the admissibility issues and give the lawyers time to produce supporting and opposing authority. This is important because non-hearsay is a concept frequently misunderstood by both lawyers and judges. The earlier the objection, the more deliberate the consideration.

Frequently more than one rule of evidence will resolve a dispute. A statement of misrepresentation may not be hearsay because it has independent legal significance and is not being offered for its truth. The statement is also an admission by the defendant when offered by the plaintiff. When a party is impeached with inconsistent answers in his deposition, the answers are also admissible as substantive evidence either as prior inconsistent statements or as party admissions. Any of these reasons will do, and having backup reasons to admit evidence is important if the first reason fails to persuade the judge.

Example 1:

This is a defamation case in which the plaintiff alleges that the defendant falsely called him a thief. In the plaintiff's case-in-chief, the plaintiff intends to call a witness to testify that the defendant said, "You're nothing but a thief," to the plaintiff. At a hearing on the defendant's motion to preclude, the following happens:

Judge: Counsel, why is this evidence inadmissible?

Defendant: Your honor, this is clearly an out-of-court statement the plaintiff is attempting to introduce at trial, and they've cited no hearsay exception to get it properly admitted. It has to stay out. Besides, we have two witnesses who will say that the defendant never said those words.

Plaintiff: Your honor, this statement, "You're nothing but a thief," is an out-of-court statement, but is not being offered for its truth. It's being offered for its falsity. Therefore, since it is not being offered for its truth, it cannot be hearsay. These are the actual words of slander, which have independent legal significance in a defamation claim.

Judge: The motion is denied. The witness will be permitted to testify to the defendant's statement.

Commentary: This ruling is correct because the statement is not hearsay to begin with. While the party admissions rule in FRE 801(d)(2)(A) would also make the statement admissible, there is no need to rely on that rule. Of course, if the judge fails to understand that words of defamation cannot be hearsay, then make the party admissions argument.

Example 2:

Defendant is charged with theft of the owner's car. Defendant's defense is that he had the owner's consent. At trial, defendant calls a witness who testifies as follows:

Q. (By defendant's lawyer) Mr. Avery, were you at the party?
A. Yes.
Q. Did you see my client, Chris Johnson, and the owner, Bobby Franklin, talking that evening?
A. Yes.
Q. Where and when was that?
A. It was around 11:00 P.M. in the kitchen. There was just me and the two of them.
Q. What did Bobby Franklin say at the time?
Prosecutor: Objection, your honor.
Judge: What's the basis for your objection?
Prosecutor: It's hearsay, your honor, and the party admissions exception does not apply to a non-party.
Judge: Overruled. The witness may answer.
A. Bobby said to Chris, "You can take my car to pick up the beer."

Commentary: Since these are words of permission or consent, they are non-hearsay. In addition, the words show why Johnson believed he had permission to take the car, also a non-hearsay use of the out-of-court statement.

Example 3:

This is a fraudulent misrepresentation case in which plaintiff is suing to rescind her purchase of defendant's property. Plaintiff in her deposition states that during negotiations over the property defendant said, "There's water under that land not more than 30 feet down." Plaintiff claims that this statement was false, that defendant knew it to be false when made, and that this statement was made to induce plaintiff to buy defendant's property. Defendant has filed a motion seeking to exclude the statement. At a hearing on the motion, the following happens:

Defendant: Your honor, this is our motion to bar at trial the plaintiff's testimony of what she claims my client stated to her. We vigorously contest that this statement was ever made in the first place, the statement was made out of court, and the testimony is totally self-serving. It violates the hearsay rule and totally lacks reliability. In addition, it's not a party admission, since it's not being offered for the truth of the words.

Plaintiff: This statement is not hearsay. It's a statement of misrepresentation. It's a verbal act offered for its falsity, so it cannot be hearsay. Plaintiff, being a person who heard defendant make the statement, is a competent witness, and whether the statement was made is a question of credibility for the jury.

Judge: The motion is denied. The issue in this case is whether defendant made a fraudulent misrepresentation of fact, and the offered statement is non-hearsay on that issue. The fact that plaintiff is the witness to the claimed statement goes to credibility, not admissibility.

Commentary: The statement cannot be hearsay, since it is being offered for its falsity. It also would be a party admission under FRE 801(d)(2)(A).

Example 4:

This is an assault prosecution in which the defendant is charged with beating his former girlfriend. The defendant calls a witness who testifies on direct examination that he never saw the defendant beat his girlfriend. On cross-examination, the following happens:

Q. (By prosecutor) Mr. Crockett, you claim that you've never seen the defendant beat his girlfriend?
A. That's right.
Q. Well, you remember talking to my investigator, John Adams, a few weeks ago, don't you?
Defendant: Objection, your honor. May we approach?
Judge: You may. [Lawyers come to the bench.] What's the basis for your objection?
Defendant: They're trying to introduce the witness's oral statement in which he said that he had seen the defendant hit his girlfriend a few times, but not recently. That's hearsay and is being improperly used as circumstantial proof of the assault.
Prosecutor: The statement is being used to impeach, so it can't be hearsay. The witness claims that he never saw the defendant hit his girlfriend, but his statement to my investigator is completely inconsistent. We're entitled to cross-examine him on the

statement and prove it up if he doesn't admit making it, since the testimony is being used to impeach.

Judge: The objection is overruled.

Commentary: A hearsay objection is never a valid objection to otherwise proper impeachment with a prior inconsistent statement.

Example 5:

This is a murder prosecution in which the defendant is charged with killing her husband. The defense is self-defense. In the defendant's case-in-chief, a witness testifies as follows:

Q. (By defendant's lawyer) Ms. Johnson, were you with the defendant, Jane Joyce, and the deceased, William Joyce, on December 1, 2015, one week before the shooting happened?

A. Yes, I was.

Q. Where did you see them?

A. I was in their home.

Q. What was going on at the time?

A. Jane and I had just come in the door.

Q. What did Mr. Joyce say at the time?

Prosecutor: Objection, your honor. This is hearsay, and the victim's not a party.

Judge: Sustained.

Defendant: Your honor, may we approach? It's important.

Judge: All right. [Lawyers come to the bench.]

Defendant: Your honor, Mr. Joyce's statement was "If you come home this late again, you're going to pay for it big time." We're offering it to show the defendant's state of mind—fear—which is highly relevant to self-defense. We're not offering it to prove that the statement is true, only that Mr. Joyce said it and the defendant heard it. If she heard it, it induced fear in her, which goes to self-defense.

Prosecutor: Same objection as before, your honor. They're trying to introduce it to dirty up the victim, who isn't here to defend himself.

Judge: I'm changing my ruling. The objection is overruled. The question goes to the defendant's state of mind, which is relevant to the claim of self-defense. Counsel, please repeat the question before the jury.

Defendant: Ms. Johnson, what did Mr. Joyce say to Jane at that time?

A. He said, "If you come home this late again, you're going to pay for it big time."

Commentary: Some judges dislike sidebar conferences and prefer to rule from the bench. The danger is that the judge will rule incorrectly, not understanding the reason the testimony is being offered. Here, the judge, after permitting the sidebar conference, correctly changed the earlier incorrect ruling. If the judge had not permitted the sidebar conference, the defendant's lawyer would have had to make a record of what the witness would have said at the earliest available opportunity in order to preserve error.

Example 6:

This is a civil commitment case in which the state is petitioning to commit an elderly man because he is senile and represents a danger to himself and others. At the hearing, the state calls a witness who testifies as follows:

Q. (By petitioner's lawyer) Mrs. Blake, where do you live?
A. I live at 234 Maple, across the street from Mr. Wilson.
Q. For how long?
A. Twenty years.
Q. Do you see Mr. Wilson very often?
A. Almost every day. He's just across the street.
Q. What do you see him doing?
A. He's frequently in the front yard and shouts at people on the sidewalk.
Q. Can you actually hear what he says?
A. Certainly. He's usually quite loud.
Q. What does he say?
A. It's always the same thing. He keeps saying. "I'm General MacArthur; prepare for the invasion."
Respondent: Objection, hearsay.
Judge: Overruled. It's not being offered for its truth.

Commentary: The case is not concerned with whether the respondent is actually General MacArthur; the statement cannot be hearsay, since it is being offered for its falsity, not its truth. If the statement is being offered to show that the person believed he is General MacArthur, this is also non-hearsay. If the judge believes — incorrectly — that the statement is being offered for its truth, the petitioner's lawyer should argue that the statement is admissible to show the declarant's present state of mind under FRE 803(3).

§6.4.   *Prior statement by witness (FRE 801(d)(1))*[5]

1.   Law

Rule 801.   Definitions

(d) **Statements That Are Not Hearsay.** A statement that meets the following conditions is not hearsay:
(1) **A Declarant-Witness's Prior Statement.** The declarant testifies and is subject to cross-examination about a prior statement, and the statement:

---

5. McCormick §251; Weinstein §§801(d)(1)[01]-801(d)(1)(C)[03]; Mueller & Kirkpatrick §§8.24-8.26; Wigmore §§1018, 1132.

(**A**) is inconsistent with the declarant's testimony and was given under penalty of perjury at a trial, hearing, or other proceeding or in a deposition;

(**B**) is consistent with the declarant's testimony and is offered:

(**i**) to rebut an express or implied charge that the declarant recently fabricated it or acted from a recent improper influence or motive in so testifying; or

(**ii**) to rehabilitate the declarant's credibility as a witness when attacked on another ground; or

(**C**) identifies a person as someone the declarant perceived earlier.

a.   *Prior inconsistent statements made under oath used for impeachment*

Under FRE 801(d)(1)(A), a prior statement used to impeach a witness during a trial or hearing is not hearsay if the statement is "inconsistent with the declarant's testimony and was given under penalty of perjury at a trial, hearing, or other proceeding or in a deposition." This means that the statement is admissible as substantive evidence, that is, for its truth.

FRE 801(d)(1)(A) represents a compromise that followed fierce debate in Congress. The conflict was between the common law distrust of out-of-court statements when offered for their truth and the more modern view that all inconsistent out-of-court statements ought to be admissible for their truth when the declarant is available for cross-examination. The rule allows as substantive evidence those prior inconsistent statements that were made under oath at a formal proceeding. Although not defined, a hearing or proceeding includes a deposition, an administrative hearing, a preliminary hearing, a grand jury proceeding, and any other hearing where witnesses testify under oath in a judicial or an administrative setting. Sworn statements to law enforcement officers during station house interrogations are not made at a "proceeding," although it has been held that a sworn, tape-recorded statement made during questioning at an immigration hearing held at a border crossing is a "proceeding."

For example, a witness testifies that "the defendant's car ran the red light." On cross-examination, the witness is asked, "Didn't you say, during your deposition, that the defendant had the green light?" and the witness admits it. The prior statement in the deposition is admissible not only for the limited purpose of impeachment (for contradiction), but also, because of FRE 801(d)(1)(A), as substantive evidence (for its truth) that the light for the defendant was green.

The prior statement must be inconsistent with the in-court testimony, but the rule does not define inconsistency. The test used is the same one applied to prior inconsistent statements under FRE 613(b). To be inconsistent, statements do not have to be diametrically opposed or logically incompatible. An evasive answer, silence, a change in position, or a change in memory can supply the inconsistency required by the rule.

What happens when the witness on the stand claims lack of memory of the event that gave rise to the prior statement? Most courts hold that the prior statement is admissible under FRE 801(d)(1)(A) if the trial judge finds that the witness is fully aware of the event and is trying to avoid a negative impact on a party, or that the witness has feigned or falsified a lack of memory, or if the witness equivocates about whether he remembers the event. If the failure of memory is found to be legitimate and in good faith, the statement does not qualify for admission because it is not "inconsistent with the declarant's testimony."

The practical effect of FRE 801(d)(1)(A) is threefold. First, when a prior inconsistent statement not made under oath at a proceeding is admitted for the limited purpose of impeachment, the court often gives the jury a limiting instruction on the proper limited use of the statement (although jury research has found that such a limiting instruction is ineffective or even counterproductive). Second, if the prior inconsistent statement used for impeachment is also admissible as substantive evidence because made under oath at a proceeding, a lawyer can directly argue in closing argument that the statement is true. Finally, a prior inconsistent statement admitted as substantive evidence can defeat a motion for a directed verdict, since that statement is substantive evidence and may prove an element of a claim or defense.

b.   Prior consistent statements

FRE 801(d)(1)(B) provides for two occasions where a declarant-witness's prior consistent statement is not hearsay but is admissible substantively, for its truth.

Under FRE 801(d)(1)(B)(i) a prior consistent statement is not hearsay if it "is offered to rebut an express or implied charge that the declarant recently fabricated it or acted from a recent improper influence or motive in so testifying."

The rule does not prescribe any particular form of prior consistent statement. It can be oral or written, under oath or not. But it must rebut an express or implied charge against the declarant of recent fabrication or improper influence or motive, and the declarant must be subject to cross-examination on the statement. The rule is satisfied if the declarant is available to be recalled for further cross-examination. In that event, some other witness may testify to the declarant's prior consistent statement.

In *Tome v. United States*, 513 U.S. 150 (1995), the Supreme Court resolved the question of whether the prior consistent statement has to be made before the event giving rise to the charge of recent fabrication or improper influence or motive. In *Tome*, the Court held that the temporal timeline must be maintained. The declarant's consistent out-of-court statements are admissible only when they were made *before* the event giving rise to the charge of recent fabrication or improper influence or motive.

For example, a witness at trial testifies that "the defendant ran the red light." On cross-examination, the witness agrees he told an investigator that "the defendant had the green light." On redirect, it is not proper to bring out any other prior statements the witness may have previously made that the defendant ran the red light. Such prior inconsistent statements are hearsay, and FRE 801(d)(1)(B)(i) does not apply.

Suppose that the witness testifies during the trial that "the defendant ran the red light." During cross-examination, the witness is asked, "Isn't it true that last month you were hired by the plaintiff company?" and the witness admits it. The witness is then asked, "So now you're telling us that the defendant ran the red light?" The clear implication is that the witness's being hired by the plaintiff one month ago caused the witness to testify that the defendant ran the red light. Under these circumstances, during redirect examination the witness can be asked about any prior consistent statement if it was made *before* the witness was hired by the plaintiff. The question on redirect — "What did you tell the police officer right after the collision?" — and the answer — "I told him that the defendant ran the red light" — are now properly admissible under FRE 801(d)(1)(B)(i).

At times, it may be difficult to pinpoint the exact moment when a particular recent fabrication or improper influence or motive happened. The charge of recent fabrication or improper influence or motive can be "express or implied" during cross-examination.

When an accomplice agrees to testify for the prosecution in return for favorable treatment, that event becomes the time of recent fabrication or improper influence or motive. Any consistent statement the witness made *before* the agreement was reached or before he had a reasonable expectation of leniency becomes admissible if he is cross-examined about the agreement and his expectations.

Some motives and influences arise slowly over a period of time. They are not necessarily triggered by a discrete event. When that is the case, careful timeline analysis is required.

For example, in *Tome*, the defendant was charged with sexually abusing his four-year-old daughter while she was in his physical custody. The alleged crime was disclosed when the child was spending summer vacation time with her mother. On cross-examination, the defendant's lawyer suggested the child was fabricating her testimony out of a desire to remain with her mother. The prosecution introduced evidence that the child told others about the abuse during the summer she was with her mother. The Court found the prior consistent statements were made *after* the motive to fabricate arose and therefore were not admissible under FRE 801(d)(1)(B)(i).

FRE 801(d)(1)(B)(ii) took effect on December 1, 2014. It provides for substantive admissibility of a witness's prior consistent statement "if it rehabilitates the declarant's credibility as a witness when attacked on another ground."

The rule does not define the scope of the word "rehabilitates." However, the Advisory Committee Note to the rule states: "The amendment does not make any consistent statement admissible that was not admissible previously — the only difference is that all prior consistent statements otherwise admissible for rehabilitation are now admissible substantively as well."

The Note thus speaks to prior consistent statements that would explain apparent inconsistencies in a witness's testimony or rebut charges of faulty memory. To be admissible for its truth, the prior consistent statement must repair the harm done by the cross-examiner to the witness's credibility. The Advisory Committee Note states: "It does not allow impermissible bolstering of a witness."

The 2014 amendment is directed to the kind of prior consistent statement that many courts allow to rehabilitate a witness's credibility, but not for the truth of the words in the statement. In those instances, trial judges usually give instructions to the jury that confine relevance of the statement to the witness's credibility and that it is not to be considered for its truth. FRE 801(d)(1)(B)(ii) was enacted in part because of the belief that juries have a difficult time understanding the limiting instruction. The Federal Rules of Evidence do not

address the non-substantive use of a prior consistent statement offered to rehabilitate a witness's credibility.

The Advisory Committee Note suggests limits for use of the amended rule:
"As before, the trial judge has ample discretion to exclude prior consistent
statements that are cumulative accounts of an event. As before, to be admissible
for rehabilitation, a prior consistent statement must satisfy the strictures of Rule
403."

Whether the amendment will be confined to the purpose stated in the
Advisory Committee Note is not yet established. Attempts to use a prior consistent statement to "rehabilitate" a witness whose credibility has been attacked
with a prior felony conviction or claims of motive, bias, or interest appear to be
outside the purview of the amended rule.

Using prior consistent statements in rebuttal is further discussed in
See 13.4.

c.   A statement of identification of a person

Finally, under FRE 801(d)(1)(C), a prior statement is not hearsay if it
"identifies a person as someone the declarant perceived earlier."

The rule is self-explanatory. It is based on the recognition that in-court
identification testimony is weak and subject to suggestion. An out-of-court identification is fresher in time, and the opportunities for exerting influence are less.

When a witness testifies to his out-of-court identification of a person it is not
hearsay. That out-of-court identification could have happened at any place and
at any time. The identification is not limited to lineups or one-man showups. It
could be in a photograph, drawing, or videotape. The statement of identification could be accomplished by pointing a finger or nodding a head.

The identification may be consistent with the witness's in-court testimony,
thus bolstering it, or inconsistent with it, thus attacking it, so long as the witness
is subject to cross-examination on the prior identification. Once the witness
testifies to making an out-of-court identification, other witnesses may testify to
observing that identification.

If the person who made the identification is not available to testify, the rule
does not authorize the testimony of others who observed the statement of identification. That is because the requirement of the declarant being "subject to
cross-examination" has not been met.

What happens when the witness does not remember the event that resulted
in the out-of-court identification statement? The Supreme Court dealt with that
situation in *United States v. Owens*, 484 U.S. 554 (1988). There, the witness, a
prison guard, had received serious head injuries and was unable to remember
the assault. But he did testify that in a lucid moment after the assault, while in his
hospital bed, he identified the defendant as his attacker.

The Supreme Court held that the witness was "subject to cross-examination" under FRE 801(d)(1)(C) and the Sixth Amendment. An accused, said the
Court, is guaranteed an opportunity for effective cross-examination, not cross-
examination that is effective. Here, the defendant could bring out the witness's
bad memory and other facts that might discredit the testimony.

Note that *Owens* does not address the FRE 801(d)(1)(A) situation where
the witness cannot remember the event that gave rise to a prior inconsistent
statement. There, the question is whether the out-of-court statement is

inconsistent with the declarant's testimony. A legitimate lack of memory on the witness stand does not establish an inconsistency.

Nor does *Owens* provide an answer to what happens when the witness cannot remember making the out-of-court identification statement. Can some other witness testify to it? Would the out-of-court declarant be subject to cross-examination? The rule does not appear to bar the testimony from someone who observed the identification statement as long as the declarant is subject to cross-examination.

2.   Practice

The rule governing prior statements of witnesses is frequently misunderstood and misused. Witnesses can make two kinds of prior statements: prior consistent statements and prior inconsistent statements. Prior consistent statements usually are hearsay. We assume that witnesses have spoken consistently in the past, and proving this does not add much of significance to the trial testimony. Prior inconsistent statements, by contrast, used for the limited purpose of impeachment, are non-hearsay and relevant.

The only exceptions to this usual analysis are contained in FRE 801(d)(1)(i) and (ii) and involve situations where the "declarant testifies and is subject to cross-examination about a prior statement."

Under subsection (A), a prior inconsistent statement is not hearsay and is admissible as substantive evidence, that is, for its truth, if the prior statement "is inconsistent with the declarant's testimony and was given under penalty of perjury at a trial, hearing, or other proceeding or in a deposition."

Under subsection (B)(i), a prior consistent statement is not hearsay if the statement "is consistent with the declarant's testimony and is offered to rebut an express or implied charge that the declarant recently fabricated it or acted from a recent improper influence or motive in so testifying." It must be a pre-motive statement. Under subsection (B)(ii) a prior consistent statement is not hearsay "if it otherwise rehabilitates the declarant's credibility as a witness."

Under subsection (C), a prior statement, regardless of whether it is consistent or inconsistent, is not hearsay if it is a statement "that identifies a person as someone the declarant perceived earlier."

In practice, then, lawyers should always make specific reference to the appropriate subsection of FRE 801(d)(1) whenever they are arguing for the admissibility of a witness's prior statement as non-hearsay and as substantive evidence.

Example 1:

This is an automobile negligence case. A witness told the police after the collision that the defendant's car ran the red light. The witness testifies on direct examination as follows:

Q. (By plaintiff's lawyer) What did you see?
A. I saw the big black car run right through the red light and crash into the other car.
Q. Is that what you told the police officer at the scene?

Defendant: Objection.
Judge: Sustained.
Q. What did you tell the officer?
Defendant: Objection, hearsay.
Judge: Sustained.
Q. Well, did you tell the officer anything different than what you told us today?
Defendant: Objection, same basis.
Judge: Sustained. Counsel, move on to something else.

Commentary: These questions are all objectionable because the questioner is attempting to bring out a prior consistent statement to bootstrap the witness's credibility. The statement is hearsay, no matter how indirectly it is elicited.

Example 2:

This is the same automobile negligence case as Example 1. The same plaintiff's witness has completed his direct examination and is now being cross-examined. The following then happens:

Q. (By defendant's lawyer) Mr. Wilbur, you say you saw the big black car run through the red light?
A. Yes.
Q. The day after the collision an investigator came to your home?
A. That's right.
Q. You talked to him about the accident?
A. Right.
Q. And you signed a one-page statement stating what you saw?
A. Right.
Q. Let me show you that statement, which has been marked Defendant's Exhibit No. 3. That's your signature on the bottom, isn't it?
A. Yes.
Q. Didn't you say in your signed statement: "I didn't really see the traffic light until afterwards, but I assume the big black car must have run the red light"?
A. That's what I said.

When the plaintiff rests, the defendant moves for a directed verdict.

Defendant: There is no evidence my client went through the red light. The only eyewitness to the accident, Mr. Wilbur, told the investigator he did not see the light until after the collision.
Plaintiff: I object to that. The statement to the defendant's investigator is not substantive evidence in this case. He can use it only to attack Mr. Wilbur's credibility. That's a question for the jury.
Judge: Sustained. The statement came in for impeachment purposes only. It cannot be used as substantive evidence. In fact, I am directing you, defense counsel, to remember the limited purpose of the impeachment when you make your final argument.

Commentary: If the statement by Mr. Wilbur had been made under oath at a proceeding, it would be admissible as substantive evidence under FRE 801(d)(1)(A).

Example 3:

(a) This is a robbery prosecution. The victim testifies on direct as follows:

Q. (By prosecutor) Ms. Adams, do you see the man who robbed you in court today?
A. Yes, I do.
Q. Please point to him and describe what he's wearing.
A. He's the man right over there [pointing to the defendant] wearing the brown pants and white shirt.
Prosecutor: May the record show that the witness has pointed to the defendant?
Judge: Yes.
Q. Ms. Adams, you also attended a lineup?
A. Yes.
Q. Did you identify anyone?
A. Yes.
Q. What did you tell the detective at the lineup?
Defendant: Objection, your honor. It's hearsay.
Judge: Overruled. The witness may answer.
A. I told the detective that the defendant, who was one of the people in the lineup, was the one who robbed me.

(b) Same case. The victim has no memory of the lineup and has been unable to identify anyone in court. The prosecution calls a detective as its next witness:

Q. (By prosecutor) Detective Peterson, you ran the lineup?
A. I did.
Q. The victim, Ms. Jackson, was present?
A. She was.
Q. What did Ms. Jackson tell you at the lineup?
Defendant: Objection, on both hearsay and confrontation grounds.
Judge: Sustained.
Q. Did Ms. Jackson point to anyone during the lineup?
Defendant: Objection, same grounds.
Judge: Sustained. Move on to another topic.

Commentary: Under FRE 801(d)(1)(C), an identification of a person "per-ceived earlier" is usually interpreted to apply to the victim, since only the victim engaged in the mental process involving perception. Accordingly, the victim can always testify to her own out-of-court identification. However, when the victim is unable to make an identification and the prosecution attempts to introduce evidence of the same identification through another witness, usually the police officer who conducted the identification procedure, most courts consider this testimony inadmissible under FRE 801(d)(1)(A).

Example 4:

This is a sexual assault prosecution. The defendant is charged with sexually assaulting his minor daughter while she was visiting him during a school vacation. The claimed assault occurred in June. The daughter first reported the assault to the police three months later, in September. In the meantime, in August, the father petitioned for custody of the daughter. On cross-examination, the following happens:

Q. (By defendant's lawyer) Mary, you want to keep living with your mother, don't you?
A. Yes.
Q. You know your father wants you to live with him, right?
A. That's what he says.
Q. And you know that your mother and father are having a fight over that, right?
A. Yes.
Q. Mary, didn't you make up this story so that you wouldn't have to live with your father?
A. No, that's not true.
Q. Didn't you make up this story to help your mother win the custody fight?
A. No, that's not true.

On redirect, the prosecution asks the following questions:

Q. (By prosecutor) Mary, you saw Dr. Johnson as a patient in his clinic in July?
A. That's right.
Q. What did you tell him at that time about your father?
Defendant: Objection, hearsay. May we be heard?
Judge: Please come to the bench. [Lawyers approach.]
Defendant: Your honor, this is hearsay. They're trying to bootstrap the victim's testimony with her out-of-court statement. That's improper.
Prosecutor: The defense's cross-examination suggested a recent fabrica- .
tion and motive to fabricate. We're simply offering her state-ment to rebut that implication.
Judge: The objection is overruled. (To the witness) You may answer the question.
A. I said that my father had come into my bedroom and fondled me when I was pretending to sleep.
Q. Did you see the doctor again?
A. Yes, I saw him again in October, three months later.
Q. What did you tell him at that time?
Defendant: Objection, your honor. Any statements made in October are improper rebuttal.
Judge: Sustained.

Commentary: This ruling is correct under *Tome v. United States,* in which the Supreme Court held that prior consistent statements offered to rebut the implication of recent fabrication and improper influence must have been made before the time·the influencing event occurred (in this case, the father's petitioning for custody).

§6.5.   *Admission by party-opponent (FRE 801(d)(2))*[6]

1.   Law

Rule 801.   Definitions

(d) **Statements That Are Not Hearsay.** A statement that meets the following conditions is not hearsay:

(2) *An Opposing Party's Statement.* The statement is offered against an opposing party and:

(A) was made by the party in an individual or representative capacity;

(B) is one the party manifested that it adopted or believed to be true;

(C) was made by a person whom the party authorized to make a statement on the subject;

(D) was made by the party's agent or employee on a matter within the scope of that relationship and while it existed; or

(E) was made by the party's coconspirator during and in furtherance of the conspiracy. The statement must be considered but does not by itself establish the declarant's authority under (C); the existence or scope of the relationship under (D); or the existence of the conspiracy or participation in it under (E).

FRE 801(d)(2) no longer uses the word "admissions" to describe the hearsay exclusions contained in subsections (A) through (E). The rule now refers to "An Opposing Party's Statement." In our text we continue to use "admissions" to describe statements offered against a party. We do so to maintain clarity. Reported cases, trial judges, and lawyers in their practice commonly refer to "admissions" or "party admissions." In addition, we seek to avoid any confusion of party opponent admissions with the declaration against interest hearsay exception in FRE 804(b)(3).

FRE 801(d)(2) establishes five kinds of admissions by a party that are not hearsay when offered against that party. These admissions do not require that the declarant testify at the trial or hearing or be subject to cross-examination.

Party admissions are treated generously by the Rules. They are a product of the adversary process and therefore do not require the usual safeguards of reliability reflected by the hearsay rules. It has always been considered fair to use whatever an opposing party says against him at trial.

---

6. McCormick §§254-267; Weinstein §§801(d)(2)[01]-801(d)(2)(E); Mueller & Kirkpatrick §§8.27-8.34; Wigmore §§1048-1087.

The usual requirement of personal knowledge does not apply. No guarantees of trustworthiness are required. The admissions can be of fact or opinion. They can be in the form of conclusions, even conclusions of law.

Only parties to a lawsuit can make admissions. A party cannot sensibly complain that his own statement is not credible or that he has been denied the right to cross-examine himself.

A party cannot offer its own prior statement as a party admission. A statement can qualify as a party admission only when the statement is offered by the opposing party. For example, a plaintiff is an adversary of a defendant, and vice versa; a defendant is an adversary of a third-party defendant. However, a co-defendant is not an adversary of another co-defendant unless there are cross-claims between those co-defendants.

An admission does not have to be overpowering or reach an ultimate issue. It can be anything offered against the party who made it, anything contrary to that party's contentions at trial. Of course, an admission must meet general relevancy standards.

Admissions by a party-opponent should not be confused with the hearsay exception for statements against interest governed by FRE 804(b)(3). The party-opponent making an admission under FRE 801(d)(2) did not have to know his out-of-court statement was against his interest at the time it was made. Indeed, it could have been self-serving at the time made.

For example, the defendant has been involved in a dispute with his neighbor over who owns a strip of land between their properties. The defendant is heard to say, "That strip is mine." Some time later the plaintiff is injured on that strip of land and sues the defendant. The defendant's statement is a party admission when offered by the plaintiff, even though when made the statement was entirely self-serving. This also means that there is no point in analyzing an opposing party's statement as a statement against interest under FRE 804(b)(3), since any statement by an opposing party that qualifies as a statement against interest will also qualify as a party admission.

The party-opponent who makes an admission does not have to be available at the time of trial. He does not have to be confronted with the admission or given a chance to explain or deny it. FRE 613(b), governing prior statements of witnesses, does not apply to party admissions.

Finally, party admissions can always be used in two ways: They can be used as admissions, and they can be used as prior inconsistent statements to impeach the party if he testifies inconsistently at trial. Using the statement one way does not preclude its use the other way. For example, if the defendant said to a police officer following an accident, "It's my fault," the plaintiff can introduce the statement in the plaintiff's case-in-chief as a party admission and can also use the statement to impeach the defendant if the defendant testifies and denies fault.

a.   A party's own admission

Under FRE 801(d)(2)(A), a party admission includes a statement that "was made by the party in an individual or representative capacity." It can be oral, or written, or non-verbal conduct.

If the admission is made by a declarant who had a representative capacity, such as an administrator, an executor, a trustee, or a guardian, the statement is admissible if it is relevant to that representation. Whether the declarant was acting in a representative capacity when he made the statement does not matter.

A party can make an admission in the course of litigation, such as by signing an interrogatory or a pleading or by saying something in a deposition. A party's factual statement in a pleading signed under oath usually is treated as a binding judicial admission.

An admission can be a party's plea of guilty to a felony charge in a criminal proceeding, but not the judgment resulting from that plea. Any words or acts by a criminal defendant before arrest are admissible against him as admissions. After arrest, constitutional principles apply, but a properly admonished defendant may, under the *Miranda* holding, waive his Fifth Amendment (self-incrimination) and Sixth Amendment (counsel) rights and make admissions. *Miranda v. Arizona*, 384 U.S. 436 (1966).

The fact that a party is in privity with a declarant, or has some joint interest with the declarant, is not a consideration under FRE 801(d)(2)(A). The declarant's statement would not be admissible as a subsection (A) admission, although it might qualify under some other section of the Rules.

b. Adoptive admissions

Under FRE 801(d)(2)(B), a party admission includes a statement that "is one made by the party manifested that it adopted or believed to be true." An adoptive admission can be made by words, conduct, or silence.

When *A* says to *B*, "I am sorry I had to shoot the bank teller, but it was the only way you and I could get the money," and *B* says "You're right" or merely nods his head, *B* adopts *A*'s statement as his own. It is not hearsay when offered against *B*.

A party who reprints a certain newspaper article and distributes it to his customers for a business purpose adopts the statements in the article. The article is not hearsay.

A party can make an admission by silence when he fails to respond to a statement. These admissions are not favored by many trial judges because there could be valid reasons for silence. Judges will look at whether the statement was heard and understood by the party, the party had an opportunity to deny the statement, the statement is something the party would be expected to deny, there was any physical or emotional obstacle to responding, the declarant was someone the party could reasonably be expected to respond to, and the statement, if untrue, would ordinarily call for a denial under the circumstances. These factors should apply to any proposed admission by silence, including the party's failure to respond to a letter containing factual assertions.

For example, after a two-car collision, when one driver approaches the other and says, "You ran that red light," the second driver's silence, if he heard the statement and was physically and emotionally able to answer, would be an admission. If *A* tells *B*, "If I am questioned by the police, I will not tell them how we robbed the bank," *B*'s silence adopts the truth of the statement.

Admissions by silence can be admitted in civil and criminal cases, although special constitutional problems arise in criminal cases once the defendant is arrested. Under *Doyle v. Ohio*, 426 U.S. 610 (1976), the post-arrest silence of a defendant who has received *Miranda* warnings may not be used against him. Under *Fletcher v. Weir*, 455 U.S. 603 (1982), post-arrest silence before the *Miranda* warnings are given may be used only to impeach the defendant if the defendant later testifies. Most courts hold that a declarant's pre-arrest, pre-*Miranda* silence cannot be used as substantive evidence of his guilt.

Some trial judges treat admissibility of admissions by silence as conditional relevance matters under FRE 104(b). The tendency in criminal cases, however, is to require a preliminary showing under FRE 104(a) as to whether the defendant heard, understood, and, despite an opportunity to deny, acquiesced in the truth of a statement. The preliminary question is whether an innocent person would have denied the statement. Then the jury decides, with proper instructions from the trial judge, whether it should accept the defendant's silence as an admission.

There is debate about whether a party can make an adoptive admission when he has no personal knowledge of the facts he is charged with adopting. None of the exclusions in FRE 802(d)(2) requires personal knowledge. Still, a few courts hold that fairness calls for a foundation of personal knowledge. Perhaps a FRE 403 objection would best address the risk of unfair prejudice when the adoptive admission is offered.

c. *Admissions by authorized persons, agents, and employees*

Under FRE 801(d)(2)(C) and (D), a party admission includes a statement that "was made by a person whom the party authorized to make a statement on the subject," and a statement that was "made by the party's agent or employee on a matter within the scope of that relationship and while it existed." Subsection (C) and (D) admissions often are considered together.

Subsection (C) requires that the agent have authority to speak on the subject. Like subsection (D), the intent of the rule is to include statements of the agent to the principal as well as to third parties. Some courts, a minority, have held that subsection (D) may be used to admit the deposition statements of an expert against the party who employed him, on the grounds that the party authorized the expert to make statements about the issues in the case.

Subsection (D) is broader and more often used. It marks a departure from the common law requirement, still alive in many states, that the particular statement had to be authorized by the principal. Obviously agents and servants are rarely authorized to make statements that damage their principals. All that is required by subsection (D) is that the statement concern a matter within the scope of the declarant's agency or employment and that it be made during the existence of that relationship. There is no requirement that the agent or servant be authorized to speak.

There are times when the existence or scope of the agency relationship is challenged. Courts ordinarily will decide the issue under FRE 104(a). The proponent of the evidence has the burden of proof. It used to be that the alleged agent's words could not be used to prove the existence or scope of the agency. That was changed by a 1997 amendment to FRE 801(d)(2). Now, the contents of the alleged agent's out-of-court statement "must be considered but does not by itself establish the declarant's authority under (C); the existence or scope of the relationship under (D); or the existence of the conspiracy or participation in it under (E)." In addition to the declarant's statement, the court must consider "the circumstances surrounding the statement, such as the identity of the speaker, the context in which the statement was made, or evidence corroborating the contents of the statement in making its determination as to each preliminary question." Advisory Committee Note to FRE 801(d)(2).

For example, the driver of a truck says, "The crash was my fault. I was doing my job for the company when this happened." The entire statement is admissible against the defendant company only if the plaintiff first proves, using evidence other than, but including, the driver's statement, that the driver was working for the company at the time of the collision and that he spoke about something within the scope of his employment. Although this is a preliminary issue of fact for the trial judge under FRE 104(a), most judges require the evidence to be presented in the presence of the jury before ruling. The plaintiff could easily do this by introducing the employee's time and dispatcher records or perhaps by calling the employee as an adverse witness. Once this has been proven, the entire statement is admissible against the employer. Put another way, the employee's statement alone cannot be used to prove employment and scope of employment. Note that naming the employee as a co-defendant does not change the requirements for imputing his statement to the employer. If the employee is a named defendant, his statement will constitute an admission as to himself, but will not be legally imputed to the employer unless the fact of employment and the scope of employment are first independently proven.

A lawyer may make an admission on behalf of his client in pleadings, on the trial court floor, or to law enforcement agents when the lawyer has been authorized by his client to speak on the matter. A lawyer's clear statement of fact during an opening statement can be a judicial admission, binding on his client.

A statement by an employee at a deposition is admissible against his employer if the matter concerns his employment and if he still is employed at the time of the deposition.

The agent or employee making the statement does not have to be identified. For example, when an unnamed store employee is heard to say, "That spot where she fell was wet and should have been cleaned up," the statement is admissible against the store when offered by the plaintiff.

The courts and commentators are divided on the question of whether an agent-declarant must have personal knowledge of the facts underlying his vicarious admissions. Most answer the question in the negative, consistent with the views expressed in the Advisory Committee's Notes. Nothing in the Rules applies the FRE 602 personal knowledge requirement to any FRE 801(d)(2) admissions, although the personal knowledge requirement does apply to the FRE 803 and 804 hearsay exceptions. A lawyer opposing an agent's statement that is not based on personal knowledge would do well to argue the policy and terms of FRE 403. That is, the probative value of an agent's unfounded conclusion or of his repetition of someone else's meritless statements is substantially outweighed by unfair prejudice and the potential for misleading the jury.

Most courts hold the out-of-court statements of law enforcement agents are not admissible against the government in criminal cases, although it has been held that an agent's statements in a sworn affidavit to a judicial officer were the government's admissions. There seems to be no obstacle to the use of government employee statements as admissions against the government in civil and administrative matters.

d.   Co-conspirator statements

Under FRE 801(d)(2)(E), a party admission includes a statement that "was made by the party's coconspirator during and in furtherance of the conspiracy."

The co-conspirator admission applies to civil and criminal cases. No actual conspiracy need be pleaded or alleged so long as the evidence reflects some kind of joint enterprise of the declarant and the party against whom the statement is offered.

Once the conspiracy has ended, in either failure or success, subsection (E) no longer applies. Ordinarily, in criminal cases, once a co-conspirator is arrested his statements cannot be considered to be in furtherance of the conspiracy. But the mere fact of an arrest does not necessarily end the conspiracy. Courts will look to the goals of the conspiracy. If it includes an agreement to conceal the goals of the illegal plan, by making false statements to the police, for example, the conspiracy might extend beyond the arrest of one of the plotters.

Co-conspirator statements made during the course of and in furtherance of a conspiracy are not prohibited by the Sixth Amendment Confrontation Clause. In *Crawford v. Washington*, 541 U.S. 36 (2004), the Supreme Court held these statements are not considered "testimonial" and therefore do not come within the protection of the Confrontation Clause.

Two preliminary facts must be established before the statement of a co-conspirator may be admitted. First, there must be evidence there was an ongoing conspiracy involving the declarant and the person the statement is offered against. Second, the statement must have been made "during and in furtherance of the conspiracy." The statement must be part of the information flow between conspirators intending to help each perform his role in the conspiracy. Casual conversation about past events would not be "in furtherance."

Until 1987, courts were divided on the question of how and when to determine those preliminary facts. The common law cases required that proof of the conspiracy be independent of the co-conspirator's statements. Bootstrapping by using the co-conspirator's statements to prove the conspiracy was not allowed.

While some states still adhere to the common law rule, the dispute about the federal rule of evidence ended with the Supreme Court decision in *Bourjaily v. United States*, 483 U.S. 171 (1987). In that case, the government offered a tape-recorded conversation between Lonardo and an FBI informant. Lonardo told the informant he had a "gentleman friend" who wanted to buy cocaine. Lonardo arranged to meet the informant at a deserted hotel parking lot. He said his friend would be waiting to complete the transaction. At the parking lot, Lonardo removed the cocaine from the informant's car and carried it to the car where Bourjaily had been waiting. The FBI then moved in and arrested Lonardo and Bourjaily, finding nearly $20,000 in cash in Bourjaily's car. On appeal, Bourjaily claimed Lonardo's "gentleman friend" statements were inadmissible because there was insufficient proof of conspiracy and because the trial judge had relied on the statement itself in determining whether the conspiracy existed.

The Supreme Court held the following, while affirming Bourjaily's conviction:

1. The trial judge must decide the preliminary questions of fact by applying the "plain meaning" of FRE 104(a).
2. The party offering the statement must prove the preliminary facts by a preponderance of the evidence: that is, that it was more likely than not that the declarant and the party the statement is offered against were members of the conspiracy when the statement was made and that the statement was made in furtherance of that conspiracy.
3. The content of the co-conspirator's statement may be used to consider whether any of the preliminary facts exist.
4. The trial judge is free to give the evidence such weight as the judge thinks appropriate. The standard of proof is a preponderance of the evidence.
5. When reaching a decision, the trial judge should consider all relevant evidence, including evidence introduced by the party the statement is offered against.

The 1997 amendment to FRE 801(d)(2) supplied the answer to a question left open in *Bourjaily*. While the trial court may consider the declarant's statement, it is not enough, standing alone, to establish the existence of the conspiracy and the participation in it of the declarant and the party against whom the statement is offered. The amendment also adopts the view that the contents of the co-conspirator's out-of-court statement may be considered along with other evidence to determine the preliminary facts required to admit the statement. That is, "The court must consider in addition the circumstances surrounding the statement, such as the identity of the speaker, the context in which the statement was made, or evidence corroborating the contents of the statement in making its determination as to each preliminary question." Advisory Committee Note to FRE 801(d)(2). *Bourjaily* holds FRE 104(a) requires that preliminary questions of fact must be established by a preponderance of the evidence.

In *Bourjaily*, the Court refused to express an opinion on the proper order of proof that trial judges should follow when determining whether the necessary preliminary facts have been established by a preponderance of the evidence.

Most judges will not stop a trial to conduct a hearing outside the presence of the jury, although some, seeking to obviate potential problems, will hold a mini-hearing before trial to give the government an opportunity to establish the conspiracy it has charged. The usual practice is to admit the co-conspirator statements conditionally, determining at the close of the government's case and again at the close of all the evidence whether the FRE 801(d)(2)(E) preliminary facts have been established. If not, the defendant's motion to strike the co-conspirator's statements will be granted and the jury instructed to disregard them.

As a safeguard, to minimize the risk of the jury hearing inadmissible, but damaging, co-conspirator statements, the trial judge should require the government to offer whatever independent conspiracy evidence it has before it presents the co-conspirator's statements, although that procedure is not required by the Rules. Since the government's burden has been substantially eased by the *Bourjaily* holding, examples of an inadequate evidentiary foundation for a co-conspirator's statements are rare.

2.   Practice

FRE 801(d)(2) establishes five kinds of admissions by a party that are not hearsay when offered against that party. These admissions do not require that the declarant testify at the trial or hearing or be subject to cross-examination.

FRE 801(d)(2), covering party admissions, is one of the most important rules of evidence. It is important for two reasons: Party admissions are commonly introduced at trial, and they have substantial influence on the jury. After all, what could be more useful than to hear what the other party said about the issues? Because of this, evidentiary issues relating to party admissions must be carefully analyzed and argued.

In civil cases, issues should be anticipated and raised before trial, since the discovery process will usually disclose statements by parties or by agents and employees of parties. In criminal cases, because of limited discovery, party admissions issues may arise for the first time during trial.

Regardless of how and when raised, arguments on the admissibility or inadmissibility of out-of-court statements by parties, or by agents or employees of parties, should always be based on the five kinds of party admissions that are not hearsay under FRE 801(d)(2).

Example 1:

This is an automobile negligence case. A witness testifies during his deposition that he was in a bar with the defendant a few days after the collision and the defendant told him, "I can't believe I fell asleep behind the wheel during the accident." The defendant moves before trial to bar the admission of this testimony. At a hearing on the motion, the following happens:

Judge: Defense, it's your motion to exclude evidence.

Defendant: Yes, your honor. We move to exclude this evidence for two reasons. First, it's hearsay, since it's an out-of-court statement offered to prove fault. Second, it's not reliable, since it was made in a bar, after the defendant had some drinks, and it would be unfair, since there is a danger that the jury may give the statement, which the defendant will deny making, undue weight.

Plaintiff: This is a garden-variety party admission, your honor, and the statement is non-hearsay under Rule 801(d)(2)(A). All the other arguments the defense makes go to weight, not admissibility.

Judge: The motion is denied. The witness will be allowed to testify to the defendant's statement. It qualifies as a party admission, and the appropriate weight the statement deserves is for the jury to decide.

Example 2:

This is a wrongful termination case. Before trial, plaintiff designates certain portions of defendant's deposition as party admissions that plaintiff will offer at trial. Defendant then designates additional portions of his deposition that should also be offered at trial. Plaintiff objects to the additional portions. At a hearing, the following happens:

Judge: Plaintiff, what is the basis for your objecting to defendant's portions of his deposition?

Plaintiff: Your honor, any part of the defendant's deposition will be admissible when the plaintiff offers it because it will be a party admission. When the defense offers the defendant's own deposition, it's hearsay, unless some other hearsay exception applies. Here, the defense has offered no hearsay exception that would apply to his own deposition, and none exists.

Judge: Defense?

Defendant: When plaintiff goes through the transcript and designates specific questions and answers, the result is that the testimony is taken out of context. That violates Rule 106 because it creates a misleading transcript. For the sake of fairness, the entire deposition should be admitted if any portion will be admitted.

Judge: The objection is sustained. However, if defendant can show me where plaintiff has designated portions of the transcript that are out of context, or are incomplete, or result in an unfairness, I will reconsider the matter. Defendant has five days in which to file a motion in which such portions of the transcript are designated and any unfairness is demonstrated.

Commentary: Parties usually designate portions of deposition testimony they wish to introduce at trial. When the entire transcript is admissible, as when the transcript qualifies as former testimony, the designation process usually occurs without serious evidentiary problems arising. When a transcript is admissible as a party admission because offered by the opposing party, that same transcript, when offered by the deposed party, will be hearsay and usually inadmissible unless FRE 106 (the "rule of completeness"), a non-hearsay rationale, or a hearsay exception applies.

Example 3:

This is a fraudulent misrepresentation lawsuit brought against defendant seller and co-defendant real estate agent. Plaintiff claims the real estate agent made false statements about the property, which induced plaintiff to purchase the property. Defendant seller moves before trial to preclude testimony about the agent's statements. At the hearing, the following happens:

Judge: I have before me the defendant's motion to preclude the testimony of the co-defendant agent's statements. Counsel, proceed.

Defendant (Seller): Thank you, your honor. In this case, the plaintiff wants to introduce testimony, presumably through the plaintiff, of the agent's alleged misrepresentations. While we have no objection to this testimony as admissions of the agent, who is a defendant, we do object to any of those statements being imputed to the co-defendant seller. There will be no evidence showing the agent was authorized to make any misrepresentations on behalf of the seller or was acting in a representative capacity for the seller when she made those alleged misrepresentations. Rule 801(d)(2)(D) requires such a showing, through independent evidence, before any such statements can properly be imputed to the seller.

Plaintiff: Your honor, defense counsel is wrong. FRE 801(d)(2) provides that you can consider the agent's statements along with other evidence when you decide the existence and scope of the agency. We intend to offer evidence of the agent's statements along with other evidence that the agent was working for the seller at the time he made the fraudulent statements and that the agent's statements were part of his employment. I can do that now, before we select the jury, or I can do it at trial.

Judge: I believe plaintiff is correct about my right to hear all the evidence before deciding existence and scope of the agency. But I won't take the time to do it now. Present your preliminary evidence during the trial, to the jury, then I will rule.

Commentary: Under FRE 801(d)(2), the judge hears evidence of the agent's statements and other evidence when determining the scope and existence of the agency relationship. There is nothing in the rules that tells the judge how much weight to give any of the preliminary evidence when deciding admissibility. The plaintiff has the burden of establishing admissibility by a preponderance of the evidence.

Example 4:

This is an automobile negligence case in which the plaintiff was injured in a collision with the defendant's delivery truck. A vice president of the trucking company was interviewed by a reporter and was quoted in the newspaper as saying that "I've heard about the accident, and we're all saddened by it. Any accident with any of our vehicles is a serious matter, and we're sorry it happened." The defendant moves before trial to preclude the vice president's statement. At a hearing, the following happens:

Defendant: Your honor, this is our motion to preclude a certain statement made by the defendant's vice president. The statement is set forth in our motion. First, there's no evidence that the vice president had authority to make such a statement. Second, the statement isn't even an admission. It's simply a statement that the company is sorry the accident happened, which can hardly be taken as an admission of fault.

Plaintiff: The statement was made by the defendant's vice president. He is a high corporate official and has inherent authority to speak on behalf of the corporation. Moreover, he's the vice president for public relations. If anyone has authority to speak to the public, he does. Rule 801(d)(2) does not require that the statement be against interest when made. In fact, it can be self-serving when made. The only requirements under the rule are that the statement be made by the party or its employee and that the opposing side offer it. Here, the plaintiff is offering a statement of the defendant's employee, a corporate officer. That's all the rule requires.

Judge: The motion is denied. As long as the defendant said it and the plaintiff offers it, the statement qualifies as a party admission, provided that there is proof of the fact of employment at trial.

Example 5:

This is an automobile negligence case. The plaintiff claims the collision happened because the defendant made an illegal left-hand turn in front of the plaintiff. At trial, the plaintiff calls an eyewitness who testifies as follows:

Q. (By plaintiff's lawyer) Right after the collision, what happened?
A. The plaintiff, Ms. Johnson, the defendant, Mr. Williams, and Mr. Williams's son got out of their cars.
Q. What did you do?
A. I walked over to the boy and asked if he was all right.
Q. Where were the others at that time?
A. They were standing a few feet away. They appeared to be talking.
Q. What did the boy say to you?
Defendant: Objection, your honor. May we approach?
Judge: Yes. [Lawyers come to bench.]
Defendant: Your honor, I believe the witness is going to say, "We saw the other car, but my Dad thought we could make it." This is not an admission by silence because there's no showing that the defendant heard the statement. Without such proof, silence means nothing.
Plaintiff: The defendant was only a few feet away, according to the testimony. The defendant was not drunk, was not injured, and must have heard the statement. His failure to deny the statement speaks volumes.
Judge: Objection is sustained. Unless there is a showing that the defendant in fact heard the statement, which this witness cannot establish, the statement is not admissible as an admission by silence.

Commentary: The witness could still testify to any admission the defendant may have made (e.g., "We can beat that car."), since this would not involve the admission by silence concept and would be admissible as a party admission.

Example 6:

Three defendants — Adam, Baker, and Cain — have been indicted for bank robbery. The prosecution presents evidence that the three defendants were friends and were seen together during the days before the robbery. A prosecution witness identifies Adam as the robber inside the bank, and another witness identifies Baker and Cain in a car parked outside the bank at the time of the robbery. The next prosecution witness testifies as follows:

Q. (By prosecutor) Mr. Smith, do you know Mr. Adam, one of the defendants?
A. Yes.
Q. Did you know him before the day of the robbery?
A. Sure. I've known him for years.
Q. When was the last time you saw him before the robbery?
A. I saw him the day before the robbery.
Q. Where?
A. At his house. We were talking on the front steps.
Q. What did you talk about?
Defendant (Baker): Objection, your honor.
Defendant (Cain): We object as well, your honor.
Judge: Members of the jury, let's take our morning break at this time. [Jury is excused.] The witness will step down. [Witness leaves.] Counsel, what's the basis of your objection?
Defendant (Baker): Your honor, we believe the witness will testify about statements by defendant Adam that will implicate the other two defendants. The statements may be admissible against Adam as a party admission, but are not admissible against us.
Judge: Prosecution, what's the witness going to say?
Prosecutor: The witness will testify that he said to Adam, "I've been seeing you hanging around with Baker and Cain. What are you guys up to?" and that Adam responded, "We're about to score big. Stick around and you will read all about it." We've already shown that there was a conspiracy and that each of the defendants was involved; now we're entitled to introduce, under Rule 801(d)(2)(E), any statements made by any co-conspirator during the course of the conspiracy.
Defendant (Cain): Your honor, they never charged a conspiracy, and there's been no evidence that a conspiracy existed. A conspiracy requires an agreement to do something illegal, and they haven't shown any agreement. Furthermore, the rule requires that the statement be made in furtherance of a conspiracy, and this alleged statement doesn't further anything, much less a conspiracy.
Prosecutor: The rule doesn't require that a conspiracy be charged, only that a conspiracy be proved. Evidence of an agreement here

is circumstantial, as is usually the case. In addition, the "in furtherance of" language has been interpreted very broadly and covers essentially any statement about the conspiracy.

Judge: The objection is sustained. I find there is sufficient proof that there was a conspiracy and proof that Adam was a member of it at the time the statement was made. However, the statement is not in furtherance of the conspiracy.

Commentary: The admissibility of co-conspirator statements is a complex subject. Whenever possible, such issues should be raised in a motion in limine.

§6.6. *Summary of hearsay analysis*

1. Examine the out-of-court statement (words or conduct) and ask: "Is it intended as an assertion"?
   a. If not, there is no hearsay issue.
   b. If yes, examine the purpose for offering the out-of-court statement:
2. Is the statement offered for truth of the matter asserted?
   a. If yes, to be admitted the statement must be FRE 801(d) non-hearsay (three kinds of prior statements or five kinds of admissions); or an exception to the hearsay rules contained in FRE 803, 804, or 807.
3. Is the statement not offered for truth of the matter asserted?
   a. If not, there is no hearsay issue.

Common examples of non-hearsay purposes:

Notice
Motive
Listener's reasons for acting
Independent legal significance (slander, contract, gift, etc.)
Impeachment
Listener's mental state
Basis for expert's opinion under FRE 703

VII

DIRECT EXAMINATION OF WITNESSES: HEARSAY EXCEPTIONS

§7.1. Introduction[1]

Trials are a search for reliable and sensible results. Therefore, trials should present only reasonably reliable information to the fact finder. If the offered evidence is hearsay, it has failed the threshold reliability test unless the particular circumstances surrounding the making of the out-of-court statement show that it is nonetheless sufficiently reliable to warrant presenting to the fact finder. If it is, the usually required guarantees of testimonial reliability — personal presence at the trial of the witness with firsthand knowledge, administration of the oath to tell the truth, and cross-examination — can be excused.

The personal presence of the witness with firsthand knowledge of the facts ensures that the fact finder receives information from the most reliable source. The oath to tell the truth makes it less likely that the witness will intentionally lie or innocently distort information. Finally, cross-examination of the witness usually is essential, since only cross-examination will expose the bases for unreliable

---

1. McCormick §§253-327; Weinstein §§801-804; Mueller & Kirkpatrick §8.35-8.92; Wigmore §§1420-1427.

testimony, such as a lack of accurate perceptions about the event, a poor memory, an inability to communicate accurately, and a motive to fabricate or distort.

1. Hearsay exceptions rationale

Hearsay exceptions generally are based on two interrelated concepts. First, some out-of-court statements, because of the circumstances under which they are made, are inherently reliable. Second, sometimes the choice is between evidence that bears some risk of unreliability and no evidence at all. In such circumstances, necessity sometimes dictates that the evidence be admitted. Otherwise, fair results may not be achieved.

When reliability and necessity co-exist, hearing directly from the out-of-court declarant, the witness with firsthand knowledge, under oath and subjecting that declarant to cross-examination, is no longer essential. The fact finder can then properly hear evidence that is hearsay. (This hearsay evidence analysis does not determine the admissibility of testimonial statements when Sixth Amendment Confrontation Clause issues are raised in criminal cases. See *Crawford v. Washington*, 541 U.S. 36 (2004).)

Hearsay exceptions should not be considered until the four non-hearsay categories discussed in the previous chapter are weighed:

1. An out-of-court declarant must intend that his oral or written words or non-verbal conduct be an "assertion." If an assertion is not intended, it is not a "statement." If it is not a statement, it cannot be hearsay. The declarant's intent controls the inquiry.

2. Statements that are offered not for their truth, but for some other relevant purpose are not hearsay. These are statements that are offered to prove the words were said or heard. These statements include words that have independent legal significance, such as words of offer and acceptance and gift-giving words; words that are offered only to show that a witness previously said or did something inconsistent with his testimony at trial; and words offered for their effect on the listener, such as words that provide notice or knowledge or otherwise explain the listener's beliefs, motives, or conduct.

3. FRE 801(d)(1) establishes four kinds of out-of-court consistent and inconsistent statements that are not hearsay but are offered for their truth. In each instance, the declarant must be subject to cross-examination on the statement at the trial or hearing:

   (A) a statement inconsistent with the declarant's testimony if the prior statement was given under oath subject to penalty of perjury at a trial, hearing, or other proceeding or in a deposition;

   (B) a statement consistent with the declarant's testimony, offered to rebut an express or implied charge against the declarant of recent fabrication or of improper influence or motive;

   (C) a statement consistent with the declarant's testimony offered to rehabilitate the declarant's credibility as a witness when attacked on another ground;

(D)   a statement of identification of a person made after perceiving the person.

4.   FRE 801(d)(2) establishes five kinds of admissions by a party that are not hearsay when offered against that party. These admissions do not require that the declarant testify at the trial or hearing or be subject to cross-examination:

    (A)   the party's own statement in either an individual or a representative capacity,

    (B)   a statement by another where the party has shown an adoption of or belief in the statement's truth,

    (C)   a statement by a person authorized by the party to make a statement concerning the subject,

    (D)   a statement by a party's agent or servant concerning a matter within the scope of the agency or employment,

    (E)   a statement by a co-conspirator of a party during the course and in the furtherance of the conspiracy.

After it has been decided that an out-of-court statement is being offered for its truth, and after all the FRE 801(d) exclusions to the hearsay definition have been considered and rejected, the only path to admissibility is a hearsay exception. Then, and only then, is it time to consider the hearsay exceptions.

Each exception represents a decision that enough reliability exists to excuse the need for the personal appearance of the witness with firsthand knowledge of the facts, the oath, and cross-examination. Some are based on exceptions established by the common law, while some are new to the law. The search for, as the decisions described them, "adequate indicia of reliability" is grounded in our common-sense notions of reliability gleaned from life experience.

2.   The FRE 803 exceptions

Most of the exceptions do not require additional findings of trustworthiness. They are said to be "firmly rooted" in the law. The only inquiry in these instances is whether the statement fits within the words of the exception. The trial judge does not make any preliminary determinations of probable reliability.

FRE 803 contains 23 such categorical hearsay exceptions, although it may be argued that the exception for business records, FRE 803(6), requires a preliminary showing that the source of the information and the method and circumstances of the record's preparation are trustworthy. FRE 807, the residual or "catchall" exception, is not a firmly rooted hearsay exception, and the trial judge must conduct an FRE 104(a) inquiry into the existence of "equivalent circumstantial guarantees of trustworthiness" that are comparable to the indicia of reliability contained in the "firmly rooted" exceptions. (Again, this analysis does not control Confrontation Clause issues.)

If the hearsay comes within one of the FRE 803 exceptions, it does not matter whether the out-of-court declarant is available to be called as a witness.

3.   The FRE 804 exceptions

FRE 804 contains four specific hearsay exceptions and a provision for forfeiture by wrongdoing of the right to object to hearsay offered under the rule. FRE 804 differs from FRE 803 in that FRE 804 requires a preliminary showing, under FRE 104(a), that the out-of-court declarant is unavailable to be called as a witness. FRE 804 is a rule of necessity and preference. In each instance, testimony by the declarant is preferred over hearsay, but hearsay that meets the strict requirements of the FRE 804 exceptions is preferred over a complete loss of the evidence.

To provide the indicia of reliability adequate to satisfy the rule against hearsay, the exceptions in FRE 804(b) must be firmly rooted in the law or have equivalent circumstantial guarantees of trustworthiness.

All of the exceptions in FRE 804(b) reflect a strong preference for the in-court presence of the declarant. That is, testimony given on the witness stand is preferred over hearsay, but hearsay, if reliable, is preferred over a complete loss of the evidence. For that reason, each FRE 804(b) hearsay exception requires that the declarant—or, to be more precise, the declarant's testimony—be "unavailable," even though the declarant might be physically present in the courtroom. The burden of showing unavailability of the declarant's testimony is on the party offering the hearsay. The question is resolved by the trial judge under FRE 104(a).

FRE 804(a) provides five categories of "unavailability as a witness." These categories are not exclusive; they are illustrative. The rule includes situations in which the declarant

(1) is exempted from testifying about the subject matter of the declarant's statement because the court rules that a privilege applies.

This situation includes any privilege recognized by the trial judge. Most often it is triggered by the Fifth Amendment privilege against self-incrimination, although other privileges, such as the marital privilege, will serve to make a witness unavailable. Most courts require an actual claim of privilege by the declarant in court and then a ruling by the judge, although some Fifth Amendment claims may be so apparent that an actual claim in open court is not required before the judge rules. The rule does not provide for the form or timing of the claim of privilege.

(2) refuses to testify about the subject matter despite a court order to do so.

A witness could refuse to testify. The trial judge might reject his claim of possible self-incrimination. A witness might have other reasons for refusing to testify, such as fear or loyalty. His testimony becomes unavailable when the trial judge orders him to testify and he persists in refusing. Unavailability is not created simply because a judge relies on the declarant's assertion that he would refuse to testify, even if ordered by the court. The witness actually must be ordered to testify. Some courts require that the declarant be warned that continued refusal to testify would be punishable as contempt, although nothing in the rule imposes that further requirement.

> (3) testifies to not remembering the subject matter.

The lack of memory must be established by the witness-declarant. The rule contemplates the witness will be on the stand, subject to cross-examination on his claim of failed memory. The lack of memory does not have to be total. It must relate to the subject matter of the statement being offered. The fact that the witness might remember other events, but not the subject matter of the statement, has no impact on the unavailability of the witness's testimony about the subject matter of the statement. It does not matter whether the witness's lack of memory is real or false. Either way, the witness's testimony becomes unavailable. This analysis does not apply to the "subject to cross" requirement of FRE 801(d)(1)(C). See *United States v. Owens*, 484 U.S. 554 (1988).

> (4) cannot be present or testify at the trial or hearing because of death or a then-existing infirmity, physical illness, or mental illness.

The rule does not require that the illness or infirmity be permanent. When it is temporary, serious scheduling problems might arise. The trial judge has to determine the nature and seriousness of the illness or infirmity and about how long it will continue. He also has to consider the importance of the testimony and weigh the need for cross-examination. Unavailability will be found when the judge determines the illness or infirmity probably will last long enough that, considering the importance of the testimony and the nature and age of the case, the trial cannot be postponed.

> (5) is absent from the trial or hearing and the statement's proponent has not been able, by process or other reasonable means, to procure (A) the declarant's attendance, in the case of a hearsay exception under Rule 804(b)(1) or (6); or (B) the declarant's attendance or testimony, in the case of a hearsay exception under Rule 804(b)(2), (3), or (4).

The proponent of an FRE 804(b) hearsay exception must demonstrate that he has attempted to bring the declarant to court or, in some instances, to obtain his testimony "by process or other reasonable means."

Different considerations apply in civil and criminal cases. In civil cases, a subpoena may be served anyplace within the trial district or within 100 miles of the place of trial. See Fed. R. Civ. Pc. 45(b)(2). In addition, the proponent of an FRE 804(b)(2), (3), or (4) exception cannot claim unavailability unless he has made a good faith effort to obtain the deposition testimony of the witness. If a witness's deposition has been taken by the proponent, the witness is not unavailable under those subsections, although the deposition transcript itself may be admissible as former testimony under FRE 804(b)(1). The term "other reasonable means" is not defined, but it is not unusual for a judge to inquire whether the proponent asked the witness to appear voluntarily. If the witness agrees to appear at trial, he is not unavailable.

In criminal cases, a witness can be served with a subpoena anyplace within the United States. See Fed. R. Crim. P. 17(e). The prosecution must do more than show it issued a trial subpoena before an absent witness's statement can qualify as an FRE 804(b) exception. The Sixth Amendment's Confrontation Clause requires that the prosecution make a good faith effort to obtain the witness's presence at trial. The good faith effort includes locating the witness and then, by process or voluntarily, getting the witness into court.

In *Barber v. Page*, 390 U.S. 719 (1968), the Supreme Court held that the prosecution did not satisfy this constitutional requirement when it did no more than determine a witness was in prison in another state. However, in *Mancusi v. Stubbs*, 408 U.S. 204 (1972), the Court held that the prosecution did all it could when it determined the witness was a prisoner in another country.

Just how far the prosecution must go to find and obtain the presence of a witness is a matter of reasonableness to be determined on a case-by-case basis. The prosecution is not required to engage in futile acts. For example, in *Ohio v. Roberts*, 448 U.S. 56 (1980), the Sixth Amendment was satisfied when the prosecution issued five subpoenas on a witness at her last known address, talked to her parents, attempted to locate her present whereabouts, and still could not find her. The test is whether the prosecution used good faith efforts.

FRE 804(a) concludes with the common-sense admonition that the party claiming unavailability of a witness cannot benefit from its own wrongdoing: "But this subdivision (a) does not apply if the statement's proponent procured or wrongfully caused the declarant's unavailability as a witness in order to prevent the declarant from attending or testifying." For example, if a party threatens a witness, causing the witness to disappear before trial, that party cannot introduce the witness's deposition testimony as former testimony at trial.

The unavailable witness situations contained in FRE 804(a) are not exclusive. For example, there may be situations where children of tender years are not available as witnesses. These situations are governed by 18 U.S.C.A. §3509.

A party who engages in wrongdoing to procure the unavailability of a witness forfeits his right to object to that person's statements on hearsay grounds. FRE 804(b)(6) establishes an additional hearsay exception: "(6) Statement Offered Against a Party That Wrongfully Caused the Declarant's Unavailability. A statement offered against a party that wrongfully caused — or acquiesced in wrongfully causing — the declarant's unavailability as a witness, and did so intending that result."

The wrongdoing need not consist of a criminal act, and the rule applies to all parties, including the government. "The usual Rule 104(a) preponderance of the evidence standard has been adopted in light of the behavior the new Rule 804(b)(6) seeks to discourage." Committee Note to FRE 804(b)(6).

4. The Sixth Amendment Confrontation Clause

The Confrontation Clause of the Sixth Amendment provides: "In all prosecutions, the accused shall enjoy the right . . . to be confronted with the witnesses against him . . . ." Until 2004, Confrontation Clause analysis paid little attention to the accused's right to cross-examine the declarant of an out-of-court statement offered for its truth. The test for admissibility was whether the statement possessed adequate indicia of reliability, as a firmly rooted hearsay exception or as an exception that contained particularized guarantees of reliability equivalent to those in the firmly rooted exceptions. If adequate indicia of reliability were present, cross-examination, said the courts, would be of marginal use. *Ohio v. Roberts*, 448 U.S. 56 (1980); see *White v. Illinois*, 502 U.S. 346 (1992).

The analytical ground shifted dramatically with the Supreme Court's opinion in *Crawford v. Washington*, 541 U.S. 36 (2004). In *Crawford*, the defendant was convicted of assault and attempted murder of the man he believed had sexually assaulted his wife. Crawford claimed he was defending himself from the alleged victim's knife assault. His wife, in response to questioning at the police station, gave a tape-recorded statement in which she said she did not see a knife in the victim's hand before he fell to the ground after being stabbed by her husband. Crawford asserted his state marital privilege, preventing Mrs. Crawford from testifying against him. The prosecution offered the tape recording of her statement as a declaration against her penal interest hearsay exception. It was admitted when the state court judge found sufficient guarantees of reliability.

In the opinion written by Justice Scalia and concurred in by six other justices, the Court held Mrs. Crawford's tape recording is the kind of statement the writers of the Sixth Amendment intended to prohibit. It was offered for its truth, it was testimonial, it was a solemn declaration, Mrs. Crawford did not testify at trial, and Mr. Crawford never had an opportunity to cross-examine her about the statement. Indicia of reliability have nothing to do with *Crawford*'s Confrontation Clause analysis. The clause reflects a judgment that reliability can best be determined "by testing in the crucible of cross-examination." Crawford's convictions were reversed and remanded.

Some *Crawford*-related matters are well-established:

(1) Confrontation Clause analysis applies only to out-of-court, unconfronted testimonial statements offered for their truth, but they do not have to have been made under oath. See *Whorton v. Bockting*, 549 U.S. 406 (2007).

(2) There is no Confrontation Clause issue when the declarant of the out-of-court statement is on the witness stand, subject to cross-examination.

(3) The Confrontation Clause does not bar the admission of the defendant's inculpatory statements.

(4) The Confrontation Clause does not bar a co-conspirator's statement made in furtherance of and in the course of the conspiracy.

(5) A defendant who intentionally obtains the absence of the declarant by wrongdoing forfeits his constitutional right to confrontation. In *Giles v. California*, 554 U.S. 353 (2008), California courts held the defendant forfeited his right of confrontation when he killed his former girlfriend, who had told the police the defendant "threatened to kill her." The Supreme Court reversed the conviction, holding the prosecution failed to show the defendant intended to prevent the witness from testifying when he killed her. The Court displayed a special concern for the impact of its decision on domestic violence cases, recognizing that "acts of violence often are intended to dissuade a victim from resorting to outside help, and include conduct designed to prevent testimony to police officers or cooperation in criminal prosecutions." For that reason,

said the Court, evidence of "earlier abuse or threats of abuse, intended to dissuade the victim from resorting to outside help, would be highly relevant in this inquiry, as would evidence of ongoing criminal proceedings at which the victim would have been expected to testify."

(6) *Crawford* requires an "adequate opportunity" to effectively cross-examine the out-of-court declarant, not actual or successful cross-examination. The defense that foregoes cross-examination of a witness at a preliminary hearing forfeits its Confrontation Clause objection when the transcript of that unavailable witness is offered at trial. If the opportunity to cross-examine is unduly limited by court ruling or by the nature of the proceeding, the opportunity to cross-examine is not adequate for Sixth Amendment purposes. The Supreme Court has not yet applied *Crawford* to the situation where the declarant takes the stand at trial but has no memory of the event at issue or of what he said about it on an earlier occasion. However, a pre-*Crawford* decision held the Confrontation Clause is satisfied when the witness remembers identifying the defendant as his attacker but does not remember the attack. *United States v. Owens*, 484 U.S. 554 (1988).

(7) When an out-of-court statement is not testimonial, and thus not barred by the Confrontation Clause, admissibility remains an issue for evidentiary hearsay law. When a defendant claims violations of the Confrontation Clause and the rule against hearsay he preserves both issues by making separate objections to the statement. Failure to make specific, separate objections creates the risk of forfeiting the ground not raised. Ordinarily, the hearsay evidence issue will be decided before any Confrontation Clause issue is considered.

The most glaring unanswered question raised by *Crawford* was left by the Court for "another day" — a case-resolving definition of "testimonial." *Crawford* did define "testimony" as a "typically solemn declaration or affirmation made for the purpose of establishing or proving some fact." At a minimum, held the Court, "testimonial" encompasses prior testimony at a preliminary hearing, testimony before a grand jury or at a prior trial, and statements made during police questioning, including accomplice confessions and witness statements against penal interest.

The Supreme Court has not decided how formal a statement must be in order to come within *Crawford* exclusion. The decision apparently does not apply to offhand, informal, or casual remarks. In *Giles v. California*, 554 U.S. 353 (2008), the Court said: "Statements to friends and neighbors about abuse and intimidation, and statements to physicians in the course of receiving treatment" are not testimonial, but are matters to be decided by evidence law.

Crawford did not say whether an out-of-court statement offered for its truth must be made to a law enforcement officer or a mandated reporter in order to be considered testimonial. Nor was it specific about time or place boundaries that might defeat consideration of a statement as testimonial. Those matters were addressed in subsequent cases.

The first post-*Crawford* attempts to define "testimonial" were the combined decisions of *Davis v. Washington* and *Hammon v. Indiana*, 547 U.S. 81 3 (2006).

The cases involved statements made to police personnel during a 911 call and to police officers at a crime scene.

In *Davis*, the declarant reported an ongoing domestic disturbance to the 911 operator. She named her attacker and described what he was doing to her and how he ran out the door and drove away. Her attacker was charged. The victim did not appear in court, but her statements were used to convict the defendant of the assault. The Court held the victim's statements, up to the point where her attacker ran out the door, were nontestimonial and did not offend the Confrontation Clause because they concerned an ongoing emergency; she was telling the operator what was happening.

In *Hammon*, there was no emergency. No argument or attack was going on when the police arrived at the victim's home. The victim and her alleged attacker, her husband, were placed in separate rooms. The victim told the police about her husband's attack. The husband was charged with battery, but his wife did not appear at his trial. Her statements to the police were used. The Court held the out-of-court statements were testimonial. Their admission violated the Confrontation Clause.

The Court used a "primary purpose" test in *Davis* and *Hammon*. It said:

> Statements are nontestimonial when made in the course of police interrogation under circumstances objectively indicating that the primary purpose of the interrogation is to enable police assistance to meet an ongoing emergency. They are testimonial when the circumstances objectively indicate that there is no such ongoing emergency, and the primary purpose of the interrogation is to establish or probe past events potentially relevant to later criminal prosecution.

It is clear that a statement cannot fall within the Confrontation Clause unless its primary purpose is testimonial. The Supreme Court offered an explanation of the primary purpose test and attempted to set the dimensions of an ongoing emergency in *Michigan v. Bryant*, 562 U.S. 344 (2011).

In *Bryant*, police officers found the victim lying on the ground next to his car at a gas station. Responding to police questions, he said he was shot by the defendant 25 minutes earlier at the defendant's home, which was about six blocks from the gas station. The defendant had not been apprehended at the time the victim was questioned. The victim died within hours of the shooting. The issue in the case was whether the police officers could testify to what the victim told them.

The answer was yes. The Court held that while the existence of the ongoing emergency at the time a statement is made to police is not "dispositive" of the testimonial inquiry, it is "among the most important circumstances informing the 'primary purpose' of an interrogation." The Court found an ongoing emergency in *Bryant*. With the shooter armed with a gun and at large, there is "a threat potentially to the police and the public."

The crucial question, said the Court, is whether the victim's words were "procured with a primary purpose of creating an out-of-court substitute for trial testimony." To answer that question, the Court objectively considered all the circumstances of the case. Among those circumstances: the weapon used, the armed shooter at large, the informality or formality of the questioning, the motives of the police officers and the victim during the questioning, the physical condition of the victim, and whether the statements were reliable hearsay exceptions. The totality of circumstances in *Bryant* convinced the Court that the primary purpose of the interrogation was not to establish evidence for the prosecution. The victim's statements were not testimonial.

Bryant was the Supreme Court's first post-*Crawford* use of hearsay reliability as a factor in Confrontation Clause analysis, although *Crawford* and *Giles* did say the firmly established, common law dying declaration hearsay exception might not be excluded by the Sixth Amendment, testimonial or not, since it was "recognized at the founding." After *Bryant,* the existence of an "ongoing emergency" has much to do with the "primary purpose" of serving as a substitute for courtroom testimony, but it does not have everything to do with it. There could be occasions where no ongoing emergency exists, but for some other reason the Confrontation Clause exclusion does not apply.

The Supreme Court repeatedly reserved the question of whether statements to persons other than law enforcement officers can come within the Confrontation Clause. That matter finally was addressed in *Clark v. Ohio*, 576 U.S. — (2015).

In *Clark*, a school teacher noticed her three-year-old student had marks on his body. She asked him: "Who did this?" His answers led to the identification and arrest of his mother's boyfriend, Carius Clark. Using Ohio law, the trial judge ruled the boy was not competent to testify. The prosecution offered the school teacher to testify about the boy's statements to her. The defendant was convicted, but the Ohio Supreme Court held the defendant's Confrontation Clause rights had been violated. The conviction was reversed. The U.S. Supreme Court agreed to hear the case. It reversed the Ohio judgment and remanded the case.

As to whether statements to persons other than law enforcement officers are subject to the Confrontation Clause, the Court opened a small affirmative window:

> Because at least some statements to individuals who are not law enforcement officers could conceivably raise confrontation concerns, we decline to adopt a categorical rule excluding them from the Sixth Amendment's reach. Nevertheless, such statements are much less likely to be testimonial than statements to law enforcement officers.

Here, said the Court, considering all relevant circumstances, the boy's statements "clearly were not made with the primary purpose of creating evidence for Clark's prosecution." To reach this conclusion, the Court noted the teacher's questioning was meant to identify the abuser and to protect the boy from future attacks. As in *Bryant*, the emergency was ongoing.

The "primary purpose" test for whether a statement is testimonial emerged intact from *Ohio v. Clark*. But it was dented. The *Clark* decision may have created a prosecutorial escape hatch from *Crawford* Sixth Amendment exclusion.

While satisfying the primary purpose test is a necessary condition for the exclusion of out-of-court statements under the Sixth Amendment, said the Court, it is not always sufficient. The Court is referring to evidence that was "regularly admitted in criminal cases at the time of the founding," like statements by the boy in this case. The Court did not offer any other examples of the kind of statement it was talking about. The dying declaration would seem to fit. Just how many other hearsay exceptions would avoid Confrontation Clause exclusion because they were allowed at the time the Sixth Amendment was adopted is unclear and must await future decisions. Also unclear is whether the "historical" approach to Confrontation Clause analysis, by itself, would be enough to support the conviction in *Clark*.

One other area of Confrontation Clause jurisprudence must be explored. It has to do with the use and admissibility of a forensic report where the author of the report is not called as a witness.

Crawford held that business and public records are "generally admissible" as hearsay exceptions without confrontation because they have been created for the "administration of an entity's affairs and not for the purpose of establishing or proving some fact at trial." But where a report or other document is prepared by an absent witness for use at a criminal trial, the Confrontation Clause is implicated. The Supreme Court has addressed the issue more than once.

In *Melendez-Diaz v. Massachusetts*, 557 U.S. 305 (2009), the trial court admitted, over objection, a sworn certificate of a state laboratory analyst to prove the substance seized from the defendant was cocaine of a certain quantity. The analyst was not called as a witness. Admission of the certificate was held to be a violation of the Confrontation Clause. Because the certificate "provides testimony" against the defendant, he is guaranteed the right to cross-examine the analyst who performed the test. Where a document is prepared "specifically for use" at a defendant's trial, held the Court, it is testimonial and subject to confrontation and the Sixth Amendment. In a 5-4 vote the defendant's conviction was reversed and the case remanded.

Next came *Bullcoming v. New Mexico*, 564 U.S. ____ (2011), a Driving While Intoxicated case. The analyst who performed the blood alcohol concentration test on Bullcoming certified his results in a report but was not called as a witness at trial. Instead, the state called another analyst to validate the report. That analyst was familiar with the testing device used to examine the defendant's blood and with the laboratory's testing procedures, but he had not participated in or observed the testing. His testimony was admitted over objection.

In a 5-4 decision, the Supreme Court held use of "surrogate testimony" violates the Confrontation Clause, saying: "The accused's right is to be confronted with the analyst who made the certification, unless that analyst is unavailable at trial, and the accused had an opportunity, pre-trial, to cross-examine that particular scientist." The conviction was reversed and remanded for a harmless error inquiry.

The Supreme Court in *Bullcoming* raised but did not answer the question of what happens when an expert offers an opinion based on out-of-court statements made by others that are not offered into evidence. The question was addressed by the Supreme Court later that year in *Williams v. Illinois*, 132 S. Ct. 2221 (2011). No clear, precedential answer was provided.

In *Williams*, a bench trial, the defendant was charged with sexual assault and robbery. After the assault, at a time when Williams was not a suspect in the crime, semen from the victim's body was sent to Cellmark, a private lab in Maryland. When the Cellmark report was sent to Illinois authorities, a crime lab analyst compared the Cellmark DNA profile to profiles in unrelated cases. A match was made. Williams was arrested and charged.

At trial, the Cellmark analyst who tested the semen taken from the victim's body was not called as a witness. The Cellmark report was never offered into evidence. Instead, using the Illinois counterpart to FRE 703, the prosecution relied on the Illinois crime lab analyst who made the match. She testified that the DNA profile from Williams' earlier arrest matched the Cellmark profile. And she testified to the contents of the Cellmark report. There was no evidence concerning the reliability of the Cellmark report.

Williams was convicted and the case eventually reached the U.S. Supreme Court. Five justices voted to affirm the conviction. But the Court's reasoning was split three ways, into a 4-4-1 plurality.

Four of the justices offered two separate reasons for their vote to affirm. First, the Cellmark report was not offered for the truth of the words contained in the report, thus keeping it outside the Confrontation Clause. Second, even if the Cellmark report had been introduced for its truth, it was "not prepared for the primary purpose of accusing a targeted individual," and thus was not a violation of the Sixth Amendment.

Justice Thomas was the fifth affirming vote. He believed the Cellmark report was offered for its truth and he did not agree with the new "targeted individual" test. He concurred in the result because the Cellmark report was not sworn to or certified, and thus was not formal or solemn enough to be testimonial within the meaning of the Confrontation Clause.

Four of the justices, the "dissenters," said the Cellmark report, admitted in evidence or not, was used for its truth when the prosecution's expert testified that the report said the victim's vaginal swab contained Williams' DNA. Since the defendant had no opportunity to cross-examine the author of the report, the Confrontation Clause was violated.

What, then, does *Williams* stand for? Since only four of nine justices signed on to the "targeted individual" test, it is not binding precedent. Some courts have adopted it. Some have refused to use it, observing that five justices held that the words of the Cellmark report were used for their truth and thus were testimonial, even though the report was not admitted into evidence.

5. Organizing hearsay exceptions

When trying to get hearsay admitted in evidence, only one hearsay exception need apply, so trial lawyers think in terms of alternative theories of admissibility. For example, if the offered evidence does not qualify as a dying declaration, it may qualify as an excited utterance. If it does not qualify as a business record, it may qualify as recorded recollection.

Since trial lawyers think in terms of alternative theories of admissibility, it makes sense to organize the common hearsay exceptions into groups that relate to each other factually, rather than using the FRE 803 and 804 distinction. This approach creates the following groups:

(a) *Spontaneous statements*
  1. present sense impression — 803(1)
  2. excited utterance — 803(2)
  3. then existing physical and mental condition — 803(3)
  4. statement for diagnosis and treatment — 803(4)
  5. dying declaration — 804(b)(2)
(b) *Prior statements*
  6. former testimony — 804(b)(1)
  7. statement against interest — 804(b)(3)
  8. statement of personal or family history — 804(b)(4)
      (Prior statement by witness — 801(d)(1) — and admission by party-opponent — 801(d)(2) — although classified as non-hearsay, should always be considered with this group.)
(c) *Records*
  9. business record — 803(6), 803(7)
  10. public record — 803(8)-803(17)
  11. recorded recollection — 803(5)
(d) *Miscellaneous commonly used exceptions*
  12. reputation evidence — 803(19)-803(21)
  13. learned treaties — 803(18)
(e) *Residual exceptions*
  14. residual exception — 807

Each of these exceptions will be discussed in this chapter.

The rule against hearsay is satisfied when the out-of-court statement fits within one hearsay exception. That is not the same as saying the hearsay is then admissible. There may be other valid reasons for excluding the evidence.

First, the evidence must always be relevant under the general relevancy rules FRE 401-402 and the special relevancy rules of FRE 404-406.

Second, there are other considerations of reliability outside the hearsay rules. The personal knowledge requirement of FRE 602 applies to every hearsay exception other than FRE 804(b)(4), which expressly provides that a statement about personal or family history does not have to be based on the declarant's personal knowledge. The statement, oral or written, must meet the authentication requirements of FRE 901 and 902. If written or recorded, the statement must satisfy the original writings rule of FRE 1001-1004.

Third, although the hearsay may be relevant and reliable, there still may be valid policy reasons to exclude it. Under FRE 403, the evidence may be excluded when its probative value is substantially outweighed by the danger of creating unfair prejudice, confusing the issues, or misleading of the jury or by considerations of undue delay, waste of time, or needless presentation of cumulative evidence. Under FRE 407-415, the evidence may violate a policy reason reflected by the Rules, and under FRE 501, the evidence may be excluded by the privileges rules.

The fact that a statement was "self-serving" when made does not affect its admissibility if it fits within a hearsay exception. The common law concept of "res gestae" was finally laid to rest by the Federal Rules, although the corpse shows signs of life on rare, and unfortunate, occasions. Objections based on these grounds are best avoided altogether.

§7.2.   Present sense impressions (FRE 803(1))[2]

1.   Law

Rule 803.   Exceptions to the Rule Against Hearsay — Regardless of Whether the Declarant Is Available as a Witness

The following are not excluded by the rule against hearsay, regardless of whether the declarant is available as a witness:

(1) *Present Sense Impression.* A statement describing or explaining an event or condition, made while or immediately after the declarant perceived it.

The theory behind this exception, according to the Advisory Committee's Note, is that "substantial contemporaneity of event and statement negative the likelihood of deliberate or conscious misrepresentation." That is, the declarant did not have time or opportunity to forget the event or condition, nor did he have time to fabricate or distort a story about it.

This exception is based in part on the leading case, *Houston Oxygen Co. v. Davis*, 161 S.W.2d 474 (Tex. 1942). In *Houston Oxygen*, the plaintiff's car passed the witness's car four or five miles from the accident scene. The witness sought to testify that at the time the other car passed, a passenger in his car said, "They must have been drunk, that we would find them somewhere in the road wrecked if they keep that rate of speed up." On appeal, the hearsay statement was held admissible.

Under FRE 803(1), the statement must describe or explain the event or condition and be "made while or immediately after the declarant perceived it." The key to establishing the exception is the length of time between the event or condition and the statement about it. The rule requires that the statement be made at the same time or "immediately thereafter." There must be no time to consider or contemplate.

No exact timeline can be drawn. As used in the rule, "immediately" should permit only a slight lapse of time. Most courts so hold, and the usual situations involve either contemporaneous statements or statements made within seconds of perceiving the event. However, a few courts have admitted statements made a substantial amount of time later. For example, in one case, the defendant directed a porter to pick up her bag (the event). They were then stopped by the police, a few questions were asked, and they walked about 100 feet to the baggage area, where the porter said, "That's the bag you gave me." The porter's statement was admitted as a present sense impression. Such cases clearly represent the outer limits of the rule.

---

2. McCormick §271; Weinstein §803(1)[01]-[03]; Mueller & Kirkpatrick §8.35; Wigmore §§1745, 1750-1751, 1767.

The party offering the statement has the burden of showing that a specific amount of time passed between the event and the statement and that this time complies with the rule. Failure to carry that burden will exclude the statement.

Sometimes the out-of-court declarant is also a witness at trial. On those occasions, he can be questioned about his own hearsay statement. However, there is no requirement that the declarant be available to testify at trial. A statement can be admitted as a present sense impression, even where the declarant denies making it, so long as another witness can properly testify about the statement. In fact, the declarant does not have to be identified, although judges are more likely to find a lack of trustworthiness when the declarant is not identified.

The personal knowledge requirement is met when the witness on the stand has personal knowledge about the making of the statement and the judge is satisfied the declarant actually perceived the event or condition. The witness can be examined on the circumstances surrounding the making of the statement, but he does not have to have any knowledge about the event. For example, if the unavailable eyewitness to a burglary describes the burglar to someone else during a telephone conversation while the burglary is taking place, the person hearing the description over the telephone may testify to it. If the conversation is tape-recorded, the recording is admissible if it is properly authenticated.

Defendants in criminal cases sometimes attempt to offer their exculpatory statements at the time of arrest as present sense impressions. These attempts are usually unsuccessful because the defendants' statements ordinarily refer to some past event. The statements are hearsay, and usually no hearsay exception applies.

Nothing in the rule requires corroboration of the fact that the statement was made while the declarant was perceiving the event or immediately thereafter. The statement itself can be sufficient, although the argument for admissibility is weakened, perhaps fatally, when the declarant also is unidentified. Fitting a statement within the strict terms of a hearsay exception sometimes is not enough for admissibility when the trial judge has serious concerns about the statement's reliability.

2.   Practice

It is usually more persuasive to call an eyewitness to the event than to introduce a hearsay statement about the event. When the exception is used, it is often because the declarant is unavailable at trial and there is insufficient credible eyewitness testimony about the event. This exception is more commonly used today, given the prevalence of cell phones.

This hearsay exception is similar to other exceptions, such as excited utterances, statements of then existing physical or mental conditions, statements made for the purpose of diagnosis and treatment, and dying declarations. Since hearsay is properly admitted whenever one hearsay exception applies, other related exception always should be considered at the same time.

Example:

This is a burglary case. The prosecution offers a tape recording of a 911 call in which a neighbor across the street calls the police about a burglary in progress and describes what is happening. At a hearing on a motion to preclude, the following happens:

Defendant: Your honor, we've moved to preclude the admission of the 911 tape. The reason is that the tape is hearsay. Moreover, the witness is available to testify. The prosecution should not get around our cross-examining the witness by the device of introducing that witness's 911 call.

Prosecutor: This is a present sense impression, your honor. The witness saw an event, and he made a contemporaneous statement about what he saw, which was recorded on a 911 tape. It falls squarely within Rule 803(1). As far as the defendant's right to examine the witness, if we don't call the witness in our case-in-chief, the defense can call him in the defense case. They have the same subpoena power that we have.

Judge: The objection is overruled. The tape recording of the 911 call will be admitted, provided that the prosecution lays a proper foundation for the tape.

Commentary: If a 911 call to the police describes something that just happened or is presently happening, it usually is admitted as a present sense impression, unless *Crawford* bars its admission.

§7.3. *Excited utterances (FRE 803(2))*[3]

1. Law

Rule 803.   Exceptions to the Rule Against Hearsay — Regardless of Whether the Declarant Is Available as a Witness

The following are not excluded by the rule against hearsay, regardless of whether the declarant is available as a witness:

(2) *Excited Utterance.* A statement relating to a startling event or condition, made while the declarant was under the stress of excitement that it caused. . . .

This hearsay exception is much broader in both subject matter and permissible time lapse between the event and the statement than the present sense impressions exception. Under FRE 803(2), the statement must be made while the declarant "was under the stress of excitement" caused by the event or condition and must be "relating to a startling event or condition."

Spontaneity is the key factor in both exceptions, but the excited utterance exception is based on the nature of the event or condition. It must be startling, such as a car crash, an explosion, or a man with a gun. It must excite the declarant. It must arouse the declarant's emotions or feelings.

---

3. McCormick §§272-272.1; Weinstein §803(2)[01]-[03]; Mueller & Kirkpatrick §8.36; Wigmore §§1745-1757.

The declarant must be excited by the event and still be excited when the statement is made, but the standard is a subjective one. Whether a reasonable person should have been startled is not the standard. A declarant who blurts out, "Look out, he's got a gun!" or "Oh my God, the car just exploded!" is making an excited utterance. Such excited utterances are considered reliable because the declarant has no time for reflection, no time to consciously fabricate, distort, or forget.

When admissibility is challenged, the trial judge conducts an FRE 104(a) inquiry. Among the factors the judge will consider are (1) the lapse of time between the event and the statement; (2) the age of the declarant; (3) the physical and mental condition of the declarant at the time of the statement; (4) the nature of the event that gave rise to the statement; (5) the subject matter and content of the statement; (6) the location of the event, as opposed to the location of the statement; and (7) whether the statement was spontaneous or was the result of questions asked of the declarant.

Two issues frequently arise with this exception. First, how much time can pass between the startling event and the excited utterance? Since the exception applies whenever the declarant is still excited by the startling event, a subjective standard, an excited utterance can be made a substantial period of time after the event. For example, consider a person who sees a homicide and is still shouting about what happened 30 minutes later. Since the person is still excited and his excitement was caused by seeing the homicide, the statement qualifies as an excited utterance. An assault victim who recovers consciousness hours later in a place far from the attack can make an excited utterance.

The prompt complaint or outcry of the victim in a sexual assault case may qualify as an excited utterance. Some courts have relaxed the time and excitement requirements of the rule in these cases, particularly where there is a suggestion by the defense that the charges have been exaggerated or fabricated. In such situations, there usually is no effective way to rebut such a suggestion other than by introducing evidence of the prompt complaint. For example, the victim's statement "I was just raped," made to a police officer 30 minutes after the assault, is frequently admitted under this exception, even though there is insufficient evidence that the statement was made while the victim was still in an excited state.

Courts also broaden the exception where a child's statement is concerned, some extending the time lapse into hours, especially in cases of sexual or other physical assault. The statement may be admitted even though the child was not competent to testify as a witness.

Second, how broad is the requirement that the statement "relate" to the startling event? When the person's statement is directly about the startling event, no problems arise. For example, in a collision case, a bystander who shouts, "My God, that car ran the red light!" is obviously making an excited utterance about the event. In a slip and fall case, the store clerk, moments after the fall, is heard to say, "That slippery stuff on the floor should have been removed hours ago!" This statement relates to the slip and fall. In a vehicle collision case brought against the driver's company, the upset driver is heard to say after the crash, "I had to call on a customer!" This statement relates to the purpose of his driving and is admissible to aid in proving the driver's agency.

However, if in a homicide case the statement is "Bobby just grabbed a gun and is going after Vito! Bobby's been threatening him for years," problems arise.

Does the latter part of this statement "relate" to the event? An argument can be made that this statement does not relate to the immediate event, which was the grabbing of a gun. In that case, this latter part of the statement should not qualify as an excited utterance. An argument also can be made that since this statement shows the declarant was able to talk about past history between the two persons, the declarant was not really excited and therefore the entire statement should be excluded. Some courts have been understandably reluctant to admit statements, or parts of statements, that sound too analytical or that recount past history, under this hearsay exception.

The mere fact that the statement was made miles from where the event happened will not defeat the exception where the state of excitement persists. Likewise, the fact that the statement was elicited in response to a question will not disqualify a statement if it was made under continuing stress of the event. For example, if the declarant is asked, "What happened?" and immediately blurts out, "He just shot the store clerk in cold blood!" the statement qualifies as an excited utterance.

Nothing in the rule excludes the excited utterance of an unidentified bystander, nor does the bystander have to be a participant in the startling event. For example, a witness may testify that after he heard a crash, a bystander said, "My God, that black Cadillac went through the red light!" Trial judges, however, are rightfully wary of these statements and will carefully examine the totality of circumstances when determining whether the declarant spoke from personal knowledge.

Claims that a statement is self-serving or that the declarant has a motive to fabricate should not defeat admissibility when the statement qualifies as an excited utterance. A statement can be admitted even where the declarant at trial denies making it. These are matters of weight appropriate for the fact finder, but do not defeat admissibility.

A mostly academic question arises when the proponent relies on an excited utterance to establish that the startling event happened. That occurs when no eyewitness testifies to seeing the startling event. For example, a caller, unavailable at trial, tells the police, "Come quick! Someone is trying to break into the building." The statement is offered to establish that the break-in took place. It does not happen very often, but nothing in the rule bars it.

Excited utterances, like present sense impressions, do not require corroboration. FRE 104(a) allows the trial judge to consider inadmissible hearsay, along with the appearance, behavior, and condition of the declarant, to determine admissibility of the statement. Personal knowledge of the declarant is the key to admissibility.

If the hearsay statement qualifies as an excited utterance, it can contain an opinion or accusation. For example, if the declarant says, "Look out! That car is speeding!" the statement is properly admissible, even though speeding is an opinion.

The excited utterance exception has been criticized on the ground that people are less precise and more prone to inaccuracy and mistake when making statements under stress. While there is substantial social science research behind this criticism, the opponents have had no success in excluding excited utterances. Whatever is lost in the declarant's power of accurate observation is gained in the admissibility of statements that are free of conscious fabrication.

2.   Practice

Excited utterances are a frequently used hearsay exception. Common issues are whether the declarant is still excited when making the statement and whether the statement properly relates to the event or improperly includes statements of past events.

Example 1:

This is a sexual assault case. The victim testifies that she went with the defendant to the movies and then to his apartment, where the sexual assault occurred. After a while, she was able to leave the apartment. The direct examination continues as follows:

Q. (By prosecutor) What time did you leave the defendant's apartment?
A. About 1:00 A.M.
Q. What did you do next?
A. I drove over to my mother's house.
Q. Where is your mother's house?
A. It's about a 30-minute drive.
Q. When did you get there?
A. Around 1:30 or 1:45 A.M.
Q. Was your mother there?
A. Yes. I woke her up, and she came to the door.
Q. How were you feeling at that time?
A. I thought I was going to explode unless I talked to her.
Q. What did you tell her?
Defendant: Objection, your honor. May we approach?
Judge: Come to the bench. [Lawyers approach.] Defense, what's the basis for your objection?
Defendant: Any statement at this time, and under these circumstances, would not be an excited utterance. At least 30 to 45 minutes had passed from the time she left the house, and longer since the claimed assault happened. She had enough presence of mind to drive a number of miles in the morning hours. There's no indication that she was still excited by that time.
Prosecutor: The issue is not how much time passed; the question is whether the witness was still under the stress of an exciting event. She just said that she was going to explode. Her statement, "Mom, I was raped," clearly falls within the exception.
Judge: The objection is overruled. The witness may answer.

Commentary: Courts have been generous in allowing initial complaints in sexual assault cases to qualify as excited utterances.

Example 2:

This is a kidnaping case. At a preliminary hearing, a witness testifies that a woman ran out of the apartment where the kidnaping occurred, yelling "Smith's got a gun and he's grabbed Jane. He's been threatening to do this for weeks now." The defendant moves before trial to preclude the statement. At a hearing on the motion, the following happens:

Judge: Defense, it's your motion to preclude.
Defendant: Yes, your honor. This statement, based on the preliminary hearing transcript, is not an excited utterance. The rule requires that the witness be excited by a startling event and make the statement while still under the stress of the event. Here, the statement itself shows that the witness was not startled because she had the presence of mind to talk about what happened in the past. She wouldn't talk about past events if she were truly still excited. For that reason, the entire statement should be excluded. In the alternative, the second statement, "He's been threatening to do this for weeks now," should be excluded, since it's not a statement directly related to the event. Just because a person may be excited doesn't mean that anything that person says is admissible under this exception.
Prosecutor: The rule requires only that the witness in fact be excited by a startling event, which is obviously the case here; that the statement be made while the witness was excited, which is also the case here; and that the statement "relate" to the startling event. The witness's statement about the past clearly relates to the event and should be admitted.
Judge: The first statement will be permitted; the second will not.

Commentary: This is a close case over which judges may differ.

§7.4.   *Then existing mental, emotional, or physical conditions (FRE 803(3))*[4]

1.   Law

Rule 803.   Exceptions to the Rule Against Hearsay — Regardless of Whether the Declarant Is Available as a Witness

The following are not excluded by the rule against hearsay, regardless of whether the declarant is available as a witness:

(3) *Then-Existing Mental, Emotional, or Physical Condition.* A statement of the declarant's then-existing state of mind (such as motive, intent, or plan) or emotional, sensory, or physical condition (such as mental feeling, pain, or bodily health), but not including a statement of memory or belief to prove the fact remembered or believed unless it relates to the validity or terms of the declarant's will.

---

4. McCormick §§273-276; Weinstein §803(3)[01]-[07]; Mueller & Kirkpatrick §§8.37-8.41; Wigmore §§1714-1740.

This exception evolved from pain and suffering origins. Substantive law sometimes makes the declarant's mental or physical condition relevant, most commonly on the issue of damages in personal injury cases, and these conditions often cannot be proven persuasively unless such statements are admitted. In addition, statements about one's condition are considered to have a sufficient degree of reliability, since a person is unlikely to misstate his present condition.

In some ways, this hearsay exception resembles present sense impressions. Both require a lack of time or opportunity to reflect or fabricate. Reliability stems from the spontaneity and probable sincerity of the statement. The declarant must be referring to his own present mental, emotional, or physical condition, not someone else's.

FRE 803(3) requires that the statement relate to a relevant state of mind, emotion, or physical condition existing at the time the statement was made. That is, it must be a present state of mind, emotion, or physical condition. For example, statements such as "I'm frightened," "I love you," and "My back is killing me" are statements of a present state of mind or condition. It is the use of the present tense that is critical. Once the statement is admitted, the mental, emotional, or physical condition may be inferred to continue into the future if the circumstances support this inference.

These statements are classified as hearsay exceptions because they are offered to prove something the declarant actually thinks, believes, feels, or intends at the time he makes the statement. For this reason, factual assertions contained in the statements are not included within the exception. For example, if the victim in an extortion case says, "I am afraid of Arthur because he uses a baseball bat to collect debts," the statement may be admissible to prove the declarant's fear, but it is not admissible to prove that Arthur actually uses a bat.

Under FRE 803(3), the declarant's statement of his present physical or mental condition can be used three ways. First, it can be direct evidence of a physical condition. For example, the declarant says, "My neck hurts."

Second, it can be direct evidence of a mental or an emotional condition. For example, the declarant says, "I'm afraid to drive the car during rush hour traffic." These kinds of statements of present mental or emotional conditions are relevant to the issue of damages in personal injury cases and are commonly admitted.

Care must be taken that the declarant's then existing state of mind is actually relevant to an issue in the case. Relevance is determined by the applicable substantive law. For example, in a tax evasion case, the defendant, trying to prove he had cash on hand at the start of the relevant time period, offers evidence that he told his accountant at that time, "I have at least $350,000 on hand to get started." The statement is not admissible under FRE 803(3) because the relevant issue in the case is whether the defendant actually had the money, not whether he believed he had it. The statement of belief cannot be used as circumstantial proof that he actually had the money. In practice, trial judges place great weight on whether the declarant had a motive to falsify at the time the statement was made.

Third, evidence of present mental condition can be used as circumstantial proof of conduct. For example, if the issue is whether the declarant was in Boston on a particular date, the declarant's statement "I am going to Boston on Christmas" makes it more likely that the declarant was actually in Boston on that date. Experience tells us that people are likely to do what they say they plan to do. This use of present mental condition, often called "state of mind" evidence, to prove the declarant's *own future* conduct is widely accepted.

However, when the declarant's statement of his present mental condition is offered to prove *someone else's* future conduct, disagreement abounds. This use of such evidence is inherently less reliable, since it requires an additional inference — that the other person went with the declarant.

The famous case of *Mutual Life Insurance Co. v. Hillmon*, 145 U.S. 285 (1892), is the origin of this part of the rule. In *Hillmon,* the insurance company wanted to prove that Walters, not Hillmon, died from an accidental gunshot wound while camping at Crooked Creek, Kansas. To prove that Walters actually went to Crooked Creek, the insurance company offered a letter Walters had written that stated: "I expect to leave Wichita on or about March the 5th with a certain Mr. Hillmon." The Supreme Court approved the admission of the declarant's letter to prove future conduct, that is, that Walters actually went to Crooked Creek and that Hillmon went with him.

This case, and the correctness of its holding that a declarant's present state of mind can be used to prove his future conduct as well as that of other persons, has been extensively discussed and debated. Many jurisdictions accepted the expansive view of *Hillmon,* while others restricted the use of such evidence to prove only the declarant's future conduct. The issue has most frequently surfaced in homicide cases, where the statements usually involve the victim's assertion of an intention to meet the defendant at a later time and place.

FRE 803(3) itself is silent on whether the expansive *Hillmon* interpretation should be followed. However, the House Judiciary Committee Report states that the committee intended to limit the holding in *Hillmon* to the declarant's own future conduct, not that of third persons, and federal case law has generally been in accord. Many states, however, continue to follow the *Hillmon* holding.

For example, if the declarant says, "I am going to Taylor Street to buy heroin tonight," the statement will be admitted to prove that the declarant went there for the stated purpose. If the declarant says, "I am going to Taylor Street tonight with Roger to buy heroin," the question whether the statement may be offered in the heroin case against Roger is more difficult. Its purpose is to prove that Roger acted in conformity with the declarant's stated purpose. Under the federal approach, most judges will exclude the statement, since it is being used to prove the future conduct of a person other than the declarant. However, some judges might allow the statement if there is some other evidence that the meeting took place or that the declarant and Roger were connected in some way, although it is difficult to see how the declarant's state of mind can be evidence of someone else's conduct.

FRE 403 plays an important role when state of mind testimony is being offered. For example, in a murder case, the prosecution offers evidence that the victim said, "I'm afraid to go home." The statement is arguably relevant if her husband's defense is that she died by accident or suicide. The trial judge should then carefully weigh the probative value of the statement against its unfair prejudice, considering whether there is a manifest need for the evidence.

Consider another example. Frank is accused of murdering Mary. He denies seeing her on the night of her death. The prosecutor offers evidence that on the day of the murder Mary told a friend, "I'll see you tomorrow. I am going out with

Frank tonight." The evidence is offered to prove she was with Frank on the night of the murder. The judge will have to weigh the probative value of the evidence against its unfair prejudice. Whether Mary had a motive to deceive her friend should not enter the balancing process. In practice, in the trial court, it often does.

Where a statement admitted under FRE 803(3) contains an additional fact, the opponent is entitled to a limiting instruction. For example, the victim in an extortion case says. "I am afraid of Rocky because he has killed people before." The statement is admitted in the case against Rocky to prove the victim's state of mind, but is not admissible to prove Rocky killed anyone. Here, too, an FRE 403 balancing analysis is appropriate. The trial judge will have to consider whether a limiting instruction can erase the danger that the jury will misuse the evidence.

Evidence of the declarant's present state of mind, offered to prove *past* conduct, is expressly inadmissible. This was the holding in another famous case, *Shepard v. United States*, 290 U.S. 96 (1933). In that case, a murder prosecution, the defendant was accused of poisoning his wife. The prosecution introduced evidence that before she died, Mrs. Shepard asked her nurse to bring a bottle of whiskey from the defendant's room. She then stated that this was the same bottle she drank from before collapsing, asked whether there was enough liquor to test for poison, and added, "Dr. Shepard has poisoned me." The Supreme Court held that the statement about past events was inadmissible under the state of mind hearsay exception (and, for other reasons, did not qualify as a dying declaration).

Declarations of memory or belief pointing backward in time would virtually destroy the rule against hearsay if allowed. FRE 803(3) incorporated the *Shepard* holding by specifically excluding "a statement of memory or belief to prove the fact remembered or believed."

FRE 803(3) has one exception to the general rule that the declarant's statement of memory or belief is not admissible to prove the fact remembered or believed. Where the "validity or terms of the declarant's will" are in issue, the rule allows proof of the testator's past declarations of his state of mind to resolve the issue. This is done out of necessity and expediency. For example, a testator's statement such as "I tore up that will" or "I never made a will" is admissible under the rule. But a statement concerning the conduct of others ("My nephew pressured me to name him") is not.

FRE 803(3) has been used to admit certain scientific survey evidence. For example, in a case involving alleged false promotional pitches to doctors by pharmaceutical representatives, the plaintiff offered results of surveys of doctors. The evidence of the doctors' statements was offered to prove their then existing state of mind — their impressions resulting from the defendant's statements to them — to prove a pattern of implied falsehood. The evidence was admissible under FRE 803(3), but the limited purpose of the rule did not extend to the doctors' memories of what was said to them during the surveys by the defendant's representatives.

2. Practice

Statements of present physical and mental condition are commonly introduced during trials, particularly in personal injury cases, where the plaintiff's physical and mental condition is relevant to the issue of damages. It is in the circumstantial use of such statements that the more difficult issues arise.

Example 1:

This is a personal injury case. Plaintiff calls a witness who testifies as follows:

Q. (By plaintiff's lawyer) Ms. Collins, around six months after the plaintiff was injured, did you visit her?
A. Yes.
Q. Did she talk to you about her present condition?
A. Yes.
Q. What did she say at that time?
Defendant: Objection, your honor. Hearsay.
Judge: Overruled.
A. She said, "My neck still hurts a lot."
Q. What else did she say?
Defendant: Objection. Same basis.
Judge: Overruled.
A. She said, "I keep having nightmares about the collision."

Commentary: The question about the plaintiff's present condition signals to the judge that the answer will fall within the present condition exception. A more general question, such as "Did she talk to you?" would probably result in an objection and a sidebar conference, where the plaintiff's lawyer would have to tell the judge what the anticipated answers are so that the judge can determine that the answers will fit within the exception.

Example 2:

John is charged with his girlfriend's murder. At trial, the victim's mother testifies as follows:

Q. (By prosecutor) Mrs. Johnson, before Mary left the house, did you talk to her?
A. Yes.
Q. Did she say what she was going to do?
Defendant: Objection, your honor. May we be heard?
Judge: Yes. [Lawyers come to the bench.] What is the witness going to say?
Prosecutor: She's going to testify that Mary said, "I'm going to the beach for a party. John's going to meet me there."
Defendant: That's the problem, your honor. They're trying to use Mary's statement to prove the defendant's conduct. That's improper under Rule 803(3).
Prosecutor: Your honor, we're offering Mary's out-of-court statement to prove future conduct. That's proper under the rule. There's nothing in the wording of Rule 803(3) that limits the proof the way the defense argues.
Judge: The objection is sustained in part. The statement "I am going to the beach for a party" will be admitted. All references to what John is going to do are inadmissible. Federal case law and the House report on the application of *Hillmon* tell us that the extensive holding of *Hillmon* has been rejected by the rule. (To the witness) Mrs. Johnson, please limit your testimony to what Mary planned to do.

Example 3:

This is a probate case. The deceased's will provides: "I give all my jewelry to my daughter." At his death, the deceased had two daughters, Karen and Helen. Shortly before his death, the deceased said to his brother, "I'm glad that Karen is getting my jewelry. She'll carry on the family tradition." Karen argues that she takes the jewelry under the will. Helen argues that the bequest is defective because it is ambiguous and that the jewelry passes through the will's residuary clause, under which the daughters share equally. At a hearing on admissibility of the statement, the following happens:

Petitioner (Helen's lawyer): Your honor, we've petitioned to declare the bequest of jewelry void, and we move to preclude testimony of the deceased's statements following the execution of the will. Any such statements are hearsay. Furthermore, such statements are directed to proving past conduct and are inherently unreliable.

Respondent (Karen's lawyer): The statement falls squarely within Rule 803(3), which permits a statement directed to past conduct if it "relates to the execution, revocation, identification, or terms of declarant's will." Here, the statement relates to the terms of his will and helps resolve an ambiguity so that the testator's intent can be carried out.

Judge: The objection is overruled.

§7.5. *Statements for purpose of medical diagnosis or treatment (FRE 803(4))*[5]

1. Law

Rule 803.   Exceptions to the Rule Against Hearsay — Regardless of Whether the Declarant Is Available as a Witness

The following are not excluded by the rule against hearsay, regardless of whether the declarant is available as a witness:

(4) *Statement Made for Medical Diagnosis or Treatment.* A statement that:

(A) is made for — and is reasonably pertinent to — medical diagnosis or treatment; and

(B) describes medical history; past or present symptoms or sensations; their inception; or their general cause.

---

5. McCormick §§277-278; Weinstein §803(4)[01]-[03]; Mueller & Kirkpatrick §8.42; Wigmore §§1719-1720.

The reliability rationale for this exception is based on a patient's strong motivation to be truthful. Spontaneity is not required. It is reasonable to assume that the patient believes the effectiveness of his medical treatment will depend in large part on the accuracy of the information he gives the health care provider, regardless of when he gives it. Reliability, then, centers on the declarant's purpose for saying the words. The exception covers statements of the patient and others made to the health care provider. The patient's statements can be in response to questions. However, it does not cover a health care provider's statements to the patient. For example, the doctor's statement "You have a broken leg" is not admissible under this exception.

FRE 803(4) substantially expands the scope of the common law exception. First, the statement need not be by the patient. In some instances, statements made by family members can be admissible if made for "medical diagnosis or treatment." If the patient is unable to speak because of age or condition, someone responsible for the patient, such as the patient's mother, can make statements that fall within the exception. For example, a parent of a young child tells the doctor, "Bobby's been complaining about his stomach hurting since this morning." This statement is made "for purposes of medical diagnosis or treatment" and falls within the exception.

Second, the statement must be "reasonably pertinent to medical diagnosis or treatment." Statements about how the patient was injured, present symptoms, the patient's pertinent medical history, and how he felt in the past are routinely admissible, since these are the things the health care provider should know in order to diagnose and treat. For example, a patient says to the doctor, "I got rear-ended by a pickup truck. My head got whipped back, and it hurts in the middle of my neck. I've never had any trouble with my neck before." All this information is useful to a doctor diagnosing and treating the patient.

While statements of fault ordinarily do not come within this exception, if the cause of the injury is "reasonably pertinent" to diagnosis and treatment it is properly admissible. However, statements of "pure fault" are not admissible, since these could not influence the diagnosis or treatment. The key question the trial judge asks is this: Is the information that is being communicated to the doctor or the medical staff the kind of statement that a doctor generally relies on to diagnose or treat? If yes, the statement is admissible. For example, the statement "The other car hit me on my driver's side door at about 35 mph" helps the doctor evaluate and treat the patient, since the speed of the other car is important to determine whether the patient might have suffered internal injuries. If the statement cannot influence the doctor's diagnosis or treatment, it is excluded. For example, the statement "The other driver ran the red light" or "The other driver was drunk" cannot possibly influence the doctor's evaluation or treatment of this patient. These are "pure fault" statements and do not fall within this exception.

Most of the recent cases concerning FRE 803(4) involve physical or sexual assaults. Clearly the victim may describe the details of the assault to the health care provider. Conclusions, such as "I was raped," are permitted. But what happens when the victim names her attacker? The answer depends on whether the information is something the health care provider reasonably relies on for diagnosis or treatment. For example, several cases have held that a child abuse victim's statement identifying the abuser as a member of the victim's household is admissible under FRE 803(4). The information is relevant to the patient's future physical and emotional health and his psychiatric treatment.

Third, the statement need not be made directly to a doctor. It can be made to any health care provider, including doctors, nurses, therapists, ambulance attendants, and chiropractors. For example, a patient tells the nurse, "My back cramped up when I bent over and picked up a beam." The nurse records the statement, which the doctor later reads. That statement helps diagnose the patient, even though not made directly to the doctor, who will make the actual diagnosis and develop a treatment plan.

Fourth, FRE 803(4) eliminates the common law distinction between treating and non-treating physicians. The common law generally excluded statements made to physicians who examined the declarant only for the purpose of testifying at trial. It was thought that the declarant, with litigation on his mind, had a motive to exaggerate or falsify his condition.

Under FRE 803(4), the examining or non-treating doctor may testify regarding statements made for medical diagnosis, even though the real purpose of the examination was to qualify the doctor to testify at trial. Under the rule, the patient's statements are admitted as substantive evidence. The rule recognizes that jurors often cannot distinguish between patient statements admitted for their truth and those testified to by experts as the bases for their opinions under FRE 703, where the underlying facts or data often are not admissible as substantive evidence. The rule also recognizes that while patients have different motivations when talking to non-treating doctors, these motivations can be adequately exposed through cross-examination and discussed during closing argument.

For example, the plaintiff in a personal injury case is examined by the defense doctor shortly before trial. The patient, knowing that the examination is being conducted so that the defense doctor can testify at trial, may exaggerate or distort his present condition, such as degree of present pain or limitations in movement. However, these motivations can be exposed during cross-examination and discussed during closing argument, so there is little danger that the jury will be misled.

2.   Practice

Patient statements, whether testified to orally or contained in medical records, are routinely admitted in personal injury trials. The rule is broad, allowing almost all statements in evidence. The only limitations are on statements of pure fault and medical history not reasonably pertinent to the present medical condition. When medical records contain statements of pure fault, an objection should be made before trial so that the record when admitted will have the inadmissible statements physically deleted.

Example 1:

This is an automobile negligence case. The plaintiff in the pretrial statement lists an ambulance driver as a witness as well as the ambulance driver's report as a business record. The report notes that the plaintiff said, "My leg hurts. I think I broke it when the other car hit me." The defendant objects to the testimony of the driver and the statements in the report on hearsay grounds. At a hearing, the following happens:

Judge: Defense, why is this statement not admissible?

Defendant: Your honor, the statement was not made to the treating doctor or the emergency room staff; it was made to an ambulance driver. The patient did not make the statement so that the driver could diagnose his condition. It doesn't qualify under Rule 803(4).

Plaintiff: The fact of the matter is that the driver reported the statement to the nurses at the emergency room, which he routinely does. The statement was passed on to the staff, and the only reason is that it would help the doctors diagnose and treat. There is no requirement in the rule that the statement be made directly to the doctor or nurse.

Judge: The objection is overruled. The driver may testify to the patient's statements, and the statement in the report will be admitted, provided a proper foundation for the report is established.

Example 2:

This is a civil battery case. Plaintiff claims that her boyfriend drugged her and that she had to be treated for a drug overdose in the hospital. The emergency room records contain plaintiff's statement "I drank some LSD. My boyfriend put the LSD in my drink." The defendant moves to preclude the statement. At a hearing, the following happens:

Defendant: Your honor, this is our motion to preclude statements plaintiff made in the emergency room. We have no objection to her statement that "I drank some LSD." That statement obviously goes to diagnosis and treatment. However, we object to her other statement: "My boyfriend put the LSD in my drink." That is a statement of pure fault, which can't possibly affect how this patient is treated, and does not fall within the exception.

Plaintiff: Your honor, the doctor will want to know how the patient got the LSD in the first place. This helps the doctor understand the circumstances surrounding the ingesting of the drug, so it does fall within Rule 803(4).

Judge: The objection is sustained. This is pure fault. The statement "I drank some LSD" will be admitted, but not the second statement.

Example 3:

This is a child molestation prosecution against the victim's stepfather. At trial, the prosecution calls the victim's treating physician. During the doctor's direct examination, the following happens:

.Q. (By prosecutor) Dr. Williams, did you talk to Mary when you examined her?

A. Yes.

Q. Tell us what Mary said.

Defendant: Objection, your honor. Sidebar?

Judge: Yes. Counsel, please approach. [Lawyers come to the bench.] What's the basis for your objection?

Defendant: Hearsay, your honor. They're attempting to get in the victim's statement that her stepfather was fondling her. That's not pertinent to diagnosis and treatment for a vaginal injury, since it makes absolutely no difference who did the alleged fondling.

Prosecutor: The doctor will say that how he treats a patient for this kind of injury is significantly influenced by whether the molester was a stranger or a member of the household. There are obvious psychiatric implications, particularly when the victim is an eight-year-old.

Judge: The objection is overruled. The doctor may answer the question.

Commentary: This example is a good illustration of how broadly courts interpret the "reasonably pertinent to diagnosis or treatment" language of FRE 803(4).

§7.6.   Statements under belief of impending death (FRE 804(b)(2))[6]

1.   Law

Rule 804.   Hearsay Exceptions; Declarant Unavailable

(b) The Exceptions.   The following are not excluded by the rule against hearsay if the declarant is unavailable as a witness: . . .

(2) *Statement Under the Belief of Imminent Death.* In a prosecution for homicide or in a civil case, a statement that the declarant, while believing the declarant's death to be imminent, made about its cause or circumstances.

At common law, this exception was known as the "dying declaration," and it still is referred to by that name, although the federal rule expands the common law exception. The underlying theory of the exception was and still is that one who believes he is about to die will not go to his maker with a lie on his lips. An alternate theory, more in keeping with the spirit of the Rules, is that one who realizes he is about to die does not have time and opportunity to reflect or fabricate. The statement may be volunteered or may be triggered by a question.

FRE 804(b)(2) applies this exception not only to homicide cases (the common law rule), but also to any civil case. A "homicide" includes any crime involving an unlawful killing, such as murder, manslaughter, or vehicular homicide.

6. McCormick §§309-315; Weinstein §804(b)(2)[01]-[03]; Mueller & Kirkpatrick §8.71; Wigmore §§1430-1452.

The declarant's statement must be made "while believing the declarant's death to be imminent." Case law usually has required that the declarant himself make a statement showing his subjective belief was that he knew he was dying. For example, the declarant says, "I know I'm dying. Vito shot me." This is a classic dying declaration. Without the key words — "I know I'm dying" — or other words showing an understanding that death is "imminent," most courts will not accept it as a dying statement.

The declarant's statement must also be limited to the "cause or circumstances" of what the declarant believed to be impending death. How strictly do courts interpret the "cause or circumstances" language? For example, the declarant says, "I know I'm dying. Vito shot me. He's been lurking around waiting for the right moment for years, and he finally found it." Many courts read the "cause or circumstances" language narrowly, limiting dying declarations to the immediate circumstances of the physical injury and excluding past historical events that explain why the present event happened. The same analysis applies to exclude exculpatory statements, such as "Johnny wasn't involved in this."

The requirement of personal knowledge applies to this exception. That means the trial judge must find the declarant was in a position to know the cause or circumstances of his death. It cannot be a guess. If there is personal knowledge, statements of opinion may come in under this exception.

Since this is an FRE 804 exception, the declarant must be unavailable under FRE 804(a). A witness is "unavailable" when he asserts a privilege, refuses to testify, has a lack of memory, is dead or too sick to testify, or will not voluntarily attend the trial and cannot be reached by compulsory process. These unavailability requirements are discussed more fully in the introduction to this chapter.

The unavailability requirement of FRE 804(a) is rarely a problem for the obvious reason that the dying declarant usually will have died. The rule does not require that the declarant be the victim of the homicide for which the accused is being prosecuted. However, the proponent must always satisfy the FRE 804(a) requirement that the declarant be shown to be unavailable as a witness at the time of the trial.

Whether the foundation requirements for an FRE 804(b)(3) exception have been established will be a matter for the trial judge under FRE 104(a). The most difficult question is whether the declarant really believed he was about to die when he made the statement. The judge may consider any pertinent fact, admissible or not. This would include the declarant's condition, his other statements, words spoken to him by others, and medical evidence.

The impact of *Crawford v. Washington* on dying declarations in criminal cases is unclear, but the decision seems to allow admissability, as does *Giles v. California*. The Court noted that "although many dying declarations may not be testimonial, there is authority for admitting even those that clearly are."

2. Practice

The most common issue with dying declarations is whether there is sufficient proof the declarant believed death was imminent.

Example 1:

This is a civil suit for money damages. The defendant is charged with recklessly causing an automobile collision, which killed the victim. In the defendant's case, an eyewitness testifies as follows:

Q. (By defendant's lawyer) Right after the two cars collided, what happened?
A. The defendant remained in his car, but the driver of the other car was thrown through the windshield and ended up on the pavement about 50 feet from his car.
Q. What did you do?
A. I ran over to the man.
Q. Did he say anything?
A. Yes.
Q. What did he say?
Plaintiff: Objection, your honor. Hearsay.
Defendant: It's a dying declaration, your honor.
Judge: Please approach the bench. [Lawyers approach.] I don't know what the witness will say, so I can't rule. What will the witness testify to?
Defendant: He's going to say that the victim said, "I'm not going to make it. Please forgive me. I ran the red light." The evidence will also be that he died before reaching the hospital.
Plaintiff: This is not enough to show that he knew death was imminent. Just because he died within a short period of time doesn't prove that he knew it would happen imminently.
Judge: The objection is overruled.

Commentary: The witness's statement that he knows he's not going to make it is enough to qualify as a dying declaration.

Example 2:

This is a murder prosecution. At the preliminary hearing, a witness testifies that he heard a shot, went outside, and saw the deceased lying on the sidewalk. He asked what happened, and the victim said, "Joe just shot me. Get an ambulance quick, or else I'm a goner." The deceased died before reaching the hospital. Before trial, the defendant moves to preclude the witness from testifying to the deceased's statement. At the hearing on the motion, the following happens:

Defendant: This is our motion to preclude, your honor. The statement "Joe just shot me" is hearsay and hence inadmissible.
Prosecutor: The statement is a dying declaration, your honor, and this is a murder prosecution.
Defendant: There's no showing, coming from the deceased, that he knew that his death was imminent. If anything, he was hoping that the ambulance would come quickly. This is hardly a statement

showing that the deceased believed that his death was inevitable.

Judge: The statement is excluded.

Commentary: The defendant also could have argued that there was no proof the declarant actually knew that Joe shot him. The prosecutor also should have argued that the statement may qualify as a present sense impression or excited utterance, two hearsay exceptions that are closely related to dying declarations. Note that no Sixth Amendment Confrontation Clause objection was made. For that reason, it was not considered and the defendant may have forfeited that issue on appeal.

§7.7. *Former testimony (FRE 804(b)(1))*[7]

1. Law

Rule 804.   Hearsay Exceptions; Declarant Unavailable

(b) The Exceptions.   The following are not excluded by the rule against hearsay if the declarant is unavailable as a witness:

(1) *Former Testimony.* Testimony that:

(A) was given as a witness at a trial, hearing, or lawful deposition, whether given during the current proceeding or a different one; and

(B) is now offered against a party who had—or, in a civil case, whose predecessor in interest had—an opportunity and similar motive to develop it by direct, cross-, or redirect examination.

Arguably, former testimony is the most reliable of the hearsay exceptions because it satisfies two of the three reasons for the rule against hearsay. The testimony was given under oath, and there was an opportunity to cross-examine. The only thing missing is the personal presence of the witness at trial. Since the jury's ability to assess credibility by directly observing the witness's demeanor always has been considered important, this exception applies only if the witness is unavailable at trial. This rule, like all FRE 804 exceptions, prefers the presence of the witness at trial.

While FRE 804(b)(1) is technical, it ensures fairness. The overriding concern is this: When is it fair to introduce, in the present proceeding, the transcript of a now unavailable witness who testified in an earlier hearing? Fairness to the party against whom the transcript is now being introduced is the key concern.

The former testimony exception has three requirements, each of which must be satisfied before a transcript of a witness's earlier testimony is properly admissible.

1. Is the out-of-court declarant "unavailable" under FRE 804(a)? A witness is "unavailable" when he asserts a privilege, refuses to testify, has a lack of memory,

7. McCormick §§301-308; Weinstein §804(b)(1)[01]-[07]; Mueller & Kirkpatrick §§8.68-8.70; Wigmore §§1330-1332, 1370-1371, 1386-1389, 1402-1417.

is dead or too sick to testify, or will not voluntarily attend the trial and cannot be reached by compulsory process. These unavailability requirements are discussed more fully in the introduction to this chapter.

2. Is the transcript of that declarant's testimony now being offered against a party that was present at the earlier hearing (or, in civil cases, was the party's "predecessor in interest" present at the earlier hearing)? In common situations, the answer to this question is easy. For example, if an eyewitness is deposed and later becomes unavailable, the deposition transcript is admissible at trial. Both parties were present at the deposition, and neither party can complain at trial if the other party chooses to introduce the deposition transcript as an exhibit.

When the parties in the earlier proceeding differ from the parties in the present proceeding, more careful analysis is required. For example, consider a vehicle collision. Adam and Baker are the driver and passenger, respectively, in a car that collides with Cain. Adam files first and goes to trial first. Adam calls X as a witness in that trial. Baker files later and goes to trial one year after Adam. In the meantime, X has died. Can Baker at trial introduce the transcript of X's earlier testimony? Yes. X's transcript is now being offered against Cain, who was a party in the first trial. (The witness is also now unavailable, and Cain had an opportunity and similar motive to cross-examine the witness during the first trial.) Hence, X's transcript is admissible. Put another way, since Cain cross-examined X in the first trial, Cain cannot complain about his inability to cross-examine X again in the second trial (where the issues are the same).

Consider the same case again. Cain calls Y as a witness in the first trial. Shortly afterward, Y dies. In the second trial, can Cain introduce the transcript of Y's earlier testimony? No. Y's transcript is now being introduced against Baker, who was not present at the first trial and had no opportunity to examine Y. Hence, Y's transcript is inadmissible.

The former testimony exception is not limited to testimony being offered against the same party it was offered against at the earlier proceeding. It also may be offered against the same party who presented it at the earlier proceeding by that party's direct or redirect examination.

For example, consider the vehicle collision case again. The defendant, Cain, calls Y as a witness in the first trial. In the second trial, the plaintiff, Baker, decides to introduce the transcript of Y's former testimony. This is proper because it is being offered against Cain and Cain had an opportunity in the first trial — during direct and redirect examination — to develop Y's testimony. Hence, Y's transcript is admissible. Put another way, since Cain examined Y in the first trial, Cain cannot complain about his inability to cross-examine Y in the second trial (where the issues are the same).

In criminal cases, the party against whom the former testimony is being offered must have been a party in the earlier hearing. In the usual situation, the prosecution offers former testimony against a defendant from an earlier hearing or trial involving that same defendant, where that defendant had an opportunity to cross-examine the declarant.

In civil cases, the party against whom the former testimony is being offered does not have to have been a party at the earlier hearing. It is enough if a "predecessor in interest" of that current party had an opportunity and a similar motive to develop the testimony at the earlier hearing.

The rule does not define "predecessor in interest," and the courts do not agree on what it means. Some define it to mean privity in the common law sense. That probably was the intent of the drafters of the Rules. For example, if a defendant in the earlier hearing dies and his estate becomes the defendant in the second proceeding, the defendant is the predecessor in interest to the defendant's estate, and FRE 804(b)(1) treats the defendant and his estate as the same party for purposes of the rule.

Whenever a corporation changes its name, or is acquired by a successor corporation, or is taken over by a trustee in bankruptcy, the party is essentially the same. Whenever an individual dies, becomes incompetent, or is no longer a minor, the name change of the party does not effect any real change. The predecessor in interest rule recognizes that because no unfairness occurs, these kinds of technical changes in the name of a party in civil cases should not alter the operation of the rule.

Many courts, however, define a "predecessor in interest" more broadly to include any party with a similar interest or motive to develop the testimony. At times, courts use the term "community of interest." For example, one court has held that the government in an anti-trust action is the "predecessor in interest" of a plaintiff in a private anti-trust action involving the same subject matter. Another court has found a sufficient "community of interest" between an injured crewman who sued a ship-owner for an assault on him by another crewman and the United States Coast Guard, which had conducted an administrative proceeding against the crewman who committed the assault. Such a broad view swallows and makes meaningless the term "predecessor in interest."

3. Did that party have "an opportunity and similar motive to develop" the witness's testimony in the earlier hearing? According to this rule, the party against whom the transcript is now being introduced must have had an "opportunity and similar motive" in the earlier hearing to "develop" the testimony by direct, cross-, or redirect examination. There is no requirement that the witness actually be examined in the earlier hearing; opportunity is all that is needed to satisfy the rule and the Confrontation Clause. For example, grand jury testimony cannot be offered against a defendant because he was not present at the grand jury hearing and had no opportunity to examine the witness. But a defendant can offer grand jury testimony against the prosecution that elicited the testimony if he can persuade the trial judge that the prosecutor had a similar motive to develop the testimony. Of course, there is no Confrontation Clause issue when the accused offers the testimony.

Because only opportunity is required, not actual examination, lawyers often are faced with difficult decisions. Since one purpose of a deposition is to preserve relevant testimony, the failure to fully cross-examine a deponent who later becomes unavailable can result in a one-sided deposition being admitted at trial. Strategic choices by a lawyer do not affect the opponent's use of the deposition as former testimony.

In criminal cases, defense lawyers at preliminary hearings might not be prepared to conduct a complete cross-examination, or they might want to save key questions for trial. Still, the opportunity to cross-examine exists. If the opportunity is not used and the witness becomes unavailable, the testimony will not be barred by the hearsay rule or by the Confrontation Clause. In short, the risk is on the opponent if the opponent decides to curtail or forego examining the witness during the deposition, preliminary hearing, or other hearing.

For example, the identification testimony of a witness at a suppression hearing would be admissible at a later trial if the witness becomes unavailable. The defendant had an opportunity to cross-examine the witness at the hearing and a similar motive at both proceedings to show that the identification was unreliable.

If cross-examination is attempted, but unduly limited at the first hearing, a judge later may be persuaded there was no opportunity for effective cross-examination. It is not unusual for the scope of cross-examination to be limited at a preliminary hearing, and the relevant issues at a hearing can materially differ from those at trial. But if the cross-examination at the hearing is not actually limited by the judge, or if the opportunity to cross-examine is not used, an argument later about the limited purpose of the hearing will not defeat the admissibility of the former testimony.

The fact that a party had a different lawyer when the former testimony was offered or that the lawyer at the earlier hearing did a poor job of examining the witness has no effect on the operation of the former testimony exception.

The requirement of a "similar motive" to develop the testimony does not mean the legal and factual issues in the two proceedings have to be identical. Substantial identity of the issues is all that is required. For example, the defendants in a state case were charged with murder; and in a later federal RICO prosecution, those charges were used as predicate acts. The court found the issues were close enough that the defendants had a similar motive to develop the testimony at the first trial.

2.   Practice

Former testimony is an important, technical hearsay exception. This exception is important because it can result in the introduction of hundreds of pages of testimony. It is technical because a close analysis of the rule is required before admissibility can be determined in complicated situations. For this reason, former testimony issues should be raised before trial whenever possible.

Example 1:

This is a civil battery case. Plaintiff in his pretrial memorandum lists the deposition transcript of a witness as a trial exhibit. Defendant objects to the admission of the transcript. At the hearing on the objection, the following happens:

Judge: Plaintiff, what's the evidentiary basis for this transcript qualifying as a hearsay exception?

Plaintiff: Your honor, the deposition transcript qualifies as former testimony. The witness will be unavailable at trial; the transcript is being offered against the defendant, who was present at the deposition and had the opportunity to ask the witness questions; and the issues at the deposition are the same as the ones that will be argued during the trial. All the requirements for the former testimony exception have been met.

Defendant: Except one, your honor. The witness has not been shown to be unavailable. Saying the witness is unavailable is not the same as being unavailable at trial.

Judge: What's the status of the witness?

Plaintiff: I've talked to the witness, your honor. In fact, he's under subpoena for trial. He says he wants no part of this trial and refuses to testify.

Defendant: That's not unavailable under the rule, your honor.

Judge: I agree. Plaintiff will have to call the witness at trial and enforce the trial subpoena if necessary. If the witness disappears or refuses to testify when in court, I will declare him unavailable, but I can't do this until the time of trial.

Example 2:

This is a robbery case. The prosecution at trial, out of the hearing of the jury, offers in evidence the preliminary hearing transcript of a witness who since has died. The following then happens:

Judge: The witness, Jones, died a few weeks ago, is that right?

Prosecutor: Yes, your honor. I informed the defendant of this when I heard about it, and I have a certified copy of the death certificate.

Judge: Defense, what's your objection? The witness is dead.

Defendant: We object for two reasons, your honor. First, we didn't cross-examine him in any detail at the preliminary hearing. Second, as your honor knows, cross-examination at preliminary hearings is so restricted and limited that we were given only a few minutes, hardly the kind of cross-examination we would do if the witness testified at trial. Letting in the preliminary hearing transcript now would be unfair.

Judge: The objection is overruled as to the preliminary hearing transcript.

Commentary: This objection is frequently made and usually overruled. If cross-examination at the preliminary hearing was so restricted as to be essentially a denial of the right to cross-examine, the objection has a better chance of succeeding.

Example 3:

This is a wrongful death case. The issue is whether the defendant's car lights were on when the defendant's car hit a pedestrian. The defendant was previously prosecuted for, and acquitted of, vehicular manslaughter arising out of the same incident. Since the criminal trial, the defendant has died, and the wrongful death case is being brought against the defendant's estate. Before trial, the plaintiff offers the transcript of a witness's testimony in the criminal case. The witness has moved to another state. At a hearing on the defendant's objection, the following happens:

Judge: I need to know two things. First, is the witness unavailable? Second, if so, is the transcript admissible against the estate? Defense, it's your objection.

Defendant: Yes, your honor. First, the witness has apparently moved to another jurisdiction. Although the witness is beyond our subpoena power, there's no indication that the witness might not voluntarily return, particularly if he were paid for his expenses. In addition, they should have subpoenaed the witness while he was still here. The risk that he might move to another state is always present, and the plaintiff should have safeguarded against such a possibility by issuing a trial subpoena earlier. The plaintiff has to make a stronger showing of unavailability before the rule is satisfied because there is a strong preference for live testimony. Second, the earlier proceeding was a criminal trial. That's a totally different creature than a wrongful death case, and the issues are quite different. Moreover, this case is brought against the estate, which was not a party in the criminal case. Attempting to introduce the transcript under these circumstances is grossly unfair.

Judge: Plaintiff?

Plaintiff: Your honor, I can't subpoena a witness who is out of state. I'm not aware of any requirement that I issue trial subpoenas to all witnesses when I first become aware of them in order to protect myself if they leave the jurisdiction or become unavailable in some other way. That's one of the purposes of taking their depositions. I've talked to the witness, and he says he testified once, at the criminal trial, and he's not voluntarily coming back a second tune. Second, the fact that this case is against the estate makes no difference. The defendant is a "predecessor in interest" to the estate, so the estate steps into the shoes of the deceased defendant for the purposes of applying the former testimony exception.

Judge: The objection is overruled. The transcript will be admitted. Counsel will designate the parts they want admitted and note objections to the other side's designations within one week, and I will rule on any objections before trial.

§7.8. Statements against interest (FRE 804(b)(3))[8]

1. Law

Rule 804

(b) The Exceptions. The following are not excluded by the rule against hearsay if the declarant is unavailable as a witness:

    (3) *Statement Against Interest.* A statement that

        (A) a reasonable person in the declarant's position would have made only if the person believed it to be true because, when made, it

---

8. McCormick §§316-320; Weinstein §804(b)(3)[01]-[05]; Mueller & Kirkpatrick §§8.72-8.76; Wigmore §§1455-1477.

was so contrary to the declarant's proprietary or pecuniary interest or had so great a tendency to invalidate the declarant's claim against someone else or to expose the declarant to civil or criminal liability; and

(B) is supported by corroborating circumstances that clearly indicate its trustworthiness, if it is offered in a criminal case as one that tends to expose the declarant to criminal liability.

This hearsay exception is based on the assumption that people do not make statements damaging to themselves unless they believe for good reason that their statements are true. That is, a reasonable person in the declarant's position, even somebody who is not especially honest, would not have made the statement unless he believed it to be true.

FRE 804(b)(3) sets out several technical requirements for this exception. First, the maker of the statement, the out-of-court declarant, must be unavailable under FRE 804(a). A witness is "unavailable" when he asserts a privilege, refuses to testify, has a lack of memory, is dead or too sick to testify, or will not voluntarily attend the trial and cannot be reached by compulsory process. These unavailability requirements are discussed more fully in the introduction to this chapter.

Second, the statement must be against the declarant's pecuniary or proprietary interest, or subject the person to civil or criminal liability, or invalidate a person's claim against another. These are often referred to as the three "Ps": pecuniary, proprietary, and penal interests.

A pecuniary interest is a financial interest. For example, the declarant says, "I owe Johnson $1,000." This statement subjects him to a possible civil claim for the money owed. As a further example, immediately after a three-car, rear-end collision, the now unavailable driver of the first car says, "I should not have jammed on my brakes without warning." In a lawsuit where the driver of the third car sues the driver of the second car, the defendant may offer the first driver's words as a statement against interest. The statement not only subjects the declarant to civil liability, but also tends to extinguish any claim he might have against the other drivers. Consider another example. The driver of the car in which the plaintiff was riding at the time of a collision later says, "I drank too much whiskey at the Ace Tavern before driving home." The statement is offered in the plaintiff's dram shop case against Ace. If the driver is unavailable at trial, the statement qualifies as a statement against interest.

A proprietary interest is an interest in property. For example, the declarant says, "I gave Mary the diamond ring as a present." This statement again subjects him to a civil claim.

A penal interest is one that subjects the declarant to possible criminal liability. For example, the declarant says, "I just robbed the bank." This statement subjects him to possible criminal arrest and prosecution.

Third, note the high admissibility standard of the rule. A statement against interest is not admissible unless "at the time of its making" it was "so contrary" to the declarant's interest that "a reasonable person in the declarant's position would have made" the statement "only if the person believed it to be true." This means that each statement must be taken on a case-by-case basis, looking at when it was made and the circumstances under which it was made.

The analysis centers on the time and circumstances of the making of the statement. Each case requires a fact-intensive inquiry into the motivations of the declarant and the circumstances surrounding the making of the statement. By definition, the declarant is not available at the time of the trial to be asked why he said the words being offered into evidence. The trial judge, at an FRE 104(a) hearing, will have to determine the declarant's motives for making the statement. Of course, a finding that the declarant's statement was based on personal knowledge is required by this hearsay exception.

When the statement was made is important because it often controls the question of whether it realistically subjected the declarant to civil or criminal liability. For example, the declarant's statement "I robbed the bank" appears to be a statement subjecting him to criminal liability. If the declarant made the statement shortly after the robbery, this would probably be true. However, if the police had arrested another person and that person was indicted and about to be tried, the declarant's statement, made at the 11th hour, does not realistically expose him to criminal liability. It is unlikely that the prosecution will dismiss the case against the other person and initiate a prosecution of the declarant.

The circumstances under which the statement was made are also important because they determine if the statement was seriously made. For example, the declarant is in a bar and pays for his beer from a large roll of bills. The bartender comments on the roll of bills, and the declarant responds, "Just robbed the bank." Under these circumstances, it is obvious that the statement was not serious and therefore would not be admissible as a statement against interest.

The high admissibility threshold — so contrary to the declarant's interest that a reasonable person would have made the statement only if the person believed it to be true — means that many statements, while facially against interest, will not qualify because they do not realistically subject the declarant to civil or criminal liability at the time and under the circumstances when the statement was made.

The subject of a statement against interest most frequently arises when it is a statement that tends "to expose the declarant to . . . criminal liability." At common law, it was called a declaration against penal interest, a description that persists in the decisions and in the literature. The statement does not have to be a full confession. The declarant did not have to realize the statement would subject him to immediate criminal prosecution. And the declarant need not actually be charged with a crime. "Tending" to expose the declarant to criminal liability is enough if the trial judge concludes a reasonable person would not have made the statement unless it was true.

A statement against penal interest can be made to anyone, such as a friend, acquaintance, family member, cellmate, or police officer. The rule contains no limitations on time or place.

There are two kinds of statements against penal interest (other than one that inculpates the declarant and no one else): the kind that exculpates someone else and the kind that inculpates someone else.

The rule has a special corroboration requirement when a statement against penal interest is offered to expose the declarant to liability in a criminal case. Evidence law has always expressed distrust and no small measure of cynicism toward such statements. FRE 804(b)(3) continues that skepticism by providing that such an exculpatory statement is not admissible "unless corroborating circumstances . . . clearly indicate the truthfulness of the statement." A 2010 amendment to Rule 804(b)(3) established a level playing field. Before then, the requirement of "corroborating circumstances" applied only to a statement offered by the defense. The rule now applies to statements offered by the defense and the prosecution. For example, the defendant is on trial for robbery. In the defense case, the defendant calls Smith to testify that while in jail his cellmate, Johnson, stated that he (Johnson) had actually committed the robbery. At the time of the trial, Johnson has been released from custody and cannot be found. Unless there is solid corroboration of Johnson's statement, Smith will not be allowed to testify to the statement.

The reported decisions have given trial judges several factors to consider when pursuing the "trustworthiness" inquiry: (1) the relationship between the declarant and the accused (The closer they are, the less likely the statement is trustworthy.); (2) the declarant's motives for making the statement (Did he have a reason to help the accused?); (3) the extent to which the statement was against the declarant's interest (The more it tended to expose him to criminal liability, the more trustworthy it becomes.); (4) the number of people who heard the statement and the specificity of their accounts of the statement; (5) the kind of person the speaker is; (6) the time and circumstances of the making of the statement (Was it spontaneous? Did he have a reason for saying it?); and (7) the existence of other evidence corroborating the statement. (This is a decisive factor for many trial judges.)

When a statement against interest is offered to inculpate an accused, the declarant's status and motivation become paramount. These statements ordinarily are made to law enforcement officers, usually after an arrest. If the declarant makes the statement to shift blame to someone else, or to curry favor with the police, or to seek leniency or other favorable treatment, or to minimize his own role in the crime, the statement lacks the reliability required by the rule and should not be admitted. Likewise, a declarant who has received immunity from prosecution cannot make a statement against his penal interest concerning the subject matter of the immunity. The credibility of the witness testifying to the statement is not a requirement for admissibility under FRE 804(b)(3).

Assuming that the trial judge finds the declarant is capable of making a statement against interest, how far does the hearsay exception reach? Obviously when the declarant says, "I didn't do the robbery. Joe did," the statement does not qualify as a statement against interest. But what happens when the declarant says, "I drove the getaway car, but Joe went inside the bank to get the money"? Clearly "I drove the getaway car" is against the declarant's penal interest and is admissible at Joe's trial. But what about "Joe went inside the bank to get the money"? Is that admissible against Joe?

The Supreme Court attempted to address the question in *Williamson v. United States*, 512 U.S. 594 (1994). In *Williamson*, the declarant was an arrested accomplice. He admitted transporting cocaine, but said he was doing it for Williamson. The Supreme Court, in an attempt to "clarify the scope of the hearsay exception for statements against penal interest," held that FRE 804(b)(3) covers only those declarations or remarks within the confession that genuinely inculpate the declarant. Statements collateral to the self-inculpatory statements are not reliable and do not come within the exception, even if made within the context of a broader narrative that is generally inculpatory, that is, a broader confession.

The case was remanded to the court of appeals to determine which statements were truly self-inculpatory, but the Supreme Court suggested the declarant's statements about transporting cocaine would qualify for admission, while his statements implicating Williamson would not. Each single remark or declaration has to be analyzed. If it poses no risk of criminal liability to the declarant, it is not reliable enough to qualify as a statement against interest.

Taken literally, then, *Williamson* means "I drove the getaway car" is admissible at Joe's trial, but "Joe went inside the bank to get the money" would not be admissible because that specific statement does not genuinely inculpate the declarant.

Williamson was an evidence rules case, and Confrontation Clause issues were not addressed. Whether the holding would apply to cases in which the statement against penal interest would exculpate, not inculpate, the accused is not clear. That is, "I drove the getaway car" would be admissible, but "Joe had nothing to do with it" is subject to the prosecution's hearsay objection, not, of course, to a confrontation objection. Since the declarant obviously was not seeking to curry favor with the prosecution, his second statement is not open to a *Williamson*-type attack. He is not attempting to shift blame to the accused, as was the declarant in *Williamson.* The analysis should center on whether both statements possess sufficient objective indicia of trustworthiness, guided by the non-exclusive criteria listed in *Chambers v. Mississippi,* 410 U.S. 284 (1970) and corroborating circumstances. The question under FRE 804(b)(3) is whether the statements were so against the declarant's penal interest that a reasonable person in his position would not have made the statements unless he believed them to be true.

In *Lilly v. Virginia,* 527 U.S. 116 (1999), the Supreme Court held a declaration against penal interest is not a firmly rooted hearsay exception for Confrontation Clause purposes. That finding is of little interest after *Crawford v. Washington,* since the reliability of the statement does not matter when a testimonial statement of an unavailable witness is offered against an accused who did not have the opportunity to cross-examine the witness. The lack of firm roots may have some impact on judges when they make a pure evidence law decision concerning an FRE 804(b)(3) hearsay exception.

Finally, statements against interest under FRE 804(b)(3) should not be confused with party admissions under FRE 801(d)(2). Party admissions do not have to be against the declarant's interest when made. Nor is any showing of unavailability required. Party admissions are not hearsay at all. Statements against interest are exceptions to the rule against hearsay. The requirement of personal knowledge applies to statements against interest, but not to party admissions.

This means that if the out-of-court statement was made by a party or an agent or employee of the party, the offering party should use the party admissions exception. If the out-of-court statement was made by a non-party, the party admissions exception cannot apply, so the statements against interest exception would be the way to offer the evidence. There is no reason to analyze statements by parties under the statements against interest exception, since party admissions is the much broader, easier to apply exception.

2.   Practice

A statement against interest is a less frequently used hearsay exception, since it applies only when the declarant is unavailable and has a difficult admissibility standard.

Example 1:

This is a medical malpractice case brought against a doctor as a result of a surgical procedure. The defendant claims the plaintiff's injuries were caused by a nurse's negligence. At trial, the defendant intends to call a witness who will testify that the nurse, immediately after the surgery, stated, "I made a big mistake in there." Before trial, the plaintiff moves to preclude the statement. At a hearing on the motion, the following happens:

Plaintiff: Your honor, this is our motion to preclude an out-of-court statement by a nurse. The statement is hearsay, and no exception or non-hearsay rationale exists to admit it.

Defendant: The statement is a statement against interest, your honor. She was heard to say, "I made a big mistake in there," right after the surgery. That's clearly a statement against her pecuniary interest, since she could have been sued.

Plaintiff: That's just the point. She wasn't sued. Moreover, your honor, there's been no demonstration that the nurse is unavailable under Rule 804(a), which this hearsay exception requires.

Judge: What's the status of the nurse, counsel?

Defendant: I've talked to her. She won't cooperate and says that she will deny the statement if forced to testify.

Plaintiff: That's not unavailable under the rule, your honor.

Judge: The motion is granted for the present time. Unavailability has not been sufficiently demonstrated under Rule 804(a). Counsel, if you subpoena the nurse and she refuses to testify at that time, I will reverse my ruling.

Commentary: Most courts require a showing at trial that the witness is "unavailable." Representing before trial that the witness is uncooperative or is threatening not to testify does not meet the requirements of the rule.

Example 2:

This is a robbery prosecution. The defense claims another person, Smith, actually committed the robbery and set up Walters, the defendant. Smith is subpoenaed for trial, but asserts his Fifth Amendment privilege against self-incrimination in court. The next defense witness is then called:

Q. (By defendant's lawyer) Mr. Gibbs, were you with Smith two days after the robbery?

A. Yes.

Q. Where?

A. Over at Smith's house.

Q. Was anyone else there with you?

A. Frankie Jones was there, too.

Q. What did Smith say to you and Mr. Jones that day?

Prosecutor: Objection, your honor. Hearsay.

Defendant: May we be heard at sidebar, your honor?

Judge: You may. Please approach. [Lawyers come to bench.] Why isn't this hearsay?

Defendant: The witness will testify that Smith said, "I set up Walters so that the police would bust him instead of me. Can't believe it worked." That's a statement against Smith's penal interest, your honor. That's not the kind of statement anyone makes in front of witnesses unless true.

Prosecutor: When he made the statement, your honor, Walters had already been arrested for the robbery, so the statement wasn't against interest at the time made. In addition, they're trying to use the statement to exculpate the defendant. This requires corroboration, and, here, there's no corroboration that the statement is true.

Defendant: We will call Jones as our next witness, your honor. He'll corroborate the fact that Smith made the statement. In addition, we'll show through this witness that Walters was a boarder at Smith's house at the time of the robbery.

Judge: The objection is overruled, provided that the defendant also calls Jones to corroborate the fact that Smith made the statement.

Commentary: FRE 804(b)(3) does not define what is meant by the requirement that the "corroborating circumstances clearly indicate the trustworthiness of the statement." Most courts hold that there must be external factual corroboration of the contents of the statement. The Supreme Court noted the issue in *Williamson v. United States*, 512 U.S. 594 (1994), but declined to address it.

§7.9.   Statements of personal or family history (FRE 804(b)(4))[9]

1.   Law

Rule 804

(b) **The Exceptions.**   The following are not excluded by the rule against hearsay if the declarant is unavailable as a witness:

(4) *Statement of Personal or Family History.* A statement about

(A) the declarant's own birth, adoption, legitimacy, ancestry, marriage, divorce, relationship by blood, adoption, or marriage, or similar facts of personal or family history, even though the declarant had no way of acquiring personal knowledge about that fact; or

(B) another person concerning any of these facts, as well as death, if the declarant was related to the person by blood, adoption, or marriage or was so intimately associated with the person's family that the declarant's information is likely to be accurate.

9. McCormick §322; Weinstein §804(b)(4)[01]-[02]; Mueller & Kirkpatrick §8.77; Wigmore §§1480-1503.

Part (A) of this exception, dealing with the declarant's own personal or family history, is a rare instance in the hearsay exception rules where personal knowledge of the declarant is not required. Personal knowledge is required by part (B), where the statement refers to other persons the declarant would be expected to have accurate information about. There is no requirement in the rule that the statement be made before the controversy at issue arose.

2. Practice

This exception is commonly used at trial, mostly without objection because lawyers fail to realize they are in hearsay territory. Whenever a witness testifies about his own age, parents, blood relatives, and other family history, it is obvious that he is testifying to facts of which he has no personal knowledge. Nevertheless, this testimony is proper under FRE 804(b)(4)(A).

Example:

This is a probate case. At a hearing, the witness testifies as follows:

Q. (By petitioner's lawyer) Mr. Johnson, let's talk about your family tree. What were your parents' names?
A. John and Mary Johnson.
Q. Any brothers and sisters?
A. Yes. One sister, Kim.
Q. Are all of them living?
A. No, my parents have passed away.
Q. When and where did they pass away?
Respondent: Objection, your honor. This is hearsay unless it is first established that the witness has personal knowledge.
Petitioner: This is family history, your honor, under Rule 804(b)(4)(B).
Judge: Overruled. The witness may answer.

§7.10. Business records (FRE 803(6), 803(7), 902(11), 902(12))[10]

1. Law

Rule 803. Exceptions to the Rule Against Hearsay — Regardless of Whether the Declarant Is Available as a Witness

The following are not excluded by the rule against hearsay, regardless of whether the declarant is available as a witness:

   (6) *Records of a Regularly Conducted Activity.* A record of an act, event, condition, opinion, or diagnosis if:

---

10. McCormick §§284-294; Weinstein §803(6)[01]-[09]; Mueller & Kirkpatrick §§8.44-8.48; Wigmore §665.

(A) the record was made at or near the time by — or from information transmitted by — someone with knowledge;

(B) the record was kept in the course of a regularly conducted activity of a business, organization, occupation, or calling, whether or not for profit;

(C) making the record was a regular practice of that activity;

(D) all these conditions are shown by the testimony of the custodian or another qualified witness, or by a certification that complies with Rule 902(11) or (12) or with a statute permitting certification; and

(E) the opponent does not show that the source of information or the method or circumstances of preparation indicate a lack of trustworthiness.

(7) *Absence of a Record of a Regularly Conducted Activity.* Evidence that a matter is not included in a record described in paragraph (6) if:

(A) the evidence is admitted to prove that the matter did not occur or exist;

(B) a record was regularly kept for a matter of that kind; and

(C) the opponent does not show that the possible source of the information or other circumstances indicate a lack of trustworthiness.

Rule 902. Evidence That Is Self-Authenticating

The following items of evidence are self-authenticating; they require no extrinsic evidence of authenticity in order to be admitted:

(11) *Certified Domestic Records of a Regularly Conducted Activity.* The original or a copy of a domestic record that meets the requirements of Rule 803(6)(A)-(C), as shown by a certification of the custodian or another qualified person that complies with a federal statute or a rule prescribed by the Supreme Court. Before the trial or hearing, the proponent must give an adverse party reasonable written notice of the intent to offer the record — and must make the record and certification available for inspection — so that the party has a fair opportunity to challenge them.

(12) *Certified Foreign Records of a Regularly Conducted Activity.* In a civil case, the original or a copy of a foreign record that meets the requirements of Rule 902(11), modified as follows: the certification, rather than complying with a federal statute or Supreme Court rule, must be signed in a manner that, if falsely made, would subject the maker to a criminal penalty in the country where the certification is signed. The proponent must also meet the notice requirements of Rule 902(11).

FRE 803(6), usually referred to as the "business record exception," recognizes the reality of business life. When information is furnished and recorded by people acting routinely, under a duty to be accurate, with an employer relying on the result, admissibility of the record should not be defeated by the rule against hearsay. If it is reliable enough for the business, it should be reliable enough for the rules of evidence. All that is needed is someone who can testify to how and for what purpose and when the particular kind of record is made and kept. Requiring the presence of other participants in the record-making process would be cumbersome and a waste of time.

The 2000 amendments to FRE 803(6) and 902(11) and (12) provide another, probably simpler, way for the proponent of the records to establish the foundation for their admission. Instead of offering a witness, the foundation can be satisfied by a declaration qualifying as a self-authenticating document. FRE 902(11) governs the form and content of the certification for domestic records of regularly conducted activity and FRE 902(12) does the same for foreign records. This procedure brings the foundation rules in line with those for public records under 803(8) and the procedure for admitting foreign business records in criminal cases set out in 18 U.S.C. §3505. The certification procedure applies to civil and criminal cases and to domestic and foreign records.

The contents of the declaration should mirror the testimony that would be given by a live foundation witness. The declaration, under oath and in writing, must certify that the record — foreign or domestic — was (A) made at or near the time of the occurrence of the matters set forth by, or from information transmitted by, a person with knowledge of those matters; (B) kept in the course of the regularly conducted activity; and (C) made by the regularly conducted activity as a regular practice.

The opponent of the record is given a chance to test the adequacy of the declaration. The proponent of the record "must give an adverse party reasonable written notice of the intent to offer the record — and must make the record and certification available for inspection — so that the party has a fair opportunity to challenge them."

The business record rule can best be understood when broken into its various components.

1. The record can be a record of an "act, event, condition, opinion, or diagnosis" so long as it was the "regular practice of that activity" to make the record.

There is no limit to the method of creation. It ranges from handwritten to typed to computer generated. Handwritten office diary entries, preprinted forms filled out by hand or typewritten, and computer printouts are all included in the definition of a record.

While the rule clearly includes computer-generated records, some courts hold that a record is a business record only if the computer's output is in the same form as the original input. If the computer is asked to search and selectively retrieve information from its data base and the resulting printout is a new document that never was put into the computer in that form, the printout is a summary under FRE 1006, not a business record under FRE 803(6). While the summary will be admissible, the requirements of FRE 1006 must be met.

It is not enough that someone engaged in a business makes a record of something. The thing he records has to do with the business, and it has to be the kind of thing that is routinely recorded. Routine recording assures accuracy. The lack of routineness raises a probability that the record-maker is not motivated by a desire to be accurate. For example, a stock brokerage purchase order contains the notation "This customer is a thief." The notation is not part of the business routine and should be excluded, although the purchase order will be admissible to prove an order was placed.

The record can contain acts, events, and conditions as well as opinions and diagnoses. To be admissible, the opinions or diagnoses in the record must be part of a report made at or near the time of the events about which the opinion or diagnosis was made. A record created merely to support or express expert opinions will not qualify under the business record exception. For example, an emergency room doctor's opinion and diagnosis are part of the report of the patient's condition and treatment. But when another doctor later sees the patient solely for the purpose of rendering an opinion, the trier of fact has a right to know that doctor's qualifications before the opinion is admitted, and that doctor's opinion letter is not admissible as a business record.

The activity recorded must be regular and routine, but that does not mean this kind of record has to be made every day. For example, if a business is burglarized, hardly a usual event, a record made by the business to reflect things lost in the burglary should qualify as a business record. Ordinarily, though, casual or isolated records will not qualify unless there are some special circumstances guaranteeing trustworthiness.

The term "business" in the rule covers any kind of business, institution, association, profession, occupation, or calling, whether or not conducted for profit. It includes illegal businesses.

The original documents rule in FRE 1002 applies to a business record and sometimes requires production of the record. The original documents rule is discussed in Sec. 10.10.

2. The record must be "made at or near the time" of the act, event, condition, opinion, or diagnosis recorded.

Courts refuse to announce any arbitrary or artificial time limits for the "made at or near" requirement. The usual standard is that the record must be made a reasonable time after the event, when the acts and events are still fresh in the mind of the person having firsthand knowledge of the facts. Much will depend on the nature of the information and how and when it is recorded. When the record-maker obviously is looking back in time to recreate a record of a past event, he is not making it at or near the time of the event. Such a record is not trustworthy.

3. The record must be made by "someone with knowledge" of the act, event, condition, opinion, or diagnosis or "from information transmitted by someone with knowledge" of the act, event, condition, opinion, or diagnosis.

Admissibility of a business record is not assured simply because an employee made it in the usual course of the business. Inquiry should be made into the source of the information, that is, who the source was, why the source was supplying the information, and whether the source actually had firsthand knowledge of the information. A conscientious judge might assume that the record-maker is on the stand and ask the following: Who is the person who gave you this information? How did he come to know the information? How often does he get it? When did he transmit the information to you? Who relies on the information and for what reason? While the record-maker's presence in court is excused by the rule, his absence should not give the record more reliability than it deserves.

Frequently the record-maker will not have personal knowledge of the event he records. He will be relying on other sources of information. The source of the information must be speaking from personal knowledge. If the information is being offered for its truth, the source must have had a "business duty" to speak accurately, although that phrase does not appear in the rule. (The "business duty" concept comes from the leading case, *Johnson v. Lutz*, 170 N.E 517 (N.Y. 1930).) If the source had no such business duty, information from that source is "double hearsay," or "hearsay within hearsay." Such information, contained in a business record, is not admissible, even though the record itself is qualified as a business record, unless the information is not hearsay or a separate hearsay exception applies to the information. The admissibility of so-called "double hearsay," or "hearsay within hearsay," is governed by FRE 805, which provides that each level of hearsay must fall within a hearsay exception before it is properly admissible.

For example, Sandra Jones reports the theft of her car to her insurance company. The car is recovered, but Jones is not available to testify against the defendant at his theft trial. The prosecution offers the insurance company report to prove that Jones owned the car and that it was stolen. Jones, not being an employee of the insurance company, did not have a business duty to speak accurately. The report is being offered for the truth of her statement to the insurance company. The report is inadmissible for that purpose.

The purpose for offering the report might change, however. Jones now sues the insurance company for the value of the car, and the company defends on the ground that she failed to report the theft to the insurance company. The report becomes admissible because it is offered not for the truth of what she said, but for the fact that she said it. Her statement to the insurance company is not hearsay at all. The report is admissible for that purpose.

Under FRE 805, each layer of the out-of-court statement must be examined, from the original source of the information who had firsthand information to the actual maker of the report. The source of the information must be (1) someone with a business duty to report accurately, or (2) someone whose statement fits within a hearsay exception, or (3) someone whose statement is not hearsay at all.

For example, when a bystander to an accident tells a police officer "The blue car went through a red light," a police report containing that statement is not admissible for the truth of the statement. The bystander is not under a business duty to report accurately. His statement is no more admissible than it would be if the police officer were on the witness stand testifying to the bystander's statement. Even if the police report itself is admissible as a record, the bystander's statement must first be deleted from the report.

But the bystander might be speaking under the stress of excitement caused by the accident when he blurts out, "Oh my God! The blue car went through the red light!" In that case, each level of hearsay has been satisfied. The report itself qualifies as a record, and the bystander's statement, contained in the report, qualifies as an excited utterance. The entire report, including the bystander's statement, is admissible, since both levels of hearsay meet separate hearsay exceptions.

Another example of qualifying each layer of an out-of-court statement under FRE 805 involves the admission of a party contained in a police report. For example, in a personal injury case, a police report contains the defendant's statement: "I ran the red light." The report itself is hearsay, but qualifies as a record. The defendant's statement, contained in the report, is not hearsay, since it is a party admission under FRE 801(d)(2)(A) when the report is offered by the plaintiff.

Ordinarily, the person with the business duty and the hearsay declarant will be the same person. But there is an exception to that general rule. The person making the record does not have to have a duty to report so long as someone has a duty to verify the information reported. For example, a prison's visitors' logbook is admissible to prove the identity of a visitor when the responsible prison official requires proof of identification that is then checked against the name and address in the book. A customer's name on a firearm purchase record is admissible when gun store employees are required to verify names with photo identification. And a bank deposit slip filled out by the customer is admissible when the bank teller verifies the accuracy of the information on the slip before accepting the deposit. The controlling fact is whether the business demands identification and verification as a regular practice.

Direct proof of personal knowledge of the record-maker or the source of the information is not always easy to obtain. It usually is inferred circumstantially from the nature of the information and from the fact that business routine required an employee to obtain firsthand information. For example, a company regularly relies on the firsthand knowledge of its shipping agent. An invoice prepared by that agent is based on his firsthand knowledge.

4. The person testifying to the foundation for the business record must be its "custodian or other qualified witness."

The rule does not require that the witness have personal knowledge of the contents of the particular record, nor does he have to have personal knowledge of how the particular record was made. Those are matters of weight for the fact finder.

The witness can be anyone who can explain the way in which records like the one in question are made and kept. There is no requirement that the witness know or identify the actual person who made the record or supplied the information. But the witness does need to know the process by which the information was obtained and the record made.

The qualifying witness does not have to have been an employee of the business at the time the record was made. It has been held that a person outside the business may testify to its records if he has sufficient personal knowledge of how the records are made and kept.

In practice, the foundation for offering business records has become casual. Some judges are satisfied with conclusory questions that mirror the language of FRE 803(6). However, many judges look beyond the mere reciting of the rule's language to determine if the requirements of the rule have actually been met. Whether judges are more or less exacting when confronted with an FRE 902(11) or (12) certification is unclear.

The fact that records are created by or stored in a computer does not cause problems. The rule does not require any special or extra foundation for computer-generated records, but some judges do. Emphasis is on the accuracy of the data compiled for computer entry. The data must have been compiled and entered into the computer at or near the time of the event. The actual printout can be made at any time. When the accuracy of computer printouts is called into question, some judges require testimony that the computer and the program it used were reliable, that the computer was in good working order, and that the computer operator possessed the knowledge and training to correctly operate the computer. The opponent of the computer record has the burden of raising the issue of lack of trustworthiness. Otherwise, there is a general presumption of admissibility. But where a web site posting appears on the Internet, the proponent of the posting must call the service's customer who put it there to establish the document's trustworthiness as an authentic business record under FRE 803(6). Calling a representative of the service is not enough.

5. The record will be excluded if "the source of information" or "the method or circumstances of preparation indicate lack of trustworthiness."

The opponent of the record has the burden of raising the question of lack of trustworthiness. The attack usually centers on some motive of the record-maker or the source of the information to misrepresent. Here, the absence of routineness plays a significant role. Records made in anticipation of particular litigation lack trustworthiness. A record created to defeat another person's legal rights is untrustworthy. An employer's written comment about an employee it has discharged may be held untrustworthy because of a motive to defend the company against a claim of wrongful discharge.

The rule does not specifically exclude records made for the purpose of litigation, but the judge may exclude a record where the circumstances "indicate a lack of trustworthiness." This "anticipation of litigation" rule comes from *Palmer v. Hoffman*, 318 U.S. 109 (1943), where the Supreme Court excluded an accident report by a since-deceased train engineer offered by the railroad in a grade-crossing collision case. The Court held that such a report, obviously written with an eye toward an expected lawsuit, was too untrustworthy under the circumstances to be admitted as a business record. The *Palmer v. Hoffman* rule has not been strictly applied, since any business record can be seen as having been made with a view toward possible future litigation. However, when litigation in a particular situation becomes a distinct possibility, a record made by a party may be too self-serving to be trustworthy, and FRE 806(6) permits its exclusion.

In each instance, the trial judge conducts an FRE 104(a) inquiry into the opponent's claim of lack of trustworthiness. Judges prefer that a claim of untrustworthiness or of other reasons for inadmissibility be raised at the earliest opportunity.

Amendments to FRE 803(6), 803(7), and 803(8) became effective December 1, 2014. The amendments reflect court decisions dealing with burdens of proof when business or official records are offered into evidence. The amendments provide that the proponent must first establish the foundational requirements of each rule. Then the burden shifts to the opponent to show by evidence or argument that the source of information or the method or circumstances of preparation indicates a lack of trustworthiness. For example, the opponent of a business record can show that it was created for the purpose of litigation.

The absence of an entry on a business record can be admissible evidence. FRE 803(7) provides: "Absence of a Record of a Regularly Conducted Activity. Evidence that a matter is not included in a record described in paragraph (6) if: (A) the evidence is admitted to prove that the matter did not occur or exist; (B) a record was regularly kept for a matter of that kind; and (C) the opponent does not show that the possible source of the information or other circumstances indicate a lack of trustworthiness."

This exception applies to matters that are routinely recorded in a business record, but were not recorded on a particular occasion. The failure to record the matter becomes evidence of its non-occurrence or non-existence. For example, a record is kept each time a bus is cleaned. There is no record of a certain bus being cleaned on a particular date. This is evidence the bus was not cleaned on that date.

The foundation for this exception tracks the FRE 803(6) foundation. The custodian or other qualified person testifies that records of the matter routinely are made and kept by the business. In this case, after a diligent search, he could not find such a record, or he did find a record that would ordinarily contain the relevant entry, but it does not contain such an entry.

Some judges simply allow testimony of the absence of an entry without admitting the record in which it should have appeared. Others require introducing the record with the missing entry. The original documents rule in FRE 1002 applies when the record itself is introduced to demonstrate absence of an entry.

2. Practice

The business record exception is one of the most important, and most frequently used, hearsay exceptions. While basic foundation issues are rare and lawyers often stipulate to the foundations of business records, lawyers frequently overlook other evidentiary objections. The most important objection is to double hearsay contained within the record, because statements from sources not having a business duty to report and record accurately are usually hearsay, and those statements are not admissible unless the statements are not offered for their truth or a separate hearsay exception applies.

Additional examples of business records are contained in the exhibits chapter, Sec. 10.6.

Example:

This is a personal injury case in which plaintiff was injured in a head-on collision with defendant. Plaintiff seeks to introduce in evidence an accident report prepared by a police officer and lists the report as an exhibit in its pretrial memorandum. The police report includes the following notations: (1) "Defendant said he was going about 45 mph and didn't realize that the roadway was icy"; (2) "Bystander said defendant was going at least 60 mph." Defendant objects to admission of the report. At a pretrial hearing, the following happens:

Defendant: Your honor, we have no objection to the report as a whole. It's obviously both a business and a public record. However, we object to the statements of the defendant and the bystander. The statements of such persons, recorded in the report, are double hearsay. The business record exception applies only to the report itself, not to the statements of other persons contained in the report. This is inadmissible and must be deleted.

Plaintiff: The statement of the defendant contained in the report is an admission by a party-opponent and is admissible, since the plaintiff is offering the report. The statement of the bystander is double hearsay, and we agree that no hearsay exception applies. We will delete the bystander's statement in the copy of the record we will introduce at trial.

Judge: I agree with the plaintiff that the defendant's statement is a party admission, which will be admissible if a proper foundation for the report is established at trial. The bystander's statement will be deleted from the report.

§7.11.   *Public records (FRE 803(8)-803(17))*[11]

1.   Law

Rule 803.   Exceptions to the Rule Against Hearsay— Regardless of Whether the Declarant Is Available as a Witness

The following are not excluded by the rule against hearsay, regardless of whether the declarant is available as a witness:

(8) *Public Records.* A record or statement of a public office if:

(A) it sets out:

(i) the office's activities;

(ii) a matter observed while under a legal duty to report, but not including, in a criminal case, a matter observed by law-enforcement personnel; or

(iii) in a civil case or against the government in a criminal case, factual findings from a legally authorized investigation; and

(B) neither the source of information nor other circumstances indicate a lack of trustworthiness.

(10) Absence of a Public Record. Testimony — or a certification under Rule 902 — that a diligent search failed to disclose a public record or statement if:

(A) the testimony or certification is admitted to prove that:

(i) the record or statement does not exist; or

(ii) a matter did not occur or exist, if a public office regularly kept a record or statement for a matter of that kind; and

(B) in a criminal case, a prosecutor who intends to offer a certification provides written notice of that intent at least 14 days before trial, and the defendant does not object in writing within 7 days of receiving notice — unless the court sets a different time for the notice or the objection.

This hearsay exception is based on the assumption that a public official will perform his duty properly, but probably will not remember details of the matters he has recorded. Part of the official's duty is to prepare accurate reports. In addition to the presumed reliability of official reports, the need to bring a public official into court to testify about matters he has recorded is avoided.

This exception resembles FRE 803(6), but there are important differences. FRE 803(8) does not require that the document be made and kept in the course of a regularly conducted activity, nor does it require that a report be made at or near the time of the event it records. The rule does retain the requirement that either the maker of the record or the source of the information speak from personal knowledge of the matter. This rule, like FRE 803(6), allows the opponent to oppose the record on the grounds that its sources of information or other circumstances indicate a lack of trustworthiness. Here, too, the various layers of information and recording should be examined under FRE 805.

---

11. McCormick §§295-300; Weinstein §901(b)(7); Mueller & Kirkpatrick §§8.49-8.59; Wigmore §§665, 1630-1684.

For example, a bystander's account of an auto accident to a police officer may be accurately reported by the officer, but the report containing the bystander's account will not be admissible in the civil case unless (1) the bystander's statement comes within an FRE 803 or 804 hearsay exception (such as excited utterance or statement against interest); (2) the bystander's statement is not being offered for its truth and therefore is not hearsay (such as notice to the officer); or (3) the bystander's statement is offered for its truth, but comes within one of the non-hearsay provisions of FRE 801(d)(2) (such as party admission).

The rule addresses three types of public information. First, FRE 803(8)(A)(i) covers information about the "office's activities." The activities reflected on the record must be reasonably necessary for the performance of the agency's duties, and the record must not be prepared for specific litigation. The requirement that the record be made by persons having a duty to report and record accurately applies to this exception.

For example, official reports containing census data fall within this part. So do deportation warrants, documents showing ownership of vehicles, records of hunting licenses issued, and agency records of serial numbers of weapons. In these situations, FRE 803(8)(A) satisfies the rule against hearsay. Under FRE 902, a certified copy of the report is self-authenticating, obviating the need to produce a foundation witness at trial.

Second, FRE 803(8)(A)(ii) covers "matters observed while under a legal duty to report." Here, as in FRE 803(6), where the person providing the information has no official duty to report, the record or report will not be admitted for its truth unless the person's statement comes within a hearsay exception under FRE 803 or 804 or is exempted from the rule against hearsay by FRE 801(d)(2).

FRE 803(8) creates a hearsay exception for records or statements of a public office. However, it contains some important exclusions. Subsection (A)(ii) refers to admissibility of matters observed while under a legal duty to report, but it expressly excludes in a criminal case "a matter observed by law enforcement personnel." The literal words of the exclusion appear to apply no matter who offers the record, prosecution or defense. However, some courts have held it was not Congress's intent to exclude defense use of the record.

Another question raised by the rule is whether the subsection (A)(ii) exclusion applies to prosecution use of all official reports containing "a matter observed by law enforcement personnel." Courts refuse to apply the exclusion to non-adversarial records prepared for ministerial or routine administrative purposes. These courts hold the subsection (A)(ii) exclusion does not apply to such matters as deportation warrants, a calibration report of a Breathalyzer maintenance operator, a computer printout listing identification numbers of stolen vehicles, a list of license numbers on vehicles crossing the border from Mexico, and a list of firearm serial numbers.

Third, FRE 803(8)(A)(iii) provides for admissibility of "factual findings from a legally authorized investigation." These factual findings are admissible in civil proceedings and against the government in criminal cases, but not against the defendant in criminal cases. Again, Sixth Amendment concerns explain the prohibition on the prosecution's use of otherwise admissible factual findings in criminal cases.

In *Chandler v. Roudebush*, 425 U.S. 840 (1976), the Supreme Court held that administrative adjudicatory findings were admissible in a later civil suit involving the same substantive matters, although that case was not analyzed under FRE 803(8). Non-adjudicatory administrative findings have received mixed receptions in the courts, the outcome depending on the trustworthiness of the underlying information.

The term "factual findings" includes statements in the form of conclusions or opinions. In *Beech Aircraft Corp. v. Rainey*, 488 U.S. 153 (1988), the Supreme Court held that a naval investigative report, concluding that pilot error was the most probable cause of an airplane crash, qualified as an admissible factual finding.

This hearsay exception, then, includes so-called evaluative reports. But admissibility is not automatic. Courts will inquire into such factors as (1) the timeliness of the investigation, (2) the investigator's skill and experience, (3) whether a hearing was held, and (4) possible bias when reports are prepared with a view to possible litigation. The conclusions or opinions must be based on a competent factual investigation and must satisfy the rule's trustworthiness requirement.

Beech Aircraft has no effect on the various federal statutes that regulate the admissibility of evaluative reports. The Supreme Court in that case declined to express an opinion on whether legal conclusions contained in an official report are admissible under FRE 803(8).

FRE 803(8)(A)(ii) expressly prohibits the prosecutor's use of official reports against defendants only for "a matter observed by law enforcement personnel" in criminal cases, but nothing in FRE 803(8) addresses the possible use of these reports under some other rule.

For example, can a police report be admitted against a criminal defendant if it qualifies as a business record under FRE 803(6)? Most courts say it cannot. These courts hold that Congress intended to bar the use of law enforcement reports under FRE 803(6) as well, since the same reliability defects and confrontation problems exist. Backdoor admission under that rule has been generally disapproved.

Can a police report be admitted against a criminal defendant if it qualifies as a recorded recollection under FRE 803(5)? The Confrontation Clause is not violated, since the maker of the report is the witness in court and is subject to cross-examination. For example, a court admitted an IRS agent's report of a telephone conversation with the defendant as recorded recollection because the agent was on the stand subject to cross-examination. In that case, said the court, the report was not being used as a substitute for the officer's testimony.

A similar issue can arise in connection with FRE 803(9). That rule establishes a hearsay exception for "a record of a birth, death, or marriage, if reported to a public office in accordance with a legal duty."

FRE 803(9), like FRE 803(6), does not contain an express bar to the use of the record against a criminal defendant. For example, the rule generally would allow admission of a cause of death in a death certificate. Whether it would be admissible against a criminal defendant is unclear, although the congressional intent expressed in FRE 803(8) would seem to bar admission.

The absence of a public record or entry can be admissible evidence. FRE 803(10) provides: "Testimony—or a certification under Rule 902—that a diligent search failed to disclose a public record or statement if the testimony or certification is admitted to prove that: (A) the record or statement does not exist; or (B) a matter did not occur or exist, if a public office regularly kept a record or statement for a matter of that kind."

This rule does not contain an exclusion for offers against criminal defendants. Nor do the cases read in such an exclusion. A diligent search of public records to reliably establish the non-existence of a record is all that is required.

FRE 803 contains several other categories of records that are hearsay exceptions. These categories, listed below, are self-explanatory and generate little litigation.

FRE 803(9) — Records of vital statistics
FRE 803(11) — Records of religious organizations
FRE 803(12) — Marriage, baptismal, and similar certificates
FRE 803(13) — Family records
FRE 803(14) — Records of documents affecting an interest in property
FRE 803(15) — Statements in documents affecting an interest in property
FRE 803(16) — Statements in ancient documents
FRE 803(17) — Market reports, commercial publications
FRE 803(22) — Judgment of previous conviction
FRE 803(23) — Judgment as to personal, family, or general history, or boundaries.

Authentication requirements for many of these document exceptions are set out in FRE 901 and 902.

2. Practice

Public records are routinely admitted in civil trials. For example, motor vehicle department records are commonly introduced in collision cases. In criminal cases, however, problems frequently arise because FRE 803(8)(A) prohibit the prosecution from introducing police reports and other investigative reports and because underlying Sixth Amendment Confrontation Clause concerns exist.

Additional examples of public records are contained in the exhibits chapter, Sec. 10.7.

Example:

This is a drug prosecution. In the prosecution's case-in-chief, the prosecutor plans to introduce a laboratory report containing the results of the analysis of the suspect drugs found in the defendant's possession when he was arrested. Before trial, the defendant moves to bar the report. At a pretrial hearing, the following happens:

Defendant: Your honor, this is our motion to preclude the admission of the lab report. The reason is that the lab analysis was done by the police department's crime lab. All the personnel in the crime lab are police officers. The person who did the actual analysis of the suspect drugs in this case is a sergeant on the police force. Rule 803(8)(A) specifically bars the admission of a report made by police officers and other law enforcement personnel. Even without the rule, admitting the report would violate the Confrontation Clause. It has to stay out.

Judge: Prosecution?

Prosecutor: Sergeant Vitullo will testify during the trial, your honor. There's no Confrontation Clause problem, since the defense can cross-examine him. As far as Rule 803(8) is concerned, that section barring police reports is intended to prevent the reports of beat officers and investigating officers from being admitted in evidence so the officers are required to appear as witnesses at trial. That section is not intended to prevent the admission of routine ministerial reports such as this.

Judge: The motion is granted. The actual report is not admissible under Rule 803(8). The lab chemist who did the analysis, of course, may be called as a witness and testify to his findings.

Commentary: Many jurisdictions create a statutory hearsay exception for certain laboratory reports. Courts sometimes hold that laboratory test reports are not matters observed by law enforcement personnel within the meaning of FRE 803(8)(A)(ii). On the Confrontation Clause issue, the Supreme Court has held that a report certified or sworn to by a laboratory technician cannot serve as a substitute for courtroom testimony by the person who prepared the report.

§7.12. *Recorded recollection (FRE 803(5))*[12]

1. Law

Rule 803. Exceptions to the Rule Against Hearsay— Regardless of Whether the Declarant Is Available as a Witness

The following are not excluded by the rule against hearsay, regardless of whether the declarant is available as a witness:

(5) *Recorded Recollection.* A record that:

(A) is on a matter the witness once knew about but now cannot recall well enough to testify fully and accurately;

(B) was made or adopted by the witness when the matter was fresh in the witness's memory; and

(C) accurately reflects the witness's knowledge.

If admitted, the record may be read into evidence but may be received as an exhibit only if offered by an adverse party.

12. McCormick §§279-283; Weinstein §803(5)[01]-[03]; Mueller & Kirkpatrick §8.43; Wigmore §§734-754, 758-764, 800.

This rule assumes that reliability is inherent in certain writings made or adopted by the declarant. To comply with the rule, the writing must (1) be made or adopted by a declarant who had personal knowledge of the recorded facts, (2) be made or adopted by the declarant at a time when the matter was fresh in his memory, and (3) accurately reflect the declarant's firsthand knowledge.

Oral testimony of the declarant is not excused unless the proponent shows the witness "now cannot recall well enough to testify fully and accurately" about the matter. This does not require a total loss of memory, just enough of a loss to inhibit full and accurate testimony. This requirement has nothing to do with the accuracy of the evidence. The Advisory Committee's Note says the rule was intended to discourage "the use of statements carefully prepared for purposes of litigation under the supervision of attorneys, investigators, or claim adjustors," but the rule does not expressly exclude writings made for the purpose of litigation.

To satisfy the insufficient recollection requirement, the witness may testify that he no longer fully remembers the event, but that he remembers making an accurate record of it. The usual procedure is to show the writing to the witness once he has testified to a failure of memory about the event it describes. If the writing does not refresh the witness's memory about the event, the proponent may proceed to authenticate the writing.

If the witness has no memory of the event or of the making of the record, he may testify he routinely makes accurate records of this kind. For example, a police officer testifies he does not remember writing a memorandum about the plaintiff's fall, but he routinely writes such memoranda describing the condition of accident scenes. That is, it is his habit or practice to record these matters accurately. This part of the rule is satisfied when a witness testifies he would not have made or signed the writing unless he believed it to be true and accurate at the time.

The recorded recollection exception applies to any memorandum or record, including notes, transcripts, memos, and inventory lists. The original documents rule in FRE 1002 applies to a recorded recollection because the content of the writing is being proved.

At common law, this exception was referred to as "past recollection recorded." The common law requirement that the writing be made at or near the time of the event was dropped in FRE 803(5). Instead, it has to be made or adopted "when the matter was fresh in the witness' memory."

Whether the writing was made or adopted "when the matter was fresh in the witness' memory" will depend on the facts of the individual case. The test is not strict. For example, FRE 803(5) has been read to admit a witness's grand jury testimony concerning conversations with the accused where the testimony was given at least 10 months after the conversations. Such cases represent the outer limits of the rule and are not typical. Of course, if the declarant is subject to cross-examination, *Crawford v. Washington* holds there will be no Confrontation Clause barrier to admissibility. Where memory lapse is probable, reliability dissipates. Whether the writing was made "when the matter was fresh in the witness' memory" is for the trial judge to determine under FRE 104(a).

The rule does not require that the writing be made by the witness who observed the events recorded. The declarant could have adopted a writing made by another person. That is, where a person perceives an event and reports it to another person, who then records the statement, the writing can qualify as an FRE 803(5) hearsay exception. The declarant must testify that he accurately reported the event to the maker of the writing and that the writing accurately reflects what he said. The matter must have been fresh in the declarant's memory at the time he adopted the writing. The writing should not be admitted if the declarant disputes its accuracy, even though the maker of the writing says it is accurate.

Because a recorded recollection is considered to be a substitute for the declarant's oral testimony, the writing itself is not admitted as an exhibit and does not go to the jury unless an adverse party offers it. Otherwise, the proof is complete once the contents of the writing are read to the jury. Another reason for not giving the writing to the jury is the concern that it might carry more weight than it deserves.

2. Practice

Recorded recollection is an infrequently used hearsay exception. The easier exceptions are business records and public records. Recorded recollection is used only when the writing cannot be qualified as a business or public record and the witness on the stand has a partial or complete memory loss.

Example:

This is a wrongful termination case. Plaintiff claims he was wrongfully fired from his job in the supply room. Defendant claims plaintiff was fired for stealing inventory. To prove there was inventory loss, defendant calls another employee at trial. The following then happens:

Q. (By defendant's lawyer) Ms. Johnson, did you conduct an inventory of the supply room?
A. Yes, I did.
Q. Is that part of your regular work?
A. No. I'm the office manager. My boss told me to do the inventory.
Q. Had you ever done an inventory of the supply room before?
A. No, that was the only time I've ever done one.
Q. Does your business regularly do an inventory of the supply room?
A. No.
Q. Ms. Johnson, what was in the supply room the day you did the inventory?
A. Gosh, I couldn't tell you from memory. There were all sorts of supplies.
[Lawyer has exhibit marked, shows it to opposing counsel, and asks permission to approach the witness.]
Q. I'm showing you what's been marked as Defendant's Exhibit No. 4. Are you familiar with it?
A. Sure, it's the inventory list I made of the supply room.
Q. Does that list refresh your memory about what was in the supply room?
A. Not really. I can remember that there were reams of paper, pens, staplers, and so on, but I can't remember any of the details, such as how much of each item was there.

Q. Ms. Johnson, when did you make the list?

A. I wrote it out as I was doing it and then immediately typed it. The typed list is that exhibit.

Q. Was it accurate when you made it?

A. Oh, yes. I was very careful when I made it.

Q. Your honor, we offer in evidence the contents of Defendant's Exhibit No. 4 and ask permission to have the witness read the list to the jury.

Defendant: Objection. It hasn't been properly qualified as a business record.

Judge: Overruled. The list is a recorded recollection. The witness may read it to the jury.

Commentary: The list is only read to the jury. The opponent has the option to have the exhibit actually admitted as an exhibit.

§7.13.   *Reputation evidence (FRE 803(19)-803(21))*[13]

1.   Law

Rule 803.   Exceptions to the Rule Against Hearsay—
Regardless of Whether the Declarant Is Available as a Witness

The following are not excluded by the rule against hearsay, regardless of whether the declarant is available as a witness:

(21) *Reputation Concerning Character.* A reputation among a person's associates or in the community concerning the person's character.

A person's reputation consists of the esteem in which that person is held by others in the community. When reputation evidence is offered for its truth, which is almost always the case, the evidence is hearsay. The Federal Rules of Evidence provide three specific exceptions to the rule against hearsay when reputation evidence is offered.

FRE 803(21) permits introducing "A reputation among a person's associates or in the community concerning the person's character." This is the most frequently used reputation rule, and there are two proper uses of such evidence.

First, character evidence in reputation form can sometimes be used as direct evidence. FRE 405 permits introducing character evidence in reputation form in both civil and criminal cases, where character is an essential element in the case. FRE 404(a) and 405(a) also permit introducing character evidence in reputation form as circumstantial proof of conduct in criminal cases. These uses of character evidence are discussed in Sec. 5.3. Second, FRE 608(a) permits introducing character evidence in reputation form to attack the truthfulness of a testifying witness or to rebut such an attack. This use of character evidence is discussed in Sec. 12.4.

13. McCormick §249; Weinstein §803(21)[01]-[03]; Mueller & Kirkpatrick §8.61; Wigmore §§1580-1626.

A person's reputation for a relevant character trait, such as peacefulness, honesty, or truthfulness, is collective hearsay because such evidence is nothing more than a summary of other people's hearsay statements about the person whose character is in issue. Therefore, the reputation witness must be properly qualified before he can testify about the other person's character. The reputation witness must testify that he has heard people in the community talk about the kind of person the other person is. The community includes the place of work as well as the place of residence.

The testimony also must be directed to the proper time frame. Under FRE 404 and 405, the relevant time frame is when the conduct involved in the case occurred. Under FRE 608, the relevant time is the time of trial.

FRE 803(19) provides: "Reputation Concerning Personal or Family History. A reputation among a person's family by blood, adoption, or marriage — or among a person's associates or in the community — concerning the person's birth, adoption, legitimacy, ancestry, marriage, divorce, death, relationship by blood, adoption, or marriage, or similar facts of personal or family history."

This rule recognizes that it may be difficult to prove personal and family history without resorting to hearsay knowledge of such matters, and that such knowledge, held by other family members, is likely to be reliable.

The witness called to testify to a reputation listed in FRE 803(19) must be from that person's family, associates, or community and must be familiar with that reputation. Trustworthiness exists because members of the particular community with personal knowledge are likely to have discussed that reputation. The rule has been used to admit testimony by a victim in a statutory rape case that she was of a certain age, to prove that a witness's son had committed suicide, and to prove that two people were married to each other. The rule does not state that the reputation had to have been discussed before the controversy on which the case is based arose.

FRE 803(20) provides: "Reputation Concerning Boundaries or General History. A reputation in a community — arising before the controversy — concerning boundaries of land in the community or customs that affect the land, or concerning general historical events important to that community, state, or nation."

This rule also recognizes that it may be difficult to prove property boundaries and matters of general history without resorting to hearsay knowledge of such matters and that such knowledge is likely to be reliable.

This exception applies only to reputation about property boundaries and general history discussed before the controversy on which the case is based arose. That does not mean that the reputation evidence has to be ancient. However, the few courts that have considered this exception have been reluctant to admit reputation evidence of recent vintage.

2. Practice

The principal issues in reputation evidence, which arise most frequently under FRE 803(21), involve whether a proper foundation has been established and whether the proper character trait has been raised. These are discussed, and additional examples given, in Sec. 5.3 and 12.4.

Example:

The following testimony is offered by the defense in a perjury case against Sam Smith:

Q. (By defendant's lawyer) Ms. Johnson, have you heard the reputation of Sam Smith in this community for truthfulness?
A. Yes.
Q. How have you learned of his reputation?
A. Mr. Smith has lived on my block for the last 10 years. I've talked to lots of neighbors, and heard them talk, over the years about the kind of person he is.
Q. Have they talked about whether he's a truthful person?
A. Many times.
Q. Ms. Johnson, what is the reputation of Sam Smith in this community for truthfulness as of December 1, 2015 [the date of the alleged perjury]?
Prosecutor: Objection, your honor. May we be heard at the bench?
Judge: Come forward. [Lawyers come to the bench.]
Prosecutor: The defendant hasn't testified. His credibility is not yet in issue. They can't bootstrap his credibility before he takes the stand.
Defendant: This is a perjury prosecution. The defendant's character for truthfulness is a pertinent character trait under Rule 404(a), whether or not the defendant ever testifies.
Judge: That's right. Objection is overruled. (To the witness) Ms. Johnson, you may answer the question.
A. His reputation is excellent. Mr. Smith is known as a truthful person.

Commentary: Confusing character traits under FRE 404 and 405 with character for truthfulness under FRE 608 is common.

§7.14. *Treatises (FRE 803(18))*[14]

1. Law

Rule 803. Exceptions to the Rule Against Hearsay — Regardless of Whether the Declarant Is Available as a Witness

> The following are not excluded by the rule against hearsay, regardless of whether the declarant is available as a witness:
> **(18)** *Statements in Learned Treatises, Periodicals, or Pamphlets.* A statement contained in a treatise, periodical, or pamphlet if:
> **(A)** the statement is called to the attention of an expert witness on cross-examination or relied on by the expert on direct examination; and

---

14. McCormick §321; Weinstein §803(18)[01]-[04]; Mueller & Kirkpatrick §8.60; Wigmore §§1690-1710.

> **(B)** the publication is established as a reliable authority by the expert's admission or testimony, by another expert's testimony, or by judicial notice.
>
> If admitted, the statement may be read into evidence but not received as an exhibit.

In both civil and criminal trials, the use of expert witnesses is commonplace. When wisely and carefully used, literature in an expert's field can be an effective method for supporting the witness's testimony on direct examination or attacking it on cross. When admitted, the literature is substantive evidence. In effect, it becomes another expert witness.

Treaties and other authoritative publications may be used during both the direct and the cross-examinations of expert witnesses. FRE 803(18) permits such use if the treatise was "relied on by the expert on direct examination" or was "called to the attention of an expert witness on cross-examination."

The most common use of treaties is on cross-examination, where the examiner usually attempts to show the witness's testimony is not consistent with something in the literature in the field. The rule does not expressly require that the treatise contradict the witness's testimony, simply that it be "called to the attention" of the expert. Judges differ on whether a treatise can be used on cross-examination for purposes other than impeachment. There is no requirement in the rule that the witness rely on or even know of the existence of the treatise.

Less common is the use of a treatise on direct examination. Failure to use a treatise on direct examination often represents a missed opportunity to corroborate the expert witness's testimony with the writing of another expert in the field. The direct examiner simply has to establish the authoritative nature of the treatise, its relevance to a fact of consequence in the case, and the witness's reliance on it when reaching his opinions or conclusions. It may then be offered and, if accepted, read to the jury.

When a treatise is used on direct examination, judges are wary about experts who rush to the library in order to form and support their opinions for specific litigation. The spirit of the rule seems to require that the literature be something the expert ordinary relies on in his professional life.

There are three ways to establish the reliability of a treatise, periodical, or pamphlet, a burden resting with the party offering it: (1) The witness on the stand recognizes the treatise as authoritative or a reliable authority in the field, whether or not he relies on it or agrees with it; (2) the judge takes judicial notice of the authoritative or reliable nature of the treatise under FRE 201, a rare occurrence; or (3) a witness already called, or to be called later, by the proponent of the evidence testifies it is a reliable authority in the field. Whether the treatise has been established as a reliable authority is for the judge to decide under FRE 104(a).

The rule expressly applies to any "statement contained in a treatise, periodical, or pamphlet if: (B) the publication is established as a reliable authority . . ." However, it also has been held to apply to safety codes and standards when they are prepared by organizations formed for the purpose of promoting safety in a particular field. While the rule is phrased in terms of writings, there seems to be no good reason why it does not encompass a visual presentation, such as a training videotape for physicians used to impeach an expert witness. One court of appeals has so held.

This exception contains a high degree of accuracy when its terms are fulfilled. The treatise, periodical, or pamphlet must have been written primarily by professionals in the field for fellow professionals. It must have been subject to scrutiny and exposure for inaccuracy by some kind of peer review process, with the reputation of the writer at stake. It is "reliable" for purposes of the rule when it is recognized as authoritative in the relevant discipline. The literature and its author, not just the journal they appear in, must be established as authoritative.

If the use of a treatise is permitted under the rule, statements from the treatise "may be read into evidence but may not be received as exhibits." An attorney cannot simply read from a publication, no matter how authoritative it is. The publication may be used only when examining an expert witness, on direct or cross. The expert must be in a position to assist the fact finder in understanding the weight, if any, to be given the literature. This means that the pertinent portions of the treatise that either support the expert on direct or contradict the expert on cross are read to the jury, but the treatise itself is not admitted as an exhibit.

Once admitted, the treatise itself does not go to the jury, although some trial judges will allow the lawyers to use admitted portions of a publication as demonstrative exhibits during the expert's examination and during final argument. This rule was implemented out of concern that the treatise would be overvalued by jurors if they had the opportunity to read and reread it during their deliberations. Whether the publication is actually received as an exhibit is unclear, but is relatively unimportant, since it will not go to the jury room in any event.

2.   Practice

The principal issue with treatises involves whether the proper procedure is used. This procedure is discussed, and additional examples are given, in Sec. 12.4.

Example:

This is a medical malpractice case. A plaintiff's doctor is testifying on direct when the following happens:

Q. (By plaintiff's lawyer) Dr. Smith, on what do you base your opinion that the obstetrician on duty that night should have used positive pressure ventilation after the infant showed signs of respiratory problems?

A. Several things. I relied on the obstetrician's hospital notes, the nurse's notes, my medical training and experience, and an obstetrics treatise.

Q. Which treatise did you rely on in reaching your opinion?

A. Saunders on Obstetrics.

Q. Is that a reliable authority on the medical treatment of infants during and after delivery?

A. Certainly. It's probably the most used text on the subject in medical schools today.

[Lawyer has exhibit marked, shows it to opposing counsel, and asks permission to approach the witness.]

Q. I'm showing you a copy of Saunders on Obstetrics, marked Plaintiff's Exhibit No. 8. Is that the treatise you relied on?

A. Yes.

Q. Do you ordinarily rely on this treatise to help you reach medical judgments in your practice?

A. I use it on a regular basis.

Q. Dr. Smith, please read the section of the treatise you relied on, and tell us what page you're reading from.

Defendant: Objection. They're trying to get before the jury a part of a treatise. This isn't really impeachment, and it's improper procedure.

Plaintiff: The doctor relied on the treatise, your honor. Rule 803(18) expressly allows this on direct examination.

Judge: The objection is overruled. The doctor may read those statements from the treatise he relied on in reaching his opinions.

Commentary: While lawyers rarely use treatises during direct examination of experts, this is a powerful trial technique expressly permitted by FRE 803(18), subject to the FRE 403 analysis when that objection is made.

§7.15. *Residual or catchall exception (FRE 807)*[15]

1. Law

Rule 807. Residual Exception

(a) **In General.** Under the following circumstances, a hearsay statement is not excluded by the rule against hearsay even if the statement is not specifically covered by a hearsay exception in Rule 803 or 804:

(1) the statement has equivalent circumstantial guarantees of trustworthiness;

(2) it is offered as evidence of a material fact;

(3) it is more probative on the point for which it is offered than any other evidence that the proponent can obtain through reasonable efforts; and

(4) admitting it will best serve the purposes of these rules and the interests of justice.

(b) **Notice.** The statement is admissible only if, before the trial or hearing, the proponent gives an adverse party reasonable notice of the intent to offer the statement and its particulars, including the declarant's name and address, so that the party has a fair opportunity to meet it.

In 1997 the contents of FRE 803(24) and FRE 804(b)(5) were combined and transferred to a new FRE 807. No change in meaning was intended. The

15. McCormick §324; Weinstein §§803(24)[01]-[03], 804(b)(5)[01]-[05]; Mueller & Kirkpatrick §§8.81-8.83.

Advisory Committee statement of purpose for the residual exception bears repeating:

> The preceding 23 exceptions of Rule 803 and the first [four] exceptions to Rule 804(b), infra, are designed to take full advantage of the accumulated wisdom and experience of the past in dealing with hearsay. It would, however, be presumptuous to assume that all possible desirable exceptions to the hearsay rule have been catalogued and to pass the hearsay rule to oncoming generations as a closed system, Exception (24) and its companion provision in Rule 804(b)[(5)] are accordingly included. They do not contemplate unfettered exercise of judicial discretion, but they do provide for treating new and presently unanticipated situations which demonstrate a trustworthiness within the spirit of the specifically stated exceptions. Within this framework, room is left for growth and development of the law of evidence in the hearsay area, consistently with the broad purposes expressed in Rule 102.

When exercising the broad discretion granted by reviewing courts in this area, judges use FRE 104(a) to determine whether the requirements of the residual rule have been satisfied. Reversible error in this area is rare. Despite congressional intention, expressed in the Senate Judiciary Committee Report, that the residual exceptions "will be used very rarely, and only in exceptional circumstances," offers of evidence under these rules have become commonplace. The exceptions continue to expand, although *Crawford v. Washington* will limit the use of FRE 807 exceptions in criminal cases. Clearly, grand jury testimony and station house statements of unavailable declarants no longer come within the rule in criminal cases.

The residual exception has been applied to such matters as prior inconsistent statements of a witness that lack the oath requirement of FRE 801(d)(1)(A), prior consistent statements that do not fit within FRE 801(d)(1)(B), former testimony where the lack of opportunity and motive to cross-examine keeps it outside FRE 804(b)(1), and records that are not quite business or public. An abused child's statement identifying the abuser, but not qualifying as an excited utterance (FRE 803(2)) or a medical treatment statement (FRE 803(4)), often has been admitted under the residual exception where it contains particularized guarantees of trustworthiness—such as spontaneity, consistency, use of terminology unexpected of a child of that age, and lack of motive to fabricate. But *Crawford v. Washington* would bar such statements if they are deemed testimonial and there has been no opportunity to cross-examine the unavailable declarant.

A few courts have held hearsay that nearly misses being a specific FRE 803 or FRE 804 exception cannot qualify as a residual exception. Most courts reject the "near miss" analysis. It is doubtful that the question arises very often in the trial courts.

It really does not matter whether the call is close or clear when hearsay is rejected under a specific exception in the rules. The offered hearsay must then be analyzed according to the terms of the residual exception.

For example, in one case, the FBI asked a lens-maker to print out an analysis of eyeglass lenses to tie the glasses to the defendant. The printout was not a business record under FRE 803(6) because it was made specifically in anticipation of litigation. It was not an official record under FRE 803(8) because it was made by a private party. Yet because the testing procedure was reliable and the results probative, the printout was admitted under FRE 803(24), now FRE 807.

Where the Confrontation Clause of the Sixth Amendment is not implicated, the residual hearsay analysis is unchanged. To be admissible under the residual hearsay exception, a statement must satisfy five criteria.

a.   Trustworthiness

The statement must have circumstantial and particularized guarantees of trustworthiness that are equivalent to those of the specific exceptions in FRE 803 and 804. The focus of inquiry is on the declarant's believability and the circumstances that exist at the time the statement is made. Judges look for other evidence at trial that corroborates the statement.

The cases have created a list of factors to be analyzed when determining trustworthiness of a statement for residual exception purposes. These are in addition to other corroborating circumstances in the case. No single factor is controlling. While not exclusive or exhaustive, the list includes the following:

1. Was the statement made under oath? A statement under oath to a law enforcement officer and sworn testimony before a grand jury indicate trustworthiness.
2. Did the declarant speak from personal knowledge? If not, the statement bears little or no trustworthiness.
3. Who is the declarant? What are his age, education, and experience? Does he ordinarily use the words contained in the statement?
4. What was the declarant's mental state? Was he under duress or some kind of pressure to make the statement? Did he have a motive to fabricate? Did he have a bias or prejudice against the person named in the statement? If the declarant was trying to gain favor or leniency, the statement's value is diminished. On the other hand, if the declarant had nothing to lose, or if he knew the truth of what he said would be investigated at his peril, trustworthiness is enhanced. Voluntary statements, especially if in the declarant's own handwriting, are thought to reflect trustworthiness. Voluntary grand jury testimony, not given under a grant of immunity or under law enforcement pressure, contains circumstantial guarantees of trustworthiness. A grant of immunity would weaken trustworthiness.
5. How was the interview conducted? Spontaneous statements are more credible. Statements in response to leading or suggestive questions lack trustworthiness. Who asked the questions? Is that person to be trusted?
6. What are the circumstances of the making of the statement? Who was there? Why were they there? The presence of the defendant's lawyer or the defendant himself adds to trustworthiness. If the declarant's lawyer elicited the statement with questions, trustworthiness is decreased. How long after the event was the statement made? The longer the time, the less trustworthy, since there is more time and opportunity to fabricate.

7. How was the statement recorded, and what were the motives of the person reporting the statement? Trustworthiness is enhanced when there is no question that the statement was made, such as when a court reporter transcript or a videotaped statement is involved.
8. Did the declarant ever recant or reaffirm his statement?
9. What is the character of the declarant for truthfulness and honesty?
10. Why is the declarant unavailable? Trustworthiness is compromised if the proponent had something to do with the declarant's unavailability.

b.   Necessity

The hearsay statement must be more probative on the point for which it is being offered than any other evidence the proponent can procure through reasonable efforts. If the declarant is available to testify, or if some other available witness can testify to the same thing, the necessity requirement is not satisfied. The statement is not "probative" if it is not clearly based on the declarant's personal knowledge. Trial judges often bar otherwise admissible residual exception evidence if it is cumulative or merely adds detail. Whether the proponent has made "reasonable efforts" to procure other evidence will depend on the circumstances of each case.

c.   Material fact

FRE 401 and 402 provide that all admissible evidence must bear on a fact of consequence. Whether the materiality requirement in the catchall exceptions means something more is not clear. Some judges hold that the statement must relate to an issue of substantial importance. Clearly it should not concern trivial or collateral matters.

d.   Satisfy general purpose of Rules and interests of justice

This requirement is a restatement of the statutory construction rule contained in FRE 102.

e.   Notice

The notice requirement is intended to avoid unfair surprise. There is no specific pretrial time requirement, but ambush advocacy is not permitted by the rule. The question is whether the opposing party has a fair opportunity to meet the evidence. Most trial judges take a flexible, rather than a strict, approach to this requirement. They will look to whether the proponent was without fault in failing to give notice. The proponent must be genuinely surprised by the need to offer the hearsay statement because sometimes the need for the statement arises during trial or just before it. Another factor to consider is whether the opposing party was aware of the proposed evidence before trial.

One way judges avoid prejudice to the opposing party is to offer additional time to prepare to meet the evidence if the matter comes up shortly before trial begins. The flexible approach to the notice requirement seems to apply to both criminal and civil trials.

The residual exception has been used to admit a wide variety of hearsay statements that do not fit any other category. Some of the statements are fairly routine; their reliability is not open to strong argument. These include a postmark to prove the date and place of mailing, foreign travel documents, prior inconsistent and consistent statements where the declarant was available for cross-examination, safety codes, government firearm forms, reliably conducted polls and surveys, and single-occasion records made by a business.

A specific prohibition against a certain kind of evidence in a specific hearsay exception is usually taken to bar admissibility under the residual exception. For example, FRE 803(8)(A) specifically bars the use of police reports against defendants in criminal cases. That exclusion usually is taken to mean the reports cannot be admitted against those defendants under any other rule, including the residual exception, although there are a few reported cases where official technical or laboratory reports were admitted under a residual exception.

Because of the trial judge's wide discretion in this area, the trial courtroom becomes the decisive arena for residual exception disputes. Nowhere else in the Rules does the question of trustworthiness play so direct and crucial a role.

2. Practice

Example:

This is a patent infringement case in which the plaintiff, a mineral water seller, sues the defendant, another mineral water seller, for using a bottle shape and label design that confused the public into believing that the defendant's product came from the plaintiff. The plaintiff lists a consumer survey as a trial exhibit on its pretrial statement. At a pretrial hearing to resolve issues, the following happens:

Judge: I see that the plaintiff intends to introduce a consumer survey in the trial, and the defendant objects on hearsay and foundation grounds. Is that still the case?

Plaintiff: Yes.

Defendant: Yes.

Judge: I take it there is no issue of notice?

Defendant: No, your honor. We've received notice through the pretrial statement, and the plaintiff has given us a copy of the survey. However, we have not received the underlying documentation.

Judge: Very well. Here's what we'll do. Just before the trial begins, we'll have a hearing on admissibility. The plaintiff will provide the defendant with all the underlying documentation for the survey within two weeks of today. That documentation will include the reports of any experts and other witnesses that the plaintiff will call as foundation witnesses during the hearing. The defense, of course, may also call witnesses at the hearing and will provide the plaintiff with any reports of experts or other witnesses the defense will call during the hearing. These reports are to be served on the plaintiff within two weeks after the plaintiff serves its documentation on the defendant. After hearing all the evidence, I will rule whether the survey was designed, administered, and analyzed in such a manner as to make it admissible under Rule 807.

§7.16.   Hearsay within hearsay (FRE 805)[16]

1. Law

Rule 805.   Hearsay Within Hearsay

Hearsay within hearsay is not excluded by the rule against hearsay if each part of the combined statements conforms with an exception to the rule.

This rule governs the admissibility of what is commonly called "hearsay within hearsay" or "double hearsay." Under FRE 805, whenever evidence that is hearsay within hearsay is offered in evidence, each level of hearsay must be qualified with a hearsay exception before the evidence will be admissible. For example, consider a police report of an accident scene that contains a bystander's comment: "That car ran right through the red light." The police report is hearsay, but fits a hearsay exception, since it qualifies as a public record under FRE 803(8). The bystander's comment, contained in the police report, is also hearsay. Unless the comment qualifies as a hearsay exception, such as an excited utterance under FRE 803(2), it is not admissible. Even though the police report is admissible, the bystander's comment contained in the report is not admissible unless it qualifies as a hearsay exception. If it does not, the bystander's comment must be deleted from the report before the report can be admitted in evidence. If it does, the entire report, including the bystander's comment, is admitted in evidence.

2. Practice

Hearsay within hearsay issues often arise with business and public records. Whenever records contain the statements of, or information derived from, a person who is not an employee of the business having a business duty to report accurately, that statement or information must be analyzed under FRE 805. It will not be admissible unless the source of the information is someone whose statement fits within a hearsay exception or whose statement is not hearsay at all.

Additional discussion and examples of hearsay within hearsay are contained in this chapter (in the business and public records sections) and in the exhibits chapter, Sec. 10.6 and 10.7.

---

16. McCormick §324.1; Weinstein §805[01]-[02]; Mueller & Kirkpatrick §8.79.

Example:

This is a contract case. Plaintiff lists a Memorandum of Meeting record on its list of exhibits. Before trial, the defendant moves to bar the admission of the record at trial. At the hearing, the following happens:

Defendant: Your honor, we object to the plaintiff's Memorandum of Meeting, which it plans to introduce at trial. That memorandum, which your honor has a copy of, records a meeting between the plaintiff and the defendant at the defendant's office. We have no objection to the memorandum itself, since it appears to be a business record. However, the memorandum contains the following notation: "Mr. Weiss stated that the delay in shipping the goods was his fault, but that it wouldn't happen again in the future." That notation is the statement of someone not an employee of the plaintiff, and the comment is clearly self-serving. It must be deleted from the memorandum before the memorandum can be admitted.

Plaintiff: The statement of Mr. Weiss is a statement by an agent of the defendant. It's contained in the plaintiff's Memorandum of Meeting. The memorandum qualifies as a business record under FRE 803(6), and the statement of Mr. Weiss qualifies as an admission of the party-opponent, since the plaintiff is offering the memorandum.

Judge: I agree. The entire report is admissible.

§7.17. *Attacking and supporting credibility of declarant (FRE 806)*[17]

1. Law

Rule 806. Attacking and Supporting the Declarant's Credibility

When a hearsay statement—or a statement described in Rule 801(d)(2)(C), (D), or (E) — has been admitted in evidence, the declarant's credibility may be attacked, and then supported, by any evidence that would be admissible for those purposes if the declarant had testified as a witness. The court may admit evidence of the declarant's inconsistent statement or conduct, regardless of when it occurred or whether the declarant had an opportunity to explain or deny it. If the party against whom the statement was admitted calls the declarant as a witness, the party may examine the declarant on the statement as if on cross-examination.

This rule recognizes that when hearsay is admitted at trial through a hearsay exception, the fact finder usually must assess the credibility of two persons: the

---

17. Wigmore §§875-881; Weinstein §806[01]-[03]; McCormick §§308, 324.2; Mueller & Kirkpatrick §8.80.

witness in court and the out-of-court declarant. The witness in court can be cross-examined, so the fact finder can directly assess his credibility. The out-of-court declarant usually does not appear in court, so the fact finder has little information from which to assess the declarant's credibility. The rule also recognizes that the opponent is disadvantaged because the opponent cannot cross-examine the out-of-court declarant during the trial.

FRE 806 attempts to remedy this situation by allowing the credibility of an out-of-court declarant to be attacked by any means that would have been proper had the declarant testified during the trial. The rule applies to hearsay statements admitted under FRE 803 or 804 as well as to non-hearsay statements admitted under FRE 801(d)(2)(C), (D), or (E). For example, if the plaintiff introduces a dying declaration, the defendant may introduce evidence that the declarant had previously been convicted of burglary. If the defendant introduces the statement of the plaintiff's employee as a party admission, the plaintiff may introduce evidence that the employee has a bad reputation for truthfulness. If the prosecution offers the statement of a co-conspirator, the defendant may introduce the co-conspirator's prior inconsistent statements.

FRE 806 recognizes that since the declarant usually will not appear as a witness during the trial, it is impossible to raise the impeaching matter while the witness is testifying. Therefore, the usual requirement, explicit in FRE 613, that the witness be given an opportunity to deny or explain a prior inconsistent statement before extrinsic evidence of the statement is admissible is specifically eliminated.

FRE 806 does not address one issue: Can the out of-court declarant be attacked with impeachment that is collateral, or must it be non-collateral? For example, an eyewitness testifies in a deposition that "I had just come from home when I saw the collision." The eyewitness becomes unavailable, and the plaintiff at trial introduces the deposition transcript as former testimony. Can the defendant, in the defense case, introduce evidence that the eyewitness told a police officer that "I had just come from my office when the collision happened?" Note that if the eyewitness had been available to actually testify at trial, he could have been cross-examined on the prior inconsistent statement. However, if the witness had denied making the statement, the defendant could not have proved up the statement with extrinsic evidence — calling the police officer — because the impeachment is collateral.

Some courts have held an attack on the credibility of an absent hearsay witness cannot include questions containing bad acts of truth-telling character under FRE 608(b). These courts reason that such evidence would be the kind of extrinsic evidence barred by FRE 608(b). Other courts have held the impeachment is proper because that is the way it would have been done had the witness testified at trial.

Some judges apply the collateral–non-collateral distinction to FRE 806 and allow only non-collateral impeachment under the rule. Other judges, interpreting the "any evidence that would be admissible" language of the rule broadly, permit both collateral and non-collateral impeachment. Still other judges, probably the majority, simply do not allow impeachment on collateral matters, so the issue never comes up. Although the rules of evidence do not bar collateral evidence, there is judicial hostility to the practice, since many judges feel that if it is not important enough to prove up, it should not come before the jury in the first place.

If the out-of-court declarant's credibility is attacked by any proper impeachment, thereafter the declarant may be accredited by any proper rehabilitation. For example, if an out-of-court declarant's excited utterance has been admitted and the opposing side has introduced evidence that the declarant has a bad reputation for truthfulness, the party that presented the excited utterance can then introduce evidence that the declarant has a good reputation for truthfulness.

Finally, FRE 806 also recognizes that when a hearsay statement has been admitted during trial, the opposing party may sometimes call the out-of-court declarant as a witness. In that situation, the witness will probably be hostile, so the witness can be examined on the statement as if on cross-examination.

2. Practice

FRE 806 is often overlooked by lawyers. It can most frequently be used when a deposition transcript of a now unavailable witness is introduced at trial as former testimony under FRE 804(b)(1). The opposing party can then introduce in evidence any impeachment that could have been introduced in evidence had the deponent appeared as a witness at trial. FRE 806 is a powerful tool and gives lawyers options as to whether to bring up impeaching matters during a deposition or at trial.

Example 1:

> This is a personal injury case. Before trial, the plaintiff is examined by Dr. Williams, an orthopedic specialist. Dr. Williams is later deposed, and during the plaintiff's case-in-chief, the deposition transcript is introduced as an exhibit and read to the jury. (The doctor is unavailable at the time of the trial.) The plaintiff rests her case-in-chief. Out of the jury's presence, the following then happens:
>
> *Defendant:* Your honor, at this time I ask permission to read to the jury a section from the treatise Orthopedics. My medical expert, Dr. Henderson, will qualify it as a reliable authority in the field of orthopedic surgery. The part I intend to read is from page 347, and I have provided the court and counsel with copies of that page. That page contradicts what Dr. Williams testified to during his deposition.
>
> *Judge:* Plaintiff, any objection?
>
> *Plaintiff:* Yes, your honor. They could have cross-examined Dr. Williams with the treatise during his deposition. For whatever reason, they didn't. They can't now attempt to impeach the doctor when they should have done it during the deposition.
>
> *Defendant:* This is specifically allowed by Rule 806, your honor. Under that rule, I have an absolute right to attack the credibility of a hearsay statement, here the deposition, by any evidence that would have been admissible as impeachment had Dr. Williams testified during this trial. I could have impeached Dr. Williams

with the treatise had he testified, so I can impeach the doctor's deposition, which the plaintiff introduced as an exhibit.

Judge: The objection is overruled. Counsel, you may read the designated portion from the exhibit.

Defendant: Your honor, we will also introduce a section from another deposition Dr. Williams gave in another case last year. His testimony in that case directly contradicts what he said in his deposition in this case. I have provided the court and counsel with copies of that other deposition. It is a prior inconsistent statement and under Rule 806 can be used to attack Dr. Williams's credibility.

Plaintiff: I object. Under Rule 613, the doctor has the right to deny or explain the making of that prior statement. Again, they should have cross-examined the doctor on that prior statement during the doctor's deposition.

Judge: That objection is overruled, since Rule 806 has an express exception to the usual Rule 613 requirements in this situation. Counsel, you may introduce the relevant part of the doctor's other deposition, provided it is properly authenticated.

Commentary: Some courts would want to determine if the prior statement was non-collateral before it could be admitted for impeachment under FRE 806.

Example 2:

This is a criminal case. The defendant is charged with bank robbery and conspiracy to commit bank robbery. During the prosecution's case-in-chief, the prosecutor introduces a co-conspirator's statement under FRE 801(d)(2)(E). In the defendant's case-in-chief, out of the hearing of the jury, the following happens:

Judge: Defense, who's your first witness?

Defendant: Your honor, we will begin by offering in evidence Defendant's Exhibit No. 2. It's a certified copy of a prior conviction of the co-conspirator. The prior conviction, which was entered three years ago, was for sale of narcotics, which is a felony. That prior conviction is automatically admissible under Rule 609.

Prosecutor: We object. The co-conspirator did not appear as a witness in this case. This is improper impeachment.

Defendant: It's entirely proper under Rule 806, your honor. That rule allows us to impeach the co-conspirator because his hearsay statement was admitted under Rule 801(d)(2)(E). Rule 806 specifically provides that the declarant can be attacked by any evidence that would have been admissible to attack credibility had the declarant testified as a witness. There's no question that if the co-conspirator had testified in person, he could have been cross-examined on the prior conviction.

Judge: I agree. Defendant's Exhibit No. 2 is admitted. Counsel, you may read or show the exhibit to the jury.

VIII

DIRECT EXAMINATION OF WITNESSES: POLICY EXCLUSIONS AND PRIVILEGES

§8.1.   Introduction to policy exclusions

Each of the exclusions in FRE 407 through 412 is intended to further some desirable social goal or conduct. Each assumes the presence of at least some relevance, albeit slight and dubious in some instances, under the liberal "any tendency" definition of FRE 401. Each assumes that proof of its existence is easily made, posing no serious questions of reliability.

FRE 407, 408, 409, and 411 by their nature apply primarily to civil cases. They reflect a concern that socially useful conduct would be used by juries as party admissions to determine fault.

For example, it is socially useful to remedy dangerous situations (FRE 407), to encourage settlements and compromises (FRE 408), to pay an injured person's medical bills (FRE 409), and to procure liability insurance (FRE 411). Permitting evidence of these matters to prove fault is not worth the social cost incurred outside the courtroom, especially in view of the tenuous relationship between the evidence and the conclusion that the acting party is at fault.

After all, there are other and very good reasons for remedial measures, offers to compromise, and payment of medical bills — reasons that have nothing to do with the actor's fault. An injury might have taken place because of pure accident or solely because of the fault of the injured person. Yet the owner of the place or instrument of injury might decide to make changes for the better. The owner might decide to compromise the dispute out of a desire to avoid costly litigation, or he might want to pay the injured person's medical bills because of sympathy or compassion or some contractual obligation.

The Rules recognize the potential for juries to overvalue such evidence, particularly in light of borderline relevance in many instances. When some issue of importance, such as ownership, control, feasibility, or witness bias and interest, becomes controverted at trial, however, the social policy rationale dissipates, relevance strengthens, and the need for the evidence dictates admissibility. In those instances, trial judges should be alert to the need to instruct juries on the limited proper purpose of the evidence. A lawyer's failure to request a limiting instruction under FRE 105 will result in waiver of the issue on appeal.

FRE 410 applies to criminal and civil cases. It reflects a decision to encourage disposition of criminal cases without trial. FRE 412 also applies to civil and criminal cases. Its purpose is to protect victims of sexual misconduct from harassment and embarrassment and to encourage them to report the crimes and testify against the offenders in court.

When a social policy rule is raised as an objection to relevant evidence, the matter is resolved by the trial judge under FRE 104(a). The issue should be raised as early as possible in the proceedings.

§8.2. *Subsequent remedial measures (FRE 407)*[1]

1. Law

Rule 407. Subsequent Remedial Measures

When measures are taken that would have made an earlier injury or harm less likely to occur, evidence of the subsequent measures is not admissible to prove:

- negligence;
- culpable conduct;
- a defect in a product or its design; or
- a need for a warning or instruction.

But the court may admit this evidence for another purpose, such as impeachment or — if disputed — proving ownership, control, or the feasibility of precautionary measures.

Under FRE 407, evidence of subsequent remedial measures is not admissible to prove negligence or fault. A subsequent remedial measure is any post-injury measure, that, if taken earlier, "would have made the earlier injury or

---

1. McCormick §267; Weinstein §407[01]-[09]; Mueller & Kirkpatrick §§4.23-4.24; Wigmore §§282-283.

harm less likely to occur." This rule applies to measures taken after the injury, not after a product causing the injury leaves the manufacturer's control.

The rationale of the rule is threefold: First, it promotes repairs, making it less likely that the same condition will cause another injury; second, such repairs and other post-accident changes may not necessarily prove negligence or fault, but there is a danger that the jury may erroneously think so; third, it takes the jury's attention away from the central issues in the case. For example, in a stairwell slip and fall case, evidence that the landlord replaced the carpeting on the stairs after the accident is not admissible to circumstantially prove that the carpeting was defective or that the stairwell was negligently maintained. This encourages the landlord to make the stairwell safe (or safer), without worrying that his repairs will be used against him at trial to suggest negligence. Remedial measures include such post-accident repairs, design changes, additions of or changes to warning labels and package inserts, firings or disciplinary actions against employees involved in the injury, and changes in policies or procedures after an injury. They do not include post-accident analyses, studies, tests, or reports.

FRE 407 applies to remedial measures taken by parties to the litigation. Most courts hold that it does not apply to non-parties, since they have no lawsuit to be concerned about. Such non-party remedial measures usually are excluded anyway, since they usually have little or no relevance to the case, while the danger of jury misuse can be high, requiring exclusion under FRE 403.

The exception to the general rule of inadmissibility is important: Subsequent remedial evidence is admissible if it is probative of an actual disputed issue other than negligence or fault. If a party contests the feasibility of changing a product's design or claims he does not own or control the vehicle or property that caused an injury, this opens the door to proof of subsequent remedial measures. The evidence is proper because it is not being used to prove negligence or fault; it is being used because it specifically proves a contested trial issue. For example, if a defendant claims that it was not feasible to change the design of a product to make it safer, it opens the door to proof that the defendant changed the product's design shortly after the plaintiff was injured using the product. If a defendant claims that he did not own or control the truck involved in the collision, it opens the door to proof that the defendant repaired the truck after the collision.

These exceptions for which evidence of remedial measures may be admissible must relate to actual issues at trial. The opponent can take these issues out of the case either by not controverting them or by not raising them at all. For example, the opponent can decide not to raise the issue of ownership or control or decide not to controvert the feasibility of design changes or precautionary measures. In such cases, the opponent should let the court and other counsel know that as soon as possible.

Remedial measures can be used to impeach a witness. For example, a gun manufacturer's expert testifies that the gun in issue not only is safe but also is the standard for guns, and the finest and safest on the market. This opens the door to evidence that the gun's safety mechanism was changed within weeks of the accident. While judges are hesitant to allow remedial measures for impeachment purposes, when a witness excessively praises the product, beyond merely calling it good, safe, or proper, or when he vehemently denies knowing of the product's dangerous condition, this may open the door to impeaching the witness with evidence of remedial measures. This issue, like all the exceptions to the policy exclusions, must be analyzed under FRE 403, and, when such evidence is admitted, a limiting instruction under FRE 105 should be requested and given. That is, the opponent of the evidence could persuade the trial judge the probative value of the limited remedial change evidence is substantially outweighed by the risk that the jury will use it as evidence of negligence, culpable conduct, product defect or design, or need for warning or instruction. Persuading an appellate court, which views the trial court ruling with an abuse of discretion standard, is a far more difficult task.

Until 1997 there was some disagreement in the federal courts as to whether the FRE 407 exclusion applied to strict liability cases. The rule was amended to make it clear that it applies to all types of strict liability cases — defects in products, defects in a product's design, or a need for warning or instruction in the use of the product. The exclusion applies only when the remedial measure is taken after the injury or harm occurs. Because the rule does not cover the time period after the product leaves the manufacturer's control but before occurrence of the injury or harm at issue, remedial changes made between those events could be admissible, subject to the rules of relevancy and the FRE 403 weighing test.

Some states do not adhere strictly to FRE 407. That is, several state courts have held the remedial change exclusion does not apply to strict liability cases. Others hold that when the principle does apply it runs from the time when the product leaves a manufacturer's control or when the design is completed. This disparity in approach raises an issue in diversity cases tried in the federal courts: Does state law apply to subsequent remedial measures or does FRE 407 apply? A few courts have held *Erie Railroad Co. v. Tompkins*, 304 U.S. 64 (1938), requires the application of state law because the issue is substantive. Most federal courts, however, have held the issue is procedural, requiring application of FRE 407.

Does the FRE 407 exclusion apply to product recalls? Most jurisdictions that have decided the issue hold that it applies to voluntary, manufacturer-initiated recalls, but not to mandatory, government-initiated recalls. The reasoning is that a manufacturer should be encouraged to voluntarily recall an unsafe product by applying FRE 407. However, if the recall is ordered by a governmental body, such as the Consumer Product Safety Commission, the fact of the recall is admissible, since its mandatory nature does not require any voluntary conduct by the manufacturer. The recall under these circumstances cannot be said to be an admission of fault.

2. Practice

Facts raising FRE 407 issues are usually unveiled during discovery, so the issues can, and therefore should, be raised before trial. These issues are important because if the evidence is properly admissible, the evidence frequently has an enormous impact on the jury.

Example 1:

This is a personal injury case. Plaintiff was injured while working at defendant's boat company. The injury happened while plaintiff was working on a dock. Defendant denies that it owns or controls the dock. Plaintiff plans to introduce evidence that the day following the injury, one of defendant's workers was seen repairing the dock. Defendant moves to preclude that evidence. At a hearing, the following happens:

Defendant: Your honor, this is our motion to preclude. Plaintiff intends to offer evidence that defendant sent a worker to repair the dock the day after plaintiff was injured. This is evidence of a subsequent remedial measure and is inadmissible under Rule 407.

Plaintiff: In defendant's answer, it denied that the dock where the injury happened was owned, operated, or controlled by the defendant. This evidence is being offered to prove ownership and control, which they deny. It's an express exception to the general rule of inadmissibility in 407.

Defendant: The evidence will be that defendant is the legal owner of the boathouse, but not of the dock on which the boathouse sits.

Judge: The motion is denied. This evidence tends to show that the dock was controlled and maintained by defendant, which could give rise to legal liability and which appears to be in issue. This ruling does not limit in any way defendant's right to present contrary evidence in defendant's case-in-chief.

Commentary: This is a good example of how the pleadings affect the admissibility of evidence at trial.

Example 2:

This is a premises liability case. Plaintiff was sexually assaulted at defendant's hotel. Plaintiff claims that the hotel's door locks were inadequate and that the hotel should have provided better security, including stronger door locks with chains. Defendant claims that removing the old locks and installing new chain locks was not economically feasible. Plaintiff plans to introduce evidence that six months after the rape defendant installed chain locks on the hotel's doors. Defendant moves to preclude this evidence. At a hearing, the following happens:

Judge: Defense, this is your motion to preclude.

Defendant: Yes, your honor. What plaintiff seeks to introduce is clearly prohibited by Rule 407. They want to introduce evidence that some six months after this incident we put different door locks on the room doors. This is classic evidence of a subsequent remedial measure, prohibited by the rule.

Judge: Plaintiff?

Plaintiff: The defense put all this in issue. Their position throughout this lawsuit—beginning with their answer, continuing through discovery, and up to their answers to requests to admit and the pretrial statement — has been to deny that the locks were inadequate and to deny that they could have done anything that was economically feasible to make hotel security better. Rule 407 creates an exception for the "feasibility of precautionary measures, if controverted." That's exactly the position they've taken here: denied that they could have provided better door locks. Under these circumstances, evidence that they later in fact provided better door locks disproves their position.

Judge: The motion is denied. The evidence will be admitted. I will give the jury a limiting instruction if you want one.

Commentary: Another approach would be for the judge to bar the introduction of this evidence in plaintiff's case-in-chief, but to permit it in plaintiff's rebuttal if the defense in defendant's case-in-chief presents evidence denying that the existing door locks could have been improved.

§8.3. *Compromise and offers of compromise (FRE 408)*[2]

1. Law

Rule 408.   Compromise Offers and Negotiations

(a) **Prohibited Uses.** Evidence of the following is not admissible — on behalf of any party — either to prove or disprove the validity or amount of a disputed claim or to impeach by a prior inconsistent statement or a contradiction:

(1) furnishing, promising, or offering — or accepting, promising to accept, or offering to accept — a valuable consideration in compromising or attempting to compromise the claim; and

(2) conduct or a statement made during compromise negotiations about the claim — except when offered in a criminal case and when the negotiations related to a claim by a public office in the exercise of its regulatory, investigative, or enforcement authority.

(b) **Exceptions.** The court may admit this evidence for another purpose, such as proving a witness's bias or prejudice, negating a contention of undue delay, or proving an effort to obstruct a criminal investigation or prosecution.

Under FRE 408, evidence of a settlement or offers to settle a disputed claim are not admissible to prove liability or damages. There must be a disputed claim, as to either liability or damages, between the parties, although it need not have reached the litigation stage or even the threat of litigation. If both sides agree on the amount owed, but one tries to offer less to settle it, FRE 408 does not apply.

---

2. McCormick §266; Weinstein §408[01]-[09]; Mueller & Kirkpatrick §§4.25-4.26; Wigmore §§283a, 1061-1062.

The rationale is twofold: First, offers to settle disputed claims are irrelevant, since there may be reasons other than fault to settle a case (such as avoiding litigation expenses or adverse publicity) before or after a lawsuit is filed; second, settlements as a matter of policy should be encouraged. The rule is broad, covering both conduct and statements made during the course of negotiations. Statements of fault made during the course of settlement negotiations are not admissible. FRE 408 is broader than the common law rule, which does not bar fact statements or conduct made during settlement negotiations. In common law states, lawyers still speak "hypothetically" about the case to avoid the possibility of any statements later being used as an admission.

The exceptions to the general rule set forth in FRE 408(b), are important. Evidence of compromise or offers of compromise is admissible for any relevant purpose other than to prove liability for, or the invalidity of, a disputed claim or its amount. The exceptions arise most commonly when a former party, which has settled before trial, testifies during the trial of the remaining parties. The fact of the settlement, and its details, are usually admissible to impeach a witness by showing bias, interest, or motive.

For example, the plaintiff sues two defendants. One defendant settles before trial. During the trial between the plaintiff and the remaining defendant, the settled defendant is called as a witness by the plaintiff to testify that the remaining defendant was negligent. On cross-examination, the witness can be questioned about the settlement with the plaintiff, since this attacks the witness's credibility by showing bias and interest. Although showing bias and interest is the most common use of settlement evidence, courts have also allowed such evidence to rebut a claim of undue delay, to prove a party's motive, and to enforce the terms of a settlement agreement.

It would be an abuse of FRE 408 to allow one party to lull the other into breaching a contract and then prevent the breaching party from explaining its actions because the lulling took place around the settlement table. That is, the breaching party is allowed to explain it converted certain accounts because it thought a settlement had been reached. The spirit and purpose of FRE 408 is to encourage settlements, not to reward trickery or deceit.

There is a danger the jury will overvalue or misuse evidence of a compromise, even though it is admitted for a proper purpose. This is particularly true when such evidence is admitted for impeachment purposes. In these situations, FRE 403 plays an important role and can result in exclusion if the probative value of the evidence for a proper purpose is low, but the danger the jury will misuse the evidence for an improper purpose is high and a limiting instruction will not be an adequate safeguard.

A loan receipt agreement, also called a "Mary Carter" agreement, is a partial settlement agreement in which a plaintiff settles with one of multiple defendants. The settled defendant pays the plaintiff a "loan" amount but remains in the case and participates in the trial to the detriment of the remaining co-defendants. A few states have ruled that such agreements are void on public policy grounds. Most states have upheld such agreements, requiring that they be disclosed during discovery, and if a settled defendant testifies during the trial, the agreement is admissible to show bias and interest.

A party cannot immunize evidence from discovery by first disclosing it during settlement negotiations. If evidence is otherwise discoverable, it is admissible (assuming no other evidentiary barriers), even though it was presented during settlement negotiations.

FRE 408 does not distinguish between civil and criminal trials, except that FRE 408(a)(2) provides that conduct or statements made in compromise negotiations regarding the claim are admissible "when offered in a criminal case and when the negotiations related to a claim by a public office in the exercise of its regulatory, investigative, or enforcement authority."

2. Practice

Since the prohibition in FRE 408 is clear and broad, issues with this rule arise infrequently. When they do arise, they most commonly involve using settlements as impeachment.

Example:

This is a personal injury case brought by the plaintiff against the manufacturer of a press that injured the plaintiff and against the installer of the press. Before trial, the plaintiff settles with the co-defendant installer for $5,000, and the installer agrees to testify against the co-defendant manufacturer. Before trial, the plaintiff moves to preclude the details of the settlement. At a hearing, the following happens:

Plaintiff: This is our motion to preclude the details of the installer's settlement agreement with us. We agree that if the installer is called as a witness at trial, the fact of his settlement is admissible under Rule 408 to attack his credibility. We agree that the fact that the settlement calls for the installer to testify at this trial is admissible for the same reason. However, we move to bar disclosure that the settlement was in the amount of $5,000. The dollar amount of the settlement does not add anything of significance. Its only purpose is to suggest that if we settled with the installer for $5,000, then our case against the manufacturer can't be worth much more. That's a misuse of this fact and should be barred by Rule 408.

Judge: Defense?

Defendant: How much the installer settled for has a lot to do with how the jury will consider the installer's testimony when he gets on the stand. The jury's entitled to know what the entire deal was that resulted in his testifying for the plaintiff. That goes to the heart of the installer's bias.

Judge: The objection is overruled. All the terms of the settlement may be used if the installer testifies at trial.

Commentary: The plaintiff should also ask for a limiting instruction telling the jury the proper limited use of the evidence. Some courts exclude the amount of the settlement on the theory that a limiting instruction on the proper limited use of this evidence would not be effective.

§8.4.   *Payment of medical expenses (FRE 409)*[3]

1.   Law

Rule 409.   Offers to Pay Medical and Similar Expenses

Evidence of furnishing, promising to pay, or offering to pay medical, hospital, or similar expenses resulting from an injury is not admissible to prove liability for the injury.

The rationale behind the rule is that such offers may be motivated by altruistic reasons, but that a jury will assume it shows fault. The rule recognizes that such offers are usually made from humanitarian impulses and motives, not from admissions of liability. It encourages providing prompt medical attention to injured persons, a good social policy.

FRE 409 does not require an actual dispute or controversy over either liability or damages at the time the offer or payment is made. It does not have express exceptions, although it is obvious that such evidence can be offered for a proper purpose other than proving liability or damages, such as proving agency, ownership, or control and impeaching someone's credibility.

FRE 409 is limited in scope. Unlike FRE 408, it does not exclude other factual statements or conduct of the person making the offer. Nor does it bar statements of fault associated with an offer to pay medical expenses. For example, a person says, "I'll pay your medical bill. It was all my fault." The latter statement is not excluded. FRE 409 also does not bar offers to pay other damages, such as offering to repair the other driver's car. For this reason, the safer practice is to make such statements and offers part of settlement negotiations, governed by FRE 408, where the protection is much broader.

2.   Practice

This is a seldom-used rule, and case law is sparse. The only issues that arise usually involve the scope of the rule's exclusion.

Example:

This is a personal injury case. Plaintiff sues her landlord for injuries sustained in the lobby of her apartment building. Plaintiff plans to introduce evidence that following the injury, the building manager, an employee of the landlord, told plaintiff, "I'm terribly sorry you slipped on the floor. That shouldn't have happened. Don't worry about your medical bills. We'll take care of them." Defendant moves to preclude these statements. At a hearing, the following happens:

---

3. McCormick §267; Weinstein §409[01]-[05]; Mueller & Kirkpatrick §4.27; Wigmore §283a.

Defendant: The last item, your honor, is our motion to preclude statements of the building manager. We're not disputing that the manager has authority to speak for the defendant. However, we object to the statement in its entirety; it is inadmissible under Rule 409, since it's an offer to pay medical expenses and similar expenses.

Plaintiff: The entire statement should be admissible. Seen in context, the statement is a party admission.

Judge: I will permit part of the statement. That part in which the manager says, "I'm terribly sorry you slipped on the floor. That shouldn't have happened," is admissible as a party admission. The rest of the statement, and other reference to paying medical bills, is precluded.

Commentary: If a statement can be bifurcated so as to make part of it admissible, many judges will take this approach. Plaintiff should probably have suggested it, rather than arguing that the entire statement was admissible.

§8.5. *Existence of liability insurance (FRE 411)*[4]

1. Law

Rule 411. Liability Insurance

Evidence that a person was or was not insured against liability is not admissible to prove whether the person acted negligently or otherwise wrongfully. But the court may admit this evidence for another purpose, such as proving a witness's bias or prejudice or proving agency, ownership, or control.

FRE 411 provides that evidence a party had liability insurance is not admissible to prove negligence or fault. The rationale is that the existence of such insurance has little or no relevance to the issue of negligence or fault and that the amount of compensatory damages the jury may award the plaintiff should not be influenced by whether the defendant had insurance (or, for that matter, by any evidence of the defendant's financial condition). Evidence of lack of insurance is not admissible for the same reason. FRE 411 applies only to the parties to the litigation, not to non-parties.

The exceptions to the general rule are important. FRE 411 does not bar such evidence if it is offered to prove something else actually in issue at trial, such as bias, interest, ownership, control, or agency. For example, in a negligence case, the defendant company denies it owned or operated the truck involved in the crash because the title of the truck is in the driver's name. The plaintiff under these circumstances may introduce evidence that the

---

4. McCormick §201; Weinstein §411[01]-[13] Mueller & Kirkpatrick §§4.30-4.31; Wigmore §282a.

company insured the truck because this is evidence that the company owned and controlled the truck. In the same case, the defendant calls its insurance company's accident investigator as a witness. On cross-examination, the plaintiff may bring out the fact that the witness works for the defendant's insurer, since this shows bias and interest.

There may be other reasons for admitting evidence of insurance, such as to show why a safety inspection was made, to prove there was or was not a contrac-tual obligation to insure, or to establish a business custom of limiting liability. In all of these situations, a limiting instruction telling the jury the limited proper purpose of this evidence should be requested and given.

A particularly troublesome situation arises when a party makes a statement that is an admission and mentions insurance. For example, the passenger says to the driver, just before the car runs off the road, "Johnny, slow down. You're going way too fast." The driver replies, "Who cares? I've got insurance." This statement can be taken as proof of recklessness, but the mentioning of insurance is also prejudicial. These situations must be analyzed on a case-by-case basis, balancing the probative value against its prejudicial effect under FRE 403. Most courts will admit such a statement mentioning insurance when the state-ment is strongly probative of something in issue, such as recklessness.

It is no longer true that any inadvertent mention of insurance by a lawyer or witness will result in a mistrial. Most people understand that being insured is a common or even usual practice. Judges will treat deliberate attempts to circumvent the rule harshly, but granting a mistrial only rewards the wrongdoer.

The question often arises whether jurors can be asked about insurance matters during the jury selection process. FRE 411 does not apply to the selec-tion process. Most courts allow general questions about whether a juror or any-one close to the juror is employed by or has an ownership interest in an insurance company.

2.   Practice

The existence of liability insurance is frequently admitted at trial because excep-tions to the general rule of exclusion are common. The most common situations involve bias and interest, and party statements that happen to mention insurance.

Example 1:

This is a railroad liability case. Plaintiff was injured in a train accident. During the defense case, defendant calls a witness who is cross-examined as follows:

Q. (By plaintiff's lawyer) Mr. Gibbons, you were asked to testify by the defense, right?
A. That's right.
Q. You now work for the Worldwide Insurance Company, isn't that also right?

Defendant: Objection, your honor. May we be heard?

Judge: You may. Approach the bench. [Lawyers come forward.] Defense, why is this improper?

Defendant: Plaintiff is trying to inject insurance into the case. Their next question is obvious: They want to bring out the fact that the witness is now employed by the same company that insured the railroad. That's improper under Rule 411.

Plaintiff: That's exactly what we intend to do, your honor, and it's proper. This witness was hired by the defendant's insurance company after the accident. This is admissible to show bias and interest, which is proper under Rule 411.

Judge: The objection is overruled.

Defendant: May we have a limiting instruction on the proper limited purpose of this evidence?

Judge: You may. I will so instruct the jury after the questions are asked and repeat it in my final instructions.

Example 2:

This is a personal injury case. The plaintiff was injured while a passenger in the defendant's car, which ran off the road. During her deposition, plaintiff states that she begged her boyfriend, the defendant, to slow down, but he said, "What's the problem? Anything happens, my insurance will cover it." The defendant moves to preclude this statement. At a hearing, the following happens:

Defendant: We move to preclude the statement, your honor, because it's irrelevant, and it mentions insurance, which is specifically inadmissible to show fault.

Plaintiff: The statement is an admission by a party-opponent that happens to mention insurance. Since the statement is a party admission and is intermingled with the mentioning of insurance, it should all come in.

Defendant: Your honor, if the statement has any relevance, it would be to an issue of recklessness. However, the plaintiff has alleged only negligence, not recklessness, and seeks only compensatory, not punitive, damages. On the issue of negligence, the statement has no probative value, and even if there is minimal probative value, it is substantially outweighed by the danger of unfair prejudice.

Judge: The statement will be excluded. It has low probative value, given the issues in the case, but the danger of unfair prejudice I find significant, so I'm excluding it on that basis.

Commentary: This is a close case, and case law is mixed. The ruling in any particular case is driven more by the facts specific to the case than by case law.

DO NOT THROW AWAY THIS CARD!

Your FREE ACCESS to the

Online Student Materials for Trial Evidence

Sixth Edition

ISBN: 978-1-4548-7002-9

To redeem your access code:

1. Log in or Create an Account at www.WKLegaledu.com.
2. Go to "Redeem an Access Code" under My Account in the top right corner.
3. Enter your code in the box provided and click submit.
4. You should then find the link to the Website materials under your "Order History" or "My Digital Library."
5. Click the ACCESS button to go to the website where you can view the materials.

TIP: Bookmark the online materials website to quickly access the materials in the future.

ACCESS CODE

MAUTRIALEVID-87SQJ1H8W

Wolters Kluwer

§8.6.   *Plea agreements and discussions (FRE 410)*[5]

1.   Law

Rule 410.   Pleas, Plea Discussions, and Related Statements

(a) **Prohibited Uses.** In a civil or criminal case, evidence of the following is not admissible against the defendant who made the plea or participated in the plea discussions:

(1) a guilty plea that was later withdrawn;

(2) a nolo contendere plea;

(3) a statement made during a proceeding on either of those pleas under Federal Rule of Criminal Procedure 11 or a comparable state procedure; or

(4) a statement made during plea discussions with an attorney for the prosecuting authority if the discussions did not result in a guilty plea or they resulted in a later-withdrawn guilty plea.

(b) **Exceptions.** The court may admit a statement described in Rule 410(a)(3) or (4)

(1) in any proceeding in which another statement made during the same plea or plea discussions has been introduced, if in fairness the statements ought to be considered together; or

(2) in a criminal proceeding for perjury or false statement, if the defendant made the statement under oath, on the record, and with counsel present.

The criminal plea discussions rule parallels the civil settlement rule: Plea negotiations and agreements are not admissible to show fault. If plea negotiations fail, nothing in those discussions is admissible during the later trial. If the defendant becomes a party in a civil case, the plea negotiations are inadmissible in the civil case. FRE 410 recognizes that plea discussions and agreements play an essential role in the administration of justice in criminal cases, although the accused can expressly waive the protection of the rule if the waiver is knowing and voluntary. See *United States v. Mezzanatto*, 513 U.S. 196 (1995).

Withdrawn pleas and nolo pleas not admitting liability are usually inadmissible in a later proceeding. A guilty plea that is not withdrawn may be used against the defendant in a civil or criminal case as an admission. Factual statements made in court during the taking of a guilty plea that later is withdrawn are not barred by the rule. If a defendant is later charged with making false or perjurious statements during the taking of a guilty plea, the rule does not bar the use of the defendant's statements in the later trial. Finally, what happens when a guilty plea is withdrawn, the defendant goes to trial, and he testifies contrary to his plea discussion statements? Can his statements be used to impeach? The courts are not in agreement on this issue.

Most plea discussions are conducted by the defendant's lawyer, and the rule covers statements made by the lawyer while bargaining for the defendant.

5. McCormick §266; Weinstein §410[01]-[10]; Mueller & Kirkpatrick §§4.28-4.29; Wigmore §§1061-1062.

The defendant, however, can also directly engage in plea discussions. The defendant must intend to engage in plea negotiations. He must be seeking a guilty plea deal, not just pursuing some hope for leniency or a reduction in the number of charges that will be filed against him. The defendant must have a reasonable expectation that he will gain something in return for his admissions.

The plea negotiations must be with the prosecuting attorney. Statements made by a defendant to police officers and law enforcement agents do not fall within the protection of the rule, although some cases hold that if an agent represents to a defendant that he is authorized by the United States Attorney to engage in plea discussions, such statements fall within the rule. Where the agent is expressly authorized to engage in plea discussions, basic fairness requires exclusion, and the cases so hold. Where the agent misrepresents his authority, the rule does not seem to compel exclusion, although the outcome may well turn on the extent of deception, and rules applicable to police inter-rogations might result in exclusion.

Statements made by a defendant after a plea agreement is reached are not covered by the rule. For example, the defendant testifies before a grand jury after entering into an agreement. Later the defendant breaks the agreement, and the case is reset for trial. The defendant's grand jury testimony is not barred by the rule from being offered at the later trial.

The exceptions to the general rule parallel those in civil cases. Whenever a co-defendant enters into a plea agreement and later becomes a witness at the trial of a remaining co-defendant, the witness may be examined about his plea agreement with the prosecution and the terms of that agreement because this shows bias. This is particularly so when the agreement provides, as is commonly the case, that the pleading defendant is willing to testify as a government wit-ness in any trial of other co-defendants. The prosecution can use the former co-defendant's statements made during his plea negotiations and the taking of his guilty plea for impeachment if his trial testimony favors the defendant.

2. Practice

Paralleling the civil rule, FRE 410 issue arise infrequently. The case law is well established that when a former co-defendant who has reached a plea agreement with the prosecution testifies at trial, all the details of the plea agreement are admissible to attack the co-defendant's credibility. However, the plea agreement is not to be considered as evidence of the remaining defendant's guilt.

Example:

The defendant is on trial for armed robbery. A co-defendant has previously pleaded guilty to the reduced charge of robbery. The former co-defendant then is called as a prosecution witness. During cross-examination, the following happens:

Q. (By defendant's lawyer) Mr. Black, you made a deal with the prosecu-tion, didn't you?
A. I entered into a plea agreement.

Q. As part of that deal, you agreed to testify for the prosecution, isn't that right?

A. I agreed to testify truthfully.

Q. Let's talk about the details of your deal. You were arrested for *armed* robbery, right?

A. Yes.

Q. But the deal you made called for you to plead guilty to just plain robbery, right?

A. That's right.

Q. If convicted of *armed* robbery, you could have been sent to the pen for as much as 25 years, right?

A. That's what my lawyer said.

Q. But under your deal, you can't be sentenced to more than two years, right?

A. That's right.

Commentary: Note that the prosecutor did not object to any of these questions. Since the details of the plea agreement are admissible to attack credibility, any objection should have been overruled.

§8.7. *Victim's past sexual behavior or alleged sexual predisposition in sex offense cases (FRE 412)*[6]

1. Law

Rule 412. Sex-Offense Cases: The Victim's Sexual Behavior or Predisposition

(a) **Prohibited Uses.** The following evidence is not admissible in a civil or criminal proceeding involving alleged sexual misconduct:

(1) evidence offered to prove that a victim engaged in other sexual behavior; or

(2) evidence offered to prove a victim's sexual predisposition.

(b) **Exceptions.**

(1) *Criminal Cases.* The court may admit the following evidence in a criminal case:

(A) evidence of specific instances of a victim's sexual behavior, if offered to prove that someone other than the defendant was the source of semen, injury, or other physical evidence;

(B) evidence of specific instances of a victim's sexual behavior with respect to the person accused of the sexual misconduct, if offered by the defendant to prove consent or if offered by the prosecutor; and

(C) evidence whose exclusion would violate the defendant's constitutional rights.

---

6. McCormick §193; Weinstein §412[01]-[03]; Mueller & Kirkpatrick §§4.32-4.34; Wigmore §§62-62.3.

(2) *Civil Cases.* In a civil case, the court may admit evidence offered to prove a victim's sexual behavior or sexual predisposition if its probative value substantially outweighs the danger of harm to any victim and of unfair prejudice to any party. The court may admit evidence of a victim's reputation only if the victim has placed it in controversy.

(c) Procedure to Determine Admissibility.

(1) *Motion.* If a party intends to offer evidence under Rule 412(b), the party must:

(A) file a motion that specifically describes the evidence and states the purpose for which it is to be offered;

(B) do so at least 14 days before trial unless the court, for good cause, sets a different time;

(C) serve the motion on all parties; and

(D) notify the victim or, when appropriate, the victim's guardian or representative.

(2) *Hearing.* Before admitting evidence under this rule, the court must conduct an in camera hearing and give the victim and parties a right to attend and be heard. Unless the court orders otherwise, the motion, related materials, and the record of the hearing must be and remain sealed.

(d) Definition of "Victim." In this rule, "victim" includes an alleged victim.

The policy purpose behind FRE 412 is to protect victims of sexual misconduct from harassment, embarrassment, and invasions of privacy, while encouraging victims to report crimes and testify against offenders. Many states have similar rules, which are commonly called "rape shield" statutes, although the scope of these rules frequently is broader than the name suggests.

FRE 412 applies to any case, civil and criminal, where sexual misconduct is an issue, even though no one is charged with sexual misconduct. The rule applies to any criminal case involving sexual misconduct, even if the witness is not the alleged victim in the case on trial. This rule was discussed in some detail in Sec. 5.3.

The past conduct that is excluded includes more than sexual acts. It includes such matters as the use of contraceptives, birth of an illegitimate child, evidence of a venereal disease, and lifestyle evidence such as short dresses and vulgar language. In an action for workplace sexual harassment, evidence of the victim's sexual behavior in the workplace probably is admissible, but non-workplace conduct would be barred by the Rule. For example, posing nude for a magazine outside work hours is irrelevant to the issue of unwelcomeness of sexual advances at work. (See Notes of Advisory Committee, 1994 Amendment to FRE 412.)

In criminal cases, FRE 412 virtually bars introducing specific instances of the victim's past sexual behavior. Such instances are admissible under FRE 412(b) in only three situations: (A) Evidence of the alleged victim's past sexual behavior is admissible to prove that someone other than the defendant was "the source of semen, injury or other physical evidence"; (B) evidence of past sexual behavior between the alleged victim and the defendant is admissible when offered by the defendant to prove consent or by the prosecution; (C) evidence must be admitted if excluding the evidence would violate the defendant's constitutional rights. Of course, nothing in FRE 412 prevents the prosecution from offering relevant evidence of specific instances of sexual conduct between the alleged victim and defendant for a proper FRE 404(b) purpose.

The "constitutional rights" referred to in FRE 412(b)(1)(C) include confrontation and due process. *Olden v. Kentucky*, 488 U.S. 227 (1988), while not interpreting a rape shield statute, did make an important point about the scope of the right to confront witnesses in sexual misconduct cases. The trial judge refused to allow evidence that the alleged rape victim, who was white, was living with a man at the time of trial in order to show her motive to lie about being raped by the defendant, who was black. The Supreme Court held that the defendant's confrontation right had been violated, and it reversed. Any possible embarrassment or prejudice to the alleged victim did not justify the exclusion, a point that should apply equally to FRE 412.

FRE 412 does not bar evidence that the alleged victim had made false claims of sexual misconduct against others on other occasions. For example, in a statutory rape case it was reversible error to refuse to allow the defendant to introduce evidence that eleven months earlier the minor admitted making up a story about being raped in order to get her mother's attention. The evidence proved the minor had a motive — getting attention — to make a false accusation. But some courts have excluded evidence of false claims where they are connected with actual sexual activity, perhaps an overly strict view of the Rule.

In civil cases, evidence of the victim's specific instances of sexual behavior are admissible if otherwise admissible and the probative value of the evidence "substantially outweighs" the danger of harm to the victim or unfair prejudice to any party. When this rule is read in conjunction with FRE 404(a)(2), it is hard to imagine a situation in a civil case where specific instances of an alleged victim's sexual conduct will be admissible. Evidence of the victim's reputation is admissible only if placed in controversy by the victim.

FRE 412(c) establishes procedures that apply when a party attempts to introduce evidence under the exceptions of subsection (b). These procedures include a written motion filed at least 14 days before trial that states the evidence being offered and the purpose for which it is offered, service of the motion on every party, notice to the alleged victim, and an in camera hearing in which the parties and alleged victim have a right to appear and be heard. These procedures, found nowhere else in the Federal Rules of Evidence, set up formidable obstacles to admission.

2. Practice

When issues arise under the rule, it is essential that the matter be raised well before trial by following the procedures detailed in FRE 412(c).

Example:

This is a rape prosecution. The defense is consent. The defendant also claims the victim was a prostitute whom he paid. The defense witness list contains three persons who will testify they also paid the victim for sex. The prosecution objects. At a pretrial hearing on the objection, the following happens:

Judge: Prosecution, what's the basis for your objection?
Prosecutor: Rule 412 specifically bars exactly the kind of evidence the defendant is trying to introduce. The rule bars "[e]vidence offered to prove any alleged victim's sexual predisposition." The rule permits other acts of the victim only when consent is raised as a defense, and then only other acts with the defendant.
Defendant: That's the general rule, your honor, but there's an exception. Subsection (b)(1)(C) provides for the admission of evidence "the exclusion of which would violate the constitutional rights of the defendant." Our defense is that this was an act of prostitution. Any rule of evidence that purports to bar any relevant evidence of prostitution must give way to the defendant's due process constitutional rights to a fair trial. The rule itself acknowledges that due process rights must prevail.
Judge: The objection is sustained. This is a close case, but I find that three prior instances are insufficient evidence to prove the claim of prostitution and the evidence is highly inflammatory. I'm keeping it out.

§8.8. Introduction to privileges

The law of evidence is based largely on logic and experience. Privileges, on the other hand, are based on policy considerations. Under certain situations, goals that are more important than the evidentiary cost of losing the relevant evidence—fostering candid communications between persons having confidential relationships and strengthening those relationships—are promoted. For example, the law creates a privilege for attorney-client communications, although those communications undoubtedly contain information highly relevant to the case. In short, privileges involve social costs, since they deny the fact finder relevant information on which to base a factually accurate trial decision.

Privileges were initially a creation of the common law. The first privilege, the attorney-client privilege, was recognized in the eighteenth century in England. Other privileges were recognized over time, were transported to the American colonies, and ultimately became part of our privileges law as well.

A more recent development is the creation of privileges by statute, rather than by court decision. In the nineteenth century, many states in the United States codified their privileges, and the expansion of privileges in those jurisdictions has been by legislative enactment, a process that remains active today.

In federal courts, by contrast, privileges have always been based on case law. When the Federal Rules of Evidence were drafted, the final approved draft that was submitted to Congress contained 13 specific privileges rules (the deleted Rules 501-513). Congress, however, was concerned that making federal privileges law statutory would stop the continuing development of privileges through case law and rejected the proposed rules. Instead, Congress enacted FRE 501, which retains the historic federal case law development of privileges.

Rule 501.   Privilege in General

The common law — as interpreted by United States courts in the light of reason and experience — governs a claim of privilege unless any of the following provides otherwise:

- the United States Constitution;
- a federal statute; or
- rules prescribed by the Supreme Court.

But in a civil case, state law governs privilege regarding a claim or defense for which state law supplies the rule of decision.

Rule 502.   Attorney-Client Privilege and Work Product; Limitations on Waiver

The following provisions apply, in the circumstances set out, to disclosure of a communication or information covered by the attorney-client privilege or work-product protection.

(a) Disclosure Made in a Federal Proceeding or to a Federal Office or Agency; Scope of a Waiver. When the disclosure is made in a federal proceeding or to a federal office or agency and waives the attorney-client privilege or work-product protection, the waiver extends to an undisclosed communication or information in a federal or state proceeding only if:

(1) the waiver is intentional;

(2) the disclosed and undisclosed communications or information concern the same subject matter; and

(3) they ought in fairness to be considered together.

(b) Inadvertent Disclosure. When made in a federal proceeding or to a federal office or agency, the disclosure does not operate as a waiver in a federal or state proceeding if:

(1) the disclosure is inadvertent;

(2) the holder of the privilege or protection took reasonable steps to prevent disclosure; and

(3) the holder promptly took reasonable steps to rectify the error, including (if applicable) following Federal Rule of Civil Procedure 26(b)(5)(B).

(c) Disclosure Made in a State Proceeding. When the disclosure is made in a state proceeding and is not the subject of a state-court order concerning waiver, the disclosure does not operate as a waiver in a federal proceeding if the disclosure:

(1) would not be a waiver under this rule if it had been made in a federal proceeding; or

(2) is not a waiver under the law of the state where the disclosure occurred.

(d) Controlling Effect of a Court Order. A federal court may order that the privilege or protection is not waived by disclosure connected with the litigation pending before the court—in which event the disclosure is also not a waiver in any other federal or state proceeding.

(e) Controlling Effect of a Party Agreement. An agreement on the effect of disclosure in a federal proceeding is binding only on the parties to the agreement, unless it is incorporated into a court order.

(f) Controlling Effect of this Rule. Notwithstanding Rules 101 and 1101, this rule applies to state proceedings and to federal court-annexed and federal court-mandated arbitration proceedings, in the circumstances set out in the rule. And notwithstanding Rule 501, this rule applies even if state law provides the rule of decision.

(g) Definitions. In this rule:

(1) "attorney-client privilege" means the protection that applicable law provides for confidential attorney-client communications; and

(2) "work-product protection" means the protection that applicable law provides for tangible material (or its intangible equivalent) prepared in anticipation of litigation or for trial.

§8.9.   *Preliminary considerations*[7]

Because privileges law is jurisdiction specific, the first question that always must be addressed whenever an issue arises is this: Which jurisdiction's law applies, the federal or forum state's privileges law? For this purpose, it is useful to think of four types of cases:

1. federal criminal cases
2. federal civil cases based on federal question jurisdiction
3. federal civil cases based on diversity jurisdiction
4. state cases

In the first two categories, FRE 501 applies the federal common law of privileges. In the last two categories, state privileges law applies. This is because in federal diversity cases FRE 501 provides that when a state law supplies the rule as to a claim or defense, the state's privileges law will apply as well. FRE 501 applies the *Erie* doctrine to privileges law in civil diversity cases. See *Erie Railroad Co. v. Thompkins*, 304 U.S. 64 (1938).

The second question logically follows: What is the applicable federal and state privileges law? Under FRE 501, the federal privileges law is the law as developed by federal courts over time, or "federal common law." Researching

---

7. McCormick §72; Weinstein §501[01]-[10]; Mueller & Kirkpatrick §5.7; Wigmore §§2190-2224.

the federal cases specific to the jurisdiction involved is essential. However, a good way to start is to review the deleted Rules 501-513. While these rules were rejected by Congress, they were approved by the Supreme Court and provide an accurate list and definitions of recognized non-constitutional federal privileges as they existed in 1975 (and most have remained unchanged since that time). They are as follows:

> Lawyer-client privilege (deleted 503)
> Psychotherapist-patient privilege (deleted 504)
> Husband-wife privilege (deleted 505)
> Communications to clergymen (deleted 506)
> Political vote (deleted 507)
> Trade secrets (deleted 508)
> Secrets of state and other official information (deleted 509)
> Identity of informer (deleted 510)

The state privileges law is the law enacted by statute or developed by case law. Most of the states have made their privileges law statutory, while a few continue with case law. The various states differ substantially in the privileges they recognize and in their definitions of a particular privilege. Researching the current law of the applicable state is essential.

Once the applicable jurisdiction's privileges law is determined, three key questions arise. First, who is the "holder" of the privilege? The holder of the privilege is the person who is intended to be benefited or protected by the privilege. For example, the client is the holder, not the lawyer; the patient is the holder, not the doctor. The identity of the holder is important because only the holder can assert or waive the privilege, since privileges are deemed personal to the holder (although a lawyer can always assert a privilege on behalf of a client).

Second, what causes a "waiver" of the privilege? Since a privilege is personal to the holder, it follows that the holder can waive the benefit of the privilege by disclosing, or not objecting to the disclosure of, privileged information. The privilege can be waived expressly or implicitly by engaging in speech or conduct that is inconsistent with the privilege. The presence of a third party waives the privilege. Although not technically a waiver, most jurisdictions also hold that a privilege will not operate in certain situations, primarily those in which eliciting privileged information is necessary to accurately resolve litigation between the parties to the privilege. For example, the attorney-client privilege does not apply when there is litigation between the attorney and the client, such as a malpractice action, since the communications between them will invariably be critical evidence. FRE 502, adopted in 2008, significantly changes the law on advertent and inadvertent waivers of the attorney-client privilege and work-product protection in federal and state litigation.

Third, when, if ever, does a "termination" of the privilege occur? Most privileges never terminate, even though the relationship on which the privilege was based has ended. For example, the attorney-client privilege continues, even if the attorney-client relationship has ended. However, some privileges do not survive the termination of the relationship.

Other difficult legal issues abound in the privileges arena. For example, can a person other than a holder (or the holder's attorney) ever raise or assert a privilege on behalf of the holder? What if the holder is not present to assert the privilege or doesn't have knowledge that some party is attempting to disclose privileged matter? What happens if privileged matter is inadvertently disclosed? Who has a right to appeal from a ruling upholding, or rejecting, the existence of a privilege? While not everyday issues, they can be critical when they arise. For that reason, jurisdiction-specific research, well before trial, is particularly important whenever a privilege issue arises. Whether a privilege exists, has been timely and properly asserted, and has been waived or terminated, as well as other issues, are questions of law decided by the judge under FRE 104(a).

The following sections will discuss the four privileges that arise most commonly during trials: the privilege to bar a spouse's testimony, the interspousal communications privilege, the attorney-client privilege, and the doctor-patient privilege.

§8.10.   Marital privilege to bar spousal testimony[8]

1.   Law

This privilege, the first of two marital privileges, is more accurately defined as a witness incompetency rule. The privilege prevents one spouse from being compelled to testify adversely against the other spouse, thereby putting strains on the marital relationship. However, the rule has been disfavored in recent years and has been narrowed or rejected entirely in many jurisdictions.

The privilege to bar a spouse's testimony applies only to criminal cases under federal law. Some states follow the federal approach; others apply the privilege in both civil and criminal cases. In those jurisdictions recognizing it, the most common rule is that the privilege is created when there is a lawful marriage between the spouses and terminates when the marriage terminates, such as by divorce or separation. If the privilege applies, it most commonly applies only to the time frame of the marriage. This approach prevents persons from marrying on the eve of trial for the purpose of creating a bar to being called as a trial witness.

Many courts also hold that the privilege applies only to a spouse's testimony that is actually adverse to the party spouse. There is no bar when a spouse is merely asked to testify to "objective facts" having no direct adverse impact on the party spouse.

The holder rules are particularly important here because the jurisdictions differ significantly. Since the Supreme Court's decision in *Trammel v. United States*, 445 U.S. 40 (1980), under federal law the testifying spouse is the holder of this privilege. This means that whenever a spouse wishes to testify against a party spouse, she can, simply by waiving the privilege. Some states follow *Trammel*'s holder rule. Many states, however, follow the common law rule and provide that the party spouse is the holder of the privilege. This means that the party spouse can, by asserting the privilege, prevent the other spouse from testifying against him as to any events occurring during the time of their marriage. The

---

8. Weinstein §505[01]-[03]; Mueller & Kirkpatrick §5.31; Wigmore §§2227-2245.

holder of the privilege may, of course, waive the privilege and permit or introduce testimony about otherwise barred matters.

The privilege to bar a spouse's testimony is usually held inapplicable in certain situations. In a criminal case between the spouses, such as an assault, or in a civil case between the spouses, such as a divorce or child custody proceeding, the privilege does not apply. The reason is that these cases can only be decided by invading the privilege, otherwise, the most relevant evidence, the testimony of a spouse, would be barred. Most jurisdictions also make the privilege inapplicable if both spouses are jointly charged with a crime, since spouses involved in joint crimes should not benefit from the rule.

Most jurisdictions hold that this privilege terminates upon the termination of the marriage. This means that if the spouses divorce or legally separate before trial, the privilege ends.

2.   Practice

Privilege issues should be raised before trial whenever possible, and important privilege issues almost always surface before trial. Privilege issues are often complicated, involving both procedural and substantive issues, and judges are understandably loathe to decide contested issues without briefs and argument from counsel and an opportunity to consider the issues without time pressures.

This is particularly true with spousal privileges, where the issues can be particularly complicated because two distinct privileges may be involved. When this occurs, the privilege to bar spousal testimony should always be considered first because if that privilege applies, it is usually unnecessary to consider the interspousal communications privilege.

Common issues with respect to the privilege to bar spousal testimony involve whether the privilege has been created or still exists and who the holder of the privilege is.

Example 1:

This is a bank robbery case brought in federal court. One week before trial, the defendant marries his girlfriend, a witness to the alleged robbery. The morning of the trial the following takes place outside the presence of the jury:

Defendant: Your honor, we have one other matter before we proceed with the opening statements. One week ago the defendant and Ms. Johnson were married. Since they are now married, we assert the privilege to bar a spouse's testimony.

Prosecutor: It's not the defendant's privilege to assert. He's not the holder of the privilege; she is.

Defendant: Of course. She has told us she will assert the privilege if called as a witness.

Prosecutor: Even if she's the holder, the privilege does not arise until the time of the marriage, and the privilege under federal law applies only to the time frame of the marriage. We certainly won't ask her about anything that happened since she married the defendant.

Judge: The defendant's wife may be called as a witness by either side. She may be asked about anything that occurred before the time she and the defendant were married. Since she is the holder of the privilege, she can waive it or assert it as she sees fit as to testifying about anything that happened since the marriage.

Commentary: Under state law, the outcome may be different. In some states, the defendant spouse is the holder of this privilege. In some states, the privilege is not limited to the time frame of the marriage.

Example 2:

This is a criminal assault case brought in state court. The defendant is charged with assaulting his wife. Under the law of this state, the party spouse is the holder of the privilege. Before trial, the defendant moves to bar his wife from testifying. At a hearing, the following happens:

Judge: Why can the defendant assert the privilege under the facts of this case?

Defendant: The defendant is the holder of the privilege, your honor, and the events on which the charge is based occurred during a time when they were validly married.

Prosecutor: This is an assault case, your honor, in which the defendant is charged with assaulting his wife. This privilege does not apply to interspousal torts and crimes.

Judge: The motion is denied. The defendant's wife may be called as a witness.

Commentary: If the privilege to bar a spouse's testimony does not apply, lawyers must then determine whether the second marital privilege, protecting interspousal communications, applies.

§8.11. *Interspousal communications privilege*[9]

1. Law

This second spousal privilege has the same rationale as most communications privileges: It promotes open, candid communications between spouses, which is a socially beneficial goal. This rationale has been questioned, since there is doubt whether such communications are affected by the privilege or whether couples even know of the privilege. More persuasive is the idea that certain

---

9. McCormick §§78-86; Weinstein §505[04]-[06]; Mueller & Kirkpatrick §5.32; Wigmore §§2332-2341.

things should remain private and driving a wedge between spouses is something the law should not do.

This privilege — covering interspousal communications — is separate and distinct from the other marital privilege — barring a spouse's testimony. The usual rule is that asserting, or waiving, one of the marital privileges has no implications as to the other privilege.

The interspousal communications privilege is recognized in all jurisdictions and usually applies to both civil and criminal cases. The most common rule is that the privilege protects confidential communications between lawfully married spouses made during the time frame of the marriage. Once created, the privilege does not terminate upon the termination of the marriage.

The holder rules vary with this privilege. In many jurisdictions, each spouse is the holder as to his or her communications to the other; in a number of others, both spouses are holders as to all communications by each spouse to the other. As with any privilege, the holder can waive the benefit of the privilege and permit the otherwise barred communication.

Problems arising with this privilege most commonly center on the meaning of "confidential communications." It is clear that the privilege will not attach if the spouses, through their conduct or words, indicate that they do not intend their communications to be confidential. For instance, if another person, even another family member, is present during a conversation between the spouses, the spouses obviously do not intend the communication to be confidential. If one spouse reads a letter she is mailing to the other spouse to another person, confidentiality is not intended. However, what happens if a communication, intended to be confidential, is intercepted by another person, such as an eavesdropper on a conversation? While historically courts took the position that privileges are to be narrowly construed, in recent years many have reacted to the harshness of that rule, and today most take the position that so long as the spouses took reasonable steps to assure confidentiality in the communication, the privilege still attaches.

The privilege to bar a spouse's testimony about communications with the party-spouse is usually held inapplicable to interspousal crimes and torts, domestic relations litigation, and joint crimes.

2.   Practice

This privilege is the more commonly applicable marital privilege, since it applies to confidential communications between married couples made during the course of the marriage and it never terminates. Common issues involve whether the communications were privileged and whether the holder can assert the privilege.

Example 1:

This is a personal injury case brought in federal court. Plaintiff calls defendant's wife as a witness during trial. Under the applicable state's law, each spouse is the holder of the privilege as to all communications between the spouses, and the state has abrogated the spousal bar privilege. The following then happens:

Q. (By plaintiff's lawyer) Mrs. Johnson, you saw your husband the evening of June 1?
A. Yes.
Q. What time?
A. He came home around 10:00 P.M.
Q. Who was home at that time?
A. Just me and the two kids.
Q. How old are they?
A. Frank is two years old, and Mary's six months old.
Q. Where were they when your husband came home?
A. In the living room, with me.
Q. Now, Mrs. Johnson, tell us what your husband said when he walked into the living room.
Defendant: Objection, your honor. This is privileged.
Judge: Approach the bench. [Lawyers come to the bench.] Counsel, state the basis for your objection.
Defendant: They're asking about an interspousal communication, your honor. They were married at the time of the communication, and the husband as well as the wife can assert the privilege under this state's law. The privilege has been timely asserted.
Judge: Plaintiff, what's your position?
Plaintiff: All of that is true, your honor, but the privilege never arose here. The statement was made in front of their children, so obviously no confidentiality was ever intended. Consequently there's no privileged communication to protect.
Judge: Objection sustained. Speaking in front of children this young does not break the privilege.

Commentary: This dispute should have been resolved before trial. The objection would have been made if the wife had been deposed, and the issue could have been presented to the judge before trial. Judges dislike having privileges issues come up in the middle of trial.

Example 2:

This is a criminal fraud case. Under the law of this state, each spouse is the holder of the privilege as to that spouse's communications to the other. During trial, the state calls the defendant's former wife as a witness. The following then happens:

Q. Ms. Avery, you were once married to the defendant?
A. Yes.
Q. But you're no longer married?
A. That's right. Our divorce became final six months ago.
Q. Ms. Avery, let's turn to January of last year, when your former husband came home from the stockholders' meeting. You remember that day?

A. Yes.

Q. What did your former husband say about the meeting?

Defendant: Objection. This is privileged matter. May we be heard at sidebar?

Judge: Yes. Please approach. [Lawyers come to the bench.] Counsel, hasn't the privilege been terminated? They're no longer married.

Defendant: No, your honor. The marital privilege to bar a spouse's testimony has terminated, but not the interspousal communications privilege. That privilege continues, even if the marriage terminates, and the communication was made when they were still married.

Plaintiff: But the former wife is willing to testify, your honor. She's waived the privilege by voluntarily testifying.

Defendant: She's only the holder of the privilege as to her communications. The husband is holder of the privilege as to his communications to the wife, and he hasn't waived. I've made a timely objection on his behalf.

Judge: That's right. The objection is sustained.

Commentary: This issue should also have been raised and decided before trial.

§8.12.   Attorney-client privilege[10]

1.   Law

The attorney-client privilege, the first recognized privilege, protects confidential communications, oral and written, between an attorney and a client relating to the rendering of legal services. The policy rationale is obvious: Such protection is necessary to ensure that the client will communicate candidly with the lawyer. The client is the holder of the privilege. The attorney can assert the privilege on behalf of the client, but only the client can waive it. Once created, the privilege does not terminate upon the termination of the relationship, and the holder's estate can assert it after the holder's death. The Supreme Court has held the privilege survives the declarant's death in criminal cases. *Swidler & Berlin v. United States*, 524 U.S. 399 (1998). As with any privilege, the holder can waive the benefit of the privilege and permit the disclosure of the contents of otherwise barred communications. When the holder is a corporation, only the board of directors or high managerial officers can waive it.

Who is the "attorney"? Recognizing that in today's world an attorney hires secretaries, clerks, paralegals, and law clerks and works with other lawyers in the firm, courts treat "attorney" broadly to include such third persons. However, when an attorney uses people outside the law firm, are they included within the protection? Most courts hold that if the outsider, such as an interpreter, an investigator, a consulting accountant, a doctor, or an engineer, is necessary

10. McCormick §§87-97; Weinstein §503[01]-[04]; Mueller & Kirkpatrick §§5.8-5.30; Wigmore §§2290-2329.

for the lawyer to communicate meaningfully with the client, is hired specifically for this litigation, and as part of his employment agreement agrees to keep client communications confidential, then the privilege is not waived.

A "confidential communication" is an oral statement, a written communication, or sometimes assertive conduct for which the attorney and the client take reasonable precautions to ensure the privacy of their communications and take reasonable steps to maintain the confidentiality of the communications after they occur. While a few jurisdictions still apply privileges law narrowly, most today hold that eavesdropping on a conversation or intercepting a letter will not break the privilege. The privilege extends to both the client's communications to the lawyer and, ordinarily, the lawyer's communications to the client. A difficult question, in the corporate setting, is whether a written communication from the corporation, which has passed through various hands in the corporation before being transmitted to counsel, is a confidential communication and therefore privileged. If the communication is merely fact-gathering done by lower employees as a routine internal business matter, not a legal matter where advice is sought, it does not become privileged just because it was eventually sent to counsel; if it is a communication from a corporate officer to help counsel in representing the corporation, it should be privileged. If a communication is initially privileged, the corporation must take reasonable steps to maintain the confidentiality of its communications, by keeping them in separate files and restricting access to corporate officers, in order to maintain the privilege.

Whether a communication is privileged or not depends on the circumstances under which it is initially made. If a communication is not privileged when made, transmitting it later to the lawyer cannot make it privileged. For example, the client sends the lawyer a letter after first showing it to a friend. The letter is not privileged, since it was voluntarily shown to someone else. Sending it to the lawyer does not alter its status. If, on the other hand, the document is privileged when made, it retains that status when the client sends it to the lawyer. Since the privilege applies only to communications, it follows that the existence of the attorney-client relationship, the identity of the client, and the basis and source of the lawyer's compensation are not privileged.

Another difficult problem arises when a lawyer inadvertently discloses a privileged communication. This most commonly occurs when a lawyer, responding to documents requests submitted by the other side during discovery, mistakenly includes a privileged document along with other records. While some jurisdictions hold that this breaks the privilege, most hold that a lawyer's mistake should not prejudice the client and that the improperly produced document must be returned and remains inadmissible during trial.

FRE 502, adopted in 2008, significantly changes the law on advertent and inadvertent waivers of the attorney-client privilege and work-product doctrine in federal and state litigation.

First, FRE 502 provides that when a disclosure is made in a federal or state proceeding and waives the attorney-client privilege or work-product protection, the waiver extends to undisclosed communications and information only if the waiver is intentional, the disclosed and undisclosed communications or information concern the same subject matter, and they in fairness should be considered together. This rule rejects the broad "subject matter waiver" rule, which was followed in a number of jurisdictions.

Second, FRE 502 provides that when an inadvertent disclosure is made in a federal proceeding, the disclosure does not operate as a waiver in a federal or state proceeding if the disclosure is inadvertent, the holder of the privilege or protection took reasonable steps to prevent disclosure, and the holder promptly took reasonable steps to rectify the error. This rule should substantially reduce the costs of privilege review, since an inadvertent disclosure alone will no longer automatically trigger a waiver.

Third, FRE 502 provides that in a state proceeding, where there is no state court order regarding waiver, a disclosure does not operate as a waiver in a federal proceeding if the disclosure would not be a waiver under this rule if the disclosure had been made in a federal proceeding, or is not a waiver under the law of the state where the disclosure occured.

Fourth, FRE 502 provides that a federal court may order that the privilege or protection is not waived by disclosure connected with the litigation pending in federal court, and the disclosure is not a waiver in any other federal or state proceeding. This rule makes a federal order regarding privilege waiver binding on parties and non-parties in other federal or state proceedings.

Fifth, FRE 502 provides that unless an agreement on the effect of disclosure in a federal proceeding is incorporated into a court order, it is binding only on the parties to the agreement.

Collectively, the changes brought about by FRE 502 should substantially reduce the costs of discovery, in particular the costs of privilege review, in the litigation process, since a federal court order limiting the effect of a waiver will be applicable to parties as well as non-parties in other federal and state proceedings.

Lawyers sometimes intentionally share information with other lawyers when the parties have agreed to a joint defense. For example, the lawyers for multiple defendants in a criminal case frequently get together to share information, including statements of their clients. If the clients expressly agree to this arrangement, the privilege remains, and any such client statements remain protected. The party claiming privilege must make a clear showing the parties have shared information because a joint defense effort or strategy has been decided on and undertaken by the parties.

What constitutes the rendering of "legal advice"? Keep in mind that only when an attorney acts as an attorney does the privilege apply. When an attorney has a personal conversation with a social friend or discusses financial matters with someone who is a business partner or associate, the lawyer is not acting in the capacity of a lawyer giving legal advice, and the attorney-client privilege will not attach.

Who is the "client"? A client is not only a person or an entity that has established a formal relationship with an attorney; it includes prospective clients, even if they never actually hire the attorney. This governs the common situation where an attorney needs to hear the prospective client's story before deciding to take the case, but the client is reluctant to talk unless the communications will be protected by the privilege. Even if the attorney rejects the case, the communication is still privileged.

The question of the extent of the attorney-client privilege is most difficult in the situations where an attorney represents multiple clients and where the client is an artificial entity, such as a corporation. If one attorney represents multiple clients, the usual rule is that the privilege attaches to each of their communications, but that if there is later litigation between those clients, the privilege is deemed waived. This is because the multiple clients, by not retaining separate counsel, show that they do not intend their communications to be confidential among themselves.

In the corporate setting, privilege issues are complex, in large part because corporate structures and conduct are complex, and corporate counsel can communicate with the corporation only through its employees and agents. Whether a communication between corporate counsel and a particular corporate employee is privileged or is merely a communication with a fact witness frequently arises. The distinction is important because the communication may be disclosable at trial and discoverable before trial if the employee is merely a fact witness. Here, the federal rule differs significantly from those in the majority of states. What kind of corporate employees can corporate counsel communicate with and have that communication protected by the attorney-client privilege? Many states still apply the "control group" test, although other tests exist. Under the control group test, only those communications between corporate counsel and the control group—officers, directors, and managerial employees with legal decision-making authority who can speak for the corporation—are protected by the privilege. Some states, concerned that the narrowness of the control group test often leaves unprotected the communications between counsel and those corporate employees most involved in the facts giving rise to the litigation, created tests that protect such communications.

Federal courts follow *Upjohn Co. v. United States*, 449 U.S. 383 (1981), which rejected the control group test as too narrow and substantially broadened the protection of the privilege in the corporate setting. Under *Upjohn*, whenever corporate counsel needs to communicate with any corporate employee for the purpose of not only making legal decisions, but also obtaining factual information about the employee's conduct and corporate duties necessary to competently represent the corporation, the confidential communications with that employee are protected and remain privileged as long as they are safeguarded and kept confidential. This means, for example, that the communications of an eyewitness-employee to corporate counsel, describing an injury that occurred on the company's premises and the employee's involvement with the incident, will probably be protected by the privilege.

If the communication is privileged, the corporation as the holder can waive the privilege and disclose the contents of the communication to persons outside the corporation. More difficult is whether the privilege is broken by disclosing the contents of the communication to other employees within the corporation. Most courts will uphold the privilege if files are reasonably safeguarded and the communications are circulated only to corporate officers with a need to know the information.

Note that the privilege applies when corporate counsel communicates with the corporate client for the purpose of providing legal advice. When corporate counsel merely provides business advice, or acts as a business negotiator, or acts as an internal corporate investigator, there is a danger that some courts may view these activities as outside the attorney-client privilege. When a lawyer does "non-legal" work and business considerations dominate over legal considerations, the communications that are part of the non-legal work may not be protected. Courts are more likely to reach this result when the corporate counsel is in-house counsel.

Note that conflicts may arise in federal court when the litigation involves both federal question claims (to which the *Upjohn* rule applies) and pendant claims based on diversity jurisdiction (to which the state rule applies).

There are times when a corporation, in self-defense, will voluntarily disclose its internal investigations to the government. Many courts have found this disclosure, partial as it might be, waives the attorney-client privilege and the work-product privilege of the report and its underlying data. For the most part, claims for selective waiver have been rejected. In the absence of voluntary disclosure, corporations conducting internal investigations often attempt to rely on a privilege for critical self-analysis when opposing parties seek discovery. These efforts, grounded mostly in the work-product doctrine, have met with limited success.

The attorney-client privilege is usually inapplicable in litigation between the attorney and the client, as when the client sues for malpractice or the attorney sues for unpaid fees. In addition, if the reason for the communication is itself improper, as when the client seeks legal advice he knows is for carrying out ongoing or future fraudulent or criminal activity, the privilege does not apply. Of course, the privilege applies when a client seeks advice from his lawyer concerning crimes or frauds already committed.

The attorney-client privilege must be kept distinct from the work-product doctrine. While the attorney-client privilege is absolute, the work-product doctrine under Federal Rule of Civil Procedure 26(b)(3) is a qualified privilege that protects an attorney's trial preparation materials unless an opposing party makes a showing of substantial need and undue hardship. Most states hold that the attorney is the holder of the work-product doctrine.

Documents used to refresh a witness's memory before the witness's deposition generally are producible on demand under FRE 612. But what if the documents are work-product? Some courts hold the documents must be produced, especially when they have had some impact on the witness's deposition testimony. Courts are split on whether production is required when the witness says the work-product documents did nothing to refresh his memory.

The work-product doctrine also protects the efforts of trial consultants from the discovery process, so long as the work is directed by an attorney and pertains to the attorney's thoughts, opinions, and impressions. Protection includes the consultant's witness preparation, as well as strategy sessions, client discussions, jury research and selection, and demonstrative evidence development.

2.   Practice

Privilege issues probably arise most frequently with the attorney-client privilege. Common issues involve whether the privilege attaches to a particular communication, whether the communication has been kept confidential, and whether the privilege applies to corporate counsel's communication with particular corporate employees.

Example 1:

This is a federal income tax evasion case. The defendant contacts a neighbor, a lawyer, and discusses the case with him over the telephone. The lawyer decides not to take the case and refers the defendant to another lawyer. Before trial, the prosecution subpoenas the lawyer who had declined the representation. That lawyer moves to quash the subpoena. At a hearing on the motion to quash, the following happens:

Judge: This is the motion of Mr. James Woods to quash a trial subpoena directed to him. Mr. Woods, are you present?

Woods: I am, your honor. I'll be representing myself.

Judge: Please proceed.

Woods: Your honor, I have moved to quash the subpoena because it appears to call for testimony that would violate the attorney-client privilege. The prosecution has indicated that it intends to question me about conversations I have had in the past with the defendant. Doing so would violate the privilege. I'm asserting the privilege on behalf of the defendant, and the defense has told me that they intend to assert the privilege as well.

Judge: Defense, is that correct?

Defense: That's correct, your honor. I'm also asserting the privilege on behalf of my client.

Judge: Prosecution, what's your position?

Prosecutor: There's no privilege to assert, your honor. These conversations took place outside of the attorney-client relationship. The defendant was not his client at the time these telephonic conversations occurred. In fact, the defendant never became his client. The relationship was never created.

Judge: Counsel, without disclosing the contents of your actual communications, were they about the possibility of representing the defendant?

Woods: They were, your honor. After exploring the possibility of representing him, I decided I was not the right person for the case and referred him to defense counsel.

Judge: The motion is granted. The prosecution may not inquire into any conversations between the defendant and Mr. Woods that concerned the possibility of retaining Mr. Woods in this matter.

Commentary: Conversations between attorney and prospective client exploring the possibility of representation are protected by the privilege.

Example 2:

This is a breach of contract case brought against the defendant corporation. The plaintiff moves to compel compliance with a documents request that calls for the defendant to produce an internal memorandum that admits late delivery of goods to the plaintiff. The defendant resists complying with the documents request on the basis that the memorandum is a privileged communication in the possession of defense counsel. At the hearing on the motion to compel, the following happens:

Plaintiff: Your honor, we moved to compel the production of this internal memorandum. The defendant admitted in other discovery that the memorandum was written by the defendant's production chief and directed to the vice president for marketing. The memorandum remained in the vice president's files until after this litigation started, after which it was sent to corporate counsel, who sent it to defense counsel. The document was not a privileged communication when it was written, and it doesn't become privileged because it was later sent to a lawyer.

Defendant: The memorandum was written after the dispute with the plaintiff arose. At that time, the corporation was already represented by counsel, its in-house general counsel. Under these circumstances, the memorandum was privileged, and we have maintained the confidentiality of the memorandum ever since.

Judge: Was this memorandum written at the direction of counsel?

Defendants: Not directly, your honor; but the company obviously knew that litigation might result from this dispute.

Judge: Was this memorandum written to counsel?

Defendant: Again, not directly, but it was obvious from the situation that the memorandum would be passed on to counsel.

Judge: The motion to compel is granted. The defendant will deliver a copy of the memorandum to the plaintiff's counsel within five days of today.

Example 3:

This is a personal injury case. Plaintiff was injured when she slipped and fell in the corporate defendant's store. Plaintiff deposes a store sales clerk who witnessed the incident. During the deposition, the clerk is asked what she told the store's lawyer when she was interviewed about the incident. Defendant's lawyer objects to these questions on the basis of attorney-client privilege and directs the clerk not to answer. Plaintiff moves to compel answers. At a hearing on the motion to compel answers, the following happens:

Plaintiff: This is our motion to compel, your honor. Defendant objected to questions at the employee's deposition on the basis of the attorney-client privilege. However, communications between the store's employee and the store's lawyer are not privileged. As you know, in this state, we follow the control group test to make that determination. The communication here was with a sales clerk, not someone with managerial responsibility who is a member of the store's control group.

Judge: Defense?

Defendant: Your honor, we needed to interview the store's employees to represent the store competently. The clerk was a critical eyewitness as well as an employee. Plaintiff has already deposed the clerk to learn everything she knows. We objected only when they tried to get her to divulge what she told the store's lawyers, who were representing the store in this matter.

Judge: The motion to compel is granted. The employee will be deposed again so that these questions will be answered.

Commentary: In federal court, following the *Upjohn* decision, the defendant's argument should prevail. Defense counsel also might have objected to these questions on the basis of the work-product doctrine, found in Rule 26(b)(3) of the Federal Rules of Civil Procedure.

Example 4:

This is a wrongful termination case brought against the plaintiff's former employer. During an investigation by the defendant's lawyer, the lawyer interviews a current employee of the defendant who provides information about the plaintiff's past work performance. At trial, the defendant calls the employee as a witness. Out of the hearing of the jury, the following happens:

Lawyer: Your honor, my name is Ralph Thomas. I represent Mr. Johnson, who has been called as the next defense witness. I am objecting to any planned testimony in which Mr. Johnson will be asked to recount what he told defense counsel during the interview. Mr. Johnson believed—in fact, was led to believe—that the interview was confidential and that this was a private conversation with a lawyer that would be kept private. Now the defense plans to use his statements at trial.

Defendant: Your honor, the store's lawyer represented the store, not the employee, and he made that clear at the time. This is not a privileged communication because the store's lawyer was not a lawyer to the clerk. There's no privilege that ever arose.

Judge: The objection is overruled.

Commentary: Note that neither the plaintiff's nor the defendant's lawyer can directly make a privilege objection, since the employee is not their client. The situation here is a common one. Corporate counsel represents only the corporate entity, not its officers or employees in their individual capacity.

§8.13. Doctor-patient privilege[11]

1. Law

The doctor-patient privilege, where it exists, protects confidential communications between a doctor and a patient relating to the rendering of medical treatment. The policy rationale is that the privilege is necessary to ensure that the patient candidly will communicate necessary information to the doctor. Many states, however, protect not only the communications, but also the results of examinations and tests. The patient is the holder of the privilege. Once created, the privilege does not terminate upon the termination of the relationship. As with any privilege, the holder can waive the benefit of the privilege and elicit or permit otherwise barred testimony.

The doctor-patient privilege must be kept distinct from medical records privacy acts, which exist in many states. Such acts usually make hospital and other medical records confidential and bar the hospital or medical office from disclosing them without the express consent of the patient. These privacy acts often are substantially broader than the usual doctor-patient privilege.

The predominant rule in federal courts is that there is no federal general doctor-patient privilege. This is because the policy rationale that underlies privileges — the need to foster candid communications between persons having certain relationships — is insufficient to warrant this privilege. After all, why would a patient not be candid with his treating physician, when the patient has a motive to be diagnosed and treated correctly?

In *Jaffee v. Redmond*, 518 U.S. 1 (1996), the Supreme Court recognized a federal absolute privilege for psychotherapist-patient communications and held that the privilege applies to communications between the patient and psychiatrists, psychologists, and licensed social workers. This decision brought uniformity to this area, since now the federal courts and every state recognize a psychotherapist-patient privilege, although the jurisdictions may differ in their definition of a psychotherapist.

Most states also recognize a general doctor-patient privilege. In those states that recognize the privilege, the scope of the privilege varies considerably, from the narrow application of communications to the broader application of general patient medical records. In the latter approach, the privilege usually covers patient communications of current conditions, medical history, and results of examinations and tests. Some states limit the privilege to psychotherapists. Some jurisdictions limit the privilege to civil cases.

Doctor-patient communications must be confidential. Most courts interpret "doctor" and "patient" broadly, holding that the doctor's medical personnel are all considered within the privilege. Likewise, a patient includes someone with a close relationship to the actual patient, such as a spouse or a parent, who communicates to the doctor or his staff, and such communications are within the privilege. However, courts have generally held that where the examination is not voluntary, such as a court-ordered physical or mental examination, the privilege will not apply.

11. McCormick §§98-105; Weinstein §504[01]-[09]; Muller & Kirkpatrick §§5.34-5.35; Wigmore §§2380-2391.

Waiver issues are common with the doctor-patient privilege. Most jurisdictions follow the rule that filing a lawsuit, putting in issue a specific medical condition, operates as a waiver of the doctor-patient privilege as to the medical records relevant to the condition. The waiver includes information regarding past treatment for the same or related conditions. Therefore, the defense can depose the plaintiff's physicians and obtain their medical records during discovery. This includes the treating physician as well as other doctors who have treated the patient for the same or similar conditions in the past. A few states require more express conduct before a waiver will occur.

2. Practice

Doctor-patient privilege issues do not arise as frequently because the federal courts and a few states do not recognize a general doctor-patient privilege, although the federal courts and every state recognize a psychotherapist-patient privilege, and because waiver situations are so common. The most common issues involve whether the privilege exists under the particular circumstances.

Example:

This is a personal injury case brought in federal court under its diversity jurisdiction. The defendant claims some of the plaintiff's claimed injuries from the collision are preexisting injuries. The defendant subpoenas the plaintiff's orthopedic doctor, who treated her for injuries that occurred before the collision, and the doctor's patient files. The plaintiff objects. At a pretrial hearing, the following happens:

Judge: Plaintiff, why is this improper?

Plaintiff: The plaintiff has not waived that doctor-patient privilege, your honor. Under the applicable state law, by filing the lawsuit she has waived the privilege only as to her treating physician following the collision. They're trying to get medical records about an injury that occurred several years before this collision. That remains privileged, and we're asserting the privilege for her.

Defendant: The plaintiff claims that her leg was injured and has not fully recovered. During her deposition, she stated that she had hurt that leg several years earlier and had been treated by an orthopedic specialist. We've subpoenaed the doctor and his records because they may support our contention that some of the plaintiff's claimed injuries were preexisting.

Plaintiff: This is just a fishing expedition, your honor. They've got to have more reason to be allowed to search through the plaintiff's medical past, trying to find something that might help them during trial.

Judge: The objection is overruled. The defendant has made an adequate preliminary showing. However, I will inspect the medical records in camera to determine if there is anything in the records that might be of use to the defense. If there is, I will release the appropriate parts of those records, and the doctor will be allowed to testify about them.

§8.14.   Other privileges[12]

The marital, attorney-client, and doctor-patient privileges and the Fifth Amendment's self-incrimination privilege are the privileges that arise most frequently during litigation. However, others recognized by various jurisdictions must always be kept in mind, such as clergy-penitent, reporter-informant, trade secrets, government secrets, and the informer's privilege. In criminal cases, the privileges for government secrets and informer identity and the Fifth Amendment privilege against self-incrimination arise constantly.

---

12. McCormick §§106-143; Weinstein §§506-509; Mueller & Kirkpatrick §§5.5, 5.33; Wigmore §§2183, 2250-2284, 2345-2379, 2394-2396. See also the deleted Rules 501-513, containing the proposed federal privileges that were approved by the Supreme Court, but that were rejected by Congress and did not become law.

IX

DIRECT EXAMINATION OF EXPERTS

§9.1.   *Introduction*

One of the goals of the Federal Rules of Evidence is to bring the realities of life into the courtroom. That, we have learned, is a reliable and principled way to resolve private and public disputes.

Judges weigh probabilities and reliability when deciding evidentiary issues, and these are based on life experience. So we look to a witness's motives and reasons for doing or saying something, to his bias or interest, to the firsthand factual foundation for whatever he proposes to say. We talk about the trustworthiness of evidence in a courtroom the same way we do about the trustworthiness of people and things in our daily lives.

As life becomes more complicated and more technical, we rely more on experts for answers and guidance. The same thing is happening in our courtrooms.

It is a rare civil trial that does not present some kind of expert, such as a doctor, an accountant, a mechanic, or an engineer. In wrongful death cases, for example, it is routine for economists to testify to the economic loss of the survivors caused by the deceased's death.

In criminal cases, too, expert witnesses are becoming commonplace, whether the issue is one of fingerprint comparisons, shoeprints, DNA analysis, firearm comparisons, or any of the other class or individual evidence matters that might arise. In drug cases, for example, it is becoming routine for law enforcement officers to testify to the kinds of equipment drug dealers possess, such as digital beepers, two-way radios, and scales, and to the amount of drugs that separates the mere user from the seller.

Expert testimony must pass several evidentiary tests, governed by FRE 702-705, before it is properly admissible. These evidentiary tests are, as always, questions of law that the judge must decide under FRE 104(a), where the proponent has the burden of proving its right to admissibility by a preponderance of the evidence.

The routine cases never have caused much of a problem for trial judges. Most experts are qualified to talk about whatever matter is the subject of their proposed testimony. Judges have no difficulty sorting out unqualified witnesses. Testimony about fault and causation and injury in the routine cases ordinarily presents matters of weight for the fact finder and does not require much effort from the trial judge, other than requiring witnesses to hue to the lines of relevance.

§9.2. Frye, Daubert, Joiner, *and* Kumho Tire[1]

1. Law

Rule 702. Testimony by Expert Witnesses

A witness who is qualified as an expert by knowledge, skill, experience, training, or education may testify in the form of an opinion or otherwise if:

(a) the expert's scientific, technical, or other specialized knowledge will help the trier of fact to understand the evidence or to determine a fact in issue;

(b) the testimony is based on sufficient facts or data;

(c) the testimony is the product of reliable principles and methods; and

(d) the expert has reliably applied the principles and methods to the facts of the case.

Rule 703. Bases of an Expert's Opinion Testimony

An expert may base an opinion on facts or data in the case that the expert has been made aware of or personally observed. If experts in the particular field would reasonably rely on those kinds of facts or data in forming an opinion on the subject, they need not be admissible for the opinion to be admitted. But if the facts or data would otherwise be inadmissible, the proponent of the opinion may disclose them to the jury only if their probative value in helping the jury evaluate the opinion substantially outweighs their prejudicial effect.

Rule 704. Opinion on an Ultimate Issue

(a) In General — Not Automatically Objectionable. An opinion is not objectionable just because it embraces an ultimate issue.

---

1. Wright & Gold, Federal Practice and Procedure: Evidence §6266; Mueller & Kirkpatrick §7.17; Advisory Committee's Notes to FRE 701-703.

(b) Exception.   In a criminal case, an expert witness must not state an opinion about whether the defendant did or did not have a mental state or condition that constitutes an element of the crime charged or of a defense. Those matters are for the trier of fact alone.

Rule 705.   Disclosing the Facts or Data Underlying an Expert's Opinion

Unless the court orders otherwise, an expert may state an opinion — and give the reasons for it — without first testifying to the underlying facts or data. But the expert may be required to disclose those facts or data on cross-examination.

Traditionally, in the more complicated or technical cases, especially where something new or novel was being proposed, judges operated in a well-established comfort zone — the *Frye* standard. That is, when the validity of a scientific principle and the conclusion based on it were challenged, the trial judge knew that "the thing from which the deduction is made must be sufficiently established to have gained general acceptance in the particular field in which it belongs." *Frye v. United States*, 293 F. 1013 (D.C. Cir. 1923). *Frye* held that a systolic blood pressure deception test was inadmissible.

While federal courts and most states adopted the *Frye* general acceptance requirement, pockets of discontent would appear from time to time. The rule was rigid. Novel or new principles were excluded. The test did not yield predictable results, nor was it uniformly applied to all types of scientific evidence.

The *Frye* test surrendered primary responsibility for admission to the relevant scientific community. Judicial determinations usually reflected the proposed expert's self-assessment, although many judges, discontented with acting as virtual rubber stamps, conducted independent examinations of the scientific validity of the proposed conclusions. The federal reviewing courts were divided regarding the proper standard for admitting expert testimony. See *United States v. Dowling*, 753 F.2d 1224 (3d Cir. 1985).

The resolution came in *Daubert v. Merrell Dow Pharmaceuticals*, 509 U.S. 579 (1993). *Daubert* applies to all federal court trials, even diversity cases that apply substantive state law.

The Supreme Court in *Daubert* held that *Frye* did not survive enactment of the Federal Rules of Evidence. *Frye* no longer was to be the decisive test, although general acceptance was retained as something for the trial judge to consider when weighing admissibility of scientific evidence.

Now primary responsibility for determining the admissibility of expert witness evidence is placed on the trial judge, whose role is to be a "gatekeeper," screening the offered evidence. When faced with a challenge to the offer of expert witness evidence, the trial judge must determine at an FRE 104(a) hearing that "an expert's testimony both rests on a reliable foundation and is relevant to the task at hand."

Daubert gives the trial judge four specific factors to use when determining whether the technique or methodology used is valid and was properly applied to the facts of the case. These are (1) whether the theory or technique in question can be and has been tested, and whether standards and controls for the operation of the theory or technique have been used and maintained; (2) whether the technique or theory has been subjected to peer review and publication; (3) the known or potential error rate of the technique or theory when applied, and the existence and maintenance of standards controlling the technique's operation; and (4) whether the technique or theory has been generally accepted in the relevant scientific community. (Additional details about these and other factors are contained in Sec. 9.4.)

The trial judge's inquiry under *Daubert* is flexible, with the focus on techniques and methodology used, not on the conclusions reached: "The inquiry is focused solely on the principles and methodology, not on the conclusions they generate." No single factor is controlling. All or none might apply.

An abuse of discretion standard applies to appellate review of rulings excluding expert testimony. That was decided in *General Electric Co. v. Joiner*, 522 U.S. 136 (1997). The appeal can be outcome determinative for litigants who win the trial but lose the appeal because of improper expert testimony. The Supreme Court has authorized federal appeals courts to reverse without remand if the loser of the appeal "has had a full and fair opportunity to present the case, including arguments for a new trial. . . ." *Weisgram v. Marley Co.*, 528 U.S. 440 (2000).

Joiner did something else. It authorized trial judges to look beyond the methodology used to the conclusion reached. The Supreme Court recognized that a reliable methodology might be improperly applied to the facts of the case. That is, ". . . conclusions and methodology are not entirely distinct from one another. . . . A court may conclude that there is simply too great an analytical gap between the data and the opinion offered."

In *Joiner*, the Supreme Court held the trial judge did not abuse his discretion when he rejected the qualified experts' reliance on animal studies and three studies of disease in humans, even though recognized scientific techniques were used.

Daubert and *Joiner* have not been read to mean that contradictory expert testimony must be seen as unreliable. Nor are experts required to use the same tests or methods to reach reliable conclusions. Still, when an expert says he has applied principles and methods in accord with professional standards, his conclusion will be suspect if it is one most experts in the field would not reach.

Daubert and *Joiner* left open the question of whether they extend beyond matters of pure science. Experts can be qualified by their training, experience in the field, and observations. Specific *Daubert* factors might not be helpful to the gatekeeper in those cases. Some courts were holding evidence too unreliable to satisfy *Daubert* was admissible as non-scientific testimony. The question was resolved in *Kumho Tire Co. v. Carmichael*, 526 U.S. 137 (1999).

Kumho Tire held the trial judge's gatekeeping obligation "applies not only to testimony based on 'scientific' knowledge, but also to testimony based on 'technical' and 'other specialized' knowledge." A nonscientific expert is not treated more permissively. He receives the same scrutiny as a scientific expert. The trial judge may consider all or none of the *Daubert* factors, or he may consider any other factor that applies to reliability. The *Daubert* factors, said the Court in *Kumho Tire*, are meant to be helpful, not definitive.

An engineer, then, can be asked how often his methodology has produced erroneous results, or whether his method is generally accepted in the relevant engineering community. The bottom line is whether the expert is using in the courtroom the same level of intellectual rigor he would use in practice.

Kumho Tire dealt with testimony from a qualified tire failure analysis expert. The trial judge excluded that testimony because the expert's methodology, pure observation, lacked a scientific basis for reaching the conclusion "regarding the particular matter to which the expert testimony was directly relevant." The Supreme Court affirmed.

Principles established in *Daubert, Joiner,* and *Kumho Tire* are reflected in the 2000 amendment to FRE 702. That is, (1) the expert's testimony must be based on sufficient facts or data, (2) the testimony must be the product of reliable principles and methods, and (3) the witness must reliably apply the principles and methods to the facts of the case.

No specific reliability factor is contained in the rule. In a comprehensive and illuminating note to FRE 702, the Advisory Committee explains:

> The trial judge in all cases of proffered expert testimony must find that it is properly grounded, well-reasoned, and not speculative before it can be admitted. The expert's testimony must be grounded in an accepted body of learning or experience in the expert's field, and the expert must explain how the conclusion is so grounded.

And,

> If the witness is relying solely or primarily on experience, then the witness must explain how that experience leads to the conclusion reached, why that experience is a sufficient basis for the opinion, and how that experience is reliably applied to the facts.

The rule states that an expert may be qualified on the basis of experience, but, according to the Advisory Committee's Note, use of the word "expert" does not mean that a jury should actually be informed that a qualified witness is testifying as an "expert."

Thus far, more than 40 states have adopted *Daubert,* although some still adhere to the distinction between scientific and nonscientific testimony. The courts in some of the most populous states, including California, New York, Illinois, and Pennsylvania, have rejected *Daubert* and retained *Frye* or some modified version of *Frye.* Even in states retaining the *Frye* test, it appears that *Daubert* has had some impact, with some courts engaging in a relevancy and reliability analysis when examining expert testimony.

There is no reason why courts should not demand of experts the same intellectual rigor that is demanded of experts in their professional work, whether *Daubert* or *Frye* is the controlling law. In turn, judges cannot be passive umpires when it comes to cutting-edge scientific evidence. As gatekeepers, they will have to be active managers, if not amateur scientists.

2. Practice

Under *Daubert*, the trial judge, to carry out his "gatekeeper" role, will have to hold a "*Daubert* hearing" when there is a challenge to the admissibility of expert testimony.

Example:

This is a negligence case brought in federal court in which the plaintiff is seeking damages for a claimed whiplash injury caused when the plaintiff's car was rear-ended by the defendant's car. The defense is based in part on there being no objective findings to support the plaintiff's claims of continuing pain. One of the plaintiff's experts is a doctor who has developed a system that he claims can determine whether the plaintiff's complaints of pain are legitimate. The defendant objects to the doctor testifying, on the ground that the testimony is based on a new and unreliable method. At a pretrial "*Daubert* hearing," the following happens:

Q. (By plaintiff's lawyer) Dr. Smith, you're a neurologist and a research scientist at the state medical college?
A. That's right.
Q. You've held that position for how many years?
A. Ten years.
Q. What area has your research focused on?
A. My area of interest is pain. I do research on how to evaluate pain in patients, how to measure the degree of pain, and how to determine whether a patient is malingering or has genuine pain. It's a fascinating field.
Q. Have you been able to develop a method for measuring neck pain or for determining if a patient is exaggerating or fabricating complaints of neck pain?
A. I have. I've spent the last three years developing and testing the method.
Q. Is that the method you used to evaluate the plaintiff's neck?
A. Yes.
Q. Doctor, describe for us what you've developed.
A. Certainly. My testing method is based on the fact that when patients experience actual pain in the muscles, it affects how they use those muscles. This effect is involuntary and is well accepted in the medical world. The difficulty has always been to develop a way to verify complaints of pain through a reliable objective testing method. What my colleagues and I have done is to develop a physical test to measure whether the neck muscles are experiencing the minute, involuntary spasms that are a reaction to using muscles that experience pain. The test involves putting headgear that has a laser light on the front of a patient. The patient is then asked to use the laser light to trace a pattern on a screen that is placed in front of the patient. The pattern requires the patient to move his head up and down, side to side, and in a circular motion to trace the pattern accurately. The headgear is

connected to computerized equipment that measures how smoothly, and to what extent, the patient is able to move the light over the entire pattern. A patient without neck pain will be able to trace the pattern smoothly. A patient with actual neck pain will have small involuntary jerking motions that are undetected by the human eye, but that are recorded quite readily by the equipment. The test results can be displayed both on a computer monitor and in digital form.

Q. Have you tested the system?

A. That's what we've been doing for the past year. We hope to make the system commercially available soon.

Q. Whom have you tested?

A. We've been testing actual patients at the hospital as well as non-patients for control purposes.

Q. Have you determined a rate of error?

A. Yes. The test must, of course, be analyzed by a trained examiner. In that sense, it's very much like a polygraph examination, which needs a trained examiner to evaluate the results. About 10 percent of our tests are inconclusive. In the others, we are able to determine if the patient has actual pain.

Q. Doctor, what about patients who are malingerers?

A. We've done controlled studies in which some subjects fake pain, others have no pain, and still others have actual pain. The method is quite accurate in identifying those who fake pain. The reason is that the neck movements of subjects faking pain are quite different, when analyzed by our computerized equipment, than the neck movements of persons with either no pain or actual pain. Again, it's very much like a polygraph exam, where a trained examiner can usually easily see when a subject is trying to disguise or exaggerate his physiological responses to certain questions.

Q. Have you published any papers about your method?

A. One so far. We published in the Journal of Chiropractic Medicine earlier this year.

Plaintiff: Your honor, I have no further foundation questions.

Judge: Defense, you may inquire.

Q. (By defendant's lawyer) Other than the one article in the chiropractic journal, have you published elsewhere?

A. Not yet, but, of course, we plan on future publications.

Q. Have you been published in any orthopedic medicine journals?

A. No.

Q. Or neurological journals?

A. No.

Q. Do you know of any other research going on that is attempting to duplicate or test your method?

A. Well, we've had inquiries since we published our first article, but I'm not aware of anyone who is presently testing our method.

Q. Have the results of your method ever been admitted in any court of law in this country?

A. No. This is the first time I've been asked.

Defendant: No further questions, your honor.

Judge: Any arguments?

Plaintiff: The issue under *Daubert* is whether the test is relevant and reliable. It's clearly relevant, and the only remaining question is whether it is reliable. Dr. Smith is a respected neurologist and research scientist. He has explained the underlying scientific validity of his method and the testing that has been done to verify its accuracy. That's enough for him to testify at trial.

Defendant: Your honor, this is novel science. The method has never been admitted in court, it has never been published outside of one article in a magazine for chiropractors, and the tests have never been verified or duplicated by anyone else. That's too uncertain to qualify under *Daubert*.

Judge: The objection is sustained at the present time. I will revisit the issue at the time of trial if the plaintiff has any additional information to submit on the issue of the method's reliability.

Commentary: Under the *Frye* "general acceptance" standard, the testimony most likely would be inadmissible. The issue under the *Daubert* analysis is a closer one, as the following sections discuss in detail.

§9.3. *Relevancy*[2]

1. Law

The first consideration in the admissibility of expert testimony must be relevancy, as prescribed by FRE 401 and 702. If the proposed evidence is not relevant to a fact of consequence, there is no need to go any further. It must be so tied to the facts of the case that it will aid the jury in resolving a factual dispute. That is, the suggested testimony must "fit" the issue that the expert proposes to testify about. The judge must determine whether the reasoning or methodology used by the expert to reach his opinions or conclusions properly can be applied to the facts of the case.

Likewise, if the proposed testimony does not "assist the trier of fact to understand the evidence or to determine a fact in issue," it should be excluded. Put another way, the proposed testimony must be helpful to the trier of fact. The Supreme Court in *Daubert* gave this example: The study of the phases of the moon may provide valid scientific knowledge about whether a certain night was dark. If darkness is a fact in issue, the knowledge will assist the trier of fact. But evidence that the moon was full on a certain night will not assist the trier of fact in determining whether an individual was unusually likely to have behaved irrationally on that night.

Expert testimony that "chooses up sides" or merely tells the jury what result to reach is not helpful. For example, an expert's opinion about the defendant's guilt or whether the defendant committed fraud is not helpful. Nor is an

---

2. Weinstein §702[03]; McCormick §203; Mueller & Kirkpatrick §§7.5-7.7, 7.12-7.13; Wigmore §§555-561.

opinion about mixed questions of law and fact unless it is clear the expert understands the proper legal standards. Experts are not helpful when they decide which trial witnesses are credible or how much weight to give their testimony. But a police gang expert is allowed to testify to a gang "code of silence" to explain why one gang member testified on behalf of a fellow gang member.

The line between helpful and not helpful is not clear. In more complex matters, experts testify that the design of a product was unreasonably dangerous or that a manufacturer's conduct was negligent, but an opinion about whether a party was negligent in a simple car accident case or whether a party breached a contract is not helpful and rarely is allowed.

The general view of the cases is that experts cannot tell a jury what the law is, such as what the meaning of federal motor vehicle safety regulations is, although some cases allow tax experts to testify to the meaning of sections of the Internal Revenue Code and safety experts to define the meaning of private industry and OSHA safety standards. Most trial judges are turf conscious and are not quick to allow experts to explain the law. Some decisions, however, require expert testimony to interpret complex statutes and regulations relied on by a party to establish a standard of care.

Courts are divided on the helpfulness of expert testimony about eyewitness identification, but many do not allow it because, they say, jurors don't need that kind of assistance. Reliability of research concerning eyewitness identification is far enough along to withstand a *Daubert* attack. The strongest argument in favor of admissibility is that the research offers a way of dispelling common misconceptions — for example, that witness certainty translates into an accurate identification. Prosecution experts tell juries what certain slang expressions mean in gambling, drug, and organized crime cases because it assists the fact finder. But a witness's testimony about the fairness of insurance settlement practices of a casualty carrier is not helpful.

Put simply, the "helpfulness" test is whether the expert proposes to testify to something the average juror would not know without the expert's help. Some cases frame the issue in terms of whether the proposed opinion is beyond the common knowledge or, more elegantly, beyond the ken of the average juror. Note, too, FRE 702 provides that an expert may share specialized knowledge with a jury without giving any opinion or reaching any conclusion.

FRE 704(a) provides that expert opinion "is not objectionable just because it embraces an ultimate issue" (except, under FRE 704(b), for mental states of defendants in criminal cases). However, FRE 702 also requires that expert testimony "help the trier of fact to understand the evidence or to determine a fact in issue." Putting the two rules together creates the proper rule: An expert may testify to "ultimate issues" if the testimony is "helpful" to the jury.

For example, an accident reconstruction expert in a personal injury case testifies that from her analysis of the evidence she concluded the defendant's car was on the plaintiff's side of the road when it collided with the plaintiff's car. This testimony is proper. Can the expert then testify that the defendant was therefore legally negligent? No. Such testimony does not assist the jury, which is just as capable of taking the expert's factual conclusions and reaching the proper legal conclusions on the issue of negligence.

The one exception to the general admissibility of expert testimony on "ultimate issues" is found in FRE 704(b), which provides that experts in criminal cases cannot, by opinion or inference, state whether the defendant possessed the mental state that is an element of the crime charged or is a defense to that charge. The exception apparently applies not only to insanity defenses, where it was primarily aimed, but also to other criminal cases where the accused's mental state is in issue, such as cases that raise questions of entrapment, or premeditation to murder, or the specific intent to commit a crime.

The decisions on the distinction between proper and improper ultimate issues testimony are not consistent. FRE 704(b) does not stop experts from giving the jury information that will help it decide the ultimate issue. In an insanity defense, for example, an expert may testify to the characteristics and effects of a mental disease, such as schizophrenia, and whether the defendant suffers from it, but not whether the defendant understood the wrongfulness of his actions at the time of the alleged crime.

For example, one court held it to be error under FRE 704(b) for an IRS agent to testify that the defendant "intentionally understated his income," but not error in another case for an IRS agent to say that the defendant "wilfully and intentionally increased his income knowing full well that he had not reported the taxes due thereon."

May a police expert testify that the defendant possessed a certain amount of drugs with the intent to distribute them? The literal language of the rule seems to bar the opinion, but the decisions are hostile to that interpretation. Some courts, but not all, find the error harmless when the question is clearly directed to the defendant's intent. Others accept the opinion as "general modus operandi" testimony, or as an opinion based on the expert's knowledge of common criminal practices, rather than some special knowledge of or familiarity with the defendant's mental processes. Some courts have suggested, but none has specifically held, that FRE 704(b) is intended to apply only to psychiatrists or other mental health professionals.

While some post-*Daubert* cases have considered relevancy as the second step of the analysis, trial judges are finding it is more sensible and more economical to make the relevancy requirement the first step and first determine whether the proposed testimony "fits" the case. If it does not, much time and effort are saved by ending the matter there, without engaging in the difficult and often time-consuming task of determining scientific validity. After all, judges are trained and equipped to determine matters of relevancy. They ordinarily are not trained as scientists.

Of course, in a broader sense, relevancy is the overriding issue, since evidence that is irrelevant cannot be helpful. Still, confining the relevancy issue to its traditional scope — helpfulness or "fit" in relation to issues of consequence — without inquiry into reliability is a better analytic method because it has clear boundaries. Evidence may be reliable but not helpful. That would make it irrelevant.

2. Practice

The first issue the judge must decide is whether the expert's testimony "will help the trier of fact to understand the evidence or to determine a fact in issue." The standard favors admissibility.

The second issue, actually part of the first, is whether the expert can testify to "ultimate issues." Such testimony is generally proper if it is "helpful" to the jury.

Example 1:

This is a negligence action brought against a beauty salon. The plaintiff was injured when she tripped over a baby crawling on the floor. During trial, the plaintiff calls a safety expert. The following then happens:

Q. (By plaintiff's lawyer) Professor Adams, are you familiar with the safety considerations that apply to retail businesses like beauty salons?
A. I am.
Q. Have you studied them?
A. Yes.
Q. Professor Adams, I'm going to ask you questions about whether a baby crawling on the floor of a busy beauty salon constitutes a safety hazard. First, . . .
Defendant: Objection, your honor. This is not a proper area for expert testimony under Rule 702.
Judge: Plaintiff, any response?
Plaintiff: Yes, your honor. The issue is whether this testimony is helpful to the jury. It will help the jury resolve the issues in this case.
Judge: The objection is sustained. This is information within the knowledge and experience of the jurors.

Commentary: This objection, frequently raised, is a judgment call. The question is whether the testimony is helpful or whether it merely brings up what jurors already know and understand. The lawyer opposing this expert testimony should have raised this issue before trial.

Example 2:

This is a civil commitment proceeding in which the state is attempting to commit Philip Marlowe because he, in the words of the commitment statute, "represents a danger to himself and others." The matter is being tried to the court. During the petitioner's case, the following happens:

Q. (By petitioner's lawyer) Dr. Adams, following your examination of the respondent, Mr. Marlowe, did you reach any diagnosis?
A. Yes. I concluded that Mr. Marlowe is a paranoid schizophrenic, undifferentiated type, with organic brain damage.
A. Doctor, does that mean that Mr. Marlowe is a danger to himself and others?
Respondent: Objection, your honor. This is improper testimony.
Judge: What's improper about it?
Respondent: This is testimony on the ultimate legal issue in the case, your honor. That invades the province of the fact finder.
Judge: The objection is overruled. I find that the doctor's answer, and reasons for it, will be very helpful in resolving the issues in the case.

Example 3:

> This is a personal injury case. A doctor called in the plaintiff's case-in-chief testifies as follows:

Q. (By plaintiff's lawyer) Doctor, describe for us the limitations in the plaintiff's right arm.

A. Certainly. He has lost about 20 percent of the range of motion in the arm. He cannot extend his arm straight out the way most people can, like this [demonstrating]. He is missing the last approximately 30 degrees of extension, this part [demonstrating]. Second, the elbow structure is much weaker. The ligaments in the joint were torn and ruptured from the injury, and they will never return to their former strength. This means that the arm cannot tolerate the kind of strain it previously could tolerate.

Q. You know he used to work as a mechanic?

A. Yes, he told me that.

Q. You know what kind of manual work that involves?

A. Yes, he described what his job was like.

Q. Doctor, in your opinion, will he ever be able to return to his job as a mechanic?

Defendant: Objection, your honor. The doctor is not qualified to give such an opinion, and it invades the province of the jury.

Judge: The objection is overruled.

§9.4. *Reliability*[3]

1. Law

Once relevancy is determined, the trial judge moves on to the reliability issue, bearing in mind that under FRE 104(a) he is not bound by the Rules of Evidence, except for the privileges rules. That means the trial judge may consider such matters as literature in the relevant field, affidavits of other experts, depositions in this case or other cases, and anything he finds helpful or informative.

The trial judge fashions an FRE 104(a) hearing to fit the issue before him, bearing in mind that the proponent of the testimony has the burden of proving by a preponderance of the evidence that admissibility is warranted. The judge as "gatekeeper" does not weigh the evidence or decide who is right and who is wrong. Just how extensive the hearing will be is within the judge's discretion. The judge, if he wishes, may allow the opponent of the testimony to cross-examine, to offer his own witnesses, or to submit pertinent exhibits.

In *Kumho Tire Co. v. Carmichael,* the Supreme Court noted FRE 104(a) hearings are not required in all cases. Judges have the discretion "both to avoid unnecessary 'reliability' proceedings in ordinary cases where the reliability of an expert's methods is properly taken for granted, and to require appropriate

---

3. Weinstein §702[03]; Wigmore §§562, 655, 1700; Mueller & Kirkpatrick §§7.5-7.11; McCormick §203.

proceedings in the less usual or more complex cases where cause for questioning the expert's reliability arises."

The first stop in the reliability analysis is a determination of whether the expert is qualified to testify about the scientific, technical, or other specialized knowledge that will assist the trier of fact. If the witness is not qualified, his testimony, of course, is not reliable.

In those few cases where the qualification issue arises, most judges prefer to determine the issue before trial. Some will wait until the witness is called before the jury. Either way, the opponent of the testimony should be given an opportunity to test the qualifications of a tendered expert before the jury hears any opinions or conclusions.

FRE 702 provides that an expert is anyone "qualified as an expert by knowledge, skill, experience, training, or education." An expert must have greater knowledge than a lay person to make his testimony "helpful" to the jury. For example, a young doctor who just graduated from medical school can be a qualified expert, even though many other doctors have superior qualifications. Once the expert is shown to have some expertise in the relevant field, the expert is qualified, and the issue becomes one of credibility, which is for the jury to decide.

FRE 702's language, "a witness qualified as an expert by knowledge, skill, experience, training, or education," recognizes two basic types of experts. Some develop expertise through formal education. These include doctors, lawyers, accountants, economists, engineers, and those engaged in other specialties for which college and graduate school education is essential. Others develop expertise principally through work experience. These include farm workers, miners, truck drivers, bricklayers, designers, and those in any occupation that develops specialized on-the-job knowledge. *Daubert* applies to all of them.

The second stop in the reliability analysis is a determination of whether the expert properly reached his opinions and conclusions. An expert's opinions or conclusions themselves are not the focus of *Daubert*. *Daubert* is concerned with the way those opinions or conclusions are reached. *Joiner* authorized trial judges to conclude "there is simply too great an analytical gap between the data and the opinion proffered." That is, the expert might use a reliable technique to reach an unfounded conclusion. He must demonstrate the reliability of the specific technique he used to perform "the task at hand."

The challenge for the trial judge is to think in terms of evidentiary reliability, which, in turn, usually will be based on scientific validity. That means the judge must make a preliminary assessment of whether the reasoning or methodology underlying the testimony is scientifically valid. If the evidence supporting the expert's opinion is insufficient to allow a reasonable juror to conclude the opinion is more likely true than not true, the judge should not let the jury hear it. For example, in defective design cases, many judges have excluded opinions where the expert did not test the alternative design he contends would have been appropriate. And trial judges regularly exclude opinions where the expert did not rule out other probable or plausible causes of an injury.

When the validity of the science underlying an expert's testimony is challenged, how must a judge analyze the issue? *Daubert* holds the evidence is scientifically valid if (1) it is grounded in the methods and procedures of science and (2) it is based on reliable information or theories. The expert's work product must be "good science," not "junk science." Judges cannot simply take an expert's word for it. There must be independent validation. Judges must be "gatekeepers."

Daubert suggested four factors for the gatekeeper's consideration:

1. Whether the theory or technique has been or can be tested. The scientific status of a theory is determined by whether it can be proved false or refuted. Scientists put forth hypotheses and then test them to see whether they can be falsified. This implies that the theory can be tested in the first place. A theory has strength if it has been tested, but cannot be proved false. The theory must be challenged in some objective sense — not simply a subjective, conclusory approach that cannot reasonably be assessed for reliability. The expert must be able to explain the data on which he relies and the methodology he used to form his opinions.

2. Whether the principle has been published in a peer-reviewed publication. The Supreme Court recognized what most scientists know: Publication is not the same thing as reliability. At the same time, "submission to the scrutiny of the scientific community is a component of 'good science,' in part because it increases the likelihood that substantive flaws in methodology will be detected." *Daubert*, 509 U.S. at 593. Of course, the nature of the publication matters. Judges may inquire into who paid for it and where it appeared.

3. Whether the known or potential error rate of a certain scientific technique has been evaluated. "Error rate" ordinarily refers to the probability that the application of a particular procedure or theory can lead to a mistake in the classification or identification of an object, event, or person. The Court cited with approval a *Frye*-based decision that permitted opinions of a spectrographic voice expert after extensive testimony about false identification and false elimination error rates. When examining the known or potential error rate of a particular scientific technique, the court must consider "the existence and maintenance of standards controlling the technique's operation." *Daubert*, 509 U.S. at 594. If standards and controls for evaluating the error rate are not adequate, reliability of the results will be called into question.

4. What the relevant scientific community is and what the particular degree of acceptance of the expert's technique or methodology is. Clinging to a vestige of *Frye*, the Court observed that general acceptance can have a bearing on the inquiry. Widespread acceptance can be an important factor in ruling particular evidence admissible. But "a known technique that has been able to attract only minimal support within the community may properly be viewed with skepticism." *Daubert*, 509 U.S. at 594. *Daubert* does not censure known techniques that fall somewhere between "minimal support" and "general acceptance." This *Frye* leftover is very much alive in *Daubert* courts.

These four factors are not exclusive or exhaustive. A trial judge is not bound by any of them. None is given any particular rank or weight. The inquiry is intended to be "flexible."

For example, in *Daubert*, the issue was whether two mothers' prenatal inges-tion of the drug Bendectin caused serious birth defects in their children. The scientific dispute centered on causation. On remand, the Ninth Circuit's anal-ysis emphasized the lack of independent research by the plaintiff's experts and the failure of the scientific community to review the experts' work in the case. Instead, the plaintiff's experts developed opinions solely for the purpose of testifying. Because there was no showing the experts' testimony was based on sound scientific principle, it was excluded.

On the other hand, another post-*Daubert* decision allowed an expert to testify that one Dexatrim, a diet pill, caused the plaintiff to have an acute hyper-tensive reaction, which, in turn, caused a serious fall. The experienced expert based his opinion on published, peer-reviewed studies, including his own, that were done before the litigation arose. A high premium will be placed on research that is not related to the litigation.

Whatever else *Daubert* means, it is clear that trial judges, when faced with an objection, must look beyond the credentials of the expert witness. Something does not become scientific knowledge just because a scientist says it is. The conclusion must be reached by scientifically valid methods, and judges are not simply to take the word of the expert on the question.

For example, one court rejected the opinion of an eminent cardiologist that a nicotine patch could have caused the plaintiff's heart attack. The expert did not offer any scientific data from which the causal relation could be inferred. That was not good science. Another court barred an expert's opinion that an anaesthesia containing halothane caused an individual to develop chronic active hepatitis. The opinion was based on one study and four case reports. That was not enough, said the court, to establish scientific validity.

Case law will continue to develop other factors for the gatekeeping judge to consider when determining reliability of expert testimony. Judges are asking these questions:

> Does the proposed testimony grow out of research conducted outside the litigation, or were opinions developed for the purpose of testifying? Of course, some areas are exclusively forensic by nature. For example, opin-ions about bite marks, fiber comparisons, and questioned hair samples almost always are reached in a forensic setting.
>
> Did the expert reach his conclusion first and then go back to find facts and data that support it?
>
> Is this a subjective opinion, one that places the expert in a bare minority because his methodology is used by few or none in the field? Is it available to other experts in the field? Does the technique rely solely on this expert's interpretation?
>
> Is the field of expertise claimed by the expert one that is known to reach reliable results? The discipline itself must possess reliability, unlike, as the Supreme Court noted in *Daubert*, "generally accepted principles of astrol-ogy or necromancy."
>
> Is the expert being as careful and thorough as he would be in his regular workplace, when not being paid to consult with a lawyer? Is he using in the courtroom the "same level of intellectual rigor that characterizes the practice of an expert in the relevant field"?

Is there some certification or licensure for the use of the technique or
methodology?
Has the expert ruled out other reasonable or plausible causes for the
condition he is testifying about? Is the unconsidered cause obvious?

None of the *Daubert* or post-*Daubert* factors is exclusive or dispositive. FRE
702 makes no attempt to codify them. Proposed experts will run into trouble if
they could have tested but did not, if they could have determined error rates but
did not, or if they ignored or were not aware of peer-reviewed literature in the
relevant field.

Some courts have warned that the trial judge's assigned role of gatekeeper is
not intended to serve as a replacement for the adversary system. Thus far, most
of *Daubert*'s impact is being felt in the unusual or complex cases, such as those
involving toxic torts and prescription drugs, where the decisive issue is causation. In *Daubert*, the Supreme Court warned against a radical shift in the fact-
finding process: "Vigorous cross-examination, presentation of contrary
evidence, and careful instruction on the burden of proof are the traditional
and appropriate means of attacking shaky but admissible evidence." Some
district courts have held FRE 104(a) hearings that are tantamount to mini-trials,
both sides presenting witnesses and extensively cross-examining the other's
experts. See, for example *Glastetter v. Novartis Pharmaceutical Corp.*, 107 F.
Supp. 2d 1015 (E.D. Mo. 2000), affirmed 252 F. 3d 986 (8th Cir. 2001),
where, after a lengthy hearing, the district judge excluded expert medical testimony, based on differential diagnosis, that a drug caused the plaintiff's stroke.

Causation is *Daubert*'s primary scientific battleground, especially in toxic
tort cases. Plaintiffs must provide answers to two causation questions. First,
the generic or general question: Is exposure to the defendant's substance capable of causing the injury claimed by the plaintiff? Second, the specific question:
Did plaintiff's exposure to the defendant's substance in fact occur and actually
cause the injury? Both questions must be answered in the affirmative if the
plaintiff's case is to survive an FRE 104(a) challenge. Some courts hold differential diagnosis alone is not sufficient to establish general or specific causation. Controlled or epidemiological studies carry more weight. Those courts that
accept differential diagnosis or, more accurately, differential etiology, pose
three questions, each requiring a "yes" answer if the expert opinion is to be
admitted: (1) Did the expert make an accurate diagnosis of the nature of the
disease? (2) Did the expert reliably rule *in* the probable or plausible cause of
the disease? (3) Did the expert reliably rule *out* the probable or plausible cause
of the disease? Ruling-in and ruling-out decisions must turn on a valid methodology, not speculation. Failure to learn how much exposure the plaintiff had
to the substance at issue often leads to a finding of speculation that excludes
the opinion. On the other hand, a close temporal relationship between exposure and injury usually is given great weight.

Frye courts generally adhere to the common law proximate cause analysis in
tort cases, requiring both cause-in-fact and legal cause evidence.

Genetic factors evidence, including DNA, should find no *Daubert* barrier
when properly presented. Polygraph evidence, regularly rejected by the courts,
now stands a better chance of admissibility, with some courts taking a fresh look
at the admissibility of "lie detector" tests. Whether handwriting comparison

evidence and the horizontal gaze nystagmus test used by police to detect drunk drivers can survive the *Daubert* call for testability and falsifiability is unclear, although the Eleventh Circuit Court of Appeals has held *Daubert* and *Kumho Tire* support a finding that a qualified handwriting analysis expert could testify a demand note left at the scene of a bank robbery was written by the defendant. Other courts have excluded handwriting identification opinions, but have allowed testimony about similarity of handwriting characteristics.

In each instance, a three-stage inquiry is required. The trial judge first considers whether the evidence is relevant, that is, helpful to the trier of fact; then considers whether the scientific evidence is reliable; and finally, if the first two requirements are met, determines whether the probative value of the evidence is substantially outweighed by the risk of unfair prejudice. Trial judges are cautioned to strike the appropriate balance in each case — admitting reliable, helpful expert testimony and excluding misleading or confusing testimony.

Intricate issues of causation, in general and relating to a specific plaintiff, no doubt will continue to be a fertile area for *Daubert* gatekeeping analysis. But as the Supreme Court pointed out, FRE 702 also includes "technical, or other specialized knowledge." There is no need to be overly concerned about the *Daubert* factors in routine cases or where the science is well established. Medical doctors will continue to testify, without impediment, to injuries and causation. Qualified experts will not be stopped from opining on defective designs and inadequate warnings. Opinions about value and cost will face few challenges on scientific validity grounds, although several courts have excluded economic testimony in anti-trust cases because of questionable methodology or inadequate facts and data.

The impact of *Daubert* on the so-called soft sciences — the social and behavioral sciences — continues to evolve. *Daubert* did not mention them. These experts testify about people and the way they behave. Expert testimony about physical and sexual abuse, especially where children are involved, has been regularly admitted under *Frye*. This includes the various kinds of syndrome testimony, where experts testify that the victim of a particular abuse behaves in a typical way. That is, a child sex abuse victim will delay reporting, will often recant his or her story, will tend to be truant and run away from home, and will give inconsistent versions of what happened. However, most courts stop short of allowing behavioral experts to say the victim is telling the truth, while the defendant is lying.

Daubert provides new arguments for challenges to social and behavioral science expert testimony. In most cases, it is difficult, if not impossible, to test the methodology for accuracy, since most opinions are experience based. There is no known or potential rate of error and no valid way to determine if the theory can be proved false. Evidence of false positives and negatives is anecdotal, at best.

It is clear now that *Daubert* does apply to social science testimony in general and to psychological evidence in particular. In a recent case, the defendant confessed to stalking, kidnapping, and murdering a teen-aged girl. At trial, he offered expert testimony that he was susceptible to certain interrogation techniques and capable of confessing to a crime he did not commit. The experts would have given the jury indicia for determining when false confessions are likely to occur, but were not allowed to testify. The conviction was reversed because the trial judge failed to conduct a *Daubert* analysis to determine the admissibility of the testimony. The court held that the *Daubert* analysis applies to human behavior and mental disorders and that such evidence may be admissible even though the expert testimony covers many of the things ordinary jurors would be expected to know anyway.

A few state courts have used the *Daubert* factors to exclude child sex abuse syndrome testimony, while others simply pronounce the syndrome testimony reliable, bypassing the falsifiability and error rate criteria. In general, it should be expected that trial judges will take a closer look at syndrome testimony to satisfy themselves that the experts are using good science.

Even if the underlying scientific tests or methods pass the *Daubert* or *Frye* test, this is not enough. The proponent must also demonstrate that the particular tests, used in the present case, were correctly conducted, following proper procedures. For example, courts routinely admit the readings of radar guns in speeding cases without obliging the proponent to first present evidence of the science underlying radar guns, since this has already been well established. However, the proponent must still demonstrate that the radar gun used was reliable and had been properly tested and calibrated and that it was operated by a qualified person when it was used to obtain the reading in the present case. If this is done, the results will be admissible.

2. Practice

Issues surrounding the qualifications of an expert to testify arise infrequently because the standard favors admissibility. The expert need only have enough expertise to make his testimony helpful to the jury. The issue then becomes one of credibility, which is for the jury.

Issues surrounding the reliability, and hence admissibility, of the expert's opinions and conclusions based on scientific tests and methods involve *Daubert*, and the judge will ordinarily hold a pretrial "*Daubert* hearing" to rule on the admissibility of challenged expert testimony. See the example of a *Daubert* hearing in Sec. 9.2.

Finally, the proponent seeking to introduce the results of scientific tests must always show that the tests were properly conducted in this case. This is the most common issue in routine expert testimony based on accepted scientific tests. Even if the tests and methods used are routinely used in that field, were they done in the proper way in the present case?

Example 1:

This is a medical negligence case. Plaintiff calls a doctor who testifies as follows:

Q. (By plaintiff's lawyer) Dr. Johnson, when did you receive your medical degree?

A. This year. I recently graduated from the medical school at the university.

Q. Are you licensed to practice medicine?

A. Not yet. I just took the exams and should know the results shortly.

Q. Where are you working now?

A. I'm in my first year of a residency in orthopedics at the university hospital.

Defendant: Your honor, may we approach?

Judge: Yes. [Lawyers come to the bench.]

Defendant: I object to this witness testifying as an expert. He's barely graduated from medical school and isn't even licensed to practice.

Plaintiff: That objection goes to weight, not admissibility, your honor. The witness clearly has enough expertise to make his testimony useful to the jury. He's merely going to testify that he examined the patient, took x-rays, and determined that she had a compound fracture of her left tibia. For this purpose, he's qualified.

Judge: The objection is overruled. The doctor may testify to his diagnosis.

Example 2:

This is a trespass case in which the plaintiff is suing for the damage caused when the defendant's nearby water tank burst, flooding the plaintiff's building. During trial, the plaintiff calls a claims adjuster, who testifies as follows:

Q. (By plaintiff's lawyer) Mr. Strong, how many years have you worked as a claims adjuster?

A. About 10 years.

Q. Have you ever inspected properties that had water damage?

A. Of course.

Q. How many times?

A. Probably once a month over the past 10 years.

Q. Have you ever had to determine the amount of damage caused by the water?

A. Sure. I've had to do that every time I've inspected properties that had water damage.

Plaintiff: Your honor, we tender Mr. Strong as an expert in the appraisal of water damage to properties.

Defendant: May I voir dire the witness?

Judge: You may.

Q. (By defendant's lawyer) The water damage you've inspected, what was the source of the water?

A. Most of the time it's caused by a rupture of water pipes, or toilets overflowing, or a leaking roof.

Q. In other words, damage caused by the building's own system and structure?

A. That's right.

Q. Have you ever inspected a building where the water damage was caused by a nearby water tank rupturing?

A. No.

Defendant: Your honor, may we approach?

Judge: Yes. [Lawyers come to the bench.]

Defendant: Your honor, the witness has no expertise in examining and appraising water damage caused by a water tank rupture. I object to him testifying in this case.

Plaintiff: He's obviously an expert in inspecting and appraising water damage in general. Where the water came from isn't critical. If anything, this goes to weight.

Judge: The objection is overruled. The witness may continue his testimony.

Example 3:

This is a speeding case being tried in traffic court. In the prosecution's case-in-chief, the arresting patrol officer is testifying. The following then happens:

Q. (By prosecutor) Officer Byrne, were you using a radar gun that day?
A. I was.
Q. Did you use it when the defendant's car went by?
A. I did.
Q. What reading did you get on the defendant's car?
Defendant: Objection. There's been no showing of the underlying reliability of the radar gun.
Judge: Objection overruled. The reliability of this method is well accepted.
Defendant: We also object on the basis that there's been no proper foundation for the particular radar gun used in this case.
Judge: That objection is sustained.
Prosecutor: May I lay a further foundation, your honor?
Judge: You may.
Q. Officer, this particular model of radar gun you used, is that a standard one used by the department?
A. Yes, it was an MR-7. That's the one most of our patrol cars have. The department has been using it for years.
Q. Has that radar gun been inspected?
A. Yes, sir. It is inspected every week, at the beginning of the week. If it's not working properly or not properly calibrated, we don't use it.
Q. That day, Officer, had you yourself tested it?
A. Yes. I always test the gun at the beginning of my shift. It was in good working order.
Q. Have you been trained to use this particular radar gun?
A. Yes, and I've been using it the past three years.
Q. Officer, what was the reading on the defendant's car?
Defendant: Objection, same basis.
Judge: Overruled. You may answer.
A. The defendant's car was going 69 in a 45 mph zone.

Commentary: This basic foundation will probably be sufficient in most jurisdictions. Some jurisdictions have specific and detailed foundation requirements for this type of evidence.

§9.5.   Sources of facts and data on which expert relies[4]

1.   Law

While *Daubert* concentrates on technique and methodology, there is another aspect of the trial judge's inquiry into the degree of reliability necessary to allow a jury to hear the expert's testimony.

FRE 703 refers to the facts or data on which an expert can base an opinion or inference. Experts, unlike lay witnesses governed by FRE 701, are not limited to opinions or inferences based on their own perceptions. There are three possible sources for the facts, data, or opinions of others that can provide the basis for the opinion or inference of an expert witness.

The first possible source is the firsthand observation of the witness. A medical doctor can base an opinion on what he observes about the patient and what the patient tells him. An engineer's opinion about the unsafe design of a machine can be based on his examination of the machine.

The second possible source is the trial or hearing itself. The expert, if permitted, may attend the trial or hearing and listen to the relevant testimony. Then he bases his opinion on what he heard, taking care not to make credibility judgments, a real problem when the testimony is in conflict. The dilemma ordinarily is left for resolution during cross-examination. Or the expert may be asked a hypothetical question based on relevant facts that have been or will be introduced into evidence.

The third possible source on which the expert can rely is "facts or data" not admissible in evidence "if experts in the particular field would reasonably rely on those kinds of facts or data in forming an opinion on the subject." The term "facts or data" may include the opinions of others if the opinions are reasonably relied on by experts in the field. This rule was designed to bring judicial practice into line with the practice of the experts when they are not in court. (See Advisory Committee's Note to FRE 703.)

For example, doctors make life-and-death decisions in reliance on hospital records, x-rays, lab reports, medical treatises, statements by patients and relatives, and reports and opinions from nurses, technicians, and other doctors. It makes no sense for the law to require the time, expense, and effort of admitting these matters into evidence. Likewise, the rule provides a way to offer public opinion poll evidence because attention is directed to the validity of the techniques used, not pointless inquiries into whether hearsay was involved. On the other hand, if an accident reconstruction expert relies on the statements of unknown bystanders or interested parties to opine about the cause of the accident, reasonable reliance would be lacking, and the opinion would not be admitted. (See Advisory Committee's Note to FRE 703.)

FRE 703 does nothing to admit in evidence facts or data that would otherwise be inadmissible. When the expert is allowed to tell the jury how he reached his opinions, his recitation of underlying facts or data does not create admissible evidence. The facts and data, otherwise inadmissible, do not achieve an independent life.

---

4. Weinstein §§702[01]-[07], 703[01]-[06]; Wigmore §§678, 1700; McCormick §§14-18, 203; Mueller & Kirkpatrick §§7.8-7.11.

Put another way, the facts and data relied on by the expert do not become substantive evidence simply because he tells the jury about them. They are admitted on direct examination for a limited purpose — to allow the expert to explain how and why he reached his conclusions. They are allowed on cross-examination of the expert to test those conclusions.

FRE 703 authorizes expert opinions based on inadmissible facts or data reasonably relied on by experts in the particular field when they form opinions or inferences on the subject. If the witness is the only expert in the world who relies on these facts or data, or if he relies on them only when called to testify, FRE 703 is violated in letter and spirit. An opinion is as trustworthy as the facts or data that support it. Of course, whether the expert is relying on a sufficient basis of information, admissible or not, is a matter of reliability controlled by FRE 702.

The Advisory Committee's Note to FRE 702 observes "there has been some confusion over the relationship between Rules 702 and 703." The confusion is understandable. Rule 702 speaks to "sufficient facts or data" as one of the required bases for the expert's opinion. When an expert relies on inadmissible information, FRE 703 requires the trial court to determine whether that information is of a type reasonably relied on by other experts in the particular field. The inquiry under FRE 703 is whether the expert can rely on the inadmissible information when he reaches an opinion. On the other hand, FRE 702 poses the question of whether the expert is relying on a sufficient basis of information — admissible or not.

Courts have disagreed on how to treat inadmissible information, usually hearsay, when it is reasonably relied on by an expert in forming an opinion or drawing an inference. That is, the expert might have a right to rely on the inadmissible information, but should he be allowed to tell the jury about it? And, if so, in what detail?

The concern is that experts are being used as conduits to deliver inadmissible and prejudicial evidence to the jury. An FBI agent has testified to hearsay from informants when opining about code language used by narcotics dealers. An expert has testified to gruesome injuries suffered by persons in a study used to reach his opinions.

Judges have used the FRE 403 balancing test to determine whether the jury should hear the inadmissible information, often relying on a limiting instruction ("Admitted to allow you to weigh the expert's opinion, but not as substantive evidence or for its truth") to tilt the balance toward admissibility. The analysis changed in 2000.

The amended FRE 703 provides a rebuttable presumption against disclosure to the jury of inadmissible information used as a basis for the expert's opinion — when the information is offered by the proponent of the opinion. It applies to reasonably relied-on information that will not be admitted during the trial. It is not intended to affect the admissibility of the expert's opinion nor stop the expert from relying on information that will not be admissible for substantive purposes.

When an objection is made, the trial judge must conduct a weighing test that is unlike that of FRE 403. First, he considers the information's probative value in assisting the jury to weigh the expert's opinion. Against that he weighs the risk of prejudice resulting from the jury's potential misuse of the information. The information may be disclosed only if the probative value of the jury hearing the inadmissible facts or data substantially outweighs their prejudicial effect, a reverse FRE 403 test. When making that determination, the trial judge will consider how effective a limiting instruction might be. Although the rule does not say who carries the burden of persuading the judge, presumably it is the proponent of the evidence.

The rule applies only to disclosure by the *proponent* of the opinion or inference. It does not stop the cross-examiner from inquiring into facts or data that the expert used or should have used. Of course, that attack on the expert's basis allows the proponent, on redirect examination, to inquire into the facts or data that were reasonably relied on by the expert, even though they were not allowed on direct examination.

The Advisory Committee's Note addresses the multiparty case: ". . . where one party proffers an expert whose testimony is also beneficial to other parties, each such party should be deemed a 'proponent' within the meaning of the amendment."

When the jury is allowed to hear the underlying facts or data, the trial judge, on request, is obligated under FRE 105 to instruct the jury that the evidence is being offered for a limited purpose — to allow it to weigh the expert's opinions, but not to consider the facts and data as admitted evidence. Lawyers ought not to be allowed to move beyond that limited purpose during the trial, especially during closing arguments, where lawyers may attempt to use such evidence for its truth. For example, a lawyer cannot argue, "The hospital note relied on by the doctor said the plaintiff was abusive to the nurses. Is that the kind of person you want to award money to?" This asks the jury to consider the hospital note as substantive evidence. FRE 703 facts and data, otherwise inadmissible, cannot be used to defeat a motion for a directed verdict, since they are not substantive evidence.

FRE 703 envisions an expert with relevant opinions or inferences to offer the jury. If his purpose is simply to sum up the evidence, admissible or not, he is not a true expert. It has been held reversible error to admit the testimony of an IRS agent who simply summed up the returns and conversations with taxpayers in the prosecution of the man who prepared the tax returns.

When reasonable reliance becomes an issue, the trial judge conducts a hearing under FRE 104(a). Until *Daubert*, great deference was given to the expert's word. If the expert said his data were the type scientists in the field typically rely on, that usually was good enough for the judge. There was great reluctance to judicially second-guess an expert's claim of reasonable reliance unless it became apparent that the facts or data were not trustworthy or were no more than speculation or unwarranted assumptions.

The decisions reflect a wide variety of unadmitted facts or data held sufficient to support an expert's opinion or inference: psychiatric reports and psychological tests by others, scientifically conducted surveys, an IRS agent's conversations with the defendant's bookkeepers and other agents, publications such as industry safety codes and public agency reports, corporate financial records, depositions not in evidence, FBI laboratory reports analyzing betting slips seized in a gambling raid, trade publications and company catalogues, learned treatises and scientific literature, and fire marshal statements to a fire investigator.

Experts in criminal cases may base their opinions on hearsay statements that would offend the Confrontation Clause if offered as substantive evidence. Despite admissibility of the expert's opinion, trial judges most likely would use the balancing test in FRE 703 to bar the witness from testifying to the contents of the constitutionally inadmissible facts or data he relied on. In *Delaware v. Fensterer*, 474 U.S. 15 (1985), the Supreme Court held an expert may testify to an opinion in a criminal case, even where the expert cannot remember the test method that was the basis for his opinion. But experts are not allowed to testify to opinions based on facts or data obtained in violation of the defendant's constitutional rights, such as evidence seized in violation of the Fourth Amendment or a defendant's statements taken in violation of *Miranda*. See *Estelle v. Smith*, 451 U.S. 454 (1981). Where a federal statute excludes from evidence certain reports, such as reports compiled to enhance safety at railroad crossings, an expert may not testify to an opinion based on those reports.

2. Practice

Problems in this area usually arise when a party attempts to "backdoor" inadmissible evidence to the jury through the guise of expert testimony.

Example:

This is a murder case. The defense is insanity. The defendant is examined by a prosecution psychiatrist, who prepares a written report finding the defendant was sane at the time of the offense. The defense files a written motion to preclude the admissibility of the psychiatrist's report and to bar the psychiatrist from testifying at trial. At a hearing on the motion, the following happens:

Defendant: The reason we filed the motion, your honor, is that the psychiatrist's report expressly states that among the sources the doctor received and considered in reaching his evaluation of the defendant is the arrest report, which includes statements of the defendant. Your honor recently suppressed those statements, since they were taken in violation of *Miranda*. Since they cannot be introduced by the prosecution, the prosecution cannot be allowed to get those statements in through the backdoor by having the doctor testify about them in support of his opinion. We're asking that the doctor be barred from testifying to his evaluation, since it is obvious from his written report that he relied on the defendant's statements in reaching his clinical evaluation.

Judge: Prosecution, what's your position?

Prosecutor: Your honor, the doctor should at least be allowed to state that among the things he considered were statements the defendant made. That's standard practice in psychiatry. Second, we don't even know if those statements were necessary to the doctor's clinical evaluation. If the doctor

> can give his opinion without relying on the defendant's state-
> ments, there's absolutely no reason why he can't testify at trial.
> *Judge:* I will hold a Rule 104(a) hearing before the witness testifies. If he
> relied in any substantial way on the excluded statements, I will bar
> his evaluation. Either way, he will not be allowed to testify to
> statements obtained in violation of *Miranda*.

Commentary: The opponent of the evidence should be sure to learn everything the expert relied on to reach an opinion or conclusion. The amended FRE
703 provides an opportunity to ask for exclusion of inadmissible evidence, even
if it is the kind of fact or data experts in the field reasonably rely on. It becomes
the burden of the proponent of the testimony to prove the probative value of the
inadmissible fact or data in assisting the jury to evaluate the expert's opinion
substantially outweighs its prejudicial effect.

§9.6. Disclosure of basis of expert's testimony[5]

1. Law

FRE 705 is directed to the way expert testimony is presented. The rule does not
require that the expert on direct examination disclose underlying facts or data
before stating an opinion or inference unless the trial judge requires it. That is,
after the expert's qualifications are established, the following can happen:

> Q. Professor, do you have an opinion, based on a reasonable degree of
> engineering certainty, whether the design of the punch press in this
> case was unreasonably dangerous?
> A. I do.
> Q. What is your opinion?
> A. It was unreasonably dangerous.
> Q. No further questions.

From an advocacy point of view, that direct examination is unwise. It seldom
happens that way, but it is permitted by the rule. The burden then shifts to the
cross-examiner to decide whether questions will be asked concerning underlying facts or data. If it turns out the facts or data are not sufficient to support the
option, the judge should strike the testimony.

The rule does not say when the trial judge should require prior disclosure of
facts or data. In practice, judges require disclosure when the expert's qualifications are minimal or when the judge has some other reason for feeling a high
level of discomfort with the anticipated testimony. In criminal cases, where
discovery is limited, judges ordinarily require prior disclosure of facts or data.

One purpose of FRE 705 is to eliminate the need to ask the expert a hypothetical question. As the Advisory Committee's Note to FRE 705 observed, "The
hypothetical question has been the target of a great deal of criticism as

---

5. Weinstein §705[01]-[03]; Wigmore §§562, 655; McCormick §§203-211; Mueller &
Kirkpatrick §§7.14-7.15.

encouraging partisan bias, affording an opportunity for summing up in the middle of the case, and as complex and time consuming."

Yet despite all the criticisms and the liberal approach of FRE 705, hypothetical questions are not barred by the Rules. When used, the hypothetical asks the expert to assume the truth of relevant facts supported by the evidence. In addition, there is no reason why the question cannot include unadmitted facts or data reasonably relied on by experts in the field. The form of the question is within the discretion of the judge, but it should contain enough facts, disputed and undisputed, to provide a helpful opinion. The cross-examiner may ask the expert to assume that other facts in evidence are true or untrue.

Lawyers should be wary of taking FRE 705 too literally in summary judgment practice. Expert witness affidavits that contain bare-bones conclusions, without supporting facts or data, tend to be disregarded by trial judges.

2.   Practice

Since requiring disclosure of the sources relied on by the expert is discretionary with the judge, objections in this area are infrequent. Careful discovery of the expert's opinions and the bases of these opinions will be necessary to provide a basis for a pretrial motion attacking the expert's testimony.

Example 1:

This is a personal injury case. A doctor called in the plaintiff's case-in-chief testifies as follows:

Q. Dr. Quinn, on what sources did you rely in reaching your diagnosis?
A. I relied on my examination of the patient, the nurse's notes, x-rays, the radiologist's report, and the lab test results.
Q. Are those the kinds of sources doctors like you customarily rely on in making diagnoses?
A. Of course.
Q. Doctor, what was your diagnosis?
Defendant: Objection, your honor. Those sources have not been offered in evidence.
Judge: Overruled. Doctor, go ahead and answer.
A. I diagnosed her as having a duodenal ulcer.

Example 2:

This is a personal injury case. A doctor called in the plaintiff's case-in-chief is on the witness stand:

Q. Dr. Williams, let's turn now to the opinions you reached in this case. Did you determine if the patient's injuries are permanent?
Defendant: Objection. The doctor has not yet testified to the sources she relied on in reaching her opinion.
Judge: Overruled. Counsel, you may cross-examine later on those sources if you wish.

Commentary: Unless the judge has serious doubts about the foundation for the expert's opinions, he will usually let the expert testify about opinions and conclusions without first stating the sources relied on to reach them.

§9.7.   Form of expert's testimony[6]

1.   Law

FRE 702 permits the expert to testify "in the form of an opinion or otherwise." For example, the expert can testify to an "opinion." The expert can testify, if appropriate, to a "conclusion." The expert can testify without expressing any opinions or conclusions. The expert still can answer a hypothetical question. This flexibility allows the expert to testify in a way that most effectively develops his testimony for the jury.

FRE 702 does not require "a reasonable degree of certainty" or any other measure of certainty. For example, an expert can state: "In my opinion, to a reasonable degree of certainty, plaintiff's scars are permanent." The expert can also state: "Plaintiff's scars are permanent. They will never go away." Trial judges are more comfortable when opinions are elicited with a reasonable degree of certainty, but the cases recognize that those words mean very little to non-lawyer experts.

All that is required is that the experts do not guess or speculate. Levels of certainty are for the jury to determine, after cross-examination. When a qualified doctor testifies he "cannot say with any medical certainty that that's the cause of her low back pain," the opinion is valid enough for the jury to hear. Another doctor can testify that "it may have exacerbated the problem and it may not have." Testimony about "other possible causes" of an injury properly rebuts the plaintiff's expert's "probable" causation opinion.

In this matter, as in all matters involving the admissibility of expert testimony, the question on appeal will be whether the trial judge clearly abused his discretion.

2.   Practice

Two objections commonly arise: the objection that the testimony is not an "opinion" and the objection that the testimony is not to a "reasonable degree of medical or scientific certainty." Under the Rules, neither is a proper objection.

Example:

This is a personal injury case. A doctor called in the plaintiff's case-in-chief testifies as follows:

Q. Doctor, after you surgically fused the patient's neck between the C-3 and C-5 cervical vertebrae, did the patient make a routine recovery?

---

6. Weinstein §702[01]-[07]; Wigmore §§678, 1700; McCormick §§14-18; Mueller & Kirkpatrick §§7.5-7.7.

A. Yes. It took several weeks, of course, but the patient made an uneventful recovery.

Q. Doctor, will the patient ever be able to move his neck in the cervical area that you fused?

Defendant: Objection, your honor. This is not in opinion form, and it is not to a reasonable degree of medical certainty.

Judge: Overruled.

A. The patient's neck will never move in the C-3 to C-5 area. Fusing that part of the neck is permanent. It will never move.

§9.8.   FRE 403[7]

1.   Law

The final step in the analysis of expert testimony assumes that the testimony has survived the relevant and reliable tests. The inquiry then moves to the balancing test contained in FRE 403.

There may be a danger juries will give expert testimony more weight than it deserves. Justified or not, experts have, for some jurors, an aura of special reliability and trustworthiness. For that reason, some judges have excluded proposed expert testimony on the reliability of eyewitness identification. Expert testimony can confuse or mislead. Too much of it in one trial can bore the jury and be a waste of time.

The trial judge has broad discretion to fashion a remedy that will do justice and maintain efficiency. He may exclude testimony, or limit it, or tailor it to its limited purpose. Under FRE 611(a), the judge can limit the number of experts, especially those saying essentially the same things. He can impose reasonable time limits on expert testimony. He can require that the expert's direct testimony be reduced to writing and read to the jury, with live cross-examination to follow.

Assessments of unfair prejudice will depend on the trial judge's view of how ordinary people react to information and how they make decisions. Judges, just like other people, weigh the good against the bad when they make decisions.

2.   Practice

FRE 403 may be the last step in analyzing expert testimony, but its importance should not be overlooked. The rule puts a great deal of power in the hands of the trial judge to fashion a result that promotes trial fairness.

---

7. Weinstein §403[01]-[08]; McCormick §13; Mueller & Kirkpatrick, §§4.9-4.10.

Example:

> This is a murder prosecution. The prosecutor plans to call a pathologist to testify to the cause of the victim's death. At a pretrial hearing, the following happens:

Defendant: Your honor, this is our motion to limit the direct examination of the prosecution's pathologist. Your honor has already granted our motion to preclude the admission of morgue photographs of the victim on Rule 403 grounds. We're asking the court to preclude the pathologist from showing any of those photographs to the jury as part of the basis of his testimony on the cause of death.

Prosecutor: Your honor, we can't keep the pathologist from using the photographs if he needs the photographs to explain his examination and opinions. That would be unfair to the pathologist as well as the jury.

Judge: The pathologist can orally describe whatever he feels is necessary to explain what he did and how he reached his opinions. However, showing the jury the victim's morgue photographs is hardly essential for these purposes. The photographs will not be used during the pathologist's testimony.

§9.9.   *Court appointed experts*[8]

1.   Law

Rule 706.   Court-Appointed Expert Witnesses

(a) **Appointment Process.**   On a party's motion or on its own, the court may order the parties to show cause why expert witnesses should not be appointed and may ask the parties to submit nominations. The court may appoint any expert that the parties agree on and any of its own choosing. But the court may only appoint someone who consents to act.

(b) **Expert's Role.**   The court must inform the expert of the expert's duties. The court may do so in writing and have a copy filed with the clerk or may do so orally at a conference in which the parties have an opportunity to participate. The expert:

(1) must advise the parties of any findings the expert makes;

(2) may be deposed by any party;

(3) may be called to testify by the court or any party; and

(4) may be cross-examined by any party, including the party that called the expert.

---

8. Weinstein §706[01]-[06]; Wigmore §§787, 1385; McCormick §§8, 17; Mueller & Kirkpatrick §7.16

> **(c) Compensation.**   The expert is entitled to a reasonable compensation, as set by the court. The compensation is payable as follows:
>
> **(1)** in a criminal case or in a civil case involving just compensation under the Fifth Amendment, from any funds that are provided by law; and
>
> **(2)** in any other civil case, by the parties in the proportion and at the time that the court directs — and the compensation is then charged like other costs.
>
> **(d) Disclosing the Appointment to the Jury.**   The court may authorize disclosure to the jury that the court appointed the expert.
>
> **(e) Parties' Choice of Their Own Experts.**   This rule does not limit a party in calling its own experts.

FRE 706 permits the court to appoint experts. It can do this on its own motion or that of any party. The rule sets out the details of how the expert will be appointed and compensated and how the expert will testify and be examined at trial.

FRE 706 was adopted in large part to address the common perception of the lawyer shopping for an expert to testify to whatever he needs at trial. The result is that trials frequently pit one side's experts against the other side's, with the jury having little guidance from impartial sources. FRE 706 gives the court the power to appoint supposedly neutral experts to assist the fact finder. The rule has been infrequently utilized by judges, although the requirement that courts hold *Daubert* hearings to determine the admissibility of new scientific methods may lead to more frequent use of the rule.

FRE 706(c) gives the trial judge discretion to disclose to the jury the fact that an expert witness was appointed by the judge.

2. Practice

The few instances where judges have appointed experts usually have involved complex areas where the expert is used to educate the judge on a particular subject matter, or where the experts on both sides are evenly matched and the judge wants to hear from neutral experts to help decide the issues.

Since *Daubert*, judges may utilize FRE 706 more frequently at the pretrial stage, particularly when deciding whether the testimony of the parties' own experts meets the *Daubert* requirements.

X

EXHIBITS

§10.1. Introduction

Trial lawyers understand the foolhardiness of relying entirely on a juror's sense of hearing. People are more attentive, understand more, and remember more when they see the thing that teaches as well as hear the words. In grade school, we had "show and tell." In the courtroom, we have exhibits. The principle is the same — the best teaching is done when students are shown something that makes the point.

In a courtroom, exhibits enhance what Wigmore referred to as the "moral force of evidence." Something happens when jurors look at exhibits. They become more attentive. They move forward in their seats. Comprehension dawns. Retention improves.

Trial judges understand ours is a visual society, conditioned by televisions and computers. They recognize that exhibits energize a trial and foster juror understanding. While judges understand that exhibits must have proper foundations to be admissible and that admissibility is, as always, determined by the judge under FRE 104, most are generous in admitting exhibits under the Rules. Broad discretion is given in this area, and judges use it in favor of admissibility.

The Federal Rules of Evidence permit the use of exhibits that satisfy the three "Rs."

First, the exhibit must be relevant. Under the FRE 401-402 analysis, an exhibit must be relevant to some fact of consequence to the case, and it must have a tendency to prove or disprove something in issue.

Second, the exhibit must be reliable. The foundation requirements in FRE 901, 902, and 1001-1008 focus on the requirement that the exhibit be properly identified as being what it purports to be.

With exhibits, the concepts of relevancy and reliability often merge, since both usually are demonstrated when an exhibit is properly authenticated or identified. For example, when a witness says that an intersection photograph is of the intersection where the collision happened, the exhibit's relevancy is established. When the witness also says that the photograph fairly or accurately shows the layout of the intersection at the time of the collision, the exhibit's reliability is established.

Third, it must be right to admit the exhibit. These are the FRE 403 concerns, which involve issues of judicial efficiency and unfair prejudice. For example a judge may exclude under FRE 403 gory photographs of a person or blood-stained clothes, even though the exhibit is relevant and reliable.

The foundations for various types of exhibits, and the common evidentiary problems that arise when exhibits are introduced at trial, are the subjects of this chapter.

§10.2.   *Foundations*[1]

Rule 106.   Remainder of or Related Writings or Recorded Statements

If a party introduces all or part of a writing or recorded statement, an adverse party may require the introduction, at that time, of any other part—or any other writing or recorded statement—that in fairness ought to be considered at the same time.

Rule 901.   Authenticating or Identifying Evidence

(a) **In General.**   To satisfy the requirement of authenticating or identifying an item of evidence, the proponent must produce evidence sufficient to support a finding that the item is what the proponent claims it is.

(b) **Examples.**   The following are examples only—not a complete list—of evidence that satisfies the requirement:

(1) *Testimony of a Witness with Knowledge.* Testimony that an item is what it is claimed to be.

(2) *Nonexpert Opinion About Handwriting.* A nonexpert's opinion that handwriting is genuine, based on a familiarity with it that was not acquired for the current litigation.

(3) *Comparison by an Expert Witness or the Trier of Fact.* A comparison with an authenticated specimen by an expert witness or the trier of fact.

(4) *Distinctive Characteristics and the Like.* The appearance, contents, substance, internal patterns, or other distinctive characteristics of the item, taken together with all the circumstances.

---

1. McCormick §§212-217; Weinstein §§901-903; Mueller & Kirkpatrick §§1.17-1.18, 9.1-9.28, 10.15-10.16; Wigmore §§1150-1169; for a detailed discussion of foundation procedures and requirements, see T.A. Mauet, Trial Techniques and Trials ch. 7 (9th ed. 2013).

(5) *Opinion About a Voice.* An opinion identifying a person's voice — whether heard firsthand or through mechanical or electronic transmission or recording — based on hearing the voice at any time under circumstances that connect it with the alleged speaker.

(6) *Evidence About a Telephone Conversation.* For a telephone conversation, evidence that a call was made to the number assigned at the time to:

(A) a particular person, if circumstances, including self-identification, show that the person answering was the one called; or

(B) a particular business, if the call was made to a business and the call related to business reasonably transacted over the telephone.

(7) *Evidence About Public Records.* Evidence that:

(A) a document was recorded or filed in a public office as authorized by law; or

(B) a purported public record or statement is from the office where items of this kind are kept.

(8) *Evidence About Ancient Documents or Data Compilations.* For a document or data compilation, evidence that it:

(A) is in a condition that creates no suspicion about its authenticity;

(B) was in a place where, if authentic, it would likely be; and

(C) is at least 20 years old when offered.

(9) *Evidence About a Process or System.* Evidence describing a process or system and showing that it produces an accurate result.

(10) *Methods Provided by a Statute or Rule.* Any method of authentication or identification allowed by a federal statute or a rule prescribed by the Supreme Court.

Rule 902.   Evidence That Is Self-Authenticating

The following items of evidence are self-authenticating; they require no extrinsic evidence of authenticity in order to be admitted:

(1) *Domestic Public Documents That Are Sealed and Signed.* A document that bears:

(A) a seal purporting to be that of the United States; any state, district, commonwealth, territory, or insular possession of the United States; the former Panama Canal Zone; the Trust Territory of the Pacific Islands; a political subdivision of any of these entities; or a department, agency, or officer of any entity named above; and

(B) a signature purporting to be an execution or attestation.

(2) *Domestic Public Documents That Are Not Sealed but Are Signed and Certified.* A document that bears no seal if:

(A) it bears the signature of an officer or employee of an entity named in Rule 902(1)(A); and

(B) another public officer who has a seal and official duties within that same entity certifies under seal — or its equivalent — that the signer has the official capacity and that the signature is genuine.

(3) *Foreign Public Documents.* A document that purports to be signed or attested by a person who is authorized by a foreign country's law to do so. The document must be accompanied by a final certification that certifies the genuineness of the signature and official position of the signer or attester — or of any foreign official whose certificate of genuineness relates to the signature or attestation or is in a chain of certificates of genuineness relating to the signature or attestation. The certification may be made by a secretary of a United States embassy or legation; by a consul general, vice consul, or consular agent of the United States; or by a diplomatic or consular official of the foreign country assigned or accredited to the United States. If all parties have been given a reasonable opportunity to investigate the document's authenticity and accuracy, the court may, for good cause, either:

(A) order that it be treated as presumptively authentic without final certification; or

(B) allow it to be evidenced by an attested summary with or without final certification.

(4) *Certified Copies of Public Records.* A copy of an official record — or a copy of a document that was recorded or filed in a public office as authorized by law — if the copy is certified as correct by:

(A) the custodian or another person authorized to make the certification; or

(B) a certificate that complies with Rule 902(1), (2), or (3), a federal statute, or a rule prescribed by the Supreme Court.

(5) *Official Publications.* A book, pamphlet, or other publication purporting to be issued by a public authority.

(6) *Newspapers and Periodicals.* Printed material purporting to be a newspaper or periodical.

(7) *Trade Inscriptions and the Like.* An inscription, sign, tag, or label purporting to have been affixed in the course of business and indicating origin, ownership, or control.

(8) *Acknowledged Documents.* A document accompanied by a certificate of acknowledgment that is lawfully executed by a notary public or another officer who is authorized to take acknowledgments.

(9) *Commercial Paper and Related Documents.* Commercial paper, a signature on it, and related documents, to the extent allowed by general commercial law.

(10) *Presumptions Under a Federal Statute.* A signature, document, or anything else that a federal statute declares to be presumptively or prima facie genuine or authentic.

(11) *Certified Domestic Records of a Regularly Conducted Activity.* The original or a copy of a domestic record that meets the requirements of Rule 803(6)(A)-(C), as shown by a certification of the custodian or another qualified person that complies with a federal statute or a rule prescribed by the Supreme Court. Before the trial or hearing, the proponent must give an adverse party reasonable written notice of the intent to offer the record—and must make the record and certification available for inspection—so that the party has a fair opportunity to challenge them.

(12) *Certified Foreign Records of a Regularly Conducted Activity.* In a civil case, the original or a copy of a foreign record that meets the requirements of Rule 902(11), modified as follows: the certification, rather than complying with a federal statute or Supreme Court rule, must be signed in a manner that, if falsely made, would subject the maker to a criminal penalty in the country where the certification is signed. The proponent must also meet the notice requirements of Rule 902(11).

Rule 903.   Subscribing Witness's Testimony

A subscribing witness's testimony is necessary to authenticate a writing only if required by the law of the jurisdiction that governs its validity.

Rule 1005.   Copies of Public Records to Prove Content

The proponent may use a copy to prove the content of an official record—or of a document that was recorded or filed in a public office as authorized by law—if these conditions are met: the record or document is otherwise admissible; and the copy is certified as correct in accordance with Rule 902(4) or is testified to be correct by a witness who has compared it with the original. If no such copy can be obtained by reasonable diligence, then the proponent may use other evidence to prove the content.

Rule 1006.   Summaries to Prove Content

The proponent may use a summary, chart, or calculation to prove the content of voluminous writings, recordings, or photographs that cannot be conveniently examined in court. The proponent must make the originals or duplicates available for examination or copying, or both, by other parties at a reasonable time or place. And the court may order the proponent to produce them in court.

Exhibits are things that are presented to the jury and usually admitted in evidence. Common examples are weapons, drugs, consumer products, diagrams, photographs, letters, checks, business records, and public records. Exhibits must be "authenticated" under FRE 901 and 902. Authentication means that the proponent must show that the offered exhibit is what it is claimed to be. In trial lawyers' language, the proponent must "lay a foundation" for the offered exhibit. The proponent must present sufficient credible evidence for the judge to determine that an adequate foundation for admission has been established, so that the exhibit may be presented to the jury for its consideration. The different foundations for the several categories of exhibits are discussed below.

Under FRE 104, the admissibility of exhibits is a question of law for the judge. Under FRE 901(a), the standard the judge must apply to the offered exhibit is whether the proponent has produced "evidence sufficient to support a finding that the item is what the proponent claims it is." This is frequently called the "prima facie" standard and must not be confused with burdens of proof (such as preponderance, clear and convincing, and beyond a reasonable doubt). The prima facie standard is met if the proponent presents sufficient evidence that the exhibit is what it purports to be. If relevant, the exhibit is then admissible unless FRE 403 concerns apply, and the weight the exhibit should be given is for the jury to determine.

The prima facie standard applies to all offered exhibits in civil and criminal cases. For example, the prosecutor in a murder case calls a credible eyewitness who testifies that an exhibit, a handgun, is the weapon the defendant used to shoot the victim. The handgun is now properly admitted in evidence, even though the defense may later call other witnesses to testify that the handgun is not the weapon that was used. In short, the fact that the opposing side may present contrary evidence about the exhibit does not prevent the proponent from getting the exhibit admitted in evidence. If the proponent has produced sufficient evidence establishing the appropriate foundation, the exhibit is properly admitted. The question then becomes one of weight, which always is a jury question.

Modern computer technology poses foundation problems not specifically addressed by evidence rules. The assumption has been it is enough for someone to say the photograph or writing or tape recording is accurate, leaving it for the cross-examiner to attack the authenticity of the evidence. But these rules were the product of a time when alteration of exhibits was difficult, expensive, and easy to detect. With the advent of digital technology, that rationale is disappearing.

Speed, pitch, and content of visual and audio recordings are easy to vary. Words and faces can be rearranged or eliminated without leaving a trace. Documents and photographs can easily be altered, leaving behind no clue of manipulation. It is sensible to predict that simple statements of accuracy by a witness will become the beginning, not the end, of judicial inquiry into admissibility. There will be more FRE 104 hearings into authenticity of exhibits, and that means more intense use of discovery tools to investigate the creation, storage, and final portrayal of manipulable exhibits.

While FRE 901 does not differentiate between civil and criminal cases, in practice there often is a difference. In civil cases, the parties have the right to extensive pretrial discovery, and pretrial conference procedures usually resolve most admissibility issues before trial. In criminal cases, by contrast, discovery usually is limited, and admissibility issues are common in trials. Judges treat authentication issues in criminal cases more seriously, particularly when the foundation requirements are established by FRE 901(b).

Courts have developed courtroom procedures that must be followed as part of the process of laying a foundation for an exhibit. While the procedures may vary from jurisdiction to jurisdiction, most courts require the following steps:

1. Have the exhibit marked (if not marked before trial).
2. Show the exhibit to opposing counsel.
3. Ask the court's permission to approach the witness (if required).
4. Show the exhibit to the witness.
5. Lay the foundation for the exhibit.
6. Offer the exhibit in evidence.
7. Have the exhibit marked in evidence (if required).

These steps ensure that an adequate appellate record is made and give the opposing party a fair opportunity to make appropriate and timely evidentiary objections to the offered exhibit.

For example, in a personal injury case, plaintiff is introducing a photograph of the accident scene. An eyewitness testifies as follows:

Q. Ms. Johnson, you saw the crash?
A. Yes, I was just a few feet away, standing on the sidewalk.
Plaintiff: Your honor, may we have this photograph marked as an exhibit?
Judge: You may. [Lawyer hands photograph to court clerk, who marks it Plaintiff's Exhibit No. 1.]
Q. May the record show that I'm showing what's been marked Plaintiff's Exhibit No. 1 to defense counsel?
Judge: It will. [Defense lawyer looks at photograph, hands it back to plaintiff's lawyer.]
Plaintiff: Permission to approach, your honor?
Judge: Yes. [Lawyer walks to witness box, hands photograph to witness.]
Q. Ms. Johnson, I'm showing you what's been marked Plaintiff's Exhibit No. 1. Do you recognize the scene in the photograph?
A. Yes, that's the intersection where the crash happened.
Q. Does that photograph fairly and accurately show the intersection as it looked at the time of the crash?
A. Yes.
Plaintiff: Your honor, we offer Plaintiff's Exhibit No. 1 in evidence.
Judge: Any objection?
Defendant: No, your honor.
Judge: Very well. Plaintiff's Exhibit No. 1 is in evidence.
Plaintiff: May the clerk mark it in evidence?
Judge: Yes. [Lawyer hands exhibit to clerk, who marks on it that the exhibit is now in evidence.]

When the offered exhibit is a writing, business record, public record, recorded recollection, or summary, FRE 106 can play an important role. Under that rule, "If a party introduces all or part of a writing or recorded statement, an adverse party may require the introduction, at that time, of any other part — or any other writing or recorded statement — that in fairness ought to be considered at the same time."

FRE 106 prevents reading something out of context. While the rule is most frequently raised when using a writing during impeachment, it is equally applicable when writings are offered as exhibits. For example, it may be unfair to offer part of a document and not other related parts of that or another document. It may be unfair to offer the front side of a printed form and not offer the back side. It may be unfair to offer part of a transcript as recorded recollection and not other parts.

The purpose of the rule is to correct a misleading impression when something is taken out of context from a written or recorded statement or, in some instances, in an oral statement. However, courts hold that the rule is not designed to make something admissible that should be excluded, such as hearsay. For example, where a part of the defendant's statement is offered by the prosecution, that would not open the door to the defendant offering other parts of his statement for their truth, although those other parts might be admissible for some non-truth purpose.

FRE 106 allows an objection to be made to the admission of an exhibit if the proponent unfairly seeks to introduce only part of what should be offered in evidence. The objection will not prevent the exhibit from being admitted, but it will force the proponent to offer all the other parts that should be offered.

All offered exhibits fall into one of several categories, and there is a standard foundation for each category:

1. real evidence
2. demonstrative evidence
3. documents and instruments
4. business records
5. public records
6. recorded recollection
7. summaries

The foundations for these categories are discussed below.

§10.3.   *Real evidence*[2]

1.   Law

Real evidence refers to tangible objects, such as a gun, drugs, products, and blood. Here, the exhibit is the actual item involved in the case. To admit real evidence, under FRE 901 the proponent must call a competent witness, one having firsthand knowledge of the relevant facts at the relevant time, to testify that the exhibit is actually the object it purports to be and that it is in the same, or substantially the same, condition now as it was at the relevant time, typically when the accident or crime occurred.

For foundation purposes, it is useful to divide real evidence into two categories: that which can be uniquely identified by the senses and that which cannot.

---

2. McCormick §212; Weinstein §901(b)(3)[05]; Mueller & Kirkpatrick §§9.4-9.5; Wigmore §§1157, 1158.

a. Sensory identification

Many things can be uniquely identified by the senses, most commonly by sight, but sometimes by smell, taste, sound, or feel. For example, in an unlawful possession of a handgun case, a police officer is called as a witness. The officer must testify that he recognizes the gun in court as the gun he took from the defendant when arrested, because of its distinctive appearance, serial number, or other marks put on it, and that the gun is in substantially the same condition now as it was when he took it from the defendant. As another example, in a products liability case involving a defective tire, the plaintiff is called as a witness. The plaintiff must testify that the shredded tire in court is the same tire that was on his car at the time of the accident; that he can identify it because of its distinctive appearance, serial number, or other marks put on it; and that the tire is in substantially the same condition now as it was immediately after the accident.

Sometimes a witness testifies that "it appears to be" or "it looks like" the object, but cannot positively identify it. Is that sufficient to admit the object in evidence? Most courts conclude that under the prima facie standard of FRE 901(a) that is sufficient for admission, the issue then being one of weight, which is for the jury to decide.

The requirement that the object be in "the same or substantially the same condition" now as it was at the relevant time ensures that the exhibit does not mislead or distort. For example, if the defendant is charged with possessing a dangerous weapon, the object alleged to be the weapon ordinarily is admitted in evidence only if it is in substantially the same condition now as it was when the defendant was arrested or if the witness can explain the reason for any difference. The gun may have been tested, and its appearance therefore altered, but it still should be admissible so long as a witness can account for the difference in condition.

b. Chain of custody

Some things cannot be uniquely identified by the senses. Common examples include drugs, blood, and other fluids. No witness can credibly testify that "this blood came from John Smith" by looking at the blood, or that "this brake fluid came from the defendant's car" by looking at the brake fluid, or that "this bullet came from the victim's body" by looking at the bullet. In these situations, a "chain of custody" needs to be established to circumstantially prove that the exhibit in court is actually what its proponent claims it to be, and the proof may involve more than one foundation witness or other exhibit.

There are two common ways a chain of custody is established. First, the proponent can establish that the evidence was in the exclusive possession of one or more persons from the time first obtained to the present time (or the time it was examined or tested by an expert). This protects the integrity of the evidence by eliminating the possibility of an unknown person tampering with the evidence or replacing it with something else.

For example, consider a drunk driving case in which lab tests were done on a blood sample. A nurse drew a blood sample from the defendant, put it in a test tube, labeled it, and hand-carried it to the lab. A lab assistant then received the test tube from the nurse and locked it in the assistant's locker, to which only the lab assistant has access. The next day the lab assistant removed the test tube from the locker and gave it to the chemist. The chemist then tested the blood for alcohol. If all three witnesses — nurse, lab assistant, and chemist — testify, there has been a credible showing that the blood the chemist tested was the defendant's blood. The blood is admissible, and the chemist can testify to the results of her test.

Second, the proponent can establish that the evidence was packaged in a way that eliminates the possibility of tampering or alteration. For example, consider an unlawful possession of cocaine case. An FBI agent seized suspected drugs from the defendant's house. He then personally carried the suspected drugs to the FBI office and put them in a plastic evidence bag, labeled it, and heat-sealed the opening. He then shipped the package to the FBI for testing. A lab technician logged in the package and assigned it to a chemist. The FBI chemist received the package some time later. When he received it, the plastic bag was labeled and sealed on one side. He cut open the opposite side of the bag, removed some of the contents, and heat-sealed the bag. He then tested the contents he had removed. He brought the resealed bag with him to court, still sealed. If two witnesses, the FBI agent and the chemist, testify to these facts, there has been a credible showing that the drugs tested came from the defendant's house. The plastic bag and its contents are admissible, and the chemist can testify to the results of her test.

There is nothing mysterious about a chain of custody. The question is this: Has the proponent presented credible evidence that the object was either handled or packaged in such a way as to circumstantially demonstrate that it was not altered, contaminated, or substituted between the time it was first obtained and the time it was tested? If so, it is admissible. It should not matter that *after* being tested the object was lost, destroyed, or consumed during the testing process.

Although FRE 901 imposes the same admissibility standard for any offered exhibit and does not differentiate between civil and criminal cases, courts have sometimes imposed a higher standard in criminal cases, particularly when a chain of custody is involved. In such cases, courts have sometimes required a showing that the exhibit in court is reasonably certain to be the same substance.

2. Practice

Issues in the admission of real evidence usually center on the adequacy of the sensory identification and the completeness of the demonstrated chain of custody. These issues arise more frequently in criminal cases.

Example 1:

This is a murder case. The prosecution in its case-in-chief seeks to introduce in evidence a shotgun found at the defendant's home. The government calls an FBI agent, and the following happens:

Q. (By prosecutor) Agent Ryan, when you entered the defendant's house, what did you see?
A. In the bedroom, leaning in a corner, was a shotgun with a sawed-off barrel.
Q. What did you do with it?
A. I took it back to the FBI office, tagged it, and logged it in with the evidence section.

[Prosecutor has exhibit marked, shows it to opposing counsel, and asks permission to approach the witness.]

Q. Agent Ryan, I'm now showing you Government Exhibit No. 1. Do you recognize it?

A. Yes.

Q. What do you recognize it to be?

A. That's the shotgun I recovered from the defendant's bedroom.

Q. How are you able to determine it's the same shotgun?

A. It looks the same, and it has the evidence tag on the trigger guard that I put on it that day.

Q. Does that shotgun look in the same, or substantially the same, condition now as it looked when you saw it in the defendant's bedroom?

A. It looks exactly the same.

Prosecutor: We offer Government Exhibit No. 1.

Defendant: Objection, your honor. There's been no showing that the agent can uniquely recognize the shotgun itself. He only recognizes the tag, which could have been removed.

Judge: Overruled. Government Exhibit No. 1 is admitted.

Commentary: It is the evidence tag that makes the item uniquely identifiable. The fact that someone could conceivably have altered or switched the evidence tag goes to weight, not admissibility. Most courts would also admit the evidence if the witness says it "looks like the shotgun" and there was no identification tag.

Example 2:

This is a rape prosecution. The prosecution in its case-in-chief seeks to introduce in evidence a wallet the victim took from the defendant's car as she was pushed out of the car following the rape. The prosecution calls the victim, and during direct examination the following happens:

Q. (By prosecutor) Ms. Johnson, as you were being pushed out of the car, what did you do?

A. I saw a wallet lying on the floor by my feet. I grabbed it as I was being pushed out.

Q. What did you do with the wallet?

A. I hung onto it until I was taken to the emergency room. I then gave it to a nurse, who put it on a counter in the examining room.

Q. Did you see the wallet after that?

A. No. I assume that the police . . .

Defendant: Objection, your honor, as to what she assumed.

Judge: Sustained.

[Prosecutor has exhibit marked, shows it to opposing counsel, and asks permission to approach the witness.]

Q. Ms. Johnson, I'm showing you State's Exhibit No. 1. Do you recognize it?

A. Well, it looks like the wallet I took from the car, but I can't say for sure.

Q. Is there anything different about this wallet and the one you took from the car?

A. No. It looks like the same wallet.

During cross-examination, the following questions were asked:

Q. (By defendant's lawyer) Ms. Johnson, how long were you in the examining room?
A. Maybe an hour. I'm not sure.
Q. During that hour, nurses were in the room?
A. Yes.
Q. And doctors were in the room?
A. Yes.
Q. About how many nurses and doctors were in the room with you during that hour?
A. I'd say maybe three or four different nurses and one or two doctors.

Later in the prosecution's case-in-chief, the prosecutor calls a police officer who testifies as follows:

Q. (By prosecutor) Officer Muldowney, when you got to the hospital emergency room, did you talk to Ms. Johnson?
A. I did.
Q. Following that conversation, what did you do?
A. I went over to the counter in the examining room and recovered a wallet lying on top of it.
Q. Officer, I'm showing you what has previously been marked State's Exhibit No. 1. Please examine it. Have you seen it before?
A. Yes, I have.
Q. When was the first time you saw it?
A. When I got it from the counter in the examining room where I talked to Ms. Johnson.
Q. What did you do with the wallet?
A. I took it to the police station, put it in an evidence bag, and had it inventoried in the evidence section.
Q. When was the next time you saw it?
A. This morning, when I got it out of the evidence section and brought it to court.
Q. Does the wallet look in the same condition today as it looked when you first got it in the examining room?
A. It does.
Prosecutor: Your honor, we offer State's Exhibit No. 1 in evidence.
Judge: Any objection?
Defendant: Yes, your honor. May we be heard at sidebar?
Judge: Yes. Please approach. [Lawyers come to the bench.]
Defendant: The victim can only say the wallet "looks like" the one she took from the car, but she can't uniquely identify it. This exhibit requires a chain of custody, but the chain has been broken. The wallet was left lying on a counter for an hour, where several people had access to it. The officer can only say he picked up a wallet from the counter, but there's been no proof it's the same wallet.
Prosecutor: Your honor, the evidence is sufficient to show that the wallet is probably the same one. We don't have to show 100 percent

certainty. This foundation is enough for admissibility. The
defense's points go to weight.

Judge: The exhibit will be admitted. There's been enough of a foundation
for admissibility. Counsel can argue the weight issue to the jury
later.

§10.4. *Demonstrative evidence*[3]

1. Law

Demonstrative evidence is evidence that is not the actual thing, but represents
the actual thing. Common examples include photographs, videotapes, diagrams, models, drawings, anatomical charts and models, maps, and computer
graphics and animations. To admit demonstrative evidence, the proponent
must call a competent witness, one having firsthand knowledge of the actual
thing at the relevant date to testify that the exhibit fairly represents or shows the
actual thing. To be relevant, the exhibit must help the jury understand some fact
of consequence to the case.

For example, in an armed robbery case, the prosecution offers a diagram of
the counter area of the convenience store where the robbery occurred. The sales
clerk who was present during the robbery is called as a witness and testifies that
the diagram fairly shows the counter area of the store at the time of the robbery.
The exhibit is admissible. As a further example, in a personal injury case, the
defendant offers a model of the intersection where the accident occurred. An
eyewitness to the accident testifies that the model accurately represents the
intersection at the time of the crash. The exhibit is admissible.

Note that the exhibit need only "fairly represent" or "fairly portray" the real
thing, although "fairly accurate" or "fairly and accurately" language is also used.
There is no legal requirement that the exhibit be "to scale." If the exhibit is not
to scale, this goes to weight, not admissibility. On the other hand, if the exhibit
does not fairly portray the real thing, or if it distorts or misleads, the court should
exclude it. Some judges exclude such an exhibit on the ground that FRE 901's
requirements have not been met; others exclude on FRE 403 grounds.

The admissibility status of demonstrative exhibits varies. What does it mean
when a judge "admits" the exhibit in evidence? Some judges permit the jury to
see such exhibits only during a witness's testimony, since the exhibit illustrates
the witness's testimony. For example, a doctor testifies and uses an anatomical
chart to explain his testimony. However, since the exhibit has no independent
value, it does not go to the jury during deliberations, although most judges allow
use of the exhibit during closing arguments. Other judges reject this limited
view of demonstrative exhibits and allow such exhibits to go to the jury during
deliberations, since it helps the jury understand the facts and decide the case.

This difference in judicial views means that when a demonstrative exhibit is
offered and "admitted" in evidence, a lawyer must determine if the judge will

---

3. McCormick §§213-214; Weinstein §§1001(1), 1001(2); Mueller & Kirkpatrick
§§9.31-9.36; Wigmore §1156.

allow the exhibit to be used only with the witness, allow it to be used during closing arguments, and allow it to go to the jury during deliberations.

Photographs present another recurring problem. Some consider them demonstrative exhibits. For example, a photograph of a robbery scene illustrates the actual scene. However, a photograph of the actual robbery in progress can be viewed as real, rather than demonstrative. Whether considered real or demonstrative evidence, the foundation remains the same. The photograph should be admitted in evidence if a competent witness says that the photograph fairly portrays the scene or fairly shows how the robbery happened. Neat categories of exhibits should not be a substitute for clear thinking or analysis.

There is no requirement that the photographer be the qualifying witness. In fact, sometimes the photographer is not a proper qualifying witness. For example, consider a personal injury case involving an intersection collision. One year later, as part of his trial preparations, the plaintiff's lawyer has a photographer take photographs of the intersection. The photographer cannot qualify the photographs for admission unless he knows that the photographs fairly show how the intersection looked at the time of the collision. If the photographer does not know this, the proper qualifying witness must be someone who knows how the intersection looked at the time of the collision.

A recurring difficulty with photographs is that while the photograph itself may be reasonably accurate in showing the location of various things, it may not accurately reproduce the lighting at the relevant time. For example, a photograph of an intersection, taken during the daytime, accurately shows how the intersection looked at the time of the collision, but does not accurately reproduce the lighting at the time of the collision, which occurred at night. In this situation, the judge may admit the photograph for a limited purpose — showing the layout of the intersection — and instruct the jury that the photograph is not to be taken as showing the lighting at the time of the collision.

Another recurring difficulty is that a photograph taken through a wide-angle or fisheye lens may show the intersection, but it distorts the appearance of the intersection sufficiently that the photograph misleads, rather than informs. Or the photograph is taken from a particular perspective or angle, so that it creates a wrong impression of the scene. Such photographs should not be admitted, either because they violate FRE 901's foundation requirements or because they violate FRE 403.

Sometimes an exhibit can be either real or demonstrative, depending on its use. For example, a photograph is usually considered demonstrative evidence, since it usually portrays the real thing or place. However, if a photograph was stolen during a burglary or is alleged to be pornographic, the photograph is real evidence and would need the foundation necessary for real evidence.

Computer-generated graphics have become realistic alternatives to two-dimensional diagrams and three-dimensional models. If a computer has a computer-assisted design program, graphics of things like machines, buildings, and body organs can be created, enlarged, moved, and rotated on a monitor. Computer-generated graphics of events like an automobile collision can recreate the event with stunning clarity.

Computer-generated graphics are usually classified as either "animations" or "simulations," although some courts use the terms loosely and even interchangeably. An animation is simply a computer-generated depiction of what a witness experienced. It is conceptually no different from a photograph or diagram. For example, if a witness says he saw the collision between two vehicles, the witness can testify that a computer-generated animation of the collision accurately shows what happened. No expert testimony is necessary to have the animation admitted in evidence.

A simulation is a computer-generated re-creation of an event based on data collected about the event. For a simulation to be admitted in evidence, there must be expert testimony showing that there was reliable and sufficient data collected about the event, the data were accurately preserved and entered into a reliable and properly functioning computer, the computer had a reliable software program based on accepted scientific methodology that is capable of using the data to create an accurate simulation of the event, and that the resulting simulation accurately shows what happened. For example, a simulation of an airplane crash, based on data obtained from the flight data recorder, will be admitted in evidence if the necessary foundation is established.

Courts sometimes differ in how they treat simulations. Some courts treat simulations like other demonstrative exhibits, meaning that ordinarily the lawyers can use the simulation during closing arguments and the jurors can see the simulation during their deliberations. Other courts, concerned that jurors may put too much weight on the simulation, permit the simulation to be shown during the expert's testimony but do not allow the jury to see the simulation again during closing arguments or the jury deliberations.

Since computer-generated simulations are recent creations, courts have not yet developed consistent approaches to the foundations for, and the admissibility of, such evidence. Most courts do require that the opposing parties have an adequate opportunity to examine such simulations before trial, including the computer software program and the data that were fed into the program, and will usually hold pretrial hearings to determine the admissibility of the simulation.

At times, the computer product will consist of charts, graphs, or summaries. In addition to the need for authentication, hearsay issues might arise. If so, the entry of the data into the computer must satisfy a hearsay exception under FRE 805 — hearsay within hearsay. If the output is the product of original computer generation — automated telephone call lists, for instance — and does not include an act of data entry by some person, there is no hearsay issue.

2. Practice

Demonstrative evidence is commonly introduced during trials. The principal issue is whether the exhibit is reasonably accurate or whether it misrepresents or distorts.

Example 1:

This is a bank robbery case. The prosecution in its case-in-chief seeks to introduce a videotape of the robbery taken by a surveillance camera.

The government calls a bank teller who was present during the robbery. The following then happens:

Q. (By prosecutor) Ms. Smith, you were there during the robbery?
A. Yes.
Q. Where were you?
A. I was right in the middle of the teller area.
[Prosecutor has exhibit marked, shows it to opposing counsel, and asks permission to approach the witness.]
Q. Ms. Smith, I'm showing you a videotape, marked Government Exhibit No. 1. Have you seen the videotape?
A. Yes, I looked at it in your office earlier this morning.
Q. Does that videotape fairly and accurately show what you saw happen during the robbery?
A. If does. The camera covered the entire teller area where I was standing when the robbery happened.
Prosecutor: We offer Government Exhibit No. 1.
Judge: Any objection?
Defendant: Yes, your honor. The witness could not possibly see everything during the robbery and can't say that the camera showed everything accurately.
Judge: The objection is overruled. It will be received.

Example 2:

In a negligence action, plaintiff offers in evidence a photograph of the intersection where the collision occurred, after establishing a standard foundation through a witness. Defendant objects to the photograph and asks for a sidebar. The following then happens:

Judge: Defense, why shouldn't this photograph be admitted?
Defendant: Your honor, we don't dispute that the witness has said the magic words "fair and accurate." However, this accident happened at midnight. This photograph is obviously a daytime photograph. The lighting conditions at the time of the collision are in issue, and this photograph may well confuse or mislead the jury about the actual lighting. In addition, this photograph was obviously taken with a wide-angle lens. Look how the curb line curves here [indicating]. The perspective is distorted, and what are clearly straight lines are curved in the photograph because of the distortion of the wide-angle lens. That again will confuse and mislead the jury.
Plaintiff: Those concerns go to weight, your honor. The witness has said the photo fairly and accurately shows the intersection. That's enough to get it in. They can bring up their points on cross.
Judge: I'm not concerned with the lighting. I can always instruct the jury not to use the photograph for the purpose of determining the lighting at the time of the accident. However, the distortion

concerns me. It looks like this photo was taken through some kind of fisheye lens, and I don't see the reason for it. I'm keeping this photograph out because its distortion may well mislead the jury. Counsel, of course, is free to offer other photographs that don't have this defect.

Example 3:

In a negligence action, defendant offers in evidence a diagram of the intersection where the collision occurred, after establishing a standard foundation through a witness. Plaintiff objects to the diagram and asks for a sidebar. The following then happens:

Plaintiff: We object, your honor, because the diagram is improperly distorting. Look at the north-south distances, and compare them to the east-west distances. The east-west scale is clearly several times greater. This makes the street look several times wider than it would if the same scale had been used in both directions. In this case, the width of the street and the distances between street lights are important. Defendant's diagram makes the street look several times wider and the street lights look several times closer than they should be. That's improper under both Rule 901 and Rule 403.

Defendant: The witness said the diagram is fairly accurate, and it will obviously help the witness explain what happened.

Judge: The objection is sustained. This exhibit does not fairly show the distances between the street lights and the width of the street.

Commentary: Misleading scales and other distortions are the primary reasons that demonstrative exhibits encounter evidentiary problems.

§10.5. Documents and instruments[4]

1. Law

Certain types of written documents and instruments have independent legal significance. Common examples are wills, contracts, ransom notes, promissory notes, checks, and letters containing the words of offer and acceptance that form a contract. They have legal significance because they were made and are non-hearsay. To admit such a document or instrument, the proponent must introduce evidence showing that the signature appearing on it, or the handwriting, is in fact that of the person it purports to be made by. Put another way, the signature or handwriting must be authenticated.

Under FRE 901, this can be done by calling a witness who either saw the person sign the instrument or is familiar with the handwriting of that person and

---

4. McCormick §§218-225; Weinstein §901(b)(4); Mueller & Kirkpatrick §§9.6-9.8; Wigmore §1156.

can identify the signature or handwriting as being of the person. However, under FRE 901(b)(2), familiarity with a person's handwriting cannot have been acquired for purposes of litigation. If a proper qualifying witness is unavailable, under FRE 901(b)(3), expert handwriting comparisons can be used, or the jury can make a comparison itself.

For example, plaintiff in a contract case seeks to introduce the promissory note purportedly signed by defendant. Plaintiff calls a witness who is familiar with defendant's signature because she has seen defendant sign his name in the past. The witness says the signature on the note is defendant's. The promissory note is admissible.

Most courts also add the requirement that there be a showing that the exhibit is in the same condition now as when executed. This showing eliminates the possibility of tampering with or alteration of the exhibit's contents. This is normally done by having the qualifying witness state that the exhibit appears to be in the "same condition" or in "substantially the same condition."

2. Practice

Lawyers sometimes confuse the foundation necessary to admit documents that are non-hearsay because they have independent legal significance with the foundation necessary to admit business records, which are hearsay. When deciding how to establish the foundation for admissibility of a document, the offering lawyer first must consider the relevant purpose of the exhibit. Sometimes a document is offered to prove that a certain person was the signatory. Simply establishing a business record foundation might be inadequate to accomplish the purpose. Most judges will require that a witness with firsthand knowledge testify to the authenticity of the signature.

For example, in a contract case brought by a loan company against a debtor, the loan company seeks to introduce in evidence the promissory note. The signature on the note, purporting to be that of the debtor, must be authenticated by a qualified witness. Establishing a business record foundation for the promissory note does not fulfill the authentication requirement of FRE 901.

A document that is offered because it was made — a non-hearsay purpose — requires that the handwriting or signature be identified as being that of the person it purports to be made by. The only common issue is whether the witness has adequate knowledge to provide the necessary foundation.

Example:

This is a contract case. The plaintiff in its case-in-chief seeks to introduce the contract. To do so, the plaintiff calls a witness who was present during the execution of the contract. The following then happens:

Q. (By plaintiff's lawyer) Ms. Roberts, where were you on June 1, 2015, at 9:00 A.M.?
A. I was in the conference room at our offices.
Q. Who else was present?
A. Mr. Able and Mr. Baker.

Q. What happened in the conference room at that time?

A. I brought in the contract I had prepared, they looked it over for a few minutes, and then they signed it.

Q. Did you actually see Mr. Able and Mr. Baker sign the contract?

A. I did. I was standing right next to them.

Q. What did you do afterward?

A. I made photocopies, gave each of them a copy, and put the original in our files.

[Plaintiff has exhibit marked, shows it to opposing counsel, and asks permission to approach the witness.]

Q. Ms. Roberts, I'm showing you what has been marked Plaintiff's Exhibit No. 1. Have you seen it before?

A. Yes, that's the contract I prepared.

Q. The signatures at the bottom, did you see them placed on the contract?

A. Yes, I saw Mr. Able and Mr. Baker sign it.

Q. Is this contract in the same condition now as it was on the date it was signed?

A. Yes, it looks exactly the same.

Plaintiff: Your honor, we offer Plaintiff's Exhibit No. 1 in evidence.

Defendant: We object, your honor. There's been no showing that the witness is familiar with the defendant's handwriting or ever saw the defendant execute any other document.

Judge: Overruled. It's admitted.

Commentary: Defendant's objection is directed to weight, not admissibility.

§10.6. *Business records*[5]

1. Law

Business records usually are hearsay. They are written, out-of-court statements, and their contents are being offered to prove matters in issue. Since business records are hearsay, they must be qualified as a hearsay exception before they can be admitted. The business records exception, FRE 803(6), spells out the foundation requirements.

A "custodian or other qualified witness" must testify that the record

1. is a "record of an act, event, condition, opinion, or diagnosis";
2. "the record was made . . . by — or from information transmitted by — someone with knowledge."
3. was "made at or near the time" of the acts and events recorded on it;
4. was made as part of the "regular practice of that activity"; and
5. was "kept in the course of a regularly conducted activity of a business."

---

5. McCormick §§284-294; Weinstein §803(6); Mueller & Kirkpatrick §§8.44-8.48; Wigmore §665.

Establishing the foundation for the admission of business records is usually a simple matter of asking an appropriate witness the qualifying questions specified in FRE 803(6). Admitting the business record eliminates the need to call the maker of the record as a witness at trial, although that person can always be called as a witness if he remembers the acts and events he recorded on the record.

The rationale behind the business record exception is the usual one: reliability. If a business depends on having accurate and complete records to run the business competently, such records are reliable enough to qualify as a hearsay exception. At a practical level, the business record usually will be more reliable than the memory of the employee who made the record.

The witness necessary to qualify the record as a business record can be the "custodian or another qualified witness." This means that any employee, or even a former employee, who is familiar with how the business generates and maintains its records can testify to the business records foundation, even if that person has no personal knowledge of the acts and events contained on the record. However, courts have generally held that non-employees, such as recipients of business records who periodically receive things such as invoices or bills of lading, are not proper qualifying witnesses for the business's records.

The 2000 changes to FRE 803(6) and FRE 902(11) and (12) recognize that production of a foundation witness often is burdensome and a waste of time. FRE 803(6) now permits the foundation requirement for the business record exception to be shown by "certification that complies with Rule 902(11) or (12), or with a statute permitting certification," unless "the source of information or the method or circumstances of preparation indicate a lack of trustworthiness."

Corresponding amendments to FRE 902 (self-authentication) provide that domestic records in all cases and foreign records in civil cases can be authenticated by the declaration of a qualified witness. The witness must certify under oath that the requirements of the business record exception are met. Admissibility of foreign business records by certification is authorized by statute in criminal cases (18 U.S.C. §3505).

FRE 902(11) and (12) require the proponent of the record to provide advance notice to all parties of its intent to prove the record through certification. And the proponent "must give an adverse party reasonable written notice of the intent to offer the record — and must make the record and certification available for inspection — so that the party has a fair opportunity to challenge them."

The "business duty" concept is encompassed by the rule, although not specifically mentioned. Since the leading case of *Johnson v. Lutz*, 170 N.E. 517 (N.Y. 1930), the law has recognized that employees have a business duty to report and record information accurately on the business's records. If the employee does an inaccurate job, the employee may lose his job. That reality is what makes business records inherently reliable and is the concept behind the requirement that the record be made "by — or from information transmitted by — someone with knowledge" of the information appearing on the record. What do the additional words "made . . . from information transmitted by a someone with knowledge" mean? The business record rule recognizes that in the real world of business the person with firsthand knowledge of the facts may not be the same person as the one physically creating the record.

For example, a shipping document contains certain information, such as the weight of the shipped box. The person with knowledge of that fact is the shipping clerk who actually weighed the box at the loading dock. However, the clerk did not personally record the weight of the box on a record. The clerk telephoned the weight to the office secretary, who typed the shipping document, which included the box's weight. The secretary, of course, has no personal knowledge of the box's weight. However, since the box's weight on the record was recorded "from information transmitted by someone with knowledge" — the shipping clerk — this information is part of the business record. The practical effect of the business duty rule is to treat all employees of the business as a single person with firsthand knowledge for purposes of the hearsay rule.

The business duty concept, however, does not apply when the person having firsthand knowledge of the facts is a non-employee of the business. The non-employee is an outsider and has no business duty to report and record accurately. Statements by or information from such non-employees appearing on a business record is called "double hearsay," or "hearsay within hearsay," the admissibility of which is governed by FRE 805. When the statement or information from the non-employee is being offered for its truth, that rule permits it to be admitted in evidence only if it qualifies as a hearsay exception.

For example, an accident investigator goes to the scene of a collision shortly after it happened. The investigator notes the condition of the vehicles, weather, and road conditions, which he puts in his accident report. The investigator also interviews an eyewitness and notes in his report "Ms. Avery says that Car #2 crossed the center line and struck Car #1." This statement is double hearsay and is not admissible as part of the business record. In other words, when the investigator's report is qualified as a business record, the eyewitness's statement must be physically deleted, or "redacted," from the report before the report is admitted and shown or read to the jury unless a separate hearsay exception applies to the eyewitness's statement. Here, no exception applies.

Consider another example. A nurse fills out an emergency room report. The report shows information that the nurse herself obtained, such as the patient's temperature, pulse, and other vital signs. The report also contains the statement "Patient says that she was struck on the driver's side door by other vehicle." This statement, made by the patient, who is not an employee of the hospital, is double hearsay. However, here, a separate hearsay exception — statements made for purposes of diagnosis and treatment — applies to that statement. The result is that the entire report, including the patient's statement, is properly admissible because the report qualifies as a business record under FRE 803(6) and the patient's statement contained in the report qualifies as a statement made for diagnosis and treatment under FRE 803(4).

These double hearsay, or hearsay within hearsay, statements contained in business records are expressly admissible under FRE 805 if each level of hearsay is qualified under a separate hearsay exception. This rule is discussed further in Sec. 7.16.

Another recurring issue under the business record exception is whether the record is limited to facts or whether it also includes opinions and other evaluative and conclusory statements. Note that FRE 803(6) expressly includes not only an "act, event, [and] condition," but also an "opinion, or diagnosis." The potential conflict emerges when the expert witness rules, FRE 702-705, are considered. No witness can testify in court as an expert unless that witness is first qualified as an expert. If qualified, the expert can then testify to an "opinion or otherwise." It follows that a qualified expert's opinion or diagnosis, contained in the business record of the business by which the expert is employed, should be admissible.

For example, a hospital emergency room report contains the doctor's notation "Patient diagnosed as having a comminuted fracture of left tibia." This report is a business record, and the doctor's diagnosis contained in the report is admissible. In short, in this situation, there is no requirement that the doctor be first qualified as an expert; his qualifications are assumed under the circumstances.

Consider another example. A police accident report states that "this collision happened because Car #2 was driving too fast under existing road conditions and crossed the center line into Car #1's lane of traffic." If the police officer is testifying in person, he ordinarily cannot be qualified as an accident reconstruction expert and will not be allowed to give his opinion on what caused the collision. If this is so, the report, insofar as it contains the officer's opinions, should not be admitted as part of a business (or public) record. The factual information on the report is admissible as part of the record; the opinion is not.

The rule does not specifically exclude records made for the purpose of litigation, but the judge may exclude a record where the "method or circumstances of preparation indicate a lack of trustworthiness." This "anticipation of litigation" rule comes from *Palmer v. Hoffman*, 318 U.S. 109 (1943), where the Supreme Court excluded an accident report by a since-deceased train engineer offered by the railroad in a grade-crossing collision case. The Court held that such a report, obviously written with an eye toward an expected lawsuit, was too untrustworthy under the circumstances to be admitted as a business record. The *Palmer v. Hoffman* rule has not been broadly applied, since any business record can be seen as having been made with a view toward possible future litigation. However, when litigation in a particular situation becomes a distinct possibility, a record made by a party may be too self-serving to be trustworthy, and FRE 803(6) permits its exclusion.

While the rule clearly includes computer-generated records, some courts hold that a record is a computer record only if the computer's output is in the same form as the original input. If the computer is asked to search and selectively retrieve information from its data base, and if the resulting printout is a new document that was never put into the computer in that form, the printout is a summary under FRE 1006, not a business record under FRE 803(6). While the summary will be admissible, the requirements of FRE 1006 must be met.

Courts will reject computerized evidence offered under FRE 803(6) when there is an insufficient showing of accuracy and trustworthiness. It does not matter that a business record is maintained in a computer rather than in company books if (1) the opposing party has an opportunity to inquire into the accuracy of the computer and the input procedures used and (2) the trial court requires the proponent of the evidence to provide a foundation that will support a finding of trustworthiness. If a sufficient foundation is established, it does not matter that the printout offered into evidence was based on data stored in the computer for a period of time. But proponents of computer printouts must introduce the actual printouts, and cannot rely only on oral testimony about the contents of the printouts without running afoul of FRE 1002, the original writing rule.

FRE 803(7) allows the absence of a record to prove the non-happening of an event. If the business practice is to make a record, or a notation on a record, whenever something specific happens, and if the business has no record or notation of such an event, it circumstantially proves that the event never happened. For example, the plaintiff claims she ordered a product over the telephone from the defendant. The defense claims that the transaction never occurred. The defense calls a supervisor in the catalogue order department who testifies that she searched her records for an order confirmation record, which is always filled out whenever a telephone order is actually placed in her department. Despite an extensive search, she found no order confirmation for the claimed transaction, nor did she find any other record of the claimed transaction.

Business records also are discussed in Sec. 7.10.

2. Practice

The business record exception is probably the hearsay exception most frequently used during trials. Basic foundation issues are rare. In civil cases, such records frequently are admitted before trial or at trial without objection. Judges often do not require the full technical foundation specified by FRE 803(6). However, lawyers frequently miss objections when they mistakenly believe that once a business record foundation has been established, no other objections can be successfully raised. This notion is wrong. Many issues remain, and the two most common are double hearsay and whether the record contains inadmissible opinions and conclusions. These issues should be raised before trial whenever possible.

Example 1:

This is a contract case. Plaintiff seeks to prove damages by introducing in evidence employee time cards of a contractor who was hired to complete a construction project. An employee of the contractor testifies as follows:

Q. (By plaintiff's lawyer) Mr. Phelps, you're the business manager of your company?

A. Yes.

Q. Are you familiar with how your company creates, uses, and maintains employee time cards?

A. Of course.

[Plaintiff has exhibit marked, shows it to opposing counsel, and asks permission to approach the witness.]

Q. Mr. Phelps, I'm showing you Plaintiff's Group Exhibit No. 5. Are you familiar with those records?

A. Yes, those are our employee time cards.

Q. Who makes those time cards?

A. The cards themselves we have printed up. The employees punch themselves in and out every day, and at the end of each week, we collect the complete cards and send them to the payroll department.

Q. When are those time cards made?

A. Each time an employee comes to or leaves work and puts the time card in the punch clock.

Q. Is that the procedure you use to record the time of every employee?

A. The employees who are paid by the hour, yes.

Q. Does your company keep and maintain those records?

A. Yes, we keep them for about two years before destroying them. In the meantime, we have all the time records put into our computer data base, and we keep the computerized time records indefinitely.

Plaintiff: Your honor, we offer in evidence Plaintiff's Group Exhibit No. 5.

Defendant: Objection. They haven't established the necessary foundation under Rule 803(6).

Judge: What's missing?

Defendant: There's been no showing that the cards were made by a person having knowledge of the facts.

Judge: Overruled. Plaintiff's Group Exhibit No. 5 is admitted.

Commentary: This is an adequate foundation, even though the precise words of FRE 803(6) were not used.

Example 2:

This is a contract case in which the principal issue involves claimed lost profits. To prove those losses, plaintiff seeks to introduce its income tax return for the year involved and lists the income tax return as an exhibit on its pretrial memorandum. Defendant objects. At a pretrial hearing, the following happens:

Defendant: Your honor, we objected to proposed Plaintiff's Exhibit No. 7, its income tax return for 2014. The reason we objected is that the tax return is not a business record of the plaintiff under Rule 803(6).

Plaintiff: Plaintiff is a company that fills out a federal corporate tax return every year. These returns are based on the company's own financial data and are prepared by our accountant. Once we make them, we keep them for years. We'll have witnesses prepared to establish that foundation at trial.

Defendant: The point is that the return is a report submitted to an agency of the government. It's not a record used by the business in conducting its business. The company records used to prepare the return may be business records, but not the return itself.

Judge: The objection is overruled. The return will be admitted if a proper foundation is established at trial.

Commentary: Modern cases usually accept the idea that reports periodically and routinely submitted by businesses to government agencies, such as income tax returns to the IRS and 10-K reports to the SEC, qualify as business records.

Example 3:

This is a personal injury case in which the plaintiff was injured in a head-on collision with the defendant. The plaintiff seeks to introduce in evidence an accident report prepared by a police officer and lists the report as an exhibit on its pretrial memorandum. The police report includes the following notations: (1) "Defendant said he was going about 45 mph and didn't realize that the roadway was icy"; (2) "This collision was caused when defendant's car crossed the center line into the plaintiff's lane of traffic." The defendant objects to the report. At a pretrial hearing, the following happens:

Defendant: Your honor, we have no objection to the report as a whole. It's obviously both a business and a public record. However, we object to the statements of the defendant and the officer's statement of fault. The statements of other persons recorded in the report are double hearsay. The defendant's statement is therefore hearsay, and the business record exception applies only to the report itself, not to the statements of other persons contained in the report. Second, the statement of the officer regarding the cause of the collision is also inadmissible. It is either a statement from another eyewitness, in which case it is double hearsay, or it is the opinion of the police officer, in which case it is opinion evidence without a showing that the officer is properly qualified to give such an opinion. In either case, it's inadmissible and must be deleted.

Plaintiff: The statement of the defendant contained in the report is not hearsay because it's an admission by a party-opponent. As to the officer's opinion, we agree that it is not admissible as contained on the report, and we will be offering a redacted copy of the report.

Judge: I agree with the plaintiff that the defendant's statements are a party admission, which will be admissible if the report itself is properly admitted. Since the plaintiff has conceded the inadmissibility of the officer's opinion, that will be redacted from the copy of the report offered at trial.

Example 4:

This is a suit brought to enforce payment of unpaid debts. Plaintiff claims defendant ordered numerous items from plaintiff's store without later paying for them. Defendant claims some of the items were not ordered or sent. Plaintiff seeks to introduce in evidence a computer print-out showing all sales to defendant for the year involved and lists the report as an exhibit in its pretrial memorandum. Defendant objects. At a pretrial hearing, the following happens:

Defendant: We object to the computer printout, your honor. It's not a business record. What they asked the computer to do is to search the data base and cull out of that data base any record of sales to the defendant. That printout is not a business record, since the printout is not in the same form as the data put into the computer. Second, such a printout is not done in the ordinary course of business; it was obviously a special printout created solely because of this litigation. Again, it can't possibly be qualified as a business record.

Plaintiff: All the information on the printout came from the company's records, your honor. All the data were put into the computer in the ordinary course of business. We simply asked the computer to search for and print out only those sales records that are relevant to this lawsuit. We regularly ask the computer to retrieve specific information from its data base. The information it retrieves is still a record of the business.

Judge: The objection is sustained. I find that the printout is not a business record under Rule 803(6). However, it may be a summary under Rule 1006. That, of course, requires a different foundation, and that matter is not before me.

Commentary: The judge here is making a suggestion that plaintiff should have made earlier. If not a business record, the printout should qualify as a summary under FRE 1006. Some courts hold that a printout from a computer data base is a business record only if the output is in the same form as the original input. When the computer is asked to selectively search and print, it is creating a summary. Offering the exhibit under FRE 1006 should also eliminate the "anticipation of litigation" argument, since exhibits prepared under that rule are usually made for use at trial. An FRE 1006 summary must be based on exhibits admissible at trial.

§10.7.   *Public records*[6]

1.   Law

The rationale for admitting public records and reports as hearsay exceptions is the same as that for business records: reliability. Public employees, just like private employees, have a "business duty" to report and record accurately. In addition, it is socially beneficial to keep public employees at their jobs, rather than asking them to repeatedly make court appearances to qualify their records in evidence.

FRE 803(8) includes in public records and reports three categories of information. First, subsection (i) includes "the office's activities." This includes routine office activities, such as issuing licenses and collecting fees.

6. McCormick §§295-300; Weinstein §901(b)(7); Mueller & Kirkpatrick §§8.49-8.52; Wigmore §§665, 1630-1684.

Second, subsection (ii) includes "matters observed while under a legal duty to report." This includes the reports of organizations like police departments, which routinely report accidents, and agricultural departments, which routinely report inspections. However, FRE 803(8)(A)(ii) specifically excludes in criminal cases "a matter observed by law enforcement personnel."

Third, subsection (iii) includes "in a civil case or against the government in a criminal case, factual findings from a legally authorized investigation." The applicability of FRE 803(8)(A)(iii) is limited, however, because few public agencies are directed by statute to investigate and make "factual findings."

For example, police departments are not statutorily directed to determine the cause of vehicle collisions, so any police report that contains a section stating the cause of the collision must be deleted before the rest of the report is admissible as a public record. On the other hand, some public agencies are specifically directed to make factual findings. For example, the National Transportation Safety Board (NTSB) is statutorily charged with determining the cause of airplane accidents, so an NTSB report that concludes that a crash was caused by weather or pilot error is admissible (unless, of course, another statute specifically bars such a finding). The Equal Employment Opportunity Commission (EEOC) is charged with determining if employees have been wrongfully terminated because of race, sex, age, or other factors, so an EEOC determination letter is admissible.

In *Beech Aircraft Corp. v. Rainey*, 488 U.S. 153 (1988), the Supreme Court gave an expansive interpretation to the "factual findings" language of FRE 803(8)(A)(iii). In that case, the Court held that a report from a Navy investigation into the cause of an airplane crash, which contained opinions and conclusions on the cause of the crash, was properly admitted under FRE 803(8)(A)(iii).

The foundation for common public records is simple. Under FRE 902 and 1005, a certified copy of the record is admissible. The exhibit is said to be "self-authenticating," which means that the proponent need only offer it in evidence. This eliminates the need to call a qualifying witness at trial. A public record is properly certified under FRE 902(4) if a copy of the record is "certified as correct by the custodian or another person authorized to make the certification."

For example, a certified copy of a motor vehicle registration will usually have a photocopy or microfilm print of the vehicle registration form and an attached form containing a signed statement of an employee of the motor vehicle department certifying that the attached document is a true and accurate copy of a vehicle registration from the agency's records. The certification usually has a blue or red ribbon and a stamped or glued seal of the agency.

FRE 902(1) and (2) have different procedures for domestic public documents under seal and those not under seal, and FRE 902(3) governs foreign public documents, which require double certification. While these kinds of public documents are not commonly introduced in trials, when they are the technical requirements must be followed.

FRE 803(10) allows the absence of a public record to prove the nonoccurrence of an event. If the agency's practice is to make a record whenever an event happens and the agency has no record of such an event, this fact is admissible to prove that the event never happened. A certified statement, complying with FRE 803(10) and 902, is admissible to prove the non-existence of a record. A 2013 amendment to the rule, section (B), provides that in a criminal case a prosecutor who intends to offer a certification under this rule must provide written notice of that intent to the defendant at least 14 days before trial; the defendant has 7 days to object in writing, unless the court sets a different time for the notice or objection.

FRE 803(9) and (11)-(17) create specific hearsay exceptions for several kinds of personal, religious, business, and governmental records that record facts such as personal, property, and market information. These records all are admissible, their foundations are set out in the rule and in FRE 901 and 902, and they rarely cause disputes at trial.

Public records also are discussed in Sec. 7.11.

2. Practice

Public records are routinely admitted when properly certified copies of the records are offered at trial. When an issue arises, it usually centers on whether the record is a public record and whether opinions and conclusions contained in the record are properly admitted.

Example 1:

This is a theft case. The defendant testifies that at the time of the theft he was attending school. In rebuttal, the prosecution intends to introduce public school attendance records. The following then happens:

[Prosecutor has exhibit marked and shows it to opposing counsel.]

Prosecutor: Your honor, we offer State's Exhibit No. 8. It's a certified copy of the Washington High School attendance records for December 1, 2015.

Defendant: May we approach, your honor?

Judge: Yes. [Lawyers approach the bench.]

Defendant: The exhibit appears to be properly certified, your honor. However, our objection is that high school records are not public records. We regularly see motor vehicle records, court records, things like that. Those are records from federal, state, or county agencies. Here, we have records from a public school, which is not a government agency in the sense Rule 803(8) speaks of them. These records need an authenticating witness. Second, I can't cross-examine this record, so admitting it in evidence violates the defendant's Confrontation Clause rights.

Prosecutor: A public school is an agency of the city, your honor. Just because we don't frequently see school records offered as public records doesn't mean that they aren't. Second, the Confrontation Clause bar applies only to subsections (ii) and (iii). This exhibit contains the routine activities of the school, which falls within subsection (i).

Judge: The objection is overruled. The exhibit will be admitted. Defense, if you wish to call as witnesses the teachers who actually made the classroom attendance reports, you may, of course, do so.

Commentary: The defendant also has a right to compulsory process. In this case, the defendant can subpoena the maker of the record if the defendant feels something can be gained.

Example 2:

This is a wrongful death action brought by the widow of a U.S. Air Force (USAF) pilot against the manufacturer of a USAF fighter plane. The pilot was killed when the aircraft he was flying crashed. Plaintiff contends the crash was caused by a manufacturing defect in that foam block insulation jammed the control stick, causing the crash. Plaintiff wishes to introduce in evidence a USAF Aircraft Accident Investigation Report that concludes "the ballistic foam used inside the airframe could indeed cause a restriction and/or jam of the flight controls." Defendant objects to this report on the ground that it is not properly admissible under FRE 803(8)(A)(iii). Plaintiff moves for a pretrial determination of admissibility. At the hearing, the following happens:

Judge: This is a hearing on the issue of admissibility of the Air Force investigation report on the cause of the crash. Defendant, please proceed.

Defendant: Thank you. Your honor, we have no objection to the factual matter contained in the report. We do object to the evaluative and opinion part of the report, particularly its conclusion that the foam insulation could cause a restriction or jam of the aircraft controls. First, this is not an investigation made from "a legally authorized investigation," which is required by Rule 803(8)(A)(iii). Second, the conclusion the report draws is based on the result of tests they conducted, and there is nothing in the report that shows how those tests were done or whether they were done in a proper, reliable manner.

Plaintiff: Three points, your honor. First, this investigation was conducted pursuant to authority. The investigation here was conducted pursuant to USAF regulation, and the investigator was duly appointed by the Air Force to conduct the investigation. Your honor has before you copies of the regulation and order directing the investigation. Second, as the report itself shows, the investigation was conducted by an Air Force colonel, himself an experienced pilot and investigator. Finally, the factual basis for the opinion is set forth in the report. While plaintiff is correct in stating that the report does not set forth in detail how the tests were actually conducted, there is more than sufficient factual basis in the report for the court to conclude that the tests were reliably conducted. Hence, the conclusion is admissible.

Judge: The report will be admitted. The defendant's concerns go to weight, not admissibility.

Commentary: This ruling is consistent with *Beech Aircraft Corp. v. Rainey,* 488 U.S. 153 (1988). If the report itself suggests a lack of trustworthiness, or if there is a question of the investigator's expertise, the judge will require a further hearing to address these objections.

§10.8.   *Recorded recollection*[7]

1.   Law

When a witness forgets an earlier event, or some detail of an earlier event, but made a record of that event or detail when the event or detail was still fresh in his mind, the record, although hearsay, is probably reliable, and it is better to admit the record than to lose the evidence altogether.

FRE 803(5) reflects this compromise. It provides that "A record that: (A) is on a matter the witness once knew about but now cannot recall well enough to testify fully and accurately; (B) was made or adopted by the witness when the matter was fresh in the witness's memory; and (C) accurately reflects the witness's knowledge" is admissible. If admitted, the record is read into evidence, but is not received as an exhibit unless an adverse party offers it in evidence.

Even if the witness has a partial or complete memory loss, the recorded recollection exception need be considered only if the exhibit does not qualify as a business record or public record. It is the unusual memorandum, not regularly prepared, that is offered as recorded recollection. For example, a bank officer suspects a car dealership is selling cars without paying off the bank liens on the cars. The officer goes to the dealership and writes down the identification number of each car on the dealership lot in a memorandum. The dealership is later charged with fraud. At trial, the bank officer cannot remember the identification numbers of the cars. The memorandum is not a business record because it is not a record that is regularly created by the bank. It will qualify as recorded recollection because the officer now has forgotten the numbers, but knows that he made the memorandum accurately when he knew the numbers. The contents of the memorandum can then be read to the jury.

Recorded recollection is the other side of the refreshing recollection coin. Refreshing recollection, governed by FRE 612, is used to jog memory. Recorded recollection is used when the witness's memory cannot be jogged and the memorandum is a substitute for the forgotten memory.

Recorded recollection and refreshing recollection also are discussed in Sec. 4.11 and 7.12.

2.   Practice

Under FRE 803(5), a witness's memory need not completely fail in order to qualify a memorandum as recorded recollection. The exception applies if the witness has insufficient recollection to enable the witness to testify "fully and accurately." After being properly qualified, the lawyer or witness may read from the memorandum, but the memorandum itself is not admissible as an exhibit unless offered by an adverse party.

---

7. McCormick §§279-283; Weinstein §803(5); Mueller & Kirkpatrick §8.43; Wigmore §§725-765.

Example:

This is a burglary prosecution. The prosecution calls a security guard as a witness. The following then happens:

Q. (By prosecutor) Mr. Wilson, you were a security guard at the warehouse the day it was burgled?
A. That's right.
Q. When you learned of the burglary inside the warehouse, what did you do?
A. I went over to the warehouse to check what was missing.
Q. You knew what was in the warehouse?
A. Sure. I check the inside of that warehouse regularly, so I know what's kept in there.
Q. What's usually stored in there?
A. It's mainly construction equipment, machines, things like that.
Q. Did you determine what items were missing?
A. Yes. I could see immediately that some of the big equipment was gone. I then got the warehouse inventory log, which shows what's supposed to be there, and did a detailed check to find out what was gone.
Q. What things were missing?
A. A lot of things.
Q. Like what?
A. Well, I remember a fork lift was missing, and some power tools.
Q. What else?
A. I don't remember the details. There were dozens of things gone. [Prosecutor has exhibit marked, shows it to opposing counsel, and asks permission to approach the witness.]
Q. Mr. Wilson, I'm showing you Prosecution Exhibit No. 7. Do you recognize it?
A. Sure, that's the list I made of the missing things.
Q. Does that list refresh your memory about the missing things?
A. Well, maybe a little, but I can't say I really remember all the things. This happened almost a year ago. There were dozens of things that were missing.
Q. Mr. Wilson, when did you make that list?
A. Right when I checked the inventory list against what was in the warehouse.
Q. Was that list accurate and complete when you made it?
A. Yes, sir. I double checked everything.
Prosecutor: Your honor, we offer Prosecution Exhibit No. 7 in evidence.
Judge: Any objection?
Defendant: Yes, your honor. It's not been qualified as a business record, and there's no showing that the witness's memory has been exhausted.
Judge: The objection is overruled. It's admitted.

Commentary: Some judges may allow the list as a business record, even though a burglary is not a regular event, if the business regularly takes an inventory whenever an unusual loss occurs.

§10.9.   Summaries[8]

1.   Law

Many trials, such as those in business, commercial, and products liability cases, involve extensive documents and records. If all that paperwork were introduced during such a trial, the jury would be overwhelmed. FRE 1006 responds to this reality by providing that "The proponent may use a summary, chart, or calculation to prove the content of voluminous writings, recordings, and photographs that cannot be conveniently examined in court. The proponent must make the originals or duplicates available for examination or copying, or both, by other parties at a reasonable time and place. And the court may order the proponent to produce them in court." This allows the other parties to check the accuracy of the summary by comparing it with the underlying documents and records. The summary is admissible, if qualified as accurate by an appropriate witness, without the underlying documents and records being introduced in evidence, although the court can order that they be produced in court.

While FRE 1006 does not expressly address it, the rule assumes that the evidence on which the summary is based would be properly presentable in court. If the opponent can show that a summary reflects or incorporates inadmissible evidence, the summary should not be admitted.

For example, consider a commercial case in which the plaintiff is suing for payment of royalties. The plaintiff calls an accountant who testifies that he examined the defendant's financial records for the appropriate time period and, based on those records, calculated the unpaid royalties. The accountant then states that the exhibit, a summary chart of the royalty calculations, accurately reflects the underlying documentation and his calculations. The summary chart is admissible, even though the underlying documentation is not in evidence.

While the admission of summaries is discretionary with the judge, most judges freely admit them, after a proper foundation has been established, when they will be helpful to the fact finder. Many judges give a limiting instruction telling the jury that a summary is simply a summary of other records or documents.

2.   Practice

Issues involving summaries usually arise in two areas. First, the dividing line between business records and summaries is sometimes blurry. Some courts take the position that printouts of computer data bases that selectively retrieve data are summaries, not business records. Second, parties sometimes dispute whether a summary is appropriate, given the number of underlying records involved. These issues are usually raised and decided before trial.

---

8. McCormick §233; Weinstein §1006; Mueller & Kirkpatrick §10.16; Wigmore §§12.30, 12.44.

Example:

This is a federal wire fraud prosecution. A government witness, an employee of the telephone company, testifies as follows:

Q. (By prosecutor) Ms. Torres, at my request did you search your computerized records for certain information?
A. Yes, you asked me to search our subscriber information records.
Q. How big are those records?
A. They're all computerized. They involve millions of records.
Q. Would you be able to bring them to court?
A. I'm sure we could if we had to, but the printouts would probably fill a good-sized truck.
Q. Did you make a chart of the pertinent information your search produced?
A. Yes.
[Prosecutor has exhibit marked, shows it to opposing counsel, and asks permission to approach the witness.]
Q. I'm showing you Government Exhibit No. 55. Do you recognize it?
A. That's the chart I made of the information I got from our subscriber data base.
Defendant: Your honor, may we approach?
Judge: All right. [Lawyers approach the bench.]
Defendant: Your honor, they're trying to get in evidence a summary. The underlying records have not been introduced in evidence. Moreover, we never received notice that they were going to introduce this summary in evidence. We've been surprised and prejudiced, and what they're doing violates Rule 1006.
Prosecutor: This is a fraud case in which telephone company records obviously play a central role. That we're introducing a summary of the records can hardly come as a surprise. We listed the underlying documentation as potential exhibits at trial. All we're doing now is giving the jury a summary of that data so they can meaningfully deal with the amount of information involved.
Defendant: They listed the underlying documents as exhibits, your honor, and we have no objection to their introduction, provided they have a proper foundation. However, they never told us they were going to introduce a summary, and they never listed a summary of those records as an exhibit on their exhibit list. That's improper because we've never had a reasonable chance to verify the accuracy of the summary. That's the whole point of Rule 1006.
Prosecutor: Judge, they can cross-examine the witness just like any other witness.
Judge: No, the rule requires giving the other party an opportunity to examine and copy the underlying records. While this was done, the point of this requirement is to give the other party, before trial, a fair opportunity to check the summary for accuracy against the underlying records. Here, the defense never had such an

opportunity, since the summary was never listed as a trial exhibit and the defense never saw the summary until now. Under these circumstances, the summary will be kept out.

Commentary: A summary, being a trial exhibit, should always be disclosed before trial so that the other party is not unfairly disadvantaged at trial and the judge can resolve any disputes. Under Rule 16 of the Federal Rules of Criminal Procedure, the prosecution must, upon request, permit the defense to inspect and copy documents and tangible objects that the government intends to use as evidence in its case-in-chief. In this case, the judge excluded the summary not on FRE 1006 grounds, but on pretrial discovery rule grounds.

If FRE 1006 were the only applicable rule, the judge could have stopped the direct examination, given the defense an opportunity to examine the summary, and recalled the witness later. The prosecutor should have suggested this approach.

§10.10.   *Original documents ("best evidence") rule*[9]

1.   Law

Rule 1001.   Definitions That Apply to This Article

In this article

(a) A "writing" consists of letters, words, numbers, or their equivalent set down in any form.

(b) A "recording" consists of letters, words, numbers, or their equivalent recorded in any manner.

(c) A "photograph" means a photographic image or its equivalent stored in any form.

(d) An "original" of a writing or recording means the writing or recording itself or any counterpart intended to have the same effect by the person who executed or issued it. For electronically stored information, "original" means any printout — or other output readable by sight — if it accurately reflects the information. An "original" of a photograph includes the negative or a print from it.

(e) A "duplicate" means a counterpart produced by a mechanical, photographic, chemical, electronic, or other equivalent process or technique that accurately reproduces the original.

Rule 1002.   Requirement of the Original

An original writing, recording, or photograph is required in order to prove its content unless these rules or a federal statute provides otherwise.

9. McCormick §§229-243; Weinstein §§1001-1004; Mueller & Kirkpatrick §§10.2-10.14; Wigmore §§1171-1282.

Rule 1003.   Admissibility of Duplicates

A duplicate is admissible to the same extent as the original unless a genuine question is raised about the original's authenticity or the circumstances make it unfair to admit the duplicate.

Rule 1004.   Admissibility of Other Evidence of Content

An original is not required and other evidence of the content of a writing, recording, or photograph is admissible if:

(a) all the originals are lost or destroyed, and not by the proponent acting in bad faith;

(b) an original cannot be obtained by any available judicial process;

(c) the party against whom the original would be offered had control of the original; was at that time put on notice, by pleadings or otherwise, that the original would be a subject of proof at the trial or hearing; and fails to produce it at the trial or hearing; or

(d) the writing, recording, or photograph is not closely related to a controlling issue.

Return to the days before photocopying machines. Documents and records were handwritten or typed. Copies had to be produced by hand, rewriting or retyping the original. Reproducing an original under these circumstances could easily create errors, resulting in inaccurate copies. Small wonder, then, that courts required that whenever a party had to prove the contents of a writing, the party had to produce the original.

Now turn to the present. This is the age of photography, photocopy machines, and computers. Machines can now make accurate copies of the contents of originals. The need for always requiring the production of an original in court no longer exists.

FRE 1001-1004, the original documents rule, reflect this technological change and have several important parts. First, the rule applies to the contents of "writings," "recordings," and "photographs," although the most common application of the rule is still to writings.

Second, the rule also uses the terms "original," "duplicate," and "other evidence." An "original" is the original itself "or any counterpart intended to have the same effect" as the original. For example, a contract is typed, and three photocopies are made. The four parties to the contract sign the typed contract and the three photocopies, so that each party has a signed, executed contract. All four contracts are considered originals. A "duplicate" is any copy of the original through any system that "accurately reproduces the original." For example, carbon copies, photographs, microfilm, and photocopies are all duplicates. Third, "other evidence" is any other evidence of the contents of a writing, recording, or photograph. For example, a preliminary draft or oral testimony is other evidence of the contents of a contract.

The original documents rule, contained in FRE 1003 and 1004, has three parts:

1. In general, "[a] duplicate is admissible to the same extent as the original." For example, in a contract case, the jury obviously needs to know what the contract terms are so it can determine if the contract was breached. The plaintiff can introduce a duplicate of the contract, since this is as useful to the jury as the original to determine the contract terms.

2. "A duplicate is admissible to the same extent as the original unless a genuine question is raised about the original's authenticity or the circumstances make it unfair to admit the duplicate." In such situations the original must be produced. For example, if in the contract case the defendant claims his signature was forged or the contract terms were altered after signing, the original must be produced, since the jury is better able to determine if there was a forgery or an alteration by seeing the original. In a products liability case, where the issue is the adequacy of the warnings on the package insert, it would be unfair to admit a black-and-white duplicate if the original warning was in color, so the original must be produced.

3. If the production of the original is required, its production is excused if (1) all originals have been lost or destroyed in good faith: (2) no original can be obtained by subpoena or other judicial process; and (3) the party against whom the original would be offered had control of the original "was at that time put on notice, by pleadings or otherwise, that the original would be a subject of proof at the trial or hearing; and fails to produce it at the trial or hearing." If production of the original is excused, "other evidence" of the contents may be introduced. For example, in a contract case, the plaintiff claims the dollar amounts and delivery dates on the contract were altered. The original's production, required under these circumstances, is excused if (1) the original was destroyed in an accidental fire, (2) the original is in Switzerland and cannot be subpoenaed or obtained through any other judicial process, or (3) the defendant is served with a request to produce the original under Rule 34 of the Federal Rules of Civil Procedure and does not produce the original. In these circumstances, the plaintiff is permitted to introduce other evidence of the contents of the contract. This might include a photocopy, an earlier corrected draft of the final contract, or oral testimony.

The original writings rule does not apply to every item of proof for which there is a writing, recording, or photograph that might constitute more persuasive proof. FRE 1004(4) applies the rule only where the contents of a writing, recording, or photograph are "closely related to a controlling issue." A "controlling issue" is an important one that the parties are actually contesting at trial. For example, in a personal injury case, the plaintiff calls a doctor. The doctor may testify that she is a medical doctor, a graduate of Harvard Medical School, and licensed in the state of Maine. The original documents rule does not apply, since whether the doctor is actually a doctor and licensed is not a real issue in the case. However, if the case involves a charge of the unauthorized practice of medicine, then a controlling issue is whether the defendant doctor is in fact a graduate of a medical school and licensed to practice. The doctor or other witness will not be allowed to testify orally to those facts and will have to introduce her medical school degree and state medical license as exhibits to prove those facts.

While the original writing rule is an unusual appellate issue, it does occur at times. For example, where a Coast Guard agent's testimony about data he saw on a boat's Global Positioning System unit was offered to prove the defendant's boat had been in Mexican territorial waters, but no printout was made or offered, admission of the evidence was reversible error because it violated FRE 1002.

A federal statute, 28 U.S.C. 1732, provides that photographic copies, microfilm, microcard, or miniature photographic copies of documents that qualify as business records may be introduced in evidence in any judicial proceeding whether or not the original documents are in existence and available. For the statute to apply, the documents must fall within the business record doctrine.

2.   Practice

Common issues involve whether an original is required under the circumstances of the case and whether the original writings rule applies to a particular issue.

Example 1:

This is a civil action on a life insurance policy. The principal issue at trial is whether a policy exclusion applies to prevent payment on the policy. The insurance company cannot find the original policy, which should have been in the policyholder's file. At a bench trial, the insurance company calls as a witness the manager of the claims department. The following then happens:

Q. (By defendant's lawyer) Ms. Walker, did you look for the executed original of the plaintiff's policy with your company?
A. I did, and the people in my department did. The executed original should be in the policyholder's file. We looked in all the places it might have been misfiled, but weren't able to locate it. I have no idea what happened to it.
[Defendant's lawyer has exhibit marked and shows it to opposing counsel.]
Q. I'm showing you Defendant's Exhibit No. 2. Please examine it for a moment. What kind of document is that?
A. It's one of our standard life insurance contracts.
Q. Was that the standard policy your company used at the time you insured the plaintiff?
A. Yes, that's our standard life insurance policy, which we've used for several years, including the year we insured the plaintiff.
Defendant: We offer Defendant's Exhibit No. 2.

Plaintiff: We object, your honor, based on the best evidence rule. They're required to produce an original or a duplicate if they want to prove the contents of a writing. They haven't shown the absence of a duplicate.

Defendant: Your honor, we've shown that the original was lost in good faith. Under the rule, we are then entitled to prove the contents by any other evidence. A copy of the standard policy being issued at that time will accurately establish the policy terms and exclusions.

Judge: The objection is overruled. The policy will be admitted.

Example 2:

This is an income tax evasion case. The defendant's tax return, admitted in evidence in the prosecution's case-in-chief, shows that the defendant took deductions for several large charitable contributions. Additional evidence shows that those charities have no records of receiving contributions from the defendant during that tax year. The defendant later testifies, and the following happens:

Q. (By defendant's lawyer) Mr. Archer, did you make the charitable contributions that you took deductions for that tax year?

Prosecutor: Objection, your honor. Best evidence rule.

Judge: Overruled.

A. Yes, I did.

Q. How did you make those contributions?

Prosecutor: Same objection.

Judge: Overruled.

A. By checks.

Q. What checks did you write?

Prosecutor: Objection, your honor. May we have a sidebar on this issue?

Judge: All right. [Lawyers approach the bench.]

Prosecutor: Your honor, they're now going into the actual contents of checks the defendant claims he wrote. That violates the best evidence rule, since the contents of the checks are in issue.

Judge: I understand. I agree that the defense is now eliciting testimony of the actual contents of the checks. The objection is sustained.

[Lawyers return. Defendant's lawyer has exhibit marked and shows it to opposing counsel.]

Q. Mr. Archer, I'm showing you what has been marked Defendant's Group Exhibit No. 1. Have you seen them before?

A. Sure, these are photocopies of checks I wrote.

Q. Whom are they signed by?

A. By me.

Defendant: We offer Defendant's Group Exhibit No. 1.

Prosecutor: Same objection, your honor.

Judge: Approach the bench. [Lawyers approach.]

Prosecutor: Your honor, we already decided that the best evidence rule applies to the contents of the checks. Now they're offering photocopies of the faces of the checks. The genuineness of these checks is in issue, since we've already proved that the charities never received contributions from the defendant. There's no way these photocopies can prove payment and receipt by the charities, since we don't have the backs of the checks, and in any event, the originals are required, and they haven't accounted for the absence of the originals.

Defendant: They made no claim that these checks were forgeries, your honor. We're entitled to introduce duplicates just like originals, to show the fact that the checks were made.

Judge: No, this is a situation that requires the production of the originals, and both sides should have known that the authenticity of these checks would be in dispute. Under FRE 1003, if they can't be produced, their absence must first be satisfactorily explained before other evidence of their contents can be admitted. The objection is sustained.

Commentary: As this example shows, the original documents rule is complex. It would have been better had the issues been raised before trial.

§10.11. *Electronic evidence*[10]

In today's digital world, it has become largely unnecessary to print documents, records, and data that have been generated electronically or converted into and stored as digital files. Electronic information is both more fragile, because it can be modified and deleted easily, and more durable, because it is usually sent to, copied, and stored in multiple locations and is difficult to erase completely. This explosion of electronic information has changed how litigation, both during discovery and at trial, is being conducted.

The Federal Rules of Civil Procedure were significantly amended in 2006 to provide a comprehensive set of procedural rules to govern the discovery of "electronically stored information" (ESI). In contrast, courts to date have considered the existing Federal Rules of Evidence adequate to deal with admissibility issues that frequently arise when electronic evidence is offered in evidence at trial.

Admissibility issues surrounding electronic evidence should be analyzed, like all other evidence, under the three "Rs" approach: Is it relevant? Is it reliable? Is it right?

The principal kinds of electronic evidence that courts frequently encounter include the following:

---

10. Weinstein §900.07; Federal Evidence, 3d. 2007, §§8.79, 9.9. Marian Riedy, Suman Beros, & Kim Sperduto, Litigating with Electronically Stored Information (2007); for an oft-cited case that extensively covers admissibility issues for electronic evidence, see *Lorraine v. Markel American Insurance Co.*, 241 F.R.D. 534 (D. Md. 2007). See also *U.S. v. Siddiqui*, 235 F.3d 1318 (11th Cir. 2000); *U.S. v. Vayner*, 769 F.3d 125 (2nd Cir. 2014).

computerized business records and data and metadata
e-mail, text messages, and instant messages
Internet/web pages and postings
GPS information
digital photographs
computer-generated animations and simulations

Of all the evidentiary issues that can arise when electronic evidence is offered in evidence, the most significant and recurring are twofold. First, is the evidence hearsay and, if so, does it fall within a hearsay exclusion or exception? Second, has the evidence been properly and adequately authenticated? The following discussion focuses on these issues and the most commonly offered types of electronic evidence.

1.   Computerized business records, data, and metadata

It has been estimated that more than 90 percent of all business records are now created in computer form, so admissibility issues surrounding electronically created records and data arise frequently. Courts routinely hold that if records qualify as business records, the fact that they are in electronic form raises no additional evidentiary issues. The fact that the record was printed out at a later time, or for use in litigation, is unimportant. What matters is that the information was entered into the computer system by an employee with knowledge "at or near the time" of the events and transactions recorded. The original documents rule will not be a barrier to admissibility, since FRE 1001(d) treats a computer printout of data as an original.

Other issues commonly arise with computerized records and data. First, are the records hearsay at all? The hearsay definition requires an assertion made by a person. If a record is automatically generated by a computer or some other device without human input, the record cannot be hearsay. For example, ATM machines automatically deduct the amount of a cash withdrawal from the account holder's bank balance. Fax machines automatically record the details of a fax transmission. Flight recorders automatically record key flight information for commercial aircraft. Since the data are entered automatically, rather than by a person, no hearsay is involved. To be sure, the system must be shown to be reliable, but that is not a hearsay issue.

Second, is the output—the printout—in the same form as the original input? Most courts take the view that when the computer is asked to print business records and data stored in the computer, the printout will be a business record if it is in the same form as the input. For example, consider a department store whose computer system records every sales transaction for each day. If the computer prints out the daily sales for a particular day, the printout is in the same form as the original input. However, if the computer is asked to search the database, retrieve all sales to a particular person over a one-year period, and organize the sales chronologically, that printout is probably not a business record. Instead, it is a summary of voluminous records and is admissible only if the requirements of FRE 1006 are met (principally, that the opponent is put on notice that a summary will be introduced at trial). In short, if output is in the same form as input, the printout will be a business record. If the database is searched and only selected information is retrieved and printed, the printout will be a summary.

2. Electronic communications — overview

This is the age of electronic communication. The messages come from many sources — e-mails, Facebook, Twitter, blog posts, digital photographs, and so on. Depending on content and the purpose for which the communications are offered, few courtroom issues activate so wide a swath of evidentiary considerations as do electronic communications.

Trial judges consider exclusion or admissibility at an FRE 104(a) hearing. At times they decide to admit proposed electronic evidence on the condition that sufficient proof be introduced at a later time (FRE 104(b)).

Relevance, as defined by FRE 401, always matters. Once relevance issues are satisfied, questions concerning reliability often arise. That is, is personal knowledge of a fact or opinion required by FRE 602 and FRE 701? Is there a hearsay issue that can be resolved by using a hearsay exception or exemption? Are the FRE 1001-1004 original writing rules an issue? Does the proposed electronic evidence raise authenticity issues requiring consideration of FRE 901 and FRE 902? In addition, privilege questions often must be addressed. And the balancing test of FRE 403 can be invoked for every offer of an electronic communication.

Special attention must be paid to hearsay issues. If the sender of the message intends to make an assertion, the question then becomes whether the words of the message are being offered for their truth. The words are not hearsay if they are offered to show a relevant state of mind of the recipient, such as knowledge, fear, or some other non-hearsay fact, such as notice of something or words having independent legal significance, such as a contract, misrepresentation, defamation, or threats.

If the message is hearsay, the proponent must find some exception or exemption to exclusion. The words could be an FRE 801(1) present sense impression, an FRE 803(2) excited utterance, or an FRE 803(3) then-existing state of mind statement. If the words are spoken by a party opponent, offered against that party, they are exempt from the rule against hearsay and are admissible for their truth as party admissions pursuant to FRE 801(d)(2). On rare occasions, hearsay may come within the residual exception of FRE 807.

When electronic messages are offered for their truth, the proponent frequently seeks to establish an FRE 803(6) business record exception. To satisfy FRE 803(6) the record must have been made at or near the time of the event recorded. A record prepared in 2015 that describes what happened in 2014 does not satisfy the rule. When the person who provides the hearsay information is an outsider to the business and thus not under a business duty to report accurately, the exception will not apply unless the business does something to adequately verify the information or has some other assurance of accuracy of the information. The business's duty to verify extends to the purported outside sender's identifying information. That is, FRE 805 requires that every layer of hearsay must meet an exception to or exemption from the hearsay rule if the record is to be admitted.

Most decisions hold that back and forth e-mails ("e-threads") between employees of a business are private conversations, not records of the business. But there are times when courts have held that a routine form sent by e-mail, such as an airline or hotel reservation confirmation, furthers the sender's business and is a business record. If a web site is for a business and contains business information, such as advertising material, product price information, or orders for goods and services, the record should qualify as an FRE 803(6) exception.

3. Authenticity of electronic communications

By far, most of the reported decisions concerning electronic communications raise the issue of authenticity. Rules 901 and, more seldom, 902, govern admissibility. There is no special set of rules for dealing with electronic communications, although a few courts have suggested there should be. Instead, FRE 901 is applied to electronic communications evidence with a measure of judicial skepticism.

Courts are aware of the potential for fabrication and falsification of electronic communications. Accounts and profiles are hacked, or misusers are sending messages under fictitious names or the names of unaware subscribers. There is a low level of security and lack of controls in the electronic messaging world. Cell phones and computers at times are left unattended by their owners, inviting misuse by others. Online providers often do not verify account information submitted to them, or they make a minimal effort to verify.

FRE 901(a) establishes a fairly low barrier for the proponent of the evidence. That is, "to satisfy the requirement of authenticating or identifying an item of evidence, the proponent must produce evidence sufficient to support a finding that the item is what the proponent says it is." The judge reviews that evidence, then determines whether there is enough of it for a jury to reasonably find the item to be authentic. If the answer is yes, it then becomes a matter of weight to be determined by the jury.

Most often the question will be whether the purported sender of the message actually is the person who sent it. Simply proving that the message came from the purported sender's e-mail address or cell phone number or social media profile page usually is not enough. How then do judges determine whether electronic communications evidence is sufficiently authentic to be admitted at trial?

Whether the communication is sent by e-mail, text message, or social media, the FRE 901(a) analysis requires examination of the context of the message and consideration of direct and circumstantial evidence. General information, widely known, is not enough to establish authentication. The more particular and distinctive the sender's characteristics, contents of the message, and surrounding circumstances, the more likely the message will be found authentic.

Among the questions to consider:

1. Is there any verification of the sender's identity on the face of the communication? Verification could include a complete name, city of residence, nickname, distinguishing use of language, abbreviations, slang, identifying symbols, or distinctive use of words and grammar.

2. Does the message contain information only the purported sender and few others would know?

3. Were the contents of the message corroborated by telephone calls or letters or other conversations with the purported sender or by the sender's actions?

4. Is there a series of ongoing electronic communications between the purported sender and the receiver of the message where the same identifying information was used?

5. Is the message at issue a timely reply to an earlier message sent to the purported sender, referring to the same subject matter?

6. Can an expert determine whether a search of the purported sender's computer hard drive shows the identity of the author?

7. Does the communication come from a web site that contains the business's trade inscription, thus making the site self-authenticating under FRE 902(7)?

8. Were the e-mails produced by a party opponent during discovery? If so, the documents should be found authentic when offered against the party who possessed and produce them.

It bears repeating: general facts, generally known, such as employment, place of birth, birth dates, and residential addresses, have been held insufficient under FRE 901 to establish identity of the author of an electronic message.

4.   Digital photographs

Digital photography has largely replaced film photography for both commercial and individual uses, because digital photography is both more convenient and flexible. With digital photography, images and underlying metadata can be stored in the camera, downloaded to a computer, transmitted to others through the computer, and printed on high-quality printers.

Digital photographs usually can be authenticated under FRE 901(b)(1). A witness who knows how the scene looked at the relevant time testifies that the digital photograph fairly and accurately portrays the scene as it appeared at that time. For example, a witness testifies that the digital photograph fairly and accurately shows how the intersection looked at the time of the collision. In short, the usual foundation for traditional photographs applies equally to digital photographs.

The more difficult issues are those of alteration and enhancement. Popular software programs such as Adobe Photoshop allow digital photographs to be altered. For example, a group photograph of several individuals can be edited to eliminate a person in the group in a way that prevents someone looking at the altered photograph from realizing that it has been altered. When an allegation of alteration is made, courts usually require that the claim be supported, either by a witness who can testify that the photograph does not fairly and accurately depict the actual scene, or through the testimony of a computer forensics expert who can demonstrate that the photograph has been altered by analyzing the digital images from which the print was made.

Finally, enhancement of photographs can be an issue that raises FRE 403 concerns. For example, what if a party offers a digital photograph that has the brightness of certain colors increased to bring out the letters of a sign, or has increased the contrast to bring out the features of a face? These kinds of changes can easily be made to digital photographs with photography software. Is this "enhanced" photograph still a "fair and accurate" photograph of the scene, or will it be unduly "confusing" or "misleading"? These kinds of arguments must be analyzed under the balancing test in FRE 403.

5.   Computer-generated animations and simulations

Litigants are increasingly using computers to present complex information at trial. Two types of computer images are frequently used: animations and simulations. While some use the terms loosely and sometimes even interchangeably, most courts use the labels to define two significantly different kinds of computer-generated information.

An animation is conceptually no different from any demonstrative exhibit such as a photograph or diagram. An animation is simply a computer-generated depiction of what a witness experienced. As long as a witness who has firsthand knowledge of an event testifies that the animation fairly and accurately depicts what the witness saw, the animation has a proper foundation. For example, if a witness who saw an accident says that the animation fairly and accurately shows the paths of the two vehicles involved, the animation has been properly authenticated.

A simulation, by contrast, is essentially like expert testimony. A simulation incorporates adequate data, analyzes the data by means of a reliable software program, and creates a computerized moving image of an event. For example, a simulation of an airplane flight moments before the airplane hit the ground will be admissible if sufficient data have been obtained from the airplane's flight data recorder and other sources, and the data had been analyzed by a software program that can produce a reliable set of graphic images.

Authenticating a simulation requires expert testimony. A properly qualified expert must testify that the data obtained were reliable and sufficient to create a simulation, the computer and software program used to create the simulation were reliable and in good working order, the data were accurately entered into the program, and the output—the simulation—accurately shows what happened. Objections to the admissibility of simulations are usually raised and ruled on before trial.

Electronic evidence need not be intimidating. It should be analyzed like all evidence: Is it relevant? Is it reliable? Is it right? Particular attention should be given to the hearsay and authentication issues, which usually determine admissibility.

XI
JUDICIAL NOTICE AND PRESUMPTIONS

§11.1.   Introduction

There are times during a trial when a judge is called on to guide the jury's consideration of evidence. The Federal Rules of Evidence address two of those times. Judicial notice involves the situation where a fact is either so well known or so readily verifiable that formal proof of the fact is unnecessary. Presumptions involve the situations where proof of a fact does not exist and controls how the jury is to deal with the absence of proof. Judicial notice and presumptions are related in that both require the judge to instruct the jury.

FRE 201, governing judicial notice, promotes trial efficiency. The rule authorizes the judge to take judicial notice of certain facts, eliminating any need to prove the facts with admissible evidence, and to instruct the jury on how to consider the judicially noticed facts.

FRE 301 and 302 govern presumptions in civil cases. These rules require an understanding of the distinction between the burden of proof and the burden of going forward with evidence, and of how these burdens relate to presumptions. They authorize the judge to instruct the jury on how to consider the absence of evidence.

§11.2.   Judicial notice

1.   Law[1]

Rule 201.   Judicial Notice of Adjudicative Facts

(a) **Scope.** This rule governs judicial notice of an adjudicative fact only, not a legislative fact.

(b) **Kinds of Facts That May Be Judicially Noticed.** The court may judicially notice a fact that is not subject to reasonable dispute because it:

(1) is generally known within the trial court's territorial jurisdiction; or

---

1. McCormick §§328-335; Mueller & Kirkpatrick §§2.1-2.13; Wigmore §§2565-2583.

(2) can be accurately and readily determined from sources whose accuracy cannot reasonably be questioned.

(c) Taking Notice. The court:

(1) may take judicial notice on its own; or

(2) must take judicial notice if a party requests it and the court is supplied with the necessary information.

(d) Timing. The court may take judicial notice at any stage of the proceeding.

(e) Opportunity to Be Heard. On timely request, a party is entitled to be heard on the propriety of taking judicial notice and the nature of the fact to be noticed. If the court takes judicial notice before notifying a party, the party, on request, is still entitled to be heard.

(f) Instructing the Jury. In a civil case, the court must instruct the jury to accept the noticed fact as conclusive. In a criminal case, the court must instruct the jury that it may or may not accept the noticed fact as conclusive.

Judicial notice is the evidentiary mechanism by which the trial judge is asked to rule that certain facts are true. Its purpose is to promote trial efficiency, sharpen issues, and permit the introduction of indisputable evidence where formal proof might be difficult and time-consuming.

FRE 201 controls the process by which courts can take judicial notice of facts. The rule is limited in scope and governs only "adjudicative facts," those facts that are in issue in the case. Judicial notice of law is covered by either Rule 44.1 of the Federal Rules of Civil Procedure or Rule 26.1 of the Federal Rules of Criminal Procedure.

Geographical locations ordinarily are considered adjudicative facts within FRE 201(b), but some matters of geography create close questions. For example, some courts of appeal hold the place where a prison sits is an element of the offense and an adjudicative fact, while others hold the location of a prison within the territorial jurisdiction of the United States is a legislative fact not within FRE 201.

The procedural aspects of judicial notice are governed by FRE 201(c)-(f). A party wishing to have the court take judicial notice of something must ask the court to take judicial notice and must supply the court with the necessary information, and the opposing party must have an opportunity to state its objections. The trial judge may take judicial notice even if it is not requested by a party.

If the court takes judicial notice, the effect differs, depending on whether the case is civil or criminal. Under FRE 201(g), in civil cases, the jury must "accept the noticed fact as conclusive." In criminal cases, the jury "may or may not accept the noticed fact as conclusive."

The judicially noticed fact is conveyed to the jury in the form of an instruction. Because of FRE 201(g), in a civil case, the court would instruct the jury: "You must accept as conclusively true the fact that. . . ." In a criminal case, the court would instruct the jury "You may, but are not required to, accept as a fact that. . . ."

Under FRE 201(b), the court can take judicial notice of a fact if it is "not subject to reasonable dispute" and falls within one of two categories. First, the fact is "generally known within the trial court's territorial jurisdiction." For example, in New York City, it is generally known that the Empire State Building is in Manhattan, and a court in New York City could take judicial notice of that fact.

Second, the fact "can be accurately and readily determined from sources whose accuracy cannot reasonably be questioned." These are the so-called almanac facts. For example, an almanac or encyclopedia can provide information on when the sun rose for a given place and date; the distance between two locations; what the annual rainfall is at a particular place; or when the tide was high at a certain location, date, and time. An atlas can provide the longitude and latitude of a city or prove that a city is within a particular county or state. An almanac can provide actuarial tables showing life expectancies. In all these kinds of situations, a reliable source, such as an encyclopedia, almanac, or government publication, can provide reliable information that is not subject to reasonable dispute. Facts that judges usually take judicial notice of include prevailing interest rates, actuarial tables, weights and measures, seasons of the year, calendar dates, and locations of highways.

Although FRE 201 does not expressly govern it, courts also commonly take what amounts to judicial notice of the reliability of scientific principles underlying accepted scientific tests. For instance, courts routinely recognize that radar machines can accurately measure speed and blood tests can accurately determine alcohol level and the possibility of paternity. Parties seeking to introduce such established scientific tests no longer need to prove the reliability of the science underlying such tests. The issue arises when a party objects to the introduction of scientific tests on the basis that the reliability of the underlying science has not been demonstrated, as required by *Daubert v. Merrell Dow Pharmaceuticals*, 509 U.S. 579 (1993), which controls in federal courts, or that the underlying science has not been demonstrated to be generally accepted by the relevant scientific community, as required by *Frye v. United States*, 293 F. 1013 (D.C. Cir. 1923), which still controls in a few states. In overruling that objection, a court is implicitly taking judicial notice that this issue has been decided in previous cases and will not be relitigated in the present case. This issue is further discussed in Sec. 9.2.

2. Practice

In practice, judicial notice is infrequently requested. If the facts are so obvious and uncontestable, the parties usually enter into written stipulations that the facts are true and not in dispute. In civil cases, such facts have usually been admitted in the pleadings, during discovery, or in a pretrial memorandum. Judicial notice usually is requested only where the opposing party is uncooperative in agreeing to the obvious.

Example 1:

This is a personal injury case. Before trial, plaintiff moves that the court take judicial notice of certain facts. At a hearing, the following happens:

Plaintiff: We're asking the court to take judicial notice that a male who is presently 40 years old has a life expectancy of 38.3 years. This projection is based on the most recent Department of Labor Life Tables. I have copies with me, which I'm giving to the court and counsel.

Judge: Any objection?

Defendant: No, your honor.

Plaintiff: I assume that the court will advise the jury of the judicially noticed fact through the usual instruction.

Judge: That's right. Just let me know when you wish to have the life expectancy instruction read to the jury.

Example 2:

In a products liability case, plaintiff, an ambulance paramedic, claims he was injured while riding in an ambulance that overturned on a highway. During plaintiff's case-in-chief, the following happens:

Plaintiff: Your honor, before the jury comes back from the break, we have one matter we'd like to take up.

Judge What is it?

Plaintiff: We are asking the court to take judicial notice of the fact that vehicles with high centers of gravity are more susceptible to roll-overs. Under Rule 201, the court can take judicial notice of facts generally known in the jurisdiction. Certainly the fact that vehicles with high centers of gravity are more susceptible to rollovers is well known.

Defendant: That's not the kind of fact that is generally known, your honor. Maybe some automotive engineers know it, but it's not the kind of fact everybody knows.

Plaintiff: We're not asking the court to judicially notice specifics, just that rollovers are more likely with vehicles that have high centers of gravity. That fact is common knowledge. It's based on simple physics.

Judge: The request is denied. Most people probably know little, if anything, of the relationship between center of gravity and sus-ceptibility to rollover. Counsel, you're going to need a properly qualified expert to establish that point.

§11.3. Presumptions

Rule 301. Presumptions in Civil Cases Generally

In a civil case, unless a federal statute or these rules provide otherwise, the party against whom a presumption is directed has the burden of pro-ducing evidence to rebut the presumption. But this rule does not shift the burden of persuasion, which remains on the party who had it originally.

Rule 302. Applying State Law to Presumptions in Civil Cases

In a civil case, state law governs the effect of a presumption regarding a claim or defense for which state law supplies the rule of decision.

The jury must know the law it will apply to the facts of the case before it deliberates to determine its verdict. The judge tells the jury what law to apply by giving the jury instructions of law. Rule 51 of the Federal Rules of Civil Procedure and Rule 30 of the Federal Rules of Criminal Procedure, which are essentially identical, govern the process under which parties request, and the judge gives, the jury instructions.

Two types of jury instructions that have evidentiary considerations are burdens of proof and presumptions. The jury always must be told who has the burden of proof on the various issues that the jury will decide, and it must be told if any presumptions apply to these issues.

1.   Burden of proof[2]

"Burden of proof" is a term that is loosely and often inaccurately used. It actually encompasses two distinct concepts: the burden of going forward and the burden of persuasion. The jury is told the pertinent burdens of proof through the jury instructions.

The "burden of going forward," also called the "burden of production," is a procedural term. It refers to the party that is legally obligated to initiate the production of evidence on a claim or defense. The plaintiff has the burden of going forward as to its claims and any affirmative defenses to the defendant's counterclaims; the defendant has the burden of going forward as to its affirmative defenses and counterclaims. This is so in both civil and criminal cases.

If a party fails to introduce any evidence to support an issue, whether a claim or an affirmative defense, on which it has the burden of going forward, the remedy is that the court will, on request, enter a directed verdict on that claim or defense against the party having the burden. If a party has met its burden of going forward and made a prima facie case, the burden of going forward with contrary evidence to disprove the issue then shifts to the other side. If the other side presents contrary evidence, the effect is to make the issue a disputed one for the jury to resolve. If the other side fails to present contrary evidence, the effect depends on the quality and quantity of the proponent's evidence: If the proponent's unrebutted evidence is so overwhelming that no reasonable minds could differ, the judge will direct a verdict on that issue in favor of the proponent; if the proponent's evidence, though unrebutted, is not so overwhelming, the effect is to make the issue one for the jury to decide.

The "burden of persuasion" refers to the standard of proof a party must meet to prevail on any issue on which it has the burden. There are three basic burdens of persuasion: "preponderance" (sometimes called "more probably true than not true"), "clear and convincing," applicable to civil cases, and "beyond a reasonable doubt," applicable to criminal cases. It is often said that the burden of persuasion never shifts. In fact, there is no reason for this burden to shift because, being a concept exclusively implemented through the instructions, there is no reason to assign it until the instructions are given.

---

2. McCormick §§235-238, 426-427, 446-447, 562-563; Mueller & Kirkpatrick §§3.1-3.3, 3.11-3.14; Wigmore §§1879, 2438.

The party with the burden of going forward usually, but not always, also has the burden of persuasion. For example, in a negligence action, the plaintiff has the burden of going forward with proof of negligence, causation, and damages and also has the burden of persuasion by a preponderance of the evidence on those issues.

On the other hand, in criminal cases, the burden of going forward is sometimes different than the burden of persuasion, particularly when affirmative defenses are involved. For example, in an assault case where the affirmative defense of self-defense is raised, many jurisdictions provide that the defense has the burden of going forward with evidence of self-defense; but once raised, the prosecution has the burden of persuasion of disproving self-defense, usually beyond a reasonable doubt.

Burdens of going forward are important because they control whether a party is entitled to a directed verdict on any element of a claim or defense and whether the jury needs to be instructed on that element. If reasonable minds could not differ on whether that element is either proved or disproved, the court will enter an appropriate directed verdict, so that the element will not be submitted to the jury as a disputed matter. If the directed verdict on an element is entered because of a failure of proof and the failure of proof on that element is fatal to the claim or defense, the court will enter an appropriate directed verdict on the entire claim or defense, and it will not be submitted to the jury as a disputed matter. If the directed verdict on an element is entered because of overwhelming evidence, in a civil case, the jury is usually instructed that it must find certain matters to be as the court directs. In a criminal case, such mandatory instructions against the defendant are not given because of due process concerns.

2.   Presumptions and inferences[3]

An inference is a logical deduction derived from another fact or set of facts. For example, if the ground was clear in the evening and is covered with snow the next morning, we infer that it snowed during the night. Over the years, we have seen snow on the ground in the morning many times and have never heard any explanation for this event other than that it snowed during the night. The inference that it snowed during the night is overwhelming.

A presumption is a legal device that affects the burden of going forward or the burden of persuasion. When inferences from a given fact are sufficiently recurring and reliable, the law sometimes elevates the inference to the status of a legal presumption. The inference then becomes mandatory, meaning that once the basic fact is established, the inference from the fact must be accepted as true by the jury unless the other side presents rebutting evidence.

For example, we know from experience that when we mail a letter, properly addressed and stamped, the letter usually gets to the addressee. The law in many jurisdictions raises this inference to the level of a presumption: The receipt of a properly addressed and stamped letter is presumed from the fact of its mailing

---

3. G.C. Lilly, Introduction to the Law of Evidence ch. 3 (2d ed. 1987); Mueller & Kirkpatrick §§3.4-3.10, 3.13-3.14; McCormick §§342-349.

in a proper mailbox. Therefore, the jury is instructed that if it finds that the letter was properly addressed, stamped, and mailed, it must find that the addressee received it, absent any rebutting evidence.

Two basic schools of thought have developed over the procedural effect of a legal presumption. The Thayer approach (named after James Thayer, a nineteenth-century evidence scholar) holds that a presumption shifts the burden of going forward to the other side. If the other side presents adequate rebuttal evidence, the presumption disappears (like a "bursting bubble"). The Morgan approach (named after Edmund Morgan, a twentieth-century evidence scholar) holds that the effect of a presumption is to assign the burden of persuasion to the party against whom the presumption operates. The Thayer approach has commanded the majority of the jurisdictions.

FRE 301 adopts the Thayer, or bursting bubble, approach in civil cases. FRE 301 provides: "In a civil case, unless a federal statute or these rules provide otherwise, the party against whom a presumption is directed has the burden of producing evidence to rebut the presumption. But this rule does not shift the burden of persuasion, which remains on the party who had it originally."

In federal civil trials, applying the FRE 301 approach, the effect of the presumption depends on the state of the relevant proof. If the proponent presents adequate undisputed evidence of the basic facts, the presumption is triggered, and the jury is instructed on the mandatory effect of the presumption. If the opponent presents rebutting evidence, the presumption disappears, and the jury receives no instruction. In the earlier mailing example, if the plaintiff presents evidence that the letter was properly addressed to the defendant, stamped, and deposited in a proper mailbox, the presumption of delivery and receipt by the defendant arises. If the defendant presents no rebutting evidence, the jury will be instructed that if it finds the letter was properly addressed, stamped, and mailed, it must find that the defendant received the letter. If the defendant presents rebutting evidence, such as the defendant testifying that he never received the letter, the presumption disappears, and no instruction is given; the question of whether the defendant actually received the letter is a disputed factual issue that the jury will have to resolve. On that issue, the plaintiff still has the burden of proof.

Operation of FRE 301 is demonstrated in *St. Mary's Honor Center v. Hicks*, 509 U.S. 502 (1993), a Title VII race discrimination case. First, the employee establishes, by a preponderance of the evidence, a prima facie case of discharge due to race. That creates a presumption that the employer unlawfully discriminated against the employee. The presumption places on the employer the burden of producing evidence that the discharge was for a legitimate, nondiscriminatory reason. The employer's evidence does not have to be persuasive; it simply must be enough to meet the presumption. If the employer carries this burden of production, the presumption raised by the prima facie case is rebutted and it drops from the case. The employee then must prove from all the evidence that the reason given for discharge was not the true reason and that race was. The point made by FRE 301 is that the presumption of unlawful discrimination does not shift the burden of proof; the plaintiff at all times bears the ultimate burden of persuasion.

FRE 302 applies to federal civil trials based on diversity jurisdiction and provides that: "In a civil case, state law governs the effect of a presumption regarding a claim or defense for which state law supplies the rule of decision." This rule incorporates the *Erie* analysis in diversity cases. This means that whenever state law determines the applicable substantive law, its law on presumptions will also apply to those claims and defenses. States follow the Thayer, the Morgan, or another approach.

Note that FRE 301 and 302 apply only to civil cases. Criminal cases raise difficult questions about the constitutionality of mandatory presumptions instructions. A mandatory presumption shifts the burden of going forward or persuasion (depending on the jurisdiction) from the prosecution to the defense. Since the Due Process Clause requires that the state prove every element of the crime charged with facts sufficient to meet the beyond a reasonable doubt standard, it follows that a mandatory presumption that has the effect of removing the obligation of the prosecution to prove any necessary element with relevant facts will probably run afoul of the Due Process Clause.

The Supreme Court has grappled with the mandatory versus permissive presumption issue in several cases.

In *Mullaney v. Wilbur*, 421 U.S. 684 (1975), the trial judge instructed the jury that if it found the accused unlawfully and intentionally killed the victim, it should presume malice aforethought unless it was convinced by the accused that he acted from sudden provocation. The Court held the instruction violated due process because it shifted to the defendant the burden of proof with regard to an element of the crime.

In *County Court of Ulster County v. Allen*, 442 U.S. 140 (1979), a gun was found in an open handbag of a passenger sitting in the front seat of a car in which four people were riding. The trial judge instructed the jury it was permissible to infer possession of the firearm by all of the occupants from their presence in the car, but that the inference was not mandatory and could be ignored. The Court upheld the instruction because the inferred fact was more likely than not to flow from the facts presented to the jury.

Later in 1979, the Court decided *Sandstrom v. Montana*, 442 U.S. 510 (1979). There, in a murder case, the trial judge instructed the jury, "the law presumes that a person intends the ordinary consequences of his voluntary acts." The Court held the instruction violated due process because the jury could have thought it had to find the required intent or that the defendant had the burden of proving he did not have the required intent. Either way, it was an impermissible mandatory presumption relating to an element of the offense.

These cases do not mean the state violates due process when it places on the accused burdens to produce evidence and to persuade. The Court has upheld a procedure that requires defendants to offer evidence in support of affirmative defenses such as insanity, provocation, and self-defense and, in some instances, imposes on the defendant the burden of proving those affirmative defenses. See *Martin v. Ohio*, 480 U.S. 228 (1987); *Patterson v. New York*, 432 U.S. 197 (1977); and *Leland v. Oregon*, 343 U.S. 790 (1952). In these instances, the burden of proving the elements of the crime does not shift to the defendant.

XII

CROSS-EXAMINATION AND
IMPEACHMENT OF LAY AND
EXPERT WITNESSES

§12.1.   Introduction

The rules of cross-examination take into consideration a view of human existence. Perception, including the ability of one person to identify another, is
unreliable, but overvalued. Memory is erratic. Honest witnesses are suggestible
and make mistakes. Others are corrupt and tell lies or withhold the truth. Bias,
interest, and motive are unavoidable human traits that affect truthfulness,
whether that result is intentional or not. When a person tells two different stories
about the same event, his credibility becomes questionable. Physical appearance
is overvalued as a determinant of believability. Some techniques of persuasion
and inquiry are non-rational and misleading.

Because there are so many obstacles to a correct conclusion about a person's
believability, the law, by rule and by decision, has established rational methods for
testing and evaluating a witness's testimony. FRE 607, 608, 609, 611, and 613 bear
directly on when, how, and by whom a witness may be cross-examined.

Lay and expert witnesses can be treated together for purposes of cross-
examination and impeachment. With the exception of treatises, which by
their nature apply only to experts, all the cross-examination and impeachment
rules apply with equal force to all witnesses.

§12.2.   Cross-examination[1]

1.   Law

Rule 611.   Mode and Order of Examining Witnesses
and Presenting Evidence

(a) **Control by the Court; Purposes.** The court should exercise reasonable control over the mode and order of examining witnesses and
presenting evidence so as to:

---

1. McCormick §§19-32; Weinstein §611[01]-[07]; Mueller & Kirkpatrick §§6.62-6.65;
Wigmore §§1365, 1367-1394, 1884-1895.

> **(1)** make those procedures effective for determining the truth;
>
> **(2)** avoid wasting time; and
>
> **(3)** protect witnesses from harassment or undue embarrassment.
>
> **(b) Scope of Cross-Examination.** Cross-examination should not go beyond the subject matter of the direct examination and matters affecting the witness's credibility. The court may allow inquiry into additional matters as if on direct examination.
>
> **(c) Leading Questions.** Leading questions should not be used on direct examination except as necessary to develop the witness's testimony. Ordinarily, the court should allow leading questions:
>
> **(1)** on cross-examination; and
>
> **(2)** when a party calls a hostile witness, an adverse party, or a witness identified with an adverse party.

Cross-examination is not necessarily an attack on the witness's believability. Some cross is friendly, aimed at eliciting information that will support the cross-examiner's position. No specific rule of evidence covers that situation. None is needed. Such a cross-examination need only adhere to the basic rules of cross-examination contained in FRE 611.

There are two basic rules governing cross-examination. First, leading questions are proper. FRE 611(c) provides: "Ordinarily, the court should allow leading questions . . . on cross-examination." For example, after the plaintiff conducts the direct examination of an eyewitness, the defendant can cross-examine that witness using leading questions. A leading question is simply a question that suggests or contains the answer desired from the witness.

Most leading questions are leading because of their suggestive wording. For example, asking the witness "You didn't expect to see an accident at that corner, did you?" is a leading question. Leading questions also can be leading by their intonation. For example, asking a witness "You were on the corner looking directly across Main Street when the two cars collided?" spoken in a questioning voice with rising intonation, is a leading question, particularly when previous questions all elicited a "yes" answer.

Second, the permissible scope of the cross-examination is determined by the scope of the direct examination. FRE 611(b) follows what is called the restricted scope of cross, or American, rule: "Cross-examination should not go beyond the subject matter of the direct examination and matters affecting the witness's credibility." The American rule, also followed by most of the states, is based on the notion that each party has the right to control the subjects brought out in its case-in-chief and the opposing party cannot inject unrelated new matters into the opponent's case. This rule permits each side to present a clear, orderly case-in-chief. What constitutes the "subject matter of the direct examination" is not defined further in the rule and is inherently imprecise.

For example, if a witness has testified about one financial transaction, but has said nothing about a second, unrelated transaction, the cross-examination can go only into the first transaction. In other situations, the line between what is beyond the scope of the direct and what is proper cross-examination is not so clear, and this issue, like so many, is addressed to the sound discretion of the trial judge.

The scope of cross rule has additional constitutional implications in criminal cases. If the defendant in a criminal case testifies, he waives his Fifth Amendment privilege not to incriminate himself to the extent of his direct examination, meaning he can be cross-examined on any subject mentioned during the direct examination. *Brown v. United States*, 356 U.S. 148 (1958). However, he retains this privilege as to all other subjects not mentioned.

What happens if the cross-examiner wishes to ask questions about a subject that is beyond the scope of the direct, yet still relevant? FRE 611(b) provides that the "the court may allow inquiry into additional matters as if on direct examination," that is, with non-leading questions. The only other possibility is that the cross-examiner later can call that witness again, when the cross-examiner next has an opportunity to call witnesses, and conduct a direct examination on the new subject. Because recalling a witness is both inconvenient and inefficient, trial judges usually have been generous in permitting the inquiry into additional matters as if on direct.

Cross-examination to bring out impeaching matter always is proper, since impeachment is one of the "matters affecting the witness's credibility" and is specifically allowed by FRE 611(b). This is an important exception to the restricted scope of cross-examination rule. Any cross-examination that attempts to bring out otherwise proper impeachment—bias, interest, and motive, prior inconsistent statements, contradictory facts, prior convictions, character for untruthfulness, conduct probative of untruthfulness, and treatises—should be allowed.

2.   Practice

The common issue is whether the scope of the cross-examination exceeds the scope of the direct examination.

Example 1:

This is a contract case. The plaintiff claims, in two separate counts, that the defendant breached two contracts to sell goods, one in 2014, the other in 2015. The witness, an employee of the plaintiff, testifies on direct examination about the execution of the first contract and how plaintiff performed its obligations under that contract. On cross-examination, the following happens:

Q. (By defendant's lawyer) Ms. Grace, the first contract was signed on June 1, 2014, right?
A. Yes.
Q. You were present when it was signed?
A. Yes.
Q. How long had you been an employee on June 1, 2014?
A. About five years.
Q. And you still work for the plaintiff?
A. No, I left the firm at the end of 2015.

Q. So you were working for the plaintiff when the second contract was executed on June 1, 2015, right?

Plaintiff: Objection. Beyond the scope.

Judge: Sustained.

Defendant: Your honor, may we approach?

Judge: You may. [Lawyers approach the bench.]

Defendant: Your honor, this witness was an employee of the plaintiff who was present when both contracts were executed. Surely I should be allowed to inquire into her knowledge of the other contract. It's the basis of count two of their complaint.

Plaintiff: That's beyond the scope. We were careful to limit Ms. Grace's testimony to the first contract.

Defendant: Your honor, the two contracts are virtually identical and deal with the same kind of sale.

Judge: The objection is sustained. However, since this witness has knowledge about the second contract, you may inquire into additional matters as if on direct. I don't want Ms. Grace to have to come back to the courtroom a second time.

Commentary: Permitting additional inquiry into new matters is discretionary with the judge. The judge balances the disruption to the presentation of the plaintiff's case with the inconvenience to the witness of having to testify twice. Here, sustaining the objection has the effect of forcing the cross-examiner to ask non-leading questions about the second contract.

Example 2:

The defendant is charged with murdering his wife on October 1, 2015. He is called as a witness in the defense case and testifies on direct examination that he was a loving, supportive husband who would never hurt his wife. On cross-examination, the following happens:

Q. (By prosecutor) Mr. Strong, on June 1, 2015, you hit your wife, didn't you?

Defendant: Objection, your honor. That's irrelevant.

Judge: Overruled.

A. No.

Q. On September 1, 2015, during a party, you got into an argument with your wife, didn't you?

Defendant: Objection, your honor. May we be heard at sidebar?

Judge: Yes. Counsel will approach the bench. [Lawyers come to the bench.]

Defendant: Your honor, they're getting into other acts evidence. This is inadmissible under Rule 404(b), since they're showing the defendant's character. That's propensity evidence, it's beyond the scope of the direct, and it's inadmissible.

Prosecutor: They opened the door on direct, your honor. The defendant claimed he was a loving, supportive husband. What we're bringing out on cross is a legitimate attack on his credibility, and we're always allowed to go into additional matters that affect credibility.

Judge: Objection is overruled. Counsel, you opened the door to this.

Commentary: This is a close case. The defendant also should have argued that under FRE 403 whatever probative value this evidence had on the defendant's credibility is substantially outweighed by the danger of unfair prejudice.

Example 3:

The defendant is charged with theft by fraudulently using a stolen credit card. In the defense case, the defendant intends to call a witness to testify to the defendant's good reputation for honesty. Before the witness takes the stand, the following happens:

Defendant: Your honor, before the jury comes out, I would like to raise an evidentiary matter that involves the next witness.

Judge: Very well. What is it?

Defendant: The next witness, Wilma Morrison, will testify to the defendant's good reputation for honesty in the community in which he lives. I believe the prosecution plans to cross-examine her about the defendant's arrest for burglary eight years ago. I object to that.

Judge: Prosecution, do you intend to go into that on cross?

Prosecutor: We certainly do, your honor. It's proper under Rule 405.

Judge: Defense, why should the prosecution be barred from raising this matter on cross? You're not disputing that the arrest happened, are you?

Defendant: No, your honor. However, there are two reasons that require exclusion here. First, this charge is for fraud, while the earlier charge was for burglary. A charge of burglary is sufficiently different from the present charge that it has little probative weight, particularly when the burglary charge was brought eight years ago and the charges were later dismissed. Under 403, your honor should keep this evidence from being raised at all. Second, this witness has been in the community for six years, and the burglary charge was brought eight years ago, so it's not something that the witness would have heard being discussed in the community.

Prosecutor: The pertinent character trait involved here is honesty. A burglary charge is relevant to honesty; therefore, it's proper to raise it under Rule 405(a). In addition, even though the witness has been around for six years, if she really has heard the defendant's reputation discussed she should have heard talk about the defendant's burglary arrest. It's relevant to show her knowledge of the defendant's community reputation.

Judge: The objection is overruled: The proposed question tests her knowledge of what people say about the defendant's honesty.

> *Defendant:* Your honor, in light of your ruling, I take it that I will be allowed to ask the witness on direct whether she has heard of the arrest, whether that fact changes her testimony, and, if not, whether the reason it does not affect the defendant's reputation is that she has also heard that the charges were dropped.
>
> *Judge:* That's correct. Those facts also legitimately go to her knowledge. Bailiff, please bring in the jury.

Commentary: After the judge's ruling, the defendant has two options. First, the defendant can decide not to call the witness. If so, the defendant has probably waived any error on appeal on the judge's ruling. Second, the defendant can "draw the sting" by bringing out the burglary arrest on direct and asking the witness whether that fact affects the defendant's reputation and, if not, why not. If so, the defendant has probably again waived any error on appeal. The only way the defendant can safely preserve any error in the judge's ruling is to have evidence of the burglary come out during the prosecution's cross-examination.

§12.3. *Impeachment procedures*[2]

1. Law

While some cross-examination is friendly, lawyers most often cross-examine to attack a witness's credibility. Cross-examination that attacks a witness's credibility is called impeachment. The attacks take many forms, some of which are governed by FRE 607, 608, 609, 611, and 613, some by case law. Since the code does not contain all the rules governing impeachment, case law in this area is particularly important.

For example, the cross-examination can raise questions about the witness's ability to perceive the events he describes at a trial or to remember and describe accurately what he now says he saw and heard. If the witness was under the influence of alcohol or drugs at the time of the event he is testifying about, or if he has vision or hearing limitations, cross-examination can properly bring them out. If the witness at the time of trial suffers from some disability that affects his ability to recall or testify accurately, cross-examination is appropriate.

Care must be taken to assure relevancy and fairness. If the witness has some disability or is being treated for a condition that affects the reliability of his testimony, that evidence can be brought out, but if it has nothing to do with the witness's ability to perceive, remember, or describe accurately, that evidence should be barred, For example, evidence that a witness is delusional is relevant, but evidence that the witness was depressed or attempted to commit suicide should be excluded.

---

2. McCormick §§33, 48; Weinstein §§607-610, 613; Mueller & Kirkpatrick §§6.18-6.48; Wigmore §§874-918.

a. "Voucher" rule rejected

Rule 607. Who May Impeach a Witness

Any party, including the party that called the witness, may attack the witness's credibility.

The law recognizes that there are times when a party must use a witness who is less than ideal. Relevant information must be gleaned from someone the calling party is reluctant to embrace. An attack on the witness's credibility by the party calling him can be part of the search for relevant and reliable facts.

At common law, when a party called a witness, he "vouched" for the credibility of that witness. A party could not impeach his own witness unless the witness was hostile or said something that surprised and damaged the party calling him.

That voucher rule is abandoned by FRE 607. The credibility of a witness now may be attacked by any party, including the party who calls the witness. The attack may come in the form of questions concerning the witness's ability to perceive and recall; bias, interest, or motive; prior convictions; prior inconsistent statements; conduct probative of untruthfulness; or by any of the other accepted methods of impeachment. When a party attacks the credibility of his own witness, the examination is subject to the rules that apply to any cross-examination.

The most perplexing problem relating to FRE 607 occurs when a party attempts to impeach a witness it calls with evidence, usually a statement, that otherwise would be inadmissible. For example, consider a cocaine delivery case where a witness has told the police he helped the defendant weigh and bag the cocaine. The witness is not being tried. Just before he takes the stand, the witness tells the prosecutor that the prior statement was untrue and that he does not know the defendant. The prosecutor calls the witness to the stand and then attempts to impeach him with his prior inconsistent statement. Defense counsel objects, correctly noting that the prior statement cannot be admissible for its truth.

The decisions suggest three approaches. First, the trial judge may require the prosecutor to make a showing of surprise and damage, the common law requirement. In the example, the prosecutor obviously is not surprised by the witness's testimony, but it would be damaging to the prosecutor's case.

Second, the trial judge may consider the offered testimony in light of the prosecutor's motives. If the prosecutor is trying to smuggle the inconsistent statement into evidence under the guise of impeachment, hoping the jury will misuse it as substantive evidence, the finding of bad faith that follows should bar the evidence. Put another way, if the prosecutor's primary purpose is to place inadmissible evidence before the jury by calling the witness only to impeach him, he should not be permitted to succeed.

When considering the offering party's motive, the trial judge will take into account such factors as surprise and damage along with the potential for jury misuse of the evidence and the efficacy of a limiting instruction. Here, subterfuge is a probable conclusion. The case becomes closer if the prosecutor did not know the witness was going to renounce his prior statement. Then the issue becomes whether the witness's testimony damages the prosecutor's case. If the witness admits to taking part in the cocaine delivery and says the defendant was not present, the prosecutor's case is damaged, and the impeachment may be allowed, subject to an FRE 403 balancing test and a limiting instruction. But if the witness testifies that because of an unrelated head injury he has no memory of the cocaine transaction, the prosecutor's case has not been damaged and the impeachment should not be allowed to take place.

Third, the trial judge may analyze the problem in terms of FRE 403 and weigh probative value against unfair prejudice. Here, too, the judge must consider whether the jury could follow an instruction that limits the statement to a consideration of the witness's credibility. The probative value of simply attacking the witness's credibility is minimal at best. No other relevant purpose is served by the impeachment. The unfair prejudice is manifest.

Most of the decisions seem to combine the second and third approaches, with emphasis on the good or bad faith of the offering party. Much depends on the potential for jury misuse, which, in turn, depends on whether the out-of-court statement pertains to a damaging fact of consequence.

Trial judges are more likely to opt for admissibility when the prosecution witness's unexpected trial testimony exculpates the defendant. In that event, the witness's credibility is highly relevant

Of course, if the prior statement is made admissible for its truth by some rule of evidence, the problem vanishes. It may be non-hearsay under FRE 801(d)(1)(A) or (C), or it may be admissible under some FRE 803 exception to the rule against hearsay. In that case, the jury may consider the prior statement as substantive evidence, and there is no danger of improper use.

For example, if the witness's prior statement implicating the defendant was made under oath before a grand jury, the statement would be admissible as non-hearsay under FRE 801(d)(1)(A). If the witness testifies that he does not recognize the defendant as the perpetrator of the crime, the witness's prior statement of identification made after viewing the defendant in a lineup is admissible non-hearsay evidence under FRE 801(d)(1)(C).

b. Impeachment methods

The Rules and case law generally recognize seven impeachment methods, although differences of opinion exist on whether these should all be characterized as true "impeachment":

1. bias, interest, and motive
2. prior inconsistent statements — FRE 613
3. contradictory facts
4. prior convictions — FRE 609
5. character for untruthfulness — FRE 608(a)
6. conduct probative of untruthfulness — FRE 608(b)
7. treatises — FRE 803(18)

Bias, interest, and motive can be anything about the relationship of the witness to any of the parties or the lawsuit that might cause a witness, consciously or unconsciously, to slant his testimony for or against a particular party. For example, evidence that the witness has another lawsuit pending against the defendant is admissible to show bias. Evidence that an expert has been paid by the plaintiff or always testifies for plaintiffs when called as an expert is admissible for the same reason. Evidence that the witness once had a dispute with the defendant is admissible to show motive. There is no express rule on bias, interest, and motive, but its use is well established by case law.

Prior inconsistent statements are statements that a witness has made, at an earlier time, that are different than what the witness is now testifying to at trial. The inconsistency can take many forms. Most inconsistencies are direct inconsistencies between what the witness says at trial and what the witness has previously said about the same topic. For example, if a witness at trial testifies that the defendant's car was going 50 mph, but told a police officer that the car was going 30 mph, the inconsistent statement can be brought out at trial.

Some inconsistencies are in the form of omissions or silence. When a witness has made a statement about an event and then, when testifying about the event at trial, adds a significant fact that was not contained in the earlier statement, that omission can be brought out at trial. For example, if a witness at trial testifies that the driver of the defendant's vehicle was drunk, but his earlier statement to an insurance investigator makes no mention of that fact, this can be brought out. When a witness testifies about an event at trial, but was silent about the event under circumstances in which the witness would have been expected to speak, the silence can be brought out. For example, if a witness testifies that he saw the defendant shoot the victim, but was silent when the police sought out eyewitnesses to the shooting, this can be brought out. Prior inconsistent statements are governed by FRE 613.

Contradictory facts, sometimes called impeachment by contradiction, comprise another impeachment method. This method permits introducing evidence that contradicts the witness's testimony at trial. For example, if a witness says he has never seen marijuana in his life, he may be cross-examined on being arrested for possessing marijuana several years ago. There is no express rule governing contradictory facts, but its use is well established by case law.

Impeachment by prior conviction is an impeachment method that is a direct attack on witness credibility. The law permits the introduction of certain kinds of criminal convictions to attack a witness's credibility. For example, when a witness testifies, he can be cross-examined on his conviction for perjury three years ago. Prior convictions are governed by FRE 609.

Impeachment by showing character for untruthfulness is a permitted, although seldom used, impeachment technique. Whenever a fact witness testifies, his credibility becomes an issue in the trial. A party can then call a character witness to testify to the fact witness's character for untruthfulness, in the form of general reputation or personal opinion. For example, if the plaintiff calls a fact witness to testify, the defendant later can call a character witness to testify that the fact witness has a bad reputation in the community for truthfulness. Character for untruthfulness is governed by FRE 608(a).

Impeachment by conduct probative of untruthfulness is another impeachment method that is a direct attack on witness credibility. The law permits cross-examination about certain prior bad acts that are probative of the witness's truthfulness. For example, a witness can be cross-examined on the fact that he submitted a false loan application to a bank last year. Prior bad acts are governed by FRE 608(b).

Finally, an expert who testifies can have his testimony contradicted by showing that a learned treatise or periodical, recognized as being authoritative, contains statements that are inconsistent with the expert's testimony. For example, if an expert testifies that the plaintiff's scar tissue should disappear in a few years, the cross-examiner can establish that an authoritative medical treatise states that scar tissue is permanent and never will disappear. Impeachment using treatises is governed by FRE 803(18). The impeaching statement becomes substantive evidence in the case.

c. The good faith requirement

Impeachment requires good faith. This requirement is based on the rules of ethics and general notions of fairness. Model Rule 3.4(e) provides: "A lawyer shall not . . . allude to any matter that the lawyer does not reasonably believe is relevant or that will not be supported by admissible evidence."

This means a lawyer cannot suggest any impeaching matters, whether during the witness's examination or later, that the lawyer does not reasonably believe are both relevant and, where necessary, admissible. The lawyer, in short, must have good faith to suggest an impeaching matter. If the judge has doubts about the impeachment, the judge might ask the lawyer, at a sidebar conference, the good faith basis for suggesting the impeaching matter to make sure the lawyer has a proper factual basis for the questions. For example, a lawyer cannot ask "You drank three double martinis just before witnessing the crash, right?" unless he has some reliable evidence that this actually happened.

d. The "confrontation" or "warning question" requirement

The common law required that a witness be confronted with his prior inconsistent statement before extrinsic evidence of the statement could be admitted. In many jurisdictions, this "confrontation" requirement was called the "warning question" requirement. This meant a party who wished to impeach a witness with a prior inconsistent statement had to bring up the inconsistency during the witness's cross-examination, where the witness would have an opportunity to admit or deny making the statement.

The rationales for the common law requirement were fairness and efficiency. The procedure was fair because the witness first had an opportunity to admit or deny the impeaching matter while on the stand before other evidence of the impeaching matter would be admissible. The procedure was also efficient, since if the witness admitted the impeaching matter while on the stand, there would be no need for other evidence of the impeaching matter.

For example, consider an eyewitness to a vehicle collision. The witness gave an oral statement to the police that he "didn't notice the traffic lights at the time of the collision." At trial, the witness testifies on direct examination that "the light was green for the Main Street traffic at the time of the collision." The common law required that the cross-examiner "confront" the witness with the prior inconsistent statement by directing the witness to the date, time, and place the statement was made and by asking the witness to admit making it. If the witness admitted making it, that ended the matter, since the impeaching matter was admitted. If the witness denied or equivocated, only then could the cross-examiner later introduce extrinsic evidence that the witness made the earlier statement.

FRE 613(b) modifies the common law's confrontation requirement. It requires only that a "witness is given an opportunity to explain or deny" the prior statement and that "an adverse party is given an opportunity to examine the witness" about it before extrinsic evidence of the prior statement is admissible. The rule does not state when this "opportunity" must be afforded, just that it is a condition that must be met before extrinsic evidence is admissible.

Trial judges are uncomfortable with the flexibility of FRE 613(b). Most prefer that the witness be confronted with a prior inconsistent statement while on the stand before extrinsic evidence of the statement will be admissible. After all, the common law requirement avoided unfair surprise to the witness, avoided possible jury confusion, elicited any explanations for the inconsistencies when the witness was still on the stand, and promoted the efficient use of courtroom time. Those judges who like the common law procedure use FRE 611(a) to require that the common law procedure be employed in impeaching with a prior inconsistent statement.

Some judges require that the common law confrontation procedure be used with other impeachment methods as well, particularly with statements reflecting bias, interest, or motive, although the Rules are silent on the question. For example, some judges require that a witness be cross-examined about his acts or statements showing bias before extrinsic evidence of such matters will be admissible, although most case law holds such confrontation is unnecessary. Again, the reasons are fairness to the witness and courtroom efficiency. The case for confrontation is weaker when the witness is to be attacked with acts, not statements, reflecting bias, interest, or motive.

Trial lawyers usually prefer the common law requirement as the more effective persuasion technique. After all, when a witness is directly confronted with an impeaching matter on cross-examination, the jury knows immediately what the point is. Then, if it later becomes necessary to introduce extrinsic evidence of the impeaching matter, the jury knows why the proof is being made.

e.   The relevancy requirement and the "collateral"– "non-collateral" dichotomy

Is the impeaching matter relevant? This is the question that always must be asked first whenever a party attempts to impeach a witness. The impeaching matter must be relevant to the issues in the case and the credibility of the witness; otherwise, it should not be raised during the trial.

For example, a witness on direct examination says, "The defendant's car was traveling 70 mph." On cross-examination, the following is asked: "Didn't you tell the police officer that the defendant's car was going 65 to 70 mph?" The difference between "70 mph" and "65 to 70 mph" is insignificant. An objection based on general relevance grounds, or on FRE 403 grounds that the evidence is misleading and a waste of time, should be sustained.

If the impeaching matter survives the relevancy analysis, the second question is whether the impeaching matter is collateral or non-collateral. It is important to keep in mind that the collateral–non-collateral dichotomy addresses only the question of whether the impeaching matter can be proven through extrinsic evidence. Evidence that is collateral cannot be proven with extrinsic evidence. This question is independent of the relevancy analysis. That is, whether a matter is collateral should have nothing to do with whether the question may be asked on cross-examination.

Consider the witness who on direct examination says, "The light was red." The cross-examiner asks, "Didn't you tell the police officer that the light was green?" If the witness says "yes," the impeaching matter has been admitted, and nothing further needs to be done on this point. If the witness says "no" or equivocates with "I don't remember" or "I'm not sure," the impeaching matter is unresolved. The jury will be wondering if the witness made that statement or not. If the unadmitted statement is important, common sense says that the conflict should be resolved one way or another. Anything less would be unfair to the jury, since it has to determine what color the light was at the time of the collision. In such a situation, the cross-examiner later may be required to prove up the impeaching matter with extrinsic evidence, that is, to introduce evidence that proves that the witness did in fact make the statement to the police officer.

When will the cross-examiner (or the direct examiner, if the impeachment occurs during a direct examination) be required to prove up the unadmitted impeaching matter with extrinsic evidence? Evidence law uses the collateral–non-collateral dichotomy to answer this question. If the impeaching matter is collateral to the issues at trial, the unadmitted impeaching matter cannot be proved up later with extrinsic evidence. On the other hand, if the impeaching matter is non-collateral, the unadmitted impeaching matter must be proved up later with extrinsic evidence. The classic definition of non-collateral impeachment is this: If the impeaching matter properly can be introduced at trial for any purpose other than merely to contradict the witness's testimony, it is non-collateral. If the impeaching matter is admissible only to contradict the witness's testimony, it is collateral.

Many judges, however, take a more flexible approach and focus more on the importance of the impeachment in light of the significance of the witness and the disputed issues in the case. Underlying the collateral–non-collateral dichotomy is the policy interest in trial efficiency. Proving up an unadmitted impeaching matter takes court time. For example, if the witness does not admit telling the police officer that the light was green, it will take additional trial time to call the police officer to testify that the witness in fact told him that the light was green. In the overall context of the trial, is this important enough to justify the expenditure of time? The critical concern then becomes this: In this case, given the issues and the importance of the witness, is the unadmitted impeaching matter important enough that it makes sense to require calling another witness or introducing another exhibit to prove up the impeaching matter? If the answer is "yes," then the unadmitted impeaching matter must be proved through the later witness or exhibit.

Evidence law has recognized some impeachment categories as always non-collateral, others as always collateral, and others as being either, depending on the case-specific circumstances. Bias, interest, and motive and prior convictions always are considered non-collateral. This means that whenever a witness does not admit an impeaching matter that shows bias, interest, or motive or a prior conviction, it must be proved up with later extrinsic evidence. Conduct probative of untruthfulness, sometimes called prior bad acts, offered during cross-examination under FRE 608(b), always is considered collateral. This means the cross-examiner must "take the witness's answer" and cannot prove up a denial or equivocation with later extrinsic evidence. Finally, prior inconsistent statements and contradictory facts are taken on a case-by-case basis and are either collateral or non-collateral, depending on the case-specific situation.

For example, Smith, a plaintiff's witness called during plaintiff's case-in-chief, testifies that she saw the defendant run the red light. On cross-examination, Smith denies telling a police officer the defendant had the green light. This difference is obviously important, or non-collateral. The cross-examiner must prove up the unadmitted prior statement with extrinsic evidence when the cross-examiner next has an opportunity to call witnesses and introduce exhibits. This means the cross-examiner, in the defense's case-in-chief, must call the police officer to testify that Smith told him the defendant had the green light.

What happens when a party tries to prove up collateral impeachment? A timely objection, on the basis that counsel is trying to introduce extrinsic evidence on a collateral matter, should be sustained.

For example, a witness on direct says he was on his way to work when he saw the collision. On cross, the witness denies telling a police officer he was on his way home when he saw the collision. This inconsistency is relevant, since it casts doubt on the witness's ability to remember. The inconsistency is also collateral and cannot be proved up later by calling the police officer to testify that the witness said he was on his way home.

What happens when a party is obligated to prove up an unadmitted non-collateral matter, but doesn't? The opposing party has two choices. First, the party can object and ask the court to instruct the jury to disregard the earlier cross-examination on that point. Second, the party can use the failure to prove up during closing arguments as ammunition against the other side. Of these two approaches, many trial lawyers prefer the second, since instructions to the jury to disregard previously heard evidence probably are ineffective. It is unlikely the jury can "unring the bell." However, if the failure to prove up is a serious matter, making the motion is essential to preserve error.

For example, the defendant in a criminal case is cross-examined about a prior conviction and denies the conviction. In the prosecution's rebuttal case, the prosecutor fails to introduce any evidence of the prior conviction. This failure is serious, and the defense lawyer must make a prompt objection and, in this situation, probably ask for a mistrial as well.

While the law recognizes the collateral–non-collateral distinction, some judges dislike impeachment on collateral matters and, relying on their power under FRE 611(a), bar its use if an objection is made. They believe such impeachment distracts the jury from the central issues in the case and is more confusing than revealing. If a witness denies the collaterally impeaching matter, the lawyer's assertion remains unproven, adding to the jury's uncertainty. Some judges believe trials are made easier on the jury by preventing such situations from happening.

2. Practice

Commonly encountered issues include whether an impeaching matter is properly raised, whether a lawyer is required to prove up unadmitted impeachment, and whether impeachment is collateral and prove-up is prohibited. Where procedural issues occur, they must be raised promptly, since otherwise the issues will almost certainly be waived for appeal.

Example 1:

This is a personal injury case arising from an intersection collision. In the plaintiff's case-in-chief, a witness, James Madison, testifies that he was "just a few feet from the intersection" when he saw the collision. In the defense case-in-chief, the following happens:

Q. (By defendant's lawyer) Officer Bright, when did you get to the scene of the accident?
A. About five minutes after receiving the call.
Q. Did you see James Madison there?
A. Yes.
Q. Did you talk to him?
A. Yes.
Q. Did he say how far from the intersection he was when he saw the collision?
A. Yes, he said. . . .
Plaintiff: Objection to this hearsay, your honor. Mr. Madison was never asked about saying anything to this police officer during his cross-examination. This is improper.
Defendant: We're just bringing out the prior statement, your honor. It's impeaching.
Judge: The objection is sustained. You should have done this when Mr. Madison testified. There will be no questions to this witness about any conversations with Mr. Madison.

Commentary: This result is not required by FRE 613. However, many judges, using FRE 611, still follow the common law's requirement that the witness first be confronted by a prior inconsistent statement before extrinsic evidence of it will be admissible. The defendant's lawyer, during cross-examination of Mr. Madison, should have asked him to admit making the statement to the police officer. (If Mr. Madison were the plaintiff, the statement to the police officer also would be an admission by a party-opponent, and the defense could have the police officer testify to the statement without a need to first confront Madison with the statement.)

Example 2:

Same case as Example 1. Another plaintiff's witness testifies. During cross-examination, the following happens:

Q. (By defendant's lawyer) Mr. Gianna, you saw the crash?
A. I did.
Q. Did you have any alcohol to drink that day?
A. No.
Q. Were you tired?
A. No.

After the defense rests, the following happens out of the jury's presence:

Plaintiff: Now that both sides have rested, your honor, we ask that the jury be instructed that the defendant never proved Mr. Gianna had drunk alcohol or was tired that day. They failed to prove it up.

Defendant: I never suggested he had been drinking or was tired, your honor. I was merely inquiring. When the witness said "no," that ended the matter, and there's nothing to prove up because nothing was suggested.

Plaintiff: But they raised it, your honor. They're now obligated to prove it up.

Judge: No, I disagree. It was raised, but there was no suggestion that those raised matters were true. There's nothing to prove up, so no instruction will be given.

Commentary: If the cross-examiner had asked, "You had two double martinis just before the crash, didn't you?" and the witness denied it, then the cross-examiner would be obligated to prove up that fact, since now the lawyer has suggested the fact was true and it is non-collateral.

Example 3:

Same case as Example 1. Mr. Madison, the eyewitness, is called in the plaintiff's case-in-chief. During cross-examination, the following happens:

Q. (By defendant's lawyer) Mr. Madison, you claim today you were just a few feet from the intersection when the accident happened?

A. That's right.

Q. Right after the crash you talked to a police officer?

A. That's right.

Q. Didn't you tell that police officer, right after the crash, that you were about half a block away when the accident happened?

A. I don't think that's what I told him.

When the plaintiff rests, the defendant also rests without calling any witnesses. The jury is sent out of the courtroom. The following then happens:

Plaintiff: Your honor, we have an evidentiary issue that has just arisen. During the cross-examination of Mr. Madison, the defendant asked him to admit a prior statement he allegedly made to a police officer, that he was about half a block away when the accident happened. Mr. Madison did not admit making that statement, which was substantially different from his testimony on direct that he was just a few feet away when the collision happened. That's non-collateral impeachment, your honor; the witness never admitted making that statement, and the defendant never proved it up. Therefore, we're entitled to an instruction to the jury that this statement was never proven and that the jury should therefore disregard it.

Defendant: The witness never denied it, your honor.

Judge: But the witness never admitted it either. You were obligated to prove it up, and you didn't. The jury will be instructed accordingly.

Commentary: The other approach plaintiff could have taken is to not ask for an instruction to disregard and to argue in closing argument the implication of defendant's failure to prove up.

Example 4:

Same case as Example 1. Another eyewitness, Jane Johnson, is called by the plaintiff and testifies that she had been on the corner about 10 minutes, waiting for a bus, when the collision happened. On cross-examination, the following happens:

Q. (By defendant's lawyer) You say you were on that corner about 10 minutes when the accident happened?
A. That's right.
Q. Ms. Johnson, weren't you actually on the corner more like 20 minutes before the accident happened?
A. No, it was more like 10 minutes.
After the plaintiff rests, the following happens:
Defendant: Your honor, we call Sharon Smith.
Plaintiff: Your honor, before Ms. Smith takes the stand, may we approach?
Judge: All right. [Lawyers come to the bench.] What's the problem?
Plaintiff: Your honor, I believe the only reason this witness is being called is to prove that Ms. Johnson was standing on the corner about 20 minutes, not the 10 minutes she testified to, before the collision happened. This is collateral and improper.
Defendant: Your honor, the witness was expressly asked to admit she was there 20 minutes and denied it. We can prove through Ms. Smith, her co-worker, that Ms. Johnson told her she had been out there 20 minutes. She's the prove-up witness, and this is important to Ms. Johnson's credibility.
Judge: No, that's collateral. We're not going to spend court time just to prove Ms. Johnson had been on the corner 20 minutes, not 10 minutes, before the crash. Call your next witness.

§12.4.   *Impeachment methods*

1.   Bias, interest, and motive[3]

a.   *Law*

A time-honored and high-impact cross-examination technique not specifically mentioned in the Rules is inquiry about a witness's bias, interest, or motive for testifying in a certain way. That is, does he believe he has something to gain or lose by testifying in a certain way? This kind of evidence always is relevant,

---

3. McCormick §39; Weinstein §607[03]; Mueller & Kirkpatrick §§6.19-6.20; Wigmore §§901, 943-969.

never collateral, and never beyond the scope of direct examination. It is, however, subject to the strictures of FRE 403.

Bias exists where a witness, through some relationship to the parties or attitude about the matter in dispute, has a frame of mind that could color his testimony. For example, a witness is the plaintiff's brother; another witness was recently fired by the defendant. The first witness may be biased in favor of the plaintiff; the second may be prejudiced against the defendant. Bias can be anything about the relationship between a party and a witness "which might lead the witness to slant, unconsciously or otherwise, his testimony in favor of or against a party." *United States v. Abel,* 469 U.S. 45 (1984). In *Abel,* the Court affirmed the admission of the fact that the defendant and a witness favorable to him were members of the same secret prison gang that required its members to commit perjury, theft, and murder on each member's behalf.

When analyzing the witness's background for areas of bias, the key moment is the time when the witness first makes the accusation he is testifying to at trial. In *Davis v. Alaska,* 415 U.S. 308 (1974), it was the witness's probationary status at the time he first identified the defendant that went to his bias and motive. That was the bias and motive that could have affected the witness's in-court identification. It did not matter whether the witness was on probation at the time of trial. His bias had been established.

Interest exists where a witness's relationship to a party or the lawsuit is such that he stands to gain or lose, usually financially, from a particular outcome to the case. For example, a witness is the plaintiff's business partner; another witness has loaned the defendant a large sum of money. Both witnesses have an interest in a particular outcome of the case. An expert can be cross-examined about compensation he has received or expects to receive in this or other cases. A witness can be cross-examined about his own pending lawsuit against one of the parties.

Similar to bias and interest is motive. People usually do things for a reason, and that reason, or motive, may color a person's testimony or explain his conduct. For example, the defendant in a robbery case may have had a motive to rob the victim if the victim had previously cheated him. In this situation, the prosecution can bring out the motive during the defendant's cross-examination if the defendant testifies during his trial. (The prosecution could also introduce evidence of motive during its case-in-chief as circumstantial evidence of conduct.)

When determining how many bias, interest, or motive questions to allow, trial judges will consider the probative value of the evidence, whether the witness merely is being harassed or embarrassed, whether the questions are confusing the issues or taking more time than they are worth, and whether the cross-examiner is being repetitive and annoying. See *Delaware v. Van Arsdall,* 475 U.S. 673 (1986). In criminal cases, trial judges tend to broaden the scope of cross-examination aimed at eliciting bias, interest, or motive.

Cross-examination of prosecution witnesses in criminal cases to show bias, interest, or motive also has constitutional implications. A defendant's rights under the Sixth Amendment Confrontation Clause are violated when the trial judge refuses to allow impeachment of an alleged rape victim's testimony with facts revealing a motive to fabricate the alleged crime. *Olden v. Kentucky,* 488 U.S. 227 (1988). In *Davis v. Alaska,* 415 U.S. 308 (1974), it was a Confrontation Clause violation to refuse to allow a defendant to cross-examine a witness about his being on juvenile probation at the time he first identified the defendant to the police. The evidence, said the Court, might "afford a basis for an inference of undue pressure because of [his] vulnerable status as a probationer." The Supreme Court held that the defendant's Confrontation Clause rights defeat the state's interest in protecting witnesses from use at trial of their juvenile convictions. In the same vein, it is proper to show the witness currently is in jail, circumstantial evidence that his testimony is being given under promise or expectation of leniency. *Alford v. United States,* 282 U.S. 687 (1931).

An accomplice witness who testifies for the prosecution may be cross-examined about his expectations of leniency or other consideration despite the absence of any specific promises by the prosecution. Because pressure or influence from authorities may be real or imagined, questions about the witness's pending or recently dismissed charges are proper.

Cross-examination of an accomplice witness who testifies for the prosecution can go into the details of any cooperation agreement the witness has with the prosecution. Because of the potential impact of that testimony, a prosecutor ordinarily will ask the witness about the agreement during direct examination to remove the sting of the cross-examination. The witness will be asked whether he understands what will happen if he does not tell the truth. He almost always will say he knows he can still be prosecuted for perjury if he does not tell the truth. A few courts hold that the questions are irrelevant because the witness's credibility has not yet been attacked. Most courts, however, allow the preemptive strike on direct examination.

b.   Practice

Bias and interest cause relatively few admissibility problems, since bias and interest, where they exist, are obviously relevant to witness credibility. Motive, on the other hand, can be more difficult to demonstrate, and its relevance is sometimes less immediately apparent.

Example 1:

This is a contract case. The plaintiff claims the defendant failed to deliver goods as required under the contract. In the plaintiff's case, a witness testifies, and on cross-examination, the following happens:

Q. (By defendant's lawyer) Mr. Curtis, last year you filed a lawsuit against the defendant, didn't you?
Plaintiff: Objection, relevance.
Judge: Overruled.
A. Yes.
Q. In that lawsuit, you claimed the defendant failed to deliver certain goods to you?
A. Yes.
Q. The defendant denied that he breached the contract, didn't he?
A. Well, that's what he claims.
Q. That lawsuit is still pending?
A. That's right.
Q. And you've asked for damages in the amount of $30,000 in that lawsuit?

Plaintiff: Objection, your honor. They've brought out the fact of the law-
    suit. They can't delve into every little detail.
Judge: Overruled.
A. That's right.
Q. So there's no love lost between the two of you, is there?
A. You could say that.

Commentary: When bias is shown, the details of the facts showing bias are admissible, since these facts go to weight.

Example 2:

This is a burglary case. The defendant claims the victim fabricated the burglary charge to retaliate for the defendant's cheating him in a card game. During the cross-examination of the victim, the following happens:

Q. (By defendant's lawyer) Mr. Jackson, you claim you saw the defendant,
    Mr. Roberts, coming out of your garage at two in the morning?
A. That's right.
Q. Of course, you were alone at the time.
A. Yes.
Q. Mr. Jackson, you don't like Mr. Roberts, do you?
A. I don't hate him.
Q. Well, he's certainly not your friend, is he?
A. That's true.
Q. In fact, a month before this claimed burglary, you were in a card game
    with Mr. Roberts, weren't you?
Prosecutor: Objection, your honor. This is other acts evidence being used
    to show character. That's improper.
Defendant: It goes to motive, your honor.
Judge: Overruled.
A. We were in a card game.
Q. You lost money in that game, right?
A. Some.
Q. That "some" was about $300 dollars, right?
A. It was something like that.
Q. And Mr. Roberts was the big winner that night, right?
A. Well, I knew he won some money.
Q. In fact, Mr. Jackson, you accused Mr. Roberts of cheating, didn't you?
A. I don't think I used the term "cheating."
Q. Didn't you tell the other people at the table that Mr. Jackson was
    winning only when he got to deal the deck?
A. I don't remember that.
Q. In fact, you and Mr. Jackson got into an argument over your accusa-
    tion, didn't you?
A. I wouldn't call it an argument.

Commentary: This is proper cross-examination, since it shows the victim's motive to retaliate by bringing the burglary charge. Since the witness did not admit the facts showing motive, and since motive, like bias and interest, is always non-collateral, the defense is obligated to prove up the fact of the accusation during the defense case by calling another person who was present at the card game.

2. Prior inconsistent statements[4]

a. Law

Rule 613.   Witness's Prior Statement

(a) **Showing or Disclosing the Statement During Examination.** When examining a witness about the witness's prior statement, a party need not show it or disclose its contents to the witness. But the party must, on request, show it or disclose its contents to an adverse party's attorney.

(b) **Extrinsic Evidence of a Prior Inconsistent Statement.** Extrinsic evidence of a witness's prior inconsistent statement is admissible only if the witness is given an opportunity to explain or deny the statement and an adverse party is given an opportunity to examine the witness about it, or if justice so requires. This subdivision (b) does not apply to an opposing party's statement under Rule 801(d)(2).

Impeachment of a witness by his prior inconsistent statement, oral or written, is a time-honored method of attacking the credibility of the witness. If a witness has previously said or written something that is inconsistent with what he says at trial, this inconsistency adversely affects the witness's credibility if the inconsistency is raised during the trial. The prior inconsistent statement usually consists of words spoken or written by the witness, but it can consist of the failure to speak about a relevant fact when it would have been natural for the witness to have said something.

The prior statement can be in the form of an opinion or the failure to respond to the statement of another when a response would be expected. A prior statement of inability to recall is inconsistent with clear recall about the same matter on the witness stand.

The prior statement, no matter the form, must be inconsistent with the witness's trial testimony. Direct inconsistency is not required. The test for any inconsistency is whether the prior statement or omission has a reasonable tendency to discredit the testimony of the witness. Evasion, bad faith lack of recall, or change of position can create inconsistency. When a witness evades or changes his testimony, the statement may be said to be inconsistent. When the witness on the stand has a clear memory of events that he could not recall in the prior statement, impeachment is appropriate. But when the reverse happens — the witness has a clear memory in the statement, but fails to recall on the stand — there is no inconsistency and nothing to impeach unless the judge finds the failure of memory is purposeful and not otherwise in good faith.

---

4. McCormick §§34-38; Weinstein §607[06]; Mueller & Kirkpatrick §§6.40-6.42; Wigmore §§902-906, 1017-1046.

Impeachment by omission is an accepted technique, but at times is misunderstood. It applies when a witness makes a statement about an event and then testifies about that event, but adds an important fact that is not contained in the prior statement. The foundation for this kind of impeachment is a showing that the omitted fact is something that the witness would reasonably be expected to have included in his prior statement. For example, if a witness testifies at trial that the robber had a revolver in his waistband, but in a statement to the police after the robbery omitted any mention of a revolver, this properly can be brought out.

Another form of impeachment by omission involves the witness's earlier silence on something he testifies to at trial. The foundation for impeachment by silence is a showing that the witness would have been expected to speak about the matter. For example, if a witness testifies at trial that he was with the defendant at the time of the robbery charged, the witness can be questioned to show he never told this to the police.

Impeachment by silence can have constitutional implications in criminal cases. A criminal defendant's pre-arrest silence may be used to impeach him if he testifies at trial. *Jenkins v. Anderson*, 447 U.S. 231 (1980). The defendant's post-arrest, but pre-*Miranda*, silence also may be used to impeach him if he testifies at trial. *Fletcher v. Weir*, 455 U.S. 603 (1982).

The Supreme Court never has decided whether the prosecution may use a defendant's post-arrest, pre-*Miranda* silence during its case-in-chief without violating the defendant's Fifth Amendment rights. Most, but not all, circuit courts of appeal have held a defendant's post-arrest, pre-*Miranda* silence cannot be used as substantive evidence.

Once a defendant is arrested and *Miranda* warnings given, the defendant's silence may not be used to impeach him, even if the defendant talked about other things. *Doyle v. Ohio*, 426 U.S. 610 (1976). But if the defendant's testimony directly conflicts with his post-*Miranda* statements, he may be impeached with those statements.

When a criminal defendant testifies, he assumes an obligation to speak truthfully and may be cross-examined on matters obtained in violation of his constitutional rights. Excluding reliable evidence from the prosecution's case-in-chief is not an opportunity for the defendant to commit perjury. Statements taken in violation of *Miranda* can be used to impeach the defendant if he testifies at trial. *Harris v. New York*, 401 U.S. 222 (1971). Statements made by the defendant to police officers after the defendant invokes his Sixth Amendment right to counsel may be used to impeach the defendant during cross-examination. *Michigan v. Harvey*, 494 U.S. 344 (1990). Statements obtained from the defendant in violation of the Fourth Amendment can be used to impeach him if he testifies differently on direct examination or during cross-examination on a matter plainly within the scope of the direct examination. *United States v. Havens*, 446 U.S. 620 (1980). But that same unlawfully seized evidence, such as the defendant's suppressed statement, may not be used to impeach the testimony of other defense witnesses. *James v. Illinois*, 493 U.S. 307 (1990).

When the prior inconsistent statement is offered only to attack a nonparty witness's credibility, it is not subject to hearsay objection because it is being offered not for the truth of the words, but merely to show they were spoken. There are times when the prior inconsistent statement can be offered both to impeach the witness and as independent substantive evidence. That happens when the prior statement is non-hearsay under FRE 801(d)(1) or an exception to the rule against hearsay under the provisions of FRE 803 or FRE 807.

When the witness also is a party, the cross-examiner has two choices in using a prior inconsistent statement. The statement can be used to impeach the party if the party testifies differently at trial. The statement also can be used as an admission of a party-opponent under FRE 801(d)(2) and can be introduced in the opponent's case-in-chief.

FRE 613 does not define the scope of cross-examination. Nor does it offer any guidance concerning the propriety of questions asked on cross-examination. Scope of cross is determined under FRE 611(b). The rules of relevance and the balancing test of FRE 403 are the bases of the trial judge's rulings on objections to cross-examination questions.

The common law decisions required a cross-examiner to show a witness his written statement before he could be cross-examined on it. FRE 613(a) abolishes "this useless impediment to cross-examination," whether the statement is oral or written. Advisory Committee's Note to FRE 613. Now the cross-examiner can use the element of surprise when questioning a witness about prior statements. But there is no right to surprise the lawyer who called the witness. On request, the contents of the prior statement, whether oral or written, must be disclosed to opposing counsel.

The mandatory disclosure requirement is designed to protect against unwarranted insinuations that a statement has been made when it has not. At times, the trial judge will become concerned that the cross-examiner's suggestion of a prior statement is more imagined than real. In those instances, the trial judge will ask the cross-examiner whether he can provide proof of the statement if the witness denies making it. Prudence and the rules of professional conduct compel an affirmative answer. In addition, when a trial judge believes the witness is being dealt with unfairly, he can require the cross-examiner to show the purportedly impeaching statement to the witness before questions about it are asked.

When a witness is confronted with a prior inconsistent statement, he ordinarily will admit making it, deny making it, or explain it. If he admits making it, the impeachment is complete. There is no reason to offer other evidence that the statement was made. Explanations for it can be made on redirect examination. FRE 403 considerations usually bar extrinsic evidence of the statement if the witness has admitted making it.

If the witness denies making the statement or equivocates about making it with responses such as "I might have," or "I could have," or "I don't remember if I did or not," the cross-examiner is obligated to offer extrinsic evidence that the statement was in fact made. Impeachment is not yet complete. If the proof is not made later, the question asked of the witness will, on request, be stricken and possible error planted in the record if the point is important.

The typical method of offering extrinsic proof is to call the person to whom the statement was made. Most trial judges allow leading questions of the extrinsic evidence witness in order to direct the witness to the statement inquired about during the earlier cross-examination.

At common law, the cross-examiner was required to confront the witness with his prior inconsistent statement before extrinsic evidence of it could be admitted. Confrontation consisted of directing the witness's attention to the date, time, and place and then to the contents of the prior statement. Without that foundation, extrinsic evidence of the statement was not allowed to complete the impeachment. This is still the practice in many courts.

FRE 613(b) modifies the common law requirement of confrontation before extrinsic evidence of the statement is allowed. The operative word is "opportunity." All the rule requires is that the witness be afforded an opportunity to explain or deny the prior statement and that the opposing party be given an opportunity to ask the witness questions about the statement. No particular time or sequence for the denial or explanation is required. It can happen at any time during the trial. The Advisory Committee's Note to FRE 613 explains: "Under this procedure, several collusive witnesses can be examined before disclosure of a joint prior inconsistent statement. . . . Also, dangers of oversight are reduced."

FRE 613(b) does not say that the cross-examiner has to be the one to afford the witness an opportunity to deny or explain the prior inconsistent statement. All that is required is that the witness be available to deny or explain. The proponent of the witness's testimony may recall the witness for denial or explanation, even on rebuttal or surrebuttal. If the proponent chooses not to recall the witness, that should be the end of the matter.

There are narrowly defined occasions when extrinsic evidence of a prior inconsistent statement may be offered even though the unconfronted witness is no longer available. That is "if justice so required." For example, the cross-examiner learns of the prior inconsistent statement after the witness testifies. The witness is no longer available, through no fault of the cross-examiner. Trial judges have the discretion to allow extrinsic evidence of the statement in that circumstance. However, if the trial judge concludes there is a worthwhile denial or explanation to be made, the interests of justice would lean toward prohibiting the extrinsic evidence.

Trial judges are uncomfortable with FRE 613(b). Most prefer that the witness be confronted with his prior inconsistent statement during cross-examination. Some judges use FRE 611(a) to insist on it. The traditional confrontation requirement avoids unfair surprise and possible jury confusion. Explanations can be made then and there, during redirect examination. Things seem more complete and more fair. Then, when the witness does not admit making the prior statement, extrinsic evidence of it is admissible. The safer course, thus, is to confront the witness with his prior statements while the witness is on the witness stand.

At the least, if the cross-examiner does not intend to confront the witness with the statement, he should inform opposing counsel of his intent to offer it later. He also might suggest that the witness be kept available for recall.

FRE 613(b) expressly provides that it does not apply to admissions of a party-opponent as defined in FRE 801(d)(2). It is clear that admissions may be admitted without concern for confrontation of the declarant or his availability.

There is some confusion about the principle that extrinsic evidence of a prior inconsistent statement concerning a collateral matter is not admissible. That principle comes from decisions that weigh the wasted time and effort and the jury confusion considerations of FRE 403. It has nothing to do with whether the witness was confronted by the prior statement or whether he was available at the time it was offered.

A fact is collateral when its only admissible purpose is to contradict the witness. The fact is not collateral if it could have been introduced in evidence for any relevant purpose other than the contradiction. For example, when an eyewitness testifies that he was coming from home when he saw the accident, but told the police that he was coming from work at the time, most courts will consider the matter collateral, but a question to the eyewitness about his prior statement to the police officer is not prohibited by FRE 613(b).

FRE 613(b) is not about cross-examination. Its only purpose is to determine when extrinsic evidence of a witness's prior inconsistent statement may be admitted. Nothing in the rule states that a witness cannot be cross-examined on a collateral matter. That is a matter for the trial judge to determine under FRE 401-403 and 611(b).

After all, collateral matters can implicate the witness's credibility, always a proper area for cross-examination under FRE 611(b). Faulty memory or the inability to perceive can be demonstrated by questions on collateral matters, such as the witness's conflicting testimony about where he lived on the day of the relevant event and what clothing he was wearing that day.

Concluding that the questions inquire into collateral matters does not mean they cannot be asked on cross-examination. "That's collateral" is not a proper objection to an otherwise relevant question. In practice, however, many trial judges, in the name of getting on with the trial and avoiding possible jury confusion, prohibit cross-examination questions that inquire into collateral matters having marginal relevance.

If a witness is asked about a relevant collateral matter, the cross-examiner must accept the witness's answer. He cannot offer extrinsic evidence to contradict it. If the matter is relevant and not collateral, the extrinsic evidence can be admitted. But the test is not as automatic as it sounds. Trial judges will look to the importance of the evidence without being bound by labels.

b. Practice

Impeachment with prior inconsistent statements is, by far, the most commonly used impeachment method. Common problems center on whether proper procedures are used, whether the impeachment itself is proper, and whether the impeachment is collateral or non-collateral.

Example 1:

This is a bank robbery case. A prosecution witness, John Jones, testifies that the bank robber was 6'4" tall, a height that fits the defendant. When the defense case begins, the investigating police officer is called. The following then happens:

Q. Did you speak to John Jones after the robbery?
A. Yes, I did. At the police station, about a half hour later.
Q. Did he tell you the robber was 5'3" tall?
Prosecutor: I object. There is no foundation for that question. Jones never was asked if he made that statement to the officer.

Defendant: Your honor, under Rule 613(b), I am not required to ask a witness if he made the inconsistent statement. I can offer evidence of it so long as the witness is available to explain or deny the statement. Jones is available. The prosecutor can call him.

Judge: That might be what 613(b) says, but Rule 611(a) allows me to control the way witnesses are questioned. I think Jones should have been asked if he made the statement before you asked the officer. Objection sustained.

Commentary: Judges differ. FRE 613(b) is a change from the common law approach, and some judges don't like it. This lawyer should have learned the judge's view on the need to first confront the witness with the prior inconsistent statement. Here, the cross-examiner should ask leave to recall Jones, either to reopen the cross-examination or as a witness in the defense case, where he can be impeached under FRE 607.

Example 2:

This is a personal injury case. An eyewitness has testified, and is now being cross-examined:

Q. (By defendant's lawyer) Ms. Hogan, you say you saw the collision when it happened?
A. That's right.
Q. You actually saw the two cars hit?
A. Yes.
Q. Right after the crash, you talked to a police officer?
A. Yes.
Q. The officer was taking notes as you spoke?
A. It looked like it, but I couldn't see what he was writing.
Q. I'm showing you what has already been marked as Exhibit No. 7, the police report. Doesn't it say in that report that . . .
Plaintiff: Objection, your honor. That's not the witness's report.
Judge: Sustained.
Q. Didn't you tell the police officer that you heard the crash, and then looked up?
Plaintiff: Objection.
Judge: Overruled.
A. I don't remember saying that to him.

Commentary: The witness cannot be directly impeached using the report because it is not this witness's statement. However, the witness did speak to the officer, so she properly can be impeached with her prior oral statement to the officer. (Only the police officer can be directly impeached with his report, since he wrote it.) This is a common mistake. Witnesses can be impeached only by their own prior statements, not by someone else's statements. Here, since the witness did not remember making the statement, defense counsel must offer evidence the statement was made.

Example 3:

This is a personal injury case. An eyewitness has testified and is now being cross-examined:

Q. (By plaintiff's lawyer) Mr. Clark, you say you were about 20 feet from the intersection when the two cars crashed?
A. Yes.
Q. Mr. Clark, you remember testifying at your deposition?
A. Yes.
Q. That's when you were in my office and you answered questions under oath?
A. Yes.
Q. Didn't you say during your deposition that you were too far away to really see the collision?
Defendant: Objection, your honor. Counsel is paraphrasing.
Judge: Sustained. Please read the answer verbatim.
Q. Weren't you asked "How far were you from the crash when it happened?" and didn't you answer "I was too far away to see it clearly?"
A. I don't remember saying that.
Q. Let me show you what previously has been marked as Exhibit No. 2. That's a copy of the questions asked, and the answers you gave, during your deposition?
A. Yes.
Q. Page 34, counsel. Weren't you asked this question: "Question. How far were you from the crash when it happened?" And didn't you give this answer: "Answer. I was too far away to see it clearly"?
Defendant: Objection, your honor. He's read only part of the answer. I insist that he read the whole answer. That's required under Rule 106.
Judge: Sustained, Counsel, please read the entire answer.
Q. Didn't you give the answer: "Answer. I was too far away to see it clearly. However, I was close enough that I could tell that the truck went through the red light"?
A. Yes.

Commentary: Paraphrasing answers, rather than reading them verbatim, and reading answers out of context are two common impeachment problems. These must be objected to promptly.

Example 4:

This is a medical malpractice case. A doctor testifies in the plaintiff's case and is cross-examined as follows:

Q. (By defendant's lawyer) Dr. Mills, you say that the plaintiff, when you first saw her in the emergency room, was complaining only of neck pain, right?
A. That's right.
Q. You actually talked to her?

A. Yes.

Q. And you wrote the emergency room report?

A. I did.

Q. Doctor, I'm showing you what has been marked as Defendant's Exhibit No. 2. That's the emergency room report?

A. Yes.

Q. You signed it at the bottom?

A. Yes.

Q. On your report, under complaints, doesn't it say . . .

Plaintiff: Objection. The report is not in evidence.

Defendant: It's the witness's signed report, your honor.

Judge: Overruled. Proceed.

Q. On your report, doesn't it say under the complaints section: "Patient complains of neck and lower back pain"?

A. I guess so.

Q. That's what it says, right?

A. Yes.

Commentary: There is no requirement that documents used to impeach be in evidence or even be admissible. Here, of course, the emergency room report is admissible as a business record of the hospital.

Example 5:

This is a criminal case. The defendant is a building inspector accused of taking a bribe. A police officer testifies as a prosecution witness. On cross-examination, the following happens:

Q. (By defendant's lawyer) Officer Barlow, you claim that when you arrested the defendant, you found $300 on him?

A. Yes.

Q. You made out an arrest report?

A. Yes.

Q. And that report should contain all the important details about what you did at the time of the arrest, isn't that right?

A. We try to summarize the important aspects of the case in the report.

Q. I'm showing you a copy of your arrest report, which has been marked Defendant's Exhibit No. 1. That's your report?

A. Yes.

Q. The report makes no mention of $300, does it?

A. It's not on this report.

Prosecutor: Objection, your honor, unless counsel also reads the pertinent parts of the inventory report.

Judge: Overruled. You can take that up on redirect.

Commentary: The "rule of completeness," found in FRE 106, only prevents unfairly reading out of context from a writing. It does not require the cross-examiner, when impeaching from one document, to read from other documents that deal with the same matter. In this example, the fact that an inventory report reflects the $300 can be brought out on redirect, but the cross-examiner is not required to bring it up when impeaching with the police report.

Example 6:

This is an aggravated assault case. The defendant testifies on direct examination that the shooting was accidental. On cross-examination, the following happens:

Q. (By prosecutor) Mr. Smith, you say the gun just went off?
A. That's what happened.
Q. The whole thing was an accident?
A. Yes.
Q. Mr. Smith, you were arrested one day after the shooting, right?
A. Yes.
Q. The police gave you the *Miranda* warnings?
A. Yes.
Q. They told you that you didn't have to talk to them, right?
A. Yes.
Q. But you did talk to them?
A. Yes, I did.
Q. In fact, you told the police that you were test-firing the gun, right?
A. Yes.
Q. But you never told the police, when you were arrested, that the gun went off accidentally, did you?
A. Well, you see, what happened was . . .
Q. Mr. Smith, my question is this: You never told the police, when you were arrested, that the gun went off accidentally, did you?
A. No, not at that time.

Commentary: Using silence to impeach a testifying defendant in a criminal case is often called a "Doyle" problem, after *Doyle v. Ohio*, 426 U.S. 610 (1976). *Doyle* and its progeny must always be researched to determine under what circumstances silence in criminal cases is properly admissible, since a mistake can easily cause a mistrial. In this example, *Doyle* does not control, since the defendant talked to the police and gave an account of how the gun went off after receiving his *Miranda* warnings.

Example 7:

This is a robbery case. During the defendant's case, a witness testifies that he was 20 feet from the cash register of a store when the robbery happened and that the defendant is not the robber. On cross-examination, the prosecutor asks the witness, "Didn't you tell the police that you were 40 feet from the cash register when the robbery happened?" The witness answers, "I don't think so." After the defense rests, the prosecution calls no witnesses in rebuttal. The following then happens:

Judge: Both sides rest?
Prosecutor: Yes, your honor.

Defendant: Yes, your honor. May we be heard on a matter after the jury takes its recess?

Judge: Yes. Let's take the lunch break a little early. Members of the jury, we'll hear the closing arguments of counsel right after lunch. [Jury is excused and leaves the courtroom.] Counsel, what did you want to raise?

Defendant: Your honor, during our case, Mr. Avery testified that he was 20 feet from the robbers at the cash register, and on cross, he denied that he said he was 40 feet away. Mr. Avery couldn't identify the defendant as the robber and is the only independent eyewitness other than the store clerk. This attempted impeachment is non-collateral, and the prosecution failed to introduce extrinsic evidence to prove he was 40 feet away at the time. We're asking that the jury be instructed that the prosecution failed to prove 40 feet and that the jury disregard it because it was unproven.

Prosecutor: This is collateral. The difference between 20 feet and 40 feet under the facts of this case is minor. I asked about it in good faith, but I'm not obligated to prove it up.

Defendant: The prosecution sure made a big deal of it when the witness was being cross-examined, your honor.

Judge: I agree that this is non-collateral. Prosecution, you should have raised the issue earlier, to get my ruling on it. I will instruct the jury to disregard any implication, brought about by the cross-examination, that the witness was 40 feet away.

Commentary: As the judge suggested, when in doubt whether unadmitted impeachment is collateral or non-collateral, the safe procedure is to ask the judge to rule on the matter before the lawyer is required to prove it up with extrinsic evidence.

3. Contradictory facts[5]

a. Law

Impeachment by contradiction occurs when a witness, usually on cross-examination, is asked to admit a fact that is inconsistent with what the witness has just testified about. For example, the witness on direct examination testifies that he was 20 feet from the collision when it happened. On cross-examination, the witness is asked to admit that he was actually 100 feet away when it happened. There is no rule governing impeachment by contradiction, but its use is firmly established through case law.

Ethical rules are important here. Model Rule 3.4(e) provides in part: "A lawyer shall not . . . allude to any matter that . . . will not be supported by admissible evidence." This means that the cross-examiner cannot suggest a

---

5. McCormick §§45, 49; Weinstein §607[05]; Mueller & Kirkpatrick §§6.43-6.48; Wigmore §§907-908, 1000-1015.

contradictory fact unless he has a good faith basis for doing so and can prove that fact when required to do so. This requirement promotes fairness to both the witness and the jury.

The contradictory fact can be raised during the witness's testimony, most commonly during cross-examination. If the witness admits the fact, the impeachment is complete, and nothing more needs to be done. If the witness denies or equivocates, the cross-examiner must prove up the contradictory fact with extrinsic evidence if the fact is non-collateral.

The contradictory fact need not be raised during the witness's testimony, however. FRE 613(b) applies only to "statements." It does not apply to impeachment with evidence of contradictory facts. See Advisory Committee's Note to FRE 613. Any competent evidence of a fact that tends to contradict or disprove a witness's testimony on a significant point is admissible without concern for confrontation. The rules of relevance, the balancing test of FRE 403, and the judge's power under FRE 611(a) control the admissibility of acts or conduct of a witness.

Contradictory facts, like prior inconsistent statements, can be either non-collateral or collateral and must be analyzed on a case-by-case basis. For example, on direct, an eyewitness says he was wearing a green shirt when the collision happened. On cross, the witness denies he was wearing a blue shirt at the time. This will be collateral, meaning that the cross-examiner cannot present extrinsic evidence of the contradictory fact. On the other hand, if on cross the witness denies that a large bush was blocking his view of the collision, this will probably be non-collateral, and the cross-examiner must present extrinsic evidence that the witness was standing behind the large bush. In the second situation, the difference between what the eyewitness said on direct and what he denied on cross is significant enough that it makes sense to require using courtroom time to hear from a prove-up witness about the large bush.

b. Practice

The principal issues are whether the cross-examination suggested a contradictory fact and whether a denial or an equivocation is collateral or non-collateral.

Example 1:

This is a personal injury case. A prosecution witness is being cross-examined, and the following happens:

Q. (By defendant's lawyer) Mr. Phelps, before you saw the crash, had you had any alcohol that day?
A. No.
Q. Were you taking any prescription medication?
A. No.
Plaintiff: Objection, your honor. May we approach?
Judge: All right. [Lawyers come to the bench.] Counsel, what's your objection?

Plaintiff: The defense is going into alcohol and drugs, and I want to know the good faith basis for these questions. I have no evidence that such things exist.

Defendant: Your honor, I'm merely asking; I'm not suggesting. That's proper.

Judge: The objection is overruled. I trust both counsel know their ethical obligations in the event a cross-examination directly suggests an impeaching matter actually exists.

Commentary: This ruling is correct. However, if the cross-examiner had asked, "You were drinking alcohol before you witnessed the collision, isn't that true?" the question would have been improper unless the cross-examiner both had a good faith factual basis to ask this suggestive question and was prepared to prove it up in the event the witness denied it.

Example 2:

This is a manslaughter case. John Smith, a prosecution witness, testifies that he was about 20 feet from the fight between the defendant and the victim when it happened. The cross-examination does not challenge this part of the testimony. In the defense case, another witness testifies as follows:

Q. (By defendant's lawyer) Mr. Kowalski, were you in the bar when the fight broke out?

A. I was.

Q. Do you know a John Smith?

A. I do.

Q. Did you see him in the bar when the fight broke out?

A. Yes.

Q. Where was he standing?

Prosecutor: Objection, your honor. This is improper.

Judge: What's wrong with it?

Prosecutor: May we come to the bench and discuss it there?

Judge: All right. [Lawyers come to the bench.]

Prosecutor: Your honor, it sounds as if the defense is using this witness to attack the testimony of Mr. Smith. Mr. Smith said he was 20 feet away from the fight. The only reason they could be asking where Mr. Smith was standing is to introduce contradictory evidence.

Judge: Defense, is that true?

Defendant: Your honor, this witness says that Mr. Smith was at the far end of the room, at least 50 feet away.

Prosecutor: They never asked Mr. Smith about this claimed 50 feet when he was testifying. They can't raise it for the first time now.

Judge: The objection is overruled. The witness may answer.

Commentary: Nothing in the Rules requires that the witness first be confronted with a contradictory fact before extrinsic evidence may be admitted, so the judge's ruling is correct. However, some judges, preferring the common law's confrontation requirement, may require that the impeaching fact first be raised while the witness is on the stand.

4. Prior convictions[6]

a. Law

Rule 609.   Impeachment by Evidence of a Criminal Conviction

(a) In General. The following rules apply to attacking a witness's character for truthfulness by evidence of a criminal conviction:

(1) for a crime that, in the convicting jurisdiction, was punishable by death or by imprisonment for more than one year, the evidence:

(A) must be admitted, subject to Rule 403, in a civil case or in a criminal case in which the witness is not a defendant; and

(B) must be admitted in a criminal case in which the witness is a defendant, if the probative value of the evidence outweighs its prejudicial effect to that defendant; and

(2) for any crime regardless of the punishment, the evidence must be admitted if the court can readily determine that establishing the elements of the crime required proving — or the witness's admitting — a dishonest act or false statement.

(b) Limit on Using the Evidence After 10 Years. This subdivision (b) applies if more than 10 years have passed since the witness's conviction or release from confinement for it, whichever is later. Evidence of the conviction is admissible only if:

(1) its probative value, supported by specific facts and circumstances, substantially outweighs its prejudicial effect; and

(2) the proponent gives an adverse party reasonable written notice of the intent to use it so that the party has a fair opportunity to contest its use.

(c) Effect of a Pardon, Annulment, or Certificate of Rehabilitation. Evidence of a conviction is not admissible if:

(1) the conviction has been the subject of a pardon, annulment, certificate of rehabilitation, or other equivalent procedure based on a finding that the person has been rehabilitated, and the person has not been convicted of a later crime punishable by death or by imprisonment for more than one year; or

(2) the conviction has been the subject of a pardon, annulment, or other equivalent procedure based on a finding of innocence.

(d) Juvenile Adjudications. Evidence of a juvenile adjudication is admissible under this rule only if:

(1) it is offered in a criminal case;

(2) the adjudication was of a witness other than the defendant;

(3) an adult's conviction for that offense would be admissible to attack the adult's credibility; and

(4) admitting the evidence is necessary to fairly determine guilt or innocence.

(e) Pendency of an Appeal. A conviction that satisfies this rule is admissible even if an appeal is pending. Evidence of the pendency is also admissible.

6. McCormick §42; Weinstein §609[01]-[13]; Mueller & Kirkpatrick §§6.29-6.39; Wigmore §§980-984.

i.   Overview of FRE 609

FRE 609 is a credibility rule. It has no other purpose. The vehicle for attacking a witness's credibility under this rule is a state or federal prior conviction. The assumption of the rule is that a witness who has violated the law has a flawed character for truth-telling. The rule requires a criminal conviction. An arrest or indictment is not admissible under this rule.

A 2006 amendment to the first sentence of FRE 609 struck the word "credibility" and replaced it with "character for truthfulness." The reason for the change was to make it clear that FRE 609 could be used for an attack on a witness's character for truthfulness only and for no other purpose. A prior conviction admitted under FRE 609 to attack the credibility of a testifying criminal defendant cannot be used to show the defendant is guilty of the crime charged. Any implication that a prior conviction admitted under FRE 609 can be used to show the defendant is not law-abiding or is the kind of person who is likely to commit a crime is a misuse of the rule.

The opponent of a conviction admitted under FRE 609 is entitled, on request, to a limiting instruction under FRE 105. Some courts have held that the trial judge always must give the limiting instruction, requested or not, when the witness is a defendant in a criminal case. That is because the risk of misuse of the evidence is grave.

When the limiting instruction is given, the jury is told that the only purpose of the prior conviction is to determine the credibility of the witness. If the witness is the defendant in a criminal case, the jury also is told that the prior conviction cannot be considered as evidence of guilt of the crime charged. Whether juries are capable of following a limiting instruction concerning a prior conviction has been the subject of intense debate, although reviewing courts seem to have little difficulty assuming the jury will follow the instruction. Social science research has studied the difficulties jurors have in disregarding or limiting the use of certain evidence, including a defendant's prior convictions. (See "Understanding the Limits of Limiting Instructions," Lieberman and Arndt, 6 Psychol. Pub. Pol'y & L. 677, September 2000.)

FRE 609 applies only when a conviction is being offered to prove a witness's untruthful character. There may be other valid reasons for offering proof of a prior conviction, reasons having nothing to do with FRE 609. For example, a prior conviction may be admissible under FRE 405(b) to prove an element of a claim, charge, or defense, as when a drug sale conviction is offered to prove predisposition to sell drugs in order to rebut a claim of entrapment. A prior conviction can be used to contradict a fact assertion of a witness, as when a marijuana possession conviction is offered to contradict the testimony of a witness that he has never seen marijuana. A prior conviction can be used under FRE 608(b) to impeach a character witness, as when a character witness who testifies that the defendant has a good character for peacefulness is cross-examined with the defendant's prior conviction for aggravated assault. A prior conviction can be used to show bias, interest, or motive, as when a witness is shown to be on juvenile probation and to have an expectation of leniency. Such uses may be proper under particular circumstances, but they do not involve FRE 609.

ii. The "general rule" of FRE 609(a)

The "general rule" of FRE 609(a) contains two separate categories of crimes that may be used to impeach a witness. Each applies to any witness in any civil or criminal case.

(a) Impeachment with felonies.   FRE 609(a)(1) refers to crimes punishable by death or imprisonment in excess of one year under the law of the jurisdiction where the witness was convicted. These crimes are commonly called felonies. "Punishable" means the punishment that might have been imposed, not the sentence that was actually imposed.

1. Balancing test for defendants who testify in criminal cases. Two different balancing tests are contained in this first category. If the witness is a defendant in a criminal case, the trial judge must determine whether "the probative value of the evidence outweighs its prejudicial effect to that defendant." The prosecution has the burden of establishing admissibility.

This special balancing test for the prior convictions of an accused is a recognition that "in virtually every case in which prior convictions are used to impeach the testifying defendant, the defendant faces a unique risk of prejudice — i.e., the danger that convictions that would be excluded under Fed. R. Evid. 402 will be misused by a jury as propensity evidence despite their introduction solely for impeachment purposes." Advisory Committee's Note to Amended Rule 609(a).

The decisions have developed a number of factors that can be considered by the trial judge when conducting the special balancing test for a defendant-witness.

a. The nature of the prior crime. The crime weighs more heavily on the probative value side of the scale when it has something to do with truth-telling. Grand theft is more probative than voluntary manslaughter. Heroin distribution or sale is more probative than heroin use or possession. Burglary is more probative than aggravated assault.

b. The age of the prior crime. The older the crime is, the less probative it is, even within the 10-year time limit established by FRE 609(b). A nine-year-old conviction does not weigh as heavily on the probative value side of the scale as a two-year-old conviction. That assumes, of course, that the defendant has not in the meantime been convicted of any other crime. The trial judge will look to a defendant's entire record to determine whether the older conviction was an isolated instance in the defendant's life. Demonstrated rehabilitation tips the prejudicial effect side of the scale away from admissibility. A lengthy criminal record, either before or after the conviction at issue, will lighten the prejudicial effect side of the scale.

c. The similarity between the prior crime and the crime for which the defendant is now charged. This factor bears the most potential for destruction of the defendant as a credible witness. If the prior conviction was for the same charge as the one for which the defendant is now on trial, or if they are very similar, it would be logical for the jury to infer that since he did it before, he must have done it again, an improper inference. FRE 609 cannot be used to prove or argue an accused's propensity to commit a crime, unless the conviction was admitted under FRE 413-415.

It would take a massive leap of faith to believe a limiting instruction would dissipate the unfair prejudice of a bank robbery conviction if the defendant were on trial for bank robbery. Yet when it appears that the trial judge has balanced relevant factors in exercising discretion, reviewing courts rarely find error when a similar or identical conviction is used. For example, decisions have affirmed the use of a robbery conviction in a bank robbery case and a possession of cocaine for sale conviction in a cocaine distribution case to attack credibility. Still, the unfair prejudice argument against use of similar or identical convictions, based on an understanding of human experience, has at least some weight when made to a trial judge. There is no way to know how often trial judges are persuaded to prohibit the use of prior convictions to attack a defendant's character for truthfulness. Such rulings do not become matters for appellate court consideration.

d. The importance of the defendant's testimony. This factor cuts both ways. Judges who believe a prior conviction will deter a defendant from testifying about a central issue in the case will use this factor as a reason to bar the conviction. Other judges believe that the more important the defendant's testimony is, the more it is necessary that the jury not be misled to believe he has lived a pure and blameless life.

e. The centrality of the credibility issue. This factor is similar to the previous one. It, too, cuts both ways. When the case turns on a credibility call between a defendant and a prosecution witness, one judge might conclude the defendant should be encouraged to testify, while another might determine this defendant's testimony should be tested by the prior conviction. Presumably any time a defendant denies committing a crime, his credibility becomes a central issue.

f. The defendant's age, occupation, family, and other life circumstances. When exercising their broad and virtually unchallengeable discretion, trial judges at times will look to the kind of person on trial. Other things being equal, a younger man who is employed and has a family will be more likely to escape conviction impeachment than somebody seen as less deserving.

No particular weight can be given to any one of these factors. Reviewing courts give trial judges extremely broad discretion in this area, insisting only that a judge recognize he does have discretion. No actual on-the-record weighing process is required by the decisions.

To succeed on an objection, the opponent of the conviction will have to overcome the trial judge's concern that the jury will be seriously misled if a defendant with a criminal record is made to appear as if he has a flawless history.

When the prior crime is something other than an unplanned act of violence, such as involuntary manslaughter, it must be given some probative value. Weighed against that probative value is the prejudicial effect of a jury's potential misuse of the conviction — as improper propensity or character evidence — or the risk of a jury's overvaluing the conviction on the issue of credibility.

When a conviction is admitted under FRE 609 the proof should be limited to the crime, date, place of conviction, and the length of confinement. It should not include details of the crime itself unless the witness's explanations or denials open the door to information about the offense and reasons why the defendant may have pleaded guilty to it.

2. The FRE 403 balancing test. The other balancing test contained in FRE 609(a)(1) applies to all witnesses in civil and criminal trials other than a criminal defendant. This is the FRE 403 balancing test. Here, the trial judge determines whether the unfair prejudice of allowing the conviction *substantially* outweighs its probative value.

When the witness is someone other than a criminal defendant, the rule makes no distinction between civil and criminal cases, nor does it matter whether the witness is called by the plaintiff or the defendant, or by the prosecution or the defense.

In practice, trial judges are reluctant to allow conviction impeachment in civil cases unless the crime relates directly to truth-telling. Criminal conviction evidence is seen as a potential diversion of the jury's attention from the issues in most civil cases unless the case contains a criminal character, such as civil fraud or violation of trust.

In criminal trials, many judges realize that impeaching a defense witness with a criminal conviction can unfairly prejudice the defendant, especially when the witness bears a special relationship to the defendant. In those instances, the impeachment is likely to have a spillover effect on the defendant. On the other hand, trial judges generally recognize the low probability that prior conviction impeachment of a prosecution witness will be unfairly prejudicial.

(b) Impeachment with crimes of dishonesty or false statement.   FRE 609(a)(2) establishes a second category of criminal convictions usable to impeach a witness. Conviction impeachment is required under this category if the crime involved dishonesty or false statement, regardless of the punishment, felony or misdemeanor. The trial judge has no discretion.

No balancing test is conducted for admission of convictions in this second category. None is needed because the nature of the crime establishes the witness's flawed character for truth-telling.

The 2006 amendment to FRE 609(a)(2) was directed at decisions that allowed impeachment under the dishonesty or false statement section that were, as the Advisory Committee's Note observes, "unduly broad." That is, the courts, with few exceptions, have agreed that crimes of violence do not qualify as crimes of dishonesty or false statement, while crimes of deception, such as counterfeiting and filing false tax returns, do. There has been no disagreement with the Congressional Conference Report on the Federal Rules of Evidence, which says that FRE 609(a)(2) "means crimes such as perjury or subornation of perjury, false statement, criminal fraud, embezzlement, or false pretense, or any other offense in the nature of *crimen falsi*, the commission of which involves some element of deceit, untruthfulness, or falsification bearing on the accused's propensity to testify truthfully."

Until 2006, the gray area in FRE 609(a)(2) concerned use of convictions for robbery, burglary, theft, and narcotics offenses to attack a defendant's character for truthfulness, especially where the defendant was dishonest or made false statements while committing the crime. The amendment was intended to eliminate the gray area. It "required that the proponent have ready proof that the conviction required the factfinder to find, or the defendant to admit, an act of dishonesty or false statement." Advisory Committee's Note to amended FRE 609(a)(2). In most cases, the trial judge will look to the statutory elements of the crime charged in the prior conviction to determine whether it is one of dishonesty or false statement. In those few cases where the statute is unclear, the trial judge may look to the charging instrument or the jury instructions to determine the nature of the prior conviction.

iii.   The 10-year rule of FRE 609(b)

FRE 609(b) establishes a barrier to using convictions that are more than 10 years old. The time frame for measuring the 10-year limit begins with the date of conviction or the date of release from confinement, whichever is later, and runs to the day the witness takes the stand. "Confinement" is construed strictly and does not include time spent on parole or probation.

The 10-year barrier is not impenetrable, but the rule does make it difficult to overcome. First, the trial judge who allows the remote conviction must make a finding on the record of the facts and circumstances he considered.

Second, the judge must find that the probative value of the conviction "supported by specific facts and circumstances substantially outweighs its prejudicial effect." This reverses the FRE 403 test used for convictions less than 10 years old. This more stringent balancing test applies to all witnesses, including the criminal defendant. It applies to all convictions, both felonies under FRE 609(a)(1) and convictions involving dishonesty and false statement under FRE 609(a)(2).

Third, the proponent of the evidence must give his opponent reasonable written notice of intent to use the evidence to allow a fair opportunity to contest it.

In practice, trial judges are not generally in favor of attempts to exceed the 10-year limit, but it does happen. When the appropriate findings are made, reviewing courts rarely intervene.

iv.   Pardons, juvenile convictions, and appeals

FRE 609(c) bars the use of convictions that have been the subject of pardons, annulments, or certificates of rehabilitation when they are based on rehabilitation of the witness and the witness has not been convicted of a later felony, or a finding of innocence. A pardon that simply restores the witness's civil rights is not, standing alone, enough to bar the conviction.

FRE 609(d) makes evidence of a juvenile conviction generally not admissible, but in a criminal case, the trial judge may admit it for a witness other than the accused if the conviction would be admissible to attack the credibility of an adult and the judge is satisfied that admission is necessary for a fair determination of the issue of guilt or innocence. This rule should not be confused with the constitutional right of an accused to cross-examine a juvenile about his criminal probation for the purpose of developing the witness's bias. See *Davis v. Alaska*, 415 U.S. 308 (1974).

FRE 609(e) provides that a witness may be impeached with a conviction that is on appeal, but the party offering the witness may show that the appeal is pending.

v.   The FRE 104(a) hearing

Whether a conviction is permitted under FRE 609 is a question that should be presented as early as possible under FRE 104(a), preferably before the trial begins. Early consideration of a motion in limine gives the trial judge an opportunity to carefully weigh the issue, while an early ruling will help frame trial strategy for the parties, particularly aiding the decision of whether to call the defendant as a witness. It should be noted, however, that the early ruling is advisory only and can be changed during the trial.

If the judge makes a final ruling at trial that the conviction is admissible, the party calling the witness may elicit the conviction on direct examination to obviate the impact of the jury first hearing about it on cross-examination. But the proponent of the witness then waives the right to claim on appeal that the trial judge was in error when he allowed the conviction. *Ohler v. United States*, 529 U.S. 753 (2000).

If the trial judge rules that evidence of the conviction will be allowed, the defendant cannot claim error on appeal unless he actually testifies and is impeached. *Luce v. United States*, 469 U.S. 38 (1984).

Proof of a prior conviction may be made by asking the witness about it or by offering a certified copy of the record of conviction in accordance with the requirements of FRE 902(4).

Ordinarily the evidence is confined to the name of the offense, the date of conviction, and the sentence received. A few courts allow a witness to go further, trying to mitigate his degree of guilt or the seriousness of the conviction. For example, the witness may try to explain that his robbery conviction was based on his grabbing someone's bicycle away from him. Or the witness may try to testify that "I pled guilty to that crime because I was guilty, but I am pleading not guilty to this offense because I am not guilty." If the court allows such further details or explanations, the door is opened for the cross-examiner to question the witness about other details of the offense. For example, the witness could be asked "Isn't it true that the real reason you pled guilty is because the police caught you coming out of the house with the stolen jewelry in your pocket?" Most courts, however, consider such details and explanations collateral to the trial and bar them entirely.

The trial judge does not have to rule on admissibility of the prior conviction before the witness takes the stand. Some do not, preferring to hear testimony before making any final ruling. The judge who will not rule on the question before trial should be asked to do so before the witness begins direct examination. Again, he may decide not to.

Refusal of the judge to rule puts the defendant-witness in a difficult situation. He has to weigh the risks. He can decline to testify, or he can take the stand not knowing whether the impeachment will be allowed. If the conviction is brought out on direct examination before any ruling, the defendant waives any possible error on appeal.

Some trial judges, recognizing the probable ineffectiveness of limiting instructions, have devised ways to "sanitize" the prior conviction. The goal is to reduce the prejudice created when the jury hears the name of the prior offense. In some places, this is called the "mere fact" approach. It applies only to felony offenses governed by FRE 609(a)(1), not to the dishonesty or false statement offenses of 609(a)(2).

It involves two basic steps. First, the judge conducts the required balancing test. Second, if the conviction survives, the jury is told the defendant has been convicted of a felony on a certain date in a certain place and what the sentence was. The jury is not told the name of the felony or anything else about it.

Ordinarily the mere fact approach is not used unless the defendant asks for it. Critics of the mere fact approach have two basic objections. First, the jury is left to speculate about what the felony was, perhaps making it worse than it really is. Second, some judges are skipping the balancing test step when they use this approach, allowing in convictions that otherwise would not survive an unfair prejudice analysis.

The prior conviction, if admissible to impeach, is usually raised during the witness's examination. Although nothing in FRE 609(a) requires that the prior conviction be raised while the witness is testifying, this is the common procedure. If the witness admits the prior conviction, the impeachment is complete, and nothing further is required (although nothing in FRE 609(a) prevents the introduction of a record of the prior conviction because the witness has already admitted it). If the witness denies or equivocates, the prior conviction must be proved up with extrinsic evidence. This is because prior convictions as a category are deemed non-collateral. The usual way of proving up the fact of a conviction is to introduce a certified copy of the record of conviction or judgment order and, if necessary, evidence that the witness is the same person as named in that record or order.

b.   Practice

Prior convictions are particularly important in criminal cases, where the use of this impeachment method is more common. The admissibility of prior convictions to impeach is usually handled in a motion in limine, since the parties need to know what will be admissible before completing their trial strategy. If the judge rules that the impeachment is admissible, the party planning to call that witness can decide not to call the witness during trial or to bring out the fact of the prior conviction during the direct examination. If he brings out the prior conviction during direct examination, he cannot claim on appeal that the conviction was inadmissible under FRE 609. *Ohler v. United States*, 529 U.S. 753 (2000).

Example 1:

The defendant is charged with armed robbery of a postal carrier. Before trial, the defense moves to bar the use of the defendant's prior convictions to impeach the defendant if he elects to testify during the trial. At the hearing, the following happens:

Defendant: Your honor, this is our motion to preclude the use of the defendant's prior convictions under Rule 609. The defendant has two prior convictions in the past 10 years: a prior conviction for attempted robbery nine years ago and a prior conviction for assault with a deadly weapon three years ago. The attempted robbery should be excluded under the balancing test of Rule 609. This conviction occurred over nine years ago, so its probative value on credibility is low, but its prejudicial effect is substantial, since it is for the same crime for which he is presently on trial. There is a grave danger the jury will use this conviction as proof of recidivism, regardless of any limiting instruction. The assault with a deadly weapon should also be excluded, but for a different reason. By its very nature, an assault conviction has little, if anything, to do with credibility, but it also carries the substantial danger the jury will misuse this conviction as proof of bad character. Its probative value is minimal, but its prejudicial impact is substantial. Both should be excluded.

Judge: Prosecution?

Prosecutor: Both of these prior convictions are felonies within 10 years. To bar these convictions to impeach means the defendant can get on the stand and misrepresent himself as an ordinary citizen, when in fact he's a twice-convicted felon. The fact

> remains that these convictions have a great deal to do with credibility.
>
> *Judge:* I will admit, for impeachment purposes, the assault with a deadly weapon. It's recent, and there's no substantial danger the jury will misuse it after being given a limiting instruction. The attempted robbery I'm keeping out. It's almost 10 years old, and there's a much greater danger the jury will use it for an improper inference.
>
> *Defendant:* Your honor, letting in either prior conviction may well keep my client from testifying during trial.
>
> *Judge:* Counsel, that's a decision you and your client will have to make. I've made my ruling.

Commentary: Case law gives a great deal of deference to the trial judge in making the analysis required by FRE 609. Most judges let in most prior felonies to impeach, even if the witness is the defendant. However, when a defendant has multiple prior convictions, many judges will bar some of the prior convictions to impeach and permit only the most probative one.

Example 2:

> This is a personal injury case. The plaintiff moves in limine to preclude the prior conviction of a plaintiff witness. At a hearing on the motion, the following happens:

> *Judge:* Plaintiff, it's your motion to preclude.
>
> *Plaintiff:* Yes, your honor. Michael Mum is one of our witnesses whom we may call in our case-in-chief. He has a prior conviction, which he received when he was a freshman in college. The conviction, for misdemeanor theft, involved using his own checking account and writing a check when the account had insufficient funds to cover the check. When he didn't immediately cover the overdraft, the bank sent the matter to the city prosecutor's office. He pleaded guilty to misdemeanor theft and was sentenced to two years' probation, with the condition that the conviction would be expunged upon successful completion of the probation period. This all happened one year ago, and he has one year to go on the probation.
>
> *Defendant:* It's a misdemeanor theft, which involves dishonesty, and it happened only one year ago. There's no balancing test that applies.
>
> *Judge:* Aren't my hands tied, counsel?
>
> *Plaintiff:* Our position is that when a person overdraws his checking account, that's not a dishonest act in the sense of Rule 609. This isn't a theft involving fraud or some morally reprehensible conduct. He overdrew his account. In any event, it should be kept out on Rule 403 grounds.
>
> *Judge:* The motion is denied.

Commentary: The cases are not uniform on the question of whether misdemeanor thefts are admissible to impeach under FRE 609. Most courts, for instance, exclude ordinary shoplifting offenses. If the misdemeanor involved dishonesty or false statement, the judge must allow it.

Example 3:

The defendant is charged with fraudulently concealing assets in a bankruptcy proceeding. The defendant moves in limine to preclude the prosecution from using a prior conviction to impeach. At the hearing, the following happens:

Defendant: Your honor, the defendant's prior conviction, for receiving stolen property, was entered 12 years ago. He was put on one-year probation, so the conviction is over 10 years old. The prosecution recently notified us that they intend to use that prior conviction to impeach if the defendant testifies during the trial. Under Rule 609(b), that prior conviction is not admissible unless the court determines that the probative value of the conviction substantially exceeds its prejudicial effect. Our position is that a conviction so long ago has little probative value on the issue of credibility, but its prejudicial effect, particularly because the conviction is for similar conduct as the present charge, is very high. Your honor should exclude it.

Prosecutor: The prior conviction was for knowingly receiving stolen property, which is just the kind of conviction that has high probative value on truthfulness. In addition, this case is essentially a swearing contest between Mr. Richardson, our principal witness, and the defendant. This makes it all the more important that the jury get all the information it needs to assess the credibility of the witnesses it will hear.

Judge: The motion is granted. I am not persuaded that this conviction's probative value on the limited issue of credibility substantially outweighs the danger that the jury will misuse the conviction to infer recidivism, even if I give a limiting instruction. I'm keeping it out.

Commentary: The judge does not have to rule in advance. He can reserve ruling until the matter comes up during the trial.

5.   Character for untruthfulness[7]

a.   Law

Rule 608.   A Witness's Character for Truthfulness or Untruthfulness

(a) **Reputation or Opinion Evidence.** A witness's credibility may be attacked or supported by testimony about the witness's reputation for having a character for truthfulness or untruthfulness, or by testimony in

---

7. McCormick §43; Weinstein §608[01]-[04]; Mueller & Kirkpatrick §§6.23-6.28; Wigmore §§920-930.

the form of an opinion about that character. But evidence of truthful character is admissible only after the witness's character for truthfulness has been attacked.

(b) Specific Instances of Conduct. Except for a criminal conviction under Rule 609, extrinsic evidence is not admissible to prove specific instances of a witness's conduct in order to attack or support the witness's character for truthfulness. But the court may, on cross-examination, allow them to be inquired into if they are probative of the character for truthfulness or untruthfulness of:

(1) the witness; or

(2) another witness whose character the witness being cross-examined has testified about.

By testifying on another matter, a witness does not waive any privilege against self-incrimination for testimony that relates only to the witness's character for truthfulness.

FRE 608 is a rule about character. The only character traits it is concerned with are truthfulness and untruthfulness. It does not apply when evidence is being offered for some proper purpose other than proving truthful or untruthful character.

The rule has two parts. Section (a) is a direct examination rule and describes when opinion or reputation evidence of truthful or untruthful character may be admitted. Section (b) is a cross-examination rule and described when specific instances of conduct probative of truthfulness or untruthfulness can be inquired into during cross-examination.

i.   Character witness testimony about the truth-telling character of a fact witness

Any witness who takes the stand to testify to a fact of consequence in a civil or criminal case is open to an attack on his character for telling the truth. This includes the defendant in a criminal case. The purpose of the attack is to prove that the fact witness is acting in conformity with that character and is more likely to be testifying untruthfully. FRE 608(a) provides two ways to attack the fact witness's character for truthfulness during the direct examination of a character witness.

First, a character witness may testify to the fact witness's negative general reputation in a particular community for truthfulness, or, as some lawyers ask, "for truth and veracity." The community can be the neighborhood where the fact witness lives, the place where he works, the school he attends, or any environment where he spends an appreciable amount of time. The reputation testimony must relate to the time of trial, or shortly before it. It must be based on people talking about the general reputation, or not talking about it when negative comments would have been made if there was a reason for them.

A reputation character witness should be asked, "Have you heard the reputation of Mr. _____ in this community for truthfulness?" on direct examination. The character witness may not be asked if he believes the fact witness's trial testimony, but some courts permit him to be asked "Would you believe him under oath?"

Second, a character witness may be asked his personal opinion of the fact witness's character for telling the truth. The opinion must be based on the character witness's personal knowledge of the fact witness. That knowledge may be acquired by personal contact in any definable sphere of the fact witness's life. The opinion must relate to the time of trial, or shortly before it. A personal opinion character witness should be asked "Do you have an opinion concerning whether Mr. _____ is a truthful person?" The character witness may not be asked if he believes the fact witness's trial testimony.

In the rare case where character for truth-telling may be an essential element of a charge, claim, or defense, a party is authorized by FRE 405(b) to present evidence of his good character for truth-telling. For example, in a defamation case where the plaintiff sues a defendant who called him a "known liar," and the defense is truth, the plaintiff's character for untruthfulness is an essential element of the defense; it may be proved by evidence of the plaintiff's reputation in a definable community, by a witness's opinion of that character for truthfulness, or by evidence of relevant specific instances of conduct.

In all other cases, evidence of a witness's good character for truthfulness may not be admitted unless it first has been attacked. The attack evidence that opens the door to good truth-telling character can come in the form of reputation, opinion, or other evidence. It may consist of impeachment by prior conviction; specific conduct probative of untruthfulness; questions showing bias, interest, or motive; a prior inconsistent statement that implies the witness is lying, rather than merely mistaken; or any other vigorous assault on the witness's credibility the trial judge believes fairly warrants a response.

Once the door is open, evidence of good character for truthfulness can be presented only by general reputation or opinion testimony. Evidence of specific instances of conduct are not allowed during direct examination of the character witness. The witness may not offer examples of the fact witness's conduct that might support the reputation or opinion. At times, the line between a permissible basis for an opinion and improper specific instance testimony is thin. For example, where a prosecution witness was called a liar during the defense cross-examination, the prosecution was allowed to call a police officer who testified he used the witness to obtain search warrants "numerous times" and found him "extremely reliable," but FRE 608(b) was violated when the officer was allowed to say he had used the informant for 65 or 66 search warrants.

General reputation testimony, whether positive or negative, is an exception to the rule against hearsay under FRE 803(21). Opinion testimony must satisfy the personal knowledge requirement of FRE 602 and the rational basis requirement of FRE 701(a).

ii.   Cross-examination of a truth-telling character witness

The scope of cross-examination of a character witness is the same as it is for other witnesses. Under FRE 611(b), cross-examination is limited to the subject matter brought out on direct and to matters affecting the credibility of the character witness. For example, in a murder case where the witness testifies to the defendant's good character for peacefulness, many, but not all, judges would find it beyond the scope for the character witness to be asked, "You were not in the tavern when the killing took place, were you?"

Cross-examination of the character witness must be directed, at least in appearance, to the credibility of that witness, not to that of the fact witness he is testifying about.

When a character witness testifies to a fact witness's general reputation for truthfulness or untruthfulness, he can be asked for the names of people who spoke about the reputation, when the discussions took place, and where they took place. Those questions and others like them test the foundation for the witness's reputation testimony.

When a character witness testifies to his opinion about the fact witness's truthfulness or untruthfulness, he may be cross-examined about how he acquired his knowledge, the extent of that knowledge, and his relationship with the fact witness.

FRE 608(b) permits two methods for injecting specific instances of conduct into cross-examination of a character witness. In either, extrinsic evidence of the conduct inquired about may not be introduced. That is, that conduct may not be "proved up." It is deemed to be collateral. The cross-examiner is bound by the answer he gets. For that reason, specific instances of conduct questions must be asked in good faith. The examiner must be ready to respond to a judge's inquiry about factual support for the questions. The rule does not address the manner in which a showing is to be made, but obviously it must be sufficient to convince the judge the questions are grounded in fact.

First, the character witness may be cross-examined about specific instances of *his own* conduct, so long as the questions are relevant to his character for truth-telling. For example, the character witness may be asked, "One year ago, didn't you attempt to cash a forged check?" The question is a permissible direct attack on the character witness's credibility. This method is discussed further in the next section.

Second, the character witness may be cross-examined about specific instances of the fact witness's untruthful conduct. These questions are asked for the sole purpose of attacking the credibility of the character witness. For example, when a lawyer-witness testifies to the good general reputation for veracity and integrity of Witten, the lawyer-defendant, the witness may be asked: "Have you heard that Mr. Witten was reprimanded by Judge Thomas last November for unprofessional conduct?" The question relates to the character witness's credibility whether the answer is "yes" or "no." Several courts have held that an FRE 608(b) question containing a factual attack on a witness's truth-telling character cannot include the consequences of those facts. That is, the witness being "fired," "convicted," "expelled," or "disciplined" for his conduct should not be part of the question.

When a character witness testifies to the defendant's good reputation for truth-telling, he may be asked on cross-examination about events, reports, arrests, and convictions relevant to the defendant's truth-telling character. For example, the question "Have you heard the defendant was arrested for obtaining money by false pretenses five years ago?" may be asked the reputation witness, since the arrest is an event people would normally comment on and speculate about. See *Michelson v. United States*, 335 U.S. 469 (1948). Likewise, in a civil insider trading case, the defendant's character witnesses may be asked whether they are aware of prior fraud suits against the defendant. If the character witnesses did not know or hear about these events, the questions attack the depth of their knowledge about the defendant. If they knew and heard about the events, but still think the defendant has a good truth-telling character, the objectivity of the character witnesses is called into question.

The boundaries of the playing field are not as clear when the character witness testifies to *his opinion* of the fact witness's truth-telling character. Some judges do not allow cross-examination questions about the character witness's knowledge of reports and arrests related to the fact witness's truth-telling, on the theory that an arrest, standing alone, has nothing to do with credibility. It would seem, however, the same rationale for allowing the questions to reputation character witnesses should apply—a test of the witness's extent of knowledge and his objectivity.

When a character witness testifies, by general reputation or opinion, to the fact witness's *bad* character for truth-telling, the cross-examiner may ask about the witness's knowledge of specific events that show good truth-telling character. For example, the character witness can be asked "Are you aware the State Bar Association last year awarded Mr. _____ a gold medal for truth and integrity?" It does not happen very often, but FRE 608(b) permits it.

Some trial judges maintain that a general reputation witness may be asked only "Have you heard . . . ?" questions, while an opinion witness may be asked only "Do you know . . . ?" questions, when the cross-examiner inquires into specific instances of conduct. But most modern reported opinions allow the crossover questions, agreeing with the Advisory Committee's observation that "these distinctions are of slight if any practical significance." Advisory Committee's Note to FRE 405.

Whenever cross-examination of a character witness inquires into specific instances of conduct by the fact witness, there is a critical need for a careful limiting instruction. The jury should be told the evidence is relevant only to its evaluation of the weight and credibility of the character witness. Whether the limiting instruction will be effective, given the risk of trial by innuendo, is something the trial judge determines under the wide discretion granted by FRE 403. Ultimately, rules of basic fairness will guide the trial judge's decision.

One other limitation is built into FRE 608(b). When a specific instance question relates only to credibility, the witness, whether the accused or anybody else, does not waive his privilege against self-incrimination.

b.   Practice

Character evidence to prove truthfulness or untruthfulness of a fact witness is seldom used at trial because of the broad scope of FRE 608(b). When used, it is more common in criminal cases. The difficult recurring issue is whether the cross-examination of a fact witness has been sufficiently hard that it suggests the witness is an untruthful person, thereby triggering the admissibility of good character for truthfulness evidence. This most frequently arises when the defendant in a criminal case is cross-examined.

Example:

The defendant is charged with robbery. The defendant testifies, and on cross-examination, the following happens:

Q. (By prosecutor) Mr. Bradley, you're a convicted felon, aren't you?
A. Well, I pleaded guilty once to a burglary charge.
Q. That makes you a convicted felon, doesn't it?
A. I guess so.
Q. Today you claim you were at your girlfriend's house when the robbery happened, right?

A. That's where I was.

Q. But that's not what you told the police when you were arrested, is it?

A. Well, see, what happened was . . .

Q. That's not what you told the police, is it?

A. No.

Q. In fact, you told the police you were at your mother's house, right?

A. Yes.

Q. And you never told the police you were at your girlfriend's house, did you?

A. No.

Q. And you can't be in two places at the same time, can you?

A. I guess not.

Prosecutor: No further questions, your honor.

Defendant: No redirect, your honor.

Judge: The witness is excused. Defense, call your next witness.

Defendant: We call Arthur Jackson. [Witness takes the stand and is sworn.]

Q. (By defendant's lawyer) Mr. Jackson, do you know the defendant, David Bradley?

A. Yes.

Q. How long have you known him?

A. Almost 10 years.

Q. Under what circumstances?

A. He's a neighbor, and I've worked with him for several years.

Q. Over those years, have you formed an opinion about whether he is a truthful person?

Prosecutor: Objection, your honor. We haven't called any character witnesses to attack the defendant's character for truthfulness. This is improper rehabilitation.

Defendant: They attacked him on cross, your honor. We're then entitled to rehabilitate under Rule 608.

Judge: That's right. The objection is overruled. Mr. Jackson, please answer the question.

A. Yes, I have an opinion.

Q. What is your personal opinion about whether Mr. Bradley is a truthful person?

A. I consider him to be a truthful person. I've never had any reason to think otherwise.

6.   Conduct probative of untruthfulness[8]

a.   *Law*

Rule 608.   A Witness's Character for Truthfulness or Untruthfulness

(b) Specific Instances of Conduct. Except for a criminal conviction under Rule 609, extrinsic evidence is not admissible to prove specific

---

8. McCormick §41; Weinstein §608[05]-[06]; Mueller & Kirkpatrick §§6.24-6.28; Wigmore §§977-988.

instances of a witness's conduct in order to attack or support the witness's character for truthfulness. But the court may, on cross-examination, allow them to be inquired into if they are probative of the character for truthfulness or untruthfulness of:

(1) the witness; or

(2) another witness whose character the witness being cross-examined has testified about.

By testifying on another matter, a witness does not waive any privilege against self-incrimination for testimony that relates only to the witness's character for truthfulness.

FRE 608(b) is a cross-examination rule. It describes when and about whom specific instances of conduct may be inquired into during cross-examination, and it flatly prohibits proof of specific instances of conduct by extrinsic evidence. It applies to the cross-examination of a character witness, discussed in the previous section, and to the cross-examination of a fact witness, including a party, which is discussed next.

FRE 608(b) permits cross-examining any witness about specific instances of conduct that tend to prove the witness's untruthfulness. Trial lawyers sometimes refer to this type of impeachment as "prior bad acts" (although this label confuses this evidence with the "other acts" rule of FRE 404(b)). This technique marks a departure from the common law and created a minefield for the unwary lawyer.

For example, a witness is asked on cross, "Didn't you submit a loan application to the First National Bank last year in which you falsely stated you had no current debts?" This is a proper question, since it raises facts that suggest a lack of truthfulness. On the other hand, asking a witness "Didn't you assault a patron in O'Malley's Pub last year?" is improper, since this conduct is not probative of untruthfulness.

When used to attack a witness's character for truthfulness, specific instances of conduct questions must be probative of untruthfulness, not of any other character trait. Conduct questions involving dishonesty or false statement are probative of untruthfulness. These questions should be directed to the witness's conduct, not to the consequences of the conduct, such as an arrest or a conviction resulting from the witness's acts. While a reputation character witness may be asked about a defendant's arrests because the questions test knowledge of that reputation, those arrests have no relevance to credibility when posed to the defendant on cross-examination. See *Michelson v. United States*, 335 U.S. 469 (1948). There is no requirement that the misconduct be definable as a crime. For example, asking "Isn't it true that on February 14 of last year you used a false identification card to cash a forged check?" is a proper question. Asking whether the witness was arrested for that conduct is improper. If there was a conviction, the question should be asked under FRE 609(a)(2).

There is no time limit in FRE 608(b) on the age of a specific act probative of truthfulness. However, an act that happened many years ago is unlikely to survive an FRE 403 analysis. Many judges use the presumptive 10-year-old bar applicable to prior convictions under FRE 609(b) and apply its logic to FRE 608(b).

The list of potential specific instances of misconduct subjects is bound only by human ingenuity: for example, using a false name, filing a false tax return, committing forgery, lying or cheating on a school examination, turning back odometers for profit, killing a witness, passing bad checks, receiving stolen property, embezzling funds from an employer, falsifying corporate books, and, if an attorney, being subjected to bar discipline for unethical conduct.

Among subjects that have not been allowed are using drugs, receiving a less than honorable military discharge for failure to wear a uniform, holding foster children unlawfully, and attempting to commit murder. The courts are divided on the propriety of asking about some other topics, such as failing to file tax returns.

The questions must relate to character for truthfulness, not to some other matter, although there might be some spillover from proper questions. For example, an accomplice witness for the prosecution may be cross-examined about threats of physical harm he made to witnesses in another case to influence their testimony. The questions bear on the witness's untruthful character even though they also establish his tendency toward violence. The most commonly held view is that FRE 608(b) encompasses questions aimed at behavior that seeks personal advantage from others in violation of their rights. Under this view, conduct that at first appears more dishonest than false may be inquired into on cross-examination.

Once the question is asked, the cross-examiner is bound by the answer. All FRE 608(b) questions are considered collateral, since their only purpose is to attack a witness's credibility. In trial lawyers' language, this means that the cross-examiner must "take the witness's answer." No extrinsic proof of matters contained in the questions is allowed.

The potential for unfair prejudice is obvious. Serious accusations can hang over the trial, even if denied by the witness. Collateral matters can prove too much and deter the jury from consideration of the substantive issues in the case.

There are two safeguards. First, the cross-examiner must have a good faith basis for asking the question. The basis does not have to be admissible evidence, but it must be something that persuades the trial judge the question is proper, such as an affidavit, a reliable record, or a potential live witness. Careful judges require the cross-examiner to give advance notice of the intent to ask such misconduct questions.

The second safeguard is FRE 403. Considerations of unfair prejudice, weighed against the probative value of the question, are particularly telling in this area of inquiry. The trial judge will consider such matters as the remoteness of the act, its potential impact on the jury, the importance of the witness's testimony, whether the witness should be protected from harassment or undue embarrassment, and whether the conduct directly relates to truth-telling. It is no accident that the rule provides that specific instances of conduct are inquired into on cross-examination "in the discretion of the court."

FRE 608(b) applies only to proof of a witness's character for telling the truth. When a fact has some other relevant purpose, the rule does not apply. Any competent evidence that tends to contradict a witness on a fact of consequence in the case is admissible.

For example, in a drug case involving an entrapment defense, the informant testifies that he saw the defendant engage in drug sales when they worked together in a factory in 2010. The defendant offers records proving they did not work together in 2010. The extrinsic evidence prohibition of FRE 608(b) does not bar admission because the records disprove a specific fact material to the defendant's defense. In a drug prosecution, the defendant testifies that he never before had seen marijuana. On rebuttal, the defendant's prior marijuana possession conviction is properly admissible.

At times, the FRE 608(b) bar against use of extrinsic evidence has been construed too broadly. It has been incorrectly read to bar extrinsic evidence relating to bias, competency, factual contradiction, and inconsistent statement impeachment. For that reason, the rule was amended in 2003. Where the word "credibility" had been used, it was replaced with "character for truthfulness." The Advisory Committee Note to the current rule states: "The amendment conforms the language of the rule to its original intent, which was to impose an absolute bar on extrinsic evidence only if the *sole purpose* for offering the evidence was to prove the witness' character for veracity." (The emphasis is ours.) It is clear, then, that admissibility of extrinsic evidence for any purpose not related entirely to FRE 608(b) is governed by FRE 402 and 403.

b. Practice

Conduct probative of untruthfulness is a seldom used impeachment method. When issues arise, they most commonly center on the question of whether the prior act is actually "probative of truthfulness."

Example:

This is a personal injury case brought by a pedestrian against a truck driver and the driver's company. One of the plaintiff's witnesses is a co-worker who testifies the defendant's truck was speeding and ignored a stop sign when it hit the plaintiff. During cross-examination, the following happens:

Q. (By defendant's lawyer) Mr. Brown, weren't you suspended from your job for 45 days in June of last year because you submitted incorrect expense forms to your company?

Plaintiff: Objection, your honor, and we'd like to be heard at sidebar.

Judge: Approach the bench. [Lawyers come to the bench.] Counsel, I assume your objection is based on Rule 608?

Plaintiff: Correct, your honor. They are bringing up a prior act that is not probative of truthfulness. The fact that these expense forms were incorrect does not prove anything other than he made a mistake. In addition, Rule 608(b) does not allow evidence of any consequences resulting from conduct that is a proper attack on character for truth-telling.

Defendant: Your honor, in his deposition the witness admitted he intentionally overstated his expenses and agreed to make restitution. In addition, he admitted he was suspended for 45 days because of it. Under these circumstances, the conduct is probative of truthfulness, and Rule 608(b) permits us to bring it out on cross-examination.

Judge: I agree that nothing in Rule 608(b) allows evidence of the suspension, but I do think he can be asked about the incorrect reimbursement forms. That will be the ruling.

Plaintiff: Will your honor give the jury a limiting instruction on the proper use of this evidence?

Judge: Yes. Let's continue with the examination.

Q. Mr. Brown, isn't it true that in June of last year you submitted to your company expense reimbursement forms that you intentionally overstated?

A. Yes.

Q. Did you repay the company for the amounts you were not entitled to?

A. Yes.

Judge: Members of the jury, you should consider this evidence solely for the purpose of assessing this witness's credibility, and for no other purpose.

Commentary: This is a close case. The question is whether this conduct is relevant to the witness's character for truthfulness. If the reimbursement claims were knowingly false, the evidence should be admissible, subject to an FRE 403 analysis. In this case, the plaintiff's lawyer made a mistake when he did not contend the risk of unfair prejudice substantially outweighed the limited probative value of the evidence. The judge was correct when he excluded evidence of the suspension. The consequences that a witness may have suffered as a result of bad conduct are not authorized by FRE 608(b).

FRE 608 causes difficulties for many lawyers and judges. This is because the rule itself is complicated. It applies to both character for truthfulness and conduct probative of truthfulness, to both fact witnesses and character witnesses, and to both direct and cross-examination of those witnesses.

This section and the previous section have divided FRE 608 according to the type of impeachment — character for untruthfulness and conduct probative of untruthfulness. For some, the rules may be easier to understand if they are organized by the kind of witness being examined — a fact witness or a character witness. Under this type of approach, FRE 608 provides as follows:

i.   The fact witness

There are three ways to use FRE 608 to attack the character for truth-telling of any fact witness, including a party, in any civil or criminal case where character is not an essential element of the charge, claim, or defense:

1. A character witness may be called to testify on direct examination that the fact witness has a bad general reputation in a defined community for truthfulness (FRE 608(a)), but may not testify to specific instances of conduct (FRE 608(b)).

2. A character witness may be called to testify on direct examination that in his personal opinion the fact witness is not a truthful person (FRE 608(a)), but may not testify to specific instances of conduct (FRE 608(b)).

3. The fact witness may be asked on cross-examination about specific instances of his conduct that are probative of his untruthfulness, but extrinsic evidence of those instances of conduct may not be introduced, regardless of the witness's answers to the questions (FRE 608(b)).

ii.   The character witness

There are four ways to use FRE 608 to attack the character for truth-telling of any character witness in any civil or criminal case where character is not an essential element of the charge, claim, or defense:

1. Another character witness may be called to testify on direct examination that the character witness has a bad general reputation in a defined community for truthfulness (FRE 608(a)), but may not testify to specific instances of conduct (FRE 608(b)).
2. Another character witness may be called to testify on direct examination that in his personal opinion the character witness is not a truthful person (FRE 608(a)), but may not testify to specific instances of conduct (FRE 608(b)).
3. The character witness may be asked on cross-examination about specific instances of his conduct that are probative of his untruthfulness, but extrinsic evidence of those instances of conduct may not introduced, regardless of the witness's answers to the questions (FRE 608(b)).
4. The character witness may be asked on cross-examination about specific instances of the *fact* witness's conduct relating to the fact witness's untruthfulness. This is allowed to test the character witness's credibility and knowledge of the fact witness's character, but extrinsic evidence of those instances of conduct may not be introduced, regardless of the witness's answers to the questions (FRE 608(b)).

7.   Treatises[9]

a.   *Law*

Rule 803.   Exceptions to the Rule Against Hearsay— Regardless of Whether the Declarant Is Available as a Witness

The following are not excluded by the rule against hearsay, regardless of whether the declarant is available as a witness:

(18) *Statements in Learned Treatises, Periodicals, or Pamphlets.* A statement contained in a treatise, periodical, or pamphlet if:

(A) the statement is called to the attention of an expert witness on cross-examination or relied on by the expert on direct examination; and

(B) the publication is established as a reliable authority by the expert's admission or testimony, by another expert's testimony, or by judicial notice.

If admitted, the statement may be read into evidence but not received as an exhibit.

---

9. McCormick §13; Weinstein §803(18)[01]-[04]; Mueller & Kirkpatrick §8.60; Wigmore §§1690-1700.

Impeachment using learned treatises is the only impeachment method that applies exclusively to experts. FRE 803(18) provides that an expert witness may be impeached by "a statement contained in a treatise, periodical, or pamphlet if . . . the publication is established as a reliable authority by the expert's admission or testimony, by another expert's testimony, or by judicial notice. If admitted, the statement may be read into evidence but not received as an exhibit." This means the cross-examiner may read the impeaching parts of the treatise to the jury, but may not introduce the treatise as an exhibit, and the jury never sees the treatise during its deliberations.

The treatise's reliability is most commonly established by asking the expert, during cross-examination, to admit that the treatise is a reliable authority in the field. If the witness refuses, the court can take judicial notice that the treatise is a recognized authority (although this rarely happens), or the cross-examiner can promise the court that he will establish the authoritativeness of the treatise through his own expert witness. This flexibility prevents the expert being cross-examined from avoiding the impeachment simply by refusing to acknowledge that the impeaching treatise is a recognized authoritative source.

After the treatise is established as a reliable authority, the impeaching portion of the treatise is read to the expert and the jury, and the expert usually is asked if he agrees with the treatise. In some jurisdictions, trial judges permit putting the impeaching portion of the treatise on a large courtroom exhibit so the jury can see as well as hear the impeaching words. While FRE 803(18) by its terms does not permit this, there seems little harm in doing so, since jurors understand better when they see as well as hear. The main purpose of the procedure is to keep the jury from getting the treatise itself during deliberations, where the jury might give it more weight than it deserves.

Treatises are hearsay, but are made a hearsay exception under FRE 803(18). Treatises are also discussed in Sec. 7.14.

b.   Practice

Using treatises to impeach experts has become a common event in trials, particularly since most trials today use expert witnesses. Issues, when they arise, usually involve whether the treatise has been shown to be an authoritative source.

Example:

This is a personal injury case. The plaintiff claims her rheumatoid arthritis was caused by trauma. The plaintiff calls a medical expert who testifies on direct examination that the plaintiff's arthritis was caused by the trauma from the vehicle collision. On cross-examination, the following happens:

Q. (By defendant's lawyer) Dr. Ginsberg, your opinion is that Mrs. Smith's rheumatoid arthritis was caused by the trauma she received from the collision is that right?

A. Yes, that's my opinion.

Q. You can make that causal connection?

A. That's what I believe.

Q. What does the word "etiology" mean?

A. It simply means the origin or cause of something.

Q. Dr. Ginsberg, are you familiar with Cecil and Loeb's Textbook of Medicine?

A. Of course.

Q. That treatise is a reliable authority on internal medicine, isn't it?

A. Yes.

Q. In fact, it's a popular textbook in medical schools?

A. Yes.

Q. The most recent edition, you would consider that authoritative, wouldn't you?

A. Yes.

Q. Dr. Ginsberg, I'm going to read a section from Cecil and Loeb's Textbook of Medicine. I'm giving you a copy of that page, as well as the court and lawyers. On page 1413, it says: "The etiology of rheumatoid arthritis has not been finally determined." Do you agree with that statement?

A. In general terms, yes.

Defendant: Your honor, we offer page 1413 in evidence.

Plaintiff: Objection, your honor. Under Rule 803(18), it's not admissible as an exhibit.

Judge: That's right. Sustained. But the jury heard the statement from the treatise, and that may be considered as evidence.

Commentary: FRE 106, the rule of completeness, applies here. The cross-examiner should read the entire portion of the treatise that in fairness should be read.

8. Impeaching out-of-court declarants[10]

a. Law

Rule 806. Attacking and Supporting the Declarant's Credibility

> When a hearsay statement — or a statement described in Rule 801(d)(2)(C), (D), or (E) — has been admitted in evidence, the declarant's credibility may be attacked, and then supported, by any evidence that would be admissible for those purposes if the declarant had testified as a witness. The court may admit evidence of the declarant's inconsistent statement or conduct, regardless of when it occurred or whether the declarant had an opportunity to explain or deny it. If the party against whom the statement was admitted calls the declarant as a witness, the party may examine the declarant on the statement as if on cross-examination.

---

10. McCormick §§370-371; Weinstein §806[01]-[02]; Mueller & Kirkpatrick §8.80; Wigmore §§884-888, 1446, 1514.

Statements of out-of-court declarants are regularly admitted during trials, since they frequently qualify for admission as non-hearsay or hearsay exceptions. Consequently, the jury hears from the declarant, but the declarant may never appear at trial and, if so, cannot be personally cross-examined or impeached.

For example, a witness testifies during a deposition, but dies before trial. The witness's deposition transcript is admitted in evidence as former testimony under FRE 804(b)(1) and is read to the jury. The jury "hears" from the witness, but the witness, since not physically present, cannot be cross-examined. That witness's credibility becomes important because his out-of-court statement is being admitted for its truth.

FRE 806 governs the impeachment of such out-of-court declarants. It provides that whenever a hearsay statement, or a non-hearsay statement under FRE 801(d)(2)(C)-(E), is admitted in evidence, "the declarant's credibility may be attacked, and then supported, by any evidence which would be admissible for those purposes if declarant had testified as a witness." FRE 806's purpose is to level the playing field by allowing any impeachment that would have been allowed had the declarant personally appeared and testified at trial.

For example, if the declarant's statement is admitted as an excited utterance, the opposing side may introduce evidence that the declarant has a felony conviction. If the declarant is a doctor whose deposition testimony is admitted as former testimony, the opposing side may read in evidence portions of a treatise that contradict the expert's testimony. If the statement of a co-conspirator is admitted in a criminal trial, the opposing side may attack the co-conspirator's character for truthfulness or offer evidence of the co-conspirator's prior inconsistent statements.

Two problems occur that are not expressly resolved by the language of FRE 806. First, the usual procedure for impeaching a witness — raising the impeaching matter during the witness's direct or cross-examination and determining whether the witness will admit the matter — is inapplicable when impeaching an out-of-court declarant; since the witness is not physically present at trial, he cannot be personally examined about the impeaching matter. The only way such impeachment can be proven under these circumstances is by introducing extrinsic evidence, either by calling an appropriate witness or by offering an appropriate exhibit. However, the usual rule is that impeachment that is collateral cannot be proven with extrinsic evidence. Does this mean an out-of-court declarant can never be impeached with collateral impeachment?

For example, assume that the deposition of an unavailable declarant has been admitted in evidence. Can that declarant be impeached by an unimportant, but relevant, prior inconsistent statement or contradictory fact or by conduct probative of untruthfulness, all of which are collateral? If the declarant testifies in person at trial, he can be cross-examined on these matters, although if the witness denies them, they cannot be proved up with extrinsic evidence because they are collateral. If the declarant is not physically present, but "testifies" through his deposition, does this mean that collateral impeachment cannot be raised? The case law is not uniform. Some courts bar such collateral impeachment of out-of-court declarants; others permit it. Some courts say the truth-telling character of an absent hearsay declarant cannot be attacked through FRE 608(b), since evidence of specific acts of conduct would be the same as introducing extrinsic evidence. Other courts disagree, since the question would be allowed if the hearsay declarant were on the witness stand.

Second, can FRE 806 be used to impeach a party who does not personally testify at trial if a statement of that party is admitted as an admission under FRE 801(d)(2)(C)-(E) or a hearsay exception? FRE 806 so provides as to a "declarant," who can be a party. However, the effect of the rule on criminal defendants may be unfair.

For example, suppose that the prosecution introduces the defendant's out-of-court statement as an admission of the party-opponent. The prosecution then seeks to introduce, under FRE 806, the defendant's prior felony conviction under FRE 609 to attack the credibility of the defendant, the out-of-court declarant. Under ordinary circumstances, the prosecution cannot introduce the defendant's prior conviction under FRE 609 unless the defendant first testifies at trial. Can the prosecution get around this bar by introducing the defendant's admission and then arguing that the defendant's credibility is in issue, permitting the admission of the felony conviction? Again, case law is not uniform. Most courts bar this use of FRE 806; some do not.

b. Practice

FRE 806 is a frequently overlooked rule. It should always be considered when important evidence from an out-of-court declarant, particularly transcripts of proceedings such as depositions or pretrial evidentiary hearings, is admitted.

Example:

> This is a personal injury case. The plaintiff plans to introduce in evidence the deposition transcript of a non-treating doctor who is unavailable for trial. At a pretrial hearing to determine what portions of the transcript will be read to the jury, the following also happens:
>
> *Defendant:* Your honor, now that we've settled on what portions of the transcript will be read, we have an additional matter that we would like to get a ruling on. Since the doctor will not appear during the trial, we intend to offer two impeaching items in the defense case. First, we will offer evidence that this doctor has testified 15 times in the past five years in personal injury cases, each time as a plaintiff's witness. Second, we intend to read a section from a medical treatise that contradicts the doctor's deposition testimony.
>
> *Judge:* Any objection?
>
> *Plaintiff:* Yes, your honor. They could have brought up those things during the doctor's deposition. If they can raise these things at trial for the first time, that's totally unfair, since the doctor won't be here to respond.
>
> *Defendant:* Rule 806 says I can impeach the doctor with anything I could impeach him with if he testified live at trial. I can certainly expose his bias as a plaintiff's witness and impeach him with an authoritative treatise.
>
> *Judge:* That evidence will be permitted, provided you lay a proper foundation at trial.

XIII

REDIRECT, RECROSS, REBUTTAL, AND SURREBUTTAL

§13.1. Introduction

The Federal Rules of Evidence refer specifically to direct examination and cross-examination of witnesses. Obviously, there is more to witness examination. This chapter covers matters not specifically referred to in the Rules, but of substantial importance.

It is generally understood that fair trials require fair opportunities to respond. When the cross-examiner opens a subject that requires a response, redirect is allowed. A redirect that touches a new area may lead to recross, although at this point in the proceedings judicial patience begins to wear thin. Some judges, under some limited circumstances, will allow re-redirect and re-recross-examinations, but the case for these extended examinations must be compelling.

Likewise, parties may offer rebuttal and, on fewer occasions, surrebuttal evidence when fairness dictates. The Rules are silent on these extensions of trial stages. Again, the trial judge's discretion will establish the boundaries.

§13.2. Redirect examination[1]

1. Law

After a witness has been cross-examined, the direct examiner is permitted to examine the witness again. This examination is called the redirect examination. Its proper purpose is to respond to new matters brought out during the cross-examination. It follows that the redirect examination cannot merely repeat matters brought out during the direct examination in an attempt to get in the last word. Redirect examination is usually considered a matter of right, but is subject to the court's power under FRE 611(a) to control "the mode

---

1. F. Lane, Goldstein Trial Technique §§21.01-21.27 (3d ed. 1984); Wigmore §§1896, 1898; McCormick §§107-109.

and order of examining witnesses," No other rule governs redirect examination, which is largely defined by case law.

Case law on redirect examination focuses on three principal areas. First, redirect examination is proper when it explains, avoids, qualifies, or develops matters raised during the cross-examination. The reason is fairness. The cross-examiner cannot raise a matter and then prevent the redirect examiner from bringing out other related details that in fairness the jury should be allowed to consider. For example, the cross-examiner brings out that the witness did not report seeing the crime for several hours after it happened. On redirect examination, the victim can testify that the reason she didn't was that she was frightened or didn't want to get involved.

Second, the redirect examination can bring out other parts of statements, recordings, events, or transactions if the cross-examiner has brought out parts of them. Again, the reason is fairness. If the cross-examiner brought out only parts of writings, statements, recordings, events, or transactions, an unfair impression may be created. The redirect examiner can bring out additional matters that put things fairly in context. (Note that FRE 106, applicable to writings and recordings, provides: "If a party introduces all or part of a writing or recorded statement, an adverse party may require the introduction, at that time, of any other part — or any other writing or recorded statement — that in fairness ought to be considered at the same time." This prevents a party from unfairly taking things out of context.)

For example, the defendant is testifying, and the cross-examiner brings out part of a conversation: "You promised to deliver the goods by June 1, didn't you?" The defendant answers "yes." On redirect examination, the defendant can be asked: "What else did you tell the plaintiff during that conversation?" The defendant can answer: "I told him that my delivery of the goods would be dependent on my getting full payment before the delivery date."

Sometimes the cross-examination may go into matters that "open the door" on redirect to matters that were previously inadmissible. For example, a prosecution witness, a former co-defendant, on cross-examination admits he made a deal with the prosecutors in which he will get a reduced sentence for his participation in the crime if he testified as a prosecution witness. On redirect, the witness can state that his agreement with the prosecutors also requires his truthful testimony subject to penalties of perjury. This testimony may have been improper on direct examination, since it attempts to accredit the witness before his credibility has been attacked.

On the other hand, a lawyer cannot allow improper matter on cross-examination without objection and expect that his failure to object will open the door to a broader redirect examination. The proper remedy to an improper cross-examination is a timely objection.

Third, where the witness has been impeached during the cross-examination, the redirect examination may bring out matters that will reduce the impact of the impeachment. Again, the reason is fairness. Where a witness has been impeached with a prior inconsistent statement under FRE 613(b), the witness on redirect may be asked the reason for the inconsistency.

For example, the witness on direct states that she saw the defendant shoot the victim. The cross-examiner brings out a statement the witness made to the police, shortly after the shooting, that she did not see who did the shooting. The witness admits making the statement. On redirect, the witness can be asked: "Why did you tell the police that?" The witness can properly answer: "Because the defendant said he'd kill me if I talked to the cops." "Why" questions are entirely proper on redirect to explain prior inconsistent statements or conduct. Under FRE 613(b), if the witness is not confronted with the prior statement during cross-examination and the statement later is introduced during the cross-examiner's case, the witness can be recalled to deny or explain the statement.

Where a witness has been cross-examined and the "express or implied charge" of the cross is that the witness's testimony is the product of recent fabrication or improper influence or motive, the redirect examination can bring out a prior consistent statement for its truth if that consistent statement was made before the time of the event triggering the claim of recent fabrication or improper influence or motive. This is expressly permitted by FRE 801(d)(I)(B)(i).

For example, the cross-examination brings out that shortly before trial the witness was hired by the defendant, a large trucking company. The cross-examiner then asks, "So *now* that you have this new job, you claim that the truck driver had the green light?" This question implies that the witness's testimony, favoring the defendant, is a result of having been recently hired by the defendant. Under these circumstances, the redirect examination can establish that at the time of the collision the witness talked to a police officer and said that the defendant's truck had the green light. It becomes substantive evidence. The key requirement, that the prior consistent statement be made before the time of the event triggering the claimed recent fabrication or improper influence or motive, was emphasized in *Tome v. United States*, 513 U.S. 150 (1995).

The usual rule is that the redirect examination must follow the same questioning rules as the direct examination. This means that leading questions are generally not permitted under FRE 611(c), except for adverse parties and hostile witnesses, for matters not in dispute, preliminary and foundational matters, and where "necessary to develop the witness's testimony." As a practical matter, judges are interested in efficient presentation of evidence and usually allow a certain amount of leading on redirect in order to get to the specific point quickly, after which non-leading questions should be used. For example, on redirect, a lawyer can lead to the subject matter of the question and ask: "Counsel asked you about a conversation you had concerning the machine guns. Where did that take place?"

2. Practice

The common problems in redirect examination center on whether the redirect properly addresses matters brought out during the cross-examination or whether it merely repeats portions of the direct examination in an attempt to get in the last word. Under FRE 611, this issue is directed to the judge's discretion.

Example 1:

This is a robbery case. A prosecution witness on direct examination testifies that the defendant was one of the robbers. On cross-examination, the defense brings out that when first questioned by the police, the witness said he knew nothing about the robbery. On redirect examination, the following happens:

Q. (By prosecutor) Mr. Phelps, why did you say you knew nothing about the robbery to the police when you were first asked about it ?

Defendant: I object, your honor. This calls for a narrative.

Judge: Overruled. A "why" question is proper here. Mr. Phelps, you may answer the question.

A. I knew that the defendant lived on the next block. I was afraid of what might happen to me or my family if he found out I could identify him, so back then I thought it was safer to keep my mouth shut.

Q. What changed your mind?

Defendant: Objection. This is improper redirect.

Judge: Overruled.

A. My wife told me I had to tell the police what really happened.

Commentary: As frequently happens, the cross-examination has gone into matters that trigger the admissibility of additional matters on redirect.

Example 2:

This is a contract case. The defendant testifies in the defense case about a particular conversation he had with the plaintiff. On cross-examination, the following happens:

Q. (By plaintiff's lawyer) Ms. Williamson, let's turn to the conversation you had with the plaintiff, Shirley Rice, on June 1, 2015. During that conversation, you never told her the unit price of the folding chairs you wanted to sell, did you?

A. No.

On redirect examination, the following happens:

Q. (By defendant's lawyer) Ms. Williamson, during that conversation on June 1, 2015, did you have further discussion with Ms. Rice about price?

Plaintiff: Objection. Beyond the scope of the cross.

Judge: Overruled. This conversation was raised during cross.

A. Yes.

Q. What else did you tell her about the price of the chairs?

A. I told her that the standard unit price was on the price list I had previously sent her and that when she decided how many folding chairs she would order from us, we might be able to negotiate a volume discount.

Q. Let's talk about your company's pricing policies . . .

Plaintiff: Objection. Beyond the scope.

Judge: Sustained.

Defendant: Your honor, may I reopen my direct examination for this one point? It'll only take a minute, and I simply forgot to cover it earlier.

Judge: All right, but make it brief.

Commentary: Since reopening a direct examination is entirely discretionary with the judge, appealing to the judge's sense of fairness, and reassuring that the examination will be brief, is the better way to proceed.

Example 3:

This is an armed robbery case. Before trial, the defendant makes a motion to suppress the fruits of a search of the defendant's apartment which is granted. In the prosecution's case-in-chief, a police officer testifies about arresting the defendant in his apartment. On cross-examination, the following happens:

Q. (By defendant's lawyer) Officer O'Connor, you arrested the defendant in his apartment, right?
A. That's right.
Q. That was how long after the robbery?
A. About one hour later.
Q. You searched him?
A. That's right.
Q. You found no gun on him?
A. That's right.
Q. In fact, you found no gun anywhere in his apartment, isn't that also right?
A. Yes.
Q. Even though you looked?
A. Yes.
On redirect, the following happens:
Q. (By prosecutor) Officer, when you looked around his apartment, did you find anything?
Defendant: Objection, your honor. This violates your pretrial ruling and order.
Prosecutor: The defense went into the search of the house, your honor. They opened the door.
Judge: That's right. The objection is overruled.
A. I did.
Q. What did you find?
A. I found bullets and a holster.
Q. Where did you find them?
A. In a dresser in the bedroom.

Commentary: "Opening the door" to previously inadmissible evidence is particularly problematic in criminal cases. If the search had produced evidence not closely related to a gun, the ruling probably would have been different. However, the lesson to the cross-examiner, particularly the defense in criminal cases, is obvious: Be extremely careful that the cross-examination does not trigger, on redirect, the admission of additional evidence, even evidence that was subject to a successful motion to suppress.

Example 4:

This is a personal injury case. A plaintiff's witness during direct examination states that he was about 50 feet from the crash when it happened. On cross-examination, he is asked to admit he told a police officer after the crash that he was about 100 feet away, and the witness admits it. On redirect, the following happens:

Q. (By plaintiff's lawyer) Mr. Jenkins, you told us earlier that you were 50 feet from the crash, but told the police officer you were 100 feet away. Is there a reason for this difference?

Defendant: Objection, your honor. This calls for a narrative.

Judge: Overruled. The witness can explain the reason for the difference if one exists.

A. When I talked to the police officer. I was standing on the front lawn of a house. From there, I was about 100 feet away. But I was right on the corner when the crash happened, and from there, it was only 50 feet. I was confused about what he was asking me.

Commentary: Witnesses always may explain the reason they spoke inconsistently in the past about a particular matter.

Example 5:

This is a murder case. The prosecution witness, an accomplice of the defendant, previously entered into a plea agreement with the prosecution for a reduced sentence. On direct examination, the witness identifies the defendant as the shooter. The witness is subjected to an extensive cross-examination, including the terms of his plea agreement, which requires that the witness testify as a prosecution witness during the defendant's trial. On redirect, the following happens:

Q. (By prosecutor) Mr. Robinson, you talked to the police when you were arrested, didn't you?

Defendant: Objection, your honor. May we have a sidebar conference?

Judge: Please approach. [Lawyers come to the bench.] What's the basis for your objection?

Defendant: It's beyond the scope, your honor. I didn't go into this on cross. Besides, it's hearsay.

Prosecutor: His cross strongly suggested that the only reason the witness implicated the defendant in court was because of the previous plea agreement. Under FRE 801(d)(2)(B), we can now bring out the witness's prior consistent statement, since it rebuts the defense's suggestion of recent fabrication and improper influence. He told the police that the defendant was the shooter.

Judge: The objection is overruled. Please repeat your question before the jury.

Q. You talked to the police when you were arrested, didn't you?

A. Yes.

Q. Did you tell them who did the shooting?

A. Yes.

Q. What did you tell the police?

A. I told them the defendant did the actual shooting.

Commentary: This is another example of how a cross-examination can trigger the admission of evidence, on redirect examination, that was previously inadmissible.

§13.3.   Recross-examination[2]

1.   Law

Recross-examination may follow the redirect examination. Some courts treat recross-examination as entirely discretionary with the judge. Others treat it as a right only where the redirect has raised new matters. What is clear is that because of FRE 611(a), recross-examination is almost entirely within the judge's discretion, and many judges routinely bar it altogether, or permit it only in unusual circumstances.

The recross-examination is conducted the same way as the cross-examination, that is, using leading questions, although FRE 611(c) gives the judge discretion to bar leading questions.

2.   Practice

Since recross-examination is discretionary, the lawyer must appeal to the judge's sense of fairness in allowing the additional examination. The judge's ruling will depend more on his sense of whether the witness has already testified to everything the witness reasonably can be expected to testify about, and whether the jury is getting restless, than on any technical analysis of scope issues.

Example

This is a robbery case. A prosecution witness on direct examination testifies that the defendant was one of the robbers. On cross-examination, the defense brings out that when first questioned by the police, the witness said he knew nothing about the robbery. On redirect examination, the witness testifies that he didn't tell the police what he knew because the defendant lived on the next block; the witness was afraid for himself and his family, so he kept his mouth shut. On recross-examination, the following happens:

Defendant: Your honor, may I have a short recross? It's on one point counsel just made.
Judge: All right, but keep it brief.
Q. (By defendant's lawyer) Mr. Phelps, the police first interviewed you several days after the robbery, right?
A. Yes.
Q. You say that you didn't tell them what you knew because you were afraid?

---

2. Wigmore §§1897, 1899.

A. That's right.

Q. But on the day the police talked to you, you knew the defendant had been arrested, right?

A. Yes.

Q. And you knew he was in jail?

A. Yes.

Commentary: This recross-examination is entirely proper because what it brought out was first made relevant by the redirect examination.

§13.4. *Rebuttal*[3]

1. Law

Rebuttal evidence is evidence that refutes, contradicts, or diminishes evidence presented by another party. Evidence introduced by the plaintiff to refute the defendant's evidence usually is called "rebuttal" evidence. Evidence introduced by the defendant to refute the plaintiff's rebuttal evidence usually is called "surrebuttal" evidence.

The admissibility of rebuttal evidence rests with the sound discretion of the judge because the judge has power under FRE 611(a) to "exercise reasonable control over the mode and order of interrogating witnesses and presenting evidence." Generally speaking, however, rebuttal evidence is properly admissible when the defendant has introduced significant new matters during the defendant's case-in-chief. Like redirect examination, the rule is based on fairness. When the defendant brings out new matters, fairness dictates that the plaintiff be given a reasonable opportunity to rebut that new evidence, since the plaintiff cannot be expected to anticipate the defendant's case. For example, the defendant, charged with theft, testifies that he had no motive to steal because he runs a successful business. In rebuttal, the prosecution may introduce evidence that the business is failing and is deeply in debt.

Rebuttal is limited to non-collateral matters first raised in the defendant's case-in-chief. This means that the plaintiff cannot recall witnesses who have already testified in the plaintiff's case-in-chief as rebuttal witnesses merely to repeat their previous testimony. This also means that the plaintiff should not be able to call new witnesses as rebuttal witnesses if the new witnesses merely repeat the same testimony as witnesses who earlier testified in the plaintiff's case-in-chief. Rebuttal evidence is not an opportunity to repeat previous testimony just to have the last word. However, if those witnesses can specifically address and refute matters first brought out in the defendant's case-in-chief, then recalling those witnesses as rebuttal witnesses is proper. The same analysis applies to exhibits offered in rebuttal.

An important issue is whether a witness or an exhibit is proper rebuttal evidence or whether that witness or exhibit should have been presented in the plaintiff's case-in-chief. Once again, fairness is the controlling concern. The defendant, in the defendant's case-in-chief, should have a fair opportunity to

3. F. Lane, Goldstein Trial Technique §§22.01-22.17 (3d ed. 1984); Wigmore §1873; McCormick §§223,233.

meet all the plaintiff's evidence. The plaintiff should not be allowed to "sandbag" by intentionally withholding evidence from his case-in-chief in the hope that the defendant, not aware of the evidence, will step into the trap and present evidence that the plaintiff later can rebut dramatically.

For this reason, many courts hold that rebuttal is not proper if it could have been presented in the plaintiff's case-in-chief. In other words, rebuttal evidence must be more than merely relevant; it must specifically address new matters raised by the defense and should be evidence that the plaintiff could not reasonably have been expected to present earlier. Other courts, however, hold that the mere fact that the evidence could have been presented in the plaintiff's case-in-chief does not bar its use in rebuttal if it otherwise properly rebuts and the defendant has the opportunity of surrebuttal. Once again, these matters are addressed to the sound discretion of the judge.

If the judge sustains an objection that plaintiff's rebuttal evidence is improper, plaintiff's last recourse is to ask the judge for permission to reopen its case-in-chief. The usual argument is that the request should be granted in the interest of fairness and trial accuracy. This request is discretionary with the judge.

Another important issue is whether evidence presented is rebuttal evidence or defensive evidence. In cases where the plaintiff has claims and the defendant has counterclaims, the plaintiff's rebuttal case, as a practical matter, may contain evidence that is true rebuttal evidence and other evidence that responds to the defendant's counterclaims. Since a counterclaims is a complaint brought by a defendant, the plaintiff has an absolute right to defend against that complaint. It follows that when the plaintiff presents evidence directed to the defendant's counterclaim, such evidence is presented as of right and should not be confused with rebuttal evidence.

For example, plaintiff sues defendant on one contract, defendant counterclaims on an entirely unrelated contract, and both claims are being tried jointly. After defendant presents evidence during the defendant's case-in-chief to prove its counterclaim (as well as other evidence directed to plaintiff's complaint), plaintiff has a right to present defensive evidence on the counterclaim, since this is not rebuttal evidence.

When a witness has been attacked, on cross-examination or during the other side's case, with evidence of bad character for truthfulness, the party calling that witness can rebut with evidence of that witness's good character for truthfulness. FRE 608(a) specifically allows such rebuttal evidence in the form of general reputation or opinion evidence. For a more detailed discussion, see Sec. 12.4.

Rebuttal evidence should be presented in the same manner as in the plaintiff's case-in-chief. The plaintiff calls its witnesses under the usual rules governing direct examinations, and the defendant may cross-examine them. As a practical matter, judges are interested in efficient presentation of evidence and usually allow a certain amount of leading during the direct examination of rebuttal witnesses in order to get to the specific point quickly, after which nonleading questions should be used.

2.   Practice

The common problems with rebuttal parallel those with redirect examination. They center on whether the rebuttal evidence properly addresses matters brought out in the defendant's case or whether it merely repeats portions of the plaintiff's case-in-chief in an attempt to get in the last word. This issue is, under FRE 611, directed to the judge's discretion.

Example 1:

This is a products liability case. The plaintiff claims he was injured when the handlebar of a snowmobile broke, causing the plaintiff's injuries. In the defendant's case-in-chief, an officer of the defendant manufacturer testifies that the handlebar was safely designed and that the company had never had a problem with that handlebar design before this accident. After the defense rests and before the plaintiff presents any rebuttal evidence, the following happens:

Defendant: Your honor, before the jury comes out and the plaintiff begins his rebuttal case, we have a motion.

Judge: What is it?

Defendant: We move to preclude a James Daly from being called as a witness in the plaintiff's rebuttal case. We believe he would testify that he was injured when the handlebar on his snow-mobile, made by us, broke during use. We object for two reasons. First, that witness is not on the plaintiff's list of witnesses, so we're surprised. Second, that witness should have been called in the plaintiff's case-in-chief, and it's unfair to let them call the witness now.

Judge: I'm not concerned about the failure to list him as a witness, since my pretrial order does not apply to either side's rebuttal witnesses. Plaintiff, what about the second argument?

Plaintiff: We were not planning to call Mr. Daly in our case-in-chief, your honor. That's why we didn't list him. However, when the defendant called one of their employees to testify that they had never had a problem with that handlebar design, for the first time it made Mr. Daly's testimony relevant. He will testify that he was injured by that handlebar and notified the defendant about it before my client's accident happened.

Judge: The motion is denied. This is proper rebuttal.

Example 2:

This is a sale of illegal drugs prosecution. The defendant testifies and states that he is a successful car dealer and has no reason to try to make money illegally. The following later happens:

Judge: Does the prosecution have any rebuttal?

Prosecutor: Yes, your honor. We call Ms. Helen Smith. [Witness takes the stand and is sworn in.]

Q. Ms. Smith, you're the defendant's accountant?

A. I do the accounting for the defendant's used car dealership, the corporation. I don't do his personal accounting.

Q. Have you seen the dealership's financial records for the fiscal year 2015?

A. Yes.

Q. That's the same fiscal year during which the defendant was arrested?

A. Yes.

Q. How did you become familiar with the financial records?

A. As the dealership's accountant. I have access to all its financial records and I prepared the tax returns for that year.

Defendant: Objection to any further testimony, your honor. May we be heard at the bench?

Judge: Yes. The lawyers will approach. [Lawyers come to the bench.]

Defendant: I object on the ground that this is improper rebuttal. The prosecutor could have, and should have, presented motive evidence, which this is, in their case-in-chief.

Judge: I'm overruling the improper rebuttal argument. The defendant himself made it relevant when he testified that he had no motive to commit the alleged crime. This offered evidence is highly relevant to rebut that testimony.

Example 3:

This is a personal injury case. A defense doctor testifies that in his opinion the plaintiff's claimed injuries are preexisting. The defense then rests, and the following happens:

Plaintiff: We call Mrs. Helen Griggs as our first rebuttal witness. [Witness takes the stand and is sworn.]

Q. Mrs. Griggs, this collision happened on June 1, 2015, right?

A. That's right.

Q. You know your husband claims that his neck was injured during that collision, right?

A. Of course.

Q. Mrs. Griggs, did your husband ever complain about his neck before June 1, 2015?

A. No.

Q. Did you ever notice your husband favoring his neck at any time before June 1, 2015?

A. No, he always seemed normal before the crash.

Q. During the years you've been married to him, have you ever noticed anything wrong, or different, about his neck?

A. No.

Q. And how long have you been married?

A. Since 2005.

Commentary: Notice that the defendant did not object to this rebuttal evidence. It was clearly proper, given the defense testimony.

Example 4:

This is a personal injury case. The defendant testifies, in the defendant's case-in-chief, "I was going five miles under the speed limit. I always drive under the speed limit." The defense then rests, and the following happens:

Judge: Any rebuttal?

Plaintiff: Yes, your honor. We offer Plaintiff's Exhibit No. 23, a certified public record.

Defendant: We object, your honor, and ask to be heard at sidebar.

Judge: Counsel, please come to the bench. [Lawyers come to the bench.] What's your objection?

Defendant: These are the defendant's motor vehicle department records, your honor, showing the defendant's citations and dispositions over the past 10 years. That's improper rebuttal.

Plaintiff: The defendant's own testimony opened the door to this, your honor. He testified that he was going under the speed limit and that he always drives under the speed limit. The defendant's driving history, which contradicts his own testimony, is now proper other acts evidence under Rule 404(b).

Defendant: That doesn't open the door to his entire driving record. In addition, it's improper under Rule 403.

Judge: The objection is sustained, except as to the defendant's conviction for speeding two years ago, where he pled guilty. The defendant's comment, that he always drives under the speed limit, was brought out on direct examination. Since the defendant himself volunteered it, the plaintiff's now entitled to rebut it. Therefore, the defendant's prior conviction for speeding is now properly admissible.

Example 5:

This is a criminal assault case based on a barroom incident that happened on September 1, 2015. The defendant testifies that he hit the victim with a beer bottle because the victim was going to attack him with a knife and that "I've never intentionally hurt anyone in my life." In the prosecution's rebuttal case, the following happens:

Prosecutor: Your honor, we call Johnny Santini. [Witness takes the stand and is sworn in.]

Q. Mr. Santini, do you know the defendant?

A. I sure do.

Q. Did you see him on June 1, 2015?

Defendant: Objection, your honor. This sounds like other acts evidence.

Judge: Counsel, please approach. [Lawyers come to the bench.] What does the prosecution intend to prove through this witness?

Prosecutor: This witness will testify that the defendant attacked him with a beer bottle, your honor. That testimony will directly refute the defendant's contention that he's "never intentionally hurt anyone."

Defendant: It's still other acts evidence being offered to prove bad character, your honor. They couldn't get this in during their case-in-chief, and they can't do it now.

Prosecutor: The defendant himself made it admissible when he lied to the jury about never having intentionally hurt anyone. His credibility is now in issue, and now we're allowed to show he wasn't telling the truth.

Judge: The objection is overruled. I will give the jury a limiting instruction that they are to consider this evidence solely as it applies to the defendant's credibility, and not as evidence of character.

   Commentary: The question of whether a defendant's "sweeping claim" opens the door to otherwise inadmissible evidence in rebuttal is a common one in criminal cases. Since the defendant volunteered the additional fact, he placed it in issue and cannot stop the prosecutor from contradicting it.

§13.5.   Surrebuttal[4]

1.   Law

Surrebuttal refers to the presentation by the defendant of additional evidence after the plaintiff has presented rebuttal evidence. Surrebuttal is discretionary with the court under FRE 611(a) and is infrequently permitted. In those instances where the plaintiff's rebuttal case has presented new matters that the defendant has not yet had a fair opportunity to address, surrebuttal should be granted.

2.   Practice

Surrebuttal is discretionary, so, like recross-examination, the lawyers must appeal to the judge's sense of fairness in allowing the additional evidence. The ruling will depend more on the judge's sense of fairness and on whether surrebuttal can realistically make a difference than on any technical analysis of scope issues.

Example

   This is a criminal case. A pretrial motion to suppress the defendant's postarrest statement is denied. The prosecution in its case-in-chief calls a detective who testifies about the defendant's statement. In the defense case, the defendant testifies that he was pressured into giving a false statement while being interrogated by the police. In rebuttal, the prosecution offers in evidence a videotape of the interrogation, which shows no coercion or other improper tactics. In surrebuttal, the following happens:

Defendant: Your honor, we recall Reggie Johnson, the defendant, to the stand.

Prosecutor: Objection, your honor. He's already testified in the defense's case.

---

4. F. Lane, Goldstein Trial Technique §§22.14-22.17 (3d ed. 1984); Wigmore §1874.

Defendant: This relates to the videotape, your honor. We saw it for the first time in the prosecution's rebuttal case.

Judge: Very well. I trust you'll get to the point quickly.

Q. (By defendant's lawyer) Reggie, you saw the videotape when it was played in the courtroom?

A. Yes.

Q. Does that videotape cover the entire time you were in that interrogation room with the detective?

A. No, it doesn't.

Q. What part of your interrogation does the videotape fail to show?

A. Probably the first half hour I was in there. The detective kept telling me it would go easier on me if I just admitted what he wanted me to admit. That part isn't on the tape at all.

XIV

CLOSING ARGUMENTS

§14.1. Introduction

The purpose of closing arguments is to give the parties a final opportunity to review with the jury the admitted evidence, discuss what it means, apply the applicable law to that evidence, and argue why the evidence and law compel a favorable verdict.

As is the case with opening statements, the trial judge has latitude in deciding what is proper in closing arguments. Differences exist among the various jurisdictions, and among judges in the same jurisdiction, on what is proper to include in a closing argument. In general, however, since closing arguments are intended to help the jury understand the facts, apply the law, and reach a considered verdict, arguments that are based on the facts, the law, and common sense are proper. Conversely, closing arguments that are designed to deflect the jury from its proper duty, such as by discussing the lawyer's personal beliefs or asking the jury to base its decision on grounds other than the facts and law, are improper.

There is no federal rule of evidence, civil procedure, or criminal procedure that governs the permissible content of closing arguments. Rule 29.1 of the Federal Rules of Criminal Procedure merely provides for the prosecution opening the argument and having the right of rebuttal. State rules are usually equally silent; if they address closing arguments at all, they usually provide only that closing arguments shall be allowed and establish the order of the arguments.

Ethical rules are general. Model Rule 3.4(e) provides that a lawyer shall not "allude to any matter that the lawyer does not reasonably believe is relevant or that will not be supported by admissible evidence, assert personal knowledge of facts in issue . . . , or state a personal opinion as to the justness of a cause, the credibility of a witness, the culpability of a civil litigant or the guilt or innocence of an accused."

Evidentiary rules regarding objections apply equally to closing arguments. An objecting lawyer can, and sometimes must, do three things: Object to the argument, ask that the comment be struck and the jury instructed to disregard it, and ask for a mistrial.

An objection must be timely made and should specify the improper argument. Otherwise, error will usually be deemed waived unless the misconduct is so egregious as to constitute "plain error." In that case, the appellate court will consider it, even if no timely objection to the misconduct was made in the trial court. If the objection is sustained, the court usually also will instruct the jury to disregard the remark. If the misconduct is serious, the court may admonish the offending lawyer. If the misconduct is particularly serious or repeated, the court on motion may declare a mistrial, although that is a rare event in federal trials.

Whether error in closing arguments is harmless or sufficiently egregious that a mistrial is the appropriate remedy depends on a number of considerations: the offending lawyer's demeanor during the impropriety, whether the impropriety is repeated, the seriousness of the impropriety considered in light of the other evidence, when during the arguments it was made, whether the court sustained the objection and gave a curative instruction or admonished the lawyer, whether the offending lawyer apologized for the impropriety, whether it was a response invited by the other side's impropriety, and whether the other side had an opportunity to respond to the impropriety. Appellate courts rarely reverse on closing argument points, except in close cases for serious improprieties.

This chapter will discuss the common evidentiary objections that are made during closing arguments, discuss the relevant law, and illustrate the factual settings in which such objections frequently occur. Procedural issues, such as the right to make closing arguments, their order, the right to rebuttal, and time limitations, are not discussed, since these are controlled by statutes and by local rules and customs and are usually jurisdiction specific.

§14.2. Mentioning unadmitted evidence[1]

1. Law

Closing arguments must be based on admitted evidence, reasonable inferences from that evidence, and matters of common knowledge. Therefore, mentioning missing, unadmitted, or inadmissible evidence is improper and objectionable.

The most common errors in this category involve mentioning facts not in evidence. Whether the fact is true or not does not matter. If the fact was not "proved" during trial by presenting admissible evidence on that point, it does not "exist" as far as the jury is concerned, and the fact cannot be mentioned during closing argument, since the jury should base its verdict only on the admitted evidence and applicable law. For example, mentioning background information about parties and witnesses on which there was no testimony is improper. Mentioning evidence that was excluded by a motion in limine or a motion to suppress is obviously improper. Referring to exhibits that were not admitted in evidence is improper. In all these situations, the impropriety is

---

1. J.A. Stein, Closing Argument §§15, 16, 19, 32, 40, 44, 47 (1969); F. Lane, Goldstein Trial Technique §§23.06, 23.11, 23.15 (3d ed. 1984); L.J. Smith, Art of Advocacy—Summation §§2.11, 2.40, 2.41, 2.44 (1991). T.A. Mauet, Trial Techniques and Trails ch. 9 (9th ed., 2013).

based on the fact that the evidence was not formally admitted during the trial, and, therefore, the lawyers may not refer to it.

The most serious situations occur when a lawyer comments on other crimes and wrongs committed by a party, most commonly a criminal defendant, when those crimes and wrongs were not properly admissible under either FRE 404(b) or 609. In these situations, the error often will result in a mistrial. For example, if the prosecutor in closing argument states that the defendant was previously convicted of burglary, and if that fact has not been proven during the trial, a mistrial is probably inevitable. Another common error occurs when a prosecutor in closing argument refers to the character of the accused or the victim when there has been no character evidence introduced during the trial under FRE 404 and 405. For example, it is improper for the prosecutor to state, "How do we know the defendant did it? We know he is a violent person, just the kind of person who would commit this kind of crime," unless character evidence about the defendant has been properly admitted during the trial.

A related problem occurs when evidence has been admitted for a limited purpose and a lawyer uses that evidence for an improper purpose. For example, a defendant's prior conviction, properly admitted under FRE 609 for the limited purpose of attacking credibility, is improperly used if the prosecutor argues that the "defendant is up to his old tricks again," suggesting that the prior conviction should be used to infer recidivism. As a further example, if the fact of the defendant's insurance coverage has been properly admitted under FRE 411 to show ownership and control, the plaintiff's lawyer cannot argue that the insurance coverage demonstrates that "the defendant can take a verdict of $100,000 without it hurting him a bit."

The problem of a defendant's post-arrest silence is an important and recurring problem in criminal cases. In *Griffin v. California*, 380 U.S. 609 (1965), the Supreme Court held that the Fifth Amendment privilege against self-incrimination, applicable to the states through the Fourteenth Amendment, barred a prosecutor from commenting on the defendant's failure to testify during his trial. What kinds of references constitute an impermissible reference to a defendant's *Griffin* right? Direct comments along the lines of "He never denied what we proved" or "If he's so innocent, why didn't we ever hear from him?" are obviously improper, and reversible error unless the error is harmless beyond a reasonable doubt.

However, more indirect comments are more problematic. The most common include arguments that the prosecution has an "uncontradicted case" and that "you have heard nothing to the contrary." Most courts hold that calling the prosecution's case uncontradicted, or using similar language, is an impermissible comment on the defendant's silence where it is apparent from the facts that the only witness who is in a position to contradict the prosecution's version of the facts is the defendant himself. In fact, some courts hold that any argument calling the prosecution's case uncontradicted is improper, since the defense has the legal right not to present any evidence at trial, whether through the defendant or any other witness.

In *Lockett v. Ohio*, 438 U.S. 586 (1978), the prosecutor in closing argument repeatedly characterized the prosecution's case as "unrefuted" and "uncontradicted." The Court held that the references, in the context of the case, did not violate the defendant's constitutional right not to present evidence. In *Lockett*, the defendant's lawyer had outlined the contemplated defense case in the opening statement and had told the court and jury near the end of the case that the defendant would be the next witness. Under these particular circumstances, the prosecutor's comments added nothing to the impression created by the defendant's refusal to testify.

The other silence problem that often occurs in criminal cases involves the defendant's assertion of his *Miranda* rights and his refusal to answer any post-arrest questions by the police. Since a defendant has a legal right to assert his *Miranda* rights, no adverse consequences can flow from asserting them, and the prosecution cannot introduce the defendant's post-arrest silence as evidence of guilt during the presentation of evidence or comment on it in any way in closing arguments. See *Doyle v. Ohio*, 426 U.S. 610 (1976); *Brecht v. Abrahamson*, 507 U.S. 619 (1993).

Courts frequently state that the lawyers may refer to matters in closing arguments that are "common knowledge." The line between what is common knowledge and what is an impermissible mentioning of facts not in evidence is elusive. Most courts permit quoting or referring to classic literature, such as the Bible, Shakespeare, and Dickens, and referring to documents such as Magna Carta and the Constitution. Many permit references to more modern sources, such as familiar movies or recent historical events. Most permit talking about an experience that has happened to everyone, such as running up to someone on the street thinking it was a friend, only to discover you were mistaken.

More problematic is lawyers telling about personal experiences in their lives, such as an experience while serving in the military, and using it to make a point in closing arguments. Some courts permit this; others do not. Many courts find personal experiences improper when they are being used as a vehicle to express the lawyer's personal beliefs.

2. Practice

Objections that the argument is based on unadmitted evidence, or is not a reasonable inference from admitted evidence, are difficult objections for judges. Judges ordinarily do not want to depend on their recollections of the evidence, since a jury's collective memory usually is better. In this situation, judges commonly sustain objections only if the argument is clearly beyond anything admitted in evidence. In a gray area, however, judges usually overrule the objection or simply advise the jury to use its collective memory to determine if there is any evidence to support the argument.

Make sure that the judge makes a ruling on the objection. Judges often say, "Proceed," or "Let's move on." That is not a ruling. Insist on a ruling so that any error is preserved for appeal.

Example 1:

This is a medical malpractice case. The plaintiff claims she was injured by the defendant doctor's negligence during surgery. During the plaintiff's closing argument, the following happens:

Plaintiff: Members of the jury, was the doctor negligent? Of course! The evidence is that he had to be.

Defendant: Objection, your honor. That is not the evidence.

Judge: Overruled. This is closing argument. The jury will determine if counsel's argument is supported by the evidence or reasonable inferences.

Plaintiff: What's that evidence? Before that elective surgery, Mrs. Thomas was healthy. Immediately afterward, when she came out of the anaesthesia, she couldn't move her legs. Who was responsible for that, folks? Obviously the doctor was. He must have done something, or failed to do something, that caused that nerve damage. Mrs. Thomas certainly didn't do it to herself!

Commentary: The judge's ruling in this situation is predictable, since judges are reluctant to substitute their recollection for a jury's. The judge's comment does remind the jury to determine if the argument is supported by the evidence.

Example 2:

This is a personal injury case brought against two defendants. One defendant settles before trial, and the fact of the settlement is admitted to show bias when that defendant testifies as a plaintiff's witness during the trial. Before closing arguments, the following happens:

Defendant: Your honor, we have a motion in limine regarding the closing arguments.

Judge: What is it?

Defendant: The settled co-defendant testified, and the fact of his settlement was admitted to show bias. I'm afraid the plaintiff may argue that the verdict amount the jury should return against us should in some way be influenced by that settlement amount. This, of course, is an improper use of the fact and terms of that settlement, which was admitted only on the issue of bias.

Plaintiff: We do not intend to use that settlement for any other purpose, your honor.

Judge: Very well. The settlement will not be argued during closing arguments except as it may relate to the credibility of the settled defendant.

Commentary: The motion and the judge's ruling have one important effect: If the plaintiff's lawyer in closing argument later misuses the fact of the settlement, this misuse cannot be claimed to be inadvertent or a mistake.

Example 3:

This is a robbery prosecution in which the issue is identification. The victim, the only eyewitness to the robbery, identifies the defendant in court. The defense presents no evidence. During the prosecutor's closing argument, the following happens:

Prosecutor: Has our evidence shown that it was the defendant? Of course! All the evidence you heard and saw, without exception, points

the finger of guilt squarely at that defendant, and you've heard
absolutely nothing to contradict that identification.
Defendant: Objection, your honor. That's an improper comment.
Judge: Overruled. Prosecution, move on to something else.

Commentary: This is a difficult situation for the defense: to make an objection based on the defendant's Fifth Amendment privilege to remain silent and not present any evidence during the trial. As in the previous example, defense counsel could raise the possibility of an improper prosecution argument, commenting on the defendant's failure to present evidence, before the closing arguments and try to get a ruling before the arguments begin. Some judges would sustain the objection.

§14.3.   *Misstating or mischaracterizing the evidence*[2]

1. Law

Another common, and also problematic, error occurs when a lawyer misstates or mischaracterizes the evidence that has been admitted during the trial. The law is that a lawyer may argue the evidence and "reasonable inferences" drawn from that evidence, but cannot misstate or mischaracterize the evidence. When does an argument cross the line between what is permissible and what is impermissible?

For example, in a contract case, plaintiff's lawyer describes a letter sent from defendant to plaintiff as a letter "that accepted plaintiff's offer." Defendant's lawyer objects on the basis that this mischaracterizes the evidence, since the letter was a counteroffer, not an acceptance. In a criminal case, the evidence is that the defendant and the victim fought and that during the fight the defendant grabbed a beer bottle and hit the victim in the face with the bottle. During closing argument, the prosecutor states that "the defendant attacked the victim with a deadly weapon." The defense objects on the basis that the prosecutor is mischaracterizing the evidence.

The difficulty with such objections is that the judge is asked to determine instantly if the comment is a misstatement or mischaracterization of the evidence or if it is simply a permissible inference from the facts. This is obviously a judgment call, and one that judges are reluctant to make. Unless the comment is clearly unsupported by evidence, most judges will overrule the objection and tell the jury that "you heard the evidence, and it is up to you to determine if counsel is accurately stating the facts and if their argument is reasonable" or give some other similar instruction.

2. Practice

These kinds of objections are particularly difficult for the judge, who will probably let the jury decide if an argument misstates or mischaracterizes the evidence unless the lawyer has clearly crossed the line.

---

2. J.A. Stein, Closing Argument §16 (1969).

Example 1:

This is a personal injury case. The plaintiff claims the defendant was under the influence of alcohol and caused the collision. The evidence is that the defendant had consumed alcohol before the collision, but that his alcohol level was below the legal intoxication level. During the plaintiff's closing argument, the following happens:

Plaintiff: Folks, when the defendant left the bar, he'd been drinking. Was he under the influence? Of course! He admitted to drinking two beers, but you can take that with a grain of salt. The officer noticed at the scene that his words were slurred and his eyes were bloodshot. Should he have been on the road? Of course not!

Defendant: Objection. This mischaracterizes the evidence.

Plaintiff: This is closing argument, your honor.

Judge: Well, the jury heard the evidence, and the jury will decide if the argument is fairly based on the evidence or if it misstates the evidence. Continue.

Commentary: The judge has not ruled, so there is no ruling to appeal from. The objecting lawyer should always ask for a ruling on the objection.

Example 2:

This is a civil rights case brought against the police for illegally searching the plaintiff's home and beating him during the search. During the search, police found several marijuana cigarettes. During the defendant's closing argument, the following happens:

Defendant: So what did the police find when they searched the house? Marijuana here, marijuana there, marijuana everywhere. All told, they found 12 marijuana cigarettes in that house. What does that make the plaintiff? There's only one conclusion, folks: That man was using marijuana and undoubtedly was dealing in marijuana as well. And now this dope dealer has the audacity to . . .

Plaintiff: Objection, your honor. There's absolutely no evidence to support this argument. We ask that the comment be struck and that the jury be instructed appropriately.

Judge: The objection is sustained, and the argument is struck. Counsel, you will refrain from engaging in name-calling when there's no evidence to support it, is that clear?

Defendant: Yes, your honor.

Judge: Members of the jury, you will disregard the last comments of counsel. There's been no evidence introduced during this trial to support it. Counsel, continue with your closing.

Commentary: The judge's tone in sustaining the objection to the improper argument is an important part of dealing with the problem.

§14.4.   *Making improper comments on missing evidence*[3]

1.   Law

Lawyers in closing arguments frequently argue the significance of missing witnesses and evidence. Typical arguments are "Why didn't the other side call Mr. Johnson? What are they so afraid of?" and "Why didn't they bring you any evidence that . . . ?"

Case law holds that such comments may be proper if the witness or exhibit is within the control of the party failing to produce it, but are improper if the witness or exhibit is equally accessible by either side and could have been subpoenaed for trial. Depending on the jurisdiction, the jury also may be given a "missing witness" instruction, which tells the jury it may draw a negative inference from the failure to produce the witness or exhibit in the control of one party. For example, the only other eyewitness to a collision is the defendant's employee and the defendant does not call him as a witness during trial, although the employee is available. The plaintiff should be able to argue that the defendant's failure to call the employee demonstrates that the testimony of the employee, had he appeared, would have been unfavorable to the defendant and to get a missing witness instruction.

In criminal cases, the defendant's privilege against self-incrimination and right not to present any evidence mean that the prosecutor may not use this argument if the defense has rested without presenting evidence. However, most jurisdictions hold that if the defense does present evidence, the prosecution can then comment on what the defense produced during the trial, although the prosecution cannot attempt to shift the burden of proof to the defense.

Lawyers never may argue that evidence was excluded by a pretrial order or the rules of evidence. Arguing that "we wanted to bring you important evidence of that, but the rules of evidence prevented us" is always improper. It follows that the other side cannot argue the significance of missing evidence if it was excluded because of the court's ruling.

2.   Practice

Since missing evidence and missing witnesses may result in the jury being instructed on that issue, whether the argument is proper can often be raised during the jury instructions conference. If not, a motion in limine should be made before the closing arguments.

Example 1:

This is a contract case. During the jury instructions conference, the following happens:

Plaintiff: Our next requested instruction, No. 12, is a missing witness instruction. This is based on the fact that John Turner, the defendant's sales manager, did not testify as a defense witness during

---

3. J.A. Stein, Closing Argument §16 (1969); F. Lane, Goldstein Trial Technique §23.12 (3d ed. 1984); L.J. Smith, Art of Advocacy—Summation §2.42 (1991).

the case, although he was available. The defendant's failure to call him, when he had a significant involvement with this case, permits the negative inference that had he testified, his testimony would have been adverse to the defendant.

Defendant: Mr. Turner is retired, your honor. He's no longer one of our employees or in our control. Plaintiff could have called him as a witness if they thought he would help them, but they didn't.

Plaintiff: Mr. Turner may be retired, your honor, but he's still getting his pension benefits from the defendant. He's hardly going to testify and say something that may jeopardize himself.

Judge: Plaintiff's requested Instruction No. 12 is denied. This witness is not sufficiently within the control of the defendant that a missing witness instruction is appropriate. And counsel will not make a missing witness argument about Mr. Turner.

Example 2:

This is a wrongful death case brought by the family of a man who committed suicide while a patient in the defendant's hospital. Plaintiff claims that the patient was known to be suicidal and that the hospital did not take adequate precautions to prevent his suicide. In the defense case, the hospital does not call the nurse who supervised the suicide watch. During closing arguments, the following happens:

Plaintiff: The hospital knew Mr. Palmer was suicidal. They made that diagnosis when he was first admitted. The attending doctor, Dr. Holmes, ordered a suicide watch to make sure that Mr. Palmer would not hurt himself. After all that, Mr. Palmer was found dead the next morning. Now you've got to be wondering, where was Nurse Johnson, the nurse who was in charge of the suicide watch? She still works there. She's still a nurse at the hospital. Why didn't they call her as a witness? Folks, there's only one possible reason: Nurse Johnson couldn't help the defense. Nurse Johnson . . .

Defense: Objection. That's an improper comment. They could have called the nurse during trial.

Judge: Overruled. This is proper under the circumstances. Counsel, limit your objections to legal grounds, and do not argue them further.

Commentary: "Speaking objections" are always improper, since they are directed to influencing the jury, rather than directed to the judge.

Example 3:

This is an assault prosecution. The defense is self-defense. The defense presents evidence during the trial, although the defendant himself does not testify. In the prosecutor's closing argument, the following happens:

Prosecutor: In this case, the defense chose to present evidence, which they have a perfect right to do. When they do, however, you have a right to analyze the quality and quantity of that

evidence. So what did they do here? They paraded in two of
the defendant's friends, and nobody else, to tell us that . . .

Defendant: Your honor, that's an improper comment on the defendant's
constitutional rights.

Judge: Well, the prosecution may comment on the significance of the two
defense witnesses, so the objection is overruled. I trust that
counsel knows where the line is and will not cross it.

Commentary: The judge's comment is a thinly veiled statement to the prosecutor not to argue directly, or suggest, that the defendant's failure to testify has
meaning or should be considered.

Example 4:

This is a burglary case. During the defendant's closing argument, the
following happens:

Defendant: There's one question they don't want you to think about: Where
are the fingerprints? The evidence is that the burglar broke in
through a window and ransacked the house. So where are the
fingerprints? The prosecution offered no evidence of any kind
about fingerprints. It's obvious that the police made no effort to
get prints, and the reason they didn't is that if they had taken
fingerprints, they wouldn't have matched the defendant's.

Prosecutor: Objection, your honor. There's absolutely no evidence at all
about this.

Judge: Sustained. Counsel, you may argue the significance of no fingerprints, but you cannot argue why the police did not get prints.

Commentary: The defendant may properly argue that the absence of evidence,
such as fingerprints, weakens the prosecution's case, but the defendant may not
argue why the evidence was not obtained without evidence being admitted to
support the argument.

§14.5. *Stating personal opinions and making personal attacks*[4]

1. Law

Closing arguments should be based on the evidence and reasonable inferences
from that evidence. It follows that lawyers may not give personal opinions about
the evidence. For example, arguments along the lines of "I just don't find that
testimony believable" or "I didn't buy it, nor should you" are improper. Phrases
like "I think" and "I believe" are best deleted from a lawyer's trial vocabulary.

It also follows that personal attacks on parties, witnesses, and opposing
lawyers are improper. For example, arguments along the lines of "They don't

---

4. J.A. Stein, Closing Argument §§24, 70 (1969); F. Lane, Goldstein Trial Technique
§§23.09, 23.16, 23.17 (3d ed. 1984); L.J. Smith, Art of Advocacy—Summation §2.43 (1991).

want you to know the truth" or "They have spent the entire trial bringing you lies and falsehoods," and other direct suggestions of lying, fabricating evidence, or acting in bad faith, usually are improper, since they ask the jury to focus on the conduct of the lawyers, rather than the evidence. If such lawyer misconduct occurs, it is for the judge to deal with, not the jury.

May a prosecutor comment on the fact that a defendant testifies after his defense witnesses? In *Portuondo v. Agard*, 529 U.S. 61 (2000), the prosecutor argued ". . . he gets to sit here and listen to the testimony of all the other witnesses before he testifies. . . . You get to sit here and think what am I going to say and how am I going to say it? How am I going to fit it into the evidence?" The Supreme Court held the argument did not violate the defendant's Fifth and Sixth Amendment rights. The argument was held to be fair comment on the defendant's credibility.

2. Practice

The difficult issues involve characterizing witnesses as liars or untruthful. While name-calling usually is improper, there may be instances where calling a witness a liar, or using some other disparaging label, is a reasonable inference from proven facts. While some judges believe that such conduct is always inappropriate, others believe that if the evidence is there, the comment is proper.

Example:

> This is a murder prosecution. The state's star witness is a former co-defendant who testifies after reaching a plea agreement with the prosecution. During the defendant's closing argument, the following happens:

> *Defendant:* What does the prosecution's case depend on? It's simple. Their whole case depends on the testimony of Bobby Adams. And what is he? A liar, plain and simple. He . . .
> *Prosecutor:* Objection to the characterization, your honor.
> *Judge:* Overruled. The jury will decide if the evidence supports the characterization.
> *Defendant:* He told the police one thing and then turns around and tells you something entirely different. Either he lied to the police, or he lied to you. That makes him a liar, and we all know you can't trust a liar. Yet that's exactly what the prosecution is begging you to do in this case.

§14.6. *Appealing to sympathy, prejudice, and passions*[5]

1. Law

Improper appeals to sympathy or prejudice and other attempts to inflame the passions or arouse the prejudices of the jury involve several common situations.

---

5. J.A. Stein, Closing Argument §§21, 22, 30, 74 (1969); F. Lane, Goldstein Trial Technique §23.23 (3d ed. 1984); L.J. Smith, Art of Advocacy—Summation §§2.51, 2.52(1991).

The most common probably occurs in criminal cases where the prosecutor suggests that the jury has a duty to deter crime, that it must protect the community, and that this can be accomplished only by returning a guilty verdict. Many courts hold that this is improper, since it asks the jury to base its verdict on outside considerations, not the evidence. Similar is the "send them a message" argument, which asks the jury to return a guilty verdict to tell other criminals that this community will not tolerate similar conduct. Most courts hold that this argument is improper, for the same reason. However, if the "send a message" argument is made by a lawyer seeking punitive damages in a civil case, it is appropriate. Another common argument, that the jury is the "conscience of the community" or that "the community will be watching," or similar language, is more problematic. Some courts permit it; others hold that it is improper.

Direct appeals based on the background characteristics of the litigants also are improper. For example, asking the jury to base its verdict on the fact that a party is a minority, foreign born, or a non-citizen, or on some other characteristic of that party, such as sexual orientation, is obviously improper. Suggesting that a wealthy party or a corporation should pay more or that a poor person should receive more, because of wealth or poverty, is improper unless an issue in the case, such as punitive damages, makes the wealth of the defendant a relevant issue. Arguing that a verdict will have collateral consequences, such as affecting a doctor's professional reputation and standing in the community or raising his insurance rates, is improper.

2. Practice

These issues are important, and judges base their rulings on whether an argument focuses on the evidence and reasonable inferences from it or whether it asks a jury to base its decision on matters outside the evidence. Particularly in criminal cases, improper arguments can lead to later reversals.

Example 1:

This is a criminal case. In the prosecutor's closing argument, the following happens:

Prosecutor: Folks, you have to decide this case, of course, but your verdict does much more than just decide this case. Your verdict is a message to the community that you will not tolerate crime and those who commit it. Your verdict is a message to all the other criminals who are thinking about preying on your community.

Defendant: Your honor, I object. This is improper argument.

Judge: Sustained. Counsel, limit your remarks to the evidence.

Commentary: This is a "send them a message" argument. Some courts permit it, since they allow arguments that dwell on the evils of crime or that urge the fearless administration of the criminal law. Other courts do not, reasoning that the argument asks the jury to consider matters outside the evidence.

Example 2:

This is a products liability case. The plaintiff was injured using the defendant's product and is seeking compensatory damages. In the plaintiff's closing argument, the following happens:

Plaintiff: So what is the proper amount of damages you should return? I can't tell you what to do. That's your job. But keep in mind that the defendant is not a simple small business struggling to stay afloat. It's a large corporation, with thousands of employees and several plants . . .

Defendant: Objection, your honor. These are improper arguments on the measure of damages.

Judge: Sustained.

Commentary: This argument, focusing on the characteristics of the defendant, rather than the damages to the plaintiff, is improper unless the jury is allowed to consider punitive damages.

Example 3:

This is a criminal case. During the prosecution's closing argument, the following happens:

Prosecutor: What is the evidence the defense brought you? Nothing but a smoke screen, a house of mirrors, which has nothing to do with the issues here.

Defendant: Objection. It's improper argument.

Judge: Overruled.

Prosecutor: And why did they bring you the smoke and mirrors? Because the defense doesn't want you to learn the truth. What they've done here is . . .

Defendant: Objection again, your honor.

Judge: Yes, this is now going too far. The objection is sustained.

Commentary: "Smoke and mirrors" and "pulling the wool over your eyes" arguments are common in criminal cases, and most judges allow them. However, when the argument goes further and suggests that the defense has improper motives, the argument is usually considered improper.

§14.7. Arguing the law[6]

1. Law

Closing arguments may discuss the law, and good ones invariably do. Since the jury's job is to apply the law to the facts and reach a verdict, good closing

---

6. J.A. Stein, Closing Argument §20 (1969); F. Lane, Goldstein Trial Technique §23.20 (3d ed. 1984).

arguments use the applicable law as stated in the court's instructions. Almost all jurisdictions permit the lawyers to quote from or accurately paraphrase the instructions during closing arguments.

Nevertheless, there are some things the lawyers cannot do. Lawyers cannot misstate, mischaracterize, or in any way distort the applicable law, such as by omitting certain requirements of proof when they discuss the elements of a claim or defense. They cannot attempt to shift the burden of proof to the other party, as when a prosecutor argues that "none of the evidence they brought you proved that he was innocent." They cannot discuss the legislative intent behind the law or explain the reasons the law was enacted, since these are matters not in evidence. In almost all jurisdictions, lawyers cannot urge jury nullification, or urge the jury to ignore applicable law.

In criminal cases, lawyers frequently attempt to define the meaning of reasonable doubt. In jurisdictions where reasonable doubt is defined in an instruction, courts usually bar lawyers from further defining reasonable doubt, although they can refer to the wording of the instruction in arguing the case. For example, a lawyer can say, "The law says that a reasonable doubt is one that would make you hesitate to act in some important matter in your life," and then argue that the evidence in this case would make one hesitate. In jurisdictions where reasonable doubt is not further defined in an instruction, courts usually bar lawyers from attempting to define it, although they usually can refer to what is not reasonable doubt. For example, a lawyer can say, "The law requires proof beyond a reasonable doubt; it does not require proof beyond all possible doubt," and then argue that the evidence in the case meets the legal standard.

2. Practice

The most serious issues here involve arguments that attempt to shift the burden of proof or to apply a higher standard of proof than the law requires.

Example 1:

This is a murder prosecution. The defense is self-defense. Under the applicable law, once the defendant has raised that defense by introducing some evidence of self-defense, the prosecution must disprove self-defense beyond a reasonable doubt. During the prosecution's closing arguments, the following happens:

Prosecutor: Folks, the defense doesn't have to prove anything, but if they decide to present evidence, you're entitled to examine what they've presented. In this case, they called witnesses to prove self-defense, but have they really proven it?

Defendant: Objection. We don't have to prove anything. The prosecution has the burden of proof.

Judge: The objection is sustained. Members of the jury, the prosecution has the burden of proving, beyond a reasonable doubt, that the defendant was not entitled to defend himself under the circumstances that existed at the time of the shooting. Counsel, continue your argument.

Commentary: When a party attempts to shift the burden of proof, many judges will instruct the jury, at that time, on the correct burden.

Example 2:

This is a contract case. The plaintiff is suing on a fire insurance policy. The defense is that the plaintiff burned down his own building. Under the applicable law, the defendant has the burden of proving arson by the preponderance of the evidence. During the plaintiff's closing argument, the following happens:

Plaintiff: The defense, of course, is claiming arson. But the law says it's not enough simply to claim it was arson. The law says this to the defendant: Prove that Mr. Potter is an arsonist. Prove it!

Defendant: Your honor, we object to counsel attempting to make this sound like a criminal case with criminal burdens of proof.

Judge: Overruled. This is a civil case. It's the defendant's burden to prove, by the greater weight of the evidence, that the plaintiff caused the fire to his own building. Counsel, you will refrain from making objections that are argumentative. Don't do it again.

§14.8. *Making improper damages arguments*[7]

1. Law

A recurring problem in personal injury cases is the application of the "Golden Rule"; that is, the lawyer asks the jury to step into the shoes of a litigant, most commonly the plaintiff or the victim. Common arguments in personal injury cases are along the lines of "If you lost your leg, how much do you think your leg is worth?" or "What would you be willing to pay to regain the use of your leg?" Such an argument is improper because it directly asks the jury to take sides, rather than impartially consider the evidence and return a reasoned verdict.

A variation of the Golden Rule problem, usually occurring on the defense side, is the argument that asks the jury to consider the impact of its verdict on everyone as taxpayers. When the defendant is a government entity, there is a possibility that a verdict may be paid by the taxpayers. However, such an argument is improper because it asks jurors to base their verdict on their own pecuniary interest as taxpayers.

The Golden Rule concept also applies to criminal cases, even though damages are not an issue. Arguments that inflame the passions or prejudices of the jury by focusing on the consequences of the crime are improper. Common arguments in criminal cases are along the lines of "Think about the victim's wife and children — the wife who will grow old alone, the children who will never again hear Daddy's voice." These arguments are improper

---

7. J.A. Stein, Closing Argument §§60, 61, 65-67, 69, 81 (1969); F. Lane, Goldstein Trial Technique §§23.19, 23.33 (3d ed. 1984); L.J. Smith, Art of Advocacy—Summation §§2.30–2.39 (1991).

because they directly ask the jury to decide the case based on the consequences to the victim's family, rather than impartially consider the evidence and decide whether the evidence has proved guilt beyond a reasonable doubt.

Numerous related arguments are improper because they ask the jury to consider facts that are not in evidence or that are speculative in nature. Common are arguments that ask the jury to consider the settlements of co-defendants or verdicts in similar cases. Also improper are arguments that ask the jury to consider the effect of a verdict on a business's continued existence, especially when the business is an important local employer, and the effect of a verdict on a person's reputation and professional standing.

In wrongful death cases, evidence that the plaintiff has remarried and arguments that the plaintiff may remarry usually are improper. This is because the fact of, or possibility of, remarriage is considered irrelevant to the loss to the plaintiff, much like the fact of insurance or other collateral sources is considered irrelevant to the issue of damages in personal injury cases.

A frequently encountered problem in tort and contract cases is the argument that asks the jury to punish the other side for claimed misconduct. Unless the jury can consider punitive damages, such an argument is improper because punishment is irrelevant to the proper measure of damages, which are solely compensatory.

Finally, the propriety of per diem or other unit of time arguments on the issue of future damages has generated substantial case law. The jurisdictions vary widely. At one extreme, a few do not permit arguments for any specific daily amount for pain and suffering. At the other, a number expressly permit per diem arguments. In the middle, other jurisdictions permit asking for specific amounts for pain and suffering and other future damages, but bar calculating the amount by a per diem or other small unit of time.

2. Practice

The propriety of many damages arguments depends on the particular jurisdiction.

Example 1:

This is a personal injury case. During the plaintiff's closing argument, the following happens:

Plaintiff: Members of the jury, in a world of healthy people, what does it mean to have lost a leg? Most of us can't imagine it, but we all know that we'd do anything, and pay anything, not to have it happen to us.
Defendant: Your honor, I object. The plaintiff is violating the Golden Rule.
Judge: Sustained.

Example 2:

This is a products liability case in which only compensatory damages are sought. The plaintiff was injured when his hand was mangled in a farm machine. During the plaintiff's closing argument, the following happens:

Plaintiff: So what kind of verdict is appropriate here? When you consider that, one thing's for sure: The defendant still doesn't get it. They still don't understand that you can't put a machine like that, without any protective screening, out in the marketplace where any unsuspecting farm worker can get seriously injured. Your verdict needs to be a wake-up call. Your verdict should be large enough that the company gets the idea . . .
Defendant: Objection, your honor. That's an improper damages argument.
Judge: Sustained. Counsel, confine yourself to arguing what damages are reasonable to compensate the plaintiff.

Commentary: When an objectionable argument is made, many judges will immediately tell the jury the legally proper basis for determining damages in this kind of case.

§14.9. *Arguing consequences of a conviction or verdict*[8]

1. Law

A central concept in jury trials is that the jury determines the facts and the judge determines the law. Included in the law are the legal consequences of a judgment. It follows, then, that the lawyers in closing arguments may not argue the consequences of the jury's verdict (except in death penalty cases). Several arguments in this area commonly occur.

Perhaps most common is lawyers in criminal cases arguing the consequences of an acquittal or the possible sentence after a conviction. Both are improper (unless the jurisdiction is one of the few where the jury determines the sentence as well as guilt or innocence), since the consequences of a conviction or an acquittal are legally irrelevant to the determination of guilt or innocence. For example, urging the jury not to convict because the sentence for the crime charged "means that he will have to do at least 25 years in the pen" is improper. Urging the jury to convict because an acquittal will mean that the defendant is "free to prey on the citizens of this community" is improper.

Lawyers sometimes try to argue what personal effect the jury's verdict will have on the victim or the defendant, or on their families. Telling the jury a conviction means the "victim and her family will be able to hold their heads high again in the community" or "if the defendant is convicted, it means he will never be able to hold a license as a real estate broker" is improper because, once again, this asks the jury to consider matters irrelevant to the jury's proper function.

In the same vein, discussing the possibilities of a pardon or parole and appeals of any verdict and judgment is improper. Such discussion asks the

8. J.A. Stein, Closing Arguments §§68, 71, 74, 76 (1969).

jury to consider the consequences of its decision, and this is irrelevant to the jury's proper and limited function, which is determining whether the defendant has been proven guilty of the crime charged.

2. Practice

Problems in this area unfortunately are common, as lawyers frequently attempt to inject improper emotions and extraneous considerations into the case.

Example 1:

>   This is a criminal case. During the prosecutor's closing argument, the following happens:

> *Prosecutor:* Members of the jury, this is your community. You get to decide who is worthy of being allowed to walk the streets of your community. You get to decide . . .
> *Defendant:* Objection, your honor, to the improper argument.
> *Judge:* Sustained. Counsel, please confine your argument to the evidence and reasonable inferences from that evidence.

Example 2:

>   This is a criminal case. During the defendant's closing argument, the following happens:

> *Defendant:* Members of the jury, one thing is obvious here. Any conviction will ruin Mr. Johnson's life. Any conviction will send him to the penitentiary . . .
> *Prosecution:* Objection, your honor. It's improper to argue consequences of a conviction.
> *Judge:* The objection is sustained. Counsel will not discuss sentencing.

   Commentary: How serious the transgression is often determines whether the judge merely will sustain the objection or also will reprimand the offending lawyer and direct him to limit his argument to proper topics.

§14.10. *Making improper rebuttal arguments*[9]

1. Law

In most jurisdictions, the party with the burden of proof (more precisely, the burden of persuasion) has the right to "open and close," which means that party has the right to argue first and to make a rebuttal argument following the other side's argument. This right to rebut has raised two recurring issues.

---

9. J.A. Stein, Closing Argument §23 (1969); L.J. Smith, Art of Advocacy — Summation §2.13 (1991).

First, most courts hold that the proper scope of a rebuttal argument is rebuttal of arguments the defense has made during its closing argument. This means that the plaintiff (the party ordinarily having the burden of persuasion) cannot raise entirely new arguments for the first time in its rebuttal argument, thereby depriving the defense of a meaningful opportunity to address these arguments. It also means that if the defense chooses to limit its closing argument to certain matters, it may effectively prevent the plaintiff from arguing anything it wants to in rebuttal. An argument that raises new matters and a proper rebuttal often are separated by a fine line. For example, in a personal injury case, may the plaintiff "save" arguing exact amounts in damages until its rebuttal argument? Will this be affected by whether the defense discusses damages in its closing argument? The answers to these questions depend to a substantial degree on the attitudes of the trial judge and local custom.

Second, the issues of invited reply and retaliation frequently arise. If one party makes an improper argument, can the other side respond and make an otherwise improper argument in response? In other words, is the responsive argument now proper because it was "invited" or the other side "opened the door"? These issues arise frequently on appeal, and courts vary on how they address them. Some hold that the proper remedy for an improper argument is a timely objection, which should stop the improper argument. Other courts are more permissive, taking the position that you can fight fire with fire.

In *United States v. Robinson*, 485 U.S. 25 (1988), the Supreme Court held that where a defense attorney argued that the defendant had not been allowed to present his side of the story (the defendant did not testify), the prosecutor in rebuttal could argue that the defendant could have taken the stand and explained things to the jury. Under the circumstances since the comment was in response to the defense argument, rather than prosecutor initiated (the situation in *Griffin v. California*, 380 U.S. 609 (1965)), the comment was fair and did not violate the defendant's constitutional right to remain silent.

The best approach is to make a timely objection. If the objection is sustained, that ends the matter. If the objection is overruled, it essentially sanctions an invited reply. A lawyer who fails to object to what he considers to be an improper argument, planning to respond to it later, runs the risk that his reply will be objected to or that an appellate court will conclude the response was improper. Failure to object waives the error on appeal.

2.   Practice

The judge's principal concern is to ensure that a party has a fair opportunity to meet the other side's argument. This means the judge will be sensitive to claims that the plaintiff's rebuttal argument raises new matters that the defendant has not had a fair opportunity to address because the plaintiff did not discuss them in the plaintiff's first closing argument.

Example 1:

This is a personal injury case. In the plaintiff's closing argument, the plaintiff principally argues the liability issue and discusses the damages without ever dealing specifically with the pain and suffering component.

The plaintiff asks for a damages amount without breaking it down into its component parts. In the defendant's closing argument, the defendant principally argues liability and on the damages issue simply states that since the plaintiff has not mentioned any specific numbers for the various components of damages, there is nothing for the defense to respond to. Before the plaintiff's rebuttal argument, the following happens:

Defendant: Your honor, before the jury comes back and the plaintiff gives the rebuttal argument, we have a motion.

Judge: What is it?

Defendant: We move to preclude the plaintiff from arguing pain and suffering in rebuttal. The plaintiff did not argue any numbers in the closing argument, so there was nothing for us to respond to. It would be unfair for the plaintiff for the first time, in rebuttal, to put suggested dollar amounts on pain and suffering, when we no longer have an opportunity to respond.

Plaintiff: It's rebuttal, your honor. They talked about damages in the defense closing. Surely we're entitled to talk about damages again in rebuttal.

Judge: I agree with the defendant. You can't argue the specifics of the damages request for pain and suffering for the first time in rebuttal, since the defendant never will have an opportunity to make a meaningful response.

Commentary: This example shows the danger of plaintiff "sandbagging" in the closing argument. Saving an argument for rebuttal may result in the argument being precluded. Some judges may permit the argument and then give the defendant an opportunity to make a surrebuttal argument on the issue.

Example 2:

This is a criminal case. During the defendant's closing argument, the following happens:

Defendant: Is this robbery charge serious? You bet it is! Bobby could get up to 10 years for it.

Prosecutor: Objection, that's improper.

Judge: Sustained. Counsel, move on to something else.

During the prosecutor's rebuttal argument, the following happens:

Prosecutor: They brought out that the defendant could get up to 10 years. He also could get probation and do no jail time at all.

Defendant: Objection. That's an improper argument.

Prosecutor: It's invited, your honor. They opened the door.

Judge: Counsel, the objection is sustained. There will be no further comments on possible sentences for this type of charge. Members of the jury, you may not consider the possibility of any sentence when you deliberate on your verdict.

Commentary: Invited replies create difficult issues for the judge. It is clear that a jury should not consider the possible sentence in determining the issue of guilt or innocence. However, once the defendant improperly mentions one possible sentence, the prosecutor naturally will want to offset the impression with another possible sentence. The alert judge will stop this at the pass, sustain the objection, and admonish counsel to move on to something else.

Appendix

FEDERAL RULES OF EVIDENCE

(as amended through December 1, 2014)

ARTICLE X. CONTENTS OF WRITINGS, RECORDINGS, AND PHOTOGRAPHS

ARTICLE XI. MISCELLANEOUS RULES

ARTICLE I.   GENERAL PROVISIONS

Rule 101.   Scope; Definitions

(a) **Scope.** These rules apply to proceedings in United States courts. The specific courts and proceedings to which the rules apply, along with exceptions, are set out in Rule 1101.

(b) **Definitions.** In these rules

(1) "civil case" means a civil action or proceeding;

(2) "criminal case" includes a criminal proceeding;

(3) "public office" includes a public agency;

(4) "record" includes a memorandum, report, or data compilation;

(5) a "rule prescribed by the Supreme Court" means a rule adopted by the Supreme Court under statutory authority; and

(6) a reference to any kind of written material or any other medium includes electronically stored information.

Rule 102.   Purpose

These rules should be construed so as to administer every proceeding fairly, eliminate unjustifiable expense and delay, and promote the development of evidence law, to the end of ascertaining the truth and securing a just determination.

Rule 103.   Rulings on Evidence

(a) **Preserving a Claim of Error.** A party may claim error in a ruling to admit or exclude evidence only if the error affects a substantial right of the party and

(1) if the ruling admits evidence, a party, on the record:

  (A) timely objects or moves to strike; and

  (B) states the specific ground, unless it was apparent from the context; or

(2) if the ruling excludes evidence, a party informs the court of its substance by an offer of proof, unless the substance was apparent from the context.

(b) Not Needing to Renew an Objection or Offer of Proof. Once the court rules definitively on the record—either before or at trial—a party need not renew an objection or offer of proof to preserve a claim of error for appeal.

(c) Court's Statement About the Ruling; Directing an Offer of Proof. The court may make any statement about the character or form of the evidence, the objection made, and the ruling. The court may direct that an offer of proof be made in question-and-answer form.

(d) Preventing the Jury from Hearing Inadmissible Evidence. To the extent practicable, the court must conduct a jury trial so that inadmissible evidence is not suggested to the jury by any means.

(e) Taking Notice of Plain Error. A court may take notice of a plain error affecting a substantial right, even if the claim of error was not properly preserved.

Rule 104.   Preliminary Questions

(a) In General. The court must decide any preliminary question about whether a witness is qualified, a privilege exists, or evidence is admissible. In so deciding, the court is not bound by evidence rules, except those on privilege.

(b) Relevance That Depends on a Fact. When the relevance of evidence depends on whether a fact exists, proof must be introduced sufficient to support a finding that the fact does exist. The court may admit the proposed evidence on the condition that the proof be introduced later.

(c) Conducting a Hearing So That the Jury Cannot Hear It. The court must conduct any hearing on a preliminary question so that the jury cannot hear it if

  (1) the hearing involves the admissibility of a confession;

  (2) a defendant in a criminal case is a witness and so requests; or

  (3) justice so requires.

(d) Cross-Examining a Defendant in a Criminal Case. By testifying on a preliminary question, a defendant in a criminal case does not become subject to cross-examination on other issues in the case.

(e) Evidence Relevant to Weight and Credibility. This rule does not limit a party's right to introduce before the jury evidence that is relevant to the weight or credibility of other evidence.

Rule 105.   Limiting Evidence That Is Not Admissible
Against Other Parties or for Other Purposes

If the court admits evidence that is admissible against a party or for a purpose—but not against another party or for another purpose—the court, on timely request, must restrict the evidence to its proper scope and instruct the jury accordingly.

Rule 106.   Remainder of or Related Writings or Recorded Statements

If a party introduces all or part of a writing or recorded statement, an adverse party may require the introduction, at that time, of any other part — or any other writing or recorded statement — that in fairness ought to be considered at the same time.

ARTICLE II.   JUDICIAL NOTICE

Rule 201.   Judicial Notice of Adjudicative Facts

(a) Scope. This rule governs judicial notice of an adjudicative fact only, not a legislative fact.

(b) Kinds of Facts That May Be Judicially Noticed. The court may judicially notice a fact that is not subject to reasonable dispute because it

    (1) is generally known within the trial court's territorial jurisdiction; or

    (2) can be accurately and readily determined from sources whose accuracy cannot reasonably be questioned.

(c) Taking Notice. The court:

    (1) may take judicial notice on its own; or

    (2) must take judicial notice if a party requests it and the court is supplied with the necessary information.

(d) Timing. The court may take judicial notice at any stage of the proceeding.

(e) Opportunity to Be Heard. On timely request, a party is entitled to be heard on the propriety of taking judicial notice and the nature of the fact to be noticed. If the court takes judicial notice before notifying a party, the party, on request, is still entitled to be heard.

(f) Instructing the Jury. In a civil case, the court must instruct the jury to accept the noticed fact as conclusive. In a criminal case, the court must instruct the jury that it may or may not accept the noticed fact as conclusive.

ARTICLE III.   PRESUMPTIONS IN CIVIL CASES

Rule 301.   Presumptions in Civil Cases Generally

In a civil case, unless a federal statute or these rules provide otherwise, the party against whom a presumption is directed has the burden of producing evidence to rebut the presumption. But this rule does not shift the burden of persuasion, which remains on the party who had it originally.

Rule 302.   Applying State Law to Presumptions in Civil Cases

In a civil case, state law governs the effect of a presumption regarding a claim or defense for which state law supplies the rule of decision.

ARTICLE IV.   RELEVANCE AND ITS LIMITS

Rule 401.   Test for Relevant Evidence

Evidence is relevant if
(a) it has any tendency to make a fact more or less probable than it would be without the evidence; and
(b) the fact is of consequence in determining the action.

Rule 402.   General Admissibility of Relevant Evidence

Relevant evidence is admissible unless any of the following provides otherwise:

* the United States Constitution;
* a federal statute;
* these rules; or
* other rules prescribed by the Supreme Court.

Irrelevant evidence is not admissible.

Rule 403.   Excluding Relevant Evidence for Prejudice, Confusion, Waste of Time, or Other Reasons

The court may exclude relevant evidence if its probative value is substantially outweighed by a danger of one or more of the following: unfair prejudice, confusing the issues, misleading the jury, undue delay, wasting time, or needlessly presenting cumulative evidence.

Rule 404.   Character Evidence; Crimes or Other Acts

(a) Character Evidence.
  (1) *Prohibited Uses.* Evidence of a person's character or character trait is not admissible to prove that on a particular occasion the person acted in accordance with the character or trait.
  (2) *Exceptions for a Defendant or Victim in a Criminal Case.* The following exceptions apply in a criminal case:
    (A) a defendant may offer evidence of the defendant's pertinent trait, and if the evidence is admitted, the prosecutor may offer evidence to rebut it;

(B) subject to the limitations in Rule 412, a defendant may offer evidence of an alleged victim's pertinent trait, and if the evidence is admitted, the prosecutor may:

(i) offer evidence to rebut it; and

(ii) offer evidence of the defendant's same trait; and

(C) in a homicide case, the prosecutor may offer evidence of the alleged victim's trait of peacefulness to rebut evidence that the victim was the first aggressor.

(3) *Exceptions for a Witness.* Evidence of a witness's character may be admitted under Rules 607, 608, and 609.

(b) Crimes, Wrongs, or Other Acts.

(1) *Prohibited Uses.* Evidence of a crime, wrong, or other act is not admissible to prove a person's character in order to show that on a particular occasion the person acted in accordance with the character.

(2) *Permitted Uses; Notice in a Criminal Case.* This evidence may be admissible for another purpose, such as proving motive, opportunity, intent, preparation, plan, knowledge, identity, absence of mistake, or lack of accident. On request by a defendant in a criminal case, the prosecutor must:

(A) provide reasonable notice of the general nature of any such evidence that the prosecutor intends to offer at trial; and

(B) do so before trial — or during trial if the court, for good cause, excuses lack of pretrial notice.

Rule 405.   Methods of Proving Character

(a) By Reputation or Opinion. When evidence of a person's character or character trait is admissible, it may be proved by testimony about the person's reputation or by testimony in the form of an opinion. On cross-examination of the character witness, the court may allow an inquiry into relevant specific instances of the person's conduct.

(b) By Specific Instances of Conduct. When a person's character or character trait is an essential element of a charge, claim, or defense, the character or trait may also be proved by relevant specific instances of the person's conduct.

Rule 406.   Habit; Routine Practice

Evidence of a person's habit or an organization's routine practice may be admitted to prove that on a particular occasion the person or organization acted in accordance with the habit or routine practice. The court may admit this evidence regardless of whether it is corroborated or whether there was an eyewitness.

Rule 407.   Subsequent Remedial Measures

When measures are taken that would have made an earlier injury or harm less likely to occur, evidence of the subsequent measures is not admissible to prove:

- negligence;
- culpable conduct;
- a defect in a product or its design; or
- a need for a warning or instruction.

But the court may admit this evidence for another purpose, such as impeachment or — if disputed — proving ownership, control, or the feasibility of precautionary measures.

Rule 408.   Compromise Offers and Negotiations

(a) **Prohibited Uses.** Evidence of the following is not admissible — on behalf of any party — either to prove or disprove the validity or amount of a disputed claim or to impeach by a prior inconsistent statement or a contradiction:

(1) furnishing, promising, or offering — or accepting, promising to accept, or offering to accept — a valuable consideration in order to compromise the claim; and

(2) conduct or a statement made during compromise negotiations about the claim — except when offered in a criminal case and when the negotiations related to a claim by a public office in the exercise of its regulatory, investigative, or enforcement authority.

(b) **Exceptions.** The court may admit this evidence for another purpose, such as proving a witness's bias or prejudice, negating a contention of undue delay, or proving an effort to obstruct a criminal investigation or prosecution.

Rule 409.   Offers to Pay Medical and Similar Expenses

Evidence of furnishing, promising to pay, or offering to pay medical, hospital, or similar expenses resulting from an injury is not admissible to prove liability for the injury.

Rule 410.   Pleas, Plea Discussions, and Related Statements

(a) **Prohibited Uses.** In a civil or criminal case, evidence of the following is not admissible against the defendant who made the plea or participated in the plea discussions:

(1) a guilty plea that was later withdrawn;

(2) a nolo contendere plea;

(3) a statement made during a proceeding on either of those pleas under Federal Rule of Criminal Procedure 11 or a comparable state procedure; or

(4) a statement made during plea discussions with an attorney for the prosecuting authority if the discussions did not result in a guilty plea or they resulted in a later-withdrawn guilty plea.

(b) **Exceptions.** The court may admit a statement described in Rule 410(a)(3) or (4)

(1) in any proceeding in which another statement made during the same plea or plea discussions has been introduced, if in fairness the statements ought to be considered together; or

(2) in a criminal proceeding for perjury or false statement, if the defendant made the statement under oath, on the record, and with counsel present.

Rule 411.   Liability Insurance

Evidence that a person was or was not insured against liability is not admissible to prove whether the person acted negligently or otherwise wrongfully. But the court may admit this evidence for another purpose, such as proving a witness's bias or prejudice or proving agency, ownership, or control.

Rule 412.   Sex-Offense Cases: The Victim's Sexual Behavior or Predisposition

(a) Prohibited Uses. The following evidence is not admissible in a civil or criminal proceeding involving alleged sexual misconduct:

(1) evidence offered to prove that a victim engaged in other sexual behavior; or

(2) evidence offered to prove a victim's sexual predisposition.

(b) Exceptions.

(1) *Criminal Cases.* The court may admit the following evidence in a criminal case:

(A) evidence of specific instances of a victim's sexual behavior, if offered to prove that someone other than the defendant was the source of semen, injury, or other physical evidence;

(B) evidence of specific instances of a victim's sexual behavior with respect to the person accused of the sexual misconduct, if offered by the defendant to prove consent or if offered by the prosecutor; and

(C) evidence whose exclusion would violate the defendant's constitutional rights.

(2) *Civil Cases.* In a civil case, the court may admit evidence offered to prove a victim's sexual behavior or sexual predisposition if its probative value substantially outweighs the danger of harm to any victim and of unfair prejudice to any party. The court may admit evidence of a victim's reputation only if the victim has placed it in controversy.

(c) Procedure to Determine Admissibility.

(1) *Motion.* If a party intends to offer evidence under Rule 412(b), the party must

(A) file a motion that specifically describes the evidence and states the purpose for which it is to be offered;

(B) do so at least 14 days before trial unless the court, for good cause, sets a different time;

(C) serve the motion on all parties; and

(D) notify the victim or, when appropriate, the victim's guardian or representative.

(2) *Hearing.* Before admitting evidence under this rule, the court must conduct an in camera hearing and give the victim and parties a right to attend and be heard. Unless the court orders otherwise, the motion, related materials, and the record of the hearing must be and remain sealed.

(d) Definition of "Victim." In this rule, "victim" includes an alleged victim.

Rule 413.   Similar Crimes in Sexual-Assault Cases

(a) Permitted Uses. In a criminal case in which a defendant is accused of a sexual assault, the court may admit evidence that the defendant committed any other sexual assault. The evidence may be considered on any matter to which it is relevant.

(b) Disclosure to the Defendant. If the prosecutor intends to offer this evidence, the prosecutor must disclose it to the defendant, including witnesses' statements or a summary of the expected testimony. The prosecutor must do so at least 15 days before trial or at a later time that the court allows for good cause.

(c) Effect on Other Rules. This rule does not limit the admission or consideration of evidence under any other rule.

(d) Definition of "Sexual Assault." In this rule and Rule 415, "sexual assault" means a crime under federal law or under state law (as "state" is defined in 18 U.S.C. §513) involving

(1) any conduct prohibited by 18 U.S.C. chapter 109A;

(2) contact, without consent, between any part of the defendant's body — or an object — and another person's genitals or anus;

(3) contact, without consent, between the defendant's genitals or anus and any part of another person's body;

(4) deriving sexual pleasure or gratification from inflicting death, bodily injury, or physical pain on another person; or

(5) an attempt or conspiracy to engage in conduct described in subparagraphs (1)–(4).

Rule 414.   Similar Crimes in Child-Molestation Cases

(a) Permitted Uses. In a criminal case in which a defendant is accused of child molestation, the court may admit evidence that the defendant committed any other child molestation. The evidence may be considered on any matter to which it is relevant.

(b) Disclosure to the Defendant. If the prosecutor intends to offer this evidence, the prosecutor must disclose it to the defendant, including witnesses' statements or a summary of the expected testimony. The prosecutor must do so at least 15 days before trial or at a later time that the court allows for good cause.

(c) Effect on Other Rules. This rule does not limit the admission or consideration of evidence under any other rule.

(d) Definition of "Child" and "Child Molestation." In this rule and Rule 415,

(1) "child" means a person below the age of 14; and

(2) "child molestation" means a crime under federal law or under state law (as "state" is defined in 18 U.S.C. §513) involving

(A) any conduct prohibited by 18 U.S.C. chapter 109A and committed with a child;

(B) any conduct prohibited by 18 U.S.C. chapter 110;

(C) contact between any part of the defendant's body — or an object — and a child's genitals or anus;

(D) contact between the defendant's genitals or anus and any part of a child's body;

(E) deriving sexual pleasure or gratification from inflicting death, bodily injury, or physical pain on a child; or

(F) an attempt or conspiracy to engage in conduct described in subparagraphs (A)–(E).

Rule 415.   Similar Acts in Civil Cases Involving Sexual Assault or Child Molestation

(a) Permitted Uses. In a civil case involving a claim for relief based on a party's alleged sexual assault or child molestation, the court may admit evidence that the party committed any other sexual assault or child molestation. The evidence may be considered as provided in Rules 413 and 414.

(b) Disclosure to the Opponent. If a party intends to offer this evidence, the party must disclose it to the party against whom it will be offered, including witnesses' statements or a summary of the expected testimony. The party must do so at least 15 days before trial or at a later time that the court allows for good cause.

(c) Effect on Other Rules. This rule does not limit the admission or consideration of evidence under any other rule.

ARTICLE V.   PRIVILEGES

Rule 501.   Privilege in General

The common law — as interpreted by United States courts in the light of reason and experience — governs a claim of privilege unless any of the following provides otherwise:

- the United States Constitution;
- a federal statute; or
- rules prescribed by the Supreme Court.

But in a civil case, state law governs privilege regarding a claim or defense for which state law supplies the rule of decision.

Rule 502. Attorney-Client Privilege and Work Product; Limitations on Waiver

The following provisions apply, in the circumstances set out, to disclosure of a communication or information covered by the attorney-client privilege or work-product protection.

(a) Disclosure Made in a Federal Proceeding or to a Federal Office or Agency; Scope of a Waiver. When the disclosure is made in a federal proceeding or to a federal office or agency and waives the attorney-client privilege or work-product protection, the waiver extends to an undisclosed communication or information in a federal or state proceeding only if:

(1) the waiver is intentional;

(2) the disclosed and undisclosed communications or information concern the same subject matter; and

(3) they ought in fairness to be considered together.

(b) Inadvertent Disclosure. When made in a federal proceeding or to a federal office or agency, the disclosure does not operate as a waiver in a federal or state proceeding if

(1) the disclosure is inadvertent;

(2) the holder of the privilege or protection took reasonable steps to prevent disclosure; and

(3) the holder promptly took reasonable steps to rectify the error, including (if applicable) following Federal Rule of Civil Procedure 26(b)(5)(B).

(c) Disclosure Made in a State Proceeding. When the disclosure is made in a state proceeding and is not the subject of a state-court order concerning waiver, the disclosure does not operate as a waiver in a federal proceeding if the disclosure:

(1) would not be a waiver under this rule if it had been made in a federal proceeding; or

(2) is not a waiver under the law of the state where the disclosure occurred.

(d) Controlling Effect of a Court Order. A federal court may order that the privilege or protection is not waived by disclosure connected with the litigation pending before the court — in which event the disclosure is also not a waiver in any other federal or state proceeding.

(e) Controlling Effect of a Party Agreement. An agreement on the effect of disclosure in a federal proceeding is binding only on the parties to the agreement, unless it is incorporated into a court order.

(f) Controlling Effect of this Rule. Notwithstanding Rules 101 and 1101, this rule applies to state proceedings and to federal court-annexed and federal court-mandated arbitration proceedings, in the circumstances set out in the rule. And notwithstanding Rule 501, this rule applies even if state law provides the rule of decision.

(g) Definitions. In this rule,

(1) "attorney-client privilege" means the protection that applicable law provides for confidential attorney-client communications; and

(2) "work-product protection" means the protection that applicable law provides for tangible material (or its intangible equivalent) prepared in anticipation of litigation or for trial.

ARTICLE VI.   WITNESSES

Rule 601.   Competency to Testify in General

Every person is competent to be a witness unless these rules provide otherwise. But in a civil case, state law governs the witness's competency regarding a claim or defense for which state law supplies the rule of decision.

Rule 602.   Need for Personal Knowledge

A witness may testify to a matter only if evidence is introduced sufficient to support a finding that the witness has personal knowledge of the matter. Evidence to prove personal knowledge may consist of the witness's own testimony. This rule does not apply to a witness's expert testimony under Rule 703.

Rule 603.   Oath or Affirmation to Testify Truthfully

Before testifying, a witness must give an oath or affirmation to testify truthfully. It must be in a form designed to impress that duty on the witness's conscience.

Rule 604.   Interpreter

An interpreter must be qualified and must give an oath or affirmation to make a true translation.

Rule 605.   Judge's Competency as a Witness

The presiding judge may not testify as a witness at the trial. A party need not object to preserve the issue.

Rule 606.   Juror's Competency as a Witness

(a) **At the Trial.** A juror may not testify as a witness before the other jurors at the trial. If a juror is called to testify, the court must give a party an opportunity to object outside the jury's presence.

(b) **During an Inquiry into the Validity of a Verdict or Indictment.**

(1) *Prohibited Testimony or Other Evidence.* During an inquiry into the validity of a verdict or indictment, a juror may not testify about any statement made or incident that occurred during the jury's deliberations; the effect of anything on that juror's or another juror's vote; or any juror's mental processes concerning the verdict or indictment. The court may not receive a juror's affidavit or evidence of a juror's statement on these matters.

(2) *Exceptions.* A juror may testify about whether

(A) extraneous prejudicial information was improperly brought to the jury's attention;

(B) an outside influence was improperly brought to bear on any juror; or

(C) a mistake was made in entering the verdict on the verdict form.

Rule 607. Who May Impeach a Witness

Any party, including the party that called the witness, may attack the witness's credibility.

Rule 608. A Witness's Character for Truthfulness or Untruthfulness

(a) **Reputation or Opinion Evidence.** A witness's credibility may be attacked or supported by testimony about the witness's reputation for having a character for truthfulness or untruthfulness, or by testimony in the form of an opinion about that character. But evidence of truthful character is admissible only after the witness's character for truthfulness has been attacked.

(b) **Specific Instances of Conduct.** Except for a criminal conviction under Rule 609, extrinsic evidence is not admissible to prove specific instances of a witness's conduct in order to attack or support the witness's character for truthfulness. But the court may, on cross-examination, allow them to be inquired into if they are probative of the character for truthfulness or untruthfulness of

(1) the witness; or

(2) another witness whose character the witness being cross-examined has testified about.

By testifying on another matter, a witness does not waive any privilege against self-incrimination for testimony that relates only to the witness's character for truthfulness.

Rule 609. Impeachment by Evidence of a Criminal Conviction

(a) **In General.** The following rules apply to attacking a witness's character for truthfulness by evidence of a criminal conviction:

(1) for a crime that, in the convicting jurisdiction, was punishable by death or by imprisonment for more than one year, the evidence:

(A) must be admitted, subject to Rule 403, in a civil case or in a criminal case in which the witness is not a defendant; and

(B) must be admitted in a criminal case in which the witness is a defendant, if the probative value of the evidence outweighs its prejudicial effect to that defendant; and

(2) for any crime regardless of the punishment, the evidence must be admitted if the court can readily determine that establishing the elements of

the crime required proving — or the witness's admitting — a dishonest act or false statement.

(b) Limit on Using the Evidence After 10 Years. This subdivision (b) applies if more than 10 years have passed since the witness's conviction or release from confinement for it, whichever is later. Evidence of the conviction is admissible only if

(1) its probative value, supported by specific facts and circumstances, substantially outweighs its prejudicial effect; and

(2) the proponent gives an adverse party reasonable written notice of the intent to use it so that the party has a fair opportunity to contest its use.

(c) Effect of a Pardon, Annulment, or Certificate of Rehabilitation. Evidence of a conviction is not admissible if

(1) the conviction has been the subject of a pardon, annulment, certificate of rehabilitation, or other equivalent procedure based on a finding that the person has been rehabilitated, and the person has not been convicted of a later crime punishable by death or by imprisonment for more than one year; or

(2) the conviction has been the subject of a pardon, annulment, or other equivalent procedure based on a finding of innocence.

(d) Juvenile Adjudications. Evidence of a juvenile adjudication is admissible under this rule only if

(1) it is offered in a criminal case;

(2) the adjudication was of a witness other than the defendant;

(3) an adult's conviction for that offense would be admissible to attack the adult's credibility; and

(4) admitting the evidence is necessary to fairly determine guilt or innocence.

(e) Pendency of an Appeal. A conviction that satisfies this rule is admissible even if an appeal is pending. Evidence of the pendency is also admissible.

Rule 610.   Religious Beliefs or Opinions

Evidence of a witness's religious beliefs or opinions is not admissible to attack or support the witness's credibility.

Rule 611.   Mode and Order of Examining Witnesses and Presenting Evidence

(a) Control by the Court; Purposes. The court should exercise reasonable control over the mode and order of examining witnesses and presenting evidence so as to

(1) make those procedures effective for determining the truth;

(2) avoid wasting time; and

(3) protect witnesses from harassment or undue embarrassment.

(b) Scope of Cross-Examination. Cross-examination should not go beyond the subject matter of the direct examination and matters affecting the witness's credibility. The court may allow inquiry into additional matters as if on direct examination.

(c) Leading Questions. Leading questions should not be used on direct examination except as necessary to develop the witness's testimony. Ordinarily, the court should allow leading questions
    (1) on cross-examination; and
    (2) when a party calls a hostile witness, an adverse party, or a witness identified with an adverse party.

Rule 612.   Writing Used to Refresh a Witness's Memory

    (a) Scope. This rule gives an adverse party certain options when a witness uses a writing to refresh memory
    (1) while testifying; or
    (2) before testifying, if the court decides that justice requires the party to have those options.
    (b) Adverse Party's Options; Deleting Unrelated Matter. Unless 18 U.S.C. §3500 provides otherwise in a criminal case, an adverse party is entitled to have the writing produced at the hearing, to inspect it, to cross-examine the witness about it, and to introduce in evidence any portion that relates to the witness's testimony. If the producing party claims that the writing includes unrelated matter, the court must examine the writing in camera, delete any unrelated portion, and order that the rest be delivered to the adverse party. Any portion deleted over objection must be preserved for the record.
    (c) Failure to Produce or Deliver the Writing. If a writing is not produced or is not delivered as ordered, the court may issue any appropriate order. But if the prosecution does not comply in a criminal case, the court must strike the witness's testimony or — if justice so requires — declare a mistrial.

Rule 613.   Witness's Prior Statement

    (a) Showing or Disclosing the Statement During Examination. When examining a witness about the witness's prior statement, a party need not show it or disclose its contents to the witness. But the party must, on request, show it or disclose its contents to an adverse party's attorney.
    (b) Extrinsic Evidence of a Prior Inconsistent Statement. Extrinsic evidence of a witness's prior inconsistent statement is admissible only if the witness is given an opportunity to explain or deny the statement and an adverse party is given an opportunity to examine the witness about it, or if justice so requires. This subdivision (b) does not apply to an opposing party's statement under Rule 801(d)(2).

Rule 614.   Court's Calling or Examining a Witness

    (a) Calling. The court may call a witness on its own or at a party's request. Each party is entitled to cross-examine the witness.
    (b) Examining. The court may examine a witness regardless of who calls the witness.

(c) Objections. A party may object to the court's calling or examining a witness either at that time or at the next opportunity when the jury is not present.

Rule 615.   Excluding Witnesses

At a party's request, the court must order witnesses excluded so that they cannot hear other witnesses' testimony. Or the court may do so on its own. But this rule does not authorize excluding
   (a) a party who is a natural person;
   (b) an officer or employee of a party that is not a natural person, after being designated as the party's representative by its attorney;
   (c) a person whose presence a party shows to be essential to presenting the party's claim or defense; or
   (d) a person authorized by statute to be present.

ARTICLE VII.   OPINIONS AND EXPERT TESTIMONY

Rule 701.   Opinion Testimony by Lay Witnesses

If a witness is not testifying as an expert, testimony in the form of an opinion is limited to one that is
   (a) rationally based on the witness's perception;
   (b) helpful to clearly understanding the witness's testimony or to determining a fact in issue; and
   (c) not based on scientific, technical, or other specialized knowledge within the scope of Rule 702.

Rule 702.   Testimony by Expert Witnesses

A witness who is qualified as an expert by knowledge, skill, experience, training, or education may testify in the form of an opinion or otherwise if
   (a) the expert's scientific, technical, or other specialized knowledge will help the trier of fact to understand the evidence or to determine a fact in issue;
   (b) the testimony is based on sufficient facts or data;
   (c) the testimony is the product of reliable principles and methods; and
   (d) the expert has reliably applied the principles and methods to the facts of the case.

Rule 703.   Bases of an Expert's Opinion Testimony

An expert may base an opinion on facts or data in the case that the expert has been made aware of or personally observed. If experts in the particular field would reasonably rely on those kinds of facts or data in forming an opinion on the subject, they need not be admissible for the opinion to be admitted. But if the facts or data would otherwise be inadmissible, the proponent of the opinion may disclose them to the jury only if their probative value in helping the jury evaluate the opinion substantially outweighs their prejudicial effect.

Rule 704. Opinion on an Ultimate Issue

(a) **In General — Not Automatically Objectionable.** An opinion is not objectionable just because it embraces an ultimate issue.

(b) **Exception.** In a criminal case, an expert witness must not state an opinion about whether the defendant did or did not have a mental state or condition that constitutes an element of the crime charged or of a defense. Those matters are for the trier of fact alone.

Rule 705. Disclosing the Facts or Data Underlying an Expert's Opinion

Unless the court orders otherwise, an expert may state an opinion — and give the reasons for it — without first testifying to the underlying facts or data. But the expert may be required to disclose those facts or data on cross-examination.

Rule 706. Court-Appointed Expert Witnesses

(a) **Appointment Process.** On a party's motion or on its own, the court may order the parties to show cause why expert witnesses should not be appointed and may ask the parties to submit nominations. The court may appoint any expert that the parties agree on and any of its own choosing. But the court may only appoint someone who consents to act.

(b) **Expert's Role.** The court must inform the expert of the expert's duties. The court may do so in writing and have a copy filed with the clerk or may do so orally at a conference in which the parties have an opportunity to participate. The expert

(1) must advise the parties of any findings the expert makes;

(2) may be deposed by any party;

(3) may be called to testify by the court or any party; and

(4) may be cross-examined by any party, including the party that called the expert.

(c) **Compensation.** The expert is entitled to a reasonable compensation, as set by the court. The compensation is payable as follows:

(1) in a criminal case or in a civil case involving just compensation under the Fifth Amendment, from any funds that are provided by law; and

(2) in any other civil case, by the parties in the proportion and at the time that the court directs — and the compensation is then charged like other costs.

(d) **Disclosing the Appointment to the Jury.** The court may authorize disclosure to the jury that the court appointed the expert.

(e) **Parties' Choice of Their Own Experts.** This rule does not limit a party in calling its own experts.

Article VIII.   Hearsay

Rule 801.   Definitions That Apply to This Article; Exclusions from Hearsay

(a) Statement. "Statement" means a person's oral assertion, written assertion, or nonverbal conduct, if the person intended it as an assertion.

(b) Declarant. "Declarant" means the person who made the statement.

(c) Hearsay. "Hearsay" means a statement that

(1) the declarant does not make while testifying at the current trial or hearing; and

(2) a party offers in evidence to prove the truth of the matter asserted in the statement.

(d) Statements That Are Not Hearsay. A statement that meets the following conditions is not hearsay:

(1) *A Declarant-Witness's Prior Statement.* The declarant testifies and is subject to cross-examination about a prior statement, and the statement

(A) is inconsistent with the declarant's testimony and was given under penalty of perjury at a trial, hearing, or other proceeding or in a deposition;

(B) is consistent with the declarant's testimony and is offered:

(i) to rebut an express or implied charge that the declarant recently fabricated it or acted from a recent improper influence or motive in so testifying; or

(ii) to rehabilitate the declarant's credibility as a witness when attacked on another ground;

(C) identifies a person as someone the declarant perceived earlier.

(2) *An Opposing Party's Statement.* The statement is offered against an opposing party and

(A) was made by the party in an individual or representative capacity;

(B) is one the party manifested that it adopted or believed to be true;

(C) was made by a person whom the party authorized to make a statement on the subject;

(D) was made by the party's agent or employee on a matter within the scope of that relationship and while it existed; or

(E) was made by the party's coconspirator during and in furtherance of the conspiracy.

The statement must be considered but does not by itself establish the declarant's authority under (C); the existence or scope of the relationship under (D); or the existence of the conspiracy or participation in it under (E).

Rule 802.   The Rule Against Hearsay

Hearsay is not admissible unless any of the following provides otherwise:

- a federal statute;
- these rules; or
- other rules prescribed by the Supreme Court.

Rule 803.   Exceptions to the Rule Against Hearsay— Regardless of Whether the Declarant Is Available as a Witness

The following are not excluded by the rule against hearsay, regardless of whether the declarant is available as a witness:

   (1) *Present Sense Impression.* A statement describing or explaining an event or condition, made while or immediately after the declarant perceived it.

   (2) *Excited Utterance.* A statement relating to a startling event or condition, made while the declarant was under the stress of excitement that it caused.

   (3) *Then-Existing Mental, Emotional, or Physical Condition.* A statement of the declarant's then-existing state of mind (such as motive, intent, or plan) or emotional, sensory, or physical condition (such as mental feeling, pain, or bodily health), but not including a statement of memory or belief to prove the fact remembered or believed unless it relates to the validity or terms of the declarant's will.

   (4) *Statement Made for Medical Diagnosis or Treatment.* A statement that:

      (A) is made for—and is reasonably pertinent to—medical diagnosis or treatment; and

      (B) describes medical history; past or present symptoms or sensations; their inception; or their general cause.

   (5) *Recorded Recollection.* A record that:

      (A) is on a matter the witness once knew about but now cannot recall well enough to testify fully and accurately;

      (B) was made or adopted by the witness when the matter was fresh in the witness's memory; and

      (C) accurately reflects the witness's knowledge.

   If admitted, the record may be read into evidence but may be received as an exhibit only if offered by an adverse party.

   (6) *Records of a Regularly Conducted Activity.* A record of an act, event, condition, opinion, or diagnosis if:

      (A) the record was made at or near the time by—or from information transmitted by—someone with knowledge;

      (B) the record was kept in the course of a regularly conducted activity of a business, organization, occupation, or calling, whether or not for profit;

      (C) making the record was a regular practice of that activity;

      (D) all these conditions are shown by the testimony of the custodian or another qualified witness, or by a certification that complies with Rule 902(11) or (12) or with a statute permitting certification; and

      (E) the opponent does not show that the source of information or the method or circumstances of preparation indicate a lack of trustworthiness.

   (7) *Absence of a Record of a Regularly Conducted Activity.* Evidence that a matter is not included in a record described in paragraph (6) if

      (A) the evidence is admitted to prove that the matter did not occur or exist;

      (B) a record was regularly kept for a matter of that kind; and

      (C) the opponent does not show that the possible source of the information or other circumstances indicate a lack of trustworthiness.

(8) *Public Records.* A record or statement of a public office if
  (A) it sets out:
    (i) the office's activities;
    (ii) a matter observed while under a legal duty to report, but not including, in a criminal case, a matter observed by law-enforcement personnel; or
    (iii) in a civil case or against the government in a criminal case, factual findings from a legally authorized investigation; and
  (B) neither the source of information nor other circumstances indicate a lack of trustworthiness.

(9) *Public Records of Vital Statistics.* A record of a birth, death, or marriage, if reported to a public office in accordance with a legal duty.

(10) *Absence of a Public Record.* Testimony — or a certification under Rule 902 — that a diligent search failed to disclose a public record or statement if:
  (A) the testimony or certification is admitted to prove that:
    (i) the record or statement does not exist; or
    (ii) a matter did not occur or exist, if a public office regularly kept a record or statement for a matter of that kind; and
  (B) in a criminal case, a prosecutor who intends to offer a certification provides written notice of that intent at least 14 days before trial, and the defendant does not object in writing within 7 days of receiving notice — unless the court sets a different time for the notice or the objection.

(11) *Records of Religious Organizations Concerning Personal or Family History.* A statement of birth, legitimacy, ancestry, marriage, divorce, death, relationship by blood or marriage, or similar facts of personal or family history, contained in a regularly kept record of a religious organization.

(12) *Certificates of Marriage, Baptism, and Similar Ceremonies.* A statement of fact contained in a certificate
  (A) made by a person who is authorized by a religious organization or by law to perform the act certified;
  (B) attesting that the person performed a marriage or similar ceremony or administered a sacrament; and
  (C) purporting to have been issued at the time of the act or within a reasonable time after it.

(13) *Family Records.* A statement of fact about personal or family history contained in a family record, such as a Bible, genealogy, chart, engraving on a ring, inscription on a portrait, or engraving on an urn or burial marker.

(14) *Records of Documents That Affect an Interest in Property.* The record of a document that purports to establish or affect an interest in property if
  (A) the record is admitted to prove the content of the original recorded document, along with its signing and its delivery by each person who purports to have signed it;
  (B) the record is kept in a public office; and
  (C) a statute authorizes recording documents of that kind in that office.

(15) *Statements in Documents That Affect an Interest in Property.* A statement contained in a document that purports to establish or affect an interest in property if the matter stated was relevant to the document's purpose — unless later dealings with the property are inconsistent with the truth of the statement or the purport of the document.

(16) *Statements in Ancient Documents.* A statement in a document that is at least 20 years old and whose authenticity is established.

(17) *Market Reports and Similar Commercial Publications.* Market quotations, lists, directories, or other compilations that are generally relied on by the public or by persons in particular occupations.

(18) *Statements in Learned Treatises, Periodicals, or Pamphlets.* A statement contained in a treatise, periodical, or pamphlet if

(A) the statement is called to the attention of an expert witness on cross-examination or relied on by the expert on direct examination; and

(B) the publication is established as a reliable authority by the expert's admission or testimony, by another expert's testimony, or by judicial notice.

If admitted, the statement may be read into evidence but not received as an exhibit.

(19) *Reputation Concerning Personal or Family History.* A reputation among a person's family by blood, adoption, or marriage — or among a person's associates or in the community — concerning the person's birth, adoption, legitimacy, ancestry, marriage, divorce, death, relationship by blood, adoption, or marriage, or similar facts of personal or family history.

(20) *Reputation Concerning Boundaries or General History.* A reputation in a community — arising before the controversy — concerning boundaries of land in the community or customs that affect the land, or concerning general historical events important to that community, state, or nation.

(21) *Reputation Concerning Character.* A reputation among a person's associates or in the community concerning the person's character.

(22) *Judgment of a Previous Conviction.* Evidence of a final judgment of conviction if

(A) the judgment was entered after a trial or guilty plea, but not a nolo contendere plea;

(B) the conviction was for a crime punishable by death or by imprisonment for more than a year;

(C) the evidence is admitted to prove any fact essential to the judgment; and

(D) when offered by the prosecutor in a criminal case for a purpose other than impeachment, the judgment was against the defendant.

The pendency of an appeal may be shown but does not affect admissibility.

(23) *Judgments Involving Personal, Family, or General History, or a Boundary.* A judgment that is admitted to prove a matter of personal, family, or general history, or boundaries, if the matter

(A) was essential to the judgment; and

(B) could be proved by evidence of reputation.

(24) [*Other Exceptions.*] [Transferred to Rule 807.]

Rule 804.   Exceptions to the Rule Against Hearsay — When the Declarant Is Unavailable as a Witness

(a) Criteria for Being Unavailable. A declarant is considered to be unavailable as a witness if the declarant

(1) is exempted from testifying about the subject matter of the declarant's statement because the court rules that a privilege applies;

(2) refuses to testify about the subject matter despite a court order to do so;

(3) testifies to not remembering the subject matter;

(4) cannot be present or testify at the trial or hearing because of death or a then-existing infirmity, physical illness, or mental illness; or

(5) is absent from the trial or hearing and the statement's proponent has not been able, by process or other reasonable means, to procure

(A) the declarant's attendance, in the case of a hearsay exception under Rule 804(b)(1) or (5); or

(B) the declarant's attendance or testimony, in the case of a hearsay exception under Rule 804(b)(2), (3), or (4).

But this subdivision (a) does not apply if the statement's proponent procured or wrongfully caused the declarant's unavailability as a witness in order to prevent the declarant from attending or testifying.

(b) The Exceptions. The following are not excluded by the rule against hearsay if the declarant is unavailable as a witness:

(1) *Former Testimony.* Testimony that

(A) was given as a witness at a trial, hearing, or lawful deposition, whether given during the current proceeding or a different one; and

(B) is now offered against a party who had — or, in a civil case, whose predecessor in interest had — an opportunity and similar motive to develop it by direct, cross-, or redirect examination.

(2) *Statement Under the Belief of Imminent Death.* In a prosecution for homicide or in a civil case, a statement that the declarant, while believing the declarant's death to be imminent, made about its cause or circumstances.

(3) *Statement Against Interest.* A statement that

(A) a reasonable person in the declarant's position would have made only if the person believed it to be true because, when made, it was so contrary to the declarant's proprietary or pecuniary interest or had so great a tendency to invalidate the declarant's claim against someone else or to expose the declarant to civil or criminal liability; and

(B) is supported by corroborating circumstances that clearly indicate its trustworthiness, if it is offered in a criminal case as one that tends to expose the declarant to criminal liability.

(4) *Statement of Personal or Family History.* A statement about

(A) the declarant's own birth, adoption, legitimacy, ancestry, marriage, divorce, relationship by blood or marriage, or similar facts of personal or family history, even though the declarant had no way of acquiring personal knowledge about that fact; or

(B) another person concerning any of these facts, as well as death, if the declarant was related to the person by blood, adoption, or marriage or was so intimately associated with the person's family that the declarant's information is likely to be accurate.

(5) [*Other Exceptions.*] [Transferred to Rule 807.]

(6) *Statement Offered Against a Party That Wrongfully Caused the Declarant's Unavailability.* A statement offered against a party that wrongfully caused — or acquiesced in wrongfully causing — the declarant's unavailability as a witness, and did so intending that result.

Rule 805.   Hearsay Within Hearsay

Hearsay within hearsay is not excluded by the rule against hearsay if each part of the combined statements conforms with an exception to the rule.

Rule 806.   Attacking and Supporting the Declarant's Credibility

When a hearsay statement — or a statement described in Rule 801 (d) (2) (C), (D), or (E) — has been admitted in evidence, the declarant's credibility may be attacked, and then supported, by any evidence that would be admissible for those purposes if the declarant had testified as a witness. The court may admit evidence of the declarant's inconsistent statement or conduct, regardless of when it occurred or whether the declarant had an opportunity to explain or deny it. If the party against whom the statement was admitted calls the declarant as a witness, the party may examine the declarant on the statement as if on cross-examination.

Rule 807.   Residual Exception

(a) In General. Under the following circumstances, a hearsay statement is not excluded by the rule against hearsay even if the statement is not specifically covered by a hearsay exception in Rule 803 or 804:

(1) the statement has equivalent circumstantial guarantees of trustworthiness;

(2) it is offered as evidence of a material fact;

(3) it is more probative on the point for which it is offered than any other evidence that the proponent can obtain through reasonable efforts; and

(4) admitting it will best serve the purposes of these rules and the interests of justice.

(b) Notice. The statement is admissible only if, before the trial or hearing, the proponent gives an adverse party reasonable notice of the intent to offer the statement and its particulars, including the declarant's name and address, so that the party has a fair opportunity to meet it.

ARTICLE IX.   AUTHENTICATION AND IDENTIFICATION

Rule 901.   Authenticating or Identifying Evidence

(a) In General. To satisfy the requirement of authenticating or identifying an item of evidence, the proponent must produce evidence sufficient to support a finding that the item is what the proponent claims it is.

(b) Examples. The following are examples only — not a complete list — of evidence that satisfies the requirement:

(1) *Testimony of a Witness with Knowledge.* Testimony that an item is what it is claimed to be.

(2) *Nonexpert Opinion About Handwriting.* A nonexpert's opinion that handwriting is genuine, based on a familiarity with it that was not acquired for the current litigation.

(3) *Comparison by an Expert Witness or the Trier of Fact.* A comparison with an authenticated specimen by an expert witness or the trier of fact.

(4) *Distinctive Characteristics and the Like.* The appearance, contents, substance, internal patterns, or other distinctive characteristics of the item, taken together with all the circumstances.

(5) *Opinion About a Voice.* An opinion identifying a person's voice — whether heard firsthand or through mechanical or electronic transmission or recording — based on hearing the voice at any time under circumstances that connect it with the alleged speaker.

(6) *Evidence About a Telephone Conversation.* For a telephone conversation, evidence that a call was made to the number assigned at the time to

    (A) a particular person, if circumstances, including self-identification, show that the person answering was the one called; or

    (B) a particular business, if the call was made to a business and the call related to business reasonably transacted over the telephone.

(7) *Evidence About Public Records.* Evidence that

    (A) a document was recorded or filed in a public office as authorized by law; or

    (B) a purported public record or statement is from the office where items of this kind are kept.

(8) *Evidence About Ancient Documents or Data Compilations.* For a document or data compilation, evidence that it

    (A) is in a condition that creates no suspicion about its authenticity;

    (B) was in a place where, if authentic, it would likely be; and

    (C) is at least 20 years old when offered.

(9) *Evidence About a Process or System.* Evidence describing a process or system and showing that it produces an accurate result.

(10) *Methods Provided by a Statute or Rule.* Any method of authentication or identification allowed by a federal statute or a rule prescribed by the Supreme Court.

Rule 902.   Evidence That Is Self-Authenticating

The following items of evidence are self-authenticating; they require no extrinsic evidence of authenticity in order to be admitted:

(1) *Domestic Public Documents That Are Sealed and Signed.* A document that bears:

    (A) a seal purporting to be that of the United States; any state, district, commonwealth, territory, or insular possession of the United States; the former Panama Canal Zone; the Trust Territory of the Pacific Islands; a political subdivision of any of these entities; or a department, agency, or officer of any entity named above; and

    (B) a signature purporting to be an execution or attestation.

(2) *Domestic Public Documents That Are Not Sealed but Are Signed and Certified.* A document that bears no seal if

(A) it bears the signature of an officer or employee of an entity named in Rule 902(1)(A); and

(B) another public officer who has a seal and official duties within that same entity certifies under seal — or its equivalent — that the signer has the official capacity and that the signature is genuine.

(3) *Foreign Public Documents.* A document that purports to be signed or attested by a person who is authorized by a foreign country's law to do so. The document must be accompanied by a final certification that certifies the genuineness of the signature and official position of the signer or attester — or of any foreign official whose certificate of genuineness relates to the signature or attestation or is in a chain of certificates of genuineness relating to the signature or attestation. The certification may be made by a secretary of a United States embassy or legation; by a consul general, vice consul, or consular agent of the United States; or by a diplomatic or consular official of the foreign country assigned or accredited to the United States. If all parties have been given a reasonable opportunity to investigate the document's authenticity and accuracy, the court may, for good cause, either

(A) order that it be treated as presumptively authentic without final certification; or

(B) allow it to be evidenced by an attested summary with or without final certification.

(4) *Certified Copies of Public Records.* A copy of an official record — or a copy of a document that was recorded or filed in a public office as authorized by law — if the copy is certified as correct by

(A) the custodian or another person authorized to make the certification; or

(B) a certificate that complies with Rule 902(1), (2), or (3), a federal statute, or a rule prescribed by the Supreme Court.

(5) *Official Publications.* A book, pamphlet, or other publication purporting to be issued by a public authority.

(6) *Newspapers and Periodicals.* Printed material purporting to be a newspaper or periodical.

(7) *Trade Inscriptions and the Like.* An inscription, sign, tag, or label purporting to have been affixed in the course of business and indicating origin, ownership, or control.

(8) *Acknowledged Documents.* A document accompanied by a certificate of acknowledgment that is lawfully executed by a notary public or another officer who is authorized to take acknowledgments.

(9) *Commercial Paper and Related Documents.* Commercial paper, a signature on it, and related documents, to the extent allowed by general commercial law.

(10) *Presumptions Under a Federal Statute.* A signature, document, or anything else that a federal statute declares to be presumptively or prima facie genuine or authentic.

(11) *Certified Domestic Records of a Regularly Conducted Activity.* The original or a copy of a domestic record that meets the requirements of Rule 803(6)(A)-(C), as shown by a certification of the custodian or another qualified person that complies with a federal statute or a rule prescribed by the Supreme Court. Before the trial or hearing, the proponent must give an adverse party reasonable written notice of the intent to offer the record — and must make the record and certification available for inspection — so that the party has a fair opportunity to challenge them.

(12) *Certified Foreign Records of a Regularly Conducted Activity.* In a civil case, the original or a copy of a foreign record that meets the requirements of Rule 902(11), modified as follows: the certification, rather than complying with a federal statute or Supreme Court rule, must be signed in a manner that, if falsely made, would subject the maker to a criminal penalty in the country where the certification is signed. The proponent must also meet the notice requirements of Rule 902(11).

Rule 903.   Subscribing Witness's Testimony

A subscribing witness's testimony is necessary to authenticate a writing only if required by the law of the jurisdiction that governs its validity.

ARTICLE X.   CONTENTS OF WRITINGS, RECORDINGS, AND PHOTOGRAPHS

Rule 1001.   Definitions That Apply to This Article

In this article
(a) A "writing" consists of letters, words, numbers, or their equivalent set down in any form.

(b) A "recording" consists of letters, words, numbers, or their equivalent recorded in any manner.

(c) A "photograph" means a photographic image or its equivalent stored in any form.

(d) An "original" of a writing or recording means the writing or recording itself or any counterpart intended to have the same effect by the person who executed or issued it. For electronically stored information, "original" means any printout — or other output readable by sight — if it accurately reflects the information. An "original" of a photograph includes the negative or a print from it.

(e) A "duplicate" means a counterpart produced by a mechanical, photographic, chemical, electronic, or other equivalent process or technique that accurately reproduces the original.

Rule 1002.   Requirement of the Original

An original writing, recording, or photograph is required in order to prove its content unless these rules or a federal statute provides otherwise.

Rule 1003.   Admissibility of Duplicates

A duplicate is admissible to the same extent as the original unless a genuine question is raised about the original's authenticity or the circumstances make it unfair to admit the duplicate.

Rule 1004.   Admissibility of Other Evidence of Content

An original is not required and other evidence of the content of a writing, recording, or photograph is admissible if

(a) all the originals are lost or destroyed, and not by the proponent acting in bad faith;

(b) an original cannot be obtained by any available judicial process;

(c) the party against whom the original would be offered had control of the original; was at that time put on notice, by pleadings or otherwise, that the original would be a subject of proof at the trial or hearing; and fails to produce it at the trial or hearing; or

(d) the writing, recording, or photograph is not closely related to a controlling issue.

Rule 1005.   Copies of Public Records to Prove Content

The proponent may use a copy to prove the content of an official record — or of a document that was recorded or filed in a public office as authorized by law — if these conditions are met: the record or document is otherwise admissible; and the copy is certified as correct in accordance with Rule 902(4) or is testified to be correct by a witness who has compared it with the original. If no such copy can be obtained by reasonable diligence, then the proponent may use other evidence to prove the content.

Rule 1006.   Summaries to Prove Content

The proponent may use a summary, chart, or calculation to prove the content of voluminous writings, recordings, or photographs that cannot be conveniently examined in court. The proponent must make the originals or duplicates available for examination or copying, or both, by other parties at a reasonable time or place. And the court may order the proponent to produce them in court.

Rule 1007.   Testimony or Statement of a Party to Prove Content

The proponent may prove the content of a writing, recording, or photograph by the testimony, deposition, or written statement of the party against whom the evidence is offered. The proponent need not account for the original.

Rule 1008.   Functions of the Court and Jury

Ordinarily, the court determines whether the proponent has fulfilled the factual conditions for admitting other evidence of the content of a writing, recording, or photograph under Rule 1004 or 1005. But in a jury trial, the jury determines — in accordance with Rule 104(b) — any issue about whether

(a) an asserted writing, recording, or photograph ever existed;

(b) another one produced at the trial or hearing is the original; or

(c) other evidence of content accurately reflects the content.

ARTICLE XI.   MISCELLANEOUS RULES

Rule 1101.   Applicability of the Rules

(a) To Courts and Judges. These rules apply to proceedings before

- United States district courts;
- United States bankruptcy and magistrate judges;
- United States courts of appeals;
- the United States Court of Federal Claims; and
- the district courts of Guam, the Virgin Islands, and the Northern Mariana Islands.

(b) To Cases and Proceedings. These rules apply in

- civil cases and proceedings, including bankruptcy, admiralty, and maritime cases;
- criminal cases and proceedings; and
- contempt proceedings, except those in which the court may act summarily.

(c) Rules on Privilege. The rules on privilege apply to all stages of a case or proceeding.

(d) Exceptions. These rules — except for those on privilege — do not apply to the following:

    (1) the court's determination, under Rule 104(a), on a preliminary question of fact governing admissibility;

    (2) grand-jury proceedings; and

    (3) miscellaneous proceedings such as

- extradition or rendition;
- issuing an arrest warrant, criminal summons, or search warrant;
- a preliminary examination in a criminal case;
- sentencing;
- granting or revoking probation or supervised release; and
- considering whether to release on bail or otherwise.

(e) Other Statutes and Rules. A federal statute or a rule prescribed by the Supreme Court may provide for admitting or excluding evidence independently from these rules.

Rule 1102.   Amendments

These rules may be amended as provided in 28 U.S.C. §2072.

Rule 1103.   Title

These rules may be cited as the Federal Rules of Evidence.

INDEX